CHAPTER

Numbers and Graphing

Theme: All About Us 1

Problem Solving
Look for a Pattern,
Estimation,
Critical Thinking,
Visual Thinking

Connections
Math at Home,
Journal, Reading for Math,
Algebra Readiness

Problem Solving
Collect and Use Data,
Estimation,
Critical Thinking

Connections
Mental Math,
Tell a Math Story,
Journal

Connections
Math in Your World,
Math and Health,
Math at Home

CHAPTER 2

Addition and Subtraction: Patterns and Concepts

Theme: The Big Picnic 37

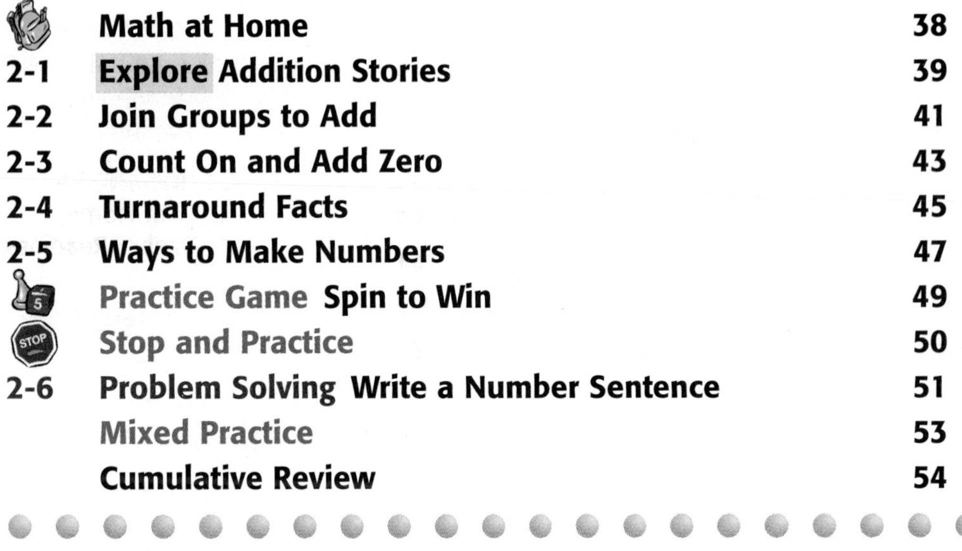

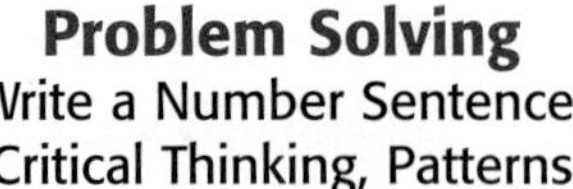

Problem Solving
Write a Number Sentence, Critical Thinking, Patterns

Connections
Math at Home, Tell a Math Story, Journal, Algebra Readiness

Problem Solving
Choose an Operation, Visual Thinking, Critical Thinking

Connections
Tell a Math Story, Reading for Math, Write About It, Journal

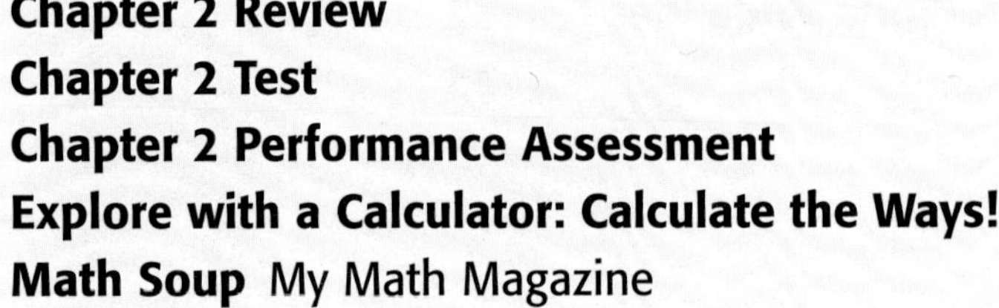

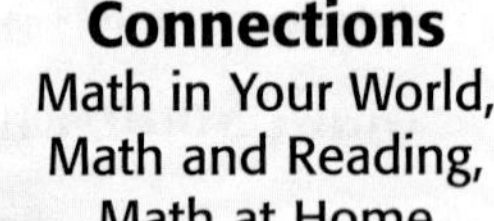

Connections
Math in Your World, Math and Reading, Math at Home

0 1 2 3 4 5 6 7 8 9 10 11 12

Addition and Subtraction Facts and Strategies

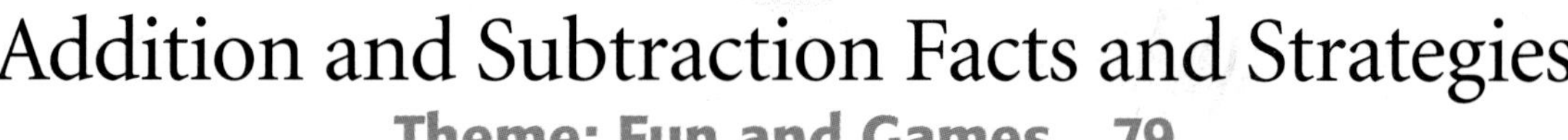

CHAPTER 4

Using Addition and Subtraction

Theme: Fun at the Fair 117

CHAPTER 5

Place Value and Patterns to 100

Theme: Colorful Collections 155

Problem Solving
Use Data from a Graph,
Critical Thinking,
Visual Thinking

Connections
Math at Home, Journal

Problem Solving
Group Decision Making,
Critical Thinking,
Estimation, Patterns,
Number Sense

Connections
Mental Math,
Reading for Math, Journal,
Algebra Readiness

Connections
Math in Your World,
Math and Social Studies,
Math at Home

CHAPTER 6

Money

Theme: What's for Sale? 197

CHAPTER 7

Time

Theme: All Around Town 231

Two-Digit Addition

Theme: What a Ride! 267

Problem Solving
Make Predictions, Patterns, Estimation, Critical Thinking

Connections
Math at Home, Reading for Math, Journal, Algebra Readiness

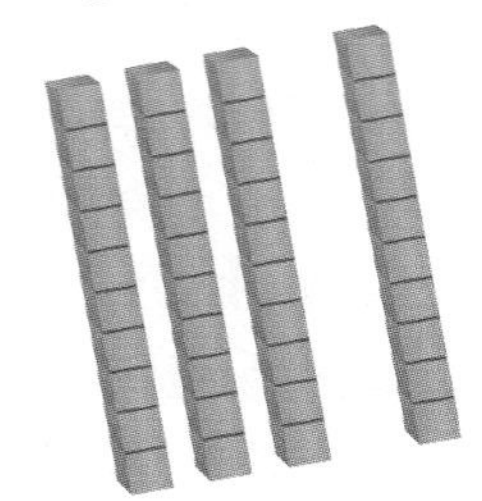

Problem Solving
Guess and Check, Visual Thinking, Critical Thinking, Estimation

Connections
Journal

Connections
Math in Your World, Math and Social Studies, Math at Home

Two-Digit Subtraction

Numbers to 1,000

Theme: Crafty Numbers 355

CHAPTER 11

Measurement

Theme: Sizing Up Your World 399

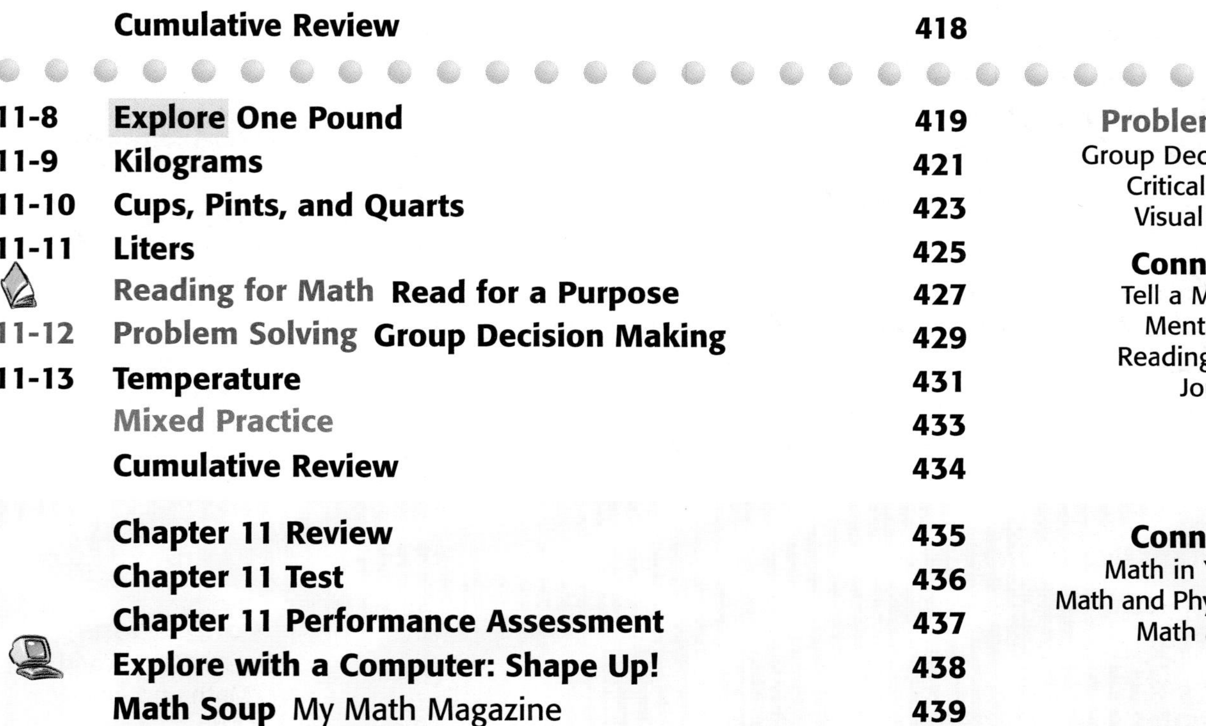

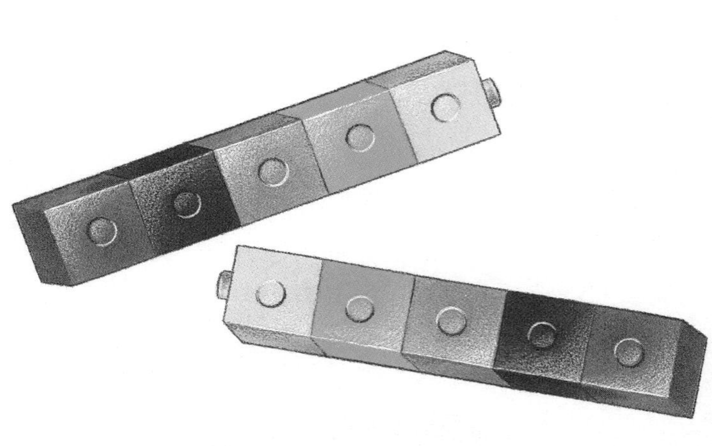

CHAPTER

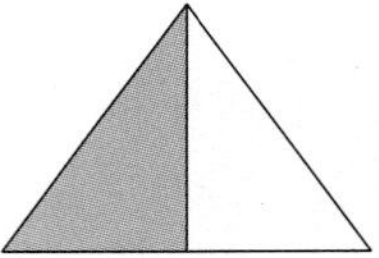

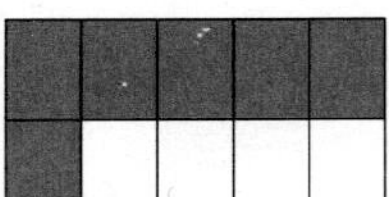

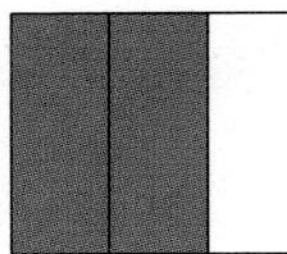

Geometry and Fractions

Theme: Food Festival 443

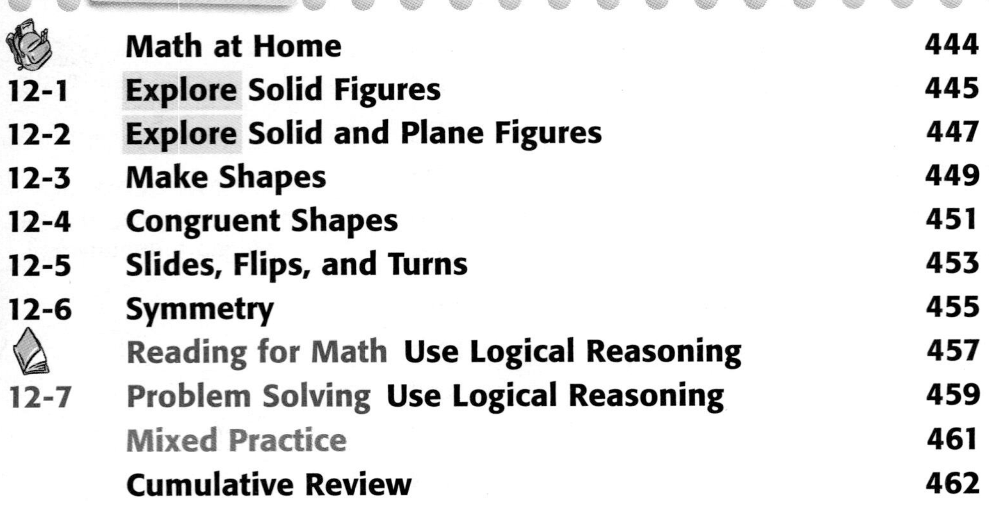

Problem Solving
Use Logical Reasoning,
Critical Thinking,
Visual Thinking, Patterns

Connections
Math at Home,
Reading for Math, Journal,
Write About It,
Algebra Readiness

Problem Solving
Make a Prediction,
Visual Thinking,
Critical Thinking

Connections
Mental Math, Journal,
Write About It

Connections
Math in Your World,
Math and Art,
Math at Home

CHAPTER 13

Multiplication and Division Concepts

Theme: Summer Fun 491

Problem Solving
Draw a Picture, Visual Thinking, Patterns, Estimation

Connections
Math at Home, Journal, Algebra Readiness

Problem Solving
Choose an Operation

Connections
Reading for Math, Journal, Tell a Math Story

Connections
Math in Your World, Math and Physical Education, Math at Home

MATHmatazz Treehouse

Welcome

CHAPTER 1

Numbers and Graphing

All About Us

Where would you put your picture?

Art	Sports	Reading	Music
	Ron Matthews		
Yasuko Masami	Nituna Totno		Rebecca Nuñez
Mark Robbins	Julia Ponti	Miguel Flores	Karen Kaspar
Anne Martin	Daniel Wozniak	Araba Stevenson	Colin Thomas

Notes for Home: Your child described what is in the pictures and what the graph shows.
Home Activity: Ask your child to tell you how many children picked reading as their favorite activity.

Dear Family,
Our class is starting Chapter 1. We will be learning about numbers, patterns, and graphing. We will count objects, compare numbers, and make different types of graphs. Together we can do these activities.

Counting Quickly

Gather 20 items, such as pennies or buttons. Have your child count to find out how many. Ask your child if he or she can think of a faster way to count the items; for example, counting by 2s.

In the News

Show your child graphs in the real world, such as those in a newspaper or magazine. Point out the title of the graph. Talk about the numbers in the graph.

Community Connection

Help your child count items outside of the home, such as the number of grocery items purchased or the number of buildings they pass on their way to school. When counting large quantities, count by 2s, 5s, or 10s.

Visit our Web site. www.parent.mathsurf.com

Name

Explore Counting and Comparing

Explore

How many girls and boys are in your class?
Use ● ○ to show how many.

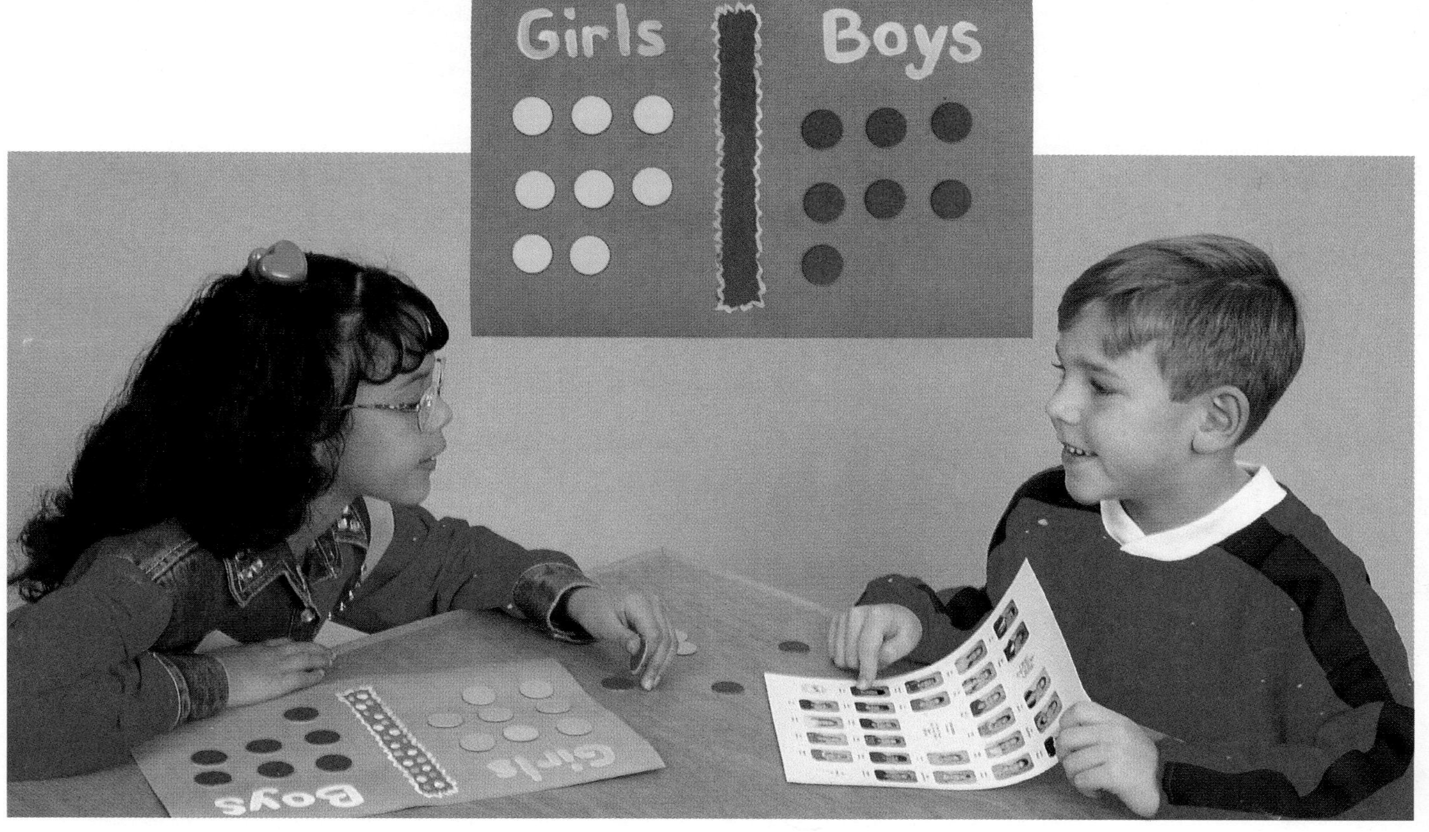

1 How many girls are in your class? ______

2 How many boys are in your class? ______

3 Which group has more? ____________

4 Which group has fewer? ____________

Share

How did you decide which group has more?

Notes for Home: Your child counted the number of boys and girls in his or her class.
Home Activity: Ask your child to find the number of objects in each of two groups. Ask which group has more.

Connect

In my class, more children walk to school. Fewer children ride.

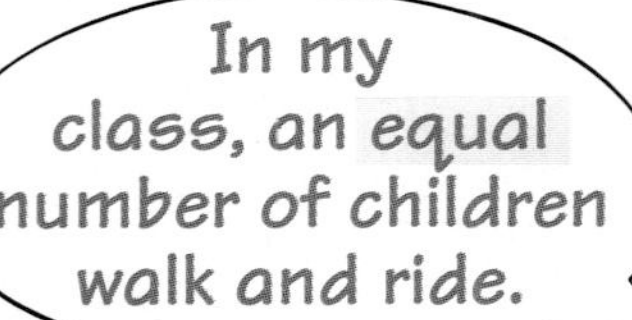

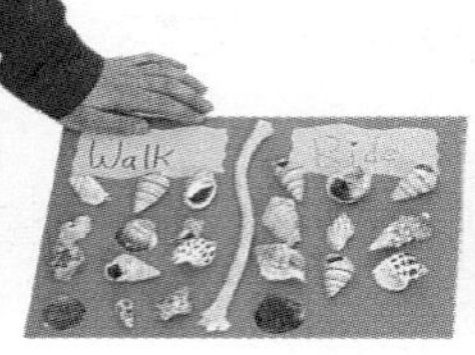

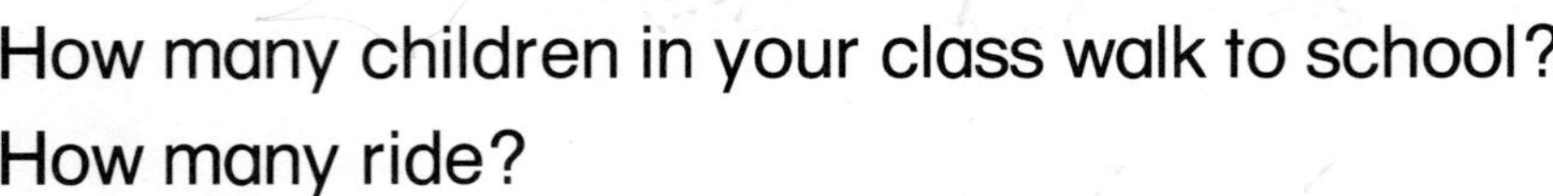

How many children in your class walk to school?
How many ride?

Use   to show how many.

5. How many children walk to school? ______

6. How many children ride to school? ______

7. Which group has more? ____________

8. Which group has fewer? ____________

Journal

9. Tell how you know if two groups are equal.

Notes for Home: Your child practiced counting and comparing numbers using more, fewer, and equal. *Home Activity:* Ask your child more, fewer and equal questions using sets of objects such as beans and buttons.

EXPLORE

Name ______________________________

Bar Graphs

Learn

Number of Letters In Our Names

1	2	3	4	5
	|	|	~~||||~~ ||	~~||||~~ |

6	7	8	9	10
|||	||	|||	|	|

I count two tally marks for 7.

Number of Letters in Our Names

Number of Children: 1 2 3 4 5 6 7

Letters in Name: 1 2 3 4 5 6 7 8 9 10

I color two boxes for 7 on the bar graph.

Check

1. How many children have 5 letters in their names? 6

2. How many spaces would you color above 8 on the graph? ______

3. How many letters does the greatest number of names have? ______

Talk About It Which numbers on the graph will have 1 space colored?

Notes for Home: Your child analyzed data using tally marks and a bar graph. *Home Activity:* Ask your child which number of letters occurs the least number of times on the chart. (1)

Practice

4 How many letters are there in the first names in your class?
Make tally marks.

Number of Letters in Our Names

1	2	3	4	5	6

7	8	9	10	11	12

5 Make a bar graph. Color one space for each tally mark.

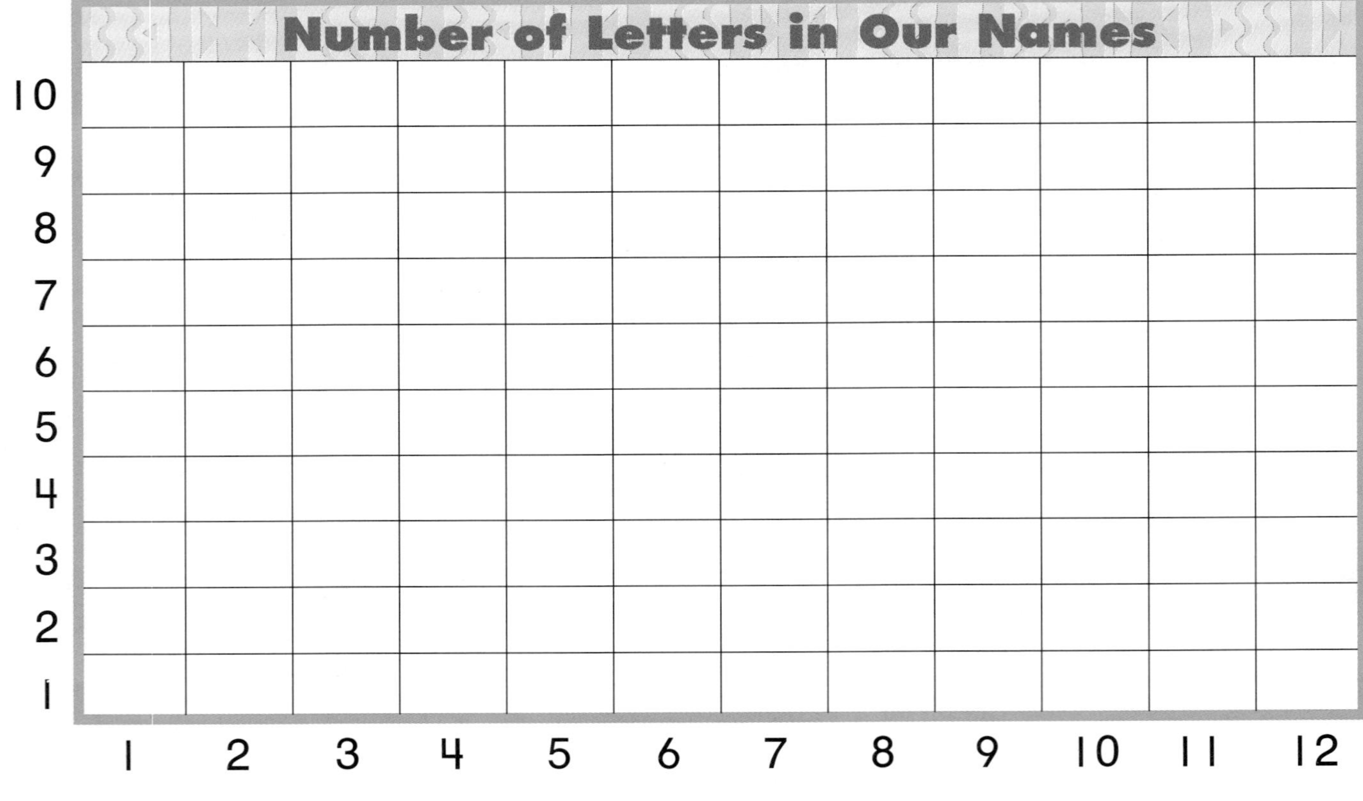

Problem Solving Critical Thinking

6 In another class, 5 children have 4 letters in their names.
Explain how you would show this on a bar graph.

Notes for Home: Your child has gathered and shown data using tally marks and a bar graph.
Home Activity: Ask your child to add the first names of people in his or her family to the graph.

For additional practice, see Skills Practice Bank, page 527, Set 3.

Name ________________________

Practice Game

Race to the Top

Players 2

What You Need

1 number cube
6 crayons in different colors

How to Play

1. Toss the number cube.
2. Color a square on the graph to show the number you rolled.
3. Use a different color crayon for each number.
4. Roll until one number is colored to the top.
   That number wins.

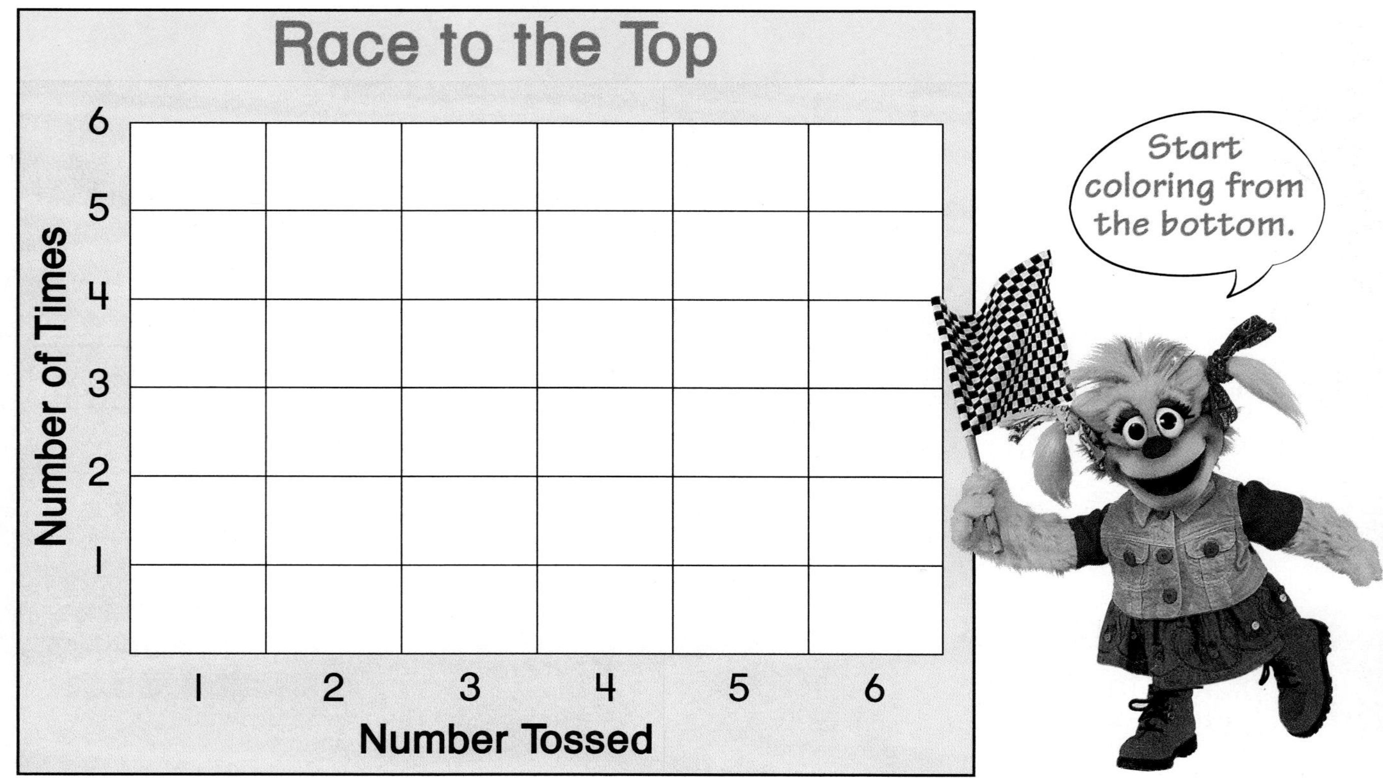

PRACTICE

Notes For Home: Your child played a game to practice graphing and comparing.
Home Activity: Ask your child to tell which number(s) was rolled the least number of times.

Name ______________________________

Compare the numbers in each group.

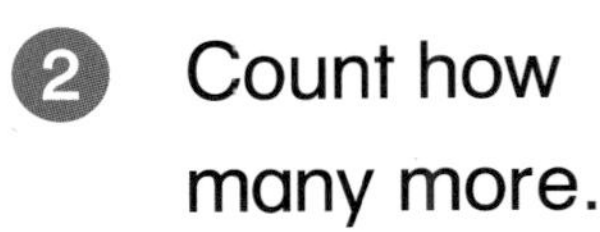

1. Are there more scissors or brushes?

   ____

2. Count how many more.

   _____ more

Count by 5s or 10s. Write the numbers.

3. 5, 10, 15, _____, _____, _____, _____, _____, _____, _____

4. 10, 20, 30, _____, _____, _____, _____, _____, _____

5. Use the tally marks. Make a bar graph.

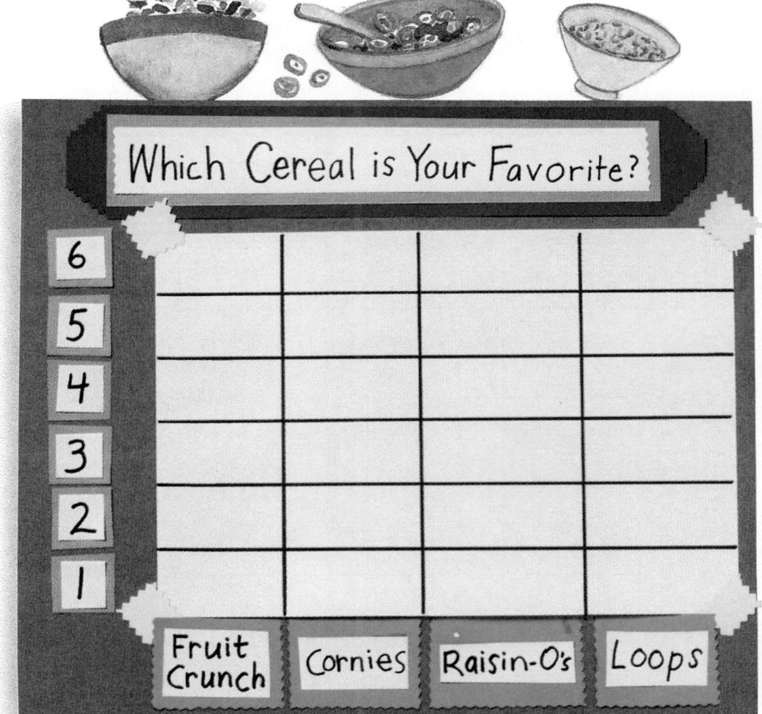

6. How many children picked Loops?

   _____

7. Which cereal was picked the least?

   ____

Notes for Home: Your child practiced comparing groups, counting, and making bar graphs.
Home Activity: Ask your child which cereal was chosen 4 times. (Cornies)

Name

Problem Solving: Collect and Use Data

Learn

PROBLEM SOLVING GUIDE

Understand • Plan • Solve • Look Back

These children showed their data using a diagram.

PROBLEM SOLVING

Check

1. How many children like both skating and biking? 3
2. How many children like skating? _____
3. How many children like skating but not biking? _____
4. How many children like biking? _____
5. How many children like biking but not skating? _____

Talk About It Do more children like skating or biking? Tell how you know.

Notes for Home: Your child studied a way to organize data. *Home Activity:* Ask your child to use the diagram to tell you what Jessie, Luisa, and Lizzie like to do. (Jessie likes skating; Luisa likes biking; Lizzie likes both skating and biking.)

PROBLEM SOLVING

Practice

6 Show data for 7 classmates using a diagram.

Do You Like Skating or Biking?

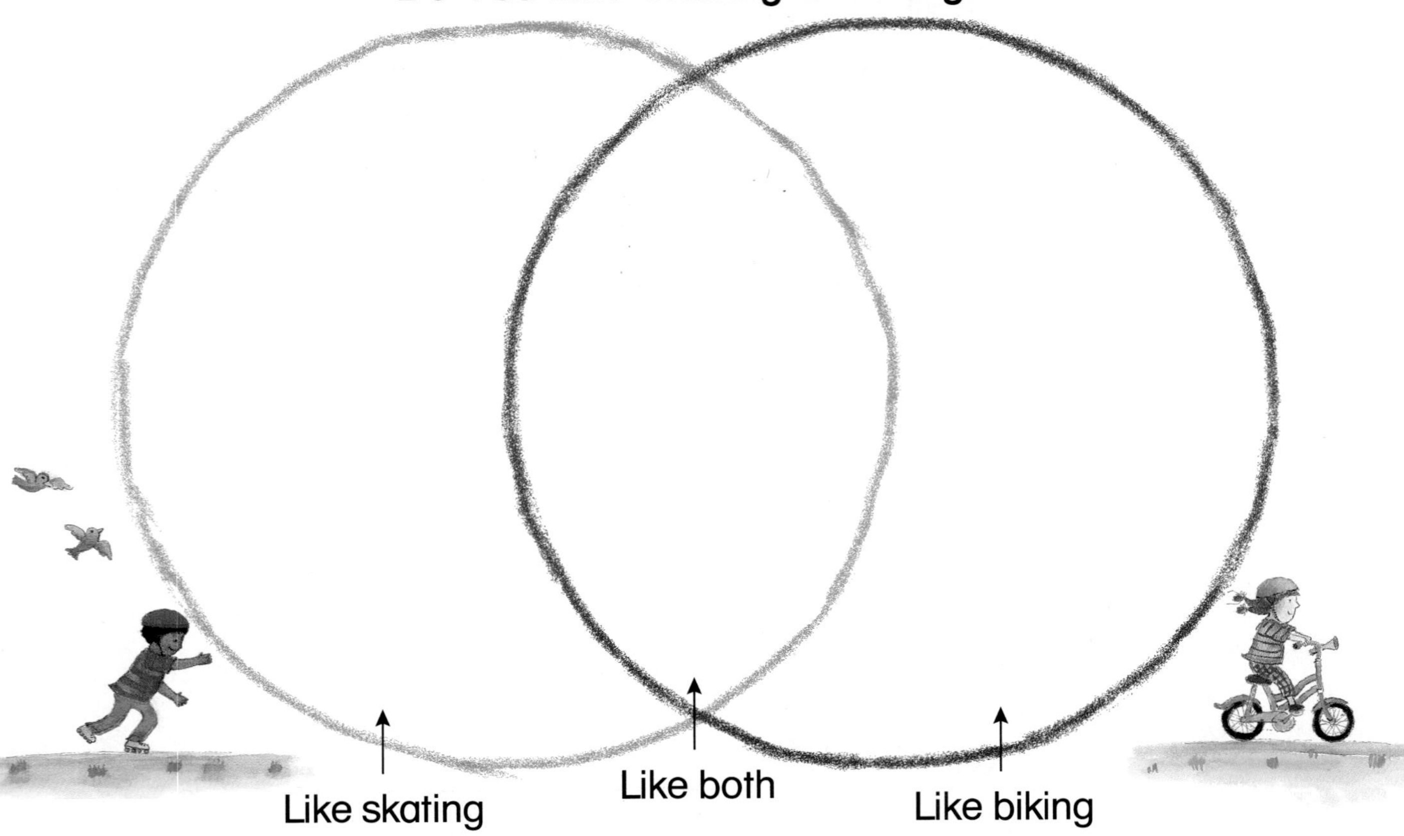

Use your diagram to answer the questions.

7 How many children like both skating and biking? _____

8 How many children like skating? _____

9 How many children like skating but not biking? _____

10 How many children like biking? _____

11 How many children like biking but not skating? _____

Tell a Math Story

12 Draw your own diagram. Ask a friend to tell a story about your diagram.

Notes for Home: Your child collected, organized, and used data to solve problems. *Home Activity:* Ask your child to place his or her name in the diagram, then ask what the placement of his or her name shows.

Name

Mixed Practice

Lessons 5–9

Concepts and Skills

Use the graph. Solve.

1 How many children liked purple best? ______

2 Did more children like green or blue? ____________

Favorite Color

Purple	🧍🧍🧍🧍🧍🧍🧍
Green	🧍🧍🧍
Red	🧍🧍🧍🧍🧍
Blue	🧍🧍🧍🧍🧍🧍

Each 🧍 means 1 child.

Use the graph to answer the questions.

3 Which pet was picked most often? ____________

4 Which pet was picked the least number of times? ____________

Favorite Pet

Dog	■	■	■	■	■	■	■	■	
Cat	■	■	■	■	■				
Fish	■	■	■						
Bird	■	■	■	■	■	■			
	1	2	3	4	5	6	7	8	9

5 How many children liked cats best? ______

Problem Solving

Look at the diagram.
Answer the questions.

Do You Like Soccer or Softball?

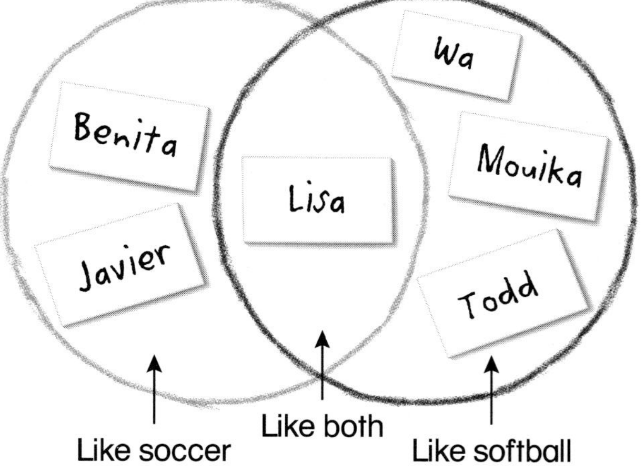

6 How many children liked softball but not soccer? ______

7 How many children liked both soccer and softball? ______

Journal

8 Write a question about the diagram. Ask a friend to answer your question.

Notes for Home: Your child practiced using graphs to compare information.
Home Activity: Ask your child to add his or her vote to the graph about a favorite color.

Name

Cumulative Review

Chapter 1

Concepts and Skills

Circle the number that is greater.

1. 4 8
2. 16 11

Circle the number that is less.

3. 15 12
4. 7 9

Problem Solving

Solve.

5. There are 6 drums.
There are 4 flutes.
Which group has more?

______

6. There are 5 guitars.
There are 8 violins.
Which group has fewer?

______

Test Prep

Fill in the ○ for the correct answer.

7. Count by 5s.
Mark the number that comes next.

5, 10, 15, 20, ____

○ 21 ○ 22 ○ 25 ○ 30

8. Count by 10s.
Mark the number that comes next.

10, 20, 30, 40, ____

○ 41
○ 42
○ 45
○ 50

Notes for Home: Your child reviewed number combinations, comparing sets, and skip counting.
Home Activity: Ask your child to find two groups of objects at home that are equal in number.

Name ______________________________

Chapter 1 Review

Vocabulary

1 Which group has more counters?

red **yellow**

2 Count how many more. ______ more

3 How many votes? Count the tally marks.

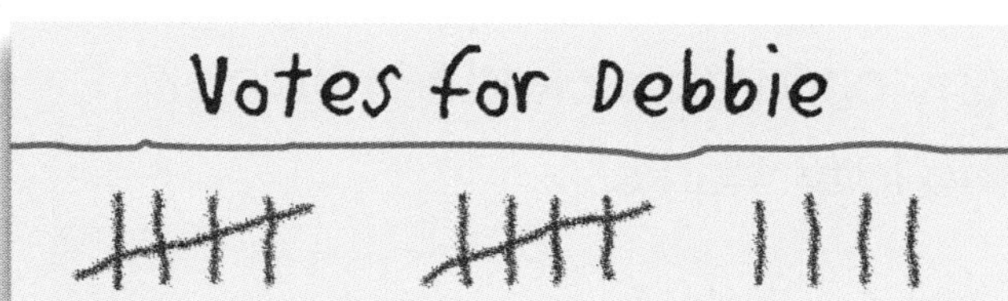

______ votes

Concepts and Skills

Count by 2s or 5s. Write the numbers.

4 2, 4, 6, ____, ____, ____, ____, ____, ____, ____

5 5, 10, 15, ____, ____, ____, ____, ____, ____, ____

Problem Solving

Use the graph.
Answer the questions.

6 How many kickball games were played?

______

7 Which game was played the most?

____

Notes for Home: Your child reviewed the vocabulary, skills, concepts, and problem solving taught in Chapter 1. *Home Activity:* Ask your child to use tally marks to count the number of windows in your home.

CHAPTER REVIEW

Name ______________________________

Chapter 1 Test

Use the graph. Answer the questions.

1 Do more children get to school by bus or bike?

____

2 How many more?

_____ more

How We Get to School

Bus	🧍🧍🧍🧍🧍🧍
Bike	🧍🧍🧍🧍
Walk	🧍🧍🧍🧍🧍

Each 🧍 means 1 child.

3 How many children picked hot lunch? Count the tally marks.

_____ children

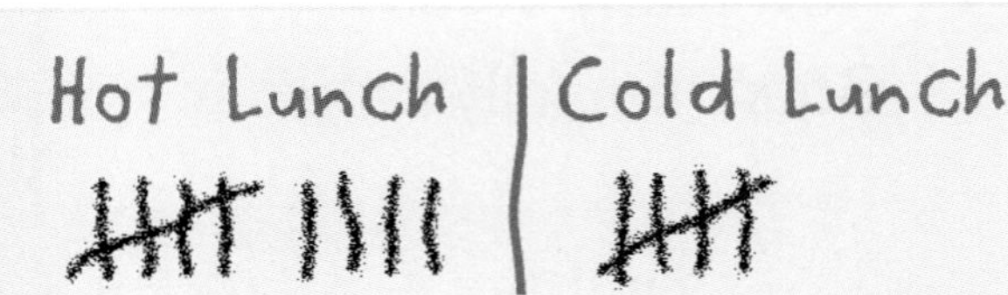

Count by 10s. Write the numbers.

4 10, 20, _____, _____, _____, _____, _____, _____, _____

Use the graph. Answer the question.

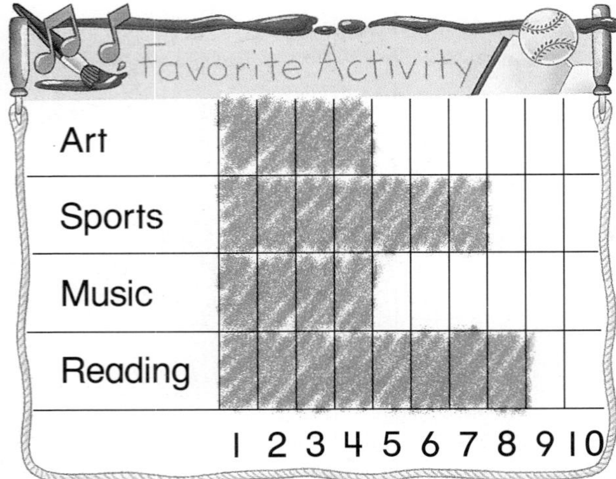

5 Which activity do most of these children like best?

____

Use the diagram. Answer the question.

Do You Like Milk or Juice?

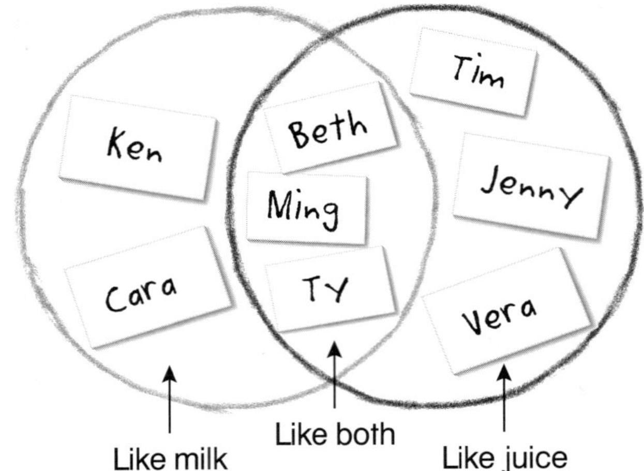

6 How many of these children like only juice?

_____

Notes for Home: Your child was tested on Chapter 1 concepts, skills, and problem solving. *Home Activity:* Ask your child to look at the diagram in Exercise 6 and name the children who like only milk. (Ken, Cara)

Name ____________________

Performance Assessment

Chapter 1

Put 1 red, 1 blue, 1 yellow, and 1 green cube in a bag.

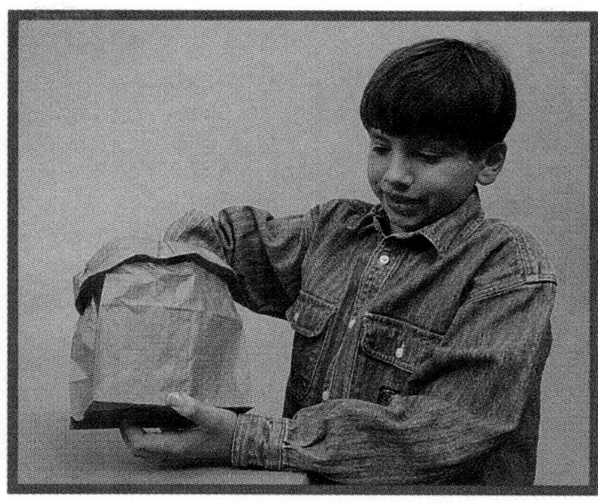

Pick a cube from the bag. What color is it?

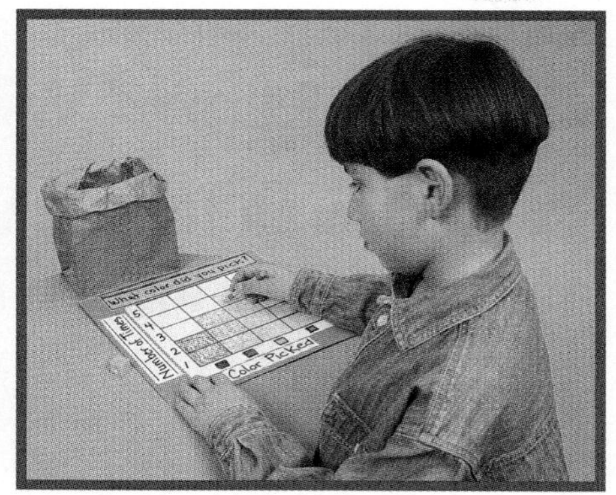

Color a box in the graph to show the cube you picked.

Put the cube back each time. Do this until one color has been picked 5 times.

1. How many times was red picked?

   ______ times

2. How many times was green picked?

   ______ times

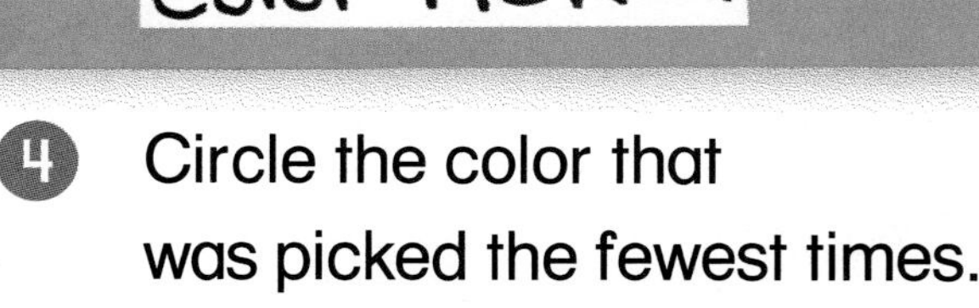

3. Circle the color that was picked the most.

   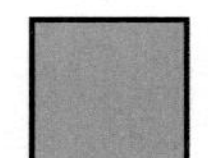

4. Circle the color that was picked the fewest times.

Problem Solving Critical Thinking

5. How else could you show which cubes you picked?

Notes for Home: Your child did an activity that assessed Chapter 1 skills, concepts, and problem solving. *Home Activity:* Ask your child to use the words <u>more</u> and <u>fewer</u> to tell about his or her graph.

Name ________________________________

Use the World Wide Web

Computer Skills You Will Need

You can use the Internet to get different kinds of information.

1. Go to: www.mathsurf.com/2. **Click** on Chapter 1.
   This activity can tell you about favorite things of second graders.
2. **Click** Forward and Backward to get from screen to screen.
3. What did you learn from this activity?

   ____

Use the information you found on the Internet.
Write 2 questions that you could ask about favorite topics.

4. ________________________________

   ____

5. ________________________________

   ____

6. Exchange your questions with a friend.
   Answer each other's questions.

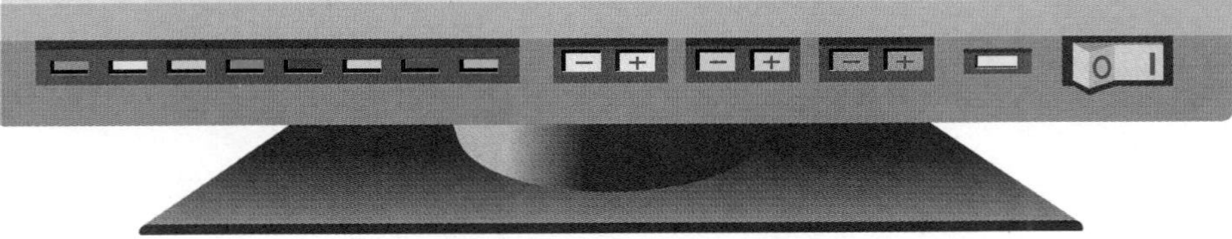

Tech Talk How is clicking Forward and Backward like turning a page in a book? How is it different?

Visit our Web site. **www.parent.mathsurf.com**

Math at Home

Mystery Jar

To win many contests, you must guess the number of things in a jar. Have your own contest at home. Make your own Mystery Jar.

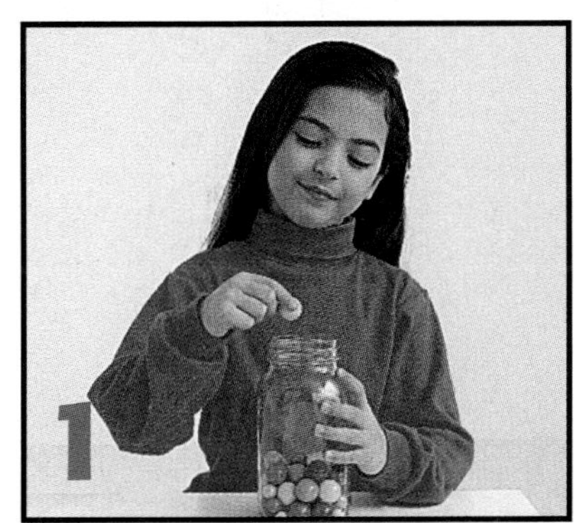

1

Fill a container with marbles. Do not count them.

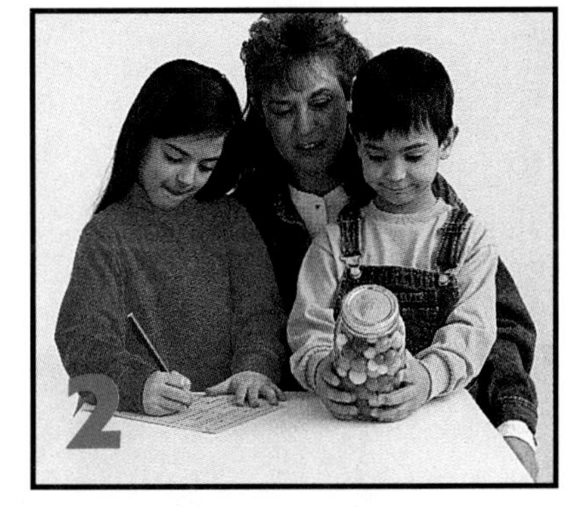

2

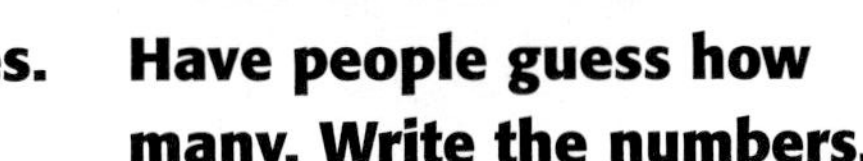

Have people guess how many. Write the numbers.

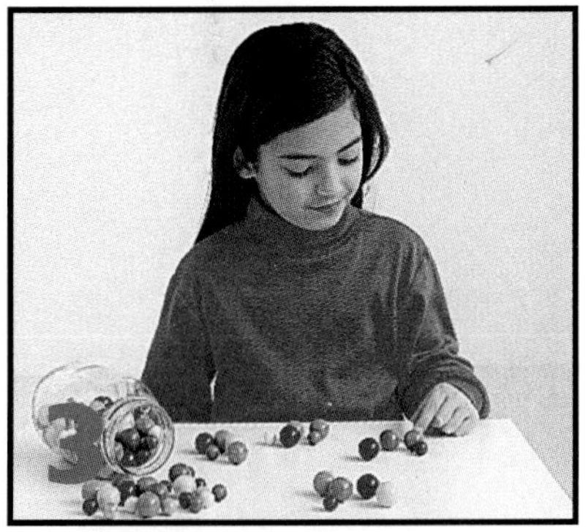

3

Count the marbles. Try counting by 2s, 5s, or 10s.

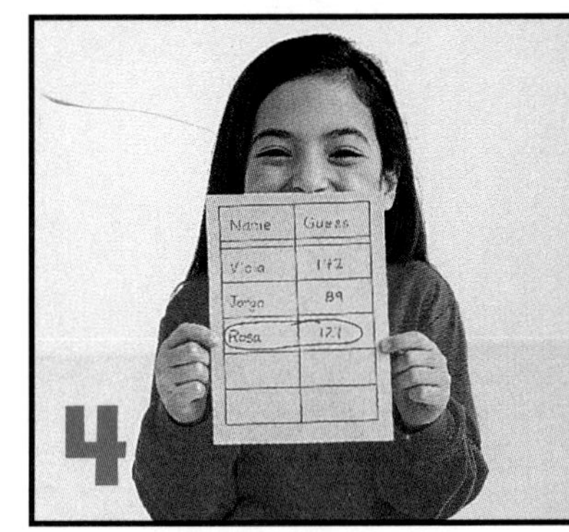

4

The nearest guess wins.

Fold down

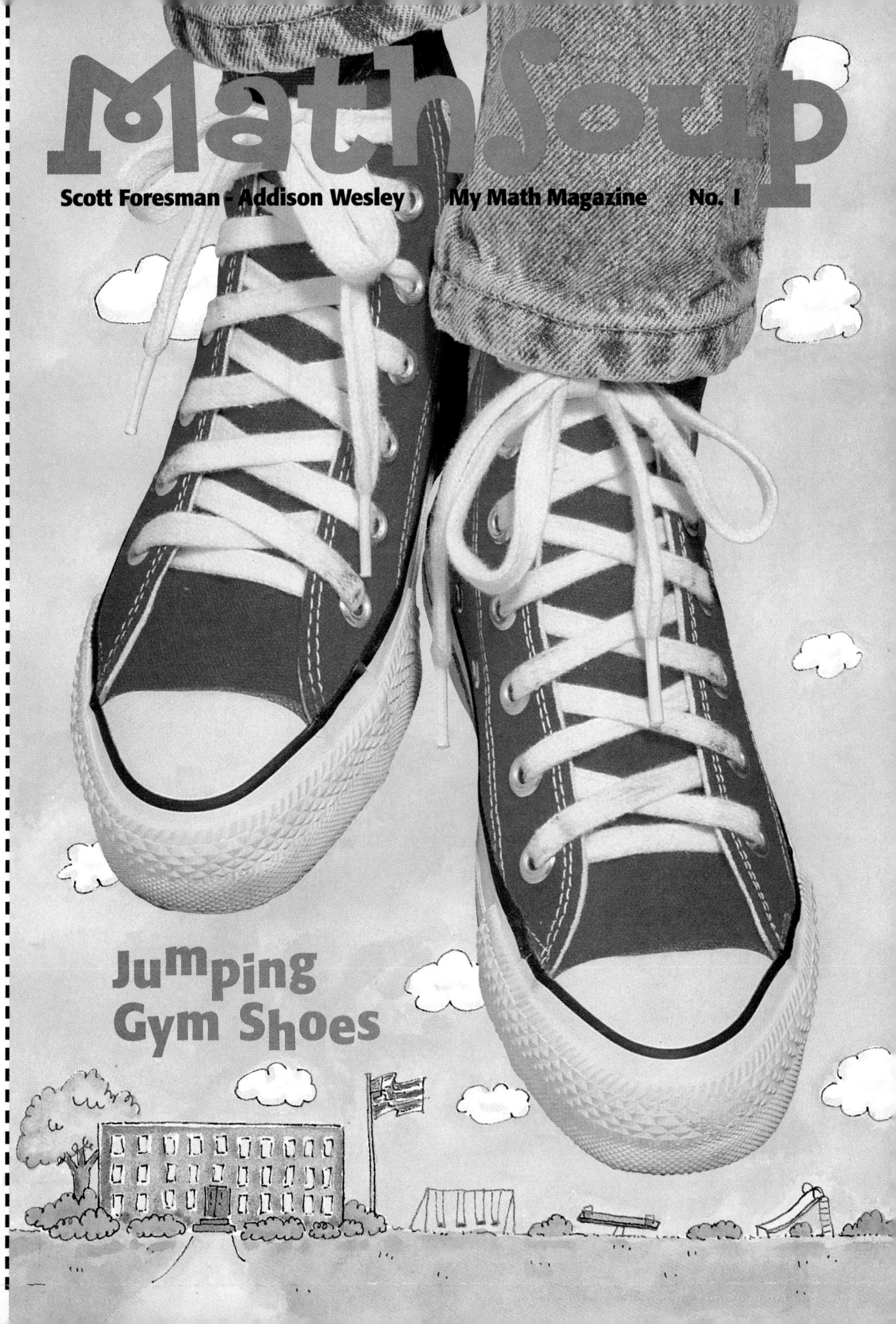

MathSoup
Scott Foresman - Addison Wesley
My Math Magazine
No. 1
Jumping
Gym Shoes

Show Your Shoes

A diagram can show all the places children wear gym shoes. Use the diagram to answer these questions.

1 How many children wear gym shoes at school, at home, and for outdoor activities?

______

2 How many children do not wear gym shoes at school?

______

Notes for Home: Your child used a diagram to solve problems. *Home Activity:* Ask your child which children on the diagram wear gym shoes only at school and at home. (Anne, Bruno)

Banana Power

Bananas help to give you energy. The graph shows how many bananas you need to do different activities. Use the graph to solve the problems.

1 How many bananas do you need to swim for 1 hour?

_____ bananas

2 How many more bananas do you need to run for 1 hour than to swim?

_____ more bananas

3 Make up your own question. Give it to a friend to answer.

Notes for Home: Your child used a graph to solve problems.
Home Activity: Ask your child which activity requires more energy from food, swimming or biking. (swimming)

Where Do You Wear Gym Shoes?

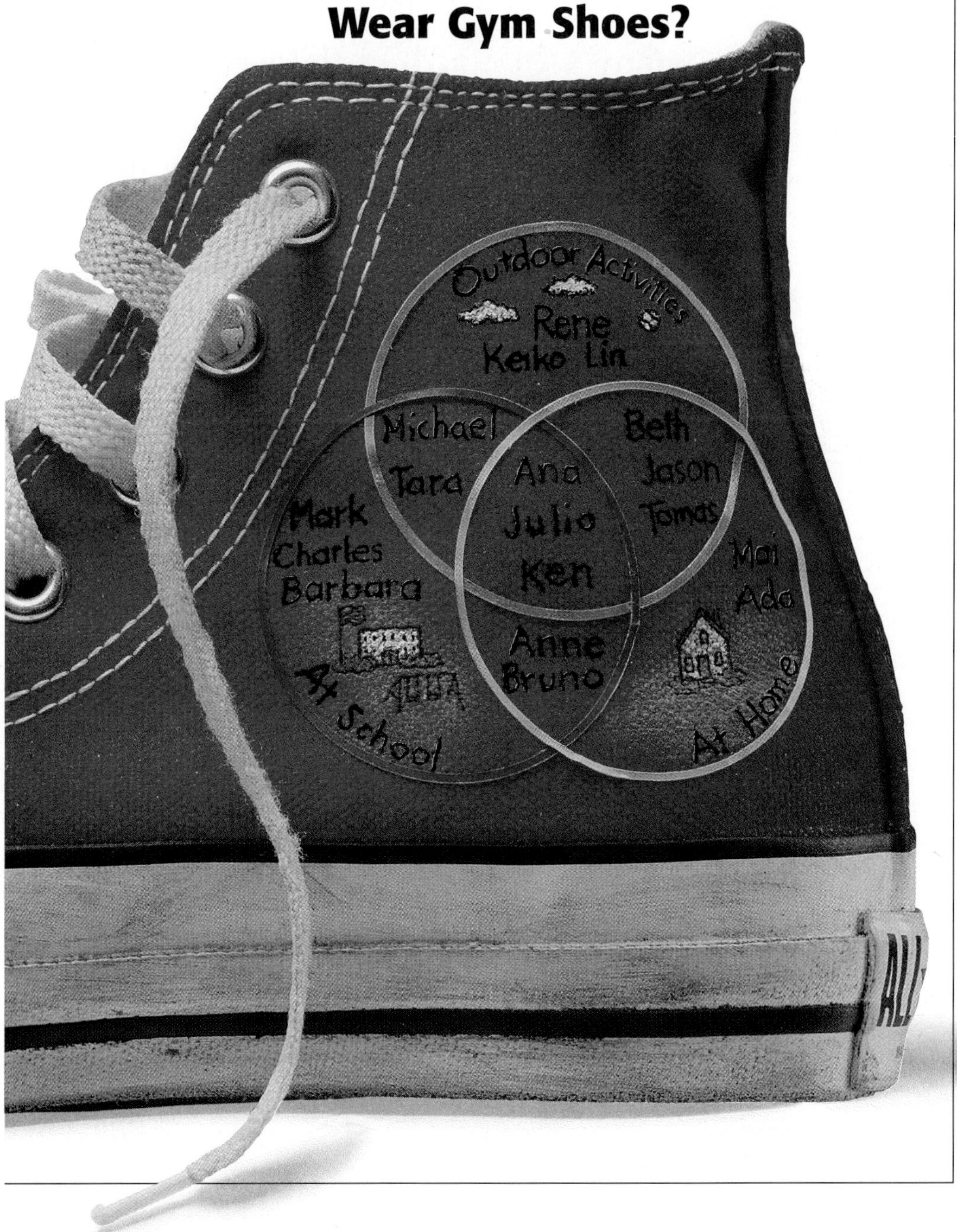

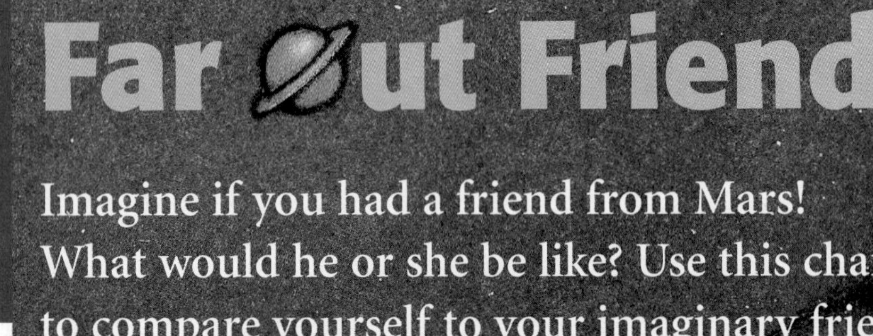

Far Out Friends

Imagine if you had a friend from Mars! What would he or she be like? Use this chart to compare yourself to your imaginary friend from Mars.

	You	Friend From Mars	Who Has More?	How Many More?
Eyes	2	5	Friend	3
Fingers				
Arms				
Noses				
Legs				

Use this space to draw a picture of yourself.

Me

Use this space to draw a picture of your friend.

My Friend From Mars

Your friend from Mars has 7 friends each with 5 eyes. How many eyes would the 7 friends have in all? Count by 5s.

Notes for Home: Your child completed a chart and used that chart to draw pictures. *Home Activity:* Ask your child how many arms 5 friends from Mars would have.

CHAPTER 2

Addition and Subtraction: Patterns and Concepts

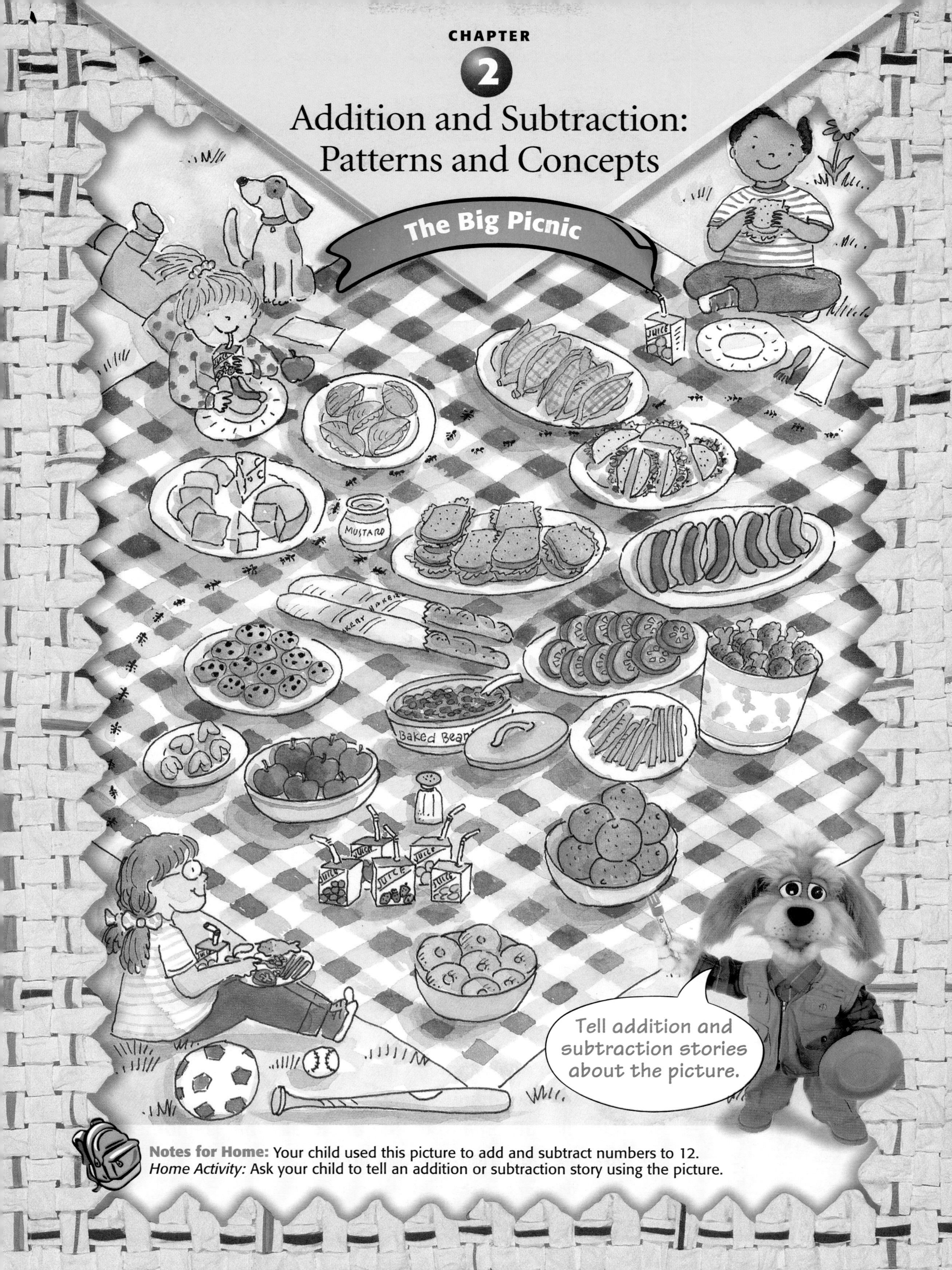

Notes for Home: Your child used this picture to add and subtract numbers to 12.
Home Activity: Ask your child to tell an addition or subtraction story using the picture.

Dear Family,
Our class is starting Chapter 2. We will learn about patterns, adding, and subtracting. We will tell math stories about numbers to 12. We can do these activities together at home.

Give and Take

Ask your child to make up addition and subtraction stories using items in your home. For example: I have 8 books on the table. I take 2 off. I have 6 left.

The Name Game

Find 8 common objects, such as spoons. Ask your child to find different ways to put the objects into two groups (for example, 2 and 6, 3 and 5). Repeat the activity with 9 objects.

Community Connection

While you are waiting in line at a store, ask your child to count how many adults and how many children are in the line. Then add to find the total. What is another way to group the people in line?

Visit our Web site. www.parent.mathsurf.com

Name

Explore Addition Stories

Explore

Use [counters] to show two groups of ants.
Tell addition stories about a picnic.
Show your story.

Share

Tell your story.

Notes for Home: Your child used counters to tell addition stories about a picnic.
Home Activity: Ask your child to tell you an addition story using small objects.

EXPLORE

Connect

5 .

4 more .

5 and 4 is 9.

Solve each problem. You can use  .

1. 3 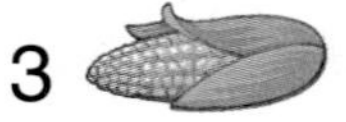 on a plate.

   4 more are added.

   How many 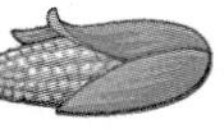 in all?

   3 and 4 is 7.

2. 6  on Mia's plate.

   4 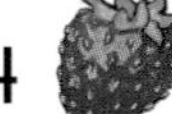 on Kayla's plate.

   How many  in all?

   _____ and _____ is _____.

3. 7  .

   Lee brings 2 more  .

   How many  in all?

   _____ and _____ is _____.

4. 3  .

   Bob brings 1 more  .

   How many  in all?

   _____ and _____ is _____.

Talk About It Tell a number story about the picture.

Notes for Home: Your child solved addition problems. *Home Activity:* Ask your child to tell you an addition story about 2 ants and 4 ants.

EXPLORE

Name

Join Groups to Add

Learn

3  on a leaf.

6  come.

How many in all?

When you add, the answer is called the **sum**.

3 and 6 is 9.

3 + 6 = 9

Check

Use   and 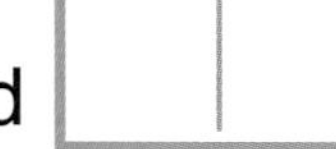 to add.

Write the number sentence.

1. 3 .

   2 more  join them.

   How many  in all?

   3 and 2 is 5.

   3 + 2 = 5

2. 5 are eating.

   5 more  come.

   How many  in all?

   _____ and _____ is _____.

   _____ + _____ = _____

3. 4  are on a leaf.

   1 more  joins them.

   How many  in all?

   _____ and _____ is _____.

   _____ + _____ = _____

Talk About It What is the greatest sum in the problems above?

Notes for Home: Your child used counters to show math stories and wrote number sentences.
Home Activity: Ask your child to use objects, such as buttons, to show you how to solve Exercise 3.

Practice

You can use   and a .

Write the number sentence. Solve.

4. 4  are near the food.

   5 more  come.

   How many  are there now?

   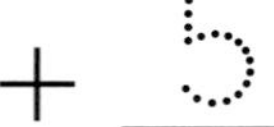 4 +  5 = 9 

5. 1  is on a flower.

   2 fly to the flower.

   How many  in all?

   ____ + ____ = ____ 

6. 7  are playing.

   2  come to play.

   How many  in all?

   ____ + ____ = ____ 

7. 6  are swimming.

   6 more  come to swim.

   How many  are swimming?

   ____ + ____ = ____ 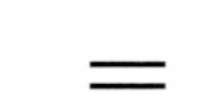 

8. Dave ate 4 .

   Sal ate 2 .

   How many  did they eat in all?

   ____ + ____ = ____ 

9. Dan has 3  .

   He finds 8 more .

   How many  does he have now?

   ____ + ____ = ____ 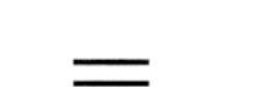 

Problem Solving Critical Thinking

Solve. You can use  .

10. There are 10 in all.

    How many  are in the basket?

    ____ 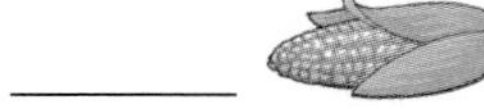

Notes for Home: Your child wrote number sentences for addition stories. *Home Activity:* Ask your child to tell you how he or she solved Exercise 8. (Sample answer: I put down 4 counters. Then I put down 2 more. 4 + 2 = 6)

Name

Turnaround Facts

Learn

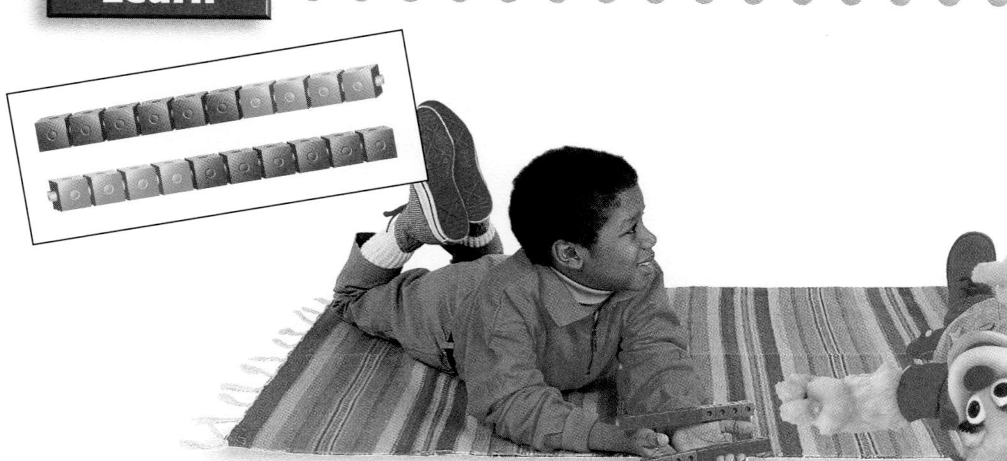

Check

Use [cubes] to make each train. Color.

1. 3 + 4 = 7

   4 + 3 = 7

2. 2 + 7 = 9

   7 + 2 = 9

3. 8 + 3 = 11

   3 + 8 = 11

4. 6 + 2 = 8

   2 + 6 = 8

Talk About It How are these alike? How are they different?

5 + 6 = 11
6 + 5 = 11

Notes for Home: Your child used turnaround facts, such as 6 + 2 and 2 + 6, to find sums.
Home Activity: Ask your child to write two addition sentences using the numbers 5, 6, and 11. (5 + 6 = 11; 6 + 5 = 11)

Practice

Write the number sentence for each train.

5 

4 + 7 = 11

7 + 4 = 11

6 

____

____

7 

____

____

8 

____

____

PRACTICE

Write the turnaround fact for each number sentence.

9 7 + 3 = 10

____

10 5 + 4 = 9

____

Problem Solving

Write the number sentence. Solve.

11 8 children were playing baseball.
4 more children joined them.
How many children were playing in all?

____ + ____ = ____ children

12 4 children were eating lunch.
8 more children came to eat.
Now how many children were eating lunch?

____ + ____ = ____ children

Notes for Home: Your child used turnaround facts to find sums to 12. *Home Activity:* Ask your child to tell you a pair of turnaround facts with the sum of 10. (Sample answer: 4 + 6 and 6 + 4)

Name

Ways to Make Numbers

Learn

You can show 5 in many ways.

Ways to Make 5
$0 + 5 = 5$
$1 + 4 = 5$
$2 + 3 = 5$
$3 + 2 = 5$
$4 + 1 = 5$
$5 + 0 = 5$

Check

Use [cubes]. Show different ways to make 6.
Write the number sentences.

1. 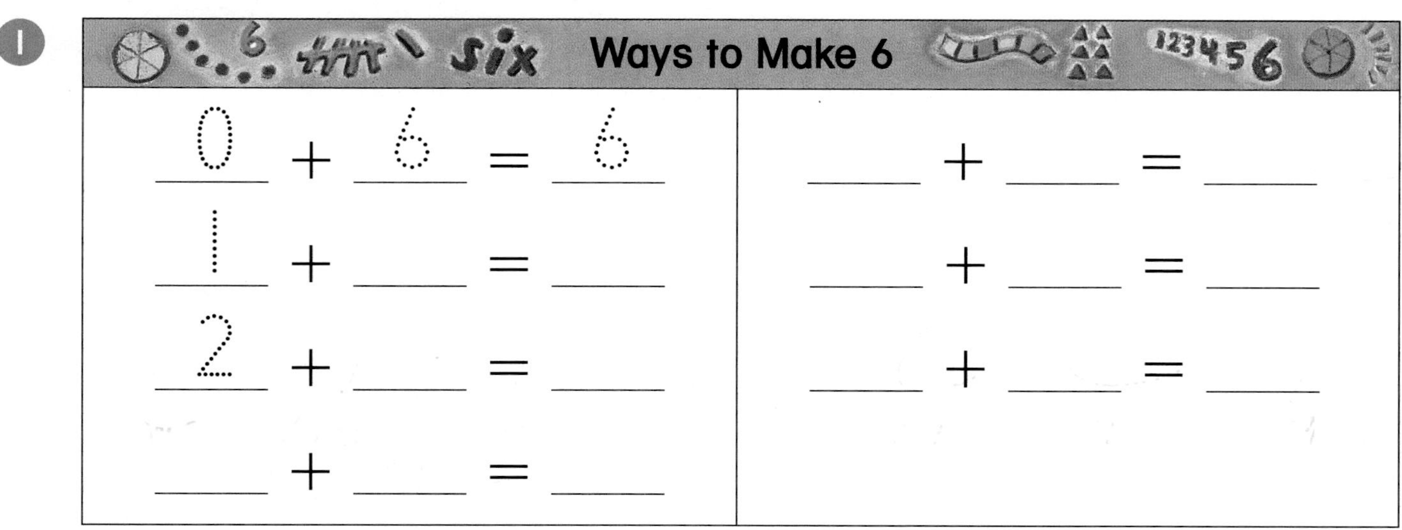

Ways to Make 6	
0 + 6 = 6	___ + ___ = ___
1 + ___ = ___	___ + ___ = ___
2 + ___ = ___	___ + ___ = ___
___ + ___ = ___	

Talk About It What patterns do you see?

Notes for Home: Your child found all the pairs of numbers that add to make 6. *Home Activity:* Ask your child to tell you one way to make 6. (Sample answer: 2 + 4 = 6)

Practice

Use [cubes]. Show different ways to make 7.
Write the number sentences.

2

Ways to Make 7	
0 + 7 = 7	___ + ___ = ___
___ + ___ = ___	___ + ___ = ___
___ + ___ = ___	___ + ___ = ___
___ + ___ = ___	___ + ___ = ___

Problem Solving Patterns

3. How many ways are there to make 5? ______

4. How many ways are there to make 6? ______

5. How many ways are there to make 7? ______

6. How many ways do you think there are to make 8? ______

7. How many ways do you think there are to make 9? ______

8. Why do you think so?

____

____

PRACTICE

Notes for Home: Your child found all the pairs of numbers that add to make 7. *Home Activity:* Ask your child what patterns he or she can find in the Ways to Make 7 chart. (Sample answer: The first number in each number sentence increases by one.)

Name ________________________________

Problem Solving: Write a Number Sentence

Learn

PROBLEM SOLVING GUIDE

Understand • Plan • Solve • Look Back

Write a number sentence. Solve.

5 children are eating lunch.
2 children join them.
How many children are eating lunch now?

5 + 2 = 7 children

Check

Write a number sentence. Solve. You can use ⚫ ⚪.

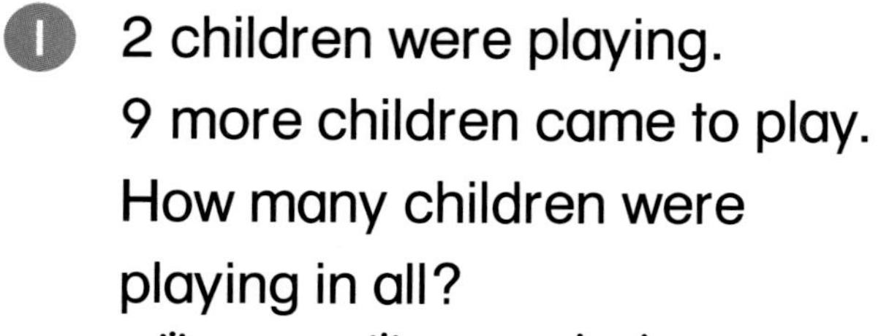

1. 2 children were playing.
9 more children came to play.
How many children were playing in all?

2 + 9 = 11 children

2. 6 children are riding bicycles.
4 children join them.
How many children are riding bicycles now?

______________ children

3. Luis found 8 sticks.
Ming found 4 sticks.
How many sticks did they find in all?

______________ sticks

4. 6 kites were stuck in the tree.
6 more kites got stuck.
How many kites are stuck now?

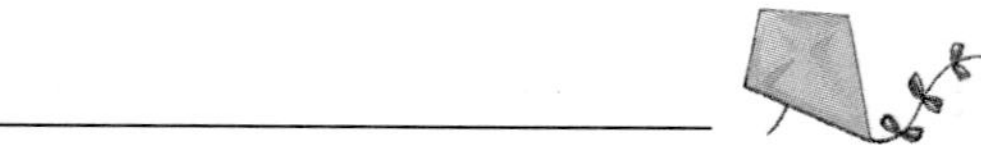

______________ kites

Talk About It What other number sentence could you use to solve the problem about bicycles?

Notes for Home: Your child wrote number sentences to solve story problems. *Home Activity:* Ask your child to make up a story problem and tell a number sentence that can be used to solve it.

Practice

Write your own. Complete each sentence.
Write a number sentence. You can use .

5 _____ are swimming.

_____ more join them.

How many are swimming now?

_______________ 

6 _____ were playing.

_____ more  joined them.

How many were playing in all?

____

7 There were _____ in a tree.

_____ more flew to the tree.

How many are in the tree now?

____

8 Pedro saw _____  in a bush

and _____  near the pond.

How many  did he see in all?

_______________ 

Tell a Math Story

9 Use the picture. Tell an addition story to a friend. Ask your friend to solve by writing a number sentence.

_____ + _____ = _____

Notes for Home: Your child practiced writing number sentences to solve story problems. *Home Activity:* Ask your child to tell you another word problem for the picture. Have your child write a number sentence that could be used to solve it.

Name ____________________

Mixed Practice

Lessons 1–6

Concepts and Skills

Add. You can use 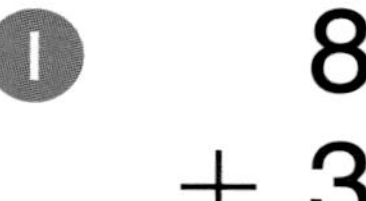 .

1.

8	6	12	4	9	7	10
+ 3	+ 4	+ 0	+ 2	+ 3	+ 2	+ 1

These pictures show turnaround facts.
Write the number sentence for each picture.

2. 

____

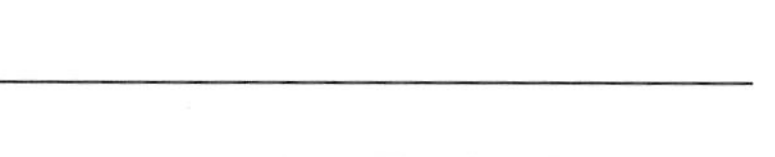

____

3. 

____

____

Problem Solving

Write a number sentence. Solve. You can use  .

4. Tara saw 5 children at the swings.
She saw 4 children at the pond.
How many children did she see in all?

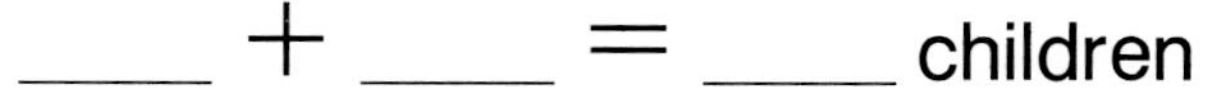

____ + ____ = ____ children

5. 2 children were playing tag.
5 more children came to play.
Now how many children were playing?

____ + ____ = ____ children

Journal

6. How can you use turnaround facts to help you find sums?

Notes for Home: Your child practiced addition and problem-solving skills. *Home Activity:* Ask your child how the number sentences in Exercise 2 are alike and how they are different. (Sample answer: They both have the same sum; the numbers are in a different order.)

For additional practice, see Basic Facts Review, page 540, Set 1.

MIXED PRACTICE

Name ____________________

Cumulative Review

Chapters 1–2

Concepts and Skills

Count by ones. Write the numbers.

1. 23, 24, 25, ____, ____, ____, ____, ____, ____, ____

Count back by ones. Write the numbers.

2. 17, 16, 15, ____, ____, ____, ____, ____, ____, ____

Problem Solving

3. Use the tally marks to make a bar graph.

Votes for Favorite Picnic Foods

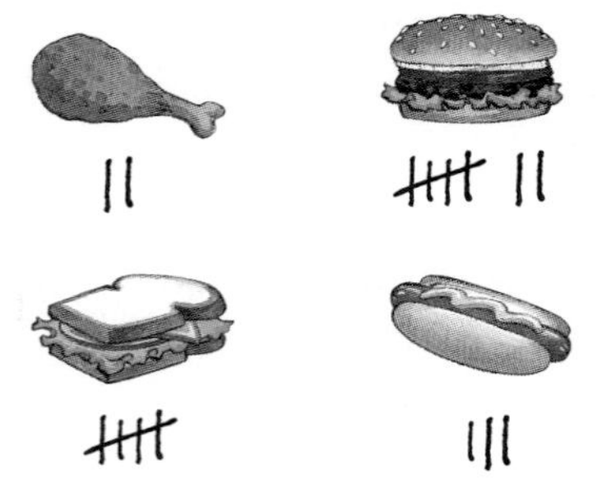

chicken: ||
hamburger: ||||/ ||
sandwich: ||||/
hot dog: |||

Favorite Picnic Foods

8				
7				
6				
5				
4				
3				
2				
1				
	chicken	hamburger	sandwich	hot dog

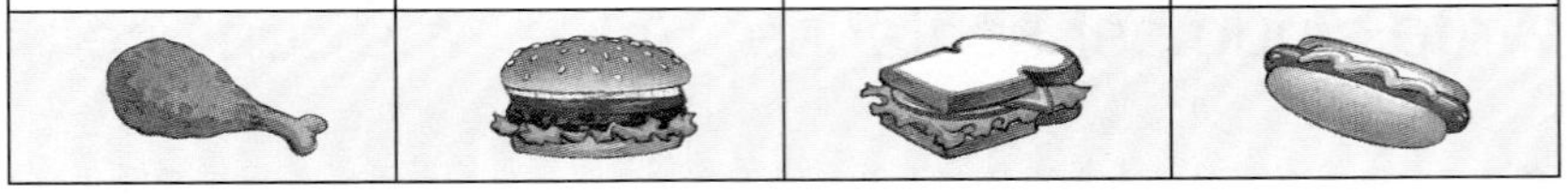

4. How many people chose ? ____ people

5. Which food was chosen the most? Circle the picture.

Test Prep

Fill in the ○ for the correct answer.
Find the missing number in the pattern.

6. 3, 6, 9, ____, 15, 18, 21, 24

○ 10
○ 11
○ 12
○ 13

Notes for Home: Your child reviewed counting, using tally marks and graphs, and finding number patterns. *Home Activity:* Ask your child to tell which food was chosen more in Exercise 3, hamburger or hot dog. (hamburger)

Name

Separate Groups to Subtract

Learn

10  are in the tree.

3  leave.

How many 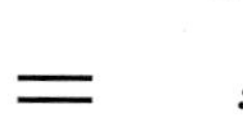 are still in the tree?

10 – 3 = 7 

Check

Use   to subtract.
Write the number sentence.

1. 9  are on a stick.
   5  fly away.
   How many  are there now?
   9 – 5 = 4  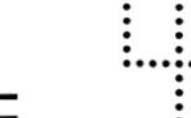

2. 8  are swimming.
   2  swim away.
   How many  are still there?
   ____ – ____ = ____ 

3. 11  are in the bush.
   2  fly away.
   How many  are still in the bush?
   ____ – ____ = ____ 

4. 12   are in the grass.
   4  hop away.
   How many  are still in the grass?
   ____ – ____ = ____ 

Talk About It What is the greatest difference in the problems above?

Notes for Home: Your child used counters and wrote number sentences to subtract.
Home Activity: Ask your child to use objects, such as pennies, to show 9 – 3 = 6.

Practice

Use counters to subtract.
Write the number sentence.

5. 7  are playing.
2  run away.
How many  are left?
7 – 2 = 5 

6. 10  are in a bowl.
Stan eats 5 .
How many 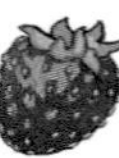 are left?
___ – ___ = ___

7. 9  are in the grass.
6  run away.
How many  are left?
___ – ___ = ___

8.  11  are on the plate.
Jo takes 4  away.
How many  are left?
___ – ___ = ___ 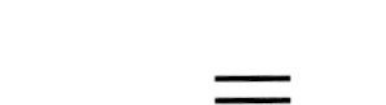

Problem Solving Visual Thinking

Draw a picture to solve.
Write the number sentence.

9. There are 8 .
3  are left on the tree.
How many  flew away?
___ – ___ = ___ 

Notes for Home: Your child used counters to subtract and then wrote number sentences.
Home Activity: Ask your child to use small objects to act out a subtraction story.

PRACTICE

Name

Explore How Many More

Explore

Use [dark counter] to show apples.
Use [light counter] to show bananas.
Tell a story about which group has more.

Use a different number of [dark counter] and [light counter] to show food.
Tell new stories about which group has more.

Draw one of your stories.

Share

Tell one of your stories.

Notes for Home: Your child told stories about comparing two groups using this picture.
Home Activity: Have your child tell you one of his or her stories.

EXPLORE

Use  to solve.

1. There are 8 on the table.
   There are 7 on the table.
   How many more are there?

   ______ more

2. There are 6 .
   There are 4 .
   How many more are there?

   ______ more

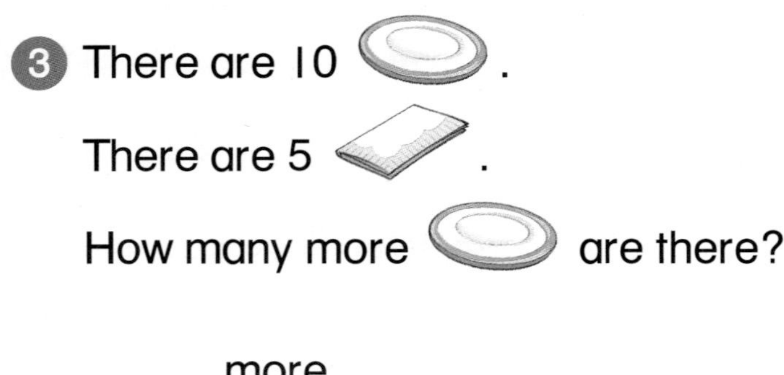

3. There are 10 .
   There are 5 .
   How many more are there?

   ______ more

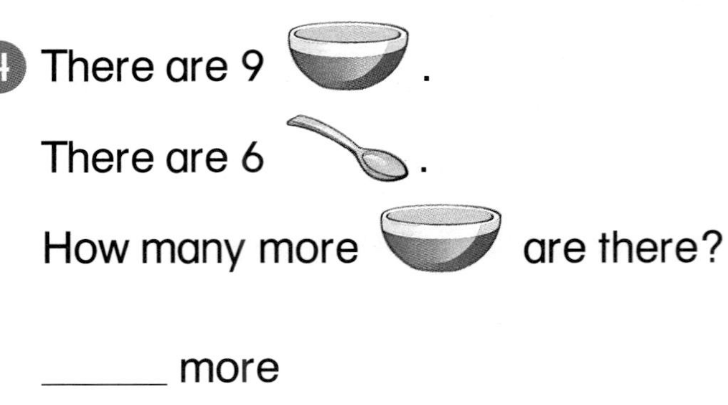

4. There are 9 .
   There are 6 .
   How many more are there?

   ______ more

Problem Solving Visual Thinking

5. How many more than ?

   ______ more

6. How many more than ?

   ______ more

Notes for Home: Your child used counters to compare groups. *Home Activity:* Ask your child to take some spoons and some forks and compare how many are in the two groups.

EXPLORE

Name

Find How Many More

Learn

How many more  than ?

Check

Write the number sentence. Solve.

You can use .

1. How many more than ?

9 − 8 = 1 more

2. How many more  than ?

___ − ___ = ___ more

3. How many more  than ?

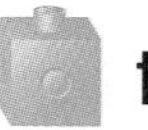

___ − ___ = ___ more

4. How many more  than ?

___ − ___ = ___ more

Talk About It Can you solve these problems without writing a number sentence? Explain.

Notes for Home: Your child used subtraction to compare groups. *Home Activity:* Ask your child to make a group of 9 objects and a group of 5 objects. Have your child write a number sentence to find which group has more. (9 − 5 = 4; 4 more)

Practice

Write the number sentence. Solve.

You can use .

5. Jan found 10 .
   Don found 3 .
   How many more  did Jan find?
   10 − 3 = 7 more

6. John had 11 .
   Ben had 5 .
   How many more  did John have than Ben?
   ____ − ____ = ____ more

7. Al saw 12 .
   Maria saw 7 .
   How many more  did Al see than Maria?
   ____ − ____ = ____ more

8. Jane saw 8 .
   Pat saw 6 .
   How many more  did Jane see?
   ____ − ____ = ____ more

PRACTICE

Problem Solving Visual Thinking

9. Draw less than 10  on the leaf.
   How many more  than ?
   Write a number sentence.
   ____ − ____ = ____ more

Notes for Home: Your child practiced using subtraction to compare groups. *Home Activity:* Show your child two groups of objects, such as 8 forks and 5 spoons. Have your child write a number sentence that tells how many more are in the larger group. (Sample answer: 8 − 5 = 3)

Name ______________________________

Relate Addition and Subtraction

Learn

You have 7 . You get 4 more.

How many  in all?

7 + 4 = 11

You have 11 . You give  away.

How many  do you have now?

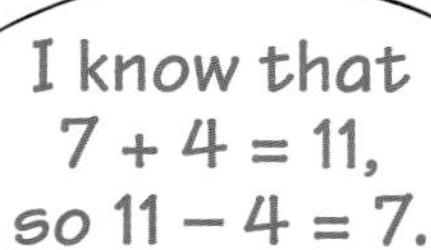

11 − 4 = 7

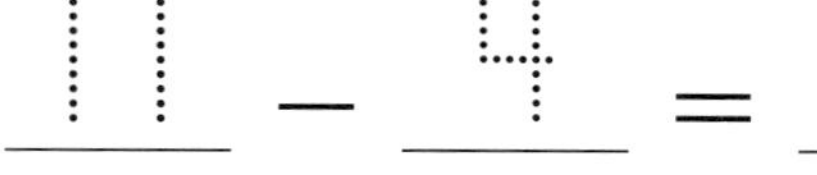

Check

Add or subtract.
Write the number sentence. Solve.

1. Sam had 5 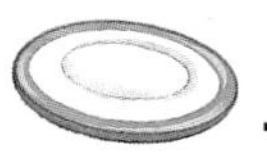.

   Carol came with 6 more.

   How many  in all?

   ___ + ___ = ___ 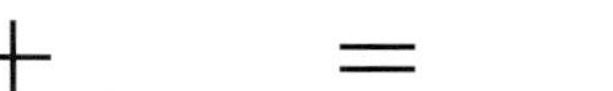

2. Sam and Carol had 11 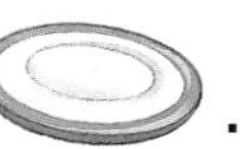.

   Carol took away 6 .

   How many  does Sam have now?

   ___ − ___ = ___ 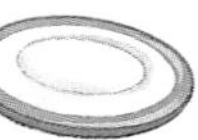

Talk About It How can you use addition to help you solve 9 − 3?

Notes for Home: Your child used related addition and subtraction facts to solve problems.
Home Activity: Use items, such as beans, to act out Exercises 1 and 2 with your child.

Practice

Add or subtract.

Write the number sentence. Solve.

3. 4 cups were on the table.

Lee came with 6 more.

How many  were there in all?

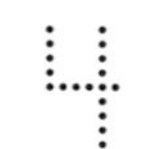    

4 + 6 = 10

4. 10 cups were on the table.

Lee took 6 .

How many  were left?

___ − ___ = ___

5. Ken found 3 .

Eva found 9 .

How many  did they find in all?

___ + ___ = ___

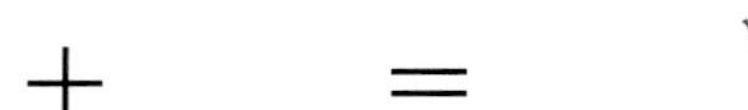

6. There were 12 .

Eva took 9 away.

How many  were left?

___ − ___ = ___ 

7. Manny found 2 .

Lisa found 9 .

How many  did they find in all?

___ + ___ = ___

8. There were 11 .

Lisa took 9 away.

How many  were left?

___ − ___ = ___ 

Tell a Math Story

Look at the picture. Tell stories to match the number sentences.

9. $2 + 5 = 7$

10. $7 - 5 = 2$

Notes for Home: Your child solved word problems. *Home Activity:* Ask your child to say a related subtraction sentence for 2 + 7 = 9. (9 − 7 = 2 or 9 − 2 = 7)

PRACTICE

Name ______________________________

Reading for Math

Compare and Contrast

Use the picture.
Tell addition stories.
Tell subtraction stories.

1. How are addition and subtraction stories alike?

____

____

2. How are addition and subtraction stories different?

____

____

Notes for Home: Your child compared addition and subtraction stories. *Home Activity:* Show your child some items, such as pens and pencils. Ask your child to make up an addition story and a subtraction story using the items.

Use the picture. Tell an addition story.

3 How do you know it is an addition story?

____

____

Tell a subtraction story.

4 How do you know it is a subtraction story?

____

____

Talk About It Tell an addition story and a subtraction story about the same group of people in the picture.

Notes for Home: Your child talked about the differences between addition and subtraction. *Home Activity:* Ask your child to draw a simple picture and tell addition and subtraction stories about it.

Name

Problem Solving: Choose an Operation

Learn

PROBLEM SOLVING GUIDE

Understand • Plan • Solve • Look Back

5 children are flying kites.
3 more children join them.
How many children are flying kites in all?

5 + 3 = 8 children

8 children are flying kites.
3 children go home.
How many children are left?

8 − 3 = 5 children

Check

Circle **add** or **subtract**. Write the number sentence.
Solve. You can use .

1. 10  are in the grass.
2  hop away.
How many  are still in the grass?

add **subtract** (circled)

10 − 2 = 8 

2. There were 6 .
3 more  came.
How many  were there in all?

add **subtract**

______ 

Talk About It How did you decide whether to add or subtract in the problem about bees?

Notes for Home: Your child chose addition or subtraction to solve problems. *Home Activity:* Ask your child to tell a math story that would be solved by adding.

PROBLEM SOLVING

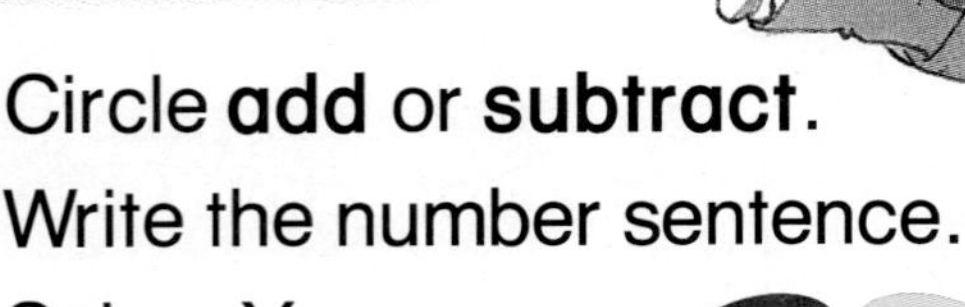

Practice

Circle **add** or **subtract**.
Write the number sentence.
Solve. You can use 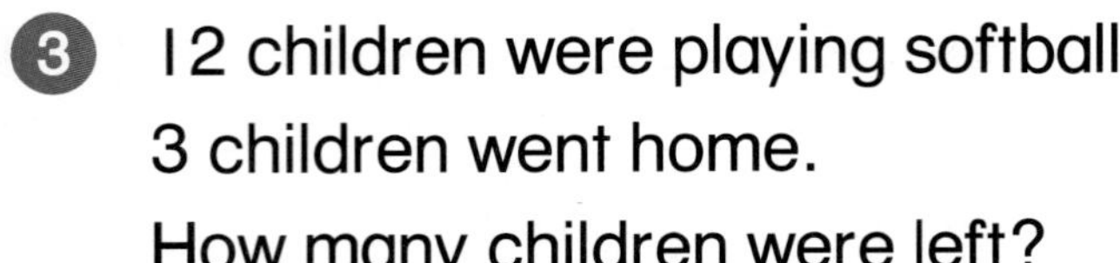.

3. 12 children were playing softball.
3 children went home.
How many children were left?

add **subtract**

12 − 3 = 9 children

4. Nora saw 2 .
Lucy saw 8 .
How many 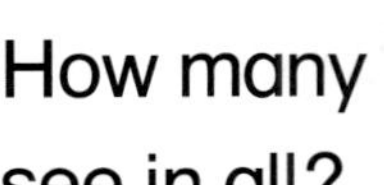 did they see in all?

add **subtract**

________________ 

5. Pam ate 7 .
Her sister ate 5 .
How many  did they eat all together?

add **subtract**

____

6. 8 children played on the swings.
8 children got off.
How many children were left?

add **subtract**

________________ children

Write About It

7. Make up your own story.
Have a friend write a number sentence to solve it.

Notes for Home: Your child practiced choosing addition or subtraction to solve problems.
Home Activity: Ask your child to make up a problem that could be solved by subtracting.

PROBLEM SOLVING

For additional practice, see Skills Practice Bank, page 528, Set 3.

Name ______________________________

Mixed Practice

Lessons 7–12

Concepts and Skills

Subtract. You can use .

5	9	4	2	12	5	11
− 1	− 3	− 4	− 1	− 3	− 3	− 0

Problem Solving

Subtract. Write the number sentence.

You can use .

 Carl found 10 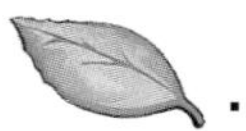.

 4 blew away.

 How many  are left?

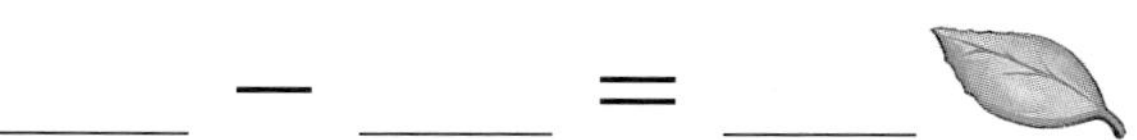

____ − ____ = ____

 8  are in the grass.

4  run away.

 How many  are left?

____ − ____ = ____

Circle **add** or **subtract**. Write a number sentence.

Solve. You can use .

 8 children are riding bicycles.
4 children join them.
How many children are riding now?

add **subtract**

__________ children

5 7 children are on the swings.
2 children get off.
How many children are left?

add **subtract**

__________ children

Journal

6 Write your own word problem using the numbers 3, 5, and 8. Would you add or subtract to solve it? Write the number sentence.

Notes for Home: Your child practiced subtraction and problem-solving skills. *Home Activity:* Ask your child to tell a story using the number sentence in Exercise 3.

For additional practice, see Basic Facts Review, page 540, Set 2.

Name ____________________

Cumulative Review

Chapters 1–2

Concepts and Skills

Write the number sentence. Solve.

 9  are on the rock.

4  jump off.

How many  are still on the rock?

 ___ − ___ = ___ 

 2  are on the table.

8 are in the basket.

How many  are there in all?

___ + ___ = ___ 

Count by ones. Write the numbers.

3. 47, 48, 49, ___, ___, ___, ___, ___, ___

Count back by ones. Write the numbers.

4. 24, 23, 22, ___, ___, ___, ___, ___, ___

Test Prep

Fill in the ○ for the correct answer.

5. Which train and number sentence show the turnaround fact for the train and number sentence below?

2 + 9 = 11

○ 
7 + 4 = 11

○ 
8 + 3 = 11

○ 
9 + 2 = 11

Notes for Home: Your child reviewed addition and subtraction skills. *Home Activity:* Ask your child to tell what the next three numbers would be in Exercise 4. (Answer: 15, 14, 13)

Name ______________________________

Chapter 2 Review

Vocabulary

1. Find the sum. $7 + 5 =$ ____

2. Find the difference. $10 - 4 =$ ____

3. Write the turnaround fact.

   $3 + 5 = 8$ ______________

Concepts and Skills

Write the number sentence. Solve.

4. 4 children are playing catch. 5 more children join them. How many children are playing now?

   ____ + ____ = ____ children

5. Ben found 10 shells. Ann found 2 shells. How many more shells did Ben find than Ann?

   ____ − ____ = ____ more

Problem Solving

Write the number sentence. Solve.

6. 12 cups are on the table. Sandy takes 5 cups away. How many cups are there now?

7. 8 children were eating lunch. 1 child finished. How many children were still eating?

   ______________ children

Notes for Home: Your child reviewed Chapter 2 vocabulary, concepts, skills, and problem solving. *Home Activity:* Ask your child to tell how he or she solved Exercise 5.

CHAPTER REVIEW

Name ______________________________

Chapter 2 Test

Write the turnaround fact. Solve.

1. 5 + 3 = 8

____

2. 9 + 1 = 10

____

Circle **add** or **subtract.**
Write a number sentence. Solve.

3. Beth found 11 .

Eric found 3 .

How many more 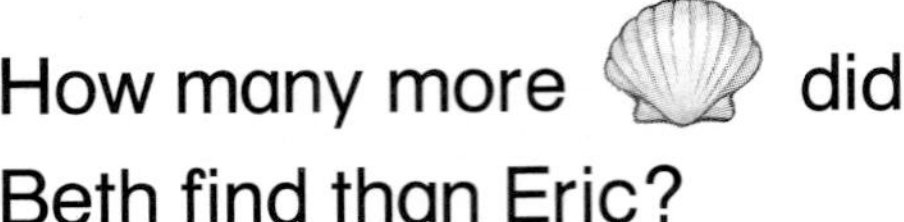 did
Beth find than Eric?

add **subtract**

______________ more

Add or subtract.

4.

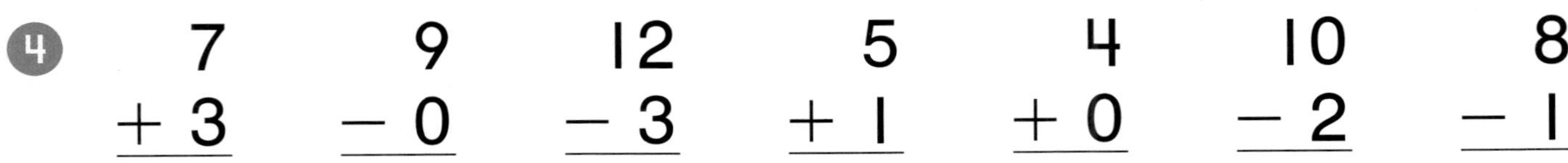

7	9	12	5	4	10	8
+ 3	− 0	− 3	+ 1	+ 0	− 2	− 1

Show two ways to make 8.

5. ____ + ____ = ____

6. ____ + ____ = ____

Write the number sentence. Solve.

7. There were 5 children on the swings. 4 more children got on. How many children were there in all?

______________ children

8. There were 9 children on the swings. 4 children got off. How many children were left?

______________ children

Notes for Home: Your child was tested on Chapter 2 concepts, skills, and problem solving.
Home Activity: Ask your child how he or she decided what number sentence to write for Exercise 8.

Name ________________________________

Show What You Know

Performance Assessment

Chapter 2

Write a story problem.

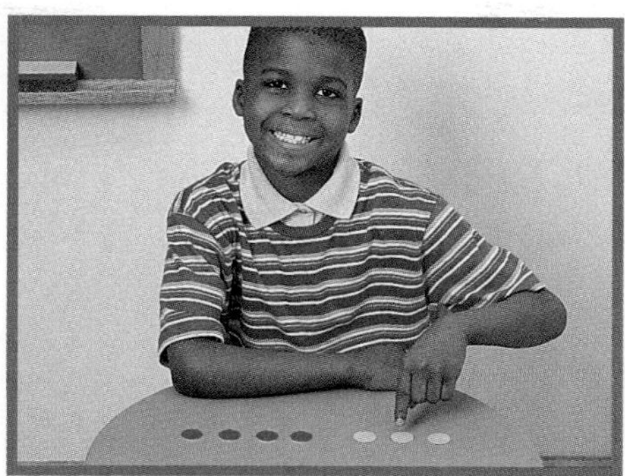

Use counters to show the problem.

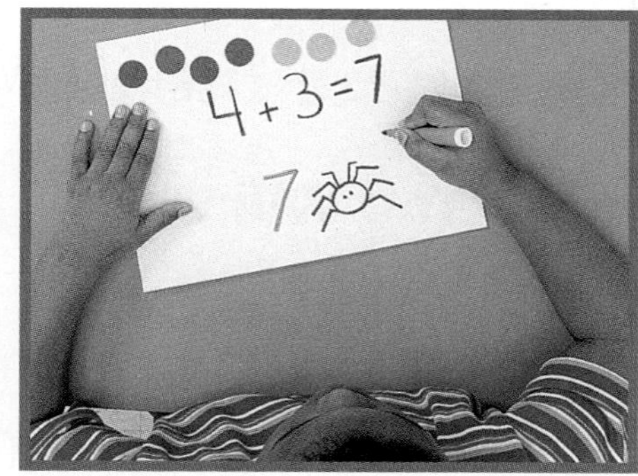

Draw your counters. Write the number sentence. Solve.

1. Write a story problem that uses addition.

____

____

____

2. Draw your counters.

3. Write the number sentence. Solve.

____ + ____ = ____

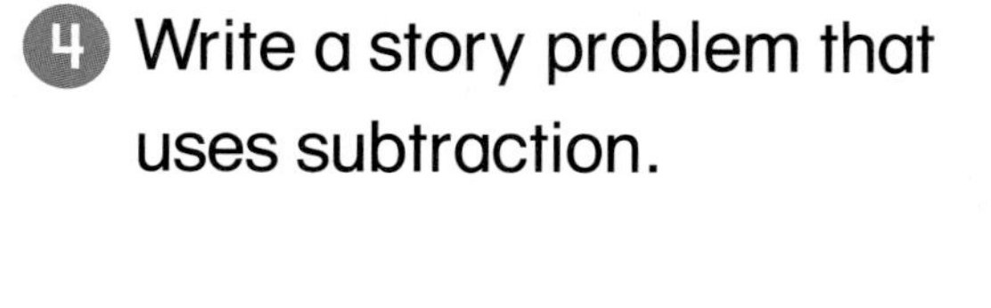

4. Write a story problem that uses subtraction.

____

____

____

5. Draw your counters.

6. Write the number sentence. Solve.

____ − ____ = ____

Critical Thinking

7. Tell another story problem using one of your number sentences.

Notes for Home: Your child did an activity that tested Chapter 2 skills, concepts, and problem solving. *Home Activity:* Ask your child to make up a story problem and write a number sentence to solve it.

Name ______________________________

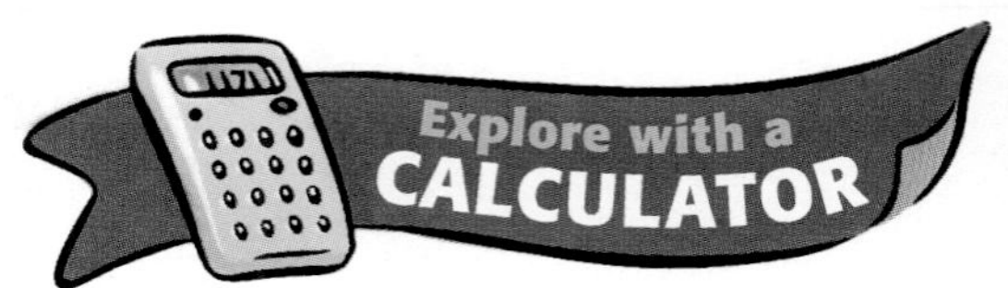

Calculate the Ways!

Keys You Will Use ON/C + =

Use your calculator to show one way to make 10.

Press ON/C 2 + 2 + 1 + 5 = 10.

Use your calculator to find more ways to make 10.

Write the number sentences.

1. 

2. 

3. 

4. 

Use your calculator to find ways to make 12.

Write the number sentences.

5. 

6. 

7. 

Tech Talk How did you find the last number in each number sentence?

Visit our Web site. **www.parent.mathsurf.com**

Number Shuffle

Players 2

What You Need

12 cards numbered 1-12

How to Play

1 Put the cards facedown. Spread them apart.
2 Turn over 3 cards. Try to make an addition or subtraction sentence using the numbers.
3 If you cannot make an addition or subtraction sentence, put the cards back. If you can make an addition or subtraction sentence, keep the cards and take another turn.
4 The player with the most cards wins!

Fold down

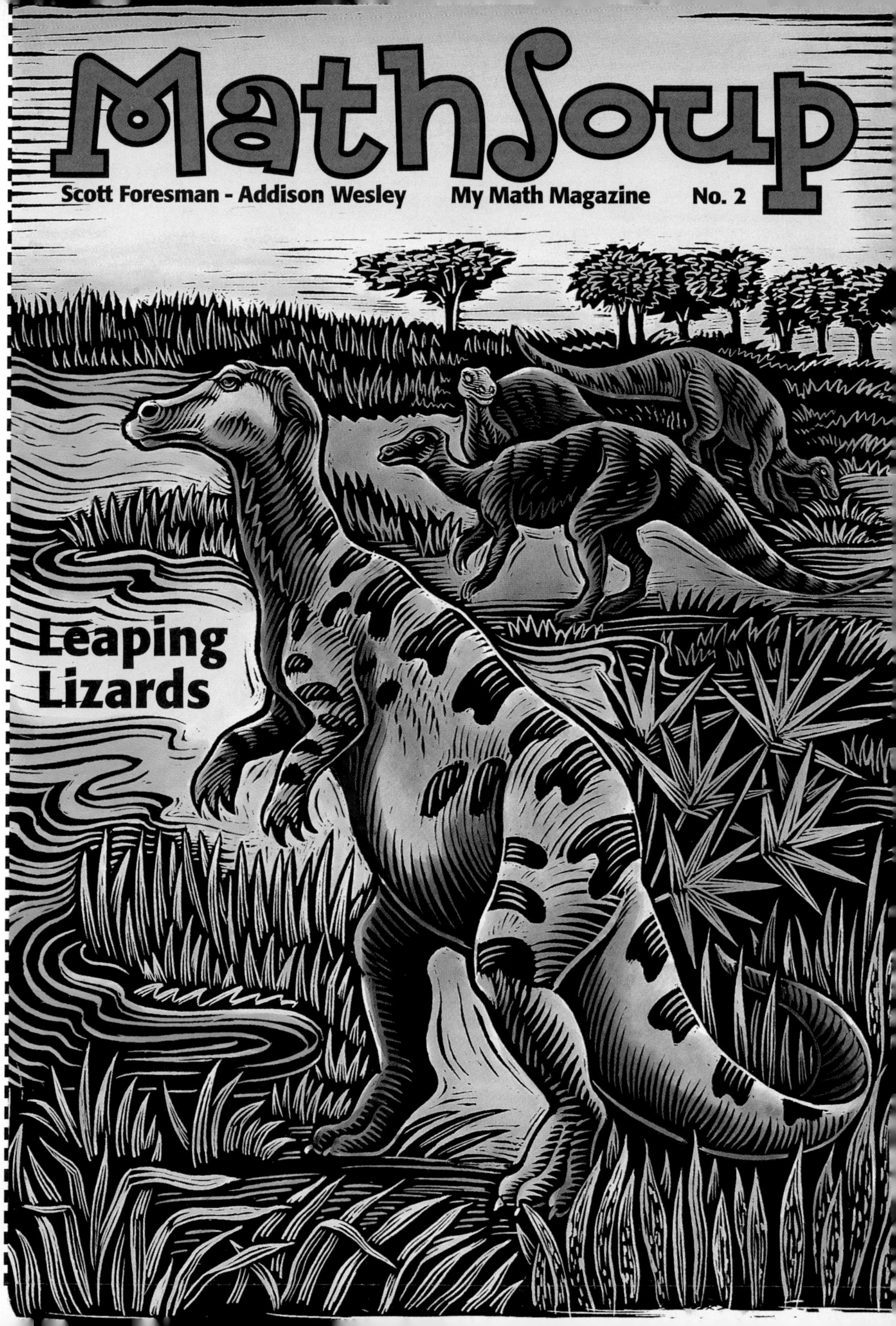

MathSoup

Scott Foresman - Addison Wesley My Math Magazine No. 2

Leaping Lizards

Math in Your World

Lizzie's Lizard

Imagine having a dinosaur named after you! That happened to nine-year-old Lizzie Williams. How did it happen? While hiking with her family in Alaska, Lizzie found some strange-looking rocks. The rocks turned out to be Hadrosaur fossils. A scientist named the fossil bones "Lizzie."

Look at these dinosaur bones.

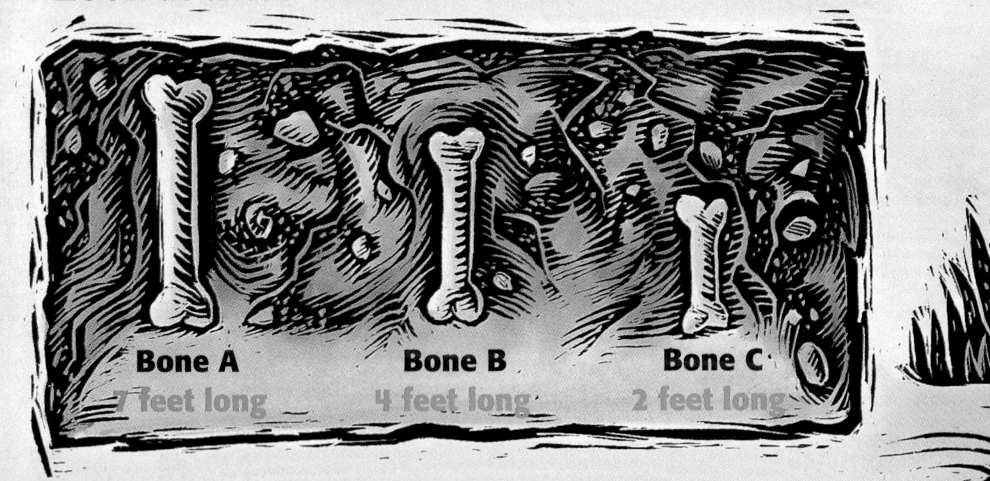

1 How much longer is Bone A than Bone B?
_____ feet

2 If Bones B and C were placed end to end, how long would they be? _____ feet

Notes for Home: Your child solved problems about dinosaur bones.
Home Activity: Ask your child to make up a story problem about the dinosaur bones, then ask him or her to solve the problem.

You can write numbers greater than 9 in Braille. To write 10, the dot patterns for 1 and 0 are shown next to each other.

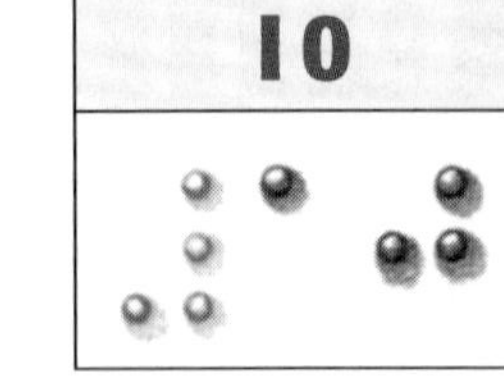

Write the numbers for these Braille dot patterns.

1 _____

2 _____

Write the dot patterns below these numbers.

3 37

4 48

5 Pick your own number and write the dot pattern for it.

Read It with Feeling

Braille is a written language for the blind. Patterns of raised dots stand for letters and numbers. People "read" the dots by touching them. This dot pattern means that a number comes next: 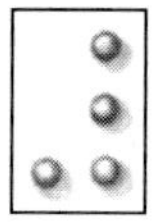 .

The dots below stand for numbers.

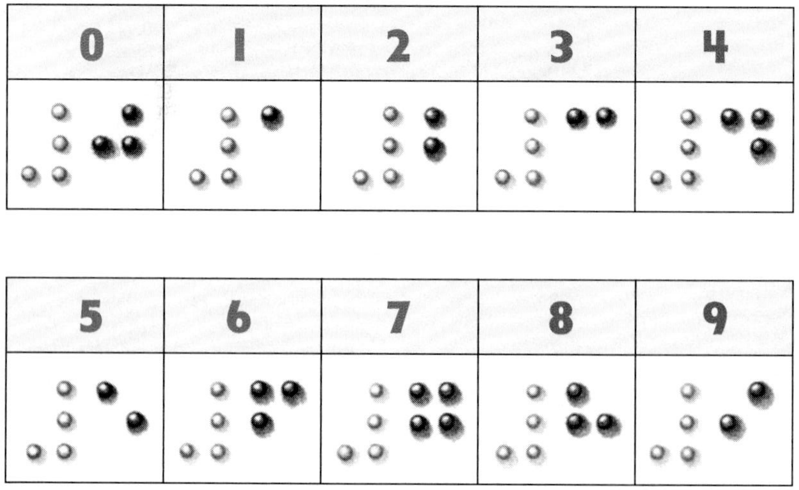

0	1	2	3	4

5	6	7	8	9

What has a long neck, three wheels, and weighs more than a ton?

Answer: A dinosaur riding a tricycle.

Notes for Home: Your child used Braille dots to read and write numbers.
Home Activity: Ask your child to write the number 25 using Braille dots.

Join the Team

This is a picture of the Troopers soccer team. Use the names and numbers in the picture to answer the riddles.

Who Am I?

I am standing. When you subtract my shirt number from 11, the difference is 6. My name is

__________.

Who Are We?

We are both sitting. The sum of our shirt numbers is 17. Our names are

__________ and __________.

Make up your own riddles using the picture. Ask a friend to solve them.

Notes for Home: Your child used logical reasoning and addition and subtraction to solve problems. *Home Activity:* Ask your child to tell you how he or she solved one of the riddles.

CHAPTER 3

Addition and Subtraction Facts and Strategies

Notes for Home: Your child told addition and subtraction stories about groups in the picture. *Home Activity:* Ask your child to tell you an addition story and a subtraction story about the children playing games.

Dear Family,
Our class is starting Chapter 3. We will add numbers with sums (totals) to 18. We will also subtract from numbers up to 18. Here are some activities we can do together.

Flash Card Fun
Make flash cards for addition and subtraction facts. Ask your child to match the addition fact with a related subtraction fact, such as 7 + 8 = 15 and 15 − 7 = 8.

Finding Facts
Help your child practice facts. Find two groups of objects, each with 1–9 objects. Add to find how many objects in all.

Community Connection

Take your child to the park. Look for situations that show addition and subtraction. For example: 6 children are playing on the slide. 4 children are swinging. How many children are playing in all?

Visit our Web site. **www.parent.mathsurf.com**

Name

Explore Doubles

Explore

You will need: 18 .

Take some cubes.
Write how many in all.

Make a train.

Try to break the train into 2 equal groups.

	How many in all?	Can you break the train into 2 equal groups?	How many in each of the 2 groups?
1	_____	yes no	_____ and _____
2	_____	yes no	_____ and _____
3	_____	yes no	_____ and _____
4	_____	yes no	_____ and _____

Share

How can you build a train that will break into two equal groups?

Notes for Home: Your child explored doubles facts (such as 6 + 6 = 12) with Snap Cubes.
Home Activity: Ask your child if a train of 8 cubes can be broken into two equal groups. (Yes; 2 groups of 4 cubes each)

EXPLORE

Connect

7 + 7 = 14

EXPLORE

Add. Write the sums. You can use .

5. 7 + 7 = 14   8 + 8 = ____   9 + 9 = ____

6. 1 + 1 = ____   2 + 2 = ____   3 + 3 = ____

7. 4 + 4 = ____   5 + 5 = ____   6 + 6 = ____

8.

3	4	5	6	7	8	9
+ 3	+ 4	+ 5	+ 6	+ 7	+ 8	+ 9

Talk About It Look at the last row of facts. What pattern do you see in the sums?

Notes for Home: Your child found the sums for doubles facts such as 6 + 6 = 12.
Home Activity: Ask your child if 8 + 7 = 15 is a doubles fact and to explain how he or she knows. (Sample Answer: No, because 8 and 7 are two different numbers.)

Name ______________________________

Name That Fact!

Players 2 to 4

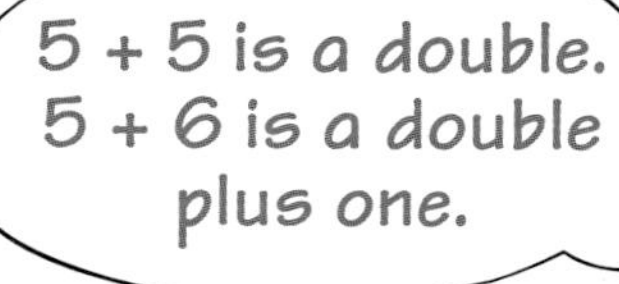

What You Need

10 counters each 

How to Play

1. Put all the counters in one pile. Take turns tossing a counter onto the gameboard.
2. Tell a fact with a sum that matches the number.
3. Take a counter each time you are correct.
4. Take an extra counter if you named a doubles or doubles plus one fact.
5. The player who gets 10 counters first, wins.

Notes for Home: Your child used addition facts to play a game. *Home Activity:* Ask your child to name two facts with the sum of 16. (Sample answers: 8 + 8 and 7 + 9)

PRACTICE

Name ______________________________

STOP and Practice

PRACTICE

Draw dots to make these doubles.
Write the number sentences.

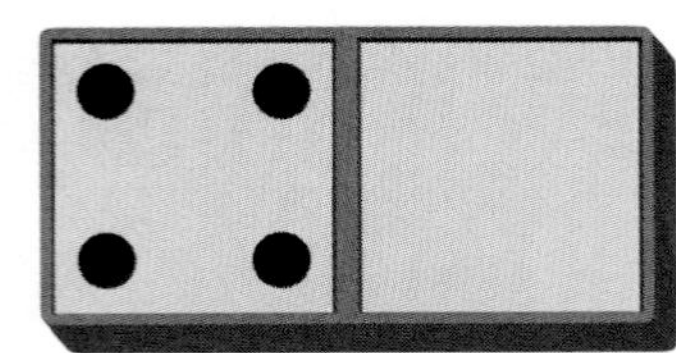

1. 4 + 4 = 8

2. ____ + ____ = ____

3. ____ + ____ = ____

4. ____ + ____ = ____

Draw dots to make doubles plus one facts.
Write the number sentences.

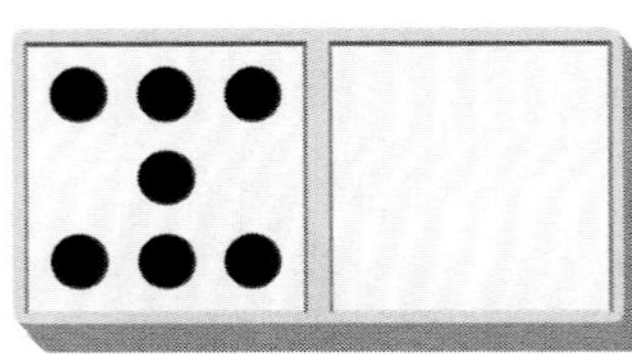

5. 7 + 8 = 15

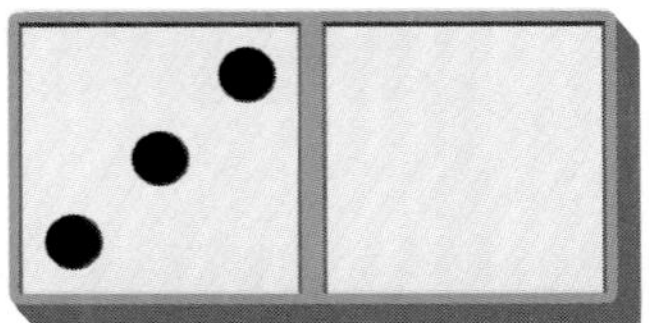

6. ____ + ____ = ____

7. ____ + ____ = ____

8. ____ + ____ = ____

Notes for Home: Your child practiced doubles such as 5 + 5 = 10 and doubles plus one facts such as 5 + 6 = 11. *Home Activity:* Ask your child to use the number 7 to make a doubles plus one fact. (7 + 8 = 15)

Name ______________________________

Explore Making 10

Explore

Draw a picture. You can use thumbprints.
Put 10 things in 2 groups. Tell fun stories.

Write a number sentence for your picture. ____ + ____ = ____

Share

Tell your story and your number sentence.

Notes for Home: Your child drew a picture of ten things and told a math story.
Home Activity: Ask your child to tell you a math story using his or her picture.

Connect

Put a picture in each empty box.
Complete the number sentence.

1. 

$6 + \_\_\_ = \_\_\_$

2. $9 + \_\_\_ = \_\_\_$

3. $7 + \_\_\_ = \_\_\_$

4. 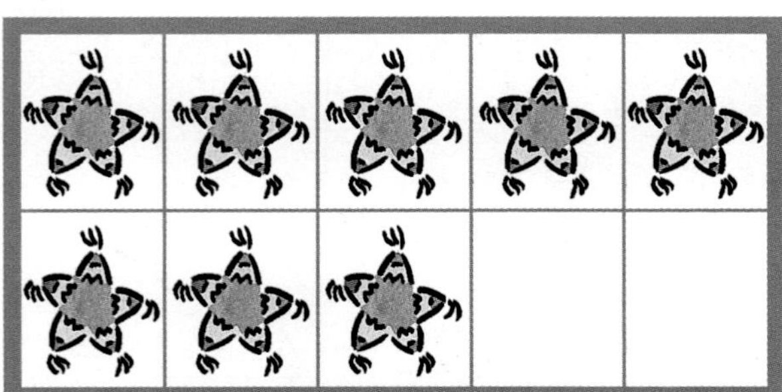

$8 + \_\_\_ = \_\_\_$

EXPLORE

Talk About It What other number sentences have a sum of 10?

Notes for Home: Your child drew pictures and wrote number sentences with the sum of 10.
Home Activity: Ask your child to draw a picture that shows 5 + 5 = 10.

Name

Make 10 When Adding 9

Learn

Find 9 + 5.
9 is close to 10.
Make a 10 to help you add.

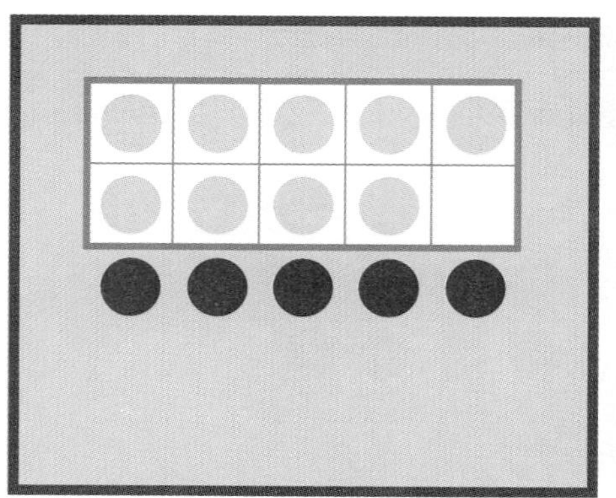

Show 9. Show 5.

Make a ten.

How many?

Check

Add. Use counters. Write the sum.

1 Show 9. Show 3.

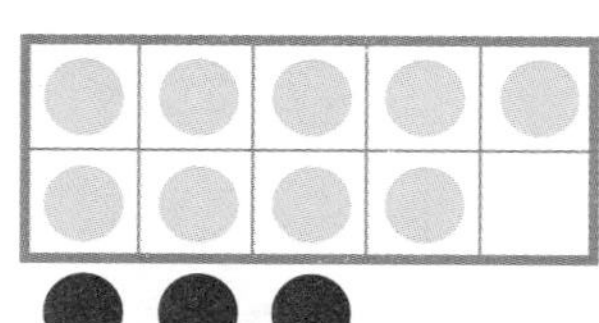

Make a ten.

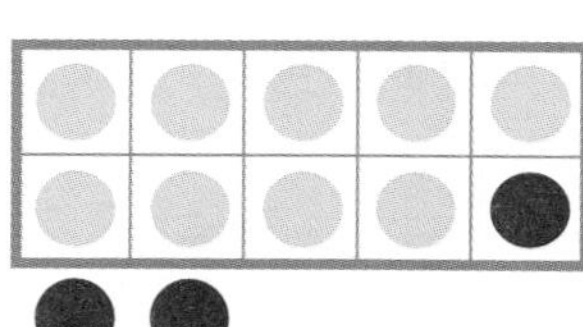

How many?

9 + 3 = 12

2 Show 9. Show 6.

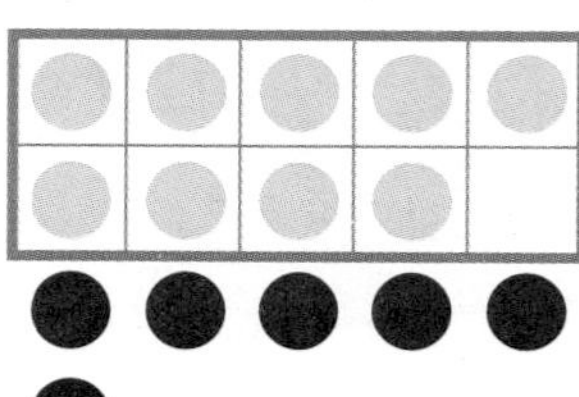

Make a ten.

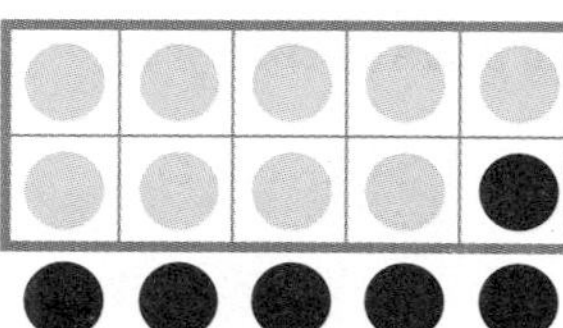

How many?

9 + 6 = ____

Talk About It Is it easier to add 9 + 6 or 10 + 5? Why?

Notes for Home: Your child added 9 to another number by first making a ten. *Home Activity:* Ask your child to explain how to add 9 + 4 by first making a ten.

Practice

Add. Write the addition sentence.

3
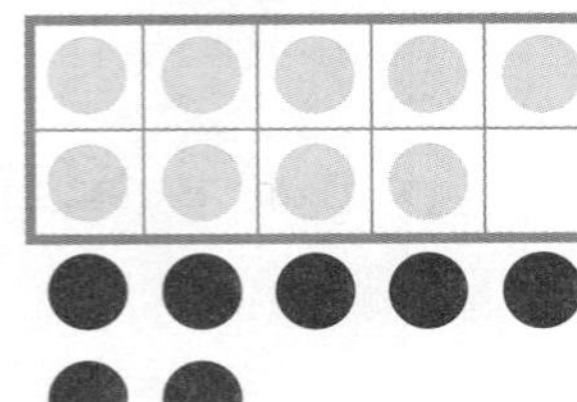

9 + 7 = 16

4
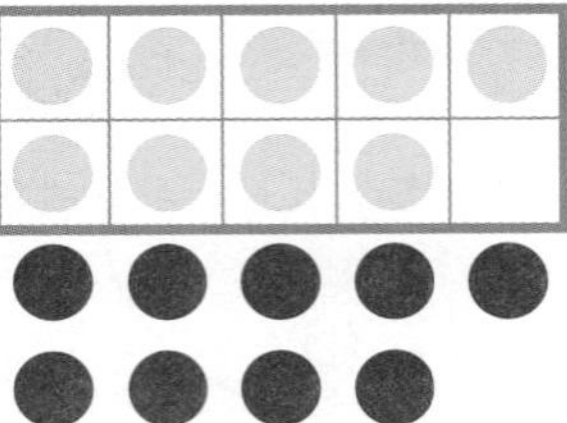

___ + ___ = ___

5
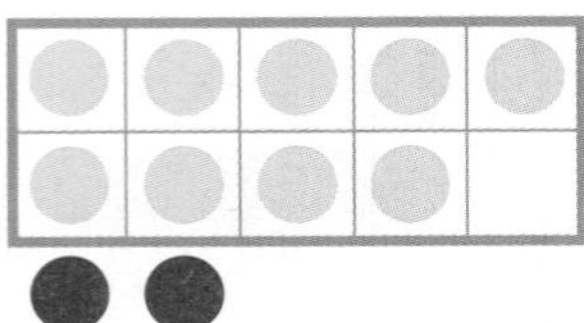

___ + ___ = ___

6
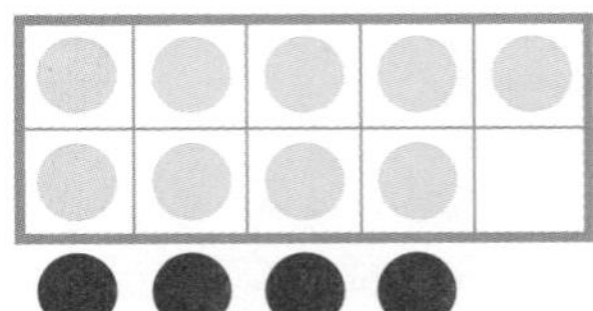

___ + ___ = ___

Add.

7

9	9	9	9	9	9	9
+ 7	+ 6	+ 4	+ 8	+ 3	+ 5	+ 9

Mixed Practice Add.

8 $6 + 6 =$ ___ $9 + 3 =$ ___ $7 + 2 =$ ___

Problem Solving **Visual Thinking**

9 Amy wants to fill this page with stickers. Josh gives her 5 more.

How many stickers will not fit on this page? ___ stickers

How many stickers does she have in all? ___ stickers

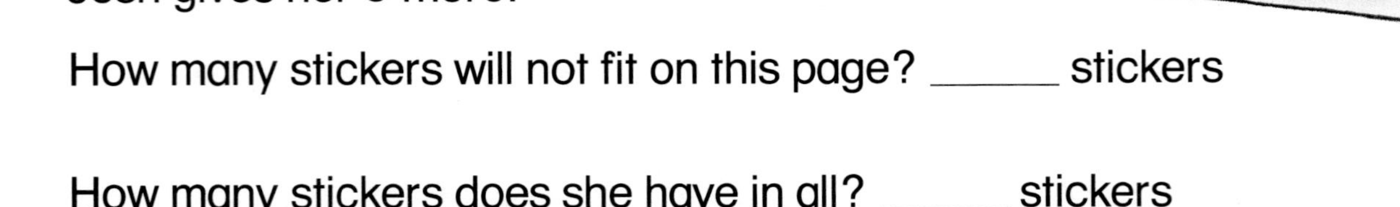

Notes for Home: Your child practiced adding 9 to another number by first making a ten.
Home Activity: Ask your child to explain how to solve Exercise 4.

PRACTICE

Name

Make 10 When Adding 6, 7 or 8

Learn

Show 8. Show 6.

Make a ten.

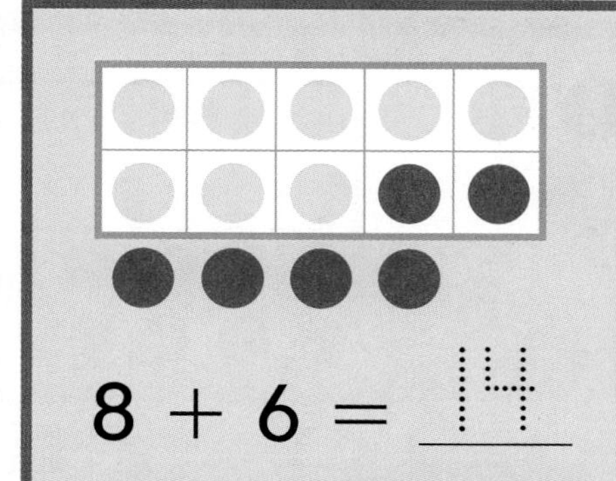

How many?

Check

Add. Use ⬤ ◯. Write the sum.

1. Show 8. Show 4.

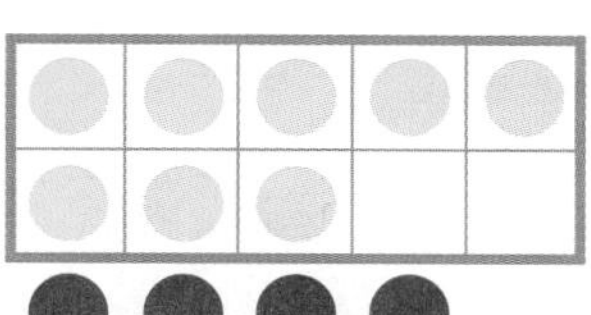

Make a ten.

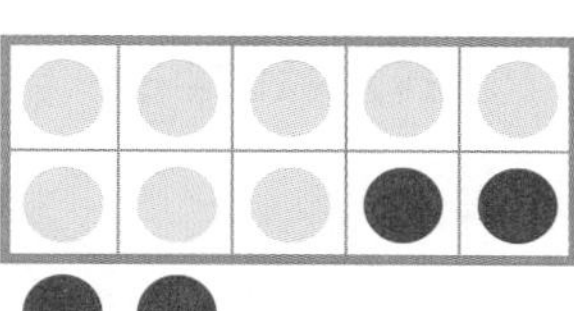

How many?

8 + 4 = 12

2. Show 6. Show 7.

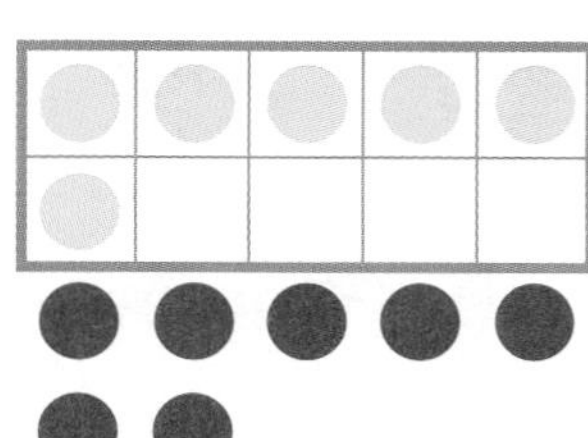

Make a ten.

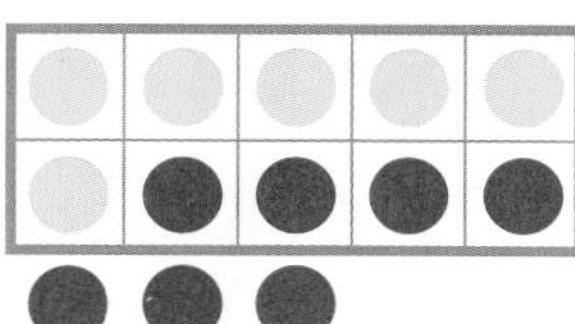

How many?

6 + 7 = ____

Talk About It Explain how to make a 10 to find 7 + 4.

Notes for Home: Your child added 6, 7, or 8 to another number by first making a ten.
Home Activity: Ask your child to explain how to make a ten when adding 7 + 4.

Practice

Add. Write the addition sentence.

3
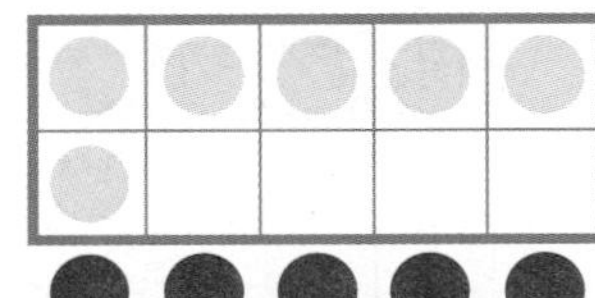

6 + 5 = 11

4
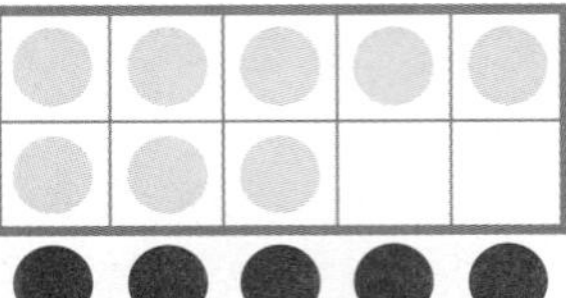

___ + ___ = ___

5
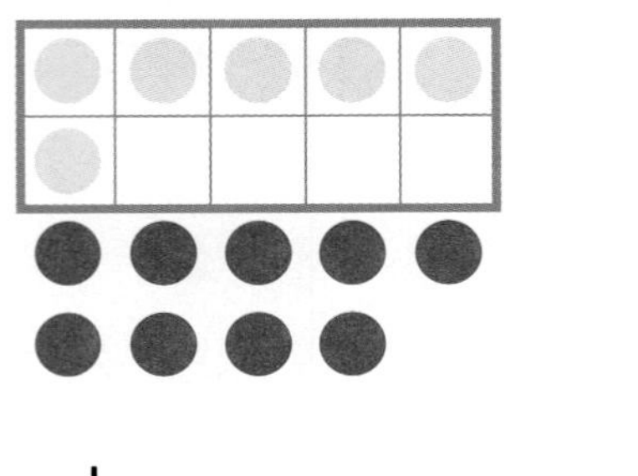

___ + ___ = ___

6
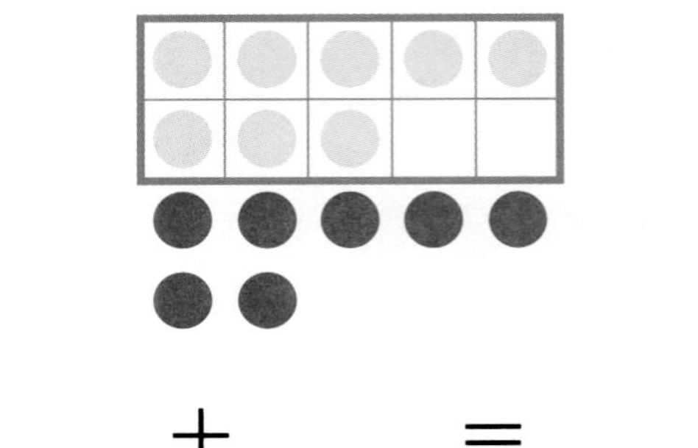

___ + ___ = ___

Add.

7

7	8	8	7	7	8	6
+ 3	+ 6	+ 9	+ 8	+ 9	+ 2	+ 7

PRACTICE

Problem Solving Critical Thinking

Carlo and Sumi played Hop-Round.
They each threw two stones into the circle.
Then they added the two numbers.

8 Carlo's score was 10. What two numbers could he have gotten?

___ and ___

9 Sumi's score was 11. What two numbers could he have gotten?

___ and ___

Notes for Home: Your child practiced adding 7 or 8 to another number by first making a ten.
Home Activity: Ask your child to explain how he or she would find 8 + 4.

For additional practice, see Skills Practice Bank, page 529, Set 1.

Name

Problem Solving: Make a List

Learn

PROBLEM SOLVING GUIDE

Understand • Plan • Solve • Look Back

Martin plays a game with stones. Find all the ways he can put 16 stones on 2 gameboards.

A gameboard holds up to 15 stones.

Use 16 cubes. Put 15 cubes on the red gameboard. Put 1  on the blue gameboard.

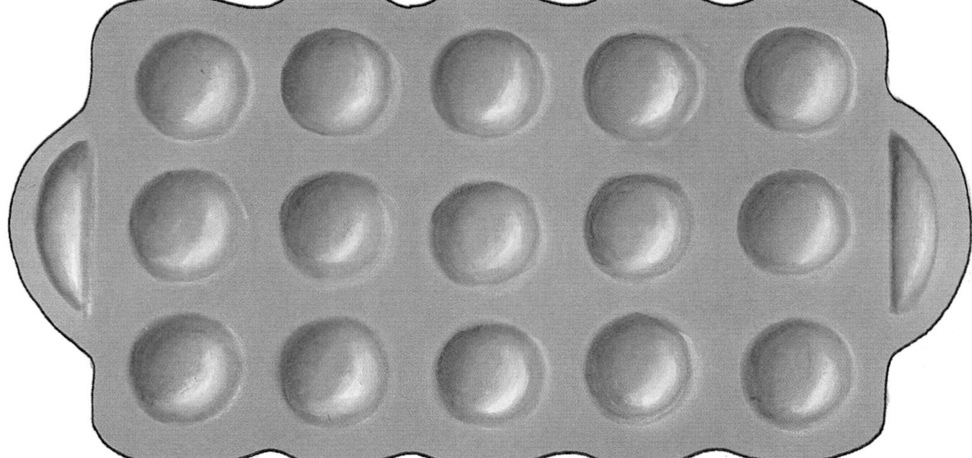

Red	Blue
15	1
14	2

Check

1. Use cubes to find all the ways. Write your numbers in the list.

Talk About It How is making a list helpful?

Notes for Home: Your child made a list to solve a problem. *Home Activity:* Ask your child to list all the ways 9 objects can be put into 2 groups. (1 and 8, 2 and 7, 3 and 6, 4 and 5, and so on)

Practice

Shauna puts her toys away.
Find all the ways she can
put 13 toys into 2 toy boxes.

2 Find all the ways. You can use ▢▢.
Write your numbers in the list.

Purple	Yellow
12	1

Patterns

3 What patterns do you see in your list?

Notes for Home: Your child practiced making a list to solve a problem. *Home Activity:* Ask your child to make a list to show all the ways that 11 children can sit in 2 train cars. (1 and 10, 2 and 9, 3 and 7, 4 and 6, 5 and 5, and so on)

For additional practice, see Skills Practice Bank, page 529, Set 2.

Name ____________________

Mixed Practice

Lessons 1–6

Concepts and Skills

Add.

1. $9 + 9 =$ ____ $8 + 8 =$ ____ $7 + 7 =$ ____

Complete the number sentences.

2. 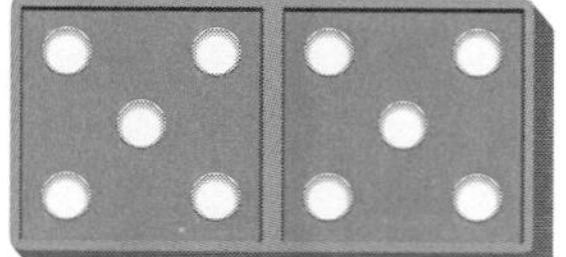 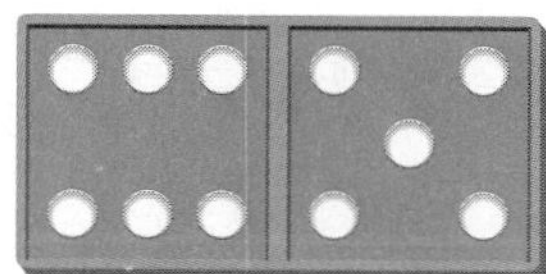

$5 + 5 =$ ____ $5 +$ ____ $=$ ____ $6 +$ ____ $=$ ____

Add. Write the number sentences.

3. 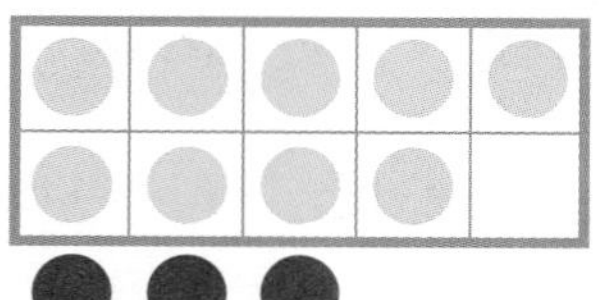

____ + ____ = ____

4. 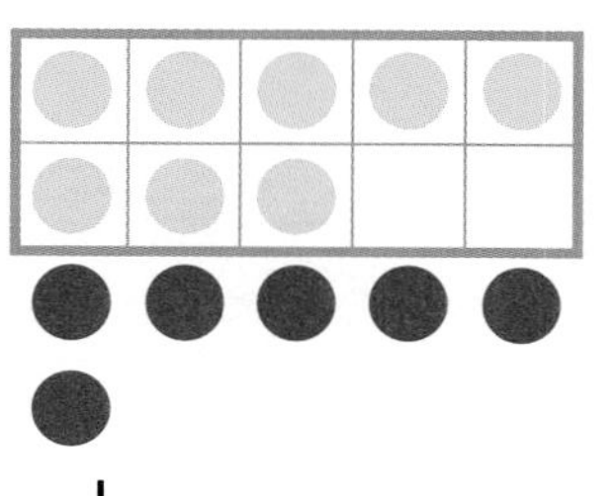

____ + ____ = ____

Problem Solving

Write a number sentence. Solve.

5. In one week, Jim read 8 books. The next week he read 7 books. How many books did he read in two weeks?

____ + ____ = ____ books

6. Kristen planted 9 daisies and 7 sunflowers. How many flowers did she plant in all?

____ + ____ = ____ flowers

Journal

7. Draw a picture to show doubles. Write a math story about your picture.

Notes for Home: Your child practiced additon facts and solving word problems.
Home Activity: Ask your child to explain how he or she would find 9 + 6.

For additional practice, see Basic Facts Review, page 541, Set 3.

Name ________________________________

Cumulative Review

Chapters 1–3

Concepts and Skills

Continue the pattern.
Write the missing numbers.

1. 3, 6, 9, ____, ____, ____
2. 5, 10, 15, ____, ____, ____

Add.

3.
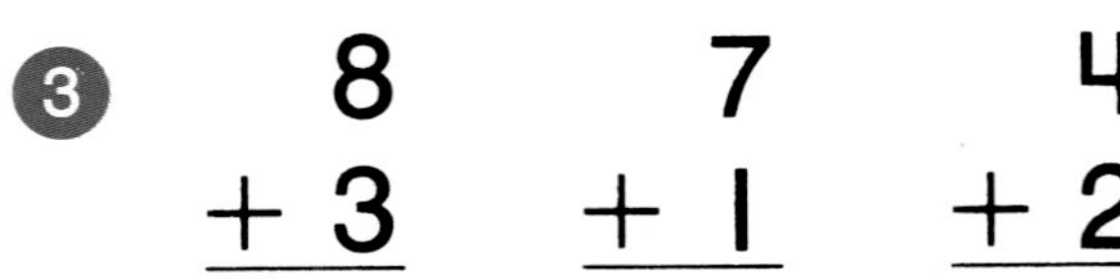

$$\begin{array}{r} 8 \\ +\,3 \\ \hline \end{array} \qquad \begin{array}{r} 7 \\ +\,1 \\ \hline \end{array} \qquad \begin{array}{r} 4 \\ +\,2 \\ \hline \end{array}$$

Problem Solving

Solve. Write a number sentence.

4. Rico had 8 crayons. Lin gave her 3 more. How many crayons did she have then?

____ + ____ = ____ crayons

Test Prep

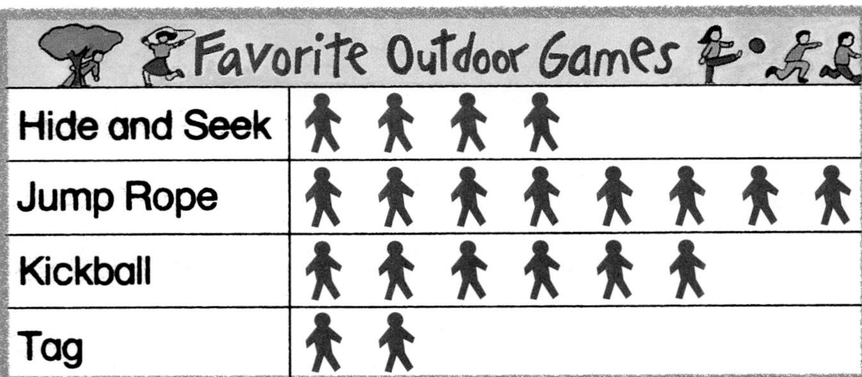

Favorite Outdoor Games	
Hide and Seek	🚶 🚶 🚶 🚶
Jump Rope	🚶 🚶 🚶 🚶 🚶 🚶 🚶 🚶
Kickball	🚶 🚶 🚶 🚶 🚶 🚶
Tag	🚶 🚶

Each 🚶 means 1 child.

Fill in the ○ to show the correct answer.

5. Which game did most children choose?

Hide and Seek ○ Jump Rope ○ Kickball ○ Tag ○

6. How many more children chose **Kickball** than **Tag**?

2 ○ 4 ○ 6 ○ 8 ○

Notes for Home: Your child reviewed number patterns, addition and subtraction facts to 12, and picture graphs. *Home Activity:* Ask your child to tell you what the next three numbers would be in Exercise 2. (35, 40, 45)

Name

Use Doubles to Subtract

Learn

$$\begin{array}{r} 6 \\ +\ 6 \\ \hline 12 \end{array} \qquad \begin{array}{r} 12 \\ -\ 6 \\ \hline 6 \end{array}$$

Check

Add. Then use doubles to subtract.

1. 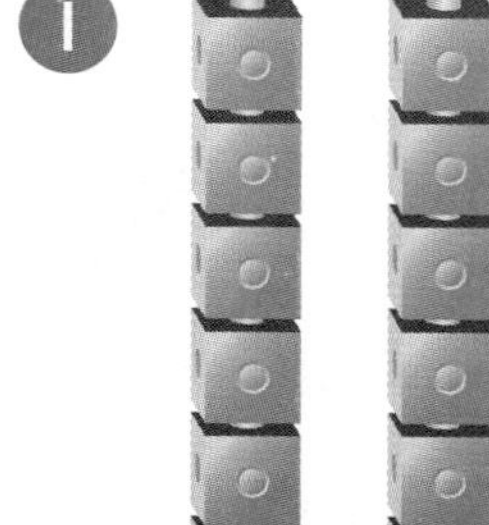

$$\begin{array}{r} 7 \\ +\ 7 \\ \hline 14 \end{array} \qquad \begin{array}{r} 14 \\ -\ 7 \\ \hline 7 \end{array}$$

2. 

$$\begin{array}{r} 5 \\ +\ 5 \\ \hline \end{array} \qquad \begin{array}{r} 10 \\ -\ 5 \\ \hline \end{array}$$

3. 

$$\begin{array}{r} 8 \\ +\ 8 \\ \hline \end{array} \qquad \begin{array}{r} 16 \\ -\ 8 \\ \hline \end{array}$$

4. 

$$\begin{array}{r} 9 \\ +\ 9 \\ \hline \end{array} \qquad \begin{array}{r} 18 \\ -\ 9 \\ \hline \end{array}$$

Talk About It How can you use doubles to help you subtract?

Notes for Home: Your child used doubles facts such as 5 + 5 = 10 to subtract. *Home Activity:* Ask your child how to use 6 + 6 = 12 to find 12 − 6.

Add or subtract.
Match each subtraction fact with a doubles fact.

5. $14 - 7 =$ 7	$6 + 6 =$ ____
6. $8 - 4 =$ ____	$3 + 3 =$ ____
7. $12 - 6 =$ ____	$7 + 7 =$ 14
8. $6 - 3 =$ ____	$4 + 4 =$ ____

Subtract. Write the double that helps.

9. $18 - 9 =$ 9   9 + 9 = 18
10. $16 - 8 =$ ____   ____ + ____ = ____
11. $12 - 6 =$ ____   ____ + ____ = ____

PRACTICE

Mental Math

Eric and his friends play kickball. Each team has the same number of players. Write the number of children on each team.

12. 12 children play in all.

____ are on one team.

____ are on the other team.

13. 10 children play in all.

____ are on one team.

____ are on the other team.

Notes for Home: Your child identified related addition and subtraction facts. *Home Activity:* Ask your child what doubles fact helps to find 14 − 7. (7 + 7 = 14)

Name ______________________________

Use Addition Facts to Subtract

Learn

$$\begin{array}{r} 6 \\ +\ 5 \\ \hline 11 \end{array} \qquad \begin{array}{r} 11 \\ -\ 5 \\ \hline 6 \end{array}$$

Check

Add. Then use the addition fact to subtract.

1. 

$$\begin{array}{r} 8 \\ +\ 5 \\ \hline 13 \end{array} \qquad \begin{array}{r} 13 \\ -\ 5 \\ \hline 8 \end{array}$$

2. 

$$\begin{array}{r} 9 \\ +\ 6 \\ \hline \end{array} \qquad \begin{array}{r} 15 \\ -\ 6 \\ \hline \end{array}$$

3. 

$$\begin{array}{r} 6 \\ +\ 8 \\ \hline \end{array} \qquad \begin{array}{r} 14 \\ -\ 8 \\ \hline \end{array}$$

4. 

$$\begin{array}{r} 8 \\ +\ 9 \\ \hline \end{array} \qquad \begin{array}{r} 17 \\ -\ 9 \\ \hline \end{array}$$

Talk About It What addition fact could you use to help you find $16 - 9$?

Notes for Home: Your child used addition facts to subtract. *Home Activity:* Ask your child to use objects such as pennies to show $7 + 8 = 15$ and $15 - 8 = 7$.

Practice

Add or subtract. Color each addition fact and the related subtraction fact the same color. Use a different color for each set of facts.

5

$\begin{array}{r}13\\-6\\\hline 7\end{array}$	$\begin{array}{r}15\\-9\\\hline\end{array}$	$\begin{array}{r}16\\-7\\\hline\end{array}$	$\begin{array}{r}11\\-2\\\hline\end{array}$
$\begin{array}{r}14\\-6\\\hline\end{array}$	$\begin{array}{r}12\\-8\\\hline\end{array}$	$\begin{array}{r}17\\-8\\\hline\end{array}$	$\begin{array}{r}18\\-9\\\hline\end{array}$

6

$\begin{array}{r}9\\+7\\\hline\end{array}$	$\begin{array}{r}8\\+6\\\hline\end{array}$	$\begin{array}{r}9\\+2\\\hline\end{array}$	$\begin{array}{r}7\\+6\\\hline 13\end{array}$
$\begin{array}{r}9\\+9\\\hline\end{array}$	$\begin{array}{r}4\\+8\\\hline\end{array}$	$\begin{array}{r}6\\+9\\\hline\end{array}$	$\begin{array}{r}9\\+8\\\hline\end{array}$

PRACTICE

Tell a Math Story

7 Tell an addition story and a related subtraction story for the picture.

Notes for Home: Your child practiced using addition facts to subtract. *Home Activity:* Ask your child to explain how 7 + 5 = 12 helps to find 12 − 5.

Name

ALGEBRA READINESS

Relate Addition and Subtraction

Learn

At the party, 9 people were dancing. 5 more joined them. How many people were dancing then?

9 + 5 = 14

14 people were dancing. 5 sat down to rest. How many people were still dancing?

14 − 5 = 9

Check

Write a number sentence. Solve.

1. Marcus and Ida made 13 tacos for the party. 6 people each ate a taco. How many tacos were left?

2. Marcus made 7 tacos. Ida made 6 tacos. How many tacos were there in all?

Talk About It How are the stories about tacos the same? How are they different?

Notes for Home: Your child wrote related addition and subtraction facts for math stories.
Home Activity: Ask your child to tell you the related subtraction fact for 9 + 5 = 14.
(Answer: 14 − 5 = 9 or 14 − 9 = 5.)

Practice

Write a number sentence. Solve.

3. There were 8 gifts on the table. Friends brought 4 more. How many gifts were there in all?

   8 + 4 = 12

4. At the party, Alex had 12 gifts. He opened 4 of them. How many were left?

   ____

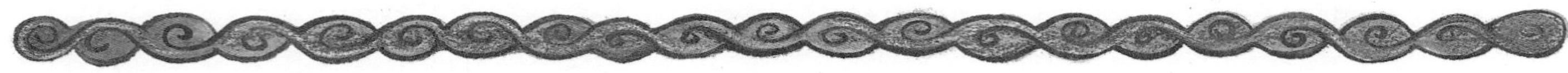

Write About It

5. Use the numbers 6, 9, and 15. Write an addition story and a related subtraction story. Write number sentences for your stories.

My Addition Story

____

____

My Number Sentence:

____

My Subtraction Story

____

____

My Number Sentence:

____

PRACTICE

Notes for Home: Your child practiced writing and solving story problems with related facts. *Home Activity:* Ask your child to write related addition and subtraction facts using these numbers: 7, 5, 12. (7 + 5 = 12 or 5 + 7 = 12 and 12 − 5 = 7 or 12 − 7 = 5)

For additional practice, see Skills Practice Bank, page 529, Set 3.

Name ______________________________

Reading for Math

Graphic Aids: Bar Graphs

You read this graph left to right.

Our Favorite Stories

Stories

Arthur's Tooth

Stone Soup

Caps for Sale

Tikki Tikki Tembo

1 2 3 4 5 6 7 8 9 10 11 12

Number of Votes

1. What is the title of the graph? ______________________
2. How many rows are there? ______
3. What is at the start of each row? ______________________
4. What do the numbers tell you? ______________________
5. How many votes did ***Stone Soup*** get? ______

Talk About It How do you know which story got 7 votes?

Notes for Home: Your child read a bar graph. *Home Activity:* Ask your child to name the stories on the graph.

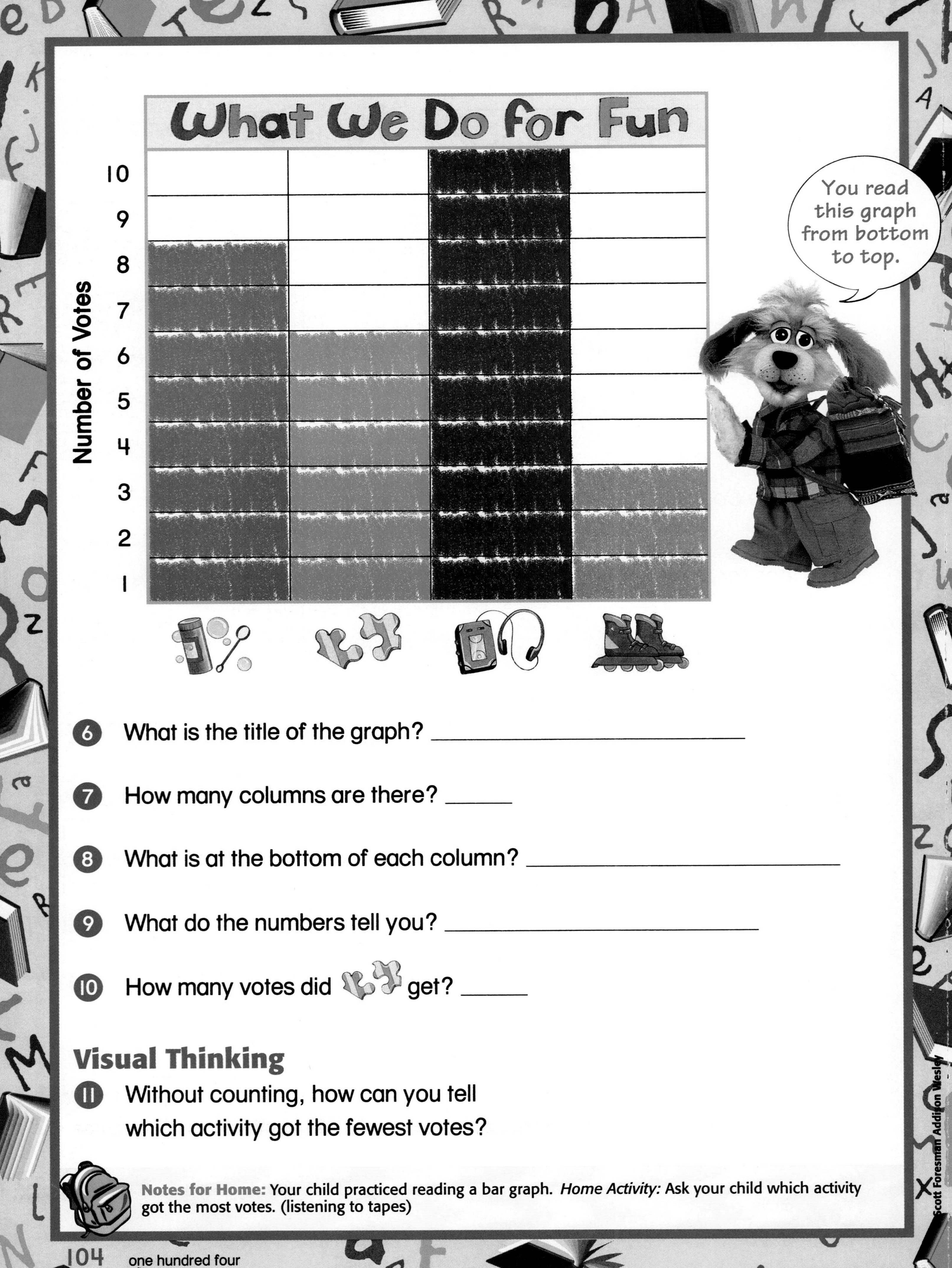

6. What is the title of the graph? ____________________

7. How many columns are there? ______

8. What is at the bottom of each column? ____________________

9. What do the numbers tell you? ____________________

10. How many votes did [puzzle pieces] get? ______

Visual Thinking

11. Without counting, how can you tell which activity got the fewest votes?

Notes for Home: Your child practiced reading a bar graph. *Home Activity:* Ask your child which activity got the most votes. (listening to tapes)

Name

Problem Solving: Group Decision Making

Learn

PROBLEM SOLVING GUIDE

Understand • Plan • Solve • Look Back

Check

Find out about a favorite topic in your class.

1. Choose a topic. Your group can use one of these topics or choose another topic.

2. Write your group's topic on the chart. Think of four choices for that topic. Ask your class to vote.

Our Topic:	How many?
Choice 1:	
Choice 2:	
Choice 3:	
Choice 4:	

Talk About It How did your group decide on the 4 choices for your topic?

Notes for Home: Your child worked in a group to take a survey. *Home Activity:* Ask your child which choice he or she voted for.

PROBLEM SOLVING

Practice

Use your information to make a bar graph.

Our Favorite ______________

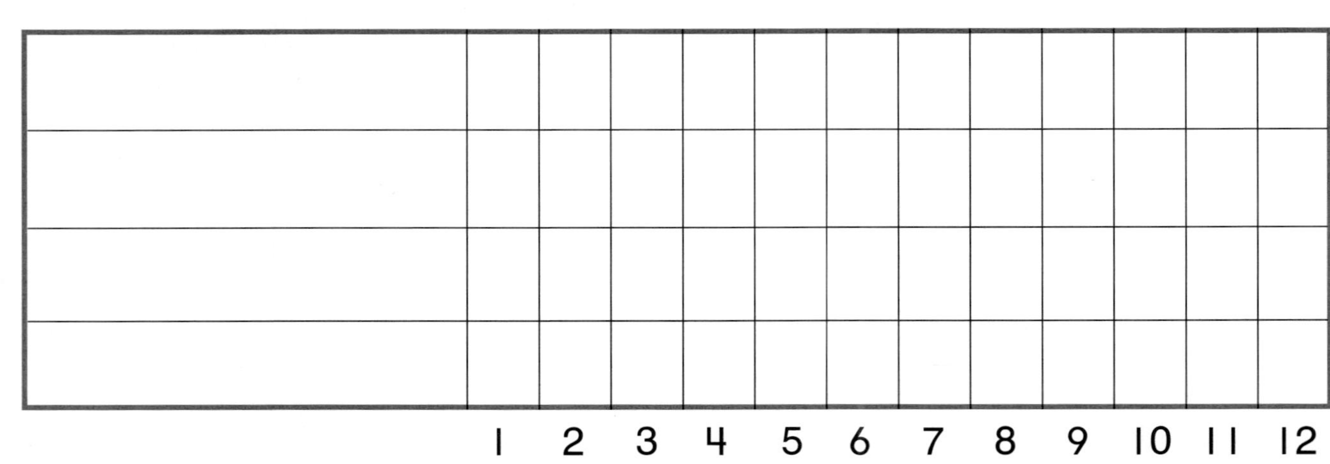

3. Write the title of your graph at the top.
4. Put a choice at the start of each row.
5. Label the side and bottom of your graph.
6. Color to show how many votes for each choice.

Write your own.

With your group, decide on 2 questions that can be answered by your graph. Write your questions.

7. ______________________________

____

8. ______________________________

____

Journal

9. What was the easiest part about working in a group? What was the hardest part?

Notes for Home: Your child made a bar graph. *Home Activity:* Ask your child to tell you the total number of votes for two choices.

PROBLEM SOLVING

Name

Mixed Practice

Lessons 7–10

Concepts and Skills

Add or subtract.

1. $\begin{array}{r} 7 \\ +\ 7 \\ \hline \end{array}$ $\begin{array}{r} 14 \\ -\ 7 \\ \hline \end{array}$

2. $\begin{array}{r} 6 \\ +\ 9 \\ \hline \end{array}$ $\begin{array}{r} 15 \\ -\ 9 \\ \hline \end{array}$

3. $\begin{array}{r} 5 \\ +\ 8 \\ \hline \end{array}$ $\begin{array}{r} 13 \\ -\ 8 \\ \hline \end{array}$

4. $\begin{array}{r} 16 \\ -\ 8 \\ \hline \end{array}$ $\begin{array}{r} 7 \\ +\ 6 \\ \hline \end{array}$ $\begin{array}{r} 9 \\ +\ 8 \\ \hline \end{array}$ $\begin{array}{r} 11 \\ -\ 6 \\ \hline \end{array}$ $\begin{array}{r} 8 \\ +\ 7 \\ \hline \end{array}$ $\begin{array}{r} 18 \\ -\ 9 \\ \hline \end{array}$ $\begin{array}{r} 15 \\ -\ 8 \\ \hline \end{array}$

Problem Solving

Write a number sentence. Solve.

5. Malinda had 9 colors of paint. Joe gave her 8 more. How many colors did she have then?

   ________________ colors

6. Malinda had 17 colors of paint. She gave Joe 8. How many colors did she have left?

   ________________ colors

Use the graph to answer the questions.

7. Which activity got the most votes?

   ____

8. How many more votes did **Reading** get than **Painting**?

   ______ more votes

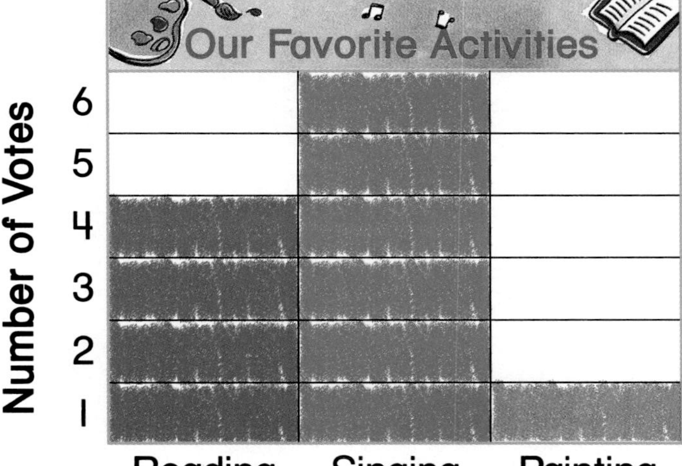

Journal

9. Draw a picture to show these related facts: $5 + 6 = 11$ $11 - 6 = 5$

Notes for Home: Your child practiced adding and subtracting related facts, reading a graph, and solving problems. *Home Activity:* Ask your child to tell you a related subtraction fact for $6 + 8 = 14$. ($14 - 8 = 6$ or $14 - 6 = 8$)

For additional practice, see Basic Facts Review, page 542, Set 4.

Name ______________________________

Cumulative Review

Chapters 1–3

Concepts and Skills

Write the number sentence. Then write the turnaround fact.

____

____

 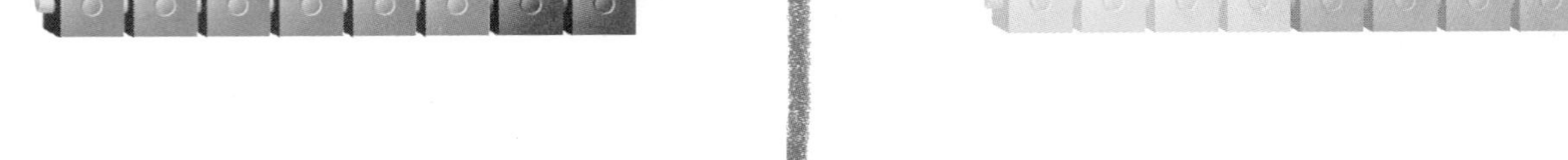

____

____

Problem Solving

Write a number sentence. Solve.

3 Dave has 5 paper planes.
He makes 5 more.
How many does he have in all?

______________________ planes

4 Camille makes 10 paper birds.
Then she gives 5 away.
How many does she have then?

______________________ birds

Test Prep

Fill in the ○ for the correct answer.

Which fact matches each picture?

5            

○ $9+2$ ○ $9-2$ ○ $6+4$ ○ $6-3$

 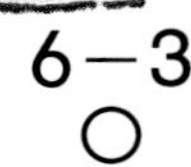

6 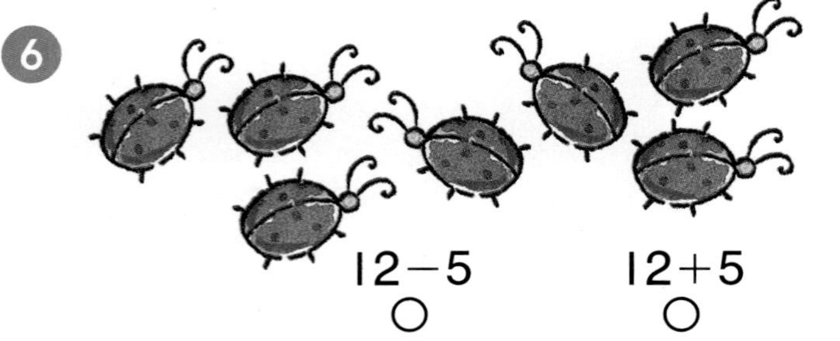 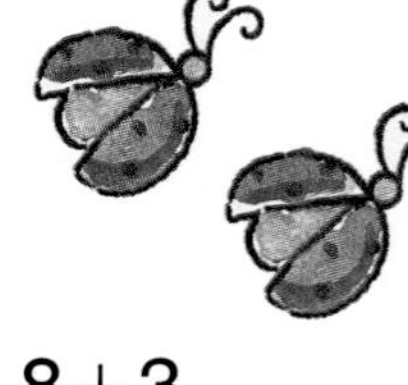 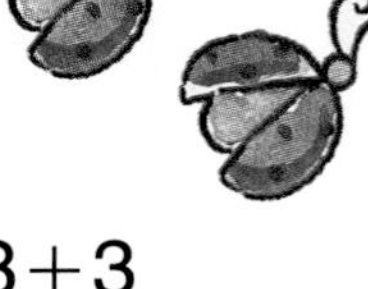 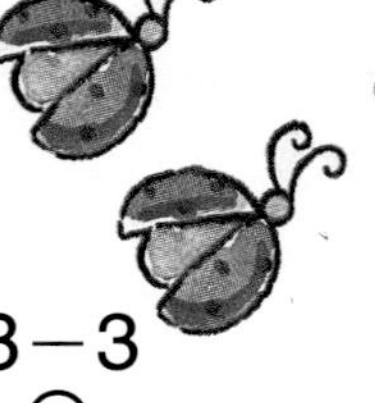 

○ $12-5$ ○ $12+5$ ○ $8+3$ ○ $8-3$

Notes for Home: Your child reviewed addition and subtraction facts to 12 and solved word problems.
Home Activity: Ask your child to tell you the turnaround fact for 8 + 3 = 11. (3 + 8 = 11)

Name ______________________________

Chapter 3 Review

Vocabulary

1. Complete the number sentence to show doubles.

   8 + ____ = ____

   Write the doubles plus one fact.

   ____ + ____ = ____

2. Add. Use the addition fact to write a related fact.

   5 + 9 = ____

   ____ − ____ = ____

Concepts and Skills

Add or subtract.

3.

9	15	13	7	18	8	14
+ 8	− 6	− 5	+ 7	− 9	+ 3	− 8

Problem Solving

Write a number sentence. Solve.

4. Jesse had 9 marbles. Louisa had 7 marbles. How many marbles did they have in all?

   ____________________ marbles

5. Jesse and Louisa had 16 marbles. Louisa took away 7 marbles. How many were left?

   ____________________ marbles

Solve.

6. Make a list.
   Show all the ways 6 can go on 2 gameboards.
   A gameboard can hold up to 5.

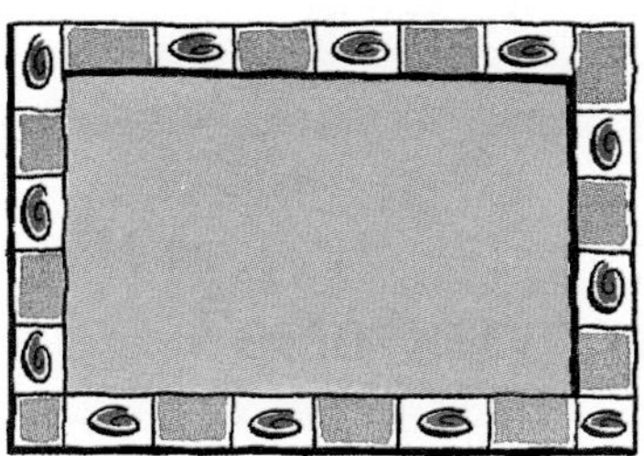

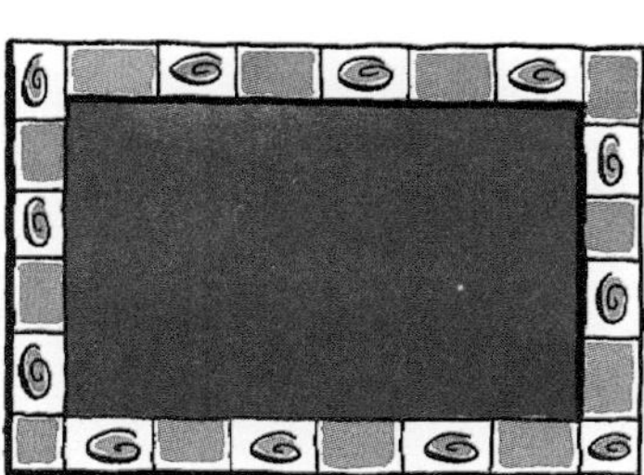

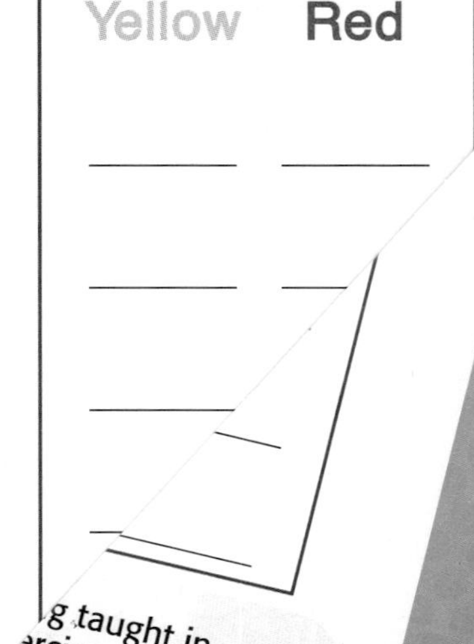

Notes for Home: Your child reviewed the vocabulary, concepts, skills ... Chapter 3. *Home Activity:* Ask your child to tell you how he or she f... g taught in ...ercise 1.

Name

Chapter 3 Test

Add.

1. $8 + 8 =$ ____ $8 + 9 =$ ____ $9 + 8 =$ ____

Add or subtract.

2.
$$\begin{array}{r} 9 \\ +\ 5 \\ \hline \end{array} \quad \begin{array}{r} 13 \\ -\ 6 \\ \hline \end{array} \quad \begin{array}{r} 18 \\ -\ 9 \\ \hline \end{array}$$

$$\begin{array}{r} 8 \\ +\ 7 \\ \hline \end{array} \quad \begin{array}{r} 15 \\ -\ 7 \\ \hline \end{array} \quad \begin{array}{r} 6 \\ +\ 4 \\ \hline \end{array}$$

3. Make a list. Show all the ways 5 children can sit in 2 boats
A boat can hold up to 4 children.

Write the number sentence. Solve.

4. Randy had 7 crayons.
Tasha had 9 crayons.
How many crayons did they have in all?

________________ crayons

5. Randy and Tasha had 16 crayons.
Tasha took away 9.
How many were left?

________________ crayons

Solve.

Which season got the most votes?

____

7. …many votes did **Winter** get?

…tes

…: Your child was tested on Chapter 3 concepts, skills, and problem solving.
…one h… your child to tell you three new things he or she learned in this chapter.

CHAPTER TEST

Name ______________________________

Performance Assessment

Chapter 3

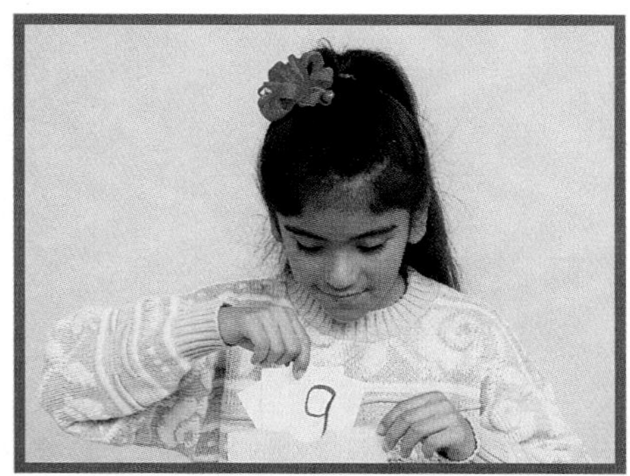

Put two sets of cards numbered 5 through 9 in a bag.

Pick 2 cards.

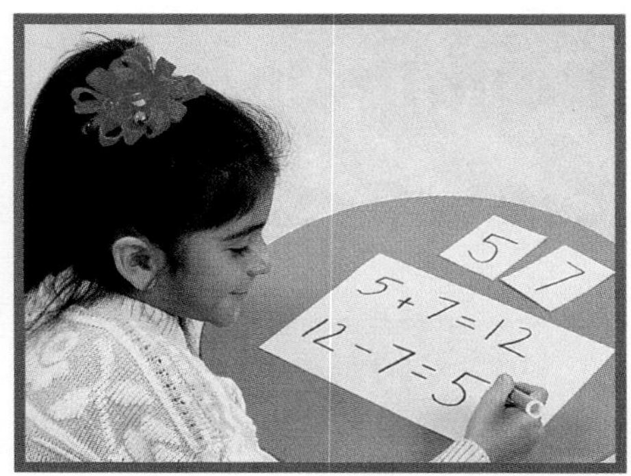

Write an addition fact. Write a related subtraction fact.

	Numbers Picked	Addition Fact	Related Subtraction Fact
1	______ and ______		
2	______ and ______		
3	______ and ______		
4	______ and ______		
5	______ and ______		

Problem Solving

6. Think of a number between 11 and 17.

Write an addition fact with that sum. ______________________________

Write a related subtraction fact. ______________________________

Tell an addition story and a subtraction story for your related facts.

Notes for Home: Your child did an activity that tested Chapter 3 skills, concepts, and problem solving. *Home Activity:* Ask your child to tell the related subtraction fact for 5 + 6 = 11. (11 − 6 = 5 or 11 − 5 = 6)

PERFORMANCE ASSESSMENT

Name ______________________________

Double Up!

Computer Skills You Will Need

1. Draw a shape using your computer's drawing program.

2. Select your drawing. Copy and paste to make two shapes.

Select all your shapes. Copy and paste. Write the double your drawing shows. Repeat the activity. Complete the chart.

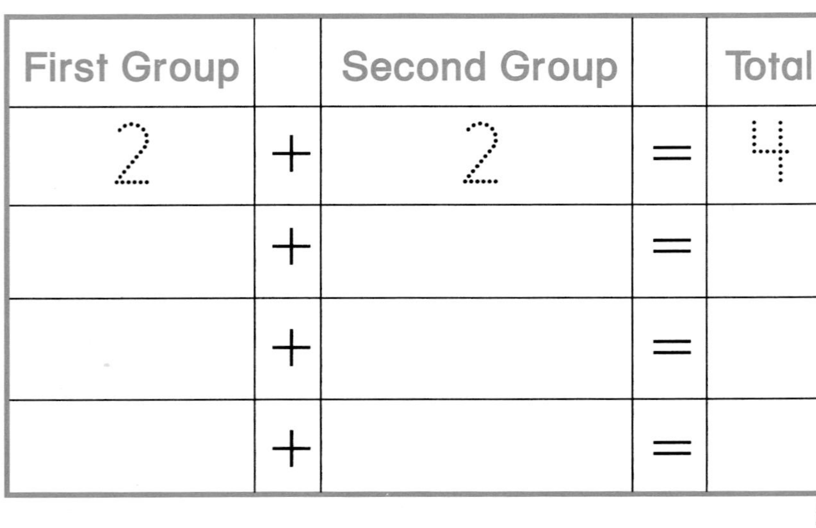

	First Group		Second Group		Total
3	2	+	2	=	4
4		+		=	
5		+		=	
6		+		=	

Tech Talk Explain how you made 8 identical shapes.

Visit our Web site. **www.parent.mathsurf.com**

Double Trouble

1 Look around your home for things that show two matching groups or doubles. Ask a family member to help you.

2 Make a doubles list for sums to 18. List the things you find and draw a picture of them.

3 Tell the family member how each group shows a double.

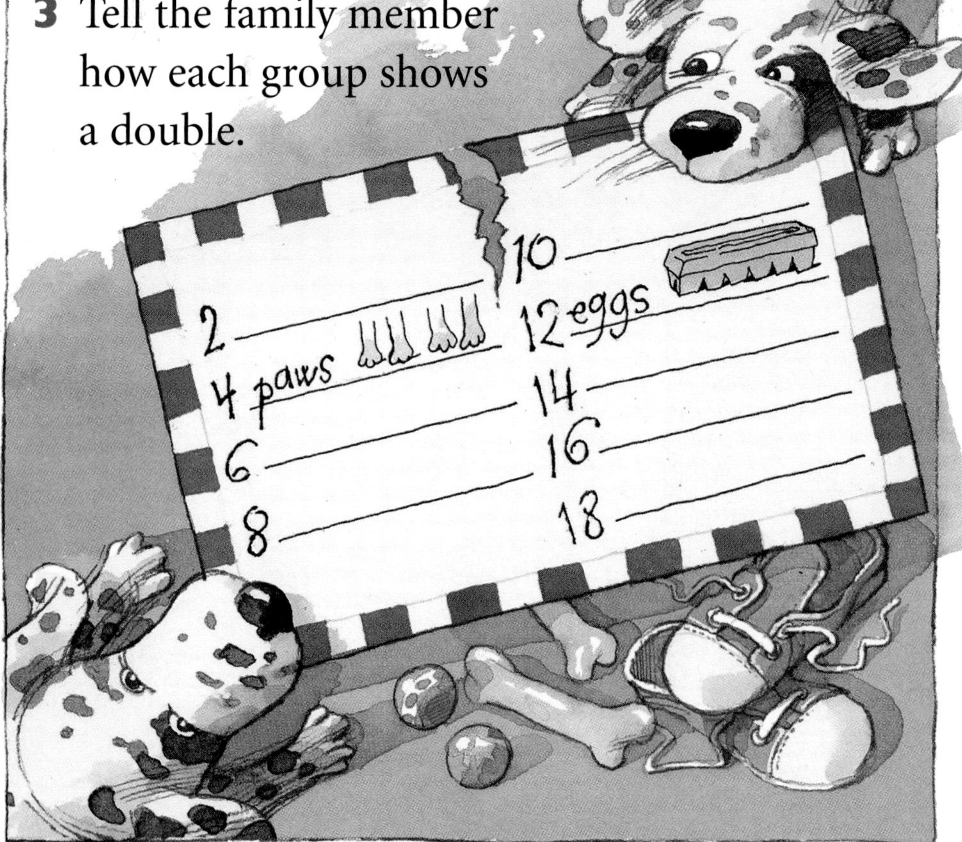

Fold down

MathSoup

Scott Foresman - Addison Wesley My Math Magazine No. 3

Meet the Champ!

Be a Mibster*

Target is one game you can play with marbles.

What You Need

2 marbles
shoe box

How to Play

1 Play with your friends.
2 Each player shoots marbles until two marbles go into any of the openings. Add the scores above the openings.
3 The player with the highest score wins!

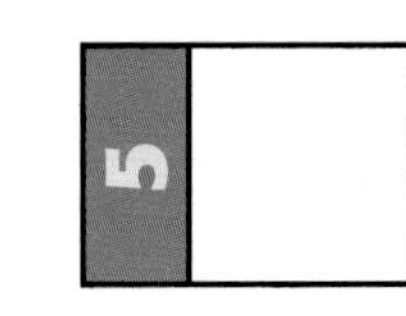

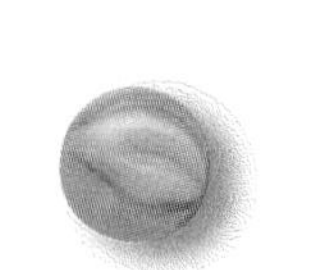

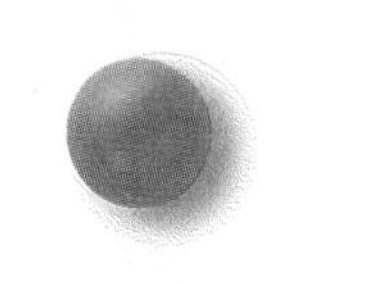
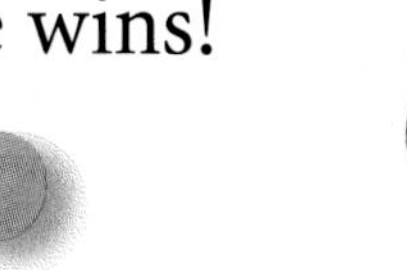

Name	Roll 1	+	Roll 2	=	Score
Chris	3	+	6	=	9
Kim		+		=	
		+		=	
				=	

Cat's-eyes marbles are very popular. Can you see why they're called cat's-eyes?

* **Marble players are called mibsters.**

Notes for Home: Your child played a marble game to practice facts.
Home Activity: Ask your child to tell you the score for 9 + 5. (14)

3 [5] [15]

Now compare the Chinese numbers for
6 and 16.
7 and 17.
8 and 18.
How are all the pairs of numbers alike?

Notes for Home: Your child wrote and compared Chinese numbers.
Home Activity: Ask your child to tell you how the Chinese numbers for 9 and 19 are alike.

A World of Numbers

People around the world write numbers in lots of different ways. These are the Chinese numbers from 1 to 20.

Write the following numbers in Chinese.

1 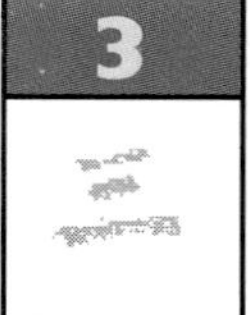

13

十三

2 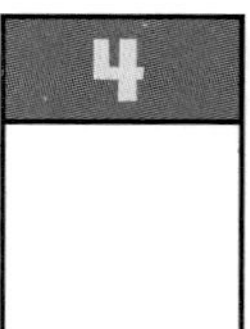 

1	一	11	十一
2	二	12	十二
3	三	13	十三
4	四	14	十四

How to Make the Target

1. Cut five openings in a cardboard box.
2. Make openings widest at the ends, narrower next to the ends, and narrowest in the middle.
3. Give the openings the scores shown above.

On a Roll!

David McGee rolled his way to winning the National Marbles Tournament.

2. Why was 6 afraid of 7?

Go Figure!

Number Noodles

Find the number words. Look across and down. How many can you find?

one
two
three
four
five
six
seven
eight
nine
ten

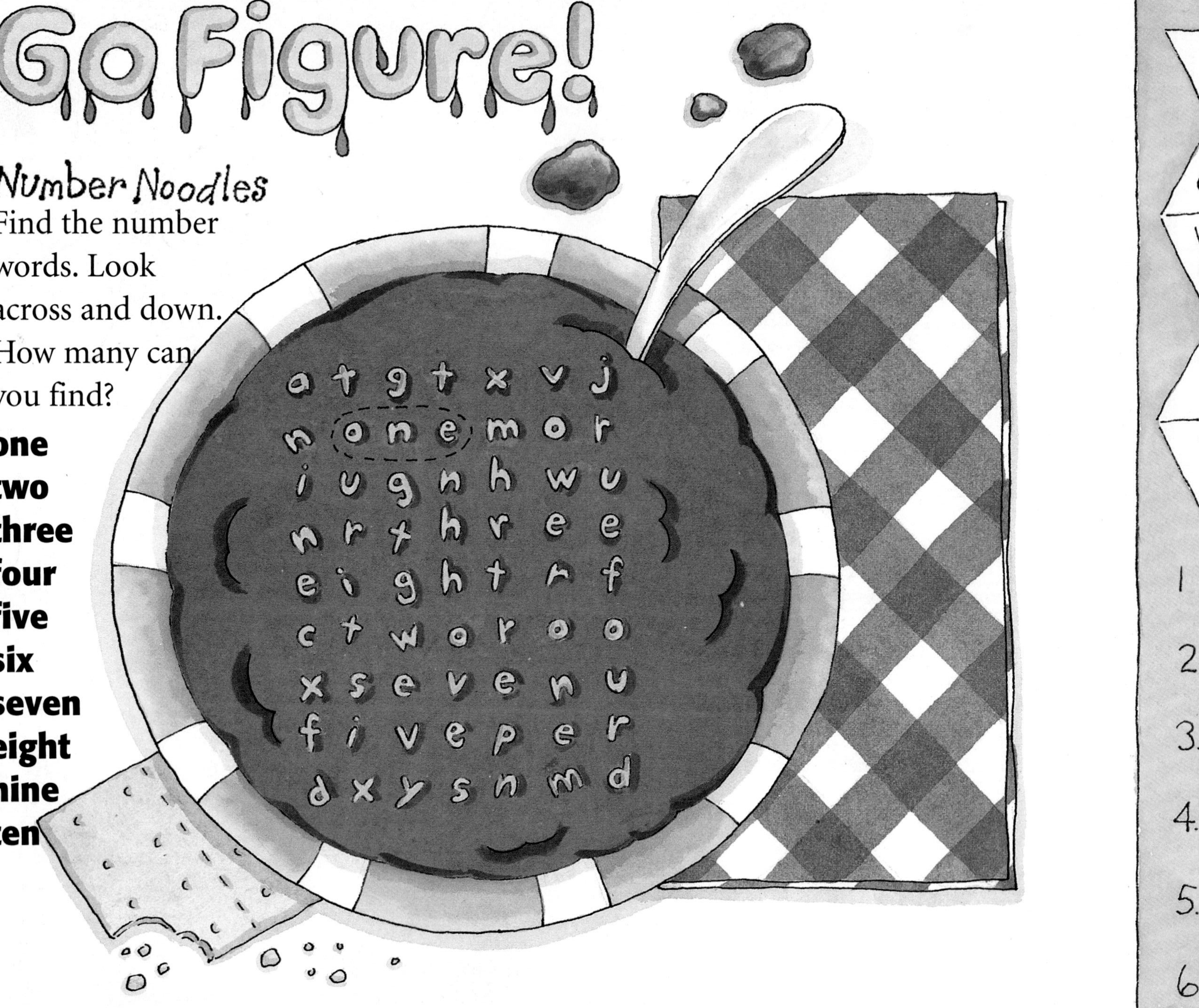

1. What kind of snake knows its numbers?

3. What is black and white and has sixteen wheels?

Break the Code

1	2	3
●	▬	◆
4	5	6
♥	▲	♣
7	8	9
■	⧗	☾
10	11	12
▱	⬢	☆

1. ▲ + ♣ = ____
2. ♥ + ♥ = ____
3. ◆ + ■ = ____
4. ⬢ - ♣ = ____
5. ⧗ - ♥ = ____
6. ☆ - ⧗ = ____

Notes for Home: Your child found number words in a puzzle and used coded numbers to write addition sentences. *Home Activity:* Ask your child to write a coded number sentence. (Example: ▬ + ▲ = 7)

Answers: 1. An adder 2. Because 7 "ate" 9 3. A zebra on rollerskates

CHAPTER 4

Using Addition and Subtraction

Fun at the Fair

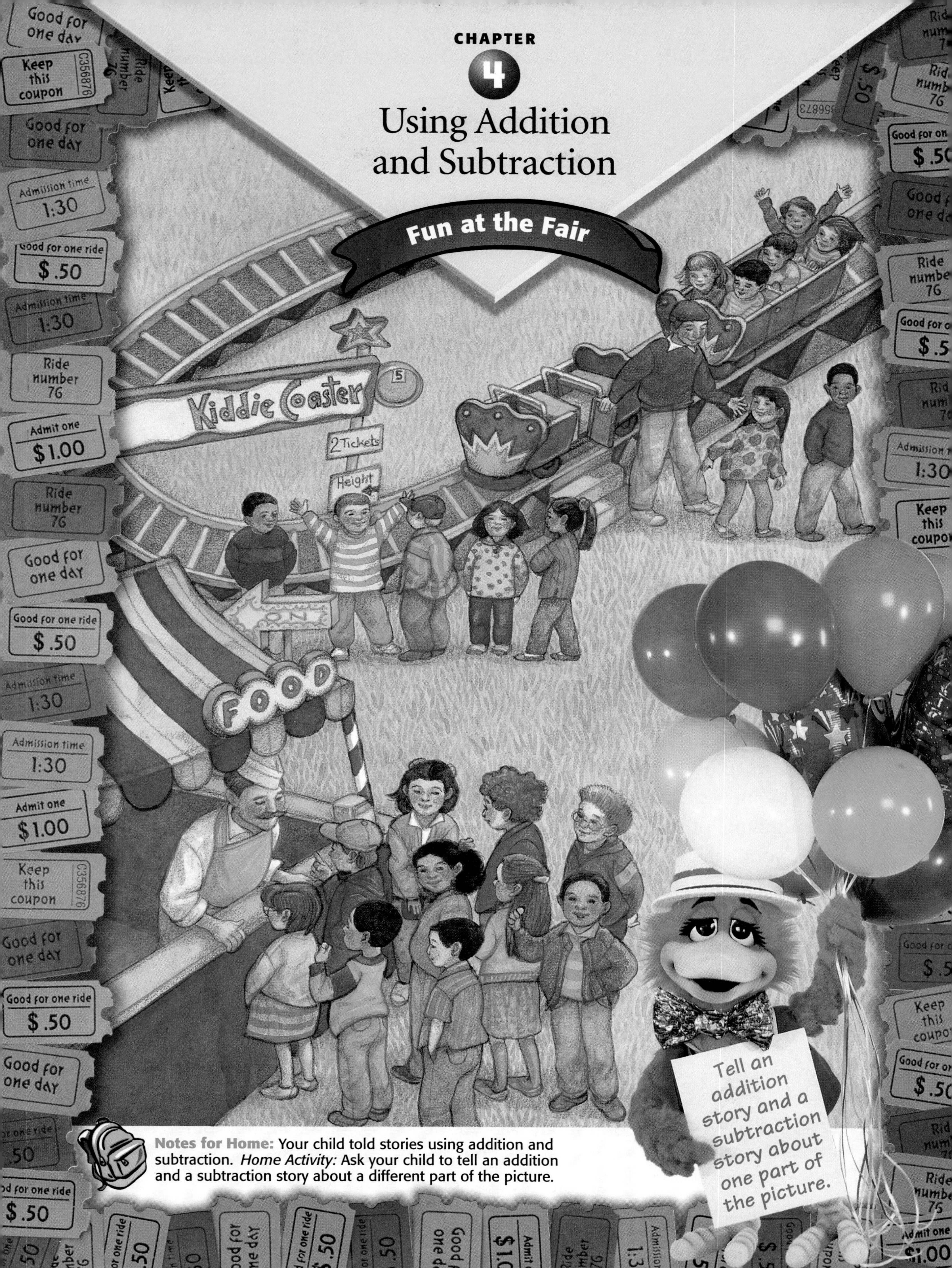

Notes for Home: Your child told stories using addition and subtraction. *Home Activity:* Ask your child to tell an addition and a subtraction story about a different part of the picture.

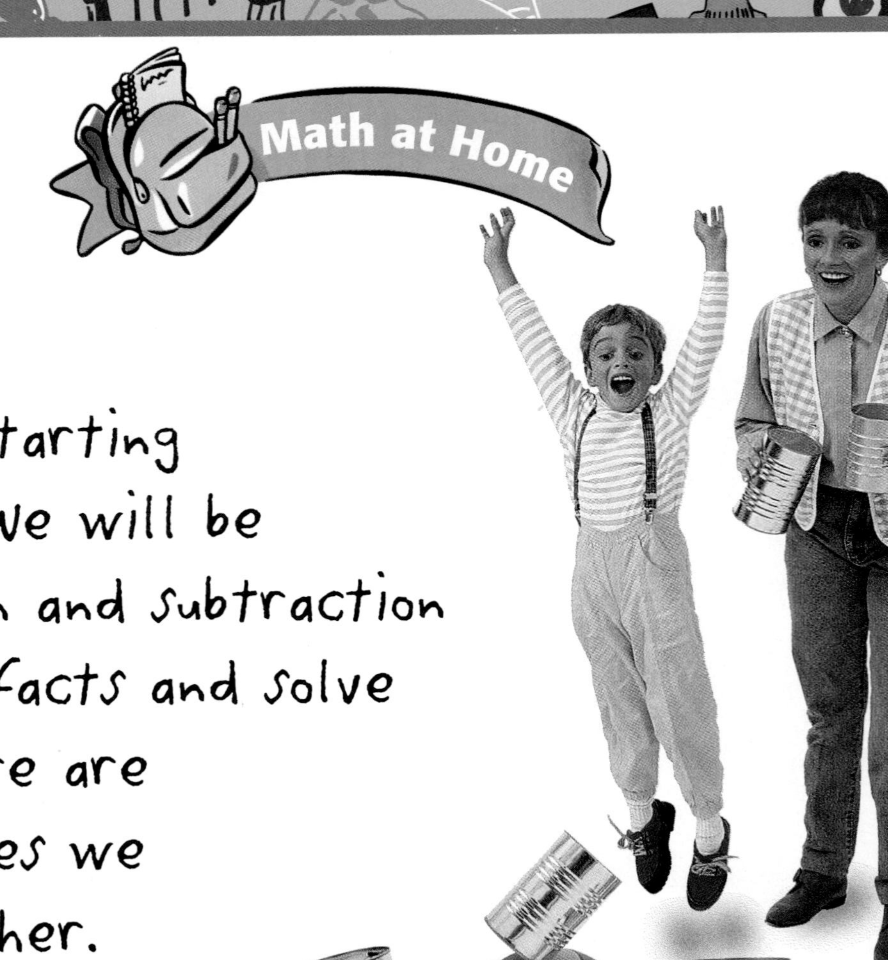

Dear Family,
Our class is starting Chapter 4. We will be using addition and subtraction as we learn facts and solve problems. Here are some activities we can do together.

Bean Counters

Use 12 to 18 objects, such as dried beans. Ask your child to count them. Put some into a cup. Show your child the remaining beans. Ask your child what number they would add to the remaining beans to equal the original number.

Knock Them Down

Use a ball and 12 to 18 empty cans. Set up the cans like bowling pins. Roll the ball at the "pins." Ask how many were knocked down and how many are left. Use the numbers to write a subtraction sentence.

Community Connection

Help your child find numbers between 12 and 18 on billboards, street signs, and in other parts of the community. Ask your child to subtract a number between 5 and 9 from the number they found.

Visit our Web site. www.parent.mathsurf.com

Name

Explore Fact Families

Explore

Use 7 [cube] and 5 [cube].

Tell addition and subtraction stories using 7, 5, and 12.

ON

OFF

Draw one of your stories.

Share

Compare your stories with a friend.

How are they the same? How are they different?

Notes for Home: Your child explored telling addition and subtraction stories about 12 objects.
Home Activity: Ask your child to use 12 objects, such as marbles or pennies, to show you two of the stories he or she told.

EXPLORE

Connect

EXPLORE

Complete each fact family.
Add or subtract.

1

$6 + 7 =$ 13 $\qquad 13 - 7 =$ 6

$7 + 6 =$ ____ $\qquad 13 - 6 =$ ____

2

$9 + 5 =$ ____ $\qquad 14 - 5 =$ ____

$5 + 9 =$ ____ $\qquad 14 - 9 =$ ____

Talk About It Tell the fact family for the numbers 4, 9, and 13.

Notes for Home: Your child added and subtracted using fact families. *Home Activity:* Give your child 17 objects, such as pennies. Ask your child to write or say number sentences for 7, 8, and 15. (7 + 8 = 15; 8 + 7 = 15; 15 − 8 = 7; 15 − 7 = 8)

Name

Use Addition to Check Subtraction

Learn

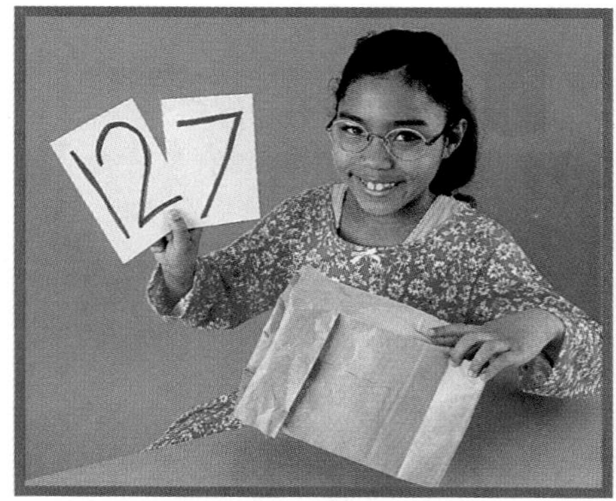

Put cards with the numbers 7 to 12 in a bag. Pick 2 cards.

Make a subtraction fact. Write the difference on a third card.

Can you use the same numbers to make an addition fact?

Hmm...If we can do this...

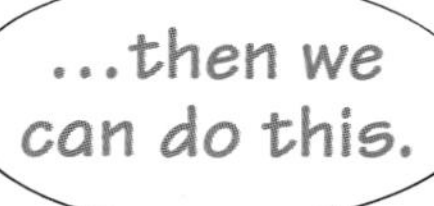

...then we can do this.

Check

	Cards Picked	Subtraction Fact	Addition Fact
1	____ and ____	____ − ____ = ____	____ + ____ = ____
2	____ and ____	____ − ____ = ____	____ + ____ = ____
3	____ and ____	____ − ____ = ____	____ + ____ = ____

Subtract. Write a related addition sentence to check your answer.

4. $14 - 6 =$ ____ ____ + ____ = ____

5. $13 - 9 =$ ____ ____ + ____ = ____

Talk About It Tell a friend a subtraction fact. Ask your friend to tell you a related addition fact.

Notes for Home: Your child subtracted and checked answers by using addition. *Home Activity:* Ask your child to explain how he or she used addition to check subtraction in Exercise 1.

Practice

Use these numbers. Write a subtraction fact.
Write an addition fact to check.

6. 15 8

15	7
− 8	+ 8
7	15

7. 5 14

8. 9 17

9. 13 7

10. 16 9

11. 8 14

PRACTICE

Problem Solving

12. Complete the number sentence.

$17 - 8 =$ ____

13. Write two related addition facts that you can use to check your answer.

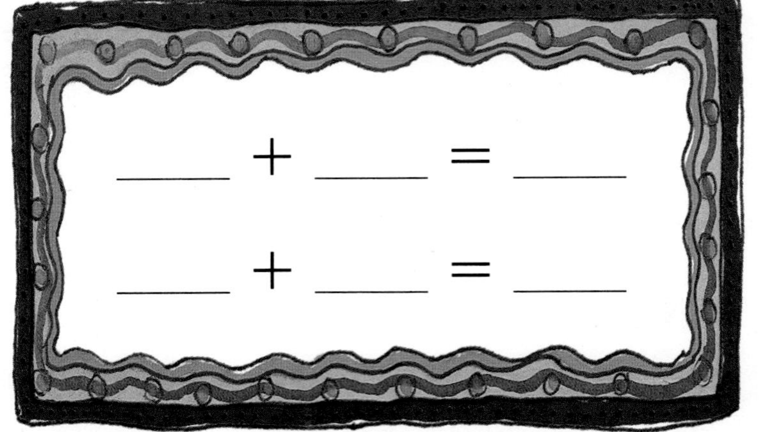

Notes for Home: Your child practiced checking subtraction using addition. *Home Activity:* Ask your child to find 14 − 9 and check the answer by adding. (14 − 9 = 5; 5 + 9 = 14 or 9 + 5 = 14)

Name

Problem Solving: Draw a Picture

Learn

PROBLEM SOLVING GUIDE

Understand • Plan • Solve • Look Back

There are 14 cans in the game. Jasmine knocked over 5 cans. On her next throw she knocked over 4 cans. How many cans are still standing?

5 cans

You can draw a picture to solve the problem.

Check

Draw a picture to solve the problem.

1. Nora's family brings 12 sandwiches to the fair. They eat 5 sandwiches at lunch. They eat 3 more sandwiches later. How many sandwiches are left?

   _____ sandwiches

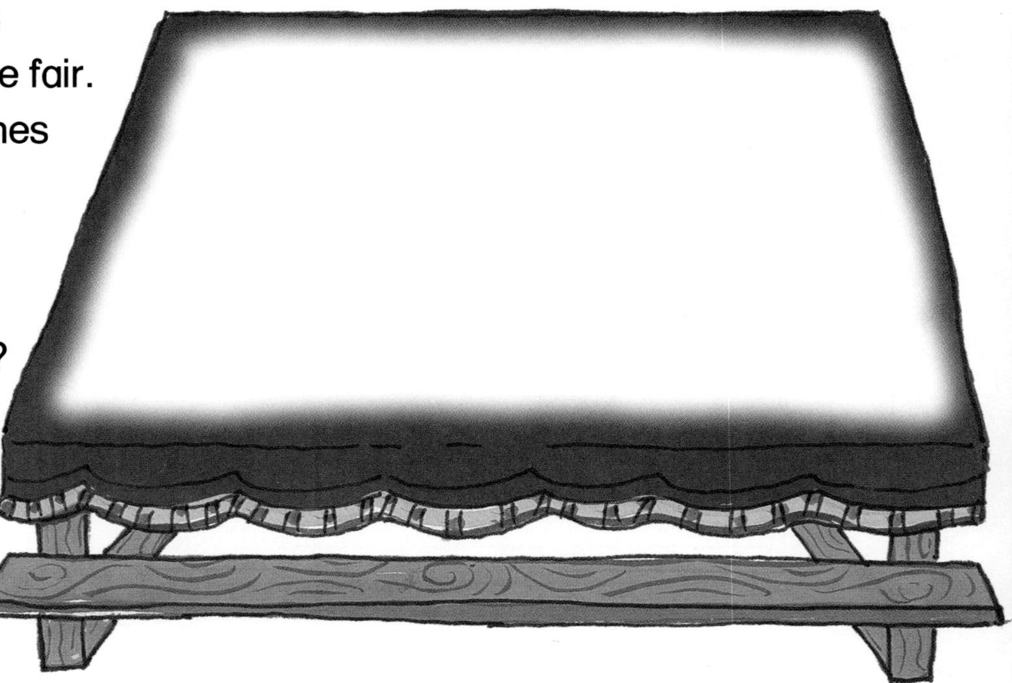

Talk About It Tell how you solved the problem about sandwiches.

Note for Home: Your child solved problems by drawing pictures. *Home Activity:* Ask your child to tell a math story for a picture of 5 objects, 4 more objects, and 3 more objects.

PROBLEM SOLVING

Practice

Draw a picture to solve the problem.

2. Josh meets his aunts, uncles, and cousins at the fair. There are 4 men, 4 women, 2 boys, and 3 girls. How many family members are there?

   _____ family members

Write About It

3. Write a problem about the fair.
   Ask a friend to draw a picture to solve it.

   ____

   ____

   ____

   ____

   ____

Notes for Home: Your child practiced drawing pictures to solve problems. *Home Activity:* Place 15 objects, such as buttons, in a cup. Remove 6 buttons, then remove 2 more. Ask your child to draw a picture to show how many buttons remain in the cup.

Name ______

Mixed Practice

Lessons 1–4

Concepts and Skills

Write the number sentences to make a fact family.

1 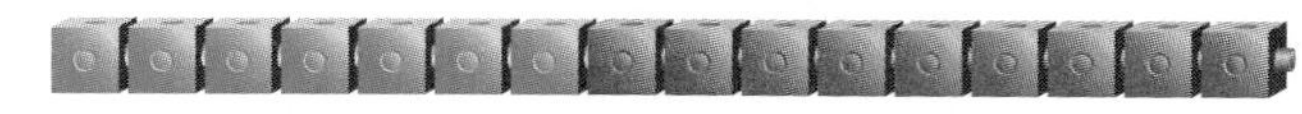

___ + ___ = ___ ___ − ___ = ___

___ + ___ = ___ ___ − ___ = ___

Subtract. Then write a related addition fact.

2 13 − 6 = ___ ___ + ___ = ___

3 15 − 9 = ___ ___ + ___ = ___

Problem Solving

Draw a picture to solve the problem.

4 Andre had 15 tickets for rides.
He gave 6 to his sister.
He gave 3 to his brother.
How many are left?

___ tickets

Journal

5 Draw a picture that shows 2 groups.
Write the fact family that your picture shows.

Notes for Home: Your child practiced addition and subtraction facts and solving problems.
Home Activity: Ask your child to write a related addition fact for 18 − 9 = 9. (9 + 9 = 18)

For additional practice, see Basic Facts Review, page 543, Set 5.

Name

Cumulative Review

Chapters 1–4

Concepts and Skills

Add.

1

7	8	9	7	6	8	8
+ 7	+ 7	+ 9	+ 6	+ 6	+ 9	+ 8

Problem Solving

Use the graph to answer the questions.

2 How many children like the Ferris Wheel best?

______ children

3 How many more children picked the Kiddie Coaster than the Ferris Wheel?

______ more children

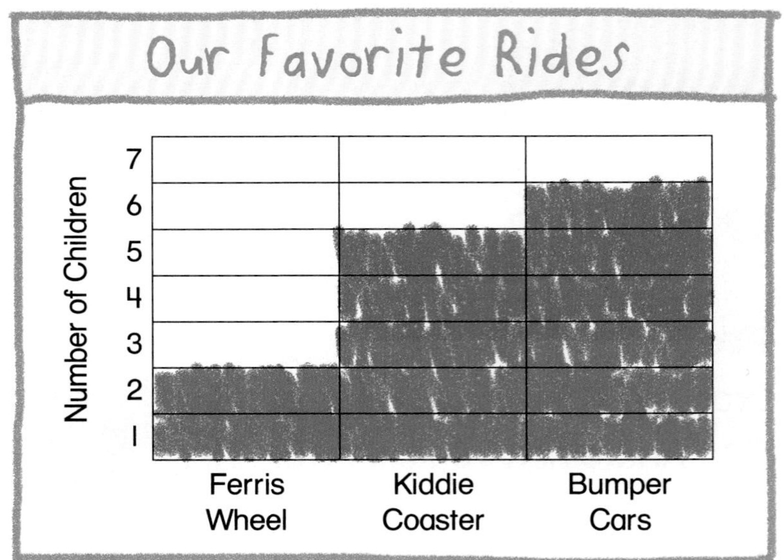

Test Prep

Fill in the ○ for the correct answer.

Solve each problem.

4 Mrs. Kim's class has 9 girls and 7 boys. How many children are in the class?

17 ○ 16 ○ 15 ○ 2 ○

5 Mr. Roy's class has 17 children. 9 are boys. How many are girls?

6 ○ 7 ○ 8 ○ 9 ○

Notes for Home: Your child reviewed addition facts, reading a graph, and solving word problems. *Home Activity:* Ask your child how many fewer children picked the Kiddie Coaster than the Bumper Cars in the graph. (1)

Name

Missing Addends

Learn

The ring toss game gives toy bears for prizes. At the end of the day, there are 4 bears left on the shelf. The shelf holds 12 bears. How many bears are needed to fill the shelf?

4 + __?__ = 12

You can use the fact family to help find the missing number!

__8__ + 4 = 12

12 − __8__ = 4

12 − 4 = __8__

8 bears are needed to fill the shelf.

Check

Find the missing numbers. Use fact families to help you.

1

16

9 | ___

9 + ___ = 16

16 − 9 = ___

___ + 9 = 16

16 − ___ = 9

2

13

___ | 5

13 − ___ = 5

5 + ___ = 13

___ + 5 = 13

13 − 5 = ___

Talk About It How would you find the missing number in 5 + ___ = 14?

Notes for Home: Your child used fact families to find missing numbers. *Home Activity:* Ask your child to describe the fact family they could use to solve 6 + ___ = 15. (15 − 6 = 9; 15 − 9 = 6; 9 + 6 = 15; 6 + 9 = 15)

Practice

PRACTICE

Find the missing numbers.
Use the fact family to help you.

3

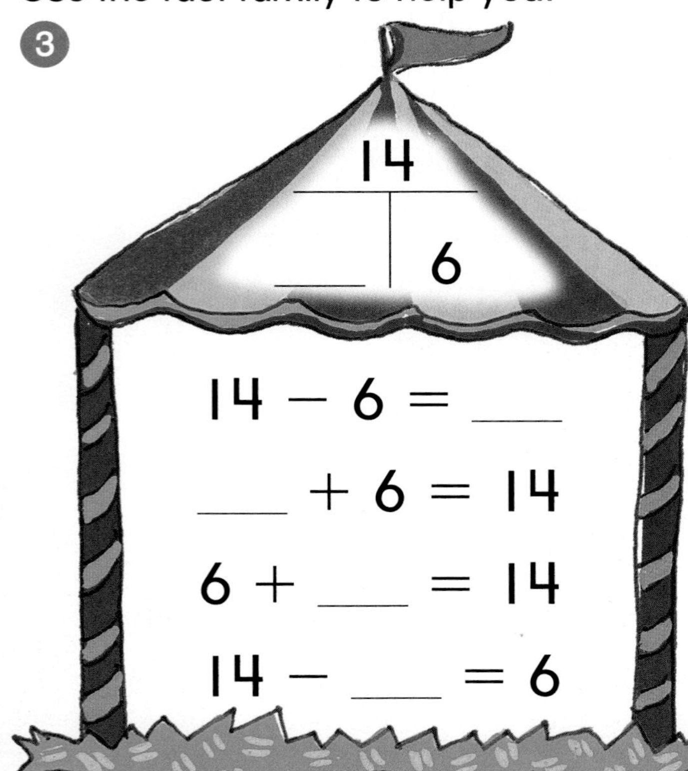

4

5 Ella won 11 prizes in all at the fair. She won 4 of the prizes in the morning. How many prizes did she win in the afternoon?

_____ prizes

6 John has 7 tickets for rides at the fair. He buys more tickets. Now he has 15. How many tickets did he buy?

_____ tickets

Problem Solving Patterns

7 Find the missing numbers. Find the pattern. Write the next fact.

$$\begin{array}{r}5\\+\square\\\hline 6\end{array}\quad\begin{array}{r}5\\+\square\\\hline 8\end{array}\quad\begin{array}{r}5\\+\square\\\hline 10\end{array}\quad\begin{array}{r}5\\+\square\\\hline 12\end{array}\quad\begin{array}{r}\square\\+\square\\\hline \square\end{array}$$

Notes for Home: Your child practiced using fact families to find missing numbers.
Home Activity: Ask your child to solve 4 + ___ = 13. (9)

Name ___________________________

Practice Game

Addition Tic-Tac-Toe

Players 2

What You Need

9 counters

paper clip

pencil

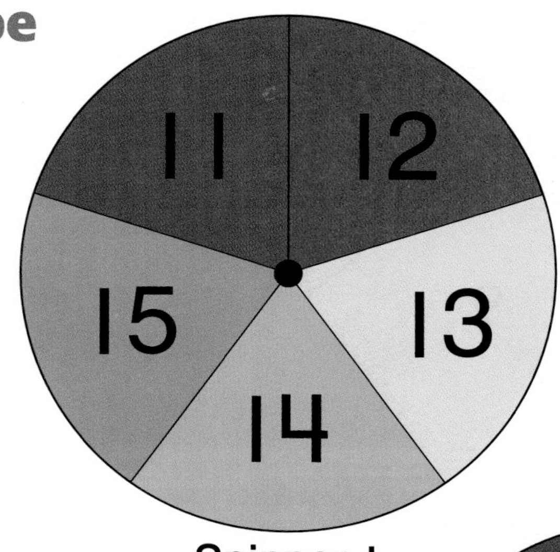

Spinner 1

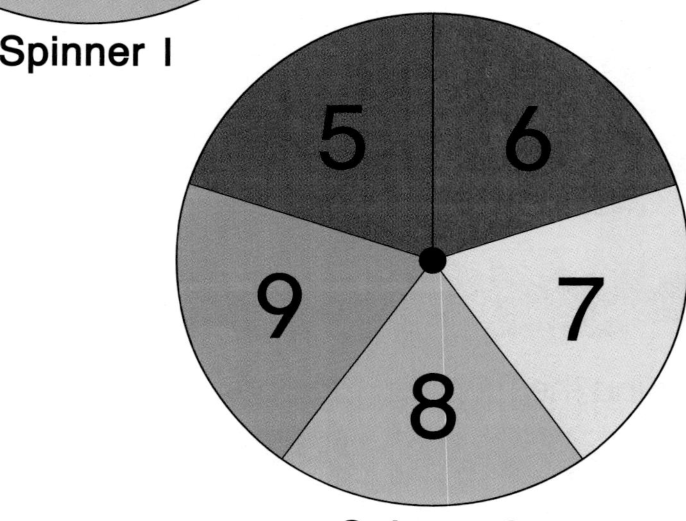

Spinner 2

How to Play

1. Spin Spinner 1. This is your target number.
2. Spin Spinner 2. What number would you add to this number to reach your target number?
3. Use a yellow counter. Cover the square on the gameboard that shows the number you added.
4. Have a friend do Steps 1–3. They should use a red counter.
5. If a number is already covered, the player's turn is over.
6. The first player with 3 in a row, wins!

Gameboard

Notes for Home: Your child played a game to practice adding numbers with sums through 15.
Home Activity: Ask your child what number he or she would add to 9 to get a sum of 15. (6)

PRACTICE

Name ___________________________

STOP and Practice

Write a fact family for each group of numbers.

1

15	
6	9

___ + ___ = ___

___ + ___ = ___

___ − ___ = ___

___ − ___ = ___

2

12	
7	5

___ + ___ = ___

___ + ___ = ___

___ − ___ = ___

___ − ___ = ___

Find the missing numbers. Finish the fact families.

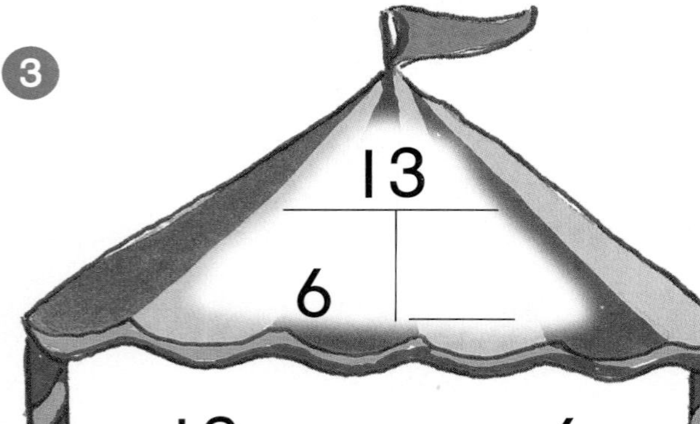

3

13	
6	___

13 − ___ = 6

___ + 6 = 13

13 − 6 = ___

6 + ___ = 13

4

11	
___	3

11 − 3 = ___

___ + 3 = 11

3 + ___ = 11

11 − ___ = 3

Notes for Home: Your child practiced addition and subtraction. *Home Activity:* Ask your child to tell you the fact family for 9, 6, and 3. (6 + 3 = 9; 3 + 6 = 9; 9 − 3 = 6; 9 − 6 = 3)

PRACTICE

Name

Three Addends

Learn

You can add in different ways.

2 + 3 + 7 = 12

2 + 3 = 5
5 + 7 = 12

Add the numbers in order.

Add the doubles first and then add the other number.

Make a ten first and then add the other number.

Check

Circle the numbers you would add first. Then add.

1

2	9	4	5	6	2	3
1	1	2	5	4	7	4
+ 8	+ 1	+ 6	+ 3	+ 1	+ 2	+ 5
11						

2 1 + 7 + 3 = ____

3 3 + 4 + 3 = ____

4 5 + 4 + 4 = ____

5 2 + 6 + 2 = ____

Talk About It Explain two ways to find 3 + 7 + 3.

Notes for Home: Your child added three numbers to find sums through 18. *Home Activity:* Ask your child to explain how he or she would add 6 + 4 + 4. (Sample answers: Find 4 + 4 = 8 and then 8 + 6 = 14; or find 6 + 4 = 10 and then 10 + 4 = 14.)

Practice

Add across.
Add down.

I add across!
5 + 4 + 3 = 12

6

3	4	6	
5	4	3	12
2	3	4	
10			

7

6	2	1	
4	3	2	
2	3	7	

8

7	0	2	
3	8	6	
1	2	1	

9

1	3	4	
5	0	4	
1	6	4	

PRACTICE

Problem Solving

10 A player needs at least 12 points to win a prize. Find each person's total score. Circle the names of the winners.

	First Toss	Second Toss	Third Toss	Total Score
Adam	5	3	5	_____ points
Iris	6	4	1	_____ points
Vern	2	3	7	_____ points
Jody	8	2	2	_____ points

Notes for Home: Your child practiced adding three numbers. *Home Activity:* Ask your child which children in the Problem–Solving chart scored exactly 12 points. (Vern, Jody)

For additional practice, see Skills Practice Bank, page 530, Set 2.

Name

ALGEBRA READINESS

Use Addition and Subtraction Rules

Learn

Follow the rule to finish the table.

Add 3.	
4	7
8	11
6	9

Check

Follow the rule. Add or subtract.

1

Subtract 2.	
18	16
10	
15	

2

Add 5.	
9	
4	
6	

3

Subtract 4.	
12	
9	
11	

Add the numbers in the first column.
Then follow the rule.

4

Add 6.	
2 + 3	11
4 + 3	
1 + 2	

5

Add 4.	
3 + 3	
6 + 1	
5 + 3	

Talk About It How do you use the rule to complete the first table on this page?

Notes for Home: Your child practiced adding and subtracting. *Home Activity:* Ask your child to explain how he or she completed the table in Exercise 4.

Practice

Follow the rule. Add or subtract.

6

Add 6.	
6	12
4	
9	

7

Subtract 3.	
10	
6	
7	

8

Subtract 5.	
10	
5	
8	

Add the numbers in the first column.
Then follow the rule.

9

Add 5.	
5 + 4	14
2 + 3	
1 + 2	

10

Add 3.	
2 + 2	
7 + 3	
8 + 1	

PRACTICE

Problem Solving

Write your own rule for each chart.
Then follow the rule. Add or subtract.

11

Add ____.	
9	
6	
8	

12

Add ____.	
5	
4	
7	

13

Subtract ____.	
12	
10	
6	

Notes for Home: Your child practiced adding and subtracting. *Home Activity:* Ask your child to choose three numbers less than 16 and then add 2 to each of them.

Name

ALGEBRA READINESS

What's My Rule?

Learn

How can you find the rule?

Add 2.	
2	4
1	3
3	5

What do you do to 2 to get 4?

What do you do to 1 to get 3?

What do you do to 3 to get 5?

Check

Write the rule. Write the missing number.

1.

Subtract 1.	
9	8
4	3
3	

2.

3	6
9	12
2	

3.

2	7
1	6
4	

4.

9	4
5	0
6	

5.

3 + 6	11
1 + 2	5
4 + 4	

Talk About It In the fourth problem, compare the numbers in each row. How do you know that you need to subtract?

Notes for Home: Your child found the rule (such as add 5 or subtract 5) for addition and subtraction tables. *Home Activity:* Have your child explain how he or she found the rule for Exercise 3.

Practice

Write the rule. Write the missing number.

6

9	5
8	4
6	2
4	

7

2 + 3	10
1 + 1	7
5 + 3	13
5 + 1	

Write your own.

Write numbers on each table that follow a rule. Ask a friend to find each rule.

8

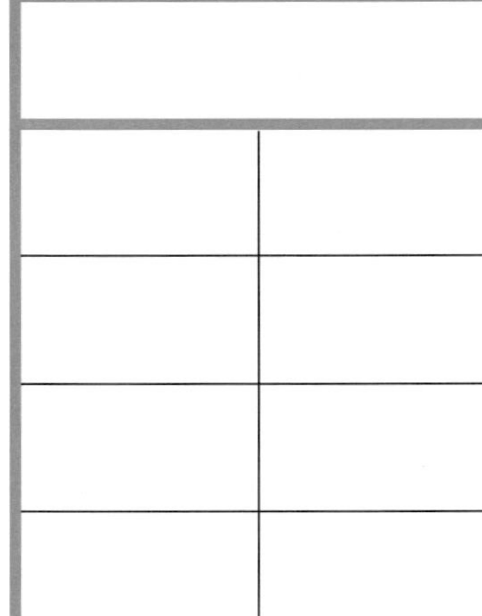

9

Problem Solving

10 Heidi has 4 tickets. Duane has 7 tickets. Alicia has 9 tickets. Each of them buys 6 more tickets. How many tickets does each have now?

Heidi: _____ tickets

Duane: _____ tickets

Alicia: _____ tickets

11 Kara has 9 tickets. Kenji has 14 tickets. Pedro has 11 tickets. After they go on a ride, Kara has 4 tickets, Kenji has 9, and Pedro has 6. How many tickets did each child use?

_____ tickets

Notes for Home: Your child practiced finding the rule (such as add 5 or subtract 4) for addition and subtraction tables. *Home Activity:* Ask your child to explain how he or she made the tables in Exercises 8 and 9.

Name ______________________________

Reading for Math

Sequencing

At the school fair, Dana won 4 goldfish.
She won 2 posters.
Then she won 1 puzzle.
How many prizes
did she win in all?

This math story has a beginning part, two middle parts, and an end part.

Draw pictures to show the parts of the math story.

Goldfish

1

Posters

2

Puzzles

3

EXIT

4

Talk About It How does knowing the beginning, middle, and end parts of a math story help you solve the problem?

Notes for Home: Your children drew the beginning, middle, and end parts of a math story. *Home Activity:* Ask your child to tell the two things that happened in the middle of the story.

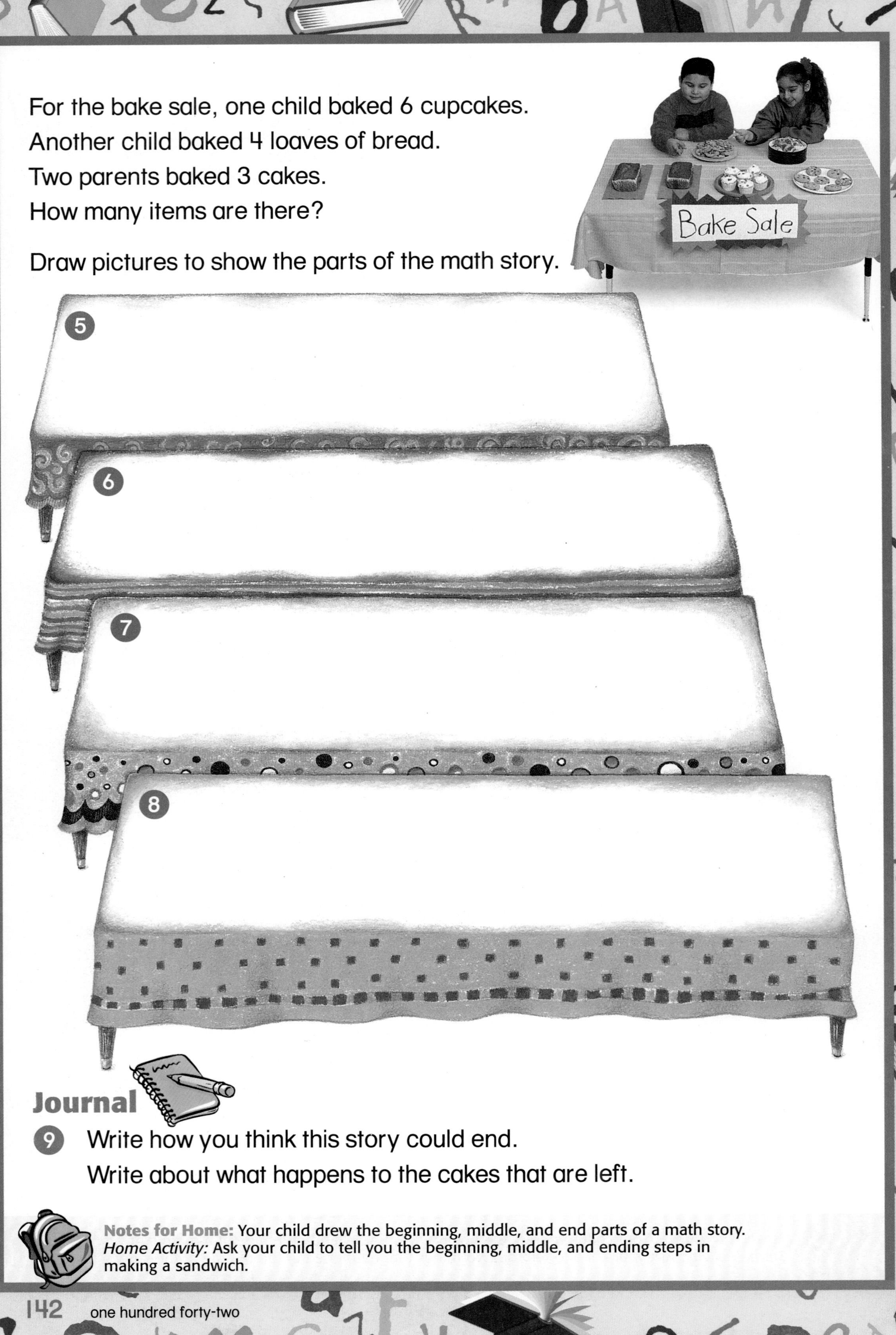

For the bake sale, one child baked 6 cupcakes.
Another child baked 4 loaves of bread.
Two parents baked 3 cakes.
How many items are there?

Draw pictures to show the parts of the math story.

5

6

7

8

Journal

9 Write how you think this story could end.
Write about what happens to the cakes that are left.

Notes for Home: Your child drew the beginning, middle, and end parts of a math story. *Home Activity:* Ask your child to tell you the beginning, middle, and ending steps in making a sandwich.

Name

Problem Solving: Multiple-Step Problems

Learn

PROBLEM SOLVING GUIDE

Understand • Plan • Solve • Look Back

Use 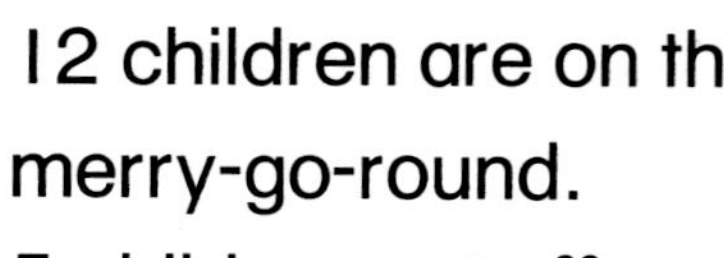.

12 children are on the merry-go-round.
5 children get off.

Step 1: Write a number sentence. Subtract since 5 got off.

$12 - 5 = 7$ children

3 children get on. How many children are on the merry-go-round now?

Step 2: Write a number sentence. Add since 3 got on.

$7 + 3 = 10$ children

Check

Use counters.
Write each number sentence.
Solve.

1 9 children are on the roller coaster.
6 more children get on.

$9 + 6 = 15$ children

7 children get off. How many children are on the roller coaster now?

__________ children

Talk About It Use $3 + 5 = 8$ and $8 - 2 = 6$ to tell a math story.

Notes for Home: Your child solved word problems. *Home Activity:* Ask your child to make up his or her own math story using $13 - 4 = 9$ and $9 + 7 = 16$.

PROBLEM SOLVING

Practice

Use (counters).
Write each number sentence. Solve.

2 At the fair, Kari bought 6 balloons. 4 flew away. $6 - 4 = 2$ balloons

She bought 6 more balloons. How many does she have now? ______ balloons

3 Jared bought 14 tickets for rides. He used 9 tickets. ______ tickets

He bought 7 more. How many tickets does Jared have now? ______ tickets

4 8 friends rode rides at the fair. 5 more friends joined them. ______ friends

6 friends left. How many friends are there now? ______ friends

Tell a Math Story

5 Tell a story problem. Include addition and subtraction in your story. Ask a friend to solve your problem.

Notes for Home: Your child practiced solving word problems. *Home Activity:* Ask your child to tell you the word problem he or she made up for Tell a Math Story.

For additional practice, see Skills Practice Bank, page 530, Set 3.

Name

Mixed Practice

Lessons 5–9

Concepts and Skills

1. Find the missing number in the fact family.

$9 + \_\_\_ = 17$

$\_\_\_ + 9 = 17$

$17 - 9 = \_\_\_$

$17 - \_\_\_ = 9$

2. Add.

$$\begin{array}{r} 7 \\ 2 \\ + 3 \\ \hline \end{array} \qquad \begin{array}{r} 5 \\ 4 \\ + 5 \\ \hline \end{array} \qquad \begin{array}{r} 3 \\ 4 \\ + 6 \\ \hline \end{array}$$

3. Follow the rule.
Write the missing numbers.

Subtract 6.	
12	
10	

4. Find the rule.
Write the rule.

9	15
7	13

Problem Solving

Write each number sentence. Solve.

5. Tammy bought 10 tickets.
She gave 6 to Don. __________ tickets

She bought 3 more tickets.
How many tickets
does Tammy have now? __________ tickets

Journal

6. Write all the ways you can solve 2 + 3 + 7.

Notes for Home: Your child practiced finding missing numbers, adding three numbers, and solving problems. *Home Activity:* Ask your child to tell you how to find the rule in Exercise 4.

For additional practice, see Basic Facts Review, page 543, Set 6.

Name ____________________

Cumulative Review

Chapters 1-4

Concepts and Skills

Add. Write the number sentence.

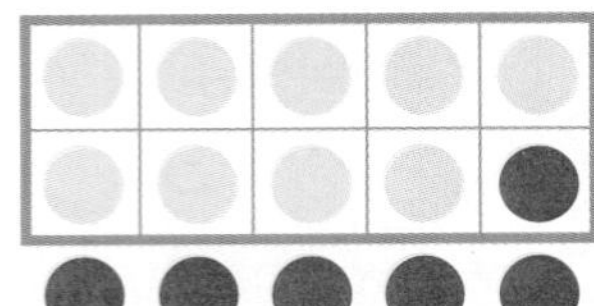

____ + ____ = ____

2

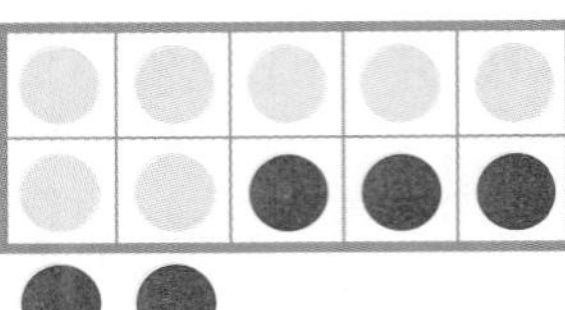

____ + ____ = ____

Problem Solving

Use the graph to answer the questions.

3 How many people visited the fair on Saturday?

____ people

4 On which day did the fewest people visit?

____

Number of People at the Fair	
Friday	🚶🚶🚶
Saturday	🚶🚶🚶🚶🚶
Sunday	🚶🚶🚶🚶

Each 🚶 means 10 people.

Test Prep

Fill in the ○ for the correct answer.

5 Which fact is shown by the picture?

6 + 5 ○ 6 + 6 ○ 6 + 7 ○ 6 − 6 ○

6 Add 8 more. How many in all?

○ 15
○ 16
○ 17
○ 18

Notes for Home: Your child reviewed numbers, used graphs to solve problems, and practiced addition facts. *Home Activity:* Ask your child to use the graph on this page to find how many people visited the fair on Sunday. (40)

Name ______________________________

Chapter 4 Review

Vocabulary

1. Complete the fact family.

$7 + 5 = \_\_\_$ $12 - 5 = \_\_\_$

$5 + 7 = \_\_\_$ $12 - 7 = \_\_\_$

Concepts and Skills

2. Find the missing numbers in the fact family.

$8 + \_\_\_ = 14$

$\_\_\_ + 8 = 14$

$14 - 8 = \_\_\_$

$14 - \_\_\_ = 8$

3. Find the rule. Write the rule.

10	4
7	1
13	7

4. Subtract. Write a related addition sentence.

$16 - 9 = \_\_\_$

$\_\_\_ + \_\_\_ = \_\_\_$

5. Add.

$$\begin{array}{r} 6 \\ 4 \\ +\ 4 \\ \hline \end{array} \qquad \begin{array}{r} 7 \\ 3 \\ +\ 2 \\ \hline \end{array} \qquad \begin{array}{r} 5 \\ 3 \\ +\ 5 \\ \hline \end{array}$$

Problem Solving

Write each number sentence. Solve.

6. 7 children are on the boat ride.
8 more children get on. ______________________ children

6 children get off. How many
children are on the boat ride now? ______________________ children

Notes for Home: Your child reviewed Chapter 4 vocabulary, concepts, skills, and problem solving. *Home Activity:* Ask your child to tell you how he or she solved Exercise 4.

CHAPTER REVIEW

Name ______________________

Chapter 4 Test

1 Find the missing number in the fact family.

4 + ___ = 13

___ + 4 = 13

13 − 4 = ___

13 − ___ = 4

2 Add.

6	5	2
4	2	4
+ 3	+ 5	+ 4

3 Follow the rule.
Write the missing numbers.

Subtract 6.	
15	
14	

4 Subtract.
Write a related addition sentence.

16 − 8 = ___

___ + ___ = ___

5 Draw a picture. Solve the problem.

12 prizes are on the shelf.
4 children win prizes.
3 more children win prizes.
How many prizes are left?

___ prizes

6 Write each number sentence. Solve.

Toni bought 14 tickets for rides.
She used 7 for the Ferris wheel.

___ − ___ = ___

She bought 3 more. How many tickets does she have now?

___ + ___ = ___

CHAPTER TEST

Notes for Home: Your child was tested on Chapter 4 concepts, skills, and problem solving.
Home Activity: Change the rule in Exercise 3 to Subtract 7. Ask your child to give the answers using this rule.

Name ______________________________

Performance Assessment

Chapter 4

Put three sets of cards numbered 3 to 5 in a bag. Pick three cards from the bag.

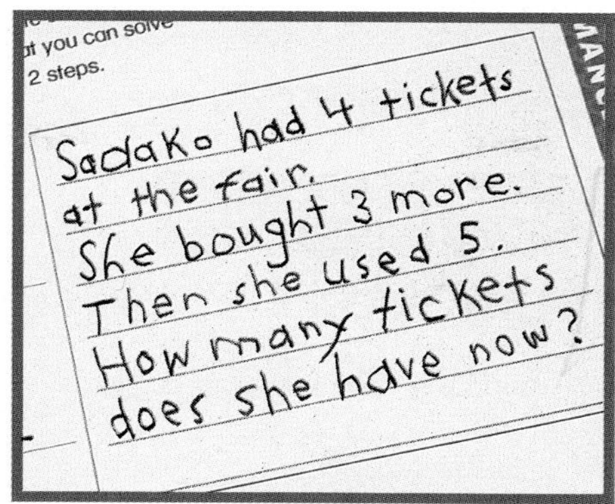

Use the numbers to write a math story that you can solve in 2 steps.

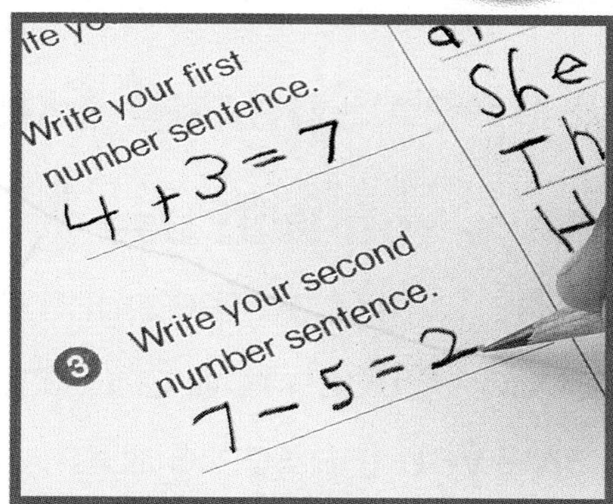

Write both of the number sentences for your story. Solve.

1. Write your math story.

2. Write your first number sentence.

   ____

3. Write your second number sentence.

   ____

Problem Solving Critical Thinking

4. Write a fact family using your first number sentence.

______________________ ______________________

______________________ ______________________

Notes for Home: Your child did an activity that tested Chapter 4 skills, concepts, and problem solving. *Home Activity:* Ask your child to write a different math story and different number sentences using the numbers picked.

Name ______________________________

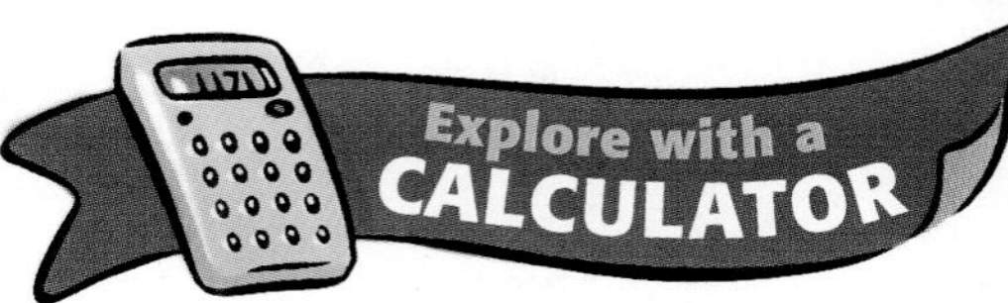

Super Special Sums!

Keys You Will Use 

When you add the numbers in this special square, each row and each column will always give you the same sum.

12	3	3	18
1	11	6	18
5	4	9	18
18	18	18	

Find the missing numbers. To find the missing number for the first row,

Press ON/C 1 2 + 3 = 15.

Then press 1 8 − 1 5 = 3.

I can use the number I found for the first row to help me find the other missing numbers.

Now try these special squares!

4	4		___
		2	___
6	8		20
___	___	___	

2

12	8		30
		15	___
9	16		___
___	___	___	

3

11	1		___
		8	___
2		4	___
15	___	15	

4

8		16	___
	12	6	___
10			___
___	32	___	

Tech Talk How does using a calculator help you to solve these special squares?

Visit our Web site. www.parent.mathsurf.com

Math Path

7	3	3	13	5	6
2	6	2	6	4	12
5	4	7	13	4	8
12	5	12	6	13	2
4	3	5	12	5	4

Draw the Math Path!

1 Find four numbers in a row. Add the first three numbers.

2 If the fourth number is the sum, circle all four numbers.

3 The first one is done for you. Find all the sums. There are 2 more going across. There are 2 going down.

Fold down

Name	Cans Crushed
Lavon	
Sonia	
Mario	
Deepak	
Kim	
Monika	

Each [can] is 1 can.

Where at the Fair?

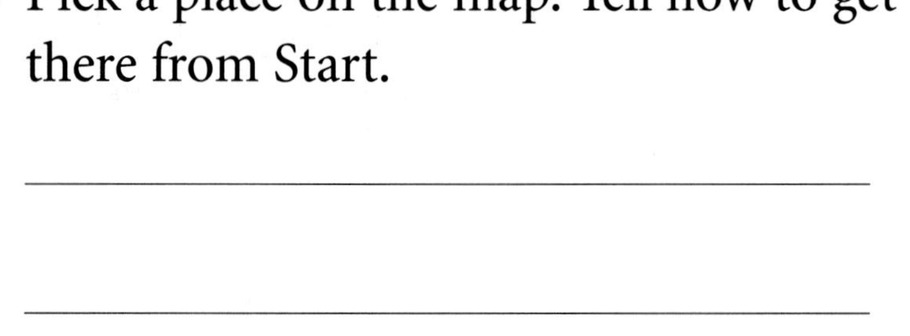

Where do you want to go at the fair?
The map shows you different places to go.

Follow these directions using the map. Always begin at **Start**. First go over and then go up. Where are you?

1 Go over 1.
Go up 4.
Where are you?

______

2 Go over 3.
Go up 2.
Where are you?

______

3 Pick a place on the map. Tell how to get there from Start.

______

______

______

Notes for Home: Your child solved problems using a map. *Home Activity:* Ask your child to use the map to make up a problem for you to solve.

Crushed!

Earth Day is celebrated every year in April. In St. Louis, Missouri, there was a big Earth Day Fair. People went on nature hikes. They learned about plants and animals.

Some children at the fair recycled cans. They crushed cans with a huge hammer. The children had fun and helped keep their city clean.

The chart shows how many cans some children crushed. Use the chart to answer the questions.

1 Sonia and Monika are sisters. How many cans did they crush in all?

2 How many cans did Mario, Deepak, and Kim crush in all?

3 Which two children crushed a total of 15 cans?

Notes for Home: Your child practiced adding numbers using a picture graph. *Home Activity:* Ask your child how many cans Lavon, Kim, and Mario crushed in all. (9 + 3 + 4 = 16)

Make 15

How to Play

1 Play with a friend. Try to make the numbers in each row and column add up to 15.

2 Choose a number between 1 and 9. Write the number in a box.

3 Have your friend write a number between 1 and 9 in a box. Cross out that number.

4 Continue playing. You can use a number more than once. Make sure rows and columns add up to 15.

5 If a player writes a number so a row or column does not equal 15, that player loses and the other player wins.

Helpful Hint
If *all* the rows and columns equal 15, both players win!

Test Your Skill!

Make 15

Notes for Home: Your child played a game to practice adding three numbers. *Home Activity:* Ask your child to tell you two different combinations of three numbers with a sum of 15.

CHAPTER 5

Place Value and Patterns to 100

Notes for Home: Your child talked about collections. *Home Activity:* Help your child start a collection of small objects, such as buttons or pennies.

Dear Family,
Our class is starting Chapter 5. We will learn about tens and ones, number patterns, and numbers up to 100. Here are some activities we can do together.

Numbers, Numbers, Everywhere!
Help your child find ways that numbers up to 100 are used in the home. For example, count all the silverware or find numbers in newspapers and magazines. Keep track of when and how numbers are used in daily life.

What's My Number?
Fill a jar with less than 100 small items, such as beans or pennies. Ask your child to guess how many are in the jar, then help him or her count to find out.

Community Connection

Look for ways that large numbers are used around your community.

Visit our Web site. www.parent.mathsurf.com

Name

Explore Estimation

Explore

Estimate. Try to take 50 ▫.
Find out how many you have.
Draw what you did.

Share

How did you find out how many  you had?

Notes for Home: Your child put items in groups to count them. *Home Activity:* Ask your child to take a handful of small objects, such as pennies, estimate how many there are, and put them into groups to count them.

EXPLORE

Connect

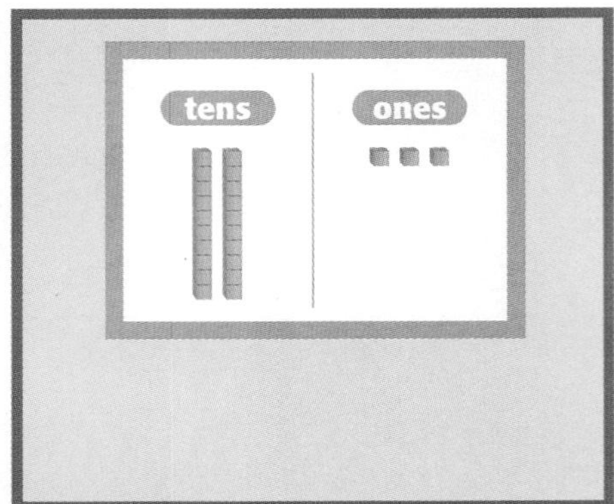

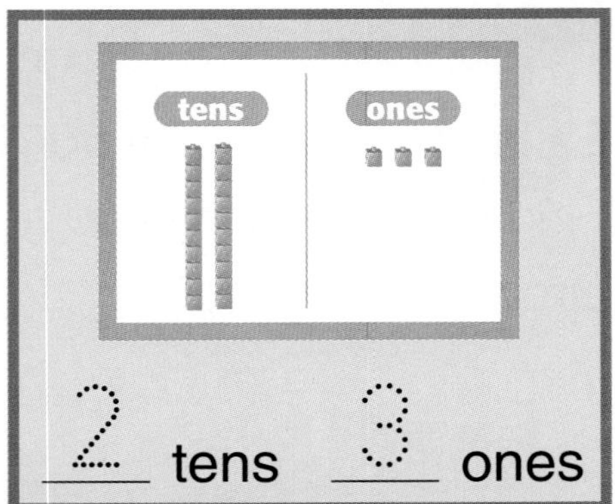

Estimate. Try to take 50 .

Use your . Make tens and ones.

Write how many tens and ones.

	Try to take this many.	Write how many you took.
1	20	______ tens ______ ones
2	30	______ tens ______ ones
3	40	______ tens ______ ones
4	50	______ tens ______ ones
5	60	______ tens ______ ones
6	70	______ tens ______ ones
7	80	______ tens ______ ones

EXPLORE

Talk About It How close did you get to your estimates? Did you get closer each time?

Notes for Home: Your child used grouping by tens to estimate and count. *Home Activity:* Put some popcorn or other small items into a pile. Ask your child to try to take 20, then have him or her put them into groups of tens and ones and count how many there are.

Name

Record Numbers

Learn

Check

Use and .

Write how many tens and ones. Write the number.

1

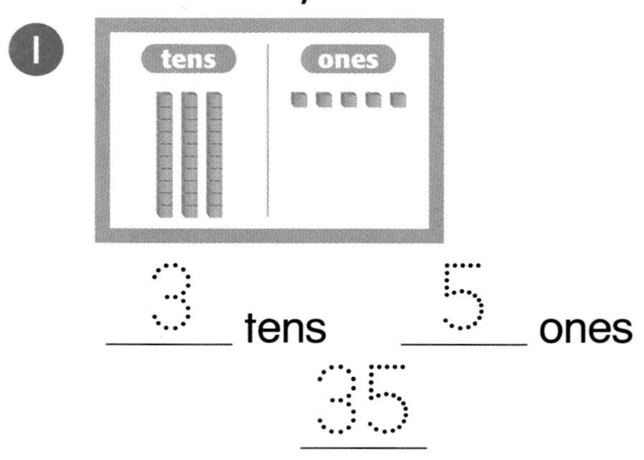

3 tens 5 ones

35

2

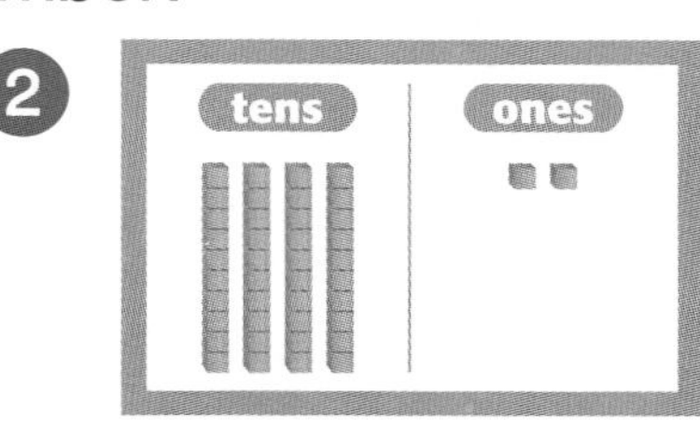

_____ tens _____ ones

_____

3

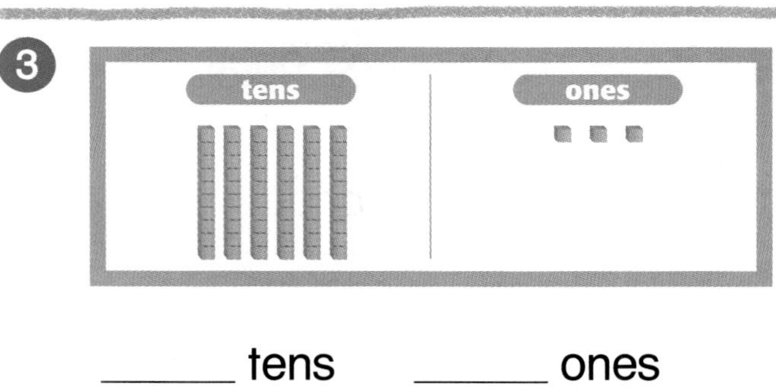

_____ tens _____ ones

_____

4

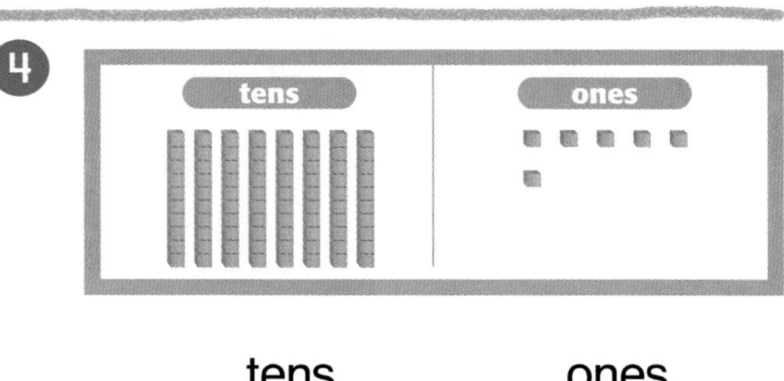

_____ tens _____ ones

_____

Talk About It How are these alike? How are they different?

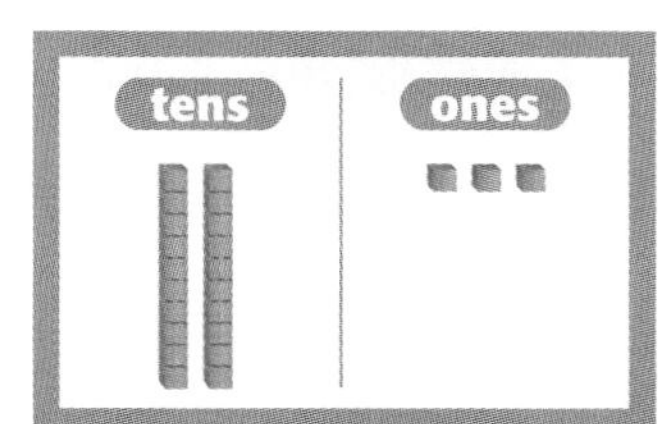

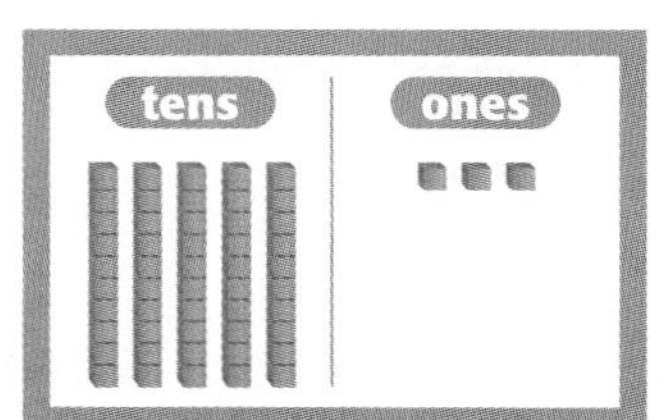

Notes for Home: Your child used tens and ones to write numbers. *Home Activity:* Ask your child to write the number that has 5 tens and 7 ones. (57)

Practice

Write how many tens and ones. Write the number.

You can use  and [ten rod and unit cubes].

5 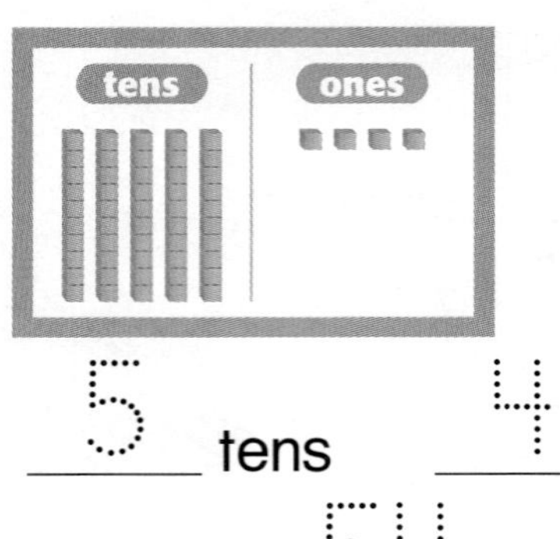

5 tens 4 ones

54

6 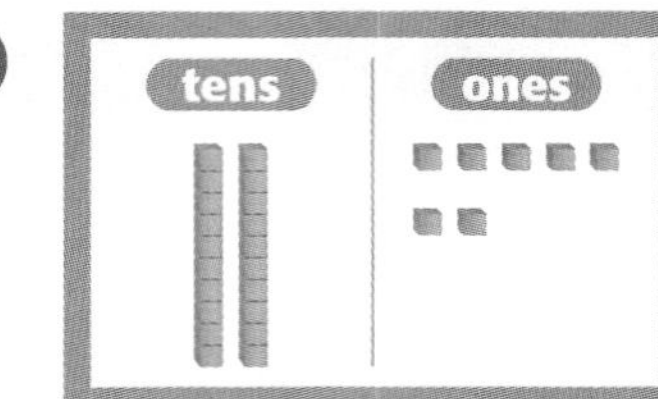

_____ tens _____ ones

_____

7 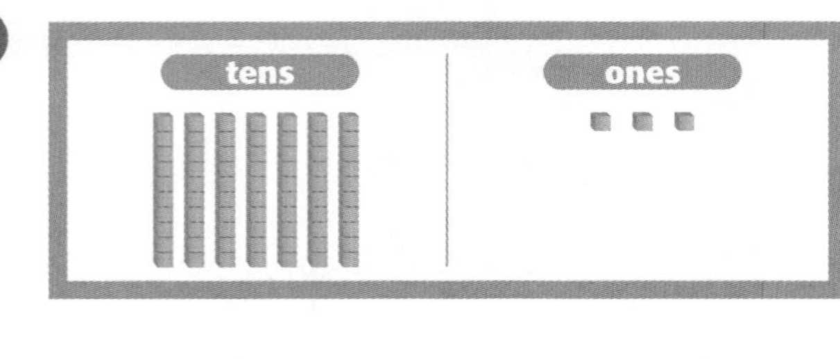

_____ tens _____ ones

_____

8 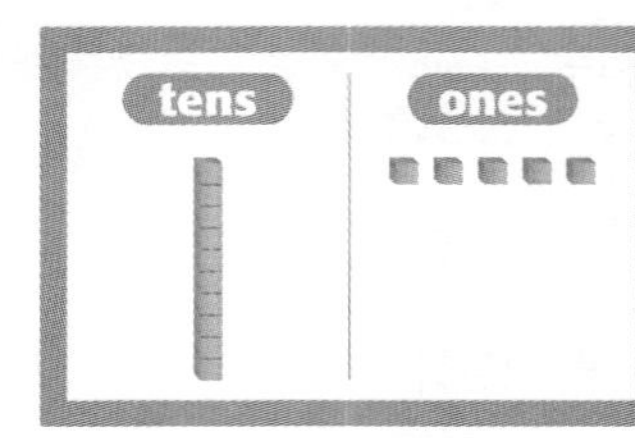

_____ ten _____ ones

_____

Write the number.

9 8 tens 7 ones

87

10 4 tens 6 ones

_____

11 9 tens 2 ones

_____

12 2 tens 9 ones

_____

Problem Solving Critical Thinking

13 How are these numbers alike? How are they different?

35 53

Notes for Home: Your child wrote numbers as tens and ones and as 2-digit numbers. *Home Activity:* Ask your child to think of a number that is less than 100 and tell you how many tens and ones it has.

Name

Number Words

Learn

You can use these to write other numbers. 48 is forty-eight.

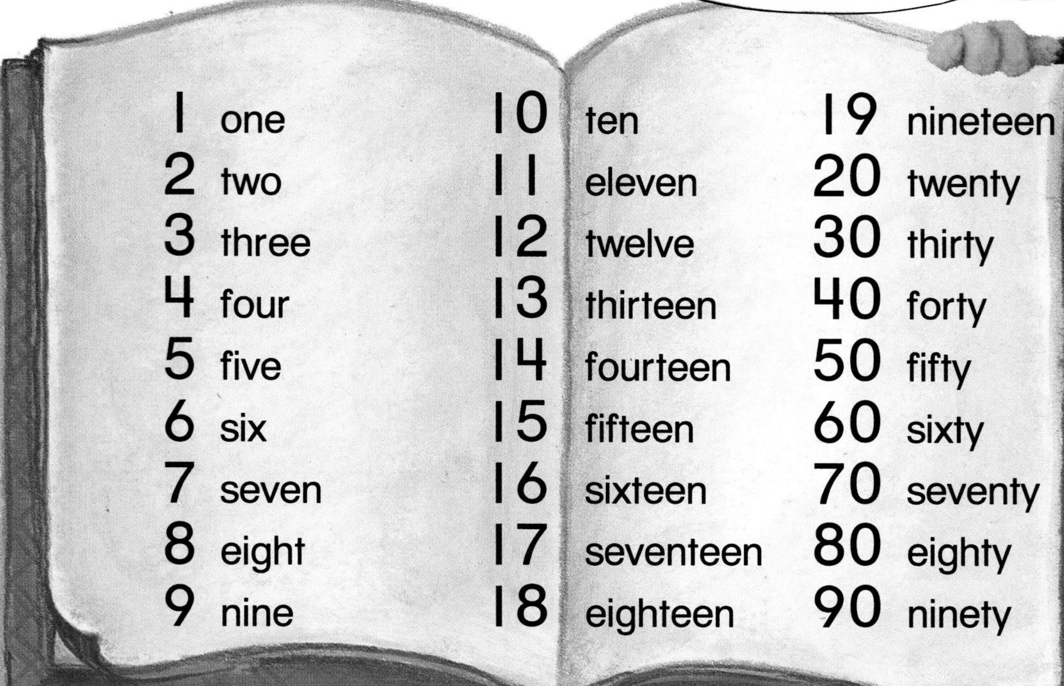

Check

Write the number.

1. three 3
2. thirteen ____
3. nineteen ____
4. forty-two ____
5. fifty-eight ____
6. fifteen ____

Write the word.

7. 4 four
8. 16 ____________
9. 36 ____________
10. 91 ____________

Talk About It What do you need to know to write the word for 61?

Notes for Home: Your child learned to read and write words for numbers up to 99. *Home Activity:* Ask your child to write the word for 62. (sixty-two) Repeat with other numbers between 20 and 99.

Practice

Write the number.

11. ninety-four 94
12. eighty-three ______
13. sixty-six ______
14. seventy ______
15. twenty-six ______
16. thirty-seven ______

17. Use the clues to write each word. Fill in the puzzle.

Across	Down
1. 4	1. 50
5. 70	2. 2
8. 9	3. 40
10. 90	4. 5
	5. 7
	6. 10
	7. 60
	9. 1

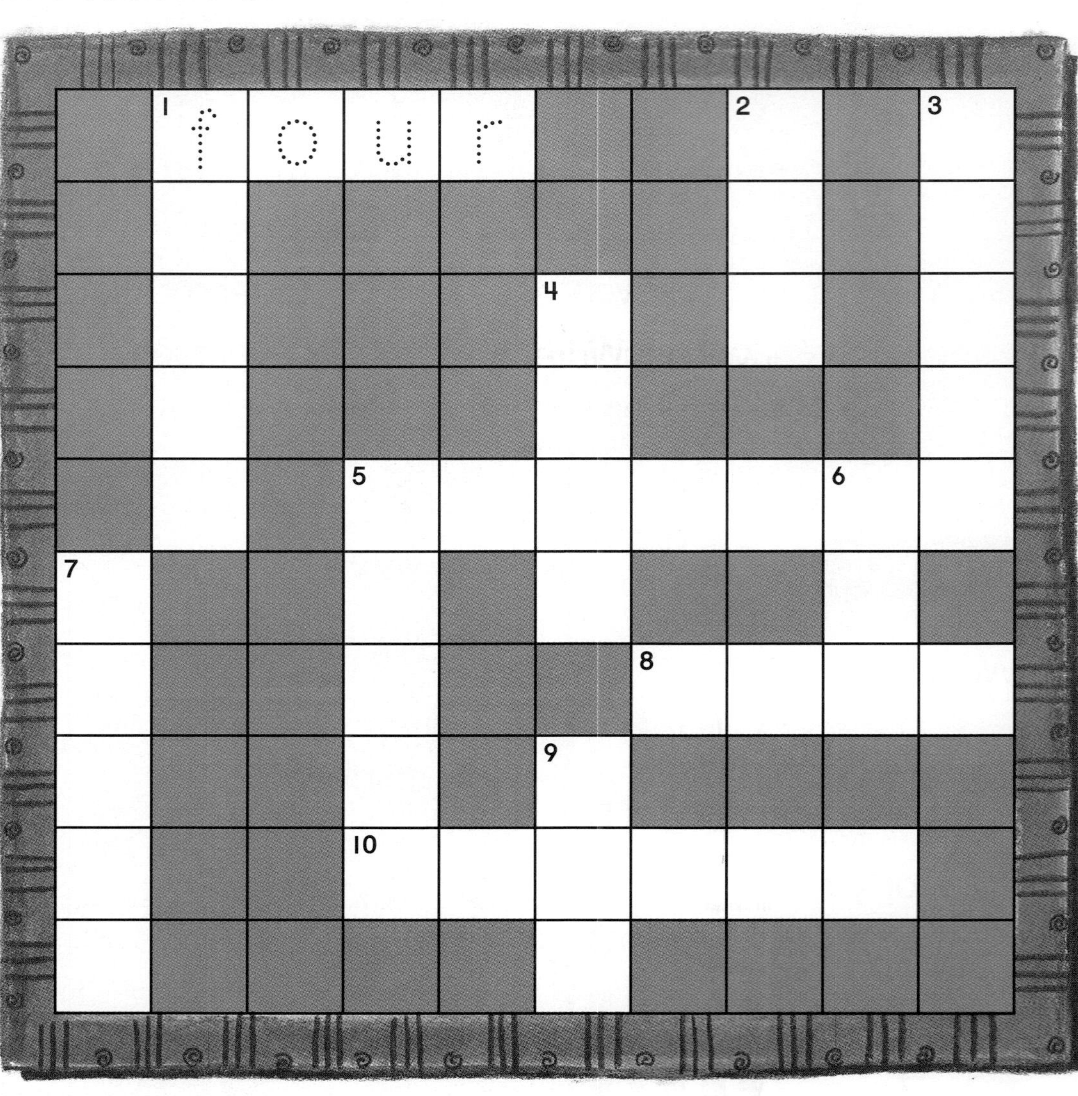

PRACTICE

Problem Solving Critical Thinking

18. Pick a number between 20 and 99. What are some ways you can show it?

Notes for Home: Your child practiced writing number words. *Home Activity:* Have your child think of a number between 20 and 99 and write the number word for it. (Sample answer: 37; thirty-seven)

For additional practice, see Skills Practice Bank, page 531, Set 1.

Name ______________________________

Tell About 100

Learn

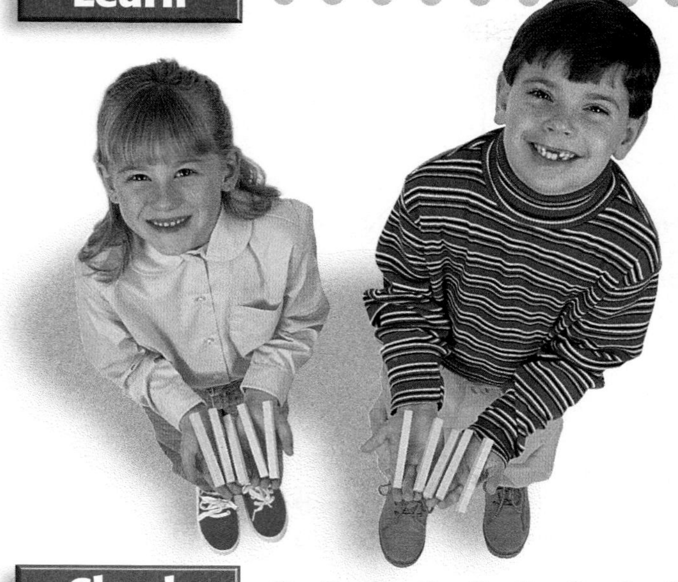

5 tens and 5 tens is 10 tens.

50 and 50 is 100.

10 tens is 100.

Check

Write how many tens. Write the numbers.

1. ______ tens and ______ tens is 10 tens.

   ______ and ______ is 100.

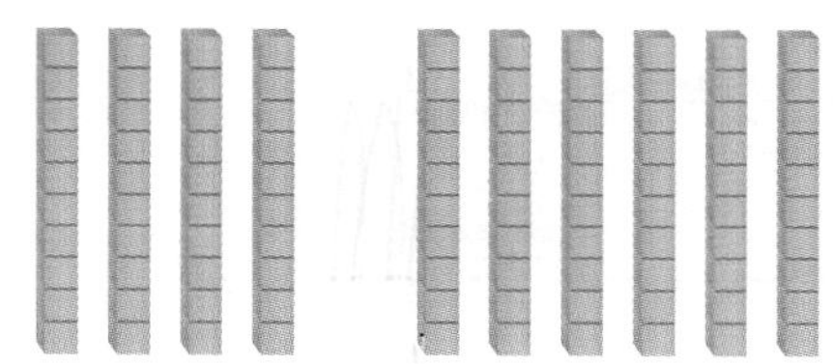

2. ______ tens and ______ tens is 10 tens.

   ______ and ______ is 100.

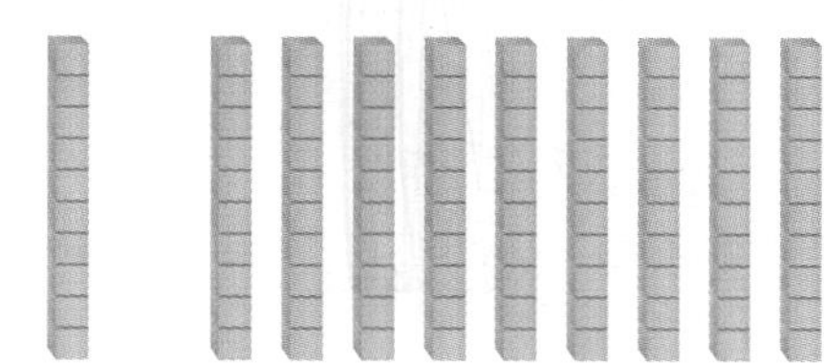

3. ______ ten and ______ tens is 10 tens.

   ______ and ______ is 100.

Talk About It How are these alike?
How are they different?

4 tens and 6 tens is 10 tens. **40 and 60 is 100.**

Notes for Home: Your child combined groups of tens to make 100. *Home Activity:* Ask your child how many tens would be added to 7 tens to make 100. (3 tens)

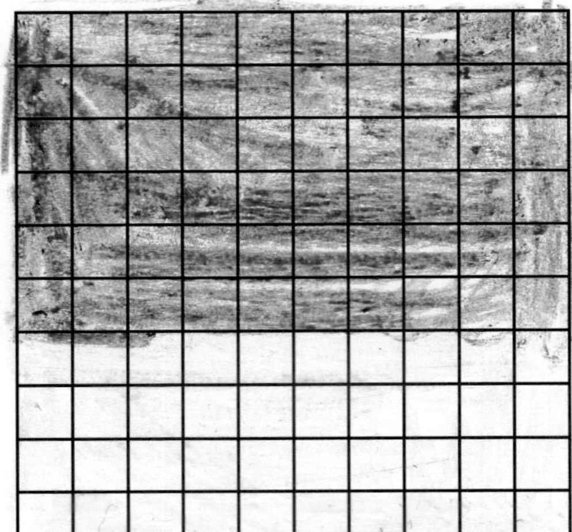

Both of these show 10 tens. Both of these show 100.

4. Color 60 red.
   Color 40 yellow.
   Write how many.

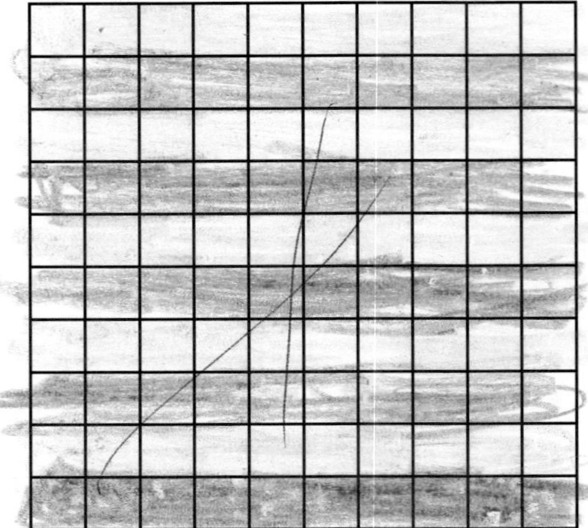

60 and 40 is 100.

Write your own.

5. Color some tens red.
   Color the rest of the tens yellow.
   Write how many.

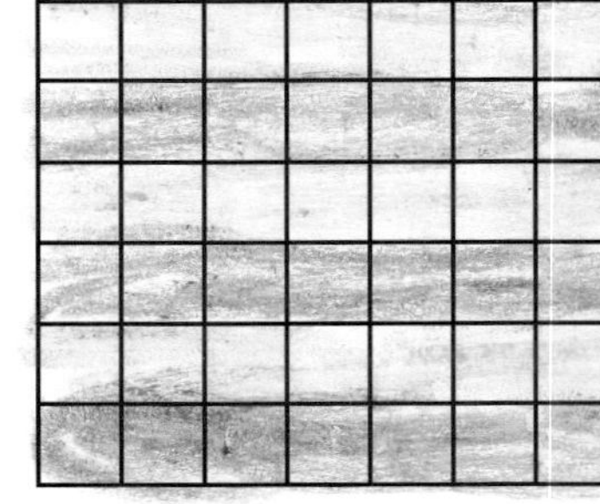

80 and 50 is 100.

Problem Solving Critical Thinking

6. How could you use 3 colors to show 100?

Notes for Home: Your child used a grid to show combinations of numbers that make 100.
Home Activity: Ask your child to tell you two numbers that can be added to make 100.

Name

Hundred Chart and Skip Counting Patterns

ALGEBRA READINESS

Learn

1	2	3	4	5	6	7	8	9	10
11	12	13	14	15	16	17	18	19	20
21	22	23	24	25	26	27	28	29	30
31	32	33	34	35	36	37	38	39	40
41	42	43	44	45	46	47	48	49	50
51	52	53	54	55	56	57	58	59	60
61	62	63	64	65	66	67	68	69	70
71	72	73	74	75	76	77	78	79	80
81	82	83	84	85	86	87	88	89	90
91	92	93	94	95	96	97	98	99	100

Counting by 2s

1	2	3	4	5	6	7	8	9	10
11	12	13	14	15	16	17	18	19	20
21	22	23	24	25	26	27	28	29	30
31	32	33	34	35	36	37	38	39	40
41	42	43	44	45	46	47	48	49	50
51	52	53	54	55	56	57	58	59	60
61	62	63	64	65	66	67	68	69	70
71	72	73	74	75	76	77	78	79	80
81	82	83	84	85	86	87	88	89	90
91	92	93	94	95	96	97	98	99	100

Counting by 5s

1	2	3	4	5	6	7	8	9	10
11	12	13	14	15	16	17	18	19	20
21	22	23	24	25	26	27	28	29	30
31	32	33	34	35	36	37	38	39	40
41	42	43	44	45	46	47	48	49	50
51	52	53	54	55	56	57	58	59	60
61	62	63	64	65	66	67	68	69	70
71	72	73	74	75	76	77	78	79	80
81	82	83	84	85	86	87	88	89	90
91	92	93	94	95	96	97	98	99	100

Counting by 3s

Check

There are lots of patterns on a hundred chart!

1 Finish counting by 4s on the chart. Shade each number.

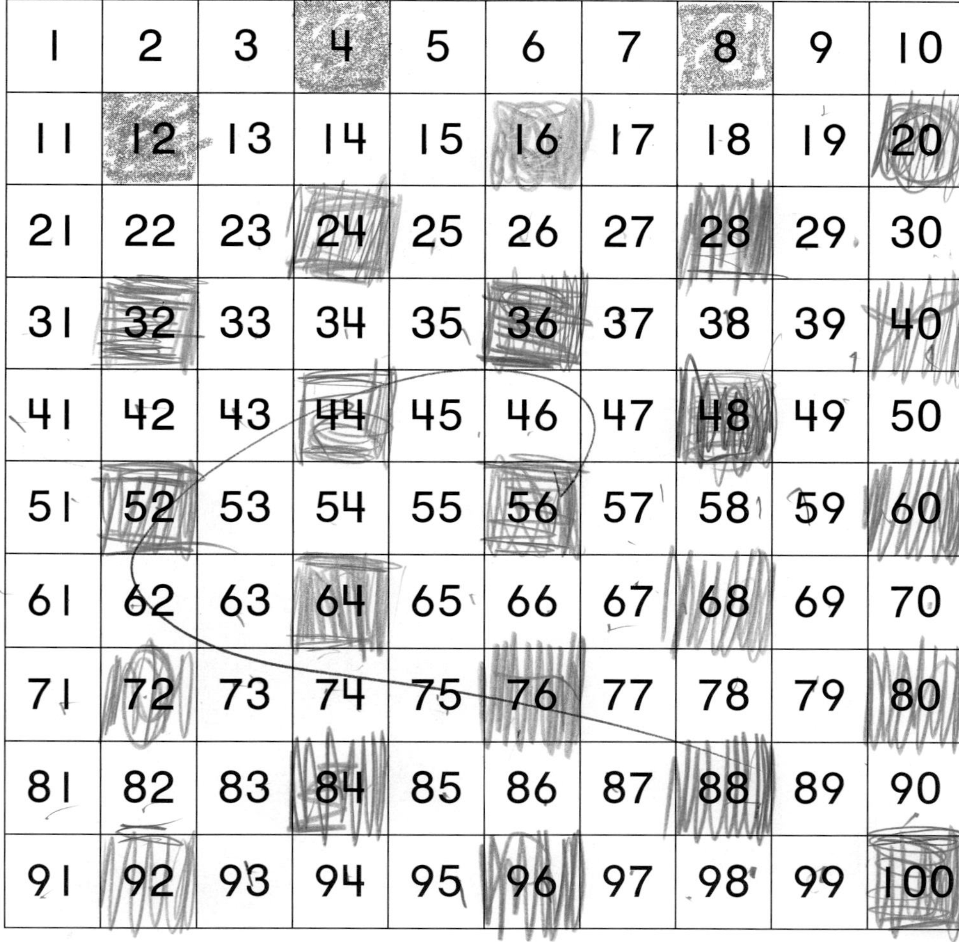

1	2	3	4	5	6	7	8	9	10
11	12	13	14	15	16	17	18	19	20
21	22	23	24	25	26	27	28	29	30
31	32	33	34	35	36	37	38	39	40
41	42	43	44	45	46	47	48	49	50
51	52	53	54	55	56	57	58	59	60
61	62	63	64	65	66	67	68	69	70
71	72	73	74	75	76	77	78	79	80
81	82	83	84	85	86	87	88	89	90
91	92	93	94	95	96	97	98	99	100

Talk About It If you counted by 8s on the chart, what pattern would you see?

Notes for Home: Your child counted by 4s to 100. *Home Activity:* Ask your child to show you how to count by 2s using the chart.

Practice

2 Complete the hundred chart. Then finish counting by 6s on the chart. Shade each number.

1	2	3	4	5	6	7	8	9	10
11	12	13	14	15	16	17	18	19	20
									40
							48		
									60
				65					
71									80
		83							
							98	99	100

3 What patterns do you see?

____

____

____

Mental Math

4 Steve has 5 toy cars in his collection.
Each car has 4 wheels.
How many wheels are there in all?

______ wheels

Notes for Home: Your child counted by 6s to 100. *Home Activity:* Ask your child to count by 3s and by 5s using the chart.

Name ____________________

Practice Game 5

The Great Toss Up

Players 2

What You Need

50 

1

How to Play

1. Take 2 handfuls of . Make tens and ones. Write your number.
2. When your partner has had a turn, write his or her number.
3. Spin the spinner to see which number wins.
4. Circle **Greater** or **Less.**
5. Circle the winning number.

Greater Wins | Less Wins

My Number	My Partner's Number	Which Number Wins?
____	____	Greater Less
____	____	Greater Less
____	____	Greater Less
____	____	Greater Less

Notes for Home: Your child played a number game. *Home Activity:* Ask your child to tell you a number greater than 30 and a number less than 30. Repeat with other numbers.

Name ______________________

STOP and Practice

1 Count by 3s on the chart. Shade each number.

1	2	3	4	5	6	7	8	9	10
11	12	13	14	15	16	17	18	19	20
21	22	23	24	25	26	27	28	29	30
31	32	33	34	35	36	37	38	39	40
41	42	43	44	45	46	47	48	49	50

Write the number that comes between.

2 32 ____ 34

3 65 ____ 67

Write the numbers in order from least to greatest.

4 27 62 54 ____ ____ ____

For each number, write the nearest ten.

5 39 ____

6 52 ____

7 34 ____

8 26 ____

9 68 ____

10 77 ____

Number Sense

11 I am a number between 20 and 30.
I am greater than 23.
I am less than 26.
I am not 24.

What number am I? ____

Notes for Home: Your child practiced showing number patterns and comparing numbers.
Home Activity: Ask your child to pick 3 numbers and put them in order from least to greatest.

PRACTICE

Name

Ordinal Numbers

Learn

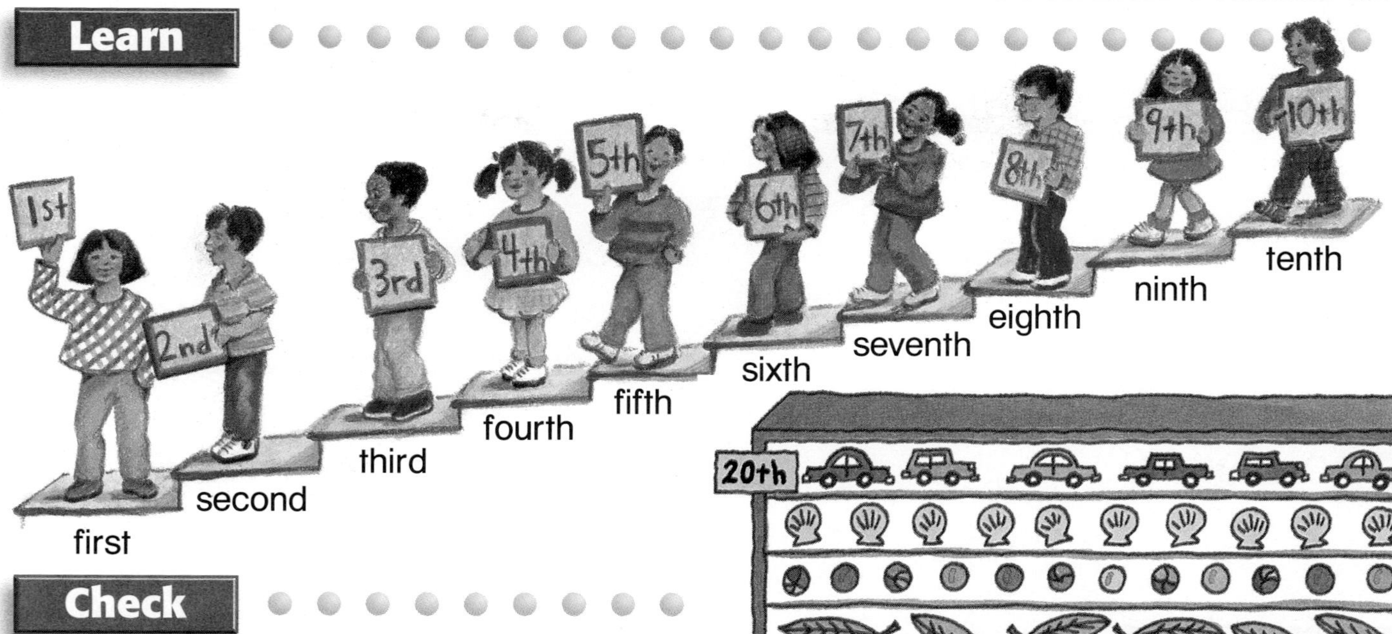

Check

Circle your answer to each question.

1 What is on the 3rd shelf?

2 What is on the 7th shelf?

3 What is on the 17th shelf?

4 What is on the 6th shelf?

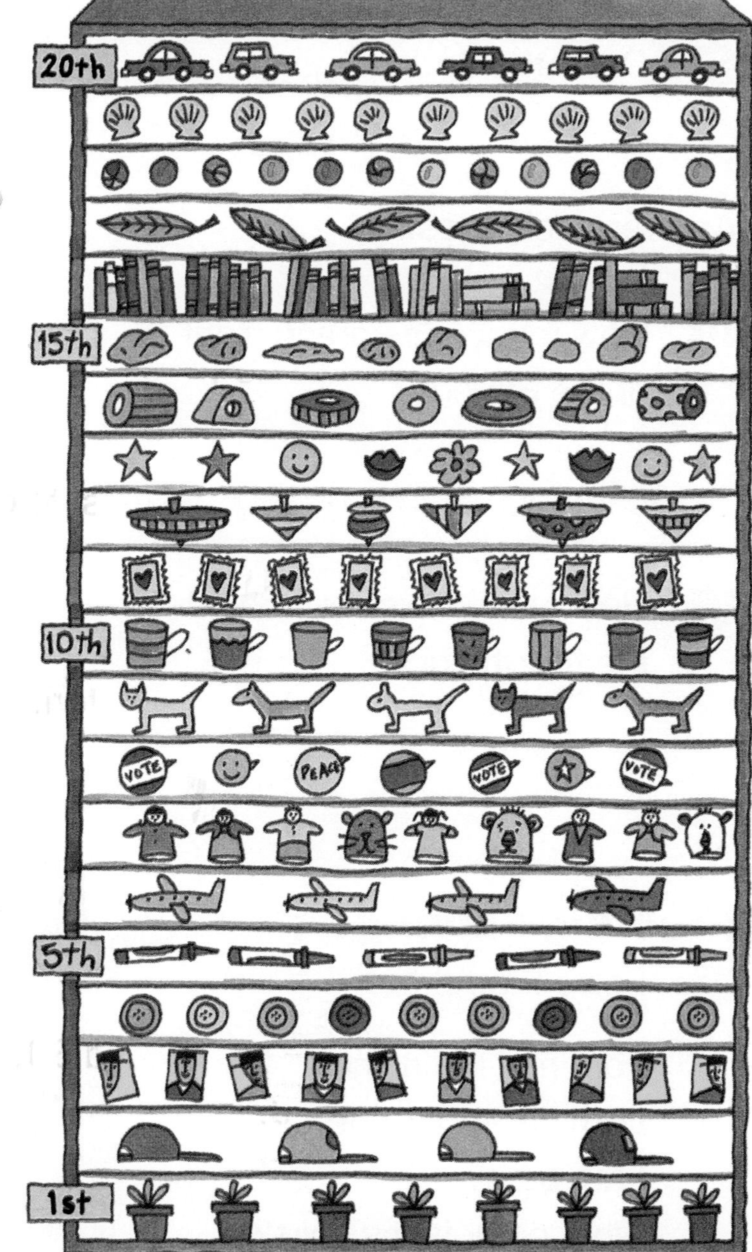

Talk About It 7 children are in line in front of you. What number are you in line?

Notes for Home: Your child used ordinal numbers from 1st through 10th. *Home Activity:* Ask your child to put four small items, such as toys, in a line and tell which is first, second, third, and fourth.

Practice

5. Color the third car red.
6. Color the 6th car purple.
7. Color the 5th car blue.
8. Color the ninth car yellow.
9. Color the 2nd car green.
10. Color the eighth car orange.

PRACTICE

Answer each question.

11. How many cars are in front of the 8th car? ______
12. How many cars are in front of the fourth car? ______
13. How many cars are behind the fourth car? ______
14. How many cars are behind the 3rd car? ______

Problem Solving

15. Solve the riddle.

I am not 1st in line.
I am not 4th in line.
I am a boy.
What color is my shirt?

____

Notes for Home: Your child used ordinal numbers from 1st through 20th. *Home Activity:* Ask your child to make up a riddle using the picture at the bottom of this page.

Name

Odd and Even Numbers

Learn

You can break 10 cubes into 2 equal parts.

10 is an even number.

You cannot break 11 cubes into 2 equal parts.

11 is an odd number.

Check

	Make a train with this many ▪.	Can you make 2 equal parts?	Is the number odd or even?
1	12	yes	even
2	13		
3	14		
4	15		
5	16		
6	17		
7	18		
8	19		

Talk About It Is 65 odd or even? How do you know?

Notes for Home: Your child learned about odd and even numbers. *Home Activity:* Ask your child to take some objects, such as pennies, count them, and tell if the number is odd or even.

Practice

Write how many in all.
Then write **even** or **odd.**

9 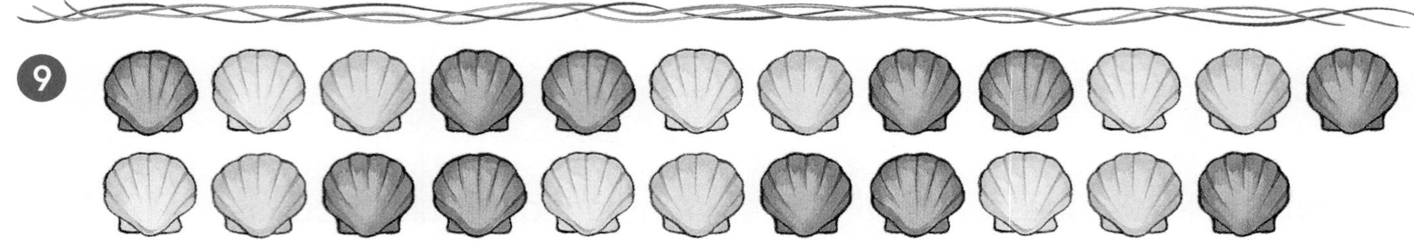

_____ __________

10 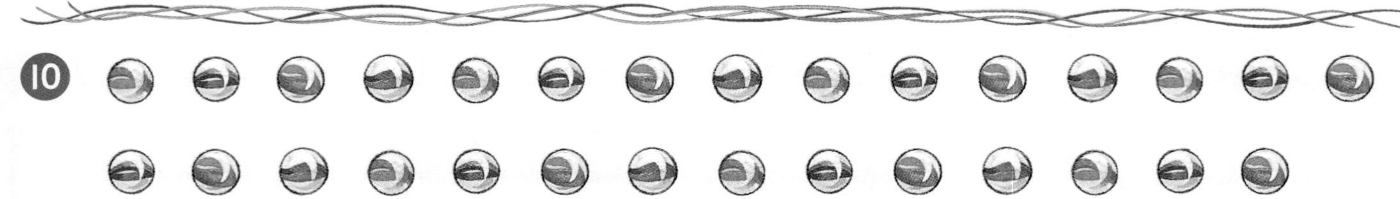

_____ __________

Write **even** or **odd**.

11 75 odd

12 32 __________

13 98 __________

14 61 __________

Write your own. Write three even numbers.
Then write three odd numbers.

15 Even numbers: _____ _____ _____

16 Odd numbers: _____ _____ _____

Problem Solving Patterns

17 Is the number 6,852 odd or even?
How do you know?

Notes for Home: Your child worked with odd and even numbers. *Home Activity:* Ask your child to think of a number and tell you if it is odd or even.

Name ______________________

Reading for Math

Classification

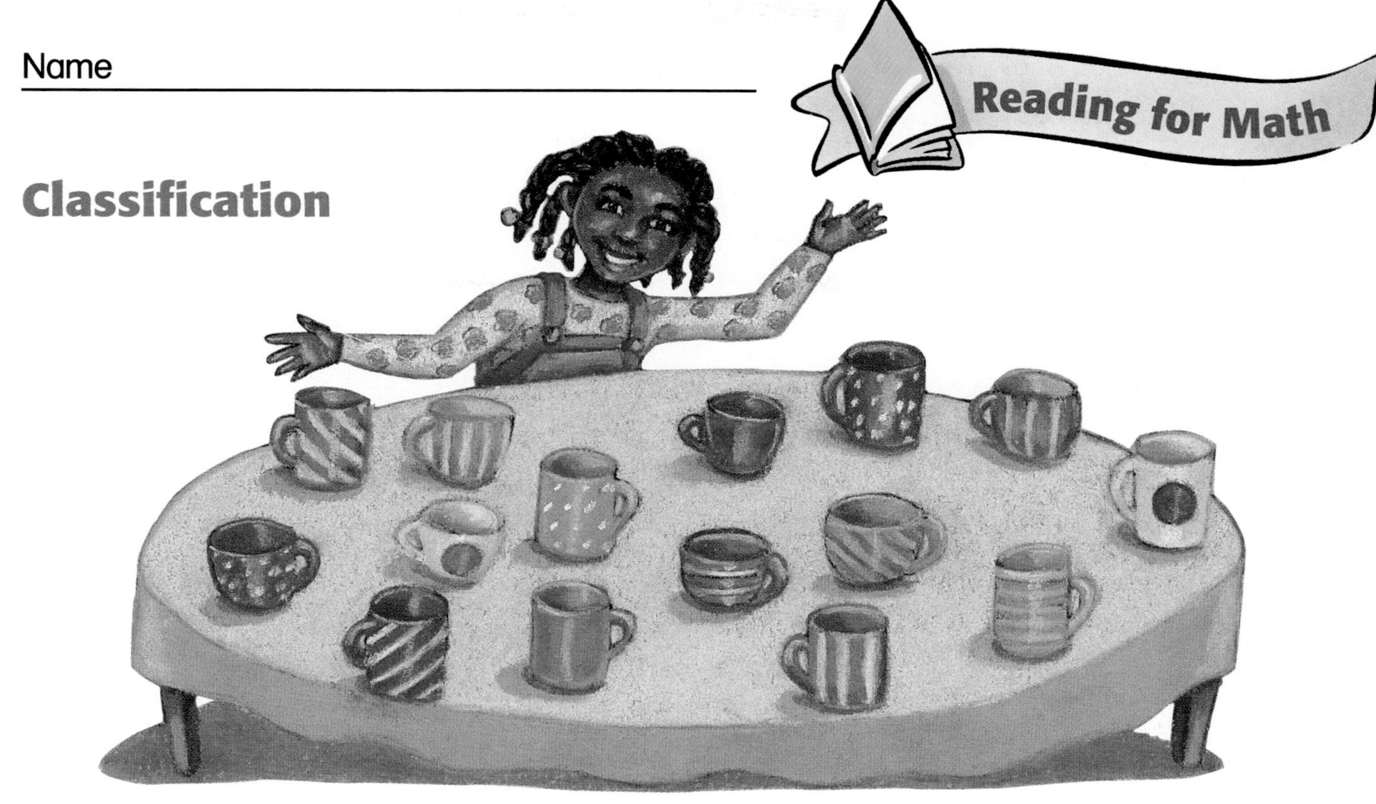

1. Tara has 15 mugs in her collection.
She wants to sort them by their designs.
Finish the chart to sort the mugs into three groups.

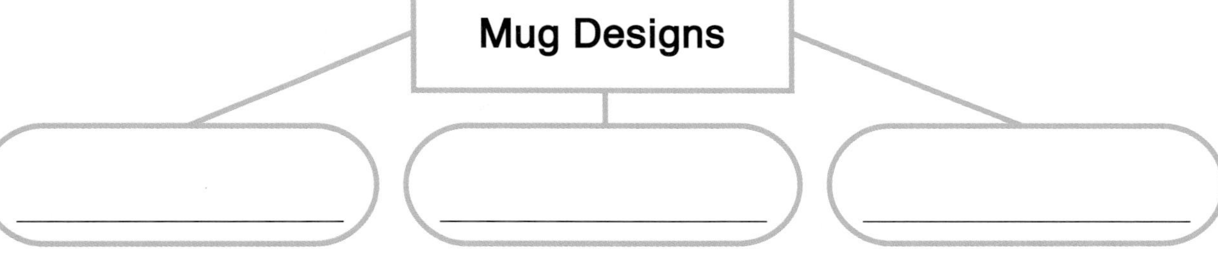

2. What other way can you sort Tara's mugs?

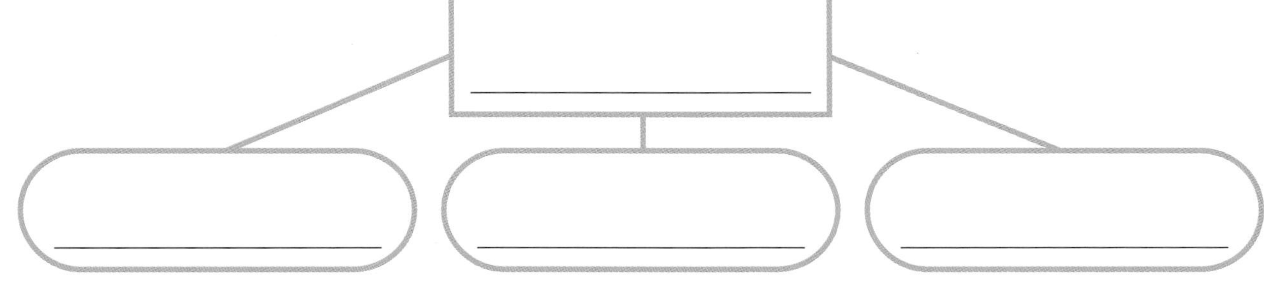

Talk About It What are some other ways you could sort Tara's mugs?

Notes for Home: Your child learned many ways to sort items. *Home Activity:* Ask your child to find two different ways to sort some coins. (Sample answers: by size, by color, by value)

3 Martin likes to collect banks.
How can Martin sort his banks?
Finish the chart to sort the banks into three groups.

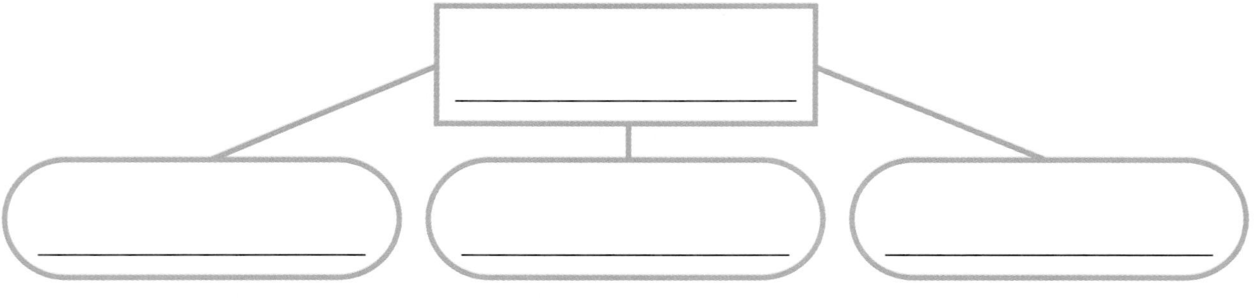

4 Find a new way to sort Martin's banks.
Finish the chart.

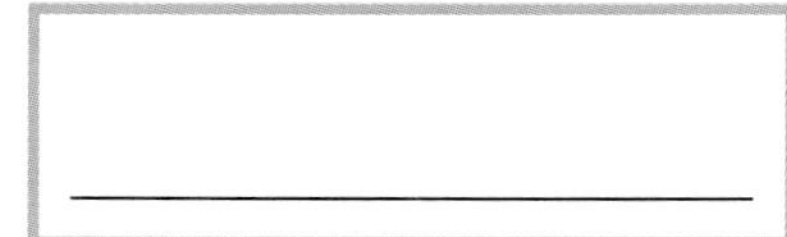

Critical Thinking

5 How would you sort the beads? Explain your reason.

     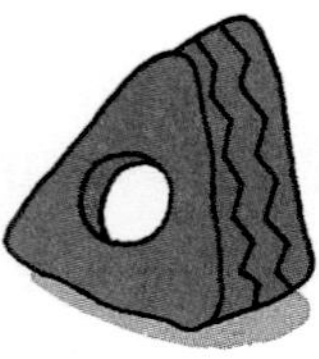

Notes for Home: Your child sorted items in different ways. *Home Activity:* Ask your child to tell you different ways to sort his or her clothing. (Sample answers: by color, by type, by weather)

Name

Problem Solving: Group Decision Making

Learn

PROBLEM SOLVING GUIDE

Understand • Plan • Solve • Look Back

Check

Work with your group.
Take items out of your desk.

1. What items did you find?

______________________ ______________________

______________________ ______________________

______________________ ______________________

2. How many ways could you sort your group's items?

______________________ ______________________

______________________ ______________________

______________________ ______________________

3. Decide as a group which way you like best. Circle it.

Talk About It How did your group decide the best way to sort the items?

Notes for Home: Your child made decisions with a group about how to sort items. *Home Activity:* Have your child gather a variety of small items and find many different ways to sort them.

PROBLEM SOLVING

Practice

4 As a group, sort your items the way you liked best.
Decide as a group how to show your sorted items.
Draw how you sorted them.

Journal

5 What was easy about working with your group?
What was hard?

Notes for Home: Your child sorted items and made decisions with a group. *Home Activity:* Help your child think of situations in daily life when groups must make decisions together. (Sample answers: what to have for dinner, what game to play at recess)

Name ____________________

Mixed Practice

Lessons 6–12

Concepts and Skills

Count by 4s. Write the numbers. You can use a hundred chart.

1. 4, 8, 12, ____, ____, ____, ____, ____, ____, ____

Write the missing numbers.

2. 

____ ____ ____ ____

For each number, write the nearest ten.

3. 53 ____
4. 78 ____
5. 37 ____

Write these numbers in order from least to greatest.

6. 91 28 74 ____ ____ ____

Problem Solving

Use the picture to answer the questions.

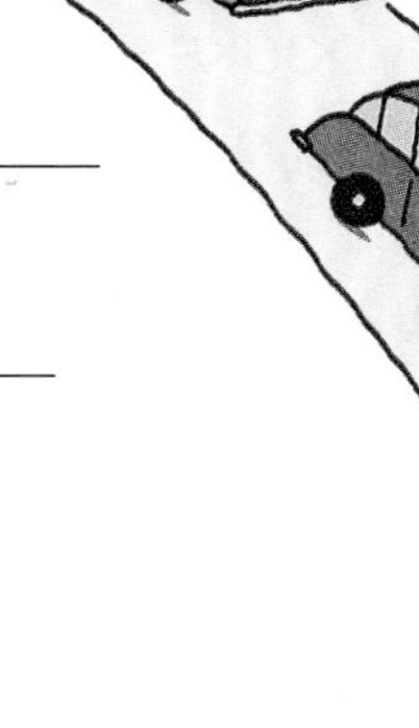

7. What color is the second car? ____________
8. What color is the fourth car? ____________

Journal

9. Are these numbers even or odd? 17 9 11 3
How do you know?

Notes for Home: Your child practiced counting by 4s, finding the nearest 10, putting numbers in order from least to greatest, and identifying the order of cars in a picture. *Home Activity:* Ask your child to think of two even numbers under 100 and tell you how he or she knows they are even.

Name ______________________________

Cumulative Review

Chapters 1–5

Concepts and Skills

Add or subtract.

1.

12	8	14	9	8	7	8
− 9	+ 5	− 6	− 5	+ 9	+ 7	+ 4

Problem Solving

Write the number sentences. Solve.

2. Milton has 10 beads.
Patti has 6 beads.
How many more beads does Milton have than Patti?

_______________ beads

3. Joan has 15 seashells.
Rob has 9 seashells.
How many more seashells does Joan have than Rob?

_______________ seashells

Test Prep

Fill in the ○ for the correct answer.

4. Nikki had 12 storybooks.
She gave away 2.
How many storybooks does she have now?

○ 12 + 2 = 14
○ 12 − 0 = 12
○ 12 − 12 = 0
○ 12 − 2 = 10

5. Mercedes had 9 toy horses.
Pablo gave her 4 more.
How many toy horses does Mercedes have now?

○ 9 − 4 = 5
○ 9 + 4 = 13
○ 13 − 4 = 9
○ 13 + 0 = 13

Notes for Home: Your child reviewed addition and subtraction facts and problem solving.
Home Activity: Ask your child to tell you an addition fact with the sum of 14.

Name ______________________________

Chapter 5 Review

Vocabulary

1. Circle the number that is greater.

   45 38

2. Circle the number that is less.

   82 79

3. Circle the odd numbers.

   21 63 54

4. Circle the even numbers.

   34 57 46

Concepts and Skills

Write how many tens and ones.

5. 38 _____ tens _____ ones

6. 74 _____ tens _____ ones

Write each number.

7. twenty-three _____

8. forty-nine _____

9. eighteen _____

Problem Solving

Use the graph to answer the questions.

10. How many books did Rosa collect? _____

11. How many more books did Rosa have than Chris? _____

12. How many books did Chris, Rosa, and Randy have in all? _____

Each [book] means 5 books.

Notes for Home: Your child reviewed vocabulary, concepts, skills, and problem solving from Chapter 5. *Home Activity:* Ask your child to pick a number and tell about it using before, between, or after. (Sample answer: 37 is between 36 and 38.)

CHAPTER REVIEW

Name

Chapter 5 Test

Write the number.

1. 2 tens 8 ones _____
2. fifty-one _____

3. Complete.

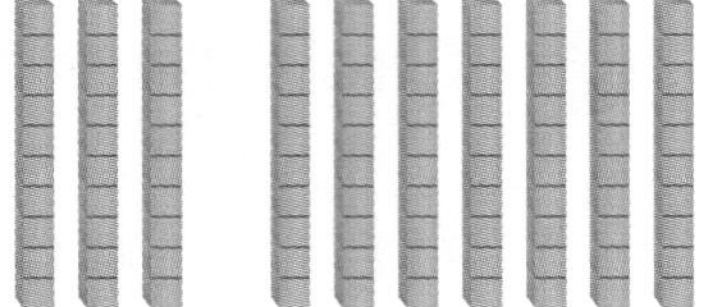

_____ and _____ is 100.

4. Write the number that comes before.

_____

5. Is 46 closer to 40 or 50?

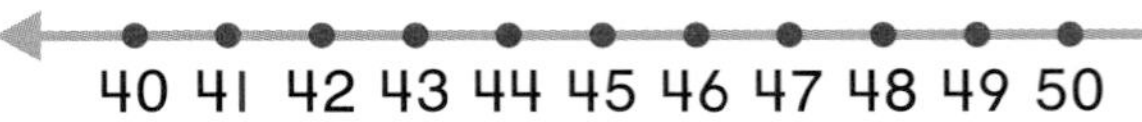

46 is closer to _____.

6. Write the numbers in order from least to greatest.

28 42 25 _____ _____ _____

7. Circle the animal that is fourth.

8. Write **odd** or **even.**

59 _____

9. Use the graph. How many more cards does Max have than Lucas?

_____

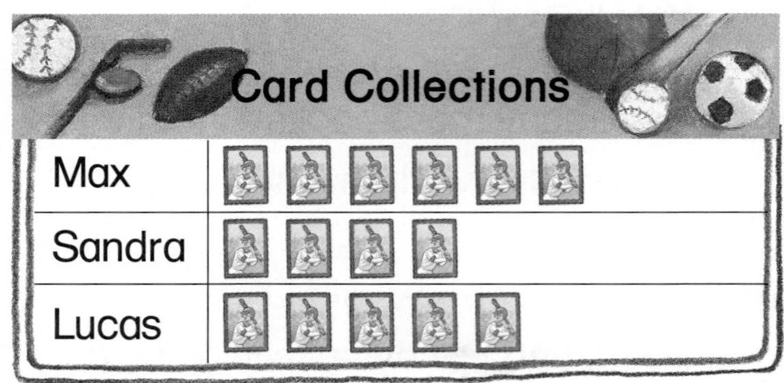

Card Collections

Max	6 cards pictured
Sandra	4 cards pictured
Lucas	5 cards pictured

Each [card] means 10 cards.

Notes for Home: Your child was tested on Chapter 5 skills, concepts, and problem solving. *Home Activity:* Ask your child to think of combinations of tens that make 100. (Sample answers: 2 tens and 8 tens; 7 tens and 3 tens; 6 tens and 3 tens and 1 ten)

CHAPTER TEST

Name ______________________________

Performance Assessment

Chapter 5

Choose 4 numbers between 30 and 60.

Tell about each of your numbers.

Fill in the chart.

	Write your numbers.	How many tens? How many ones?	Write the nearest ten.	Is your number odd or even?
1	31	3 tens 1 ones	30	odd
2		____ tens ____ ones		
3		____ tens ____ ones		
4		____ tens ____ ones		
5		____ tens ____ ones		

6. Write the numbers you chose in order from least to greatest.

31 ____ ____ ____ ____

Critical Thinking

7. Write sentences about some of your numbers.
Use these words: **before, after, between.**

Notes for Home: Your child did an activity that tested Chapter 5 skills and concepts.
Home Activity: Ask your child to choose a new number and answer the questions in the chart.

Name ___________________________

Hit the Target!

Keys You Will Use 

You can use your  to count by any number.

Press these keys to count by 3s.

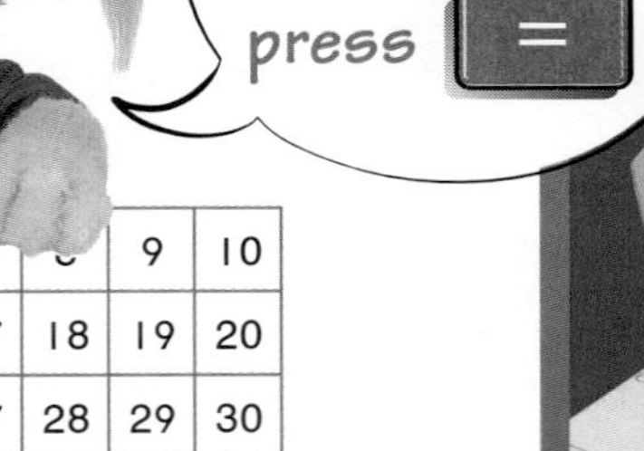

To add the same number again, I can press = !

1	2	3	4	5	6	7	8	9	10
11	12	13	14	15	16	17	18	19	20
21	22	23	24	25	26	27	28	29	30
31	32	33	34	35	36	37	38	39	40
41	42	43	44	45	46	47	48	49	50
51	52	53	54	55	56	57	58	59	60
61	62	63	64	65	66	67	68	69	70
71	72	73	74	75	76	77	78	79	80
81	82	83	84	85	86	87	88	89	90
91	92	93	94	95	96	97	98	99	100

How to Play

1. Player One chooses a target number between 30 and 100.
2. Player Two counts by 3s, 4s, 5s, or 10s to try and hit the target number. Use the chart to decide what number to count by.
3. If Player Two hits the target number exactly, he or she takes another turn. If Player Two misses, then Player One takes a turn. Pick a different target number each time.
4. Record your turns in this chart.
5. The first player to hit the target number 5 times wins!

Target Number	15									
Skip Count by:	3									
Hit Target?										

Tech Talk How would you use a calculator to count by 12s?

Visit our Web site. **www.parent.mathsurf.com**

The Winner Is...

One school held a contest for unusual collections and awarded prizes. Use the clues, then write each child's name on the correct line below.

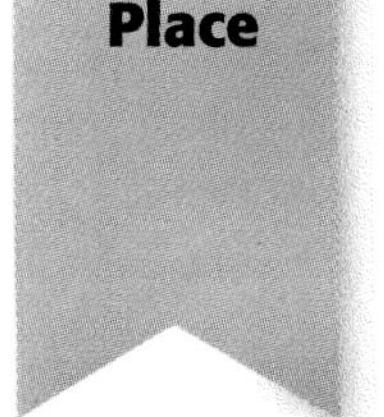

__________ __________ __________

Jesse did not come in first place. His ribbon is not yellow.

Helen did not come in third place.

Duane's ribbon is not blue.

Fold down

MathSoup

Scott Foresman - Addison Wesley My Math Magazine No. 5

Collections

How Many Is a Million?

A second-grade class in Teaneck, New Jersey, wanted to collect one million things. They collected **tea** tags — the little tags attached to tea bags. They began in 1982. Each year, a new class added more. Now they have more than 4 million tea tags!

The graph shows how many tags the class collected in one week. Use the graph to answer the questions.

1 How many tags were collected on Monday?

2 Which two days add up to 100 tags?

Notes for Home: Your child used a graph and counted by tens.
Home Activity: Ask your child how many tags were collected on Friday. (80)

UNITED STATES

A B C

D E F

G H I

Stampers*

Many people collect different types of stamps. Every stamp has a price printed on it. Use the stamp collection. Answer these questions by writing the letters of the stamps.

1 Find 2 stamps that equal sixty cents.

_________ and _________

2 Find 3 stamps that equal thirteen cents.

_________, _________, and _________

What did the stamp say to the letter?

I'm stuck on you.

* Stamp collectors are called stampers.

Notes for Home: Your child read number words and found sums.
Home Activity: Ask your child to find 3 stamps that equal fifteen cents.

Tags Collected in One Week

Monday	TEA TEA TEA TEA TEA TEA
Tuesday	TEA TEA TEA
Wednesday	TEA TEA TEA TEA TEA
Thursday	TEA TEA TEA TEA
Friday	TEA TEA TEA TEA TEA TEA TEA TEA
	Each TEA means 10 tags.

Clever Collections

People collect all kinds of things. What do you and your friends collect?

Ask at least 10 people you know what they collect. If you have a collection, include yourself. Ask people how many things are in their collections. Use tallies to fill in the chart.

How Many Things Are in Collections

Number of People with More Than 50	Number of People with Fewer Than 50

What is the strangest thing someone collected?

Max Watson, a boy in California, collects snow domes!

Robert McMath collects products that didn't sell.

Louise Mesa collects anything shaped like a frog!

Tracy has a collection of nutcrackers.

Notes for Home: Your child surveyed people about their collections. *Home Activity:* Ask your child to tell you how many people had more than 50 items in their collections and how many people had less than 50 items.

CHAPTER 6

Money

Notes for Home: Your child used this picture to talk about different amounts of money.
Home Activity: Ask your child to tell you the value for three of the groups of coins.

Dear Family,
Our class is starting Chapter 6. We will be learning about amounts of money through $1.00. Here are some activities we can do at home.

Sell, Sell, Sell!

Help your child set up a make-believe store. Pick items at home to pretend to sell. Make price tags and sale signs showing amounts less than $1.00.

Coin Count

Put some coins, such as pennies, nickels, and dimes, into a bag. Have your child take out 3 coins. Count to find the total value of the coins.

Community Connection

After making a purchase at a store, help your child count to find the total value of the coins you received as change.

Visit our Web site. www.parent.mathsurf.com

Name ________________________________

Coin Bingo

Players 2 to 4

What You Need

Coins 

Crayon (green)

Paper clip

Pencil

How to Play

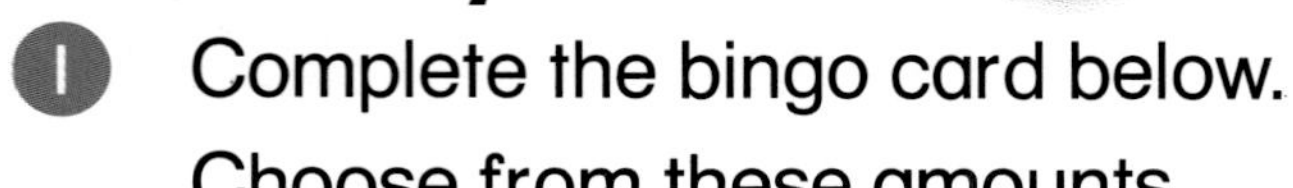

1. Complete the bingo card below.
   Choose from these amounts.
2. Spin 3 times. Take the coin shown by each spin.
3. Count your coins. Color the box showing that amount.
4. The first player to fill in his or her gameboard wins!

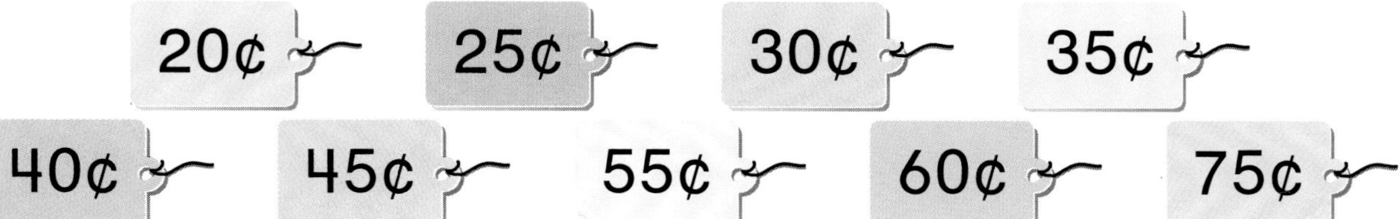

15¢		
	Free	

Notes for Home: Your child played a game with quarters, dimes, and nickels.
Home Activity: Have your child practice counting quarters, dimes, nickels, and pennies in different combinations up to a total of $1.00.

PRACTICE

Name ___________________________

STOP and Practice

Use coins to show each amount.
Draw the coins.

1

2

3

4

5

6

Number Sense

7 What other coins could you use to show 75¢?
Compare your answer with a friend's.

Notes for Home: Your child practiced, showing coins for different amounts of money. *Home Activity:* Ask your child to show you two different ways to make 36¢. (Sample answers: 1 quarter, 1 dime, and 1 penny; 3 dimes, 1 nickel, and 1 penny)

PRACTICE

Name ______________________________

Dollar Bill

Learn

Check

Use coins to show $1.00. Draw the coins. Write how many.

1. Use all quarters.
2. Use all dimes.

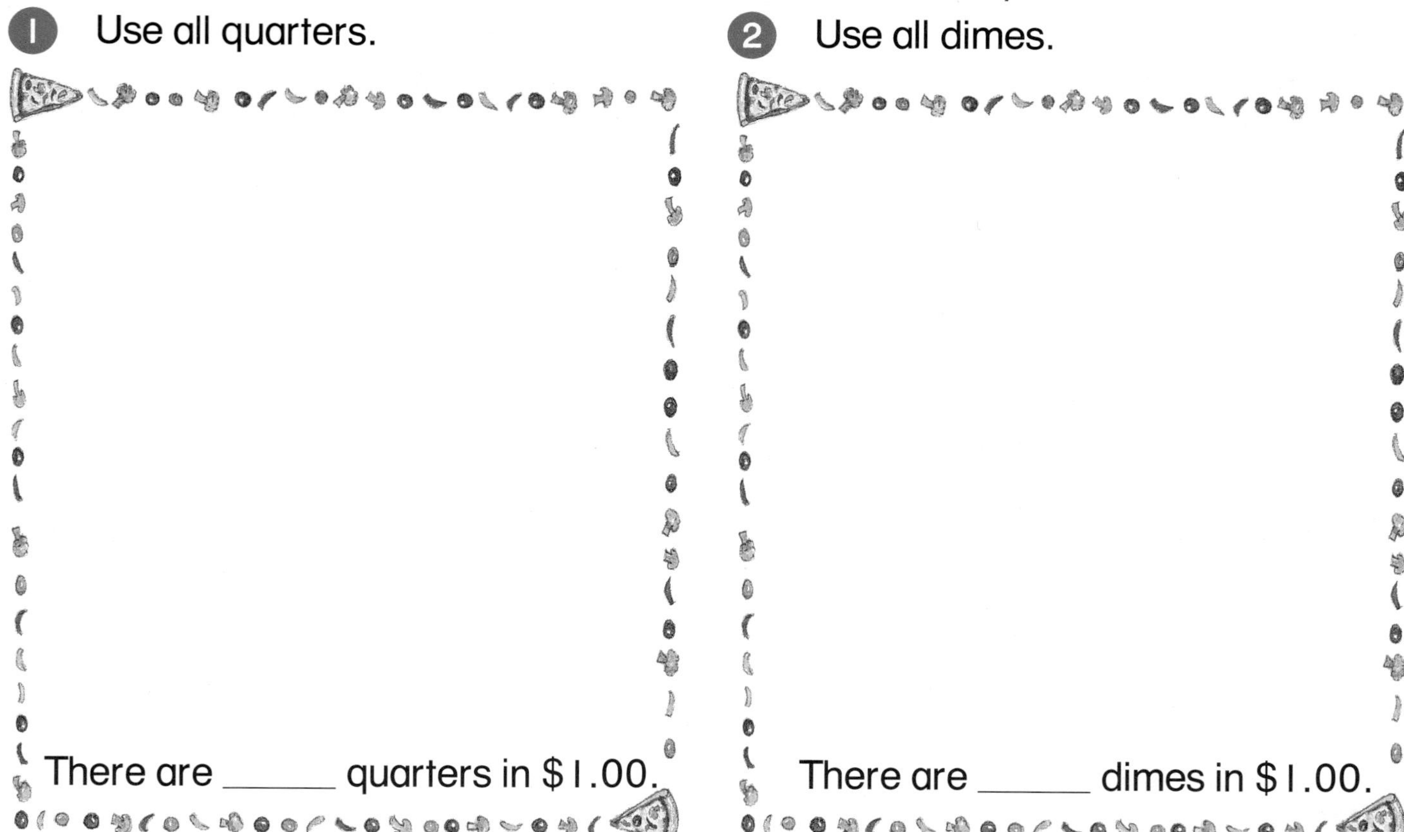

Talk About It Would it take more nickels or more dimes to make $1.00? How do you know?

Notes for Home: Your child learned some coin combinations that total $1.00.
Home Activity: Ask your child to show $1.00 using all nickels. (20 nickels)

Practice

Use half dollars, quarters, dimes, and nickels.
Find different ways to make $1.00.
Draw your coins.

3. 50¢ 50¢

4.

5.

6.

7.

8.

PRACTICE

Journal

9. Some children earn money by doing chores.
What are some ways children could earn $1.00?

Notes for Home: Your child made different coin combinations for $1.00. *Home Activity:* Ask your child how many pennies it takes to make $1.00. (100)

For additional practice, see Skills Practice Bank, page 532, Set 2.

Name ____________________

Practice Game

Race to $1.00

Players 2 to 4

What You Need

Number cube

Coins

How to Play

1. Each player gets 5 turns.
2. Toss the number cube, and take that many coins.
   You must take all dimes or all nickels or all pennies.
3. For each turn, record the value of the coins you took.
4. After each turn, count your total amount of money.
   If your total goes over $1.00, you are out of the game.
5. The person with the total closest to $1.00 wins!

Number Tossed	Coins Taken	Amount of Money for this Turn	Total Amount of Money

Notes for Home: Your child played a game using coins up to $1.00. *Home Activity:* Give your child some coins to count. Keep the total amount less than $1.00.

PRACTICE

Name ______________________

STOP and Practice

Draw the coins in each bank to solve the riddle. You can use coins to help.

1

2

I have 2 coins. The total amount is 55¢.

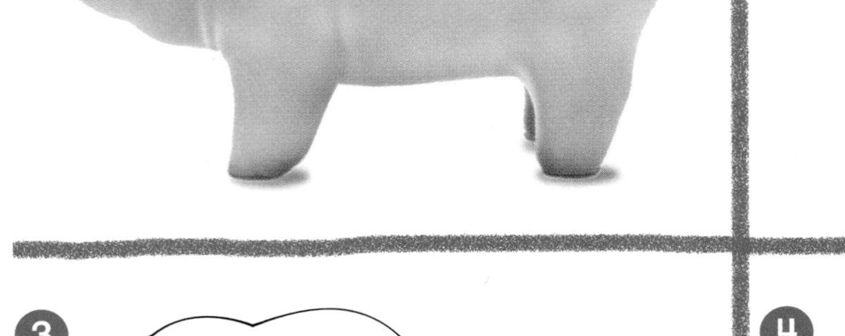

3

I have 4 coins. The total amount is 62¢.

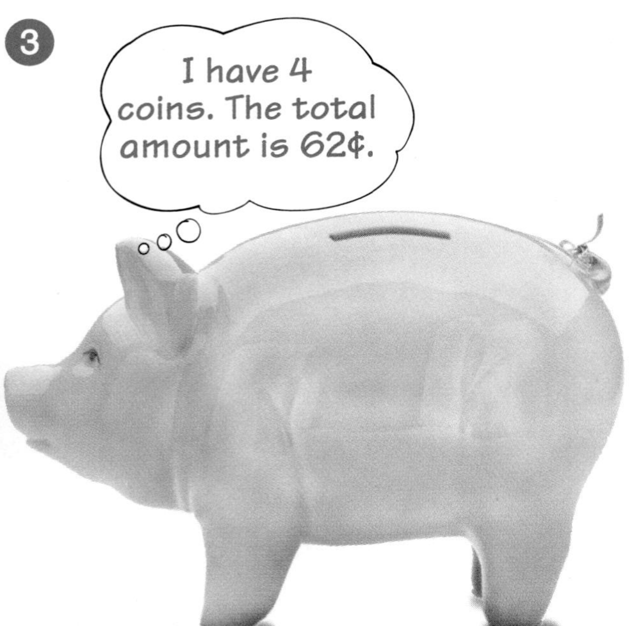

4

I have 3 coins. The total amount is 76¢.

Riddle

5 Make up a riddle for a friend to solve.

Notes for Home: Your child used coin combinations to solve the riddles on this page.
Home Activity: Ask your child what 3 coins make 12¢. (1 dime, 2 pennies)

PRACTICE

Name ______________________________

Retell the Story

Read the story.

The Choice

Sean could hardly wait until Saturday. That was the day of the big garage sale. He had 7 dimes and wanted to buy a great toy. On Saturday, Sean got to the sale early. He saw a soccer ball for 69¢ and a sled for 67¢. He wanted both of them, but he had money for only one. While he was trying to decide which toy to buy, a girl came and bought the ball. Sean quickly bought the sled and got 3¢ change. That afternoon, it began to snow. "I'm sure glad I bought the sled!" Sean said.

Work with a partner.
Retell the story. Use coins to act it out.

Fill in the blanks.

1. Sean wanted to buy a soccer ball and a ________________.
2. He bought the sled for _____ cents.
3. Sean paid with _____ dimes.
4. He got _____ cents change.
5. Sean was glad he bought the sled because it ________________.

Notes for Home: Your child retold a story about buying a toy and used coins to act it out. He or she made a book about the story. *Home Activity:* Ask your child to read the book to you.

6 Cut on the purple line. Fold your paper to make a book. Draw pictures or write sentences to retell the story.

Name

Problem Solving: Act It Out

Learn

PROBLEM SOLVING GUIDE

Understand • Plan • Solve • Look Back

Check

Take turns buying and selling. Use dimes to pay for items. Use pennies to make change.

	Cost	Amount Paid	Change
1	68¢	7 dimes	2¢
2			
3			
4			

Talk About It Nancy buys this toy. She pays with a quarter. How can you find the change?

Notes for Home: Your child used coins to make change. *Home Activity:* Use pennies and dimes. Ask your child to show you how to make change for an item in the picture.

PROBLEM SOLVING

Practice

I'm paying with 3 dimes. What's my change?

25¢ 18¢ 58¢ 57¢ 15¢ 67¢ 76¢ 48¢ 97¢ 25¢ 89¢ 39¢ 41¢

PROBLEM SOLVING

Take turns buying and selling. Use dimes to pay for items.
Use pennies to make change.

	Cost	Amount Paid	Change
5	25¢	3 dimes	5¢
6			
7			
8			
9			

Critical Thinking

10. Use the picture. Name 2 items you could buy with 9 dimes.
How do you know you could buy them?

Notes for Home: Your child practiced using coins to make change. *Home Activity:* Ask your child to point out the highest priced item in the picture and tell how many dimes he or she would need to pay for it. (teddy bear; 10 dimes)

Name

Mixed Practice

Lessons 5–7

Concepts and Skills

Use the fewest coins to show this amount.

Draw the coins.

1

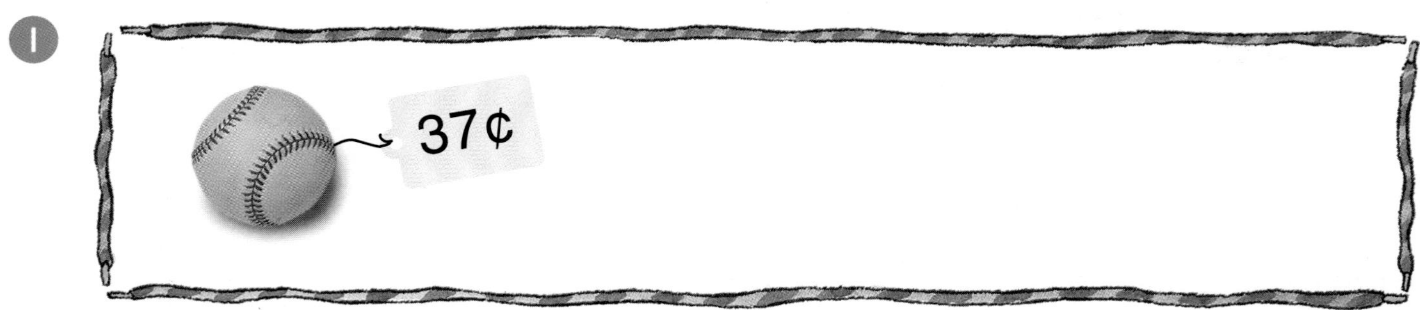

Use half dollars, quarters, dimes, and nickels.

Show 2 ways to make $1.00.

Draw the coins.

Problem Solving

4 Calvin has 6 dimes. He buys a ball at the flea market for 56¢. How much change does he get back?

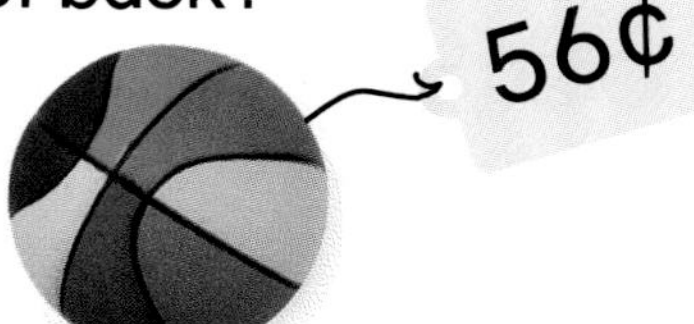

______

Journal

5 What coins could you use to pay for a book that costs 78¢? What change would you get back?

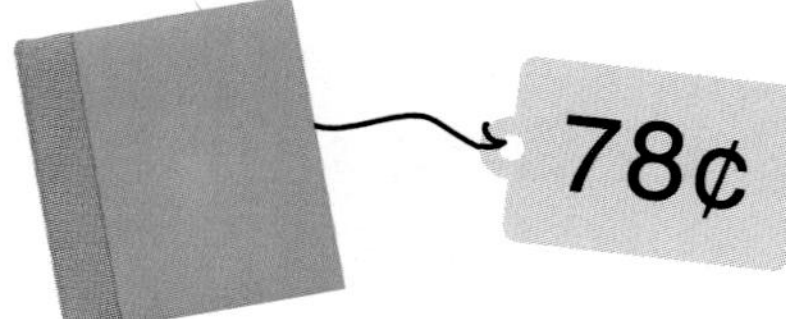

Notes for Home: Your child practiced choosing coins to show amounts of money and making change to solve problems. *Home Activity:* Ask your child to draw another way to make $1.00.

Name ______________________________

Cumulative Review

Chapters 1–6

Concepts and Skills

For each number, write the nearest ten.

1. Is 78 closer to 70 or 80?

   78 is closer to ______.

2. Is 43 closer to 40 or 50?

   43 is closer to ______.

Write the numbers in order from least to greatest.

3. 97 39 62

   ______ ______ ______

4. 73 96 44

   ______ ______ ______

Problem Solving

Solve the riddles.

5. I am between 48 and 55.
   I have 4 ones.

   What number am I? ______

6. I am greater than 78.
   I have 7 tens.

   What number am I? ______

Test Prep

Fill in the ○ for the correct answer.

7. Which sentence tells about the picture?

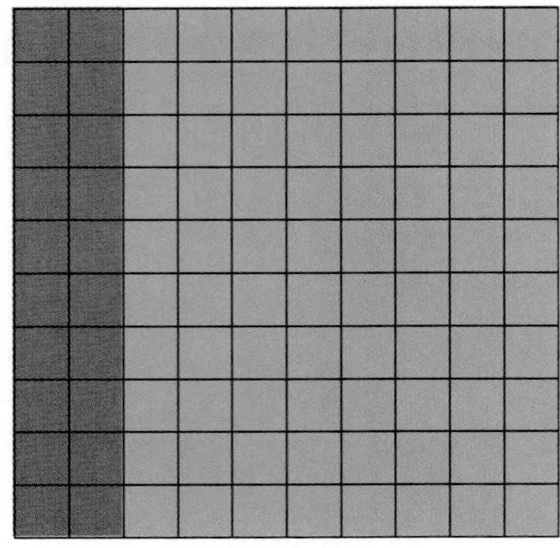

○ 50 and 50 is 100.
○ 25 and 75 is 100.
○ 20 and 80 is 100.
○ 95 and 5 is 100.

Notes for Home: Your child reviewed comparing numbers, finding the nearest ten for a number, and solving problems. *Home Activity:* Ask your child to put 72, 46, and 53 in order from least to greatest. (46, 53, 72)

Name ____________________

Chapter 6 Review

Vocabulary

Use half dollars, quarters, dimes, and nickels to make 1 dollar. Show 2 ways.
Draw the coins.

1 2

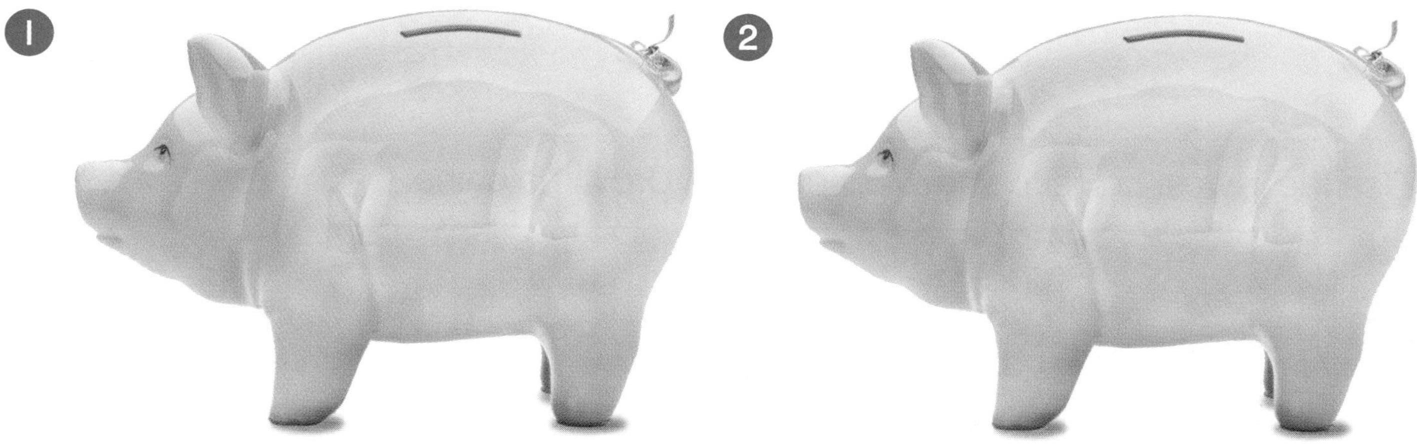

Concepts and Skills

Count the money. You can use coins. Write the total amount.

3 4

Problem Solving

Solve.

5 Kendra buys a pencil. She pays with 3 dimes. How much change does she get back?

______

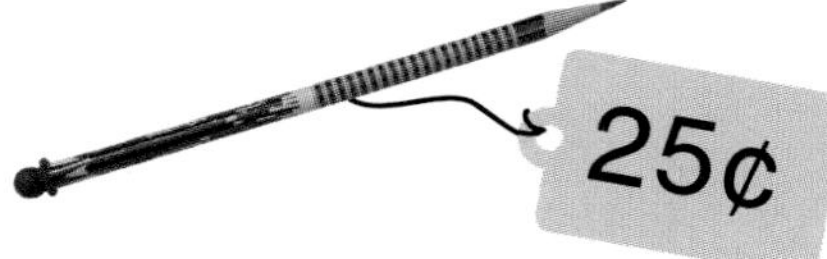

6 Webster buys a notebook. He pays with 5 dimes. How much change does he get back?

______

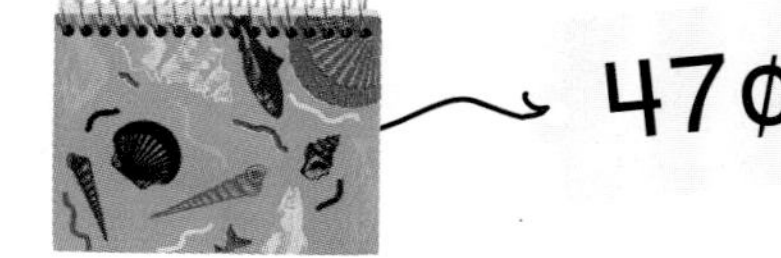

Notes for Home: Your child reviewed Chapter 6 vocabulary, concepts, skills, and problem solving.
Home Activity: Ask your child to name the coins that are worth 1¢, 5¢, 10¢, and 25¢. (penny, nickel, dime, and quarter)

CHAPTER REVIEW

Name

Chapter 6 Test

Count the money. You can use coins. Write the total amount.

Use the fewest coins to show this amount. Draw the coins.

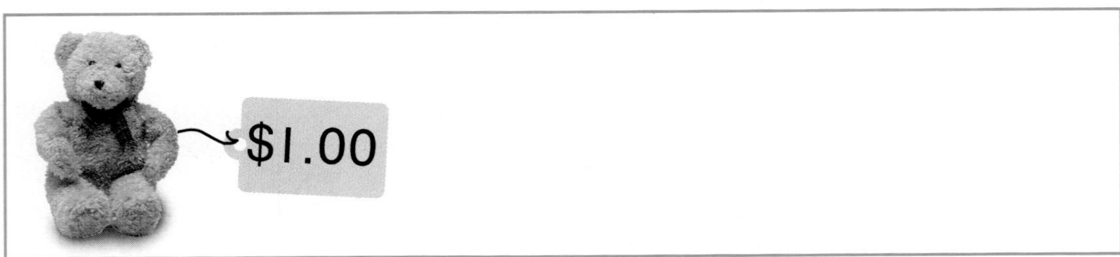

Solve. You can use coins.

3 Ina has 9 dimes. She bought a puppet at the flea market for 85¢. How much change should she get back?

_____

4 Jay has 7 dimes. He bought a kite for 68¢. How much change should he get back?

_____

5 Damir has 20¢ in his bank. He has no pennies.

Find all the ways to make 20¢ using dimes and nickels. Make a list.

dime	nickel

Notes for Home: Your child was assessed on Chapter 6 concepts, skills, and problem solving. *Home Activity:* Ask your child to tell you how many dimes he or she would need to pay for something that costs 27¢. (3 dimes)

CHAPTER TEST

Name

Performance Assessment

Chapter 6

Put these coins in a bag:

1 

1 

5 

5 

5 

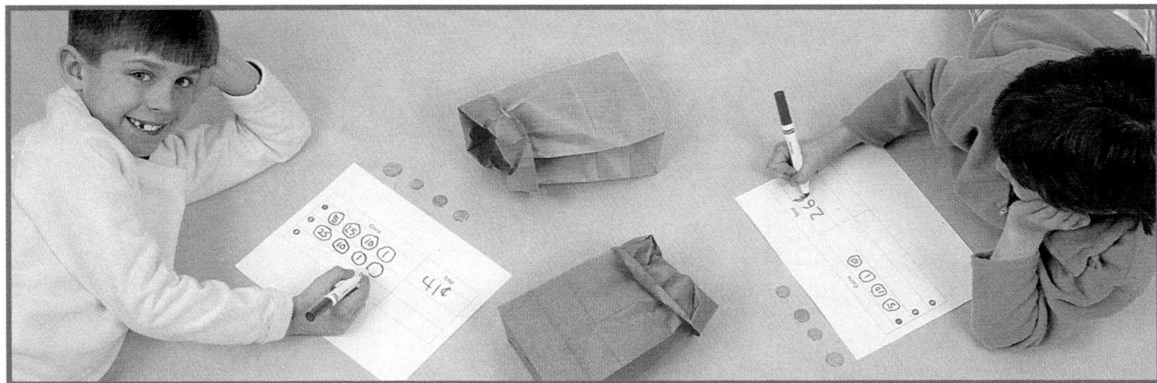

Take 4 coins. Draw your coins. Write the total amount. Repeat the activity.

	Coins	Total
1		
2		
3		

Choose one of your totals from the table above. Use coins to find 2 new ways to show that amount. Draw your coins.

4	
5	

Problem Solving Critical Thinking

Use coins from the bag.

6. What is the greatest amount you can make if you use 4 different coins? the least amount?

Notes for Home: Your child did an activity that tested Chapter 6 skills, concepts, and problem solving. *Home Activity:* Have your child think of an amount less than $1.00 and show it using many different combinations of coins.

Name ____________________

Calculate Your Costs!

Keys You Will Use 

79¢ is the same as $.79, so I press • 7 9.

You can use your calculator to find the total cost of all the items you are buying.

How much would it cost to buy a bear, a tablet, and bubbles?

Find 79¢ + 47¢ + 25¢. Press these keys.

= 1.51

The total cost of all three items is $1.51.

Use a sale flyer and your calculator.

Choose items to buy. Find the total cost.

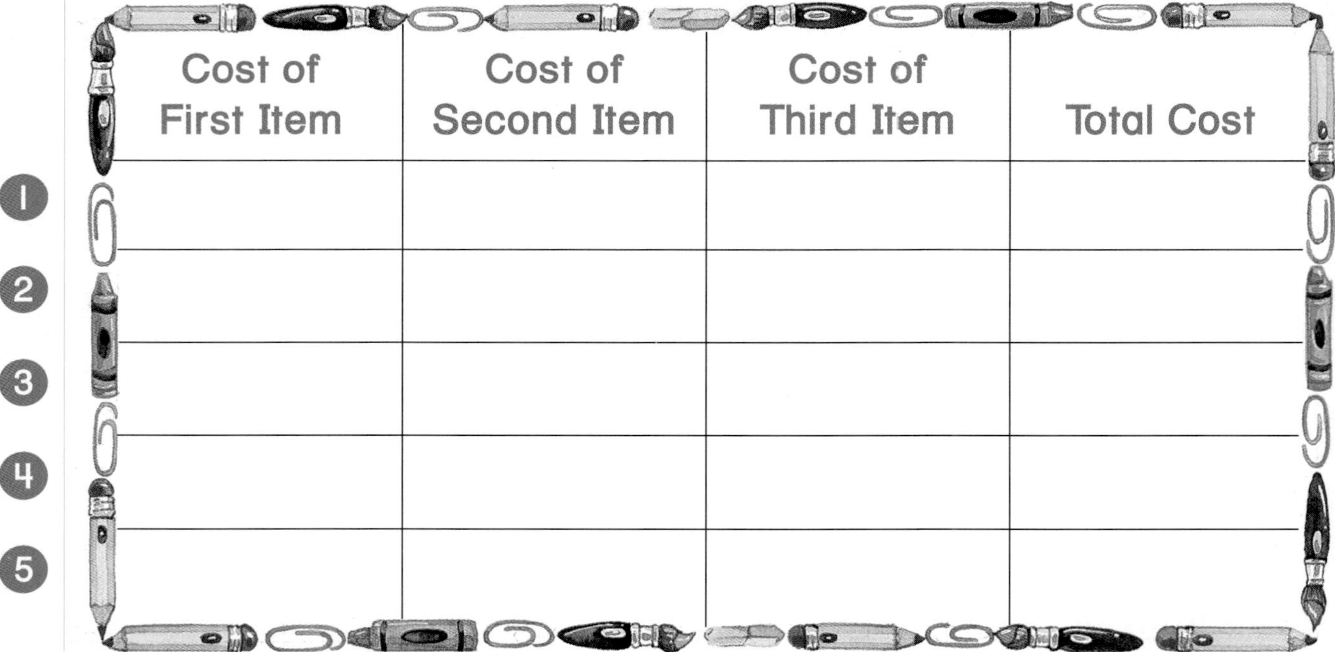

	Cost of First Item	Cost of Second Item	Cost of Third Item	Total Cost
1				
2				
3				
4				
5				

Tech Talk Your calculator displays 34.15. How many dollars and how many cents does this show? How do you know?

Visit our Web site. www.parent.mathsurf.com

Penny Power

Different machines use different amounts of electricity. The chart below shows about how much it costs to run these machines for one hour.

Machine	Electricity Cost (1 hour)
Microwave	one dime
Television	one penny
Computer	two pennies

1 How would you spend 25¢ on electricity? Pick different machines from the chart. Tell how long you would use them.

2 Ask another person how they would spend 25¢ on electricity. Compare your answers.

Fold down

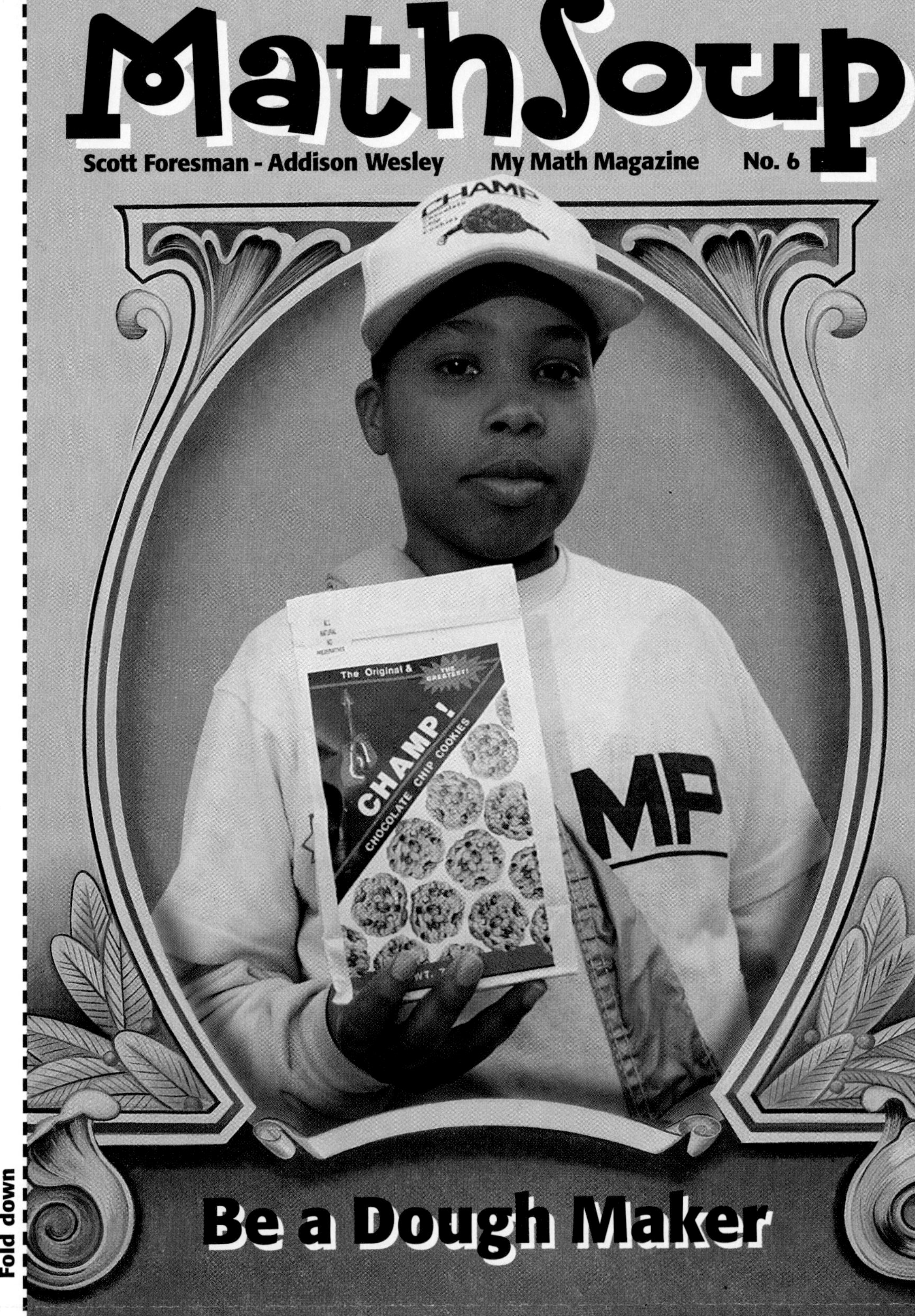

Making Dough

Number of Cookies	Price
	10¢
	25¢
	50¢

The chart above shows prices for different packages of cookies. Find how many cookies you could buy with

1 40¢. ______ cookies

2 60¢. ______ cookies

3 Choose an amount of money between 20¢ and 80¢. Ask a friend how many cookies he or she could buy.

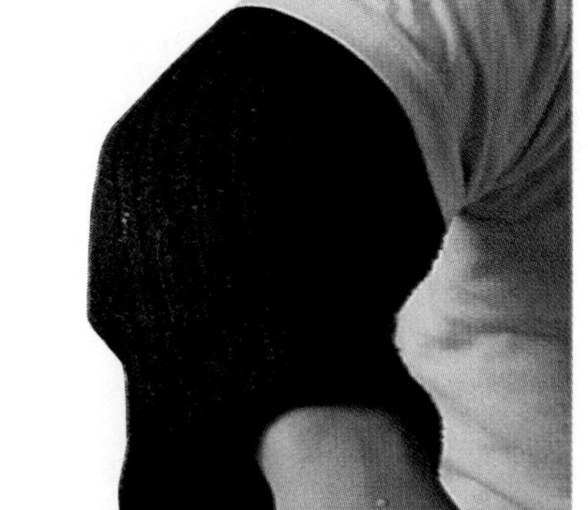

Draw your own "money" using objects such as paper clips, rubber bands, or marbles. Decide how much each object stands for.

______ cents	______ cents	______ cents

1 Show a friend your money. Ask your friend to choose any two objects. How much are they worth in all?

______

2 Pick an item you would like to buy. Decide how much it should cost. Show how you would pay for it using your money.

Notes for Home: Your child learned about quantities available at different prices. *Home Activity:* Ask your child how many cookies could be purchased for 35¢. (7)

Making Money

Long ago, many people did not use coins. They used other kinds of money to get things that they needed.

In China, people used shells.

Many Native Americans and settlers used wampum.*

Some people in Ethiopia used bars of salt.

*** Wampum is made of beads strung together.**

Notes for Home: Your child learned about some items that early civilizations used as money. *Home Activity:* Ask your child to tell you the value of three of the objects you drew.

A teacher in Washington, D.C. and his students began a company called Champ Cookies & Things. The children learned to run a business as they had fun!

The students at Champ Cookies & Things bought supplies, made cookie dough, baked cookies, and then sold them!

Making Cents

Use the triangle of nickels on the next page to answer the following questions.

1 How much is the triangle worth?

______

2 Suppose you used dimes instead of nickels. How much would the triangle be worth?

______

3 Suppose you added a row of 4 nickels to the bottom of the triangle. How much would the triangle be worth?

______

4 Suppose you made the triangle out of four rows of dimes. How much would it be worth?

______

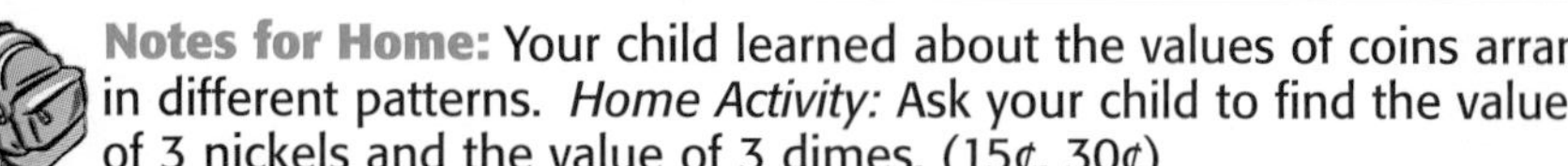

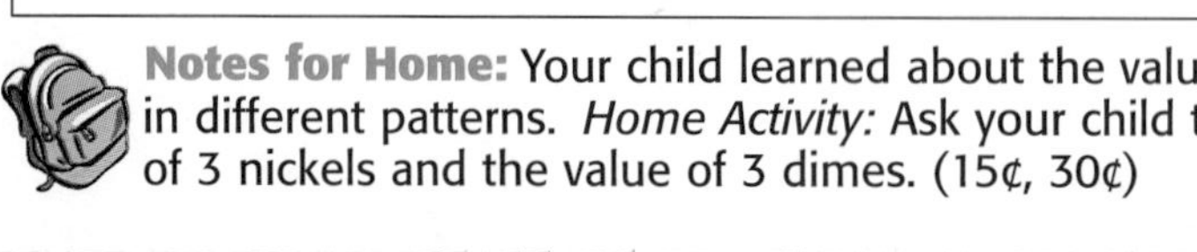

Notes for Home: Your child learned about the values of coins arranged in different patterns. *Home Activity:* Ask your child to find the value of 3 nickels and the value of 3 dimes. (15¢, 30¢)

CHAPTER 7

Time

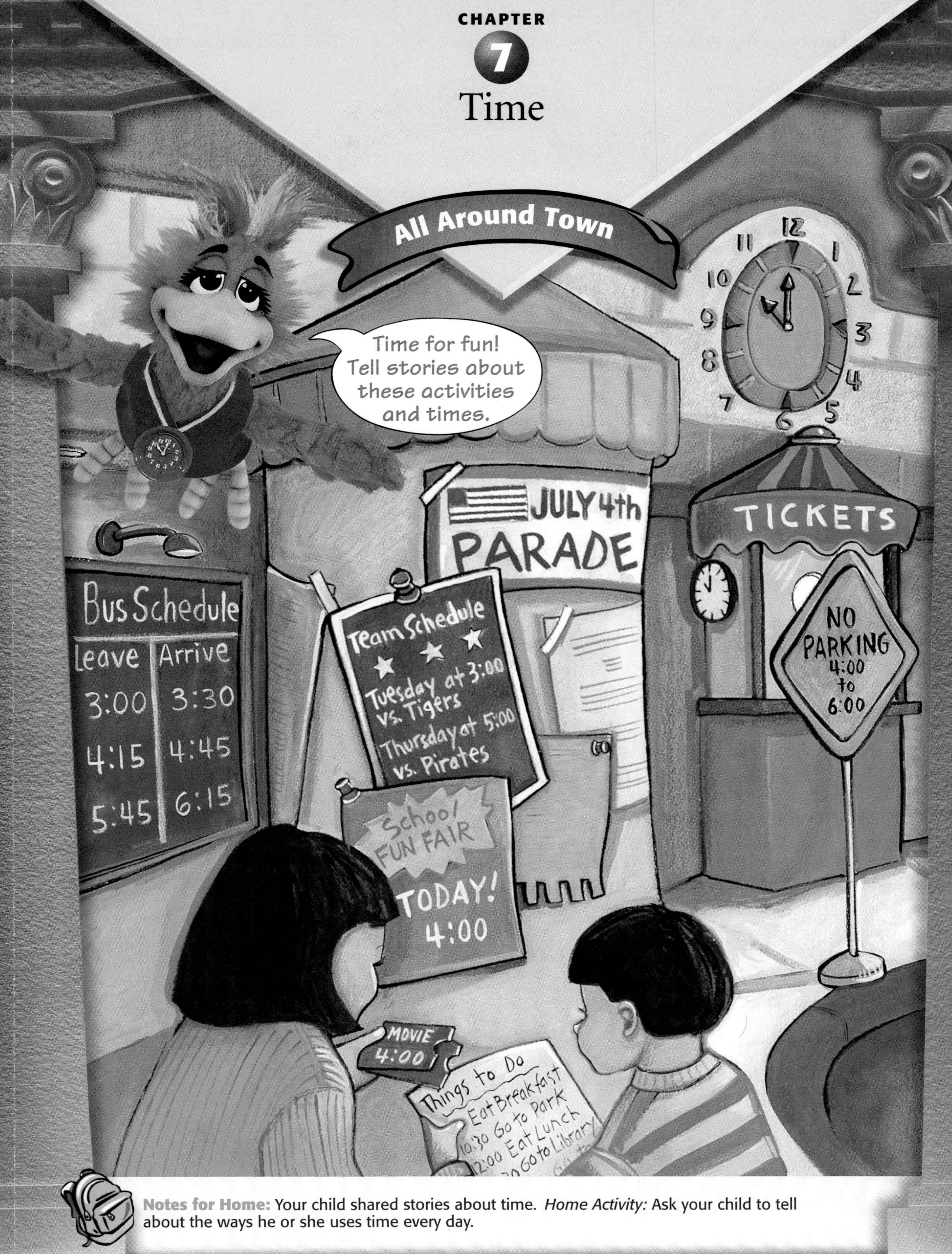

Notes for Home: Your child shared stories about time. *Home Activity:* Ask your child to tell about the ways he or she uses time every day.

Saturday Schedule

8:00 Eat breakfast.
10:30 Go to park.
12:00 Eat lunch.
1:30 Go to library to return books.
3:00 Go to store.

Dear Family,
Our class is starting Chapter 7. We will learn to tell time and solve problems about time. Together we can do these activities.

It's Story Time

Create story problems about things you do as a family. For example: It is 12:00. Lunch will be ready in 30 minutes. At what time will we eat? Work with your child to solve the problem.

Table Talk

Make a list of things to do for a weekend day. Make a schedule, listing the activities along with their starting times. As you go about the day together, talk about the schedule.

Community Connection

Look for examples of how time is used in the community. Talk about clocks that you see and signs that show time, for example, store hours and parking signs.

Visit our Web site. www.parent.mathsurf.com

Name

Explore One Minute

Explore

What could you do that takes about one minute?
Your teacher will time you as you try it.
Write and draw what you could do.

1

Share

Did your activity take more than, less than, or about one minute?

Notes for Home: Your child explored what can be done in about one minute. *Home Activity:* Ask your child what activities he or she does at home that take about one minute.

EXPLORE

Connect

How many times can you do each activity in one minute?
Estimate. Then do the activity. Write how many.

2. Write your first name.

   Estimate: ______ times

   How many? ______ times

3. Draw happy faces.

   Estimate: ______ times

   How many? ______ times

4. Hop on one foot.

   Estimate: ______ times

   How many? ______ times

5. Clap your hands.

   Estimate: ______ times

   How many? ______ times

Talk About It What activity did you do the most times? the fewest times? Compare your answers with a friend.

Notes for Home: Your child estimated how many times he or she could do an activity in one minute. Then your child timed the activity to check. *Home Activity:* Ask your child to do one of the activities again as you time the activity.

Name

Estimate Time

Learn

Check

Estimate whether the activity takes **more** or **less** than one minute. Then try it to check.
Complete the table.

	Activity	Estimate	Check
1	Say this sentence. Tim tickled the turtle's toes.	________ than one minute	________ than one minute
2	Read a story.	________ than one minute	________ than one minute
3	Sharpen a pencil.	________ than one minute	________ than one minute

Talk About It Name an activity that you do that takes less than one minute. Name an activity that takes more than one minute.

Notes for Home: Your child estimated whether an activity would take less than one minute or more than one minute. *Home Activity:* Ask your child to tell you daily activities that take less than one minute and more than one minute.

Practice

Draw or write an activity you can do in each amount of time.

4. Less than one minute

5. About one minute

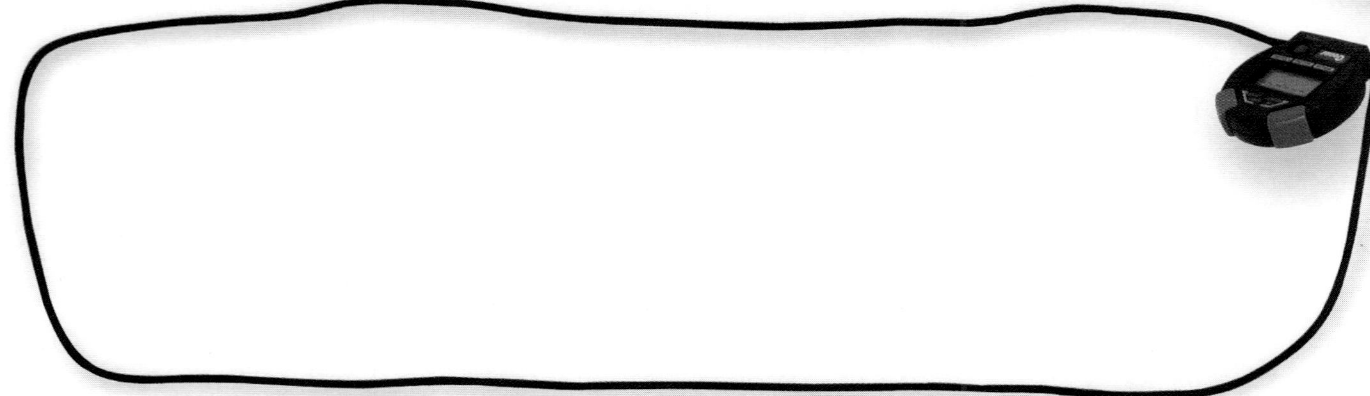

6. More than one minute

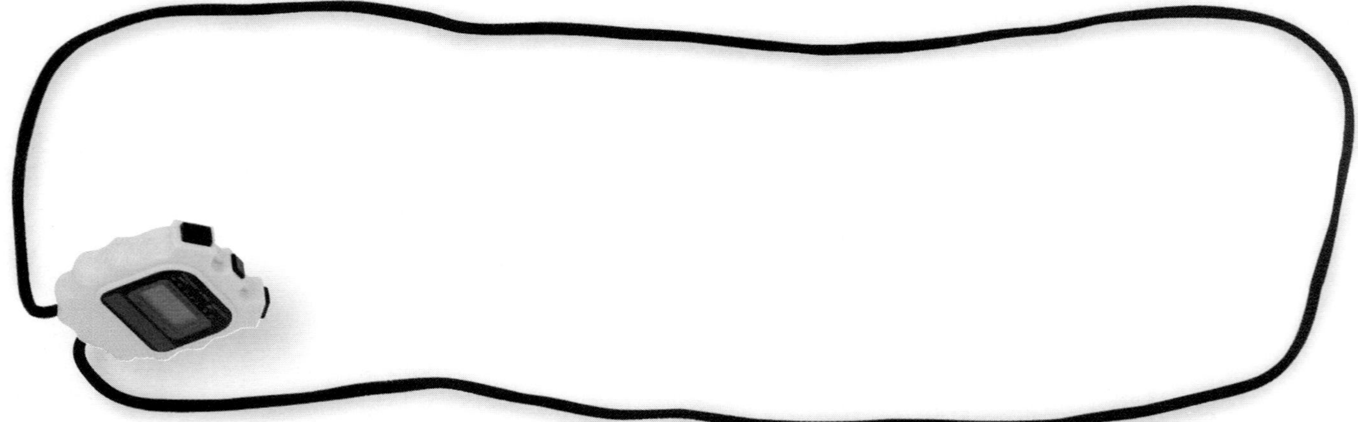

Tell a Math Story

7. You have one minute to tell someone about yourself. What would you say?

Notes for Home: Your child drew a picture of an activity that would take less than, more than, and about one minute. *Home Activity:* Ask your child to name daily activities that take about a minute.

PRACTICE

Name

Elapsed Time

Learn

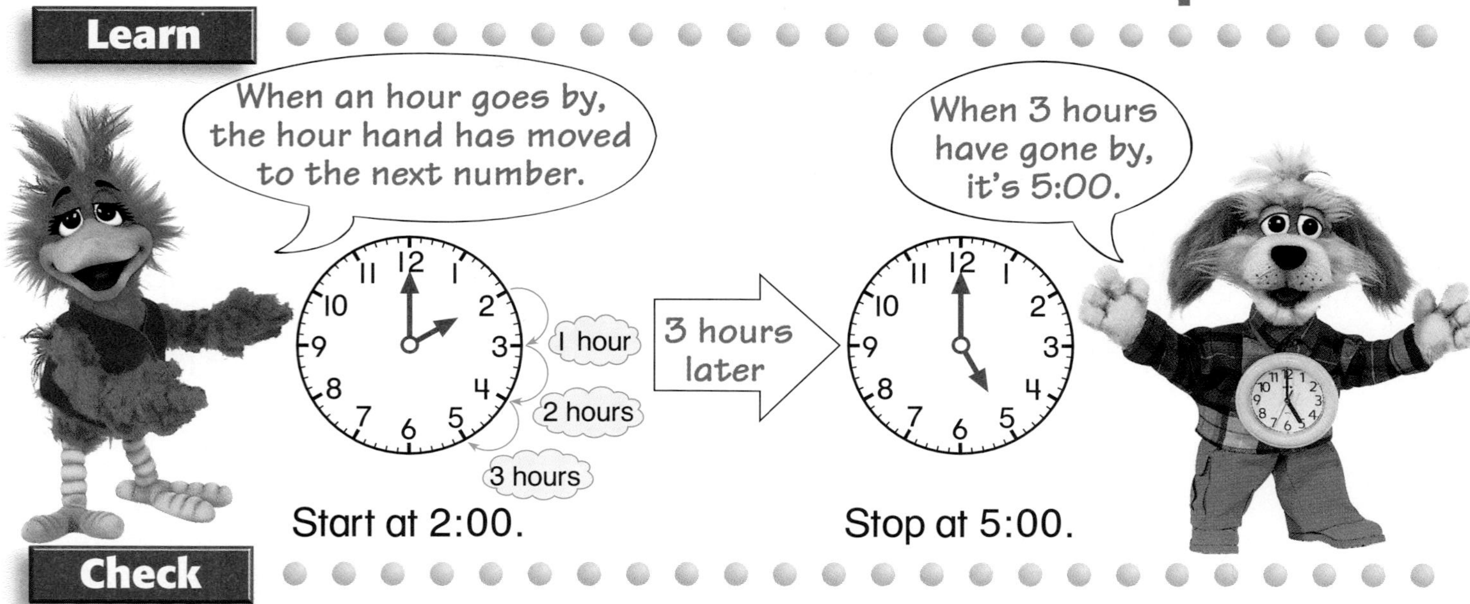

Check

Draw the clock hands. Write the ending times. You can use a clock.

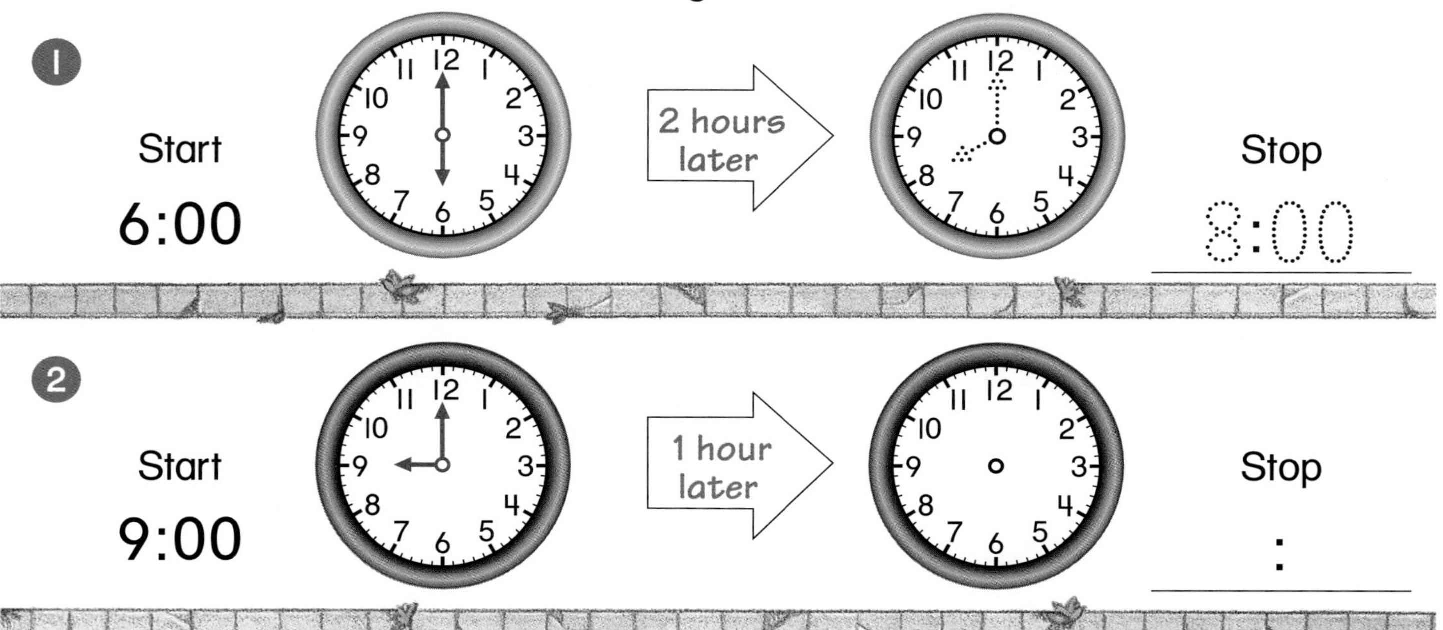

Read both clocks. How many hours have gone by?

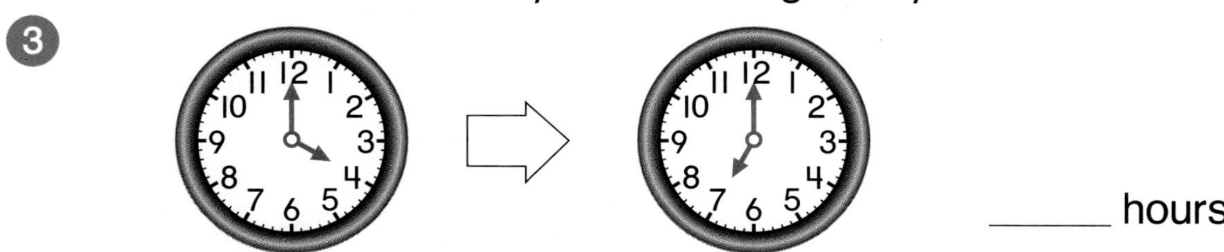

_____ hours

Talk About It Tell how you can look at the clock and know when it will be 2 hours later.

Notes for Home: Your child learned how to tell the number of hours that have gone by. *Home Activity:* Point out the clock when it shows time to the hour. Ask your child to explain how a clock shows that an hour has gone by.

Practice

Draw the clock hands. Write the ending times.
You can use a clock.

Start
4:00

3 hours later

Stop
7:00

5

Start
2:00

Stop
___:___

PRACTICE

When will each activity end? Write the ending time.
You can use a clock.

6 Dena goes to a movie at 7:00. The movie is over in 2 hours. The time is

___:___

7 Juan leaves home at 11:00. He meets a friend 1 hour later. They play in the park for 2 more hours. The time is

___:___

Problem Solving Critical Thinking

8 Tina stopped fishing at 8:00. She fished for 2 hours.

What time did she start fishing? ___:___

Notes for Home: Your child solved problems involving the passing of time. *Home Activity:* Ask your child to tell you how many hours have gone by between 1:00 and 3:00 in the afternoon. (2 hours)

For additional practice, see Skills Practice Bank, page 533 Set 1.

Name ________________________________

Practice Game

Tic-Tac-Time

Make a clock spinner.

Players 2

What You Need

2 paper clips

pencil

crayon

How to Play

1. Player One spins both spinners.
2. Use the paper clip as hour hands. Find the hour that each paper clip is closest to. Read each time.
3. Find how many hours passed from the time on Spinner 1 to the time on Spinner 2.
4. Color in the matching space on the gameboard.
5. Player Two completes Steps 1–4 using a different color. If a space on the gameboard is already colored in, a player's turn is over.
6. Continue taking turns. The first player to complete a row or column wins!

Spinner 1

Spinner 2

1 hour	2 hours	3 hours	4 hours
5 hours	6 hours	7 hours	8 hours
9 hours	10 hours	11 hours	12 hours

Gameboard

Notes for Home: Your child played a game to practice finding elapsed time. *Home Activity:* Ask your child to show you a time on a clock, and then explain how to find the time that is 5 hours later. (Sample answer: 2:00 and 7:00)

PRACTICE

Name ______________________

STOP and Practice

Does the activity take more or less than one minute?
Estimate. Then try it to check.
Complete the table. Write **more** or **less.**

	Activity	Estimate	Check
1	Write number words from 1 to 5.	______ than one minute	______ than one minute
2	Count backward from 50 to 0.	______ than one minute	______ than one minute

3. Write the time in two different ways.

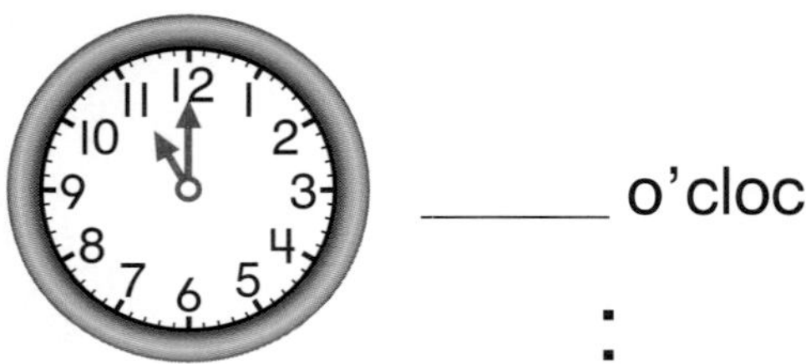

______ o'clock

______ : ______

4. Draw the clock hands to show the time.

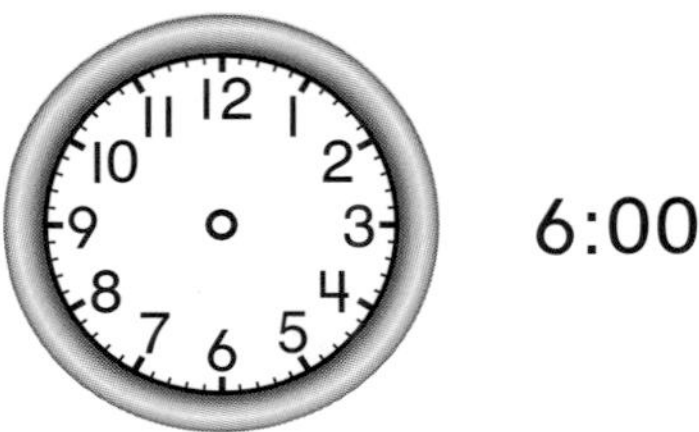

6:00

Draw the clock hands. Write the ending times.

5.

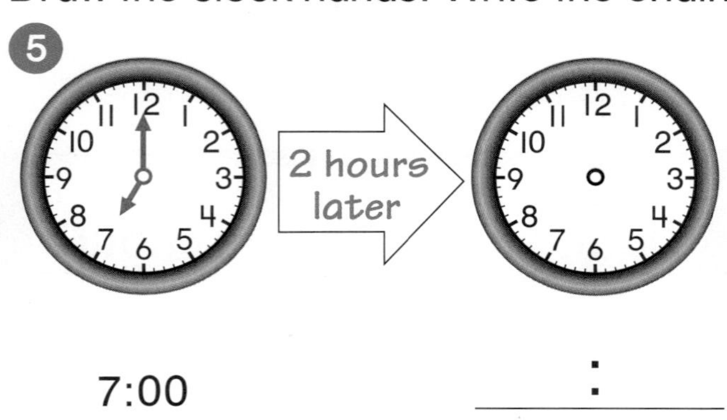

7:00 ______ : ______

6.

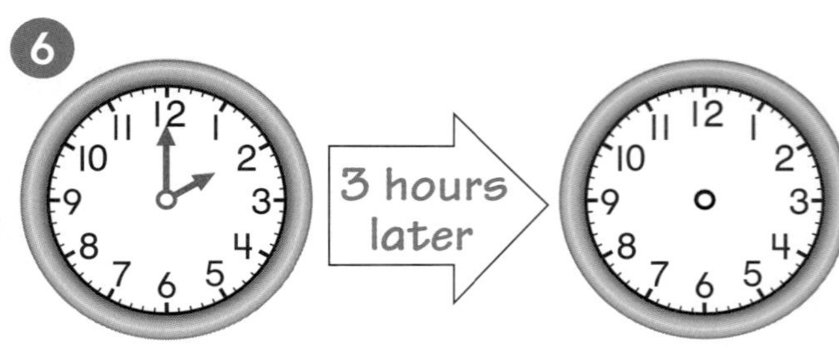

2:00 ______ : ______

Number Sense

7. Would you ever use the number 61 to tell time? Explain your answer.

Notes for Home: Your child practiced estimating time, telling time to the hour, and calculating elapsed time. *Home Activity:* Ask your child what the time will be 3 hours after 9:00. (12:00)

PRACTICE

Name

Problem Solving: Use Data from a Table

Learn

PROBLEM SOLVING GUIDE

Understand • Plan • Solve • Look Back

Saturday Classes

Class	Starts	Ends
Arts and Crafts	1:00	4:00
Basketball	1:00	3:00
Bike Safety	10:00	11:00
Cooking	10:00	12:00
Sing Along	3:00	5:00
Puppets and Plays	9:00	11:00

Check

Use the table to answer the questions.

1. What class starts at 9:00? Puppets and Plays
2. How long does **Arts and Crafts** last? ______ hours
3. What class starts 2 hours later than **Basketball**? ______________
4. What class ends after 1 hour? ______________
5. What class ends at the same time as **Puppets and Plays**? ______________

Talk About It Tell how you can look at the table and know which class lasts 3 hours.

Notes for Home: Your child used a table to solve problems about time. *Home Activity:* Ask your child to tell you what time the cooking class shown in the table ends. (12:00)

PROBLEM SOLVING

PROBLEM SOLVING

Practice

After-School Classes

Class	Starts	Ends
Book Club	4:00	5:00
Clay Play	4:00	6:00
Computer	5:00	6:00
Sports	4:00	6:00

Use the table. Solve the problems.
Write each answer.

6. Miles gets out of school 1 hour before **Sports** starts. At what time does he get out of school?

   3:00

7. Felipe takes **Clay Play**. How long is he in class?

   ______ hours

8. Tran eats dinner 1 hour after the **Book Club** ends. At what time does he eat dinner?

   ___ : ___

9. Keisha takes another class after the **Book Club** ends. What class starts at this time?

   ____

Journal

10. What class would you add to the table? What time would it start? How long would it last?

Notes for Home: Your child practiced using a table to solve problems. *Home Activity:* Ask your child to tell what class starts 1 hour after Clay Play. (Computer)

For additional practice, see Skills Practice Bank, page 533, Set 2.

Name

Tell Time to the Half Hour

Learn

Shante gets on the bus at 8:00.

The bus arrives at school at 8:30. A half hour has gone by.

After a half hour, the minute hand moves the from 12 to the 6.
The hour hand moves between the 8 and the 9.

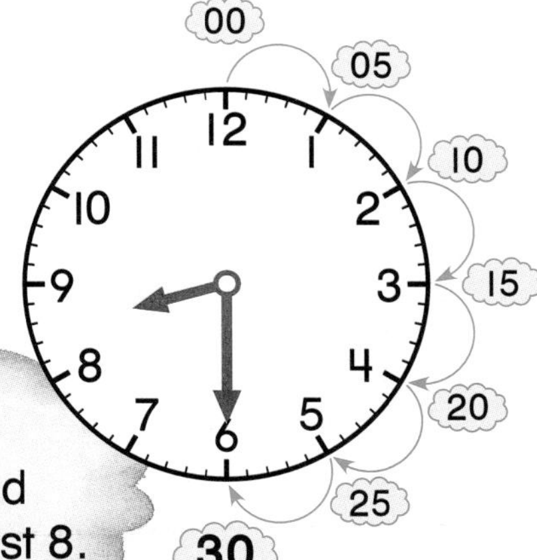

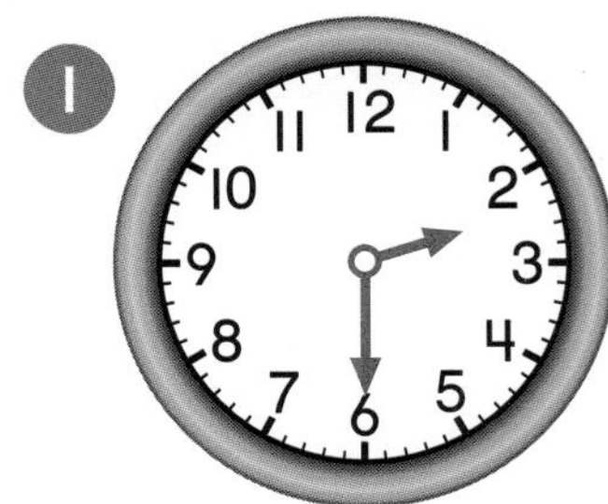

The minute hand has moved halfway around the clock. It is half past 8.

Check

Write the time shown on each clock. You can use a clock.

1. 2:30 half past ____
2. ____:____ half past ____
3. ____:____ half past ____
4. ____:____ half past ____

Talk About It What activities do you do that take about a half hour?

Notes for Home: Your child learned how to tell time to the half hour. *Home Activity:* Ask your child to tell time at home when a clock shows time to the half hour.

Practice

Write the time shown on each clock. You can use a clock.

5. 1:30 ____
half past ____

6. ____ : ____
half past ____

7. ____ : ____

8. ____ : ____
half past ____

9. 
____ : ____
half past ____

10. 
____ : ____

11. 
____ : ____
half past ____

12. 
____ : ____

PRACTICE

Write your own.

Write a time using a half hour.
Draw a picture showing what you do at that time.

____ : ____

half past ____

Problem Solving Patterns

13. Write the times to continue the pattern.

12:00, 12:30, 1:00, ____ : ____, ____ : ____, ____ : ____

Notes for Home: Your child practiced telling time to the half hour. *Home Activity:* Ask your child where the minute hand and the hour hand point at 4:30. (The minute hand points at the 6; the hour hand points between the 4 and 5.)

Name

Organize Information

A Day at School

Subject	Time
Reading	8:30–9:30
Art	9:30–10:00
Math	10:00–11:00
Lunch	11:00–11:30
Language Arts	11:30–12:30
Recess	12:30–1:00
Science	1:00–2:00

Use the rows and columns to find each answer.

1. How many subjects come before lunch?

   3

2. How many subjects come after lunch?

   ______

3. Which subjects last for one hour? Write two of them.

   ______

   ______

4. What are children doing at 10:45?

   ______

Talk About It Why are tables useful?

Notes for Home: Your child learned how to read a table. *Home Activity:* Ask your child which subject ends at 10:00 and which subject begins at 10:00. (Art ends; Math begins.)

Saturday Activities

Activity	Time
Breakfast	9:30-10:00
Library	10:00-11:00
Haircut	11:00-11:30
Lunch	11:30-12:00
Park	12:00-1:00
Movie	1:00-3:00
Shopping	3:00-4:00

This table shows the order of activities for a Saturday.

5. How much time is spent at the library?

   1 hour

6. How long does the movie last?

   ______

7. Which activities last for a half hour? Write two of them.

   ______

   ______

8. How many hours pass from the beginning of breakfast until the beginning of lunch?

   ______ hours

Journal

9. What would you like to do after school? Make your own table. Include your favorite activities.

Notes for Home: Your child practiced reading a table. *Home Activity:* Ask your child which activities in the table last for one hour. (Library, Park, Shopping)

Name ______________________________

Chapter 7 Review

Vocabulary

Choose from these words to solve the riddles.

hour	minute	half hour

1. There are 60 of me in one hour.

   I am one ____________.

2. I am 30 minutes long.

   I am a ____________.

Concepts and Skills

Write the time shown on each clock. You can use a clock.

3. 

   ____ : ____

4. 

   ____ : ____

5. 

   ____ : ____

6. 

   ____ : ____

7. Does it take **more** or **less** than one minute to close a door? ____________

Problem Solving

Use the table.
Write the answer.

8. Travis leaves school one hour after gym class ends. At what time does he leave school?

   ____ : ____

Class Schedule

Class	Starts	Ends
Music	8:00	9:00
Art	10:00	11:00
Gym	1:00	2:00

Notes for Home: Your child reviewed the vocabulary, skills, concepts, and problem solving taught in Chapter 7. *Home Activity:* Ask your child to look at a clock, tell the time, and then tell what the time will be one hour later.

CHAPTER REVIEW

Name

Chapter 7 Test

Write each time in two different ways. You can use a clock.

1 

___ : ___

half past ___

2 

___ : ___

___ minutes after ___

3 

___ : ___

___ minutes after ___

4 Draw the clock hands.
Write the ending time.

3 hours later

8:00

___ : ___

5 Circle the activity that takes more than one minute.

baking muffins

counting to 10

6 Use the calendar to complete the table. Find how many dates are in the column below each day of the week. Make tallies to show the number of dates.

January						
S	M	T	W	T	F	S
1	2	3	4	5	6	7
8	9	10	11	12	13	14
15	16	17	18	19	20	21
22	23	24	25	26	27	28
29	30	31				

Sunday	Monday	Tuesday	Wednesday	Thursday	Friday	Saturday

Notes for Home: Your child was assessed on Chapter 7 concepts, skills, and problem solving. *Home Activity:* Ask your child to look at the calendar and tell you the date of the third Sunday in the month. (15)

CHAPTER TEST

Name

Performance Assessment

Chapter 7

Pick one card from each bag.

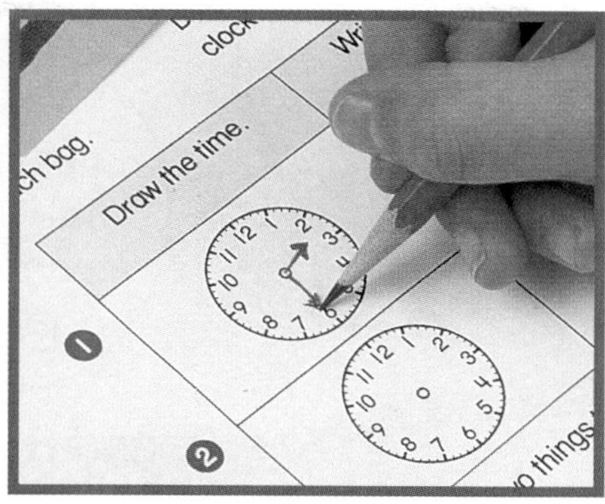

Draw the clock hands to show the time.

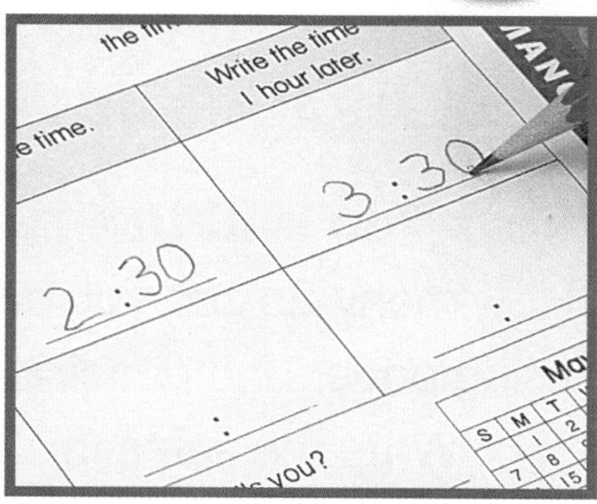

Write the time. Then write the time one hour later.

	Draw the clock hands to show the time.	Write the time.	Write the time one hour later.
1	12 1 2 3 4 5 6 7 8 9 10 11	___:___	___:___
2	12 1 2 3 4 5 6 7 8 9 10 11	___:___	___:___

3. What are two things this calendar tells you?

____

____

May						
S	M	T	W	T	F	S
	1	2	3	4	5	6
7	8	9	10	11	12	13
14	15	16	17	18	19	20
21	22	23	24	25	26	27
28	29	30	31			

Problem Solving Critical Thinking

4. Look at a calendar for this month.
How is it like this calendar for May? How is it different?

Notes for Home: Your child did an activity that assessed Chapter 7 skills, concepts, and problem solving. *Home Activity:* Ask your child to tell you the earliest time that they wrote for Exercises 1–2.

Name ______________________________

Add Again and Again!

Is it quicker to use a calculator or pencil and paper?

Keys You Will Use 

How many 2s can you add in one minute using paper and pencil?

1. Write the sums for 2 + 2, 4 + 2, 6 + 2, and 8 + 2.
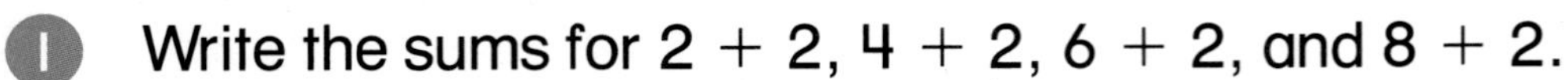
2. Now predict what your sum would be after one minute. ______
3. Start over. Have your partner time you. What is your final sum? ______
4. Compare your prediction to your final sum. Was your prediction **greater** or **less** than your final sum?

____

How many 2s can you add in one minute using your  ?

5. Press these keys.

6. Think about how many times in one minute you could add 2. Predict your final sum. ______
7. Start over. Have your partner time you. What is your final sum? ______
8. Compare your prediction to your final sum. Was your prediction **greater** or **less** than your final sum?

____

Tech Talk Repeat the activity by adding 5s. Do you think your sum will be greater or less than when you added 2s? Explain.

Visit our Web site. www.parent.mathsurf.com

Fun Time!

What if you could do anything you wanted to do for one day?

Make a table to show the activities you would most like to do.

Time	Activity
12:00–1:00	Lunch

1 Which activity would take longest?

2 How much time would you spend doing the longest activity?

Fold down

MathSoup

Scott Foresman - Addison Wesley My Math Magazine No. 7

It's About Time!

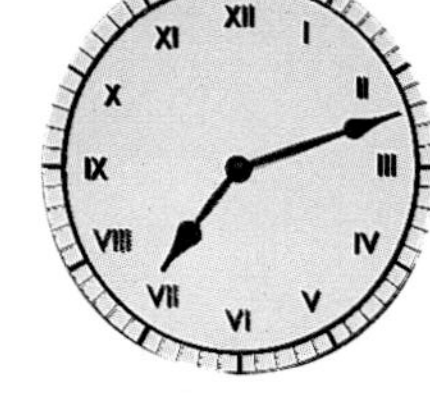

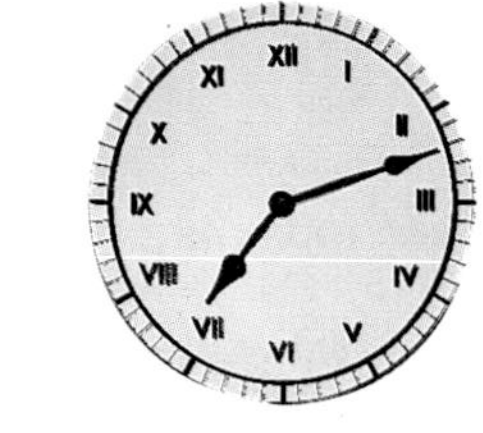

Make a Move

How do you spend your time on a rainy day? One seven-year-old from Oregon, Joshua White, spent a rainy day inventing a board game! He created Dinomite, a board game about dinosaurs. A company decided to make his game and sold it in stores all over the United States!

Use the diagram to answer the questions.

1 How many hours later is it in New York than in San Francisco?

_____ hours

2 How many hours earlier is it in Chicago than in Cairo?

_____ hours

Notes for Home: Your child practiced calculating elapsed time and making a schedule. *Home Activity:* Ask your child to calculate the time intervals for the activities on his or her "rainy day schedule."

Time Travels

When you are getting out of school, children in England may be fast asleep in bed! When it is 3:00 in the afternoon in your town, it's a different time in other parts of the United States and the world!

The diagram shows different times for some cities.

1 Suppose you decided to play Dinomite. Use the clock to find how long it took to play.

Start

End

It took _____ hours.

2 Suppose you were staying inside on a rainy day. Make a schedule to show what you would do.

Time	Activity

Notes for Home: Your child learned about different times in cities around the world. *Home Activity:* Ask your child what time it is in London when it is 6:00 in New York. (11:00)

Sands of Time

Make your own time machine!

What You Need

2 paper cups   clock with a second hand
pencil   piece of paper   sand

What You Do

1 Poke a hole through the bottom of one paper cup.

2 Fill the other paper cup with sand.

3 Pour sand into the cup with the hole, over the paper.

4 Time how long it takes for the cup to empty.

1 Record the time. Was your time more than one minute or less than one minute?

2 Repeat the activity. How can you make the time closer to one minute?

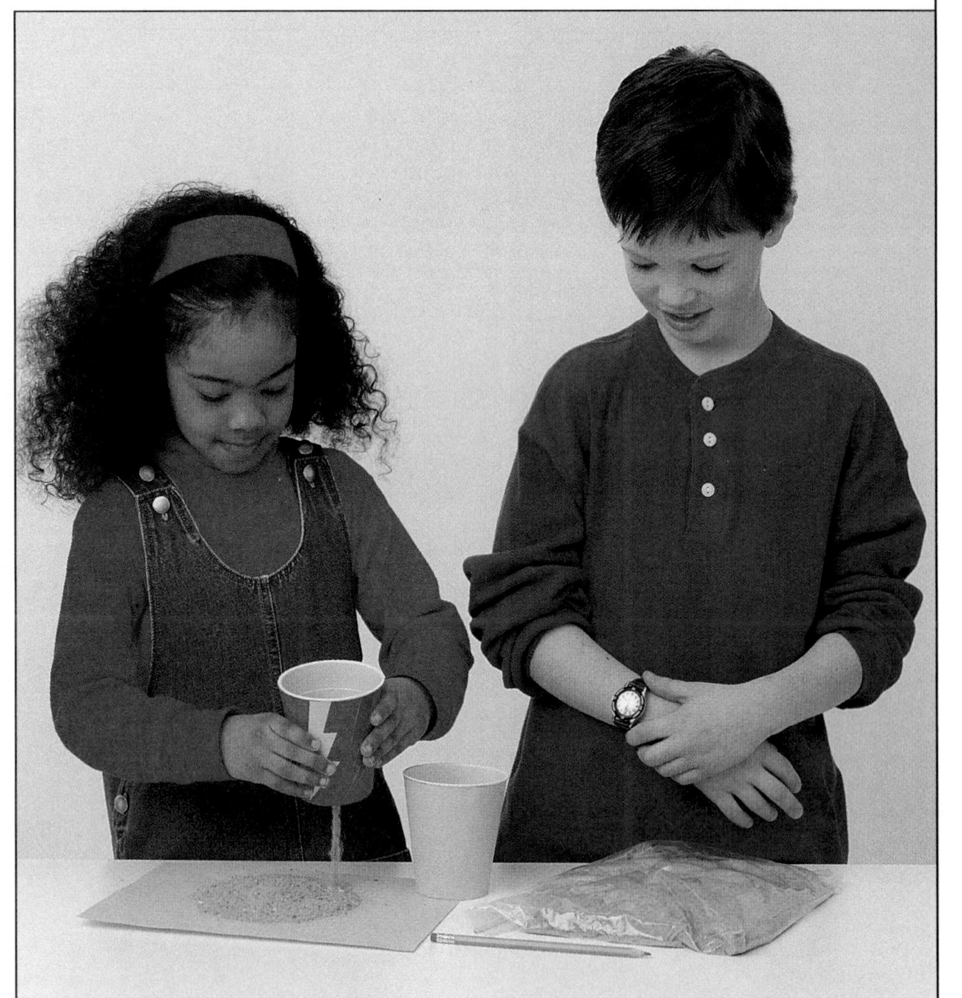

Notes for Home: Your child learned to make a sand clock and practiced estimating time. *Home Activity:* Ask your child to do the activity at home, using water rather than sand. Do the activity over a sink to avoid spills.

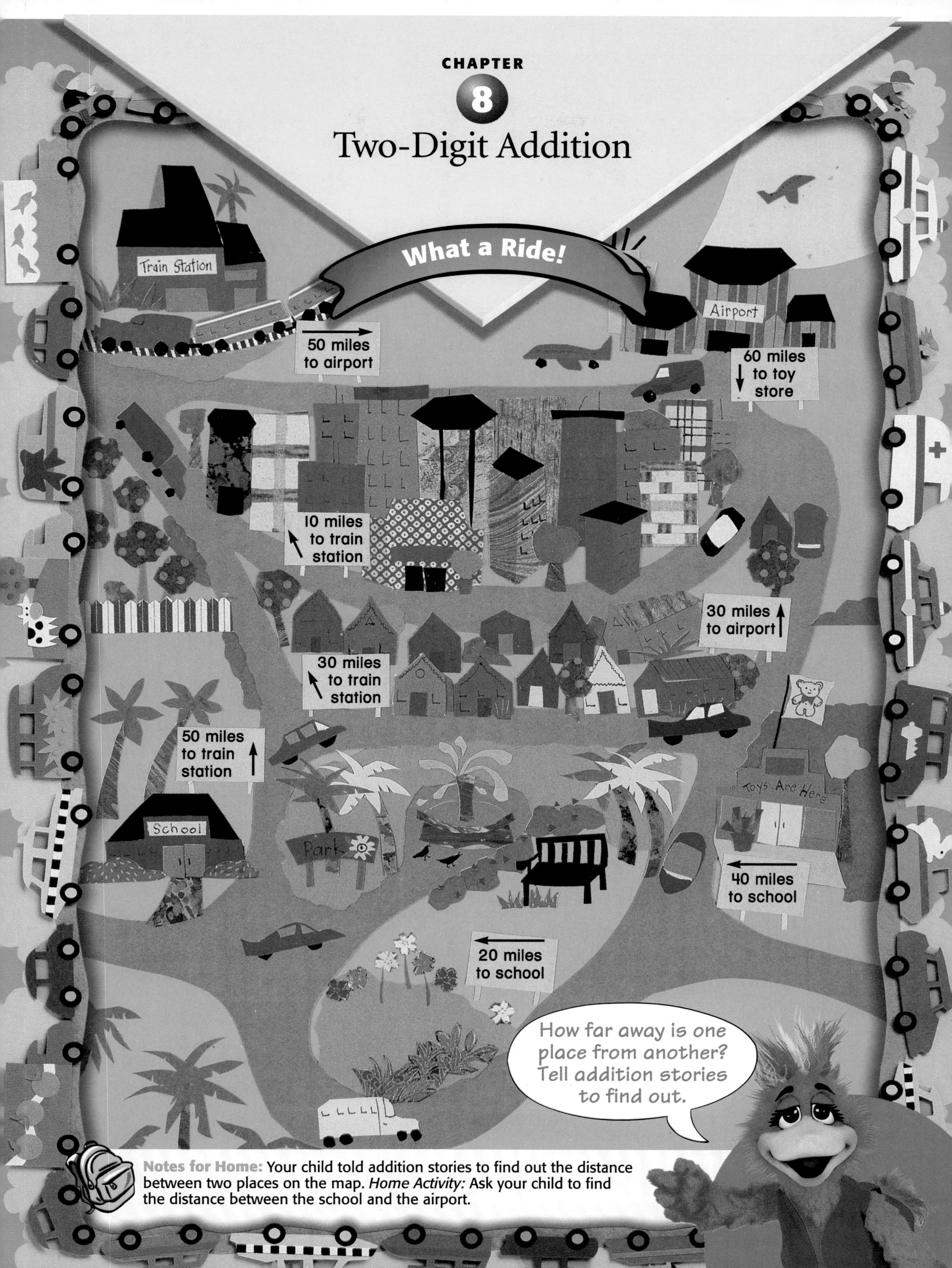

Notes for Home: Your child told addition stories to find out the distance between two places on the map. *Home Activity:* Ask your child to find the distance between the school and the airport.

Dear Family,
Our class is starting Chapter 8. We will be learning about adding two-digit numbers. You can help me practice addition at home. Together we can have fun doing these activities.

Backward Fun!
Play a game called *What's My Question?* Begin the game by saying the answer. For example: The sum is 33. Have your child say the question. For example: What is 10 plus 23? Repeat using other numbers.

Adding to Meals
Tell stories about mealtimes. For example: It took 10 minutes to fix lunch. It took us 15 minutes to eat lunch. How much time did it take altogether?

Community Connection

Take your child to the grocery store. Point out an item that costs less than 50¢. Ask your child how much two of the items would cost.

Visit our Web site. www.parent.mathsurf.com

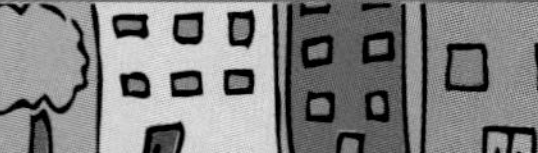

Name

Explore Adding Tens

Explore

Use [tens block] to find different ways to load the truck. Do not go over 100 pounds. Draw one of your ways.

Share

Compare your ways with those of your classmates.

Notes for Home: Your child explored ways to add tens. *Home Activity:* Ask your child to explain how to use tens to show 60. (Sample answer: 2 tens and 4 tens)

EXPLORE

Connect

How many in all?

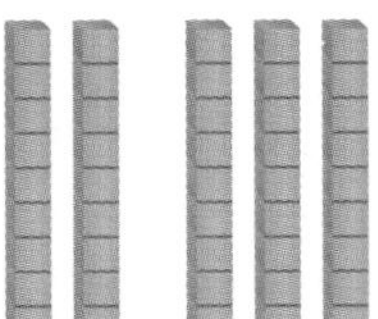

2 tens + 3 tens = 5 tens

20 + 30 = 50

Use  to find how many in all.

1

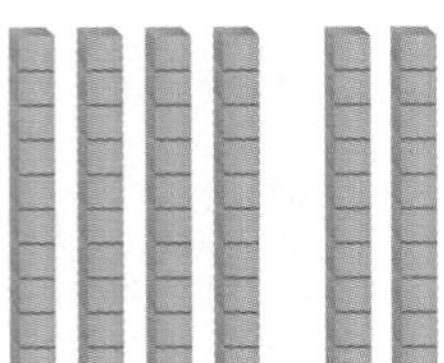

____ tens + ____ tens = ____ tens

____ + ____ = ____

2

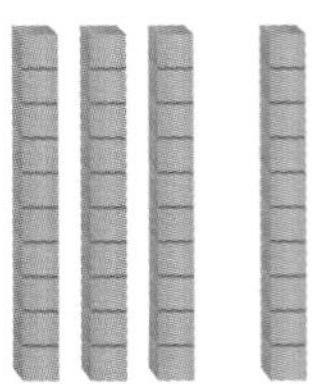

____ tens + ____ ten = ____ tens

____ + ____ = ____

Write your own problems about adding tens.

Draw the you use.

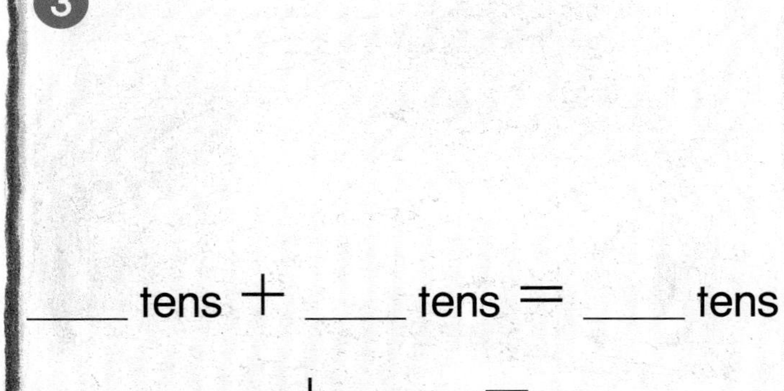

3

____ tens + ____ tens = ____ tens

____ + ____ = ____

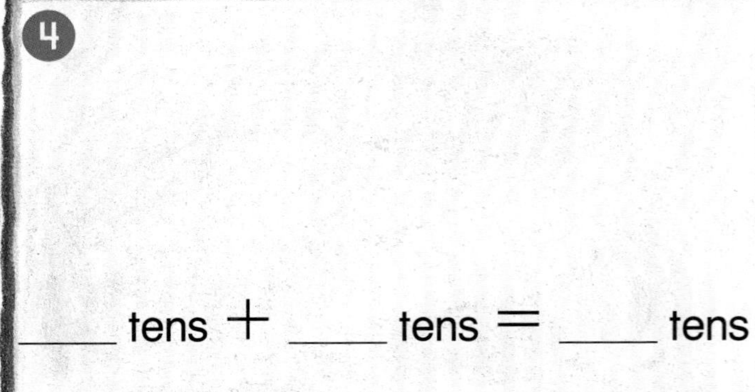

4

____ tens + ____ tens = ____ tens

____ + ____ = ____

Talk About It How is 5 + 3 like 50 + 30? How is it different?

Notes for Home: Your child used materials to add tens. *Home Activity:* Ask your child to explain how to find 3 tens + 5 tens. (3 tens + 5 tens = 8 tens; 8 tens = 80)

EXPLORE

Name

Add Tens with a Hundred Chart

Learn

There are 24 people with bikes on the path. 30 more people with bikes join them. How many bikes are on the path now?

24 + 30 = 54

There are 54 bikes on the path.

Use a hundred chart to add tens. Move down 3 rows because each row is 10.

1	2	3	4	5	6	7	8	9	10
11	12	13	14	15	16	17	18	19	20
21	22	23	24	25	26	27	28	29	30
31	32	33	34	35	36	37	38	39	40
41	42	43	44	45	46	47	48	49	50
51	52	53	54	55	56	57	58	59	60
61	62	63	64	65	66	67	68	69	70
71	72	73	74	75	76	77	78	79	80
81	82	83	84	85	86	87	88	89	90
91	92	93	94	95	96	97	98	99	100

Check

Use the hundred chart to add.

1. 24 + 10 = 34
2. 56 + 30 = ____
3. 60 + 20 = ____
4. 73 + 20 = ____
5.

49	80	32	45	50	11	34
+ 10	+ 10	+ 30	+ 20	+ 20	+ 40	+ 60

Talk About It Explain how you would use the hundred chart to find 53 + 10 + 20.

Notes for Home: Your child used a hundred chart to add tens. *Home Activity:* Ask your child how he or she would add 37 + 40 using the chart.

Practice

The hundred chart can help you add!

Add. You can use the hundred chart.

1	2	3	4	5	6	7	8	9	10
11	12	13	14	15	16	17	18	19	20
21	22	23	24	25	26	27	28	29	30
31	32	33	34	35	36	37	38	39	40
41	42	43	44	45	46	47	48	49	50
51	52	53	54	55	56	57	58	59	60
61	62	63	64	65	66	67	68	69	70
71	72	73	74	75	76	77	78	79	80
81	82	83	84	85	86	87	88	89	90
91	92	93	94	95	96	97	98	99	100

6. $54 + 30 = 84$ $68 + 20$

7. $71 + 20$ $59 + 40$

8. $23 + 40$ $39 + 50$

9. $62 + 10$ $26 + 30$ $60 + 10$ $57 + 40$ $33 + 20$ $74 + 20$ $41 + 10$

PRACTICE

Problem Solving Patterns

10. Add. What patterns do you see?

50 + 20 = ____

51 + 20 = ____

52 + 20 = ____

53 + 20 = ____

54 + 20 = ____

Write your own number sentences to make a pattern.

____ + ____ = ____

____ + ____ = ____

____ + ____ = ____

____ + ____ = ____

____ + ____ = ____

Notes for Home: Your child practiced adding tens. *Home Activity:* Ask your child to show you how to add 53 + 30, 54 + 30, and 55 + 30.

Name

Add Using Mental Math

Learn

The bicycle costs $53. The skateboard costs $20. What is the total cost of the bicycle and the skateboard? Find 53 + 20.

Think: Add the tens.

50 + 20 = 70

Then add the ones.

70 + 3 = 73

53 + 20 = $73

Check

Add. Use mental math.

1. 44 + 20 = 64

   Think:

   40 + 20 = 60

   60 + 4 = 64

2. 36 + 40 = ____

   Think:

   ____ + ____ = ____

   ____ + ____ = ____

3. 52 + 30 = ____

   Think:

   ____ + ____ = ____

   ____ + ____ = ____

4. 29 + 30 = ____

   Think:

   ____ + ____ = ____

   ____ + ____ = ____

Talk About It What other ways can you add 53 + 20 in your head?

Notes for Home: Your child used mental math to add. *Home Activity:* Ask your child how he or she would find 70 + 20 using mental math.

Practice

Use mental math to add.

5. 18 + 40 = 58   53 + 30 = ____   72 + 20 = ____

6. 46 + 20 = ____   27 + 40 = ____   56 + 30 = ____

7. 24 + 30 = ____   64 + 30 = ____   42 + 50 = ____

Problem Solving Patterns

Add. Use mental math. Then write the number sentences to continue the patterns.

8. 11 + 20 = ____
   11 + 30 = ____
   11 + 40 = ____
   ____ + ____ = ____
   ____ + ____ = ____

9. 37 + 10 = ____
   37 + 20 = ____
   37 + 30 = ____
   ____ + ____ = ____
   ____ + ____ = ____

10. Describe the patterns you see.

____

____

Notes for Home: Your child practiced using mental math to add. *Home Activity:* Ask your child to choose a number less than 50 and add 30 to it.

PRACTICE

Name

Estimate Two-Digit Sums

Learn

The bus for a field trip holds 60 children.
One class has 27 children. Another class has
21 children. Can all the children fit on one bus?

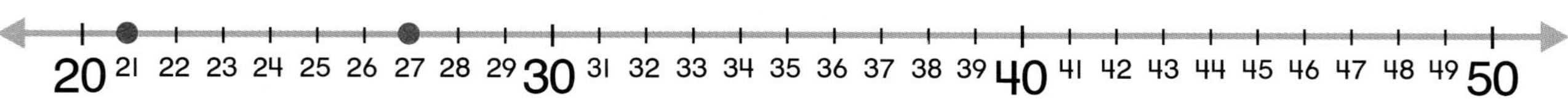

$$\begin{array}{r} 27 \\ +\ 21 \\ \hline \end{array}$$

27 is closer to 30.

21 is closer to 20.

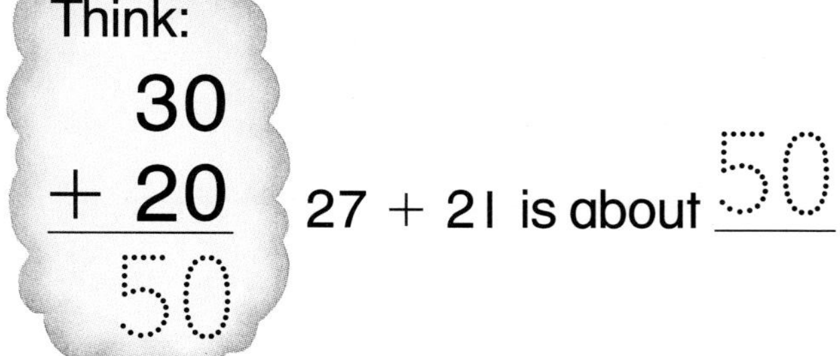

27 + 21 is about 50.

There are about 50 children.

They can fit on one bus.

I don't need an exact answer. I can use the nearest ten to estimate!

Check

Find the nearest ten. Estimate the sum.

1

$$\begin{array}{r} 51 \\ +\ 28 \\ \hline \end{array}$$

51 is closer to ____.

28 is closer to ____.

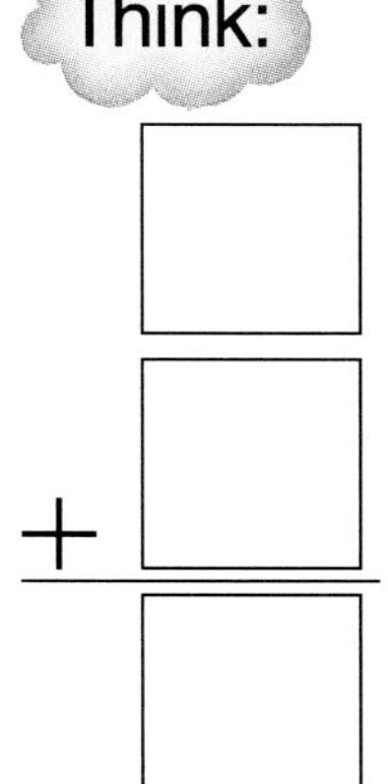

51 + 28 is about ____.

Talk About It Explain how you would estimate the sum for this problem.

$$\begin{array}{r} 25 \\ +\ 42 \\ \hline \end{array}$$

Notes for Home: Your child estimated sums. *Home Activity:* Ask your child to estimate 52 + 19. (70)

Practice

Find the nearest ten. Estimate the sum.

2

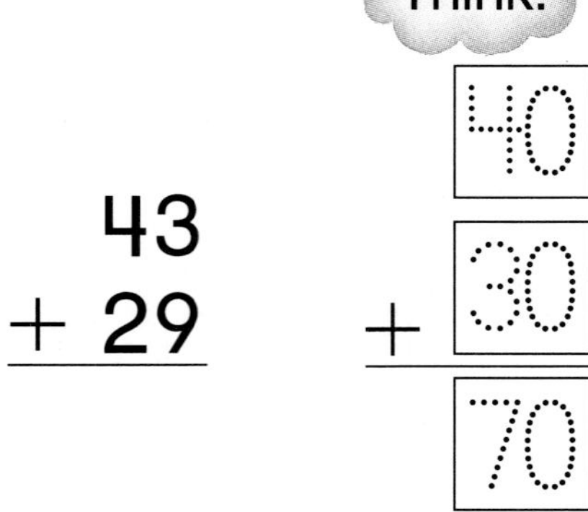

43 + 29 is about 70.

3

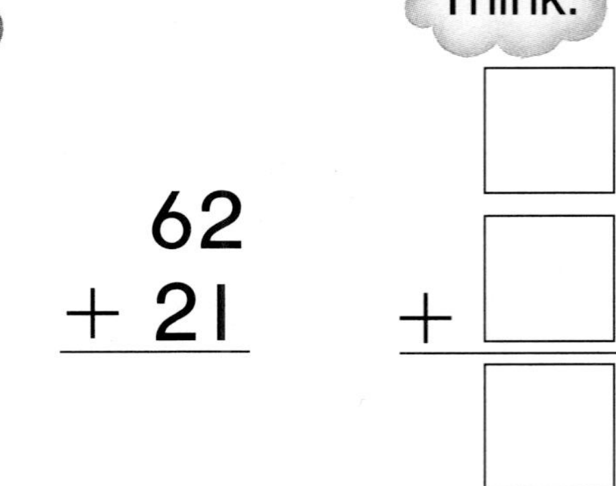

62 + 21 is about _____.

4

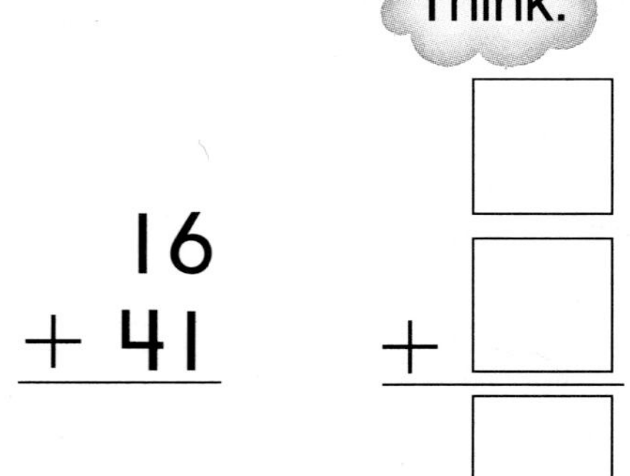

16 + 41 is about _____.

5

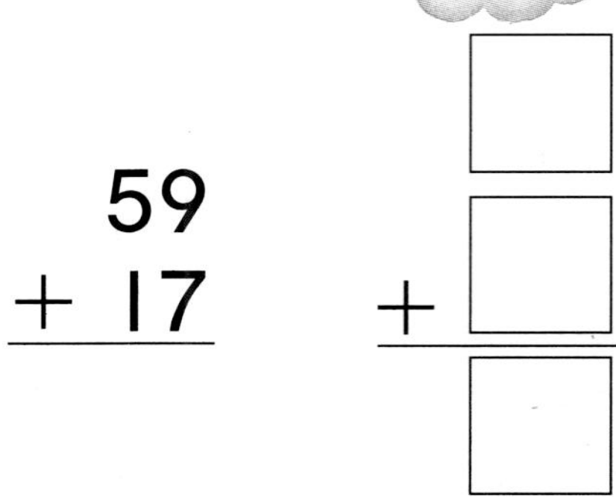

59 + 17 is about _____.

PRACTICE

Problem Solving Estimation

6 Mrs. Borke's class went to the museum. Mr. Reed's class saw a play. About how many children went on the two field trips?

about _____ children

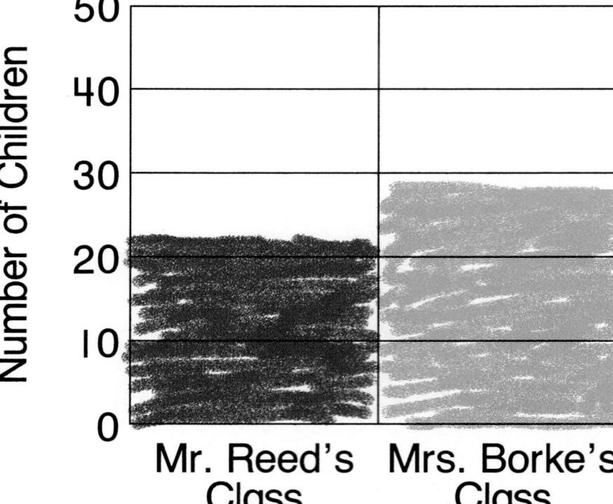

Notes for Home: Your child estimated sums by finding the nearest ten. *Home Activity:* Ask your child to explain how he or she solved Exercise 6.

Name ______________________

Reading for Math

Make Predictions

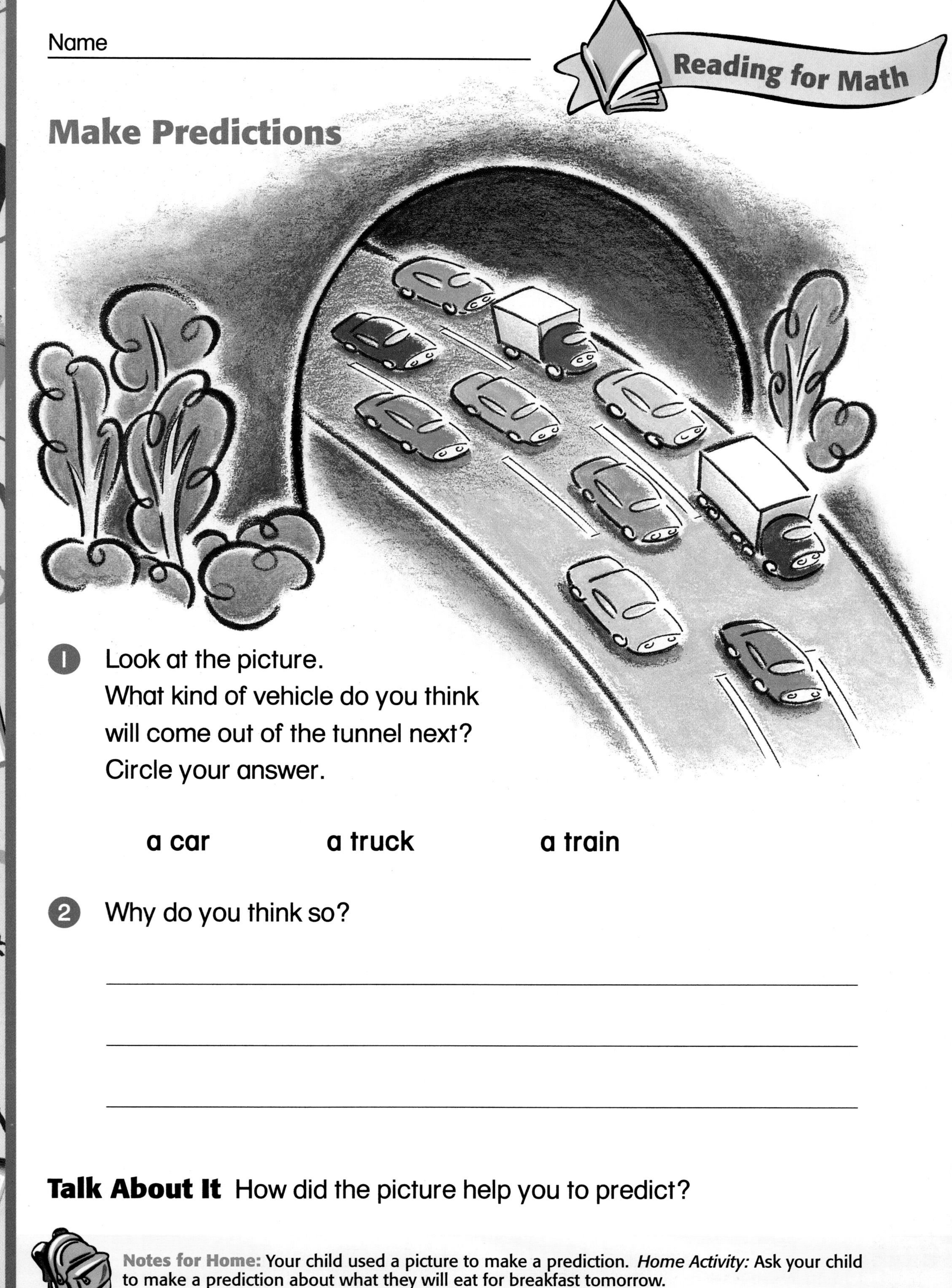

1. Look at the picture.
   What kind of vehicle do you think will come out of the tunnel next?
   Circle your answer.

   a car **a truck** **a train**

2. Why do you think so?

   ____

   ____

   ____

Talk About It How did the picture help you to predict?

Notes for Home: Your child used a picture to make a prediction. *Home Activity:* Ask your child to make a prediction about what they will eat for breakfast tomorrow.

3. Look at the picture.
Who do you think will get on next?
Circle your answer.

an adult **a child** **a dog**

4. Why do you think so?

___

___

___

Critical Thinking

5. Can you think of a place where a dog would be next?

Notes for Home: Your child used a picture to predict who would get on a bus next.
Home Activity: Ask your child to predict what color clothes he or she will wear tomorrow.

Name ______________________________

Problem Solving: Make Predictions

Learn

PROBLEM SOLVING GUIDE

Understand • Plan • Solve • Look Back

Think of a car that someone you know has.

What color is it? ____________

Share what color you wrote with your class.

Fill in the chart for your class.

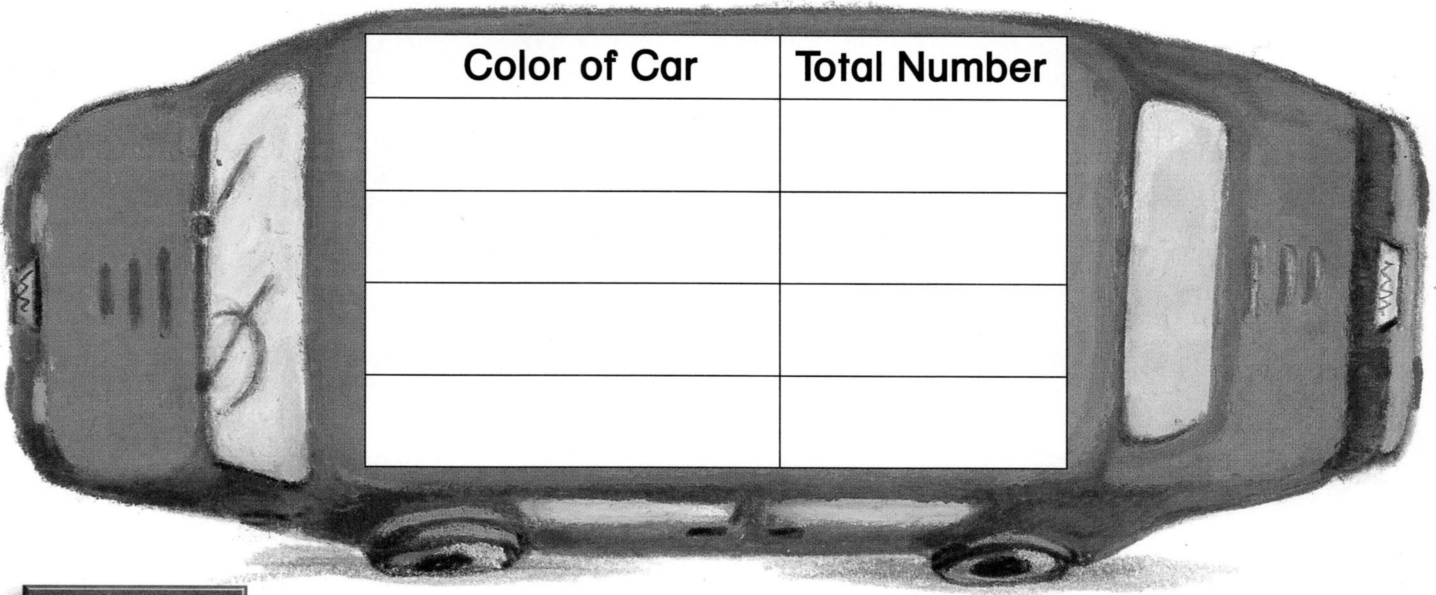

Color of Car	Total Number

Check

1. Predict. On your way home from school today, what color car do you think you will see most often?

   ____

2. Why do you think so?

   ____

   ____

   ____

Talk About It How does using what we know help us to predict?

Notes for Home: Your child make predictions about the color of car they would see going home from school. *Home Activity:* Ask your child to predict what time he or she will eat dinner tomorrow.

Practice

3. Predict. If you watched the cars that go by, which color car would you see most often?

4. Why do you think so?

____

____

5. Watch cars go by for 5 minutes. Record the results.

Color of Car	Tally	Total

6. Was your prediction close? ______________

Critical Thinking

7. If you did this activity again on another day, would you make the same prediction? Why or why not?

Notes for Home: Your child predicted the color of car they would see most often, and then did an activity to check that prediction. *Home Activity:* Ask your child to tell you the order in which the colors of the cars were seen most often.

Name

Explore Addition With or Without Regrouping

Explore

Do this activity with a partner.

1. Use cards numbered 1–9. Put the cards facedown.
2. Take turns. Draw a card and take that many .
   Then put the number card back.
3. Continue taking turns.
   Trade for a whenever you can.
   Keep your and on the chart.
4. The first player to get 100 wins!

tens	

Share

How did you know when to trade for ?

Notes for Home: Your child did an activity to group tens and ones. *Home Activity:* Ask your child how to group 7 ones and 5 ones as tens and ones. (1 ten 2 ones)

EXPLORE

Connect

18 children ride the bus to school.
6 children ride their bikes.
How many children ride to school in all?

Add 6 to 18.

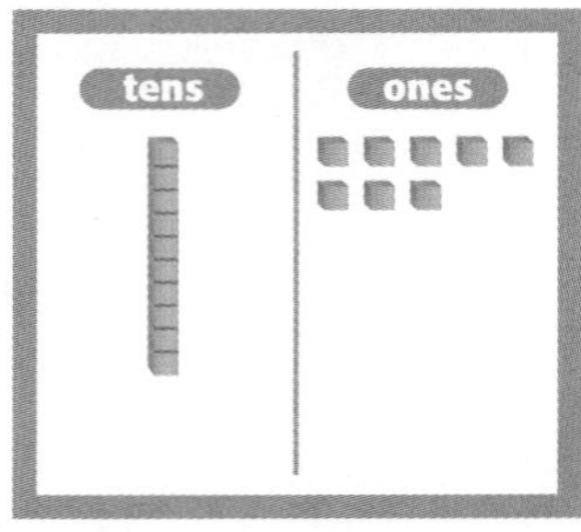

Start with 18.

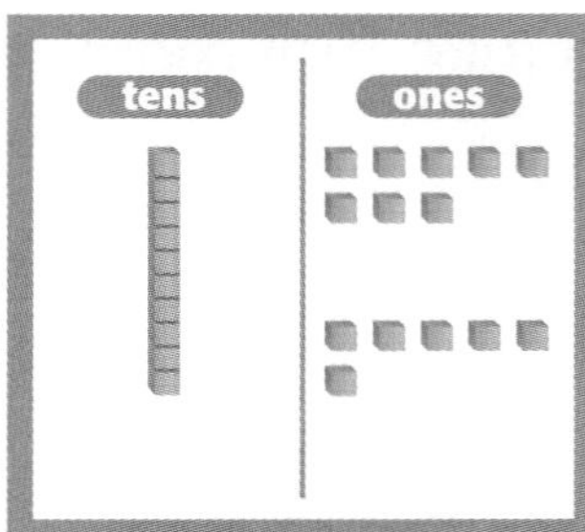

Add 6.

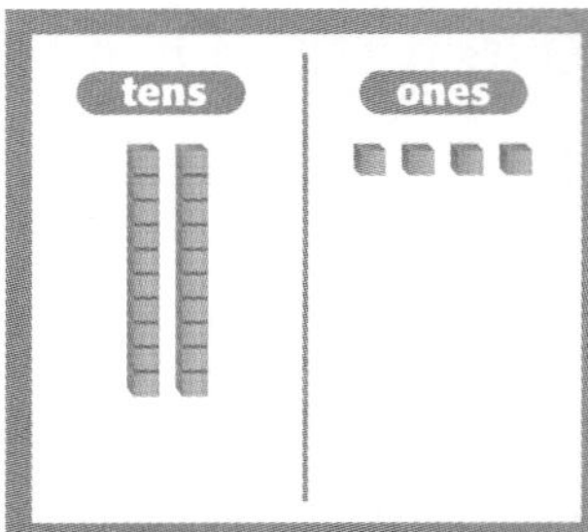

Regroup 10 ones as 1 ten.

24 in all

Regroup means changing the way you group your tens and ones.

Use , , and  .

5. Show 39. Add 4.
How many in all?

_____ tens _____ ones

_____ in all

6. Show 46. Add 7.
How many in all?

_____ tens _____ ones

_____ in all

7. Show 14. Add 6.
How many in all?

_____ tens _____ ones

_____ in all

8. Show 24. Add 8.
How many in all?

_____ tens _____ ones

_____ in all

Talk About It Why is it helpful to regroup?

Notes for Home: Your child added two numbers and wrote the answer as tens and ones.
Home Activity: Ask your child to explain how he or she did Exercise 6.

EXPLORE

Name

Add With or Without Regrouping

Learn

Do you need to regroup to add?

24 + 8 = 32

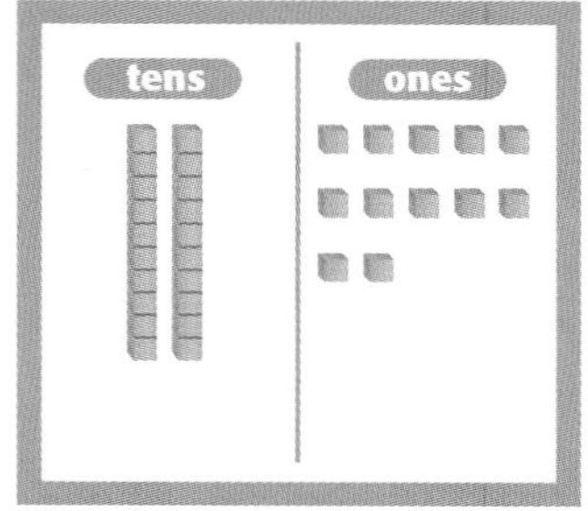

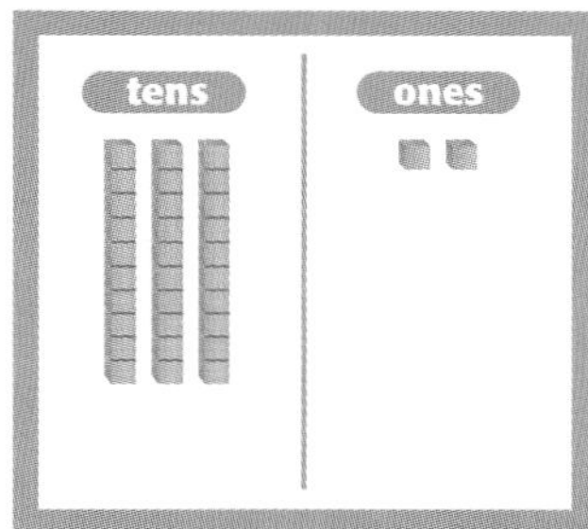

Start with 24. Add 8. You have more than 10 ones.

You need to regroup.

23 + 3 = 26

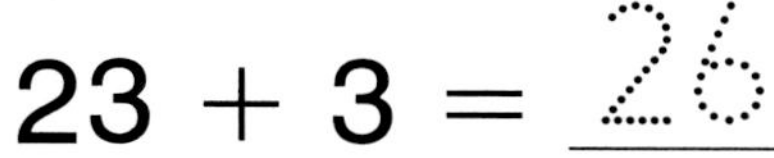

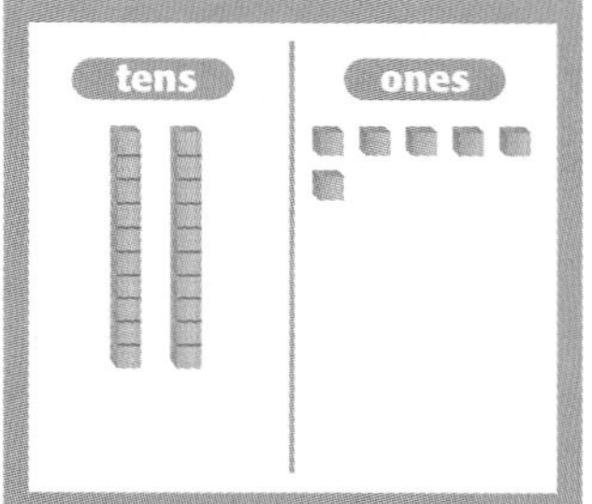

You have less than 10 ones. You do not need to regroup.

Check

Use [place-value mat], [tens rod], and [ones cube].

	Show this many.	Add this many.	Do you need to regroup?	Add.
1	36	7	yes	36 + 7 = 43
2	23	4		23 + 4 = ____
3	19	5		19 + 5 = ____

Talk About It Start with 17. Tell an addition problem. Explain how you would solve your problem.

Notes for Home: Your child determined if regrouping was needed to add two numbers.
Home Activity: Ask your child if regrouping is needed to do these problems: 49 + 15; 67 + 11. (yes, no)

Practice

Use [place-value mat], [tens rod], and [ones cube].

	Show this many.	Add this many.	Do you need to regroup?	Solve.
4	22	4	no	22 + 4 = 26
5	43	9		43 + 9 = ____
6	56	5		56 + 5 = ____
7	34	6		34 + 6 = ____
8	12	7		12 + 7 = ____
9	21	7		21 + 7 = ____
10	37	5		37 + 5 = ____

PRACTICE

Problem Solving Critical Thinking

11. What numbers less than 10 can you add to the number 16 without needing to regroup? How do you know?

Notes for Home: Your child decided if regrouping was needed before adding two numbers. *Home Activity:* Ask your child to tell you an addition problem that requires regrouping and one that does not.

Name

Record Addition

Learn

Find 27 + 8.

Add the ones.
7 ones + 8 ones = 15 ones.
Regroup before you
add the tens.

tens	ones
2	7
+	8

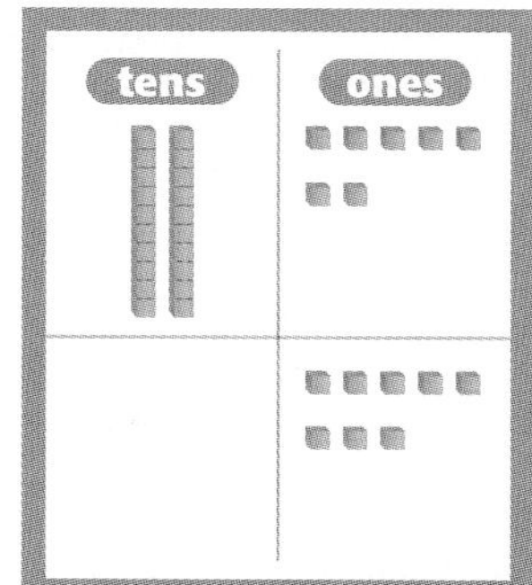

Regroup 15 ones
as 1 ten and 5 ones.
Write 5 ones.
Write 1 to show 1 ten.

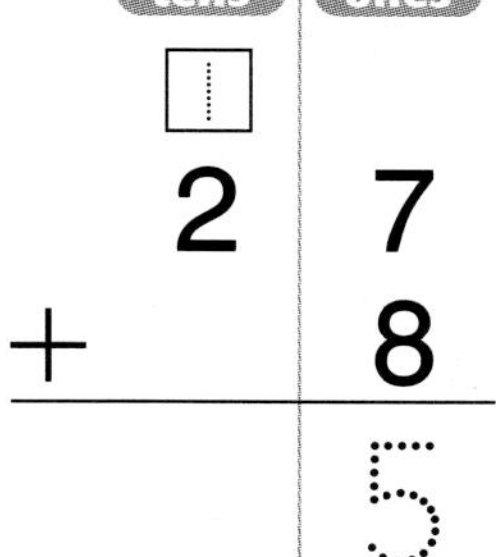

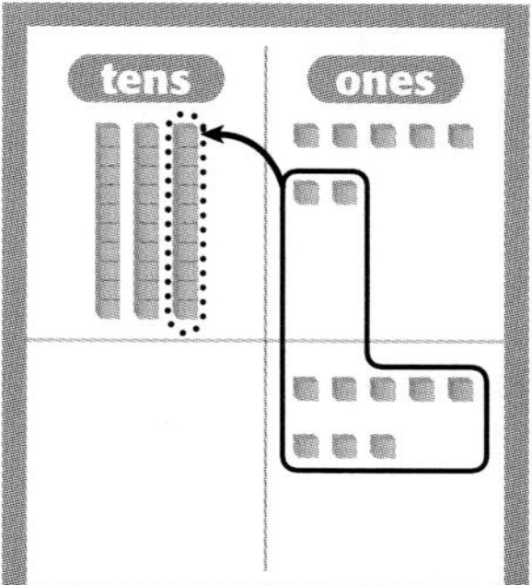

Add the tens.
1 ten + 2 tens = 3 tens.
Write 3 to show the tens.
The sum is 35.

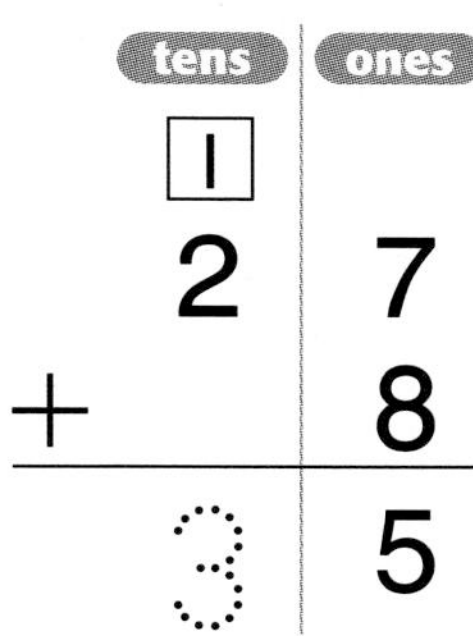

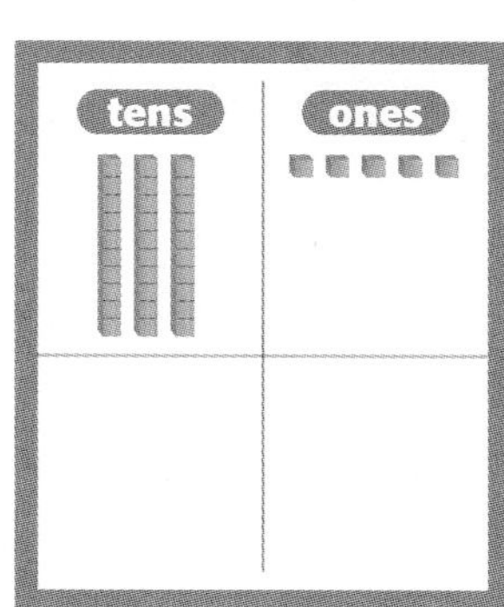

Check

Use 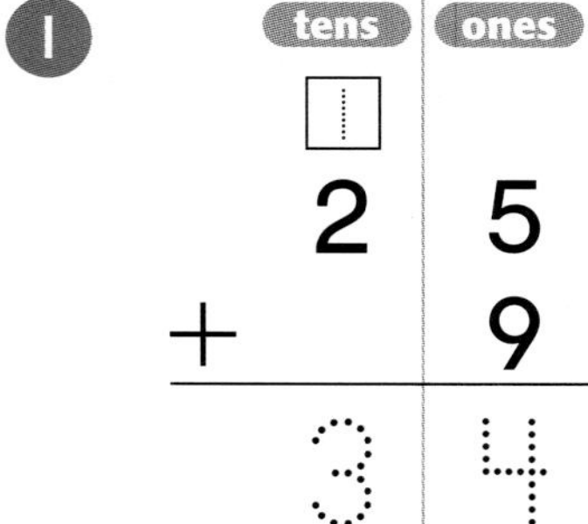, , and . Add.

1

tens	ones
1	
2	5
+	9
3	4

tens	ones
□	
3	7
+	5

tens	ones
□	
7	4
+	3

tens	ones
□	
8	2
+	9

Talk About It How do you show regrouping 10 ones as 1 ten?

Notes for Home: Your child recorded sums to addition problems which involved regrouping.
Home Activity: Ask your child to explain the steps he or she would do to find 67 + 19.

Practice

Add. Then circle the sum if you regrouped.

You can use 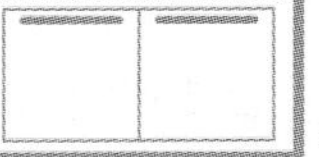, 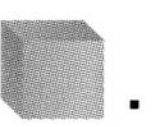, and .

2

tens	ones
1	
3	4
+	6
4	0

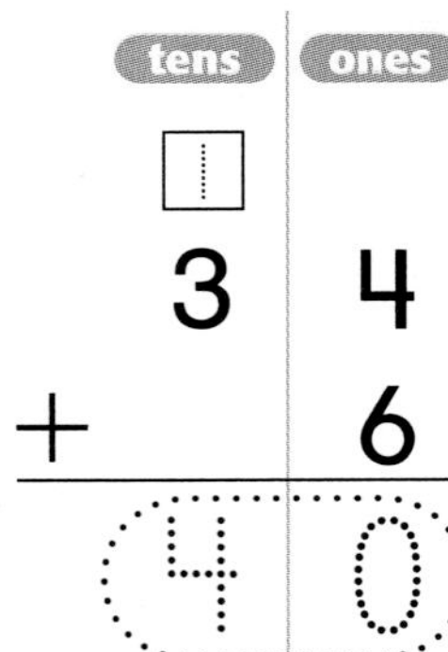

3

tens	ones
2	2
+	7

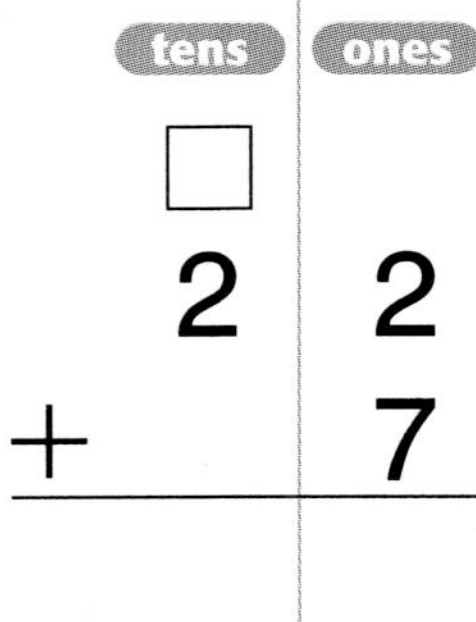

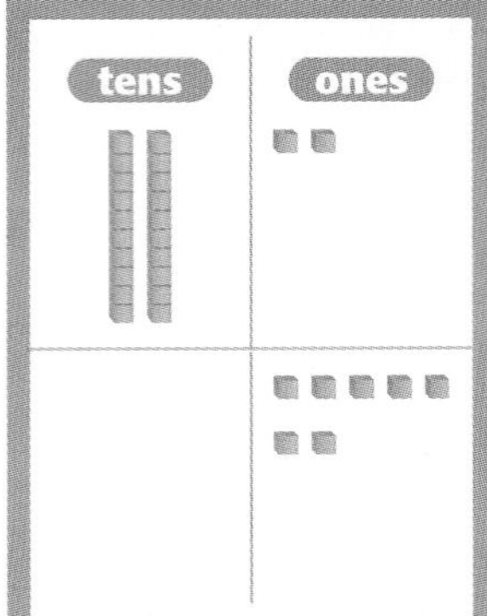

4

tens	ones
7	3
+	9

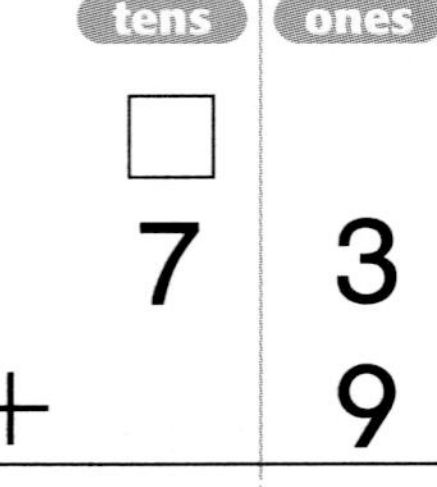

tens	ones
6	3
+	5

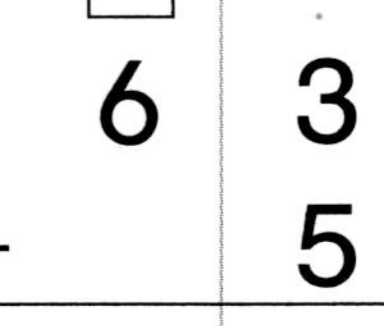

tens	ones
4	7
+	5

tens	ones
5	7
+	3

5

tens	ones
5	9
+	7

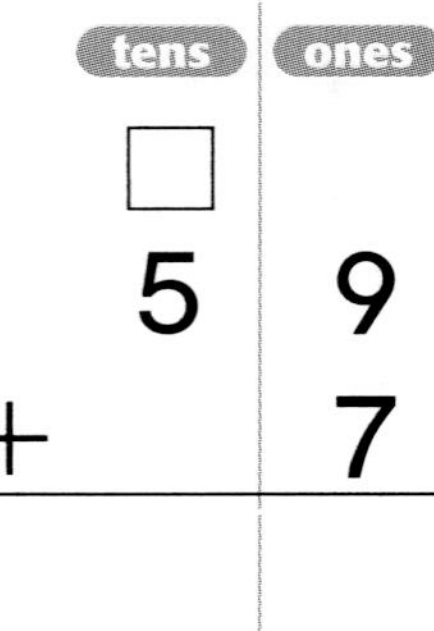

tens	ones
1	2
+	5

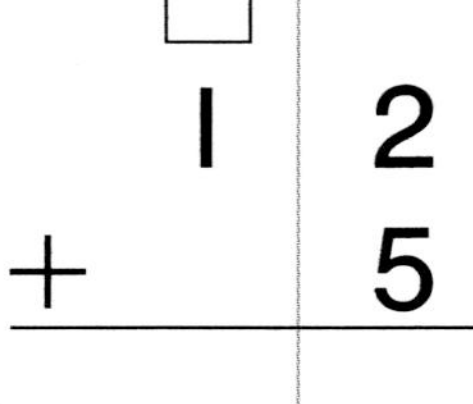

tens	ones
2	8
+	2

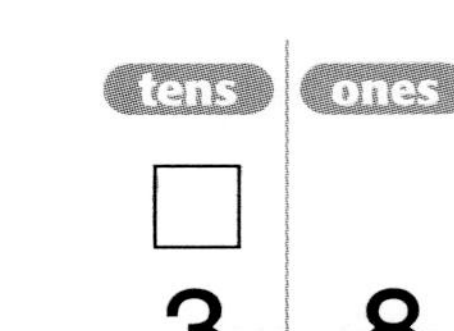

tens	ones
3	8
+	6

Problem Solving Critical Thinking

6 Leon's dog walked on his math paper.
Now Leon can't read some of the numbers.
What could the missing numbers be?
How do you know?

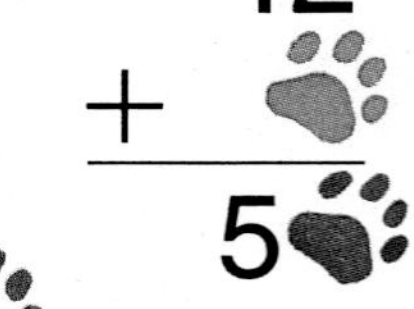

Notes for Home: Your child added two numbers and identified sums which involved regrouping. *Home Activity:* Ask your child to explain why he circled three of the sums in the exercises.

PRACTICE

For additional practice, see Skills Practice Bank, page 534, Set 1.

Name

Mixed Practice

Lessons 1–8

Concepts and Skills

1 Estimate the sum.

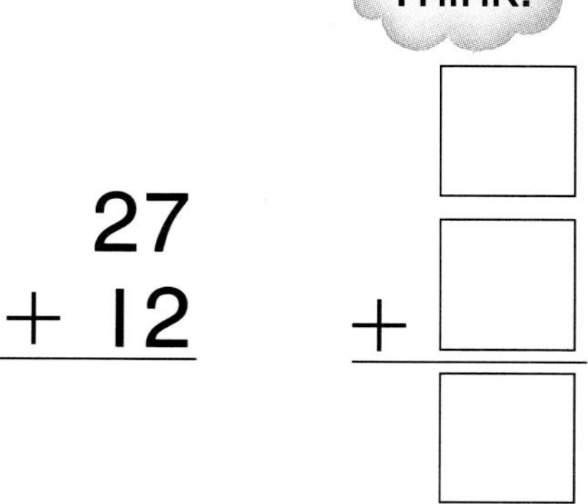

$$\begin{array}{r} 27 \\ +\ 12 \\ \hline \end{array}$$

27 + 12 is about _____.

2 Add. Use mental math.

27 + 40 = ___

47 + 30 = ___

56 + 20 = ___

73 + 20 = ___

Problem Solving

3 Complete the chart. Fill in the totals.

Color of Socks	Tally	Totals
red	卌	
blue	卌 II	
green	I	

Use the chart to predict.

4 Mrs. Jacob's second-grade class made a chart to show the color of socks worn by the students. What color of socks would you predict to see most often in Mrs. Baker's second-grade class? ____________

Journal

5 Write two addition problems. Explain how you would estimate to find each sum.

Notes for Home: Your child practiced adding tens, using mental math, estimating sums, and solving problems. *Home Activity:* Ask your child to explain how to find 54 + 30 using mental math.

MIXED PRACTICE

Name ______________________________

Cumulative Review

Chapters 1–8

Concepts and Skills

Add or subtract.

1. $7 + 7$ $14 - 7$
2. $9 + 9$ $18 - 9$
3. $5 + 5$ $10 - 5$
4. $6 + 6$ $12 - 6$
5. $8 + 8$ $16 - 8$
6. $4 + 4$ $8 - 4$

Write how many. Then write **even** or **odd**.

7. 

_____ __________

8. 

_____ __________

Fill in the ○ for the correct answer.

Use the picture to answer the questions.

9. Which car is blue?
   - ○ first
   - ○ second
   - ○ third
   - ○ fourth

10. Which car is red?
    - ○ second
    - ○ fifth
    - ○ third
    - ○ first

11. Which car is yellow?
    - ○ fourth
    - ○ fifth
    - ○ second
    - ○ first

Notes for Home: Your child reviewed related addition and subtraction facts, even and odd numbers, and ordinal numbers. *Home Activity:* Ask your child which color car in the picture is second. (yellow)

Name

Add Two-Digit Numbers With or Without Regrouping

Learn

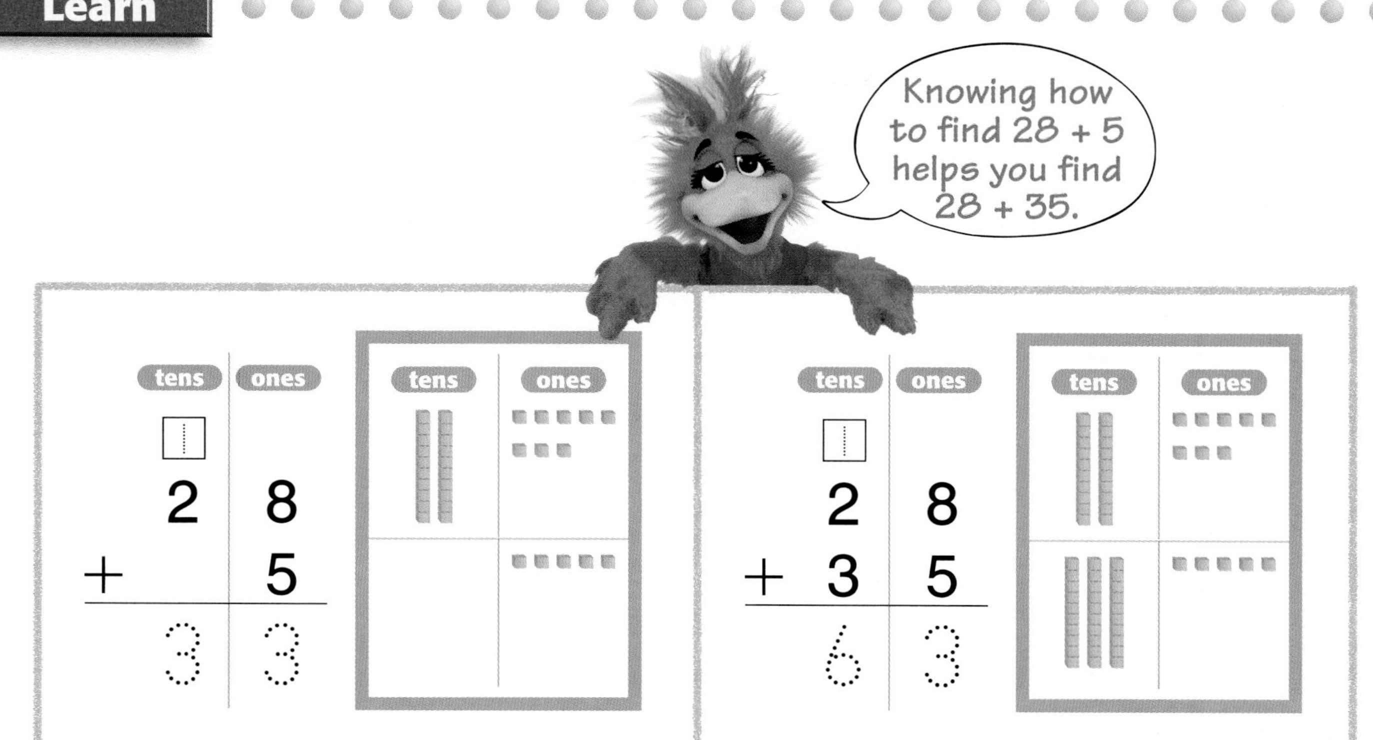

Check

Add. Use , , and .
Regroup if you need to.

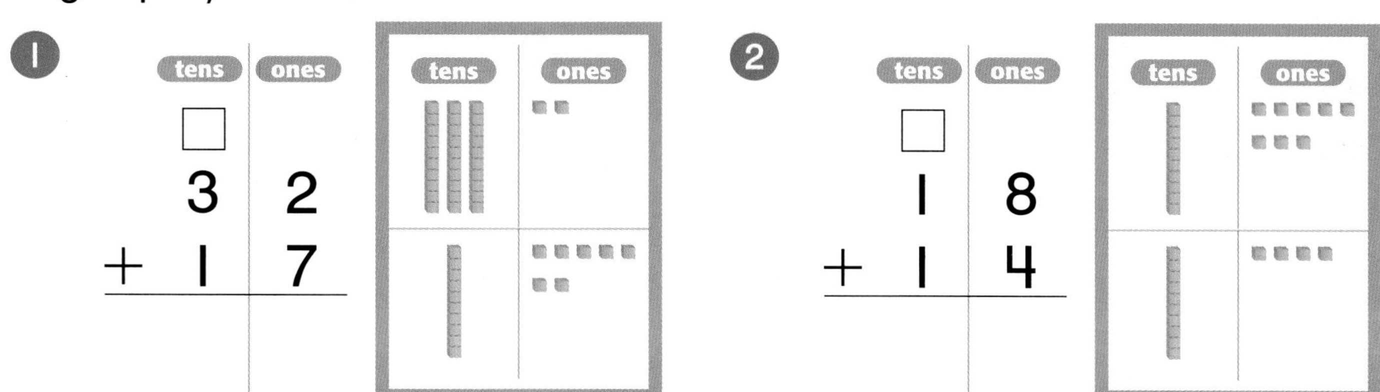

Talk About It How are these problems alike? How are they different?

$$\begin{array}{r} 46 \\ +\ 2 \\ \hline \end{array} \qquad \begin{array}{r} 46 \\ +\ 12 \\ \hline \end{array}$$

Notes for Home: Your child added two numbers involving regrouping. *Home Activity:* Ask your child to explain how the two problems in the Learn section are alike and how they are different.

Practice

Add. Use [tens/ones mat], [tens rod], and [ones cube].
Regroup if you need to.

3

tens	ones		tens	ones		tens	ones		tens	ones
☐			☐			☐			☐	
3	7		5	6		2	4		2	5
+ 1	6		+ 2	0		+ 1	7		+ 3	5
5	3									

4

tens	ones		tens	ones		tens	ones		tens	ones
☐			☐			☐			☐	
4	9		3	8		7	5		7	7
+ 2	3		+ 2	7		+ 1	4		+ 1	4

5

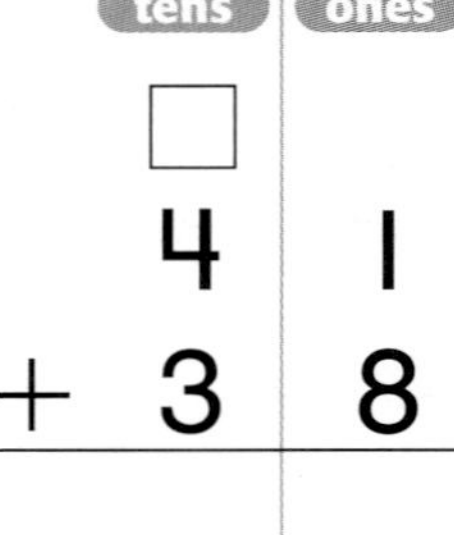
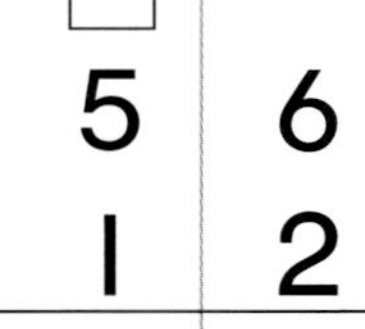

tens	ones		tens	ones		tens	ones		tens	ones
☐			☐			☐			☐	
4	1		5	6		6	2		6	8
+ 3	8		+ 1	2		+ 1	9		+ 2	1

Problem Solving Visual Thinking

6 We started with this: | Now we have this: | Draw what was added.

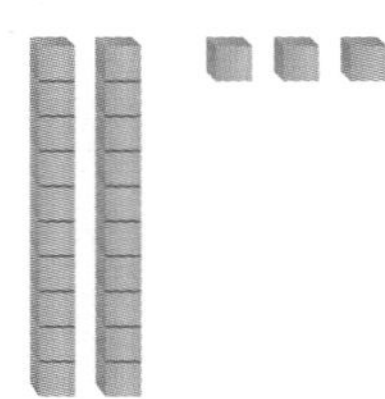
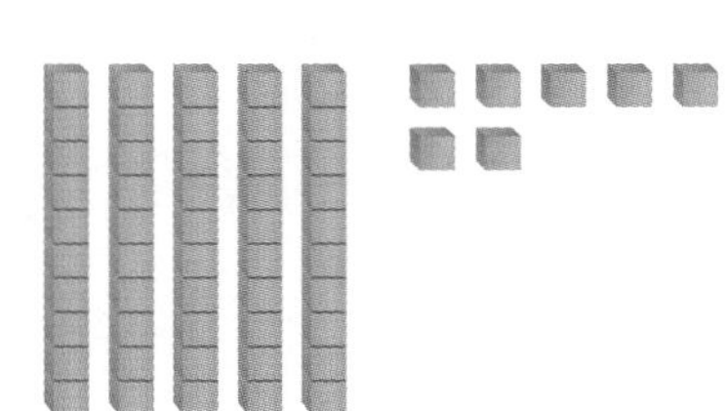

Notes for Home: Your child added two numbers. *Home Activity:* Ask your child to identify two problems in Exercise 3 which involved regrouping. (the first, third, or fourth exercise)

Name

Add Two-Digit Numbers

Learn

Don't forget to add the ten you made!

Find 28 + 25.

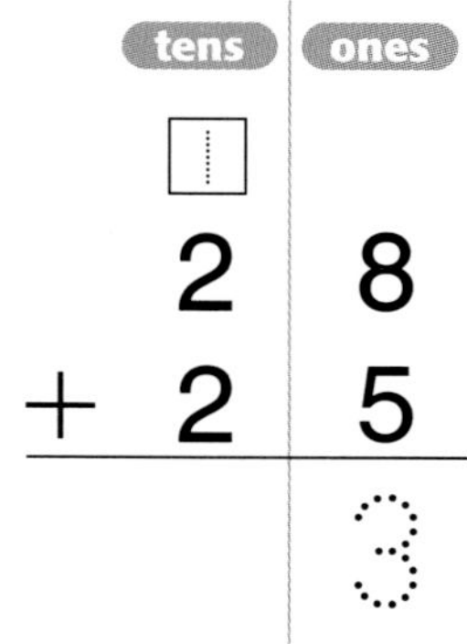

tens	ones
1	
2	8
+ 2	5
	3

Add the ones.
Regroup if you need to.

tens	ones
1	
2	8
+ 2	5
5	3

Add the tens.

Check

Add. Regroup if you need to.

1

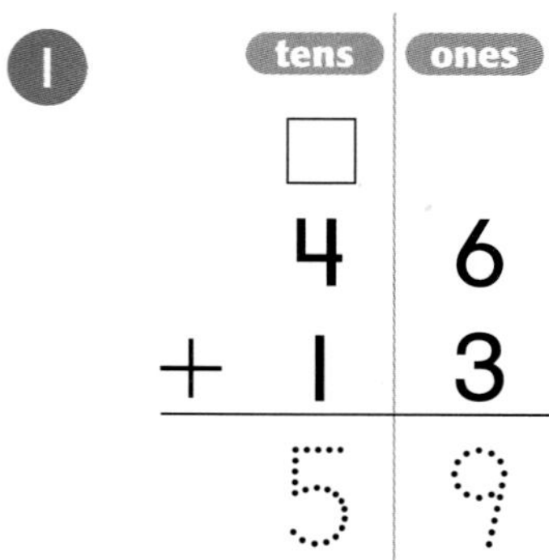

tens	ones
☐	
4	6
+ 1	3
5	9

tens	ones
☐	
5	8
+ 2	3

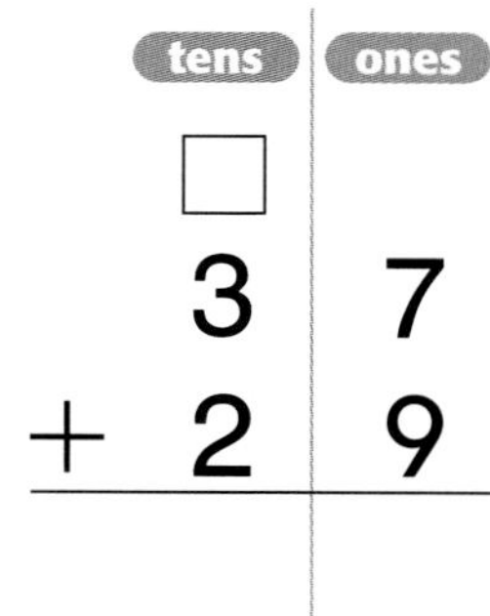

tens	ones
☐	
3	7
+ 2	9

tens	ones
☐	
2	5
+ 4	5

Talk About It Use the nearest ten to estimate:

27 + 39 is about _____.

Now add to find the exact sum.

How close was your estimate to your exact answer?

$$\begin{array}{r} 27 \\ +\ 39 \\ \hline \end{array}$$

42 + 33 is about _____.

Now add to find the exact sum.

How close was your estimate to your exact answer?

$$\begin{array}{r} 42 \\ +\ 33 \\ \hline \end{array}$$

Notes for Home: Your child used regrouping to add two numbers. *Home Activity:* Ask your child to estimate 27 + 32 and then find the exact sum. (30 + 30 = 60; 59)

Practice

PRACTICE

Add. Regroup if you need to.

2	51 + 17 68	59 + 32	39 + 15	47 + 21	28 + 6	43 + 32
3	52 + 21	63 + 17	45 + 38	37 + 21	29 + 23	38 + 41
4	81 + 15	74 + 18	68 + 23	62 + 14	27 + 31	19 + 18

Problem Solving

5 Kate's luggage weighs 35 pounds. Circle her two pieces of luggage.

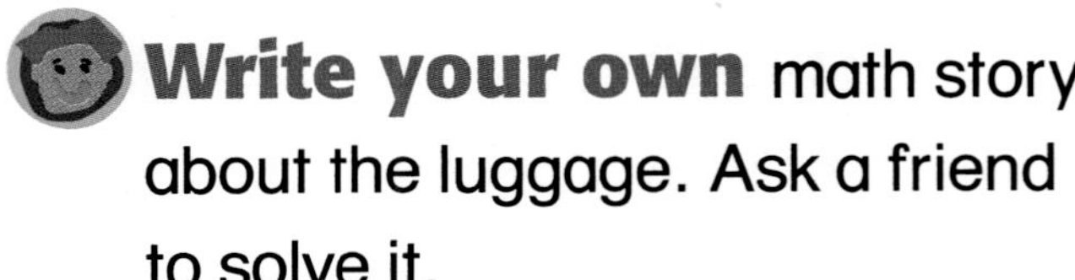

Write your own math story about the luggage. Ask a friend to solve it.

____

____

____

____

____

Notes for Home: Your child found sums for addition problems. *Home Activity:* Ask your child to show you two pieces of luggage in Exercise 6 that have a total weight of 33 pounds. (the red suitcase and the blue suitcase)

Name ___________________________

Practice Game

Sum It Up!

Players 2–4

What You Need

Paper clip

Pencil

How to Play

1. Take turns. Spin each spinner two times.
2. Record the numbers you spin in the squares below. Add.
3. The player with the highest sum wins!
4. Play again.

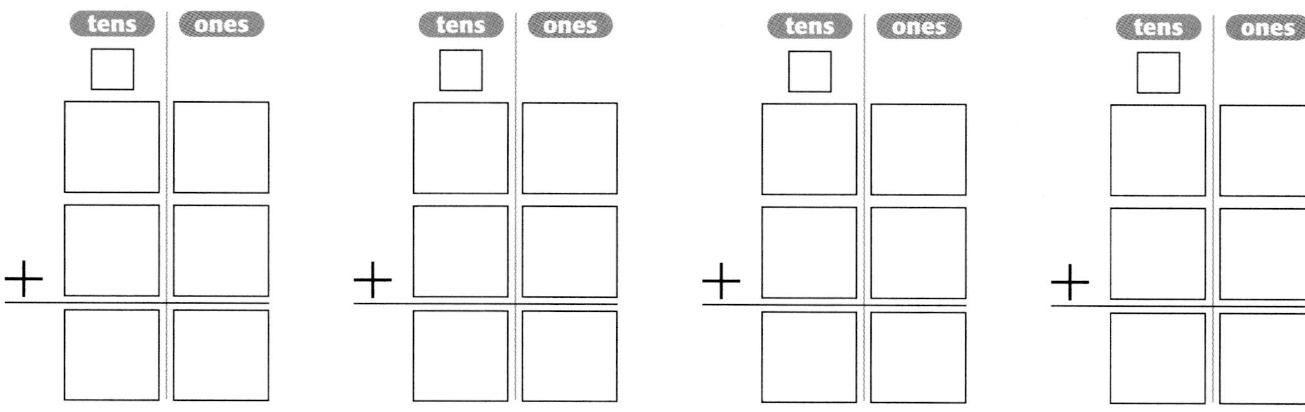

Notes for Home: Your child played a game to practice adding numbers. *Home Activity:* Ask your child to explain how he or she found one of the sums at the bottom of the page.

PRACTICE

Name ______________________

Add. Use mental math.

1. 20 + 60 = ____
2. 40 + 30 = ____
3. 50 + 40 = ____
4. 38 + 20 = ____
5. 56 + 10 = ____
6. 29 + 20 = ____

Estimate. Use the nearest ten to help.

7. 59 + 28 is about ____.
8. 21 + 68 is about ____.
9. 42 + 41 is about ____.
10. 79 + 11 is about ____.
11. 39 + 12 is about ____.
12. 19 + 33 is about ____.

Add.

13.

24	47	52	64	39	18
+ 35	+ 6	+ 29	+ 12	+ 41	+ 4

PRACTICE

Riddle

14. I have two missing numbers. Each missing number is greater than 10. The sum is 87. What could the missing numbers be?

____ and ____

Notes for Home: Your child practiced finding estimates and adding numbers. *Home Activity:* Ask your child to tell you a second pair of numbers that could solve the riddle.

Name

Add Three Numbers

Learn

You can add three numbers in different ways.

Check

Add. Circle the numbers that you added first.

1.

51	27	16	24	48	12
23	48	20	32	21	25
+ 13	+ 13	+ 6	+ 13	+ 2	+ 51
87					

2.

32	56	63	30	34	29
15	27	12	24	13	23
+ 42	+ 4	+ 14	+ 20	+ 5	+ 11

Talk About It How is adding three numbers different from adding two numbers? How is it the same?

Notes for Home: Your child added three numbers. *Home Activity:* Ask your child to show you the steps he or she used to add one of the exercises on this page.

Practice

Add.

3

34	54	13	22	15	43
13	12	10	13	24	10
+ 44	+ 16	+ 6	+ 42	+ 13	+ 23
91					

4

35	28	47	38	54	46
21	11	12	23	11	21
+ 25	+ 30	+ 7	+ 12	+ 14	+ 2

5

62	26	18	32	27	32
14	31	21	41	32	13
+ 3	+ 16	+ 4	+ 22	+ 3	+ 42

PRACTICE

Problem Solving Critical Thinking

6 The engine cannot pull more than 70 tons.
How many tons could be in the first car of the train?

Notes for Home: Your child found the sum of three numbers. *Home Activity:* Ask your child to explain how he or she solved the Problem Solving exercise.

For additional practice, see Skills Practice Bank, page 534, Set 2.

Name

Problem Solving: Guess and Check

Learn

PROBLEM SOLVING GUIDE
Understand • Plan • Solve • Look Back

Chen has 93¢. Which two toys could he buy?

These toys cost too much. I'll try a toy that costs less.

I'm closer, but it is still too much. I'll try a toy that costs even less.

I did it! I have enough to buy two toys.

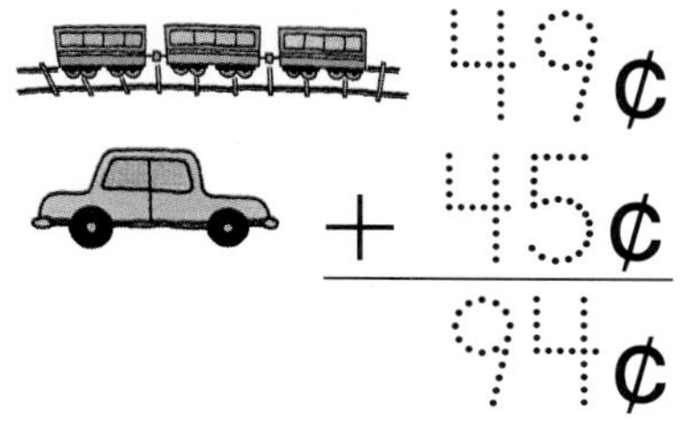

Chen can buy the train and the bike.

Check

Solve. Show and check each guess.

1. Sofia has 86¢.
She wants to buy two toys.
What can she buy?

Sofia can buy the ____________ and the ____________.

Talk About It Which other two toys can Chen buy with 93¢?

Notes for Home: Your child solved problems by guessing possible solutions and then checking them. *Home Activity:* Ask your child to find two toys that could be bought with 90¢. (bike and car, bike and truck, bike and train)

PROBLEM SOLVING

Practice

42¢ 49¢ 35¢ 25¢ 29¢ 30¢

Solve. Show and check each guess.

2 Brea has 69¢.
She wants to buy two toys.
What can she buy?

Brea can buy the ____________ and the ____________.

3 Which other two toys can
Brea buy with 69¢?

Brea can buy the ____________ and the ____________.

4 Habib has 60¢.
He wants to buy two toys.
What can he buy?

Habib can buy the ____________ and the ____________.

5 Which other two toys can
Habib buy with 60¢?

Habib can buy the ____________ and the ____________.

PROBLEM SOLVING

Estimation

6 Brea wants to buy three toys. Does she have enough money? How do you know?

Notes for Home: Your child solved problems by guessing possible solutions and then checking those solutions. *Home Activity:* Ask your child if it is possible to buy 3 of the toys pictured with 90 cents. (Yes; the bike, the motorcycle, and the train)

For additional practice, see Skills Practice Bank, page 534, Set 3.

Name ______________________________

Mixed Practice

Lessons 9–13

Concepts and Skills

Add. Regroup if you need to.

1	43 + 25	38¢ + 16¢	52 + 19	21 + 62	64¢ + 17¢	75 + 12
2	36 + 21	19¢ + 65¢	24¢ + 6¢	15 + 37	62 + 8	75¢ + 13¢
3	24 10 + 34	37 25 + 23	49 12 + 11	13 36 + 23	52 15 + 12	48 26 + 12

Problem Solving

Solve. Show and check each guess.

4 Sam has 65¢.
He wants to buy two toys.
Which two toys could he buy?

He can buy the ______________ and the ______________.

Journal

5 How did you decide which numbers to try in the problem about toys? Explain.

Notes for Home: Your child practiced adding numbers with and without regrouping, adding three numbers, and solving problems. *Home Activity:* Ask your child how much money would be needed to buy the two most expensive toys in Exercise 4. (35¢ + 36¢ = 71¢)

MIXED PRACTICE

Name ______________________________

Cumulative Review

Chapters 1–8

Concepts and Skills

Circle the numbers you would add first. Look for doubles and numbers that make ten. Add.

1

4	3	5	2	7	6
2	4	5	1	8	8
+ 6	+ 4	+ 3	+ 8	+ 3	+ 6

Draw coins. Show two different ways to make $1.00.

2 

3

Draw coins. Show two different ways to make 50¢.

4 

5 

Test Prep

Fill in the ○ for the correct answer.
Which group of numbers is in order from the least to the greatest?

6
- ○ 65, 42, 37, 19
- ○ 10, 24, 39, 52
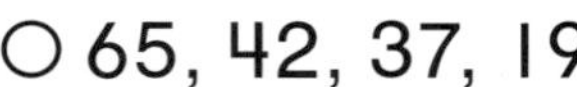
- ○ 23, 47, 15, 32
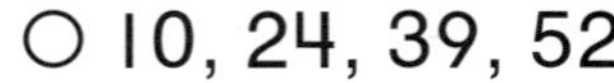
- ○ 36, 71, 49, 83

7
- ○ 62, 43, 16, 50
- ○ 97, 23, 46, 17
- ○ 18, 32, 71, 60
- ○ 39, 57, 83, 94

Notes for Home: Your child reviewed adding three numbers, finding coin combinations that equal 50¢ and $1.00, and putting numbers in order from least to greatest. *Home Activity:* Ask your child to think of four numbers between 10 and 100 and put them in order from least to greatest.

Name ______________________________

Chapter 8 Review

Vocabulary

Add. Then circle the sum if you regrouped.

1

					63	24
23	18	46	17	35	12	12
+ 14	+ 7	+ 25	+ 2	+ 27	+ 23	+ 36

Concepts and Skills

Add. Use mental math.

2 $20 + 30 =$ ____

3 $52 + 20 =$ ____

Use the nearest ten to estimate.

4 $31 + 42$ is about ____.

5 $9 + 21$ is about ____.

Problem Solving

Use the chart.

6 Which color bike do you think you would see most often next Monday?

____

7 Why do you think so?

____

____

Bikes at School on Monday

Bike colors	Tally	Totals
Blue	卌 IIII	9
Red	IIII	4
Green	II	2

Notes for Home: Your child reviewed Chapter 8 vocabulary, concepts, skills, and problem solving. *Home Activity:* Ask your child to explain how he or she regrouped to solve one of the problems in Exercise 1.

CHAPTER REVIEW

Name

Chapter 8 Test

Add. Use mental math.

1. $40 + 30 =$ ____ $20 + 70 =$ ____ $50 + 10 =$ ____

2. $56 + 20 =$ ____ $39 + 10 =$ ____ $42 + 40 =$ ____

Estimate.

3. $63 + 21$ is about ____.
4. $38 + 41$ is about ____.

Add. Regroup if you need to.

5. $\begin{array}{r} 14 \\ +\ 23 \\ \hline \end{array}$ $\begin{array}{r} 37 \\ +\ 6 \\ \hline \end{array}$ $\begin{array}{r} 12 \\ 52 \\ +\ 29 \\ \hline \end{array}$ $\begin{array}{r} 48 \\ +\ 3 \\ \hline \end{array}$ $\begin{array}{r} 24 \\ 64 \\ +\ 11 \\ \hline \end{array}$ $\begin{array}{r} 27 \\ +\ 34 \\ \hline \end{array}$ $\begin{array}{r} 38 \\ 24 \\ +\ 32 \\ \hline \end{array}$

Problem Solving

Use the chart.

Vehicles in Parking Lot on Monday		
Vehicles	**Tally**	**Totals**
Cars	𝍸 𝍸 ||||	14
Trucks	𝍸	5
Motorcycles	𝍸 |	6

6. Which vehicle do you think you would see most in the parking lot next Monday?

____

7. Why do you think so?

____

____

Notes for Home: Your child was tested on Chapter 8 skills, concepts, and problem solving. *Home Activity:* Ask your child to use the chart to tell you how many more cars were seen than motorcycles. (8)

Name ____________________

Performance Assessment

Chapter 8

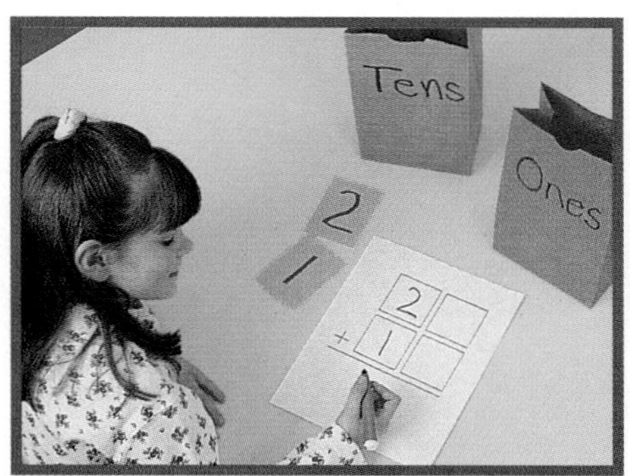

Pick 2 cards from the tens bag. Write the numbers in the tens place.

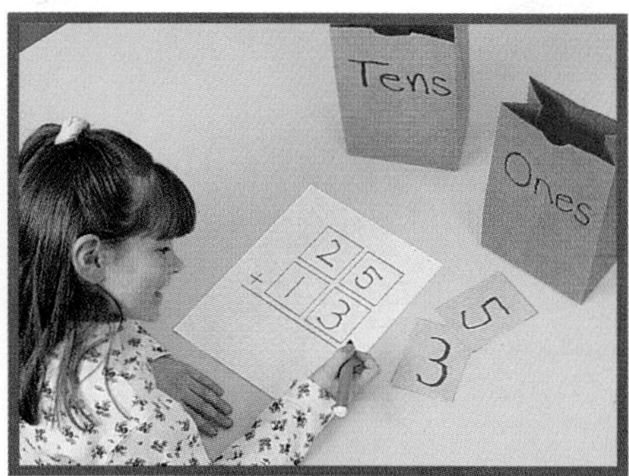

Pick 2 cards from the ones bag. Write the numbers in the ones place.

Add the numbers.

Repeat the activity. Circle your answer if you needed to regroup.

1 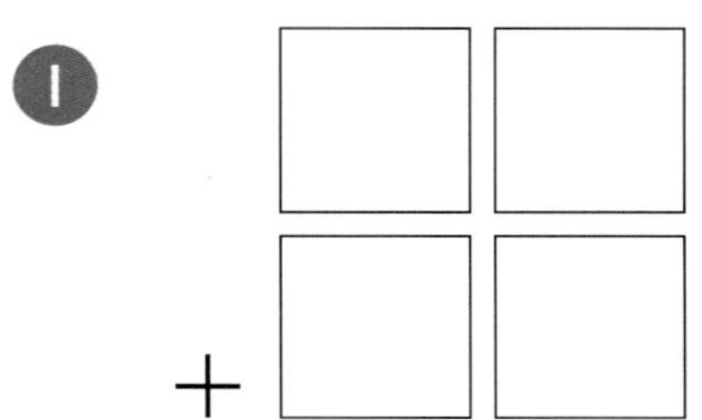 

2 

3 

4 

5 

6 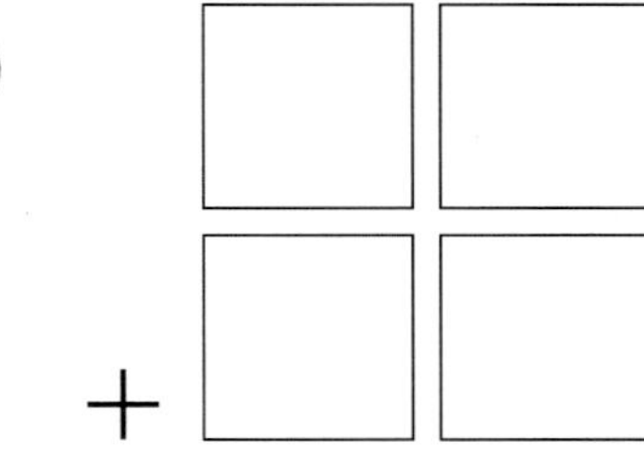

Problem Solving Critical Thinking

7 Cecelia found 3 pairs of numbers that each have a sum of 99. What 3 pairs of numbers could she have found?

Notes for Home: Your child did an activity that tested Chapter 8 skills, concepts, and problem solving. *Home Activity:* Ask your child to tell you the greatest and the least sum on the page.

Name ______________________________

Use the World Wide Web

Computer Skills You Will Need 

You can use the Internet to get different kinds of information.

1. Go to: **www.mathsurf.com/2** **Click** on Chapter 8. This activity can tell you about different forms of transportation used by second graders.

2. **Click** Forward and Backward to get from screen to screen.

3. What did you learn from this activity?

____

Use the information you found on the Internet. Write 2 questions that you could ask about different forms of transportation.

4. ______________________________

____

5. ______________________________

____

6. Exchange your questions with a friend. Answer each other's questions.

Tech Talk Do you think the information at this Web site will always be the same? Why or why not?

Visit our Web site. **www.parent.mathsurf.com**

Keep on Truckin'

What You Need

2 players 2 game pieces 9 cards

How to Play

1 Place each player's game piece on a truck labeled "Start."

2 Number the cards by 10s from 10 through 90.

3 Place the cards facedown. Turn over 3 cards. Try to make an addition sentence using the cards.

4 If you can make an addition sentence, move your game piece forward one space. Put back the cards facedown.

5 Take turns. The first player to reach **End**, wins!

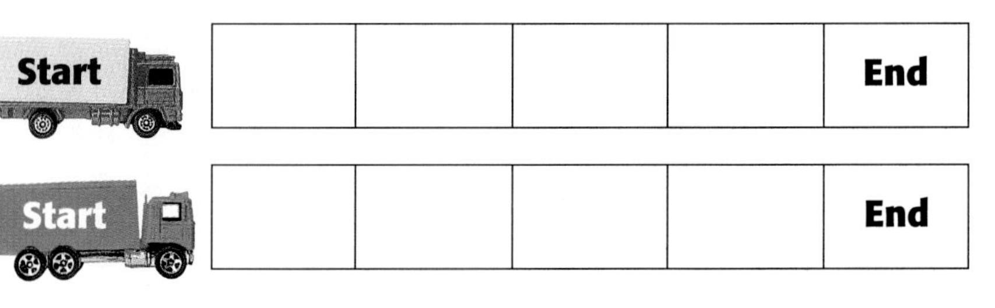

Fold down

MathSoup

Scott Foresman - Addison Wesley My Math Magazine No. 8

Ride the Fun Bus!

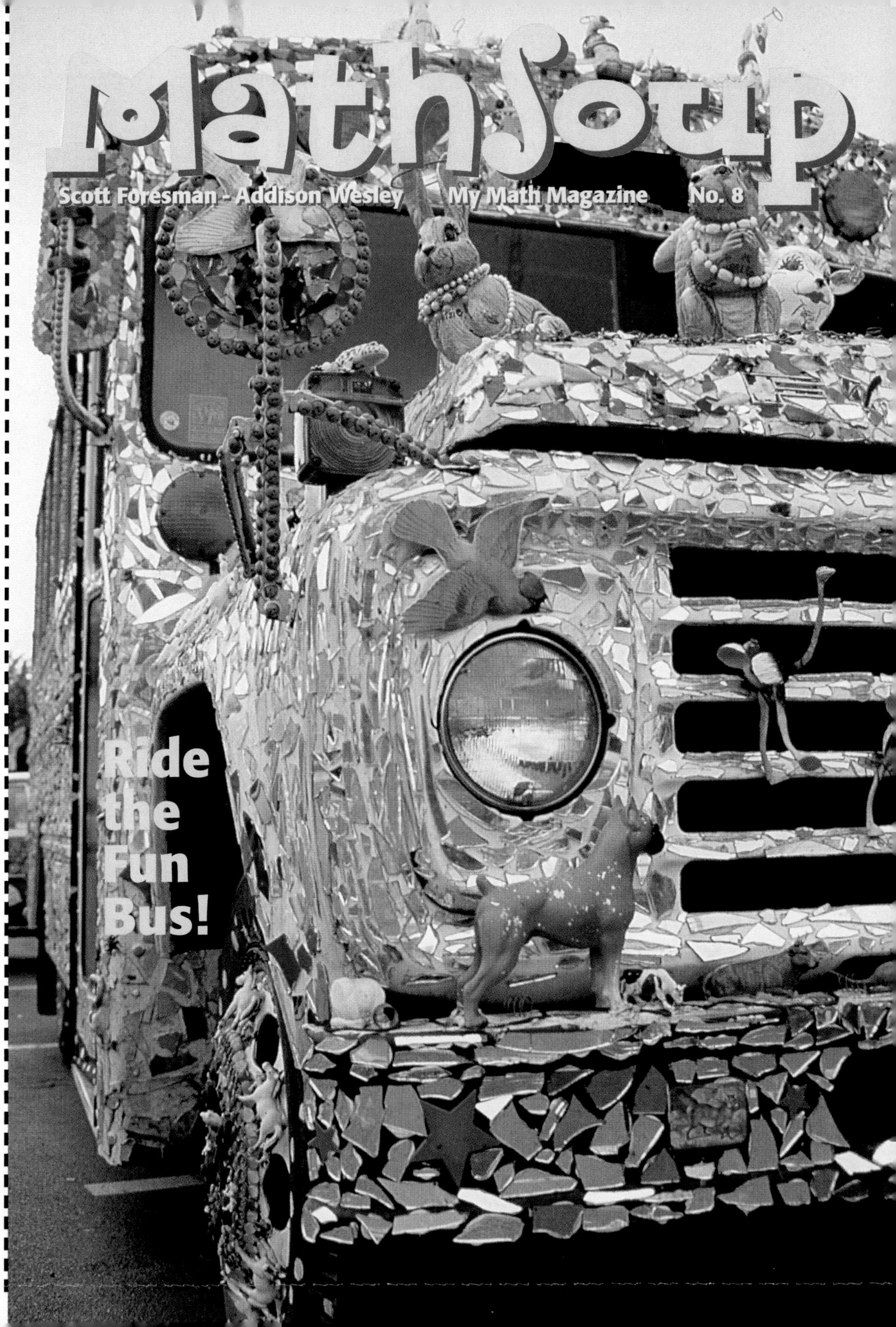

Buckle Up

Since he was 8 years old, Aaron Gordon has been trying to get seat belts installed on school buses. Aaron is currently studying the safety of different belts.

1 One school wants to install seat belts on its 2 buses. One bus holds 72 children. The other bus holds 22 children. How many seat belts should they install?

_____ seat belts

2 Two classes are going on a field trip. One class has 34 children. The other class has 27 children. How many children in all will ride the bus to the field trip?

_____ children

Notes for Home: Your child practiced two-digit addition.
Home Activity: Ask your child to add 57 + 39. (96)

How Fast Did They Go?

Machine	Speed (mph)
Steamboat	5
Airplane	
Model T car	
Airship	

▲ The Model T car's top speed was about 15 miles per hour faster than the first airplane.

▲ Giant airships used to carry people. They went about 23 miles per hour faster than the Model T.

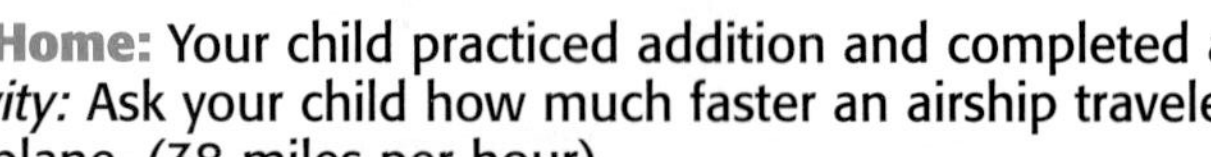

Notes for Home: Your child practiced addition and completed a table.
Home Activity: Ask your child how much faster an airship traveled than the first airplane. (38 miles per hour)

Life in the Fast Lane

For many years, people have built machines so they could travel faster and faster. Look at these pictures of different machines. Use the clues to complete the table that shows how fast they traveled.

▲ **The first steamboat traveled about 5 miles per hour.**

The first airplane traveled about 25 miles per hour faster than the steamboat. ▼

Fun-Mobiles

Each year in Houston, Texas, there is a parade of cars. People come to see cars that are decorated with all sorts of things. Some cars are covered with toys. One car even looks like a giant shark! These "art cars" are as fun to make as they are to watch!

1 This car is covered with dolls! Suppose there are 34 dolls on the hood and 46 dolls on the roof. How many dolls is this?

_____ dolls

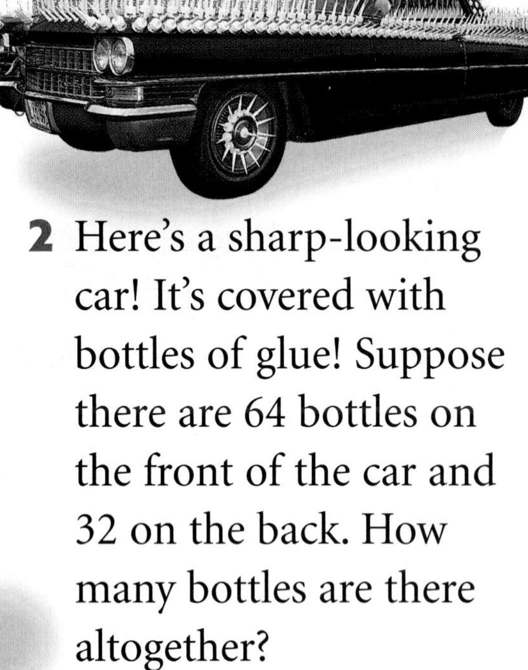

2 Here's a sharp-looking car! It's covered with bottles of glue! Suppose there are 64 bottles on the front of the car and 32 on the back. How many bottles are there altogether?

_____ bottles

Notes for Home: Your child practiced adding two-digit numbers. *Home Activity:* Ask your child to name two numbers less than 50, and then find their sum.

CHAPTER
9
Two-Digit Subtraction
Creatures and Critters
How much more does one animal weigh than another? Tell a subtraction story.
Red King Crab
about 10 pounds
Giant Octopus
about 50 pounds
Commersons Dolphin
about 90 pounds
Bluefish
about 30 pounds
Hawksbill Turtle
about 70 pounds
Ray
about 20 pounds
Notes for Home: Your child told subtraction stories using the picture. Home Activity: Ask your child to tell you one of his or her stories.

Dear Family,
Our class is starting Chapter 9. We will learn about subtraction with two-digit numbers. Together we can do these activities.

Weather Watch
With your child, listen for the day's high and low temperatures on the weather report. Work with your child to find the difference between the high and low temperatures.

Family Differences
Make a list of some family members, along with their ages. Pick out two of the family members. Help your child find the difference in their ages.

Community Connection

Look for mileage signs as you travel on roads or highways. Help your child find the distance between two locations given on one sign.

Visit our Web site. **www.parent.mathsurf.com**

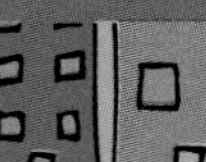

Name

Explore Subtracting Tens

Explore

The caretaker feeds the animals in the morning and in the afternoon.

Use a [tens block] to stand for 10 pounds of food. Show the total pounds each group of animals will get. Take away some [tens blocks] to show how much each group will get in the morning. Find out how many pounds each group will get in the afternoon.

	Animal	Total Food Each Day	Morning Amount	Afternoon Amount
1	Zebras	50 pounds		
2	Monkeys	40 pounds		
3	Birds	30 pounds		
4	Giraffes	70 pounds		
5	Elephants	90 pounds		

EXPLORE

Share

How did you find out how much food to give the giraffe in the afternoon?

Notes for Home: Your child explored subtracting tens. *Home Activity:* Ask your child to explain how he or she found how much food the elephants ate in the morning and in the afternoon.

EXPLORE

Connect

Subtract. Use [tens rod] to find how many are left.

6 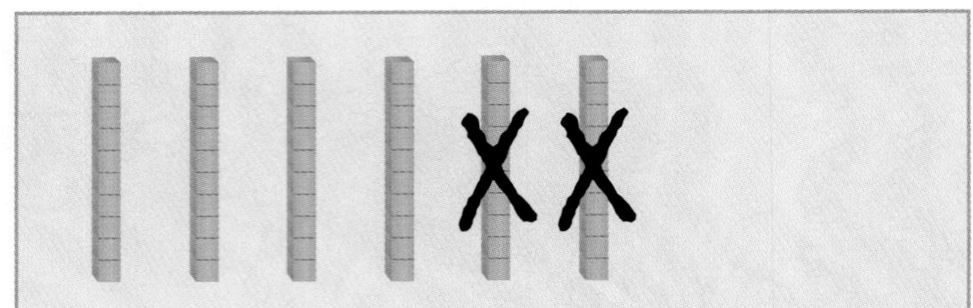

6 tens	60
− 2 tens	− 20
4 tens	40

7 

4 tens	40
− 1 ten	− 10
tens	

8 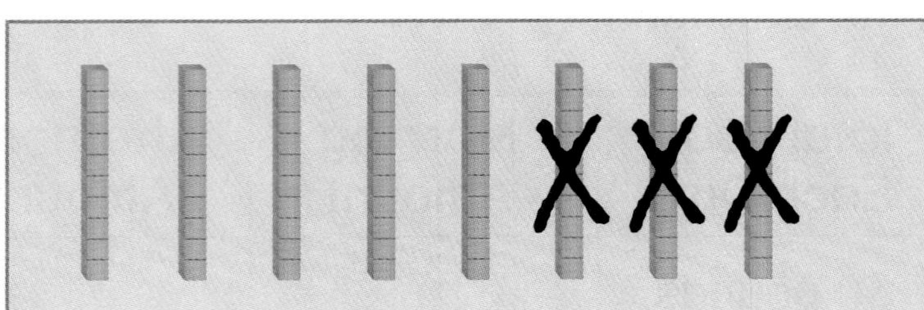

8 tens	80
− 3 tens	− 30
tens	

Subtract. You can use [tens rod] to help.

9

9 tens	90
− 3 tens	− 30

10

7 tens	70
− 5 tens	− 30

Talk About It How does finding 6 − 2 help you find 60 − 20?

Notes for Home: Your child subtracted tens. *Home Activity:* Ask your child to find 8 tens − 5 tens and 80 − 50. (3 tens, 30)

Name

Explore Subtraction With or Without Regrouping

Explore

1. Start with 5 on your chart.
2. Take turns spinning the spinner.
3. Take away that many .

   Trade a for 10 whenever you need to.
4. The first player to get to zero wins!

tens	ones

Share

How did you know when to trade for  ?

Notes for Home: Your child explored subtraction with regrouping. *Home Activity:* Ask your child how he or she would take 7 ones away from 2 tens and 4 ones. (Sample answer: Trade 1 ten for 10 ones. Take 7 ones away. You have 1 ten and 7 ones left.)

Connect

The Senegal bush baby found a nest of 30 bugs. It ate 6 bugs. How many more bugs were left in the nest?

Subtract 6 from 30.

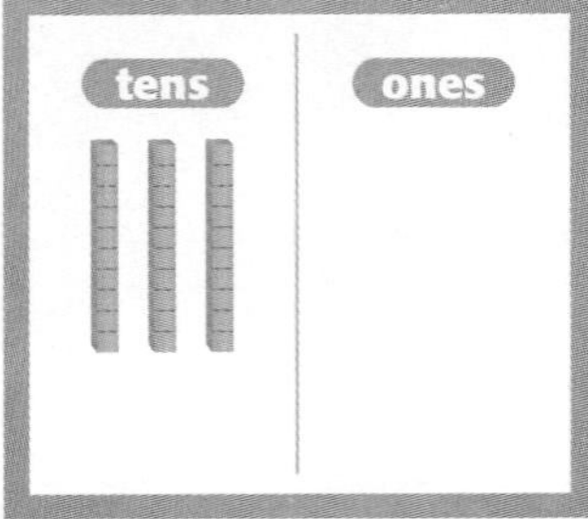

Start with 30.

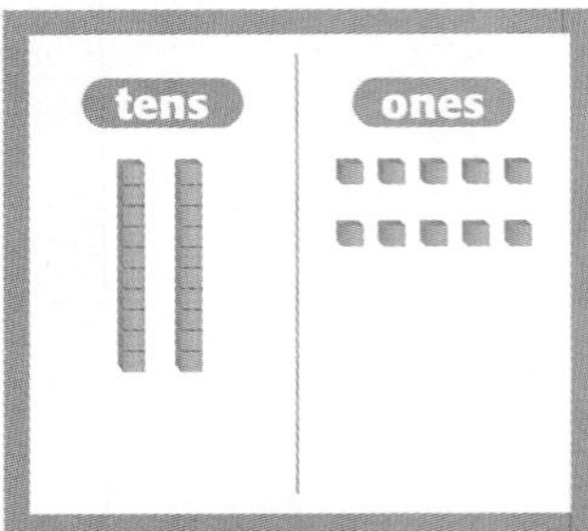

Regroup 1 ten as 10 ones.

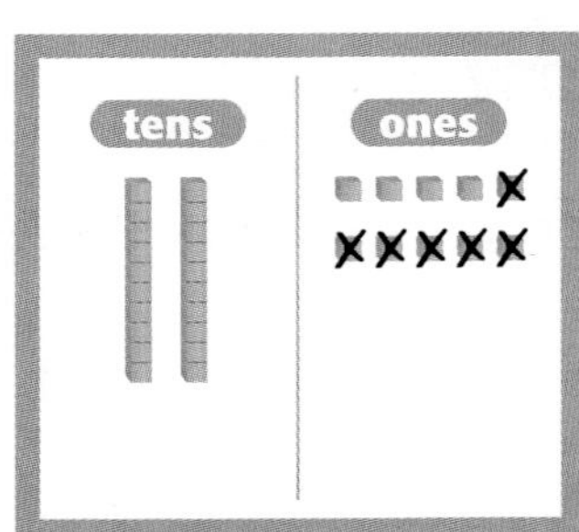

Subtract 6.

24 bugs were left.

EXPLORE

Use [tens-ones mat], [tens rod], and [ones cube].

Find how many are left.

5. Show 23. Subtract 5.

1 tens 8 ones

18

6. Show 45. Subtract 8.

______ tens ______ ones

7. Show 34. Subtract 6.

______ tens ______ ones

______

8. Show 28. Subtract 9

______ tens ______ ones

______

Talk About It Why did you need to regroup each time?

Notes for Home: Your child did subtraction with regrouping. *Home Activity:* Ask your child to explain how he or she found the answer to Exercise 7.

Name

Subtract With or Without Regrouping

Learn

Do you need to regroup to subtract?

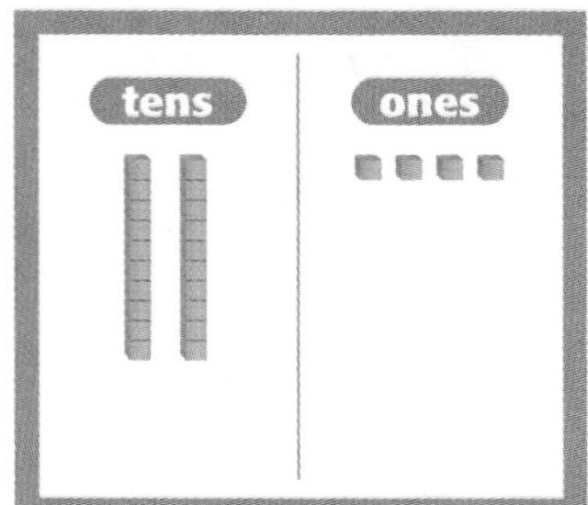

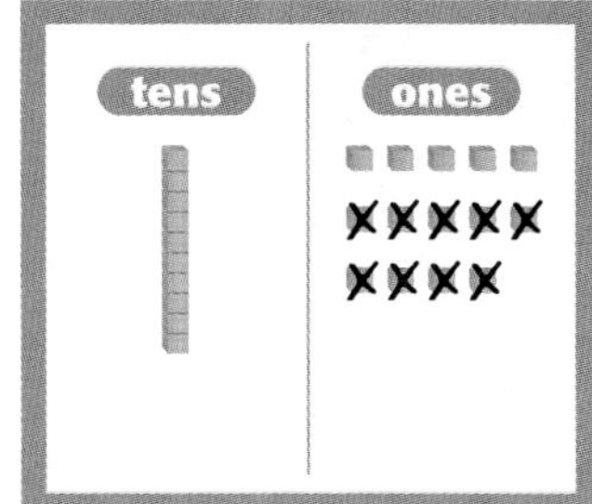

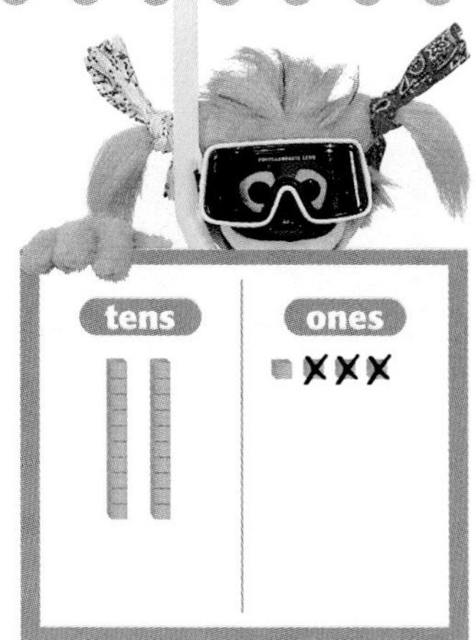

$24 - 9 =$ 15

You need to regroup to subtract the ones.

$24 - 3 =$ 21

You do not need to regroup to subtract the ones.

Check

Use , , and .

	Show this many.	Subtract this many.	Do you need to regroup?	Solve.
1	45	8	yes	$45 - 8 =$ 37
2	27	5		$27 - 5 =$ ___
3	32	4		$32 - 4 =$ ___

Talk About It Start with 36 fish. Tell a subtraction problem. Explain how you would solve your problem.

Notes for Home: Your child determined if regrouping was needed before subtracting. *Home Activity:* Ask your child if regrouping is needed to find $83 - 7$ and $59 - 6$. (Yes, no)

Practice

Use [ten-frame workmat], [tens rod], and [ones cube].

	Show this many.	Subtract this many.	Do you need to regroup?	Solve.
4	46	4	no	46 − 4 = 42
5	39	4		39 − 4 = ____
6	44	8		44 − 8 = ____
7	26	5		26 − 5 = ____
8	49	6		49 − 6 = ____
9	42	7		42 − 7 = ____
10	23	7		23 − 7 = ____
11	34	4		34 − 4 = ____
12	31	5		31 − 5 = ____

PRACTICE

Problem Solving Critical Thinking

13. Which numbers less than ten can you subtract from 35 without needing to regroup? For which numbers would you need to regroup? How do you know?

14. Which number less than ten can you subtract from 30 without needing to regroup? Explain.

Notes for Home: Your child determined if regrouping was needed before finding differences for subtraction problems. *Home Activity:* Ask your child to write one subtraction problem that uses regrouping and one problem that doesn't.

Name

Problem Solving: Choose a Computation Method

Learn

PROBLEM SOLVING GUIDE
Understand • Plan • Solve • Look Back

22 parrots fly through the jungle. 16 more parrots join them. Then 12 parrots fly away. Now how many parrots are there?

There is more than one way to solve this problem.

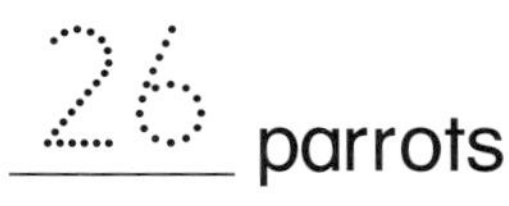

26 parrots   26 parrots

Check

Choose a way to solve the problem. Draw the place-value blocks or write a number sentence.

1. 31 Canada geese are on a lawn. 14 fly away. 8 fly back. How many Canada geese are there now?

   ______ Canada geese

Show your work here.

Talk About It Explain how you solved the problem about geese.

Notes for Home: Your child used place-value materials or a calculator to solve subtraction problems. *Home Activity:* Ask your child to explain the two steps needed to solve the problem about parrots. (Find 22 + 16. Then find 38 − 12.)

PROBLEM SOLVING

PROBLEM SOLVING

Practice

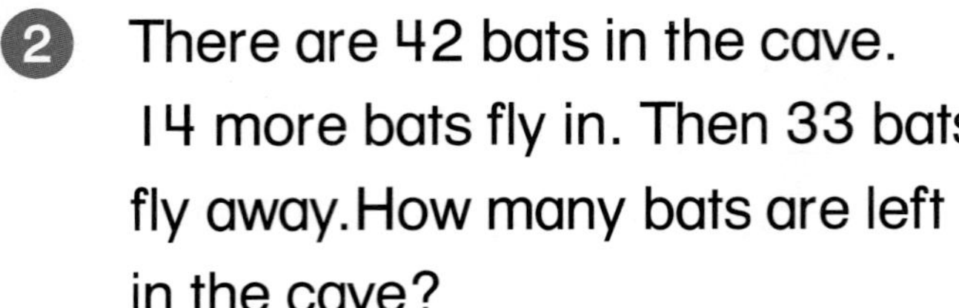

Choose a strategy to solve the problems.
Draw the blocks or write the number sentence.

2. There are 42 bats in the cave. 14 more bats fly in. Then 33 bats fly away. How many bats are left in the cave?

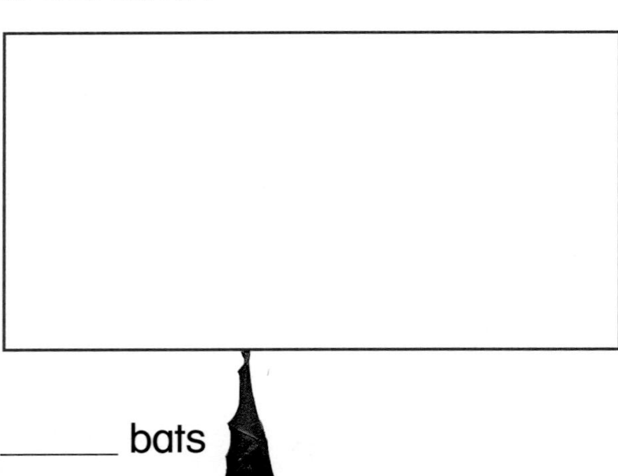

_____ bats

3. The ranger counted 17 penguins in the water. 23 more jumped in. Later, 17 more came. How many penguins were in the water?

_____ penguins

Visual Thinking

4. Write a story problem for the picture.

Notes for Home: Your child solved subtraction problems by using place-value materials or a calculator.
Home Activity: Ask your child to write two number sentences for Exercise 3. (17 + 23 + 40; 40 + 17 = 57)

Name

Explore Subtracting Two-Digit Numbers

1. Choose a number from each box.
   Use and to subtract
   the lesser number from the greater number.
   Draw a picture to show what you did.

   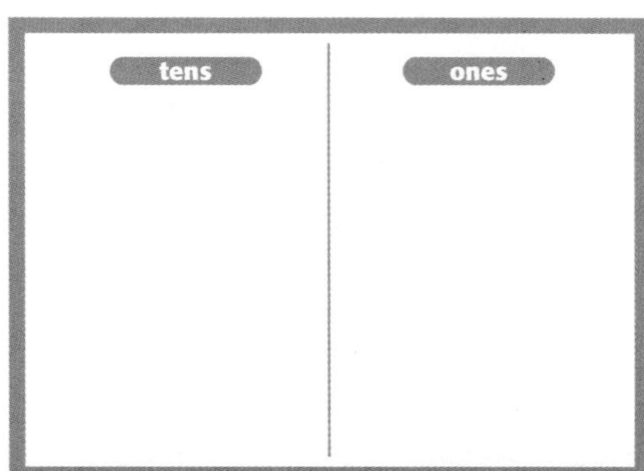

   Write a number sentence.

   _____ − _____ = _____

Choose numbers from each box to make up two more subtraction problems. Use and to solve. Write the number sentences.

2. _____ − _____ = _____

3. _____ − _____ = _____

Share

Using one number from each box, what subtraction problem can you make that can be solved without regrouping? How do you know?

Notes for Home: Your child subtracted two-digit numbers using materials. *Home Activity:* Ask your child to choose another number from each box at the top of the page, write a subtraction problem using those numbers, and tell you if regrouping is needed to solve his or her problem.

Connect

Find 42 − 17.

Before I can subtract, I need to regroup.

Take 42.

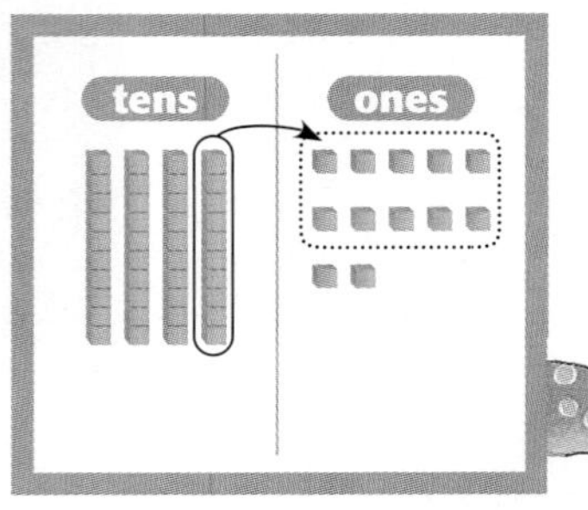

Regroup 1 ten as 10 ones.

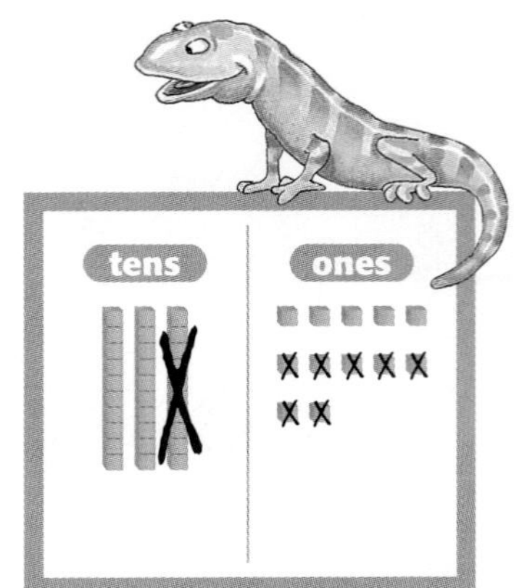

Subtract 17. Write the difference.

42 − 17 = 25

Use [tens] and [ones] to subtract.

	Show this many.	Subtract this many.	Solve.
4	55	34	55 − 34 = ____
5	36	27	36 − 27 = ____
6	84	39	84 − 39 = ____
7	27	9	27 − 9 = ____
8	68	46	68 − 46 = ____

Talk About It How can you tell if you will need to regroup?

Notes for Home: Your child used place-value materials to solve subtraction problems.
Home Activity: Ask your child which exercises on this page required regrouping. (Exercises 5, 6, and 7)

EXPLORE

Name

Subtract Two-Digit Numbers With or Without Regrouping

Learn

Knowing how to find 53 − 9 helps you find 53 − 19.

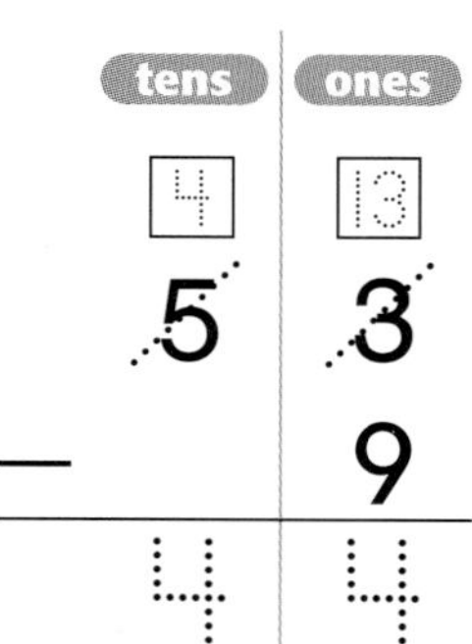

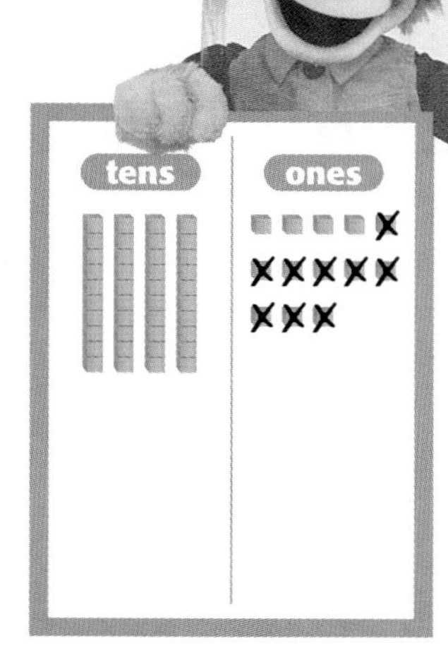

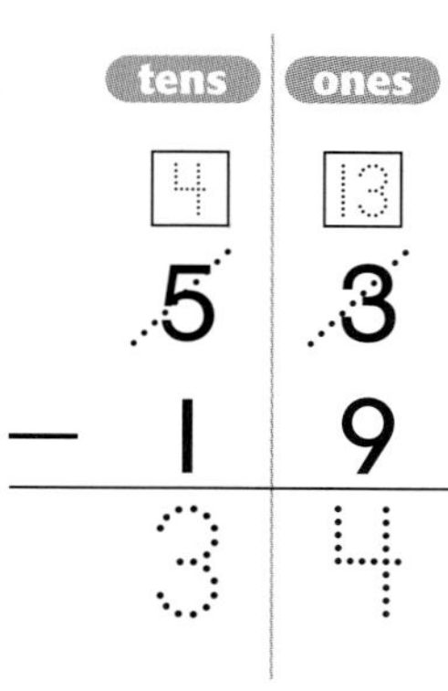

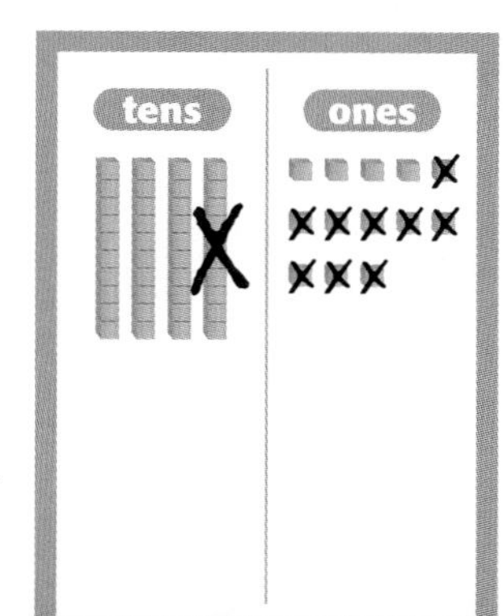

Check

Subtract. Use 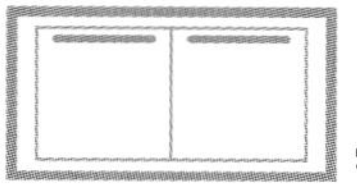, , and .
Regroup if you need to.

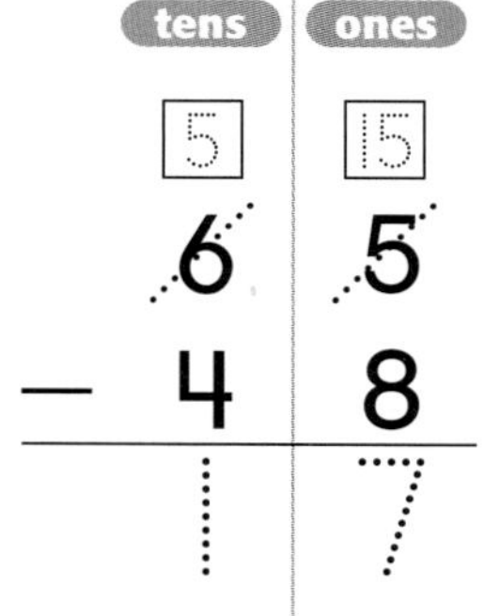

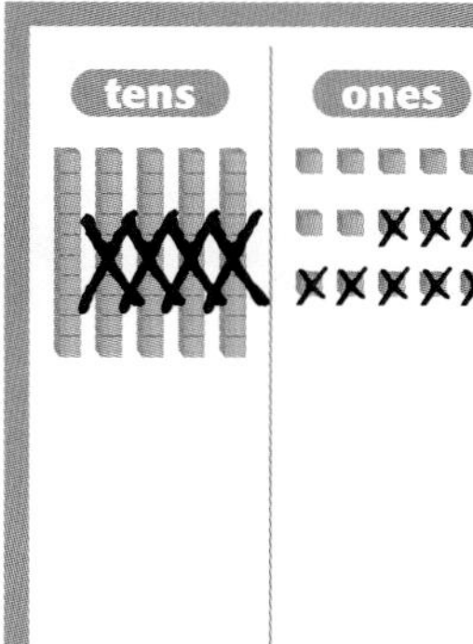

2

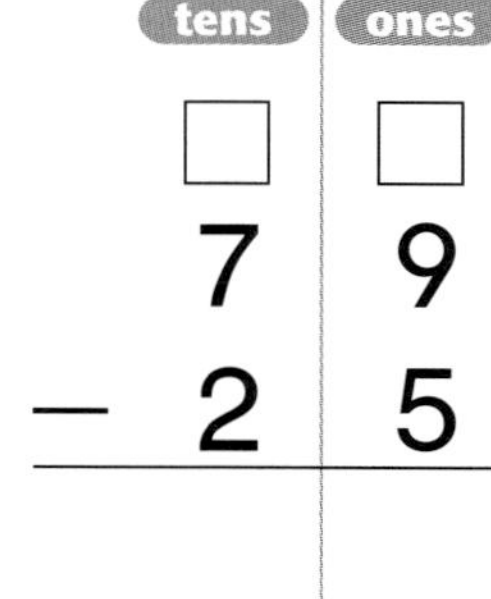

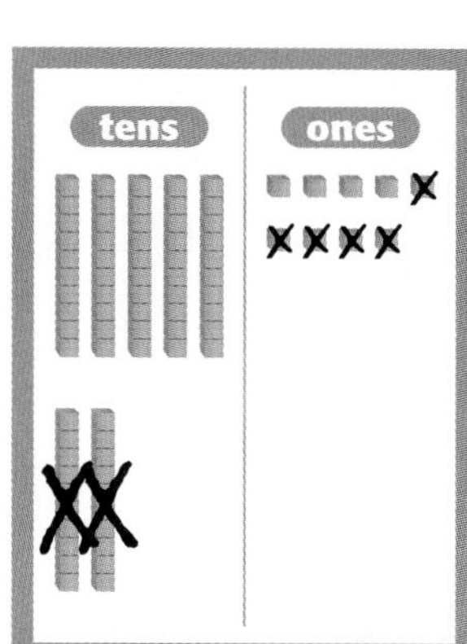

Talk About It How are the pairs of problems alike? How are they different?

$$\begin{array}{r} 85 \\ -\ \ 3 \\ \hline \end{array} \quad \begin{array}{r} 85 \\ -23 \\ \hline \end{array} \qquad \begin{array}{r} 83 \\ -\ \ 5 \\ \hline \end{array} \quad \begin{array}{r} 83 \\ -25 \\ \hline \end{array}$$

Notes for Home: Your child subtracted two-digit numbers with or without regrouping.
Home Activity: Ask your child to explain how to solve Exercise 2.

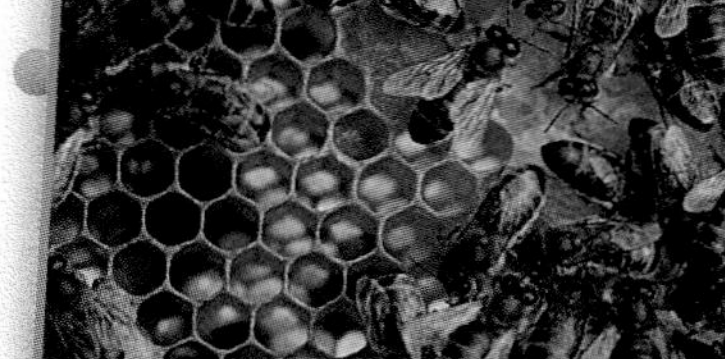

Practice

Subtract. Use 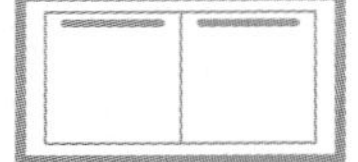, [ten rod], and [one cube].
Regroup if you need to.

3

	tens	ones
	5	11
	~~6~~	~~1~~
−	3	7
	2	4

	tens	ones
	7	4
−	2	1

	tens	ones
	6	3
−	4	8

	tens	ones
	2	8
−	1	9

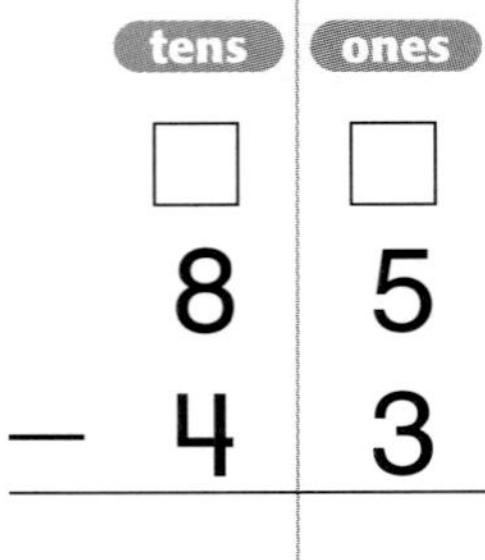

4

	tens	ones
	8	5
−	4	3

	tens	ones
	9	6
−	5	7

	tens	ones
	6	2
−	1	5

	tens	ones
	4	5
−	2	6

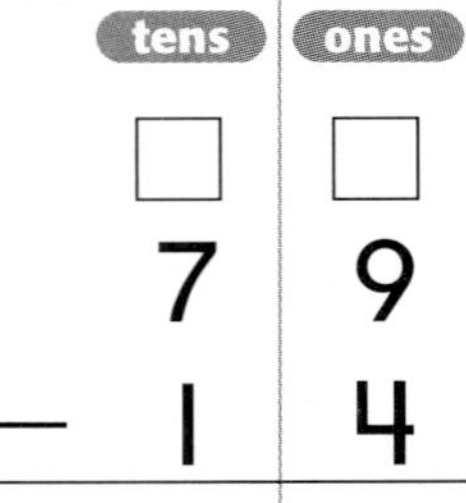

5

	tens	ones
	7	9
−	1	4

	tens	ones
	3	7
−	1	2

	tens	ones
	6	4
−	3	9

	tens	ones
	5	2
−	3	6

PRACTICE

Problem Solving Visual Thinking

6 We started with this:

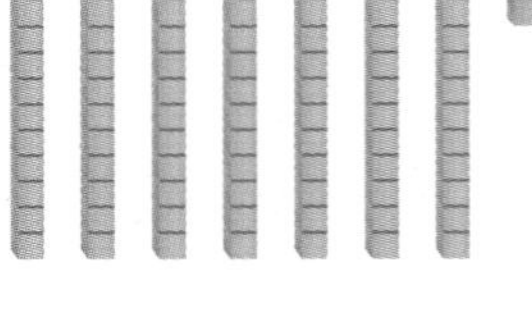

Now we have this:

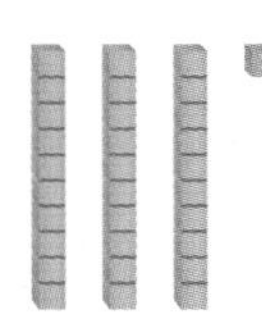

Draw what was subtracted.

Notes for Home: Your child used place-value materials to solve subtraction problems.
Home Activity: Ask your child to tell you which problems required regrouping in Exercise 4. (96 − 57, 62 − 15, and 45 − 26)

Name

Subtract Two-Digit Numbers

Learn

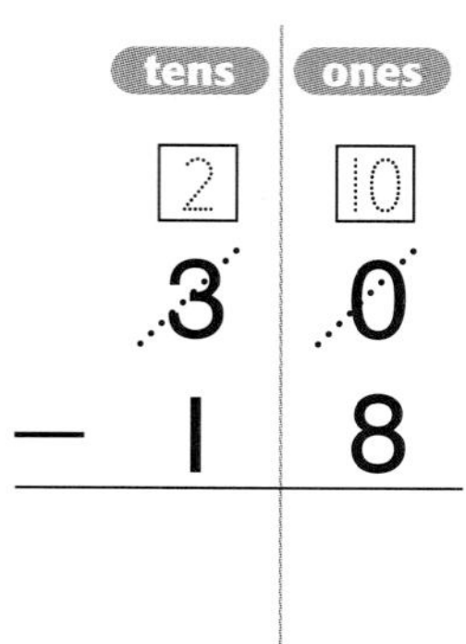

tens	ones
2	10
~~3~~	~~0~~
− 1	8
1	2

Regroup if you need to.

Subtract the ones. Then subtract the tens.

Check

Subtract. Regroup if you need to.

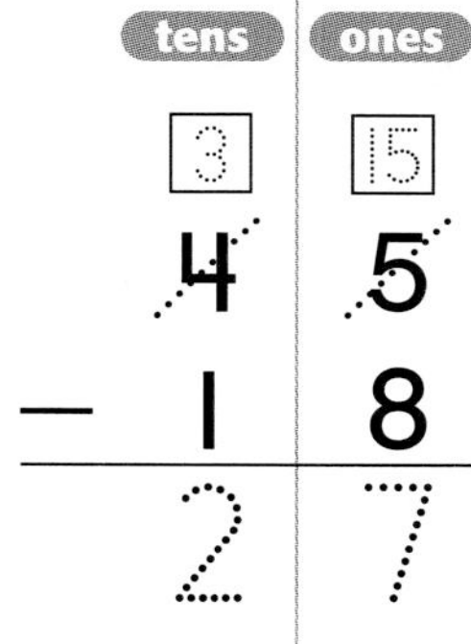

tens	ones
3	15
~~4~~	~~5~~
− 1	8
2	7

tens	ones
☐	☐
5	0
− 3	4

tens	ones
☐	☐
6	8
− 4	7

tens	ones
☐	☐
2	0
− 1	4

2

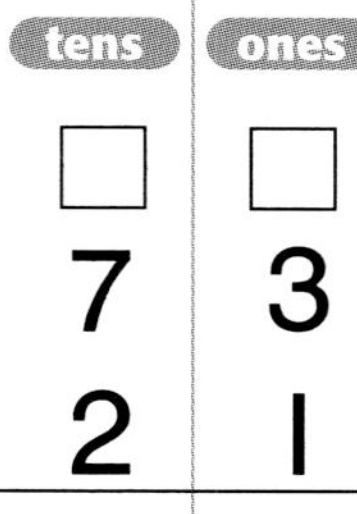

tens	ones
☐	☐
7	3
− 2	1

tens	ones
☐	☐
8	7
− 5	7

tens	ones
☐	☐
9	0
− 7	0

tens	ones
☐	☐
3	2
− 1	4

Talk About It Do you always have to regroup when there's a zero in the ones place? Why or why not?

Notes for Home: Your child found differences for subtraction problems. *Home Activity:* Ask your child to explain the two steps in the Learn section.

Practice

Subtract. Regroup if you need to.

3.
$\overset{4\ 12}{\cancel{52}} - 37 = 15$	$93 - 61$	$54 - 29$	$60 - 13$	$85 - 20$	$42 - 19$

4.
$83 - 24$	$60 - 40$	$39 - 12$	$57 - 38$	$20 - 13$	$46 - 25$

5.
$40 - 25$	$37 - 14$	$56 - 47$	$70 - 21$	$84 - 39$	$92 - 51$

Follow the rule. Subtract.

6.
Subtract 15.	
60	
45	
30	
15	

Find the rule. Write the missing number.

7.
Subtract ______.	
80	68
60	48
40	28
20	8

Problem Solving Critical Thinking

8. Julia's dog ate her math paper! This is all that was left. What could the missing numbers be? How do you know?

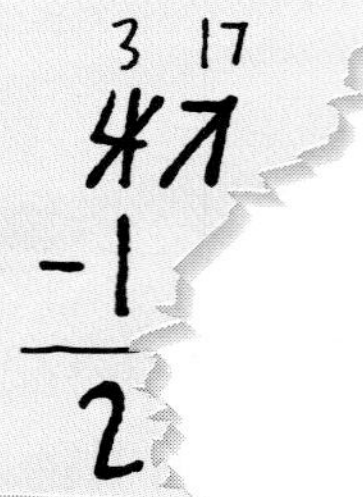

Notes for Home: Your child solved subtraction problems. *Home Activity:* Ask your child to explain how he or she found the rule in Exercise 7.

For additional practice, see Skills Practice Bank, page 534, Set 2.

Name

Use Addition to Check Subtraction

Learn

There are 55 frogs in the pond. 17 of the frogs are green. The rest are orange. How many frogs are orange?

1
38 orange frogs
+ 17 green frogs
55 frogs in the pond

Check

Subtract. Add to check.

1

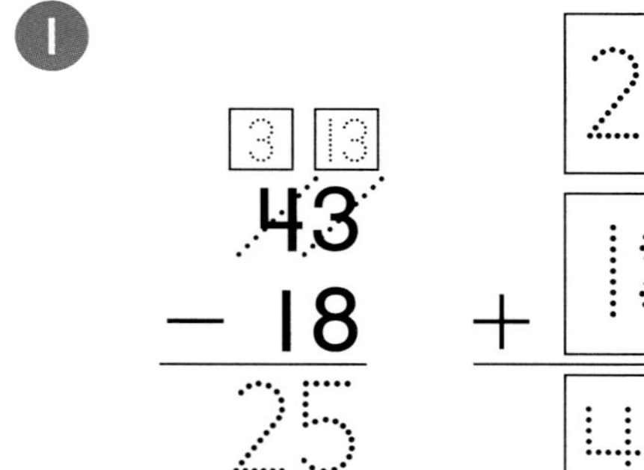

61
− 47

+ ☐ ☐ ☐

38
− 29

+ ☐ ☐ ☐

4 12
52
− 38
24

1
24
+ 38
62

Talk About It Susan solved this subtraction problem and used addition to check her work. What mistake did she make?

Notes for Home: Your child used addition to check the differences for subtraction problems. *Home Activity:* Ask your child to pick a problem in Exercise 1. Have him or her explain how the addition problem shows if the subtraction problem has been done correctly.

Practice

Subtract. Write an addition problem to check.

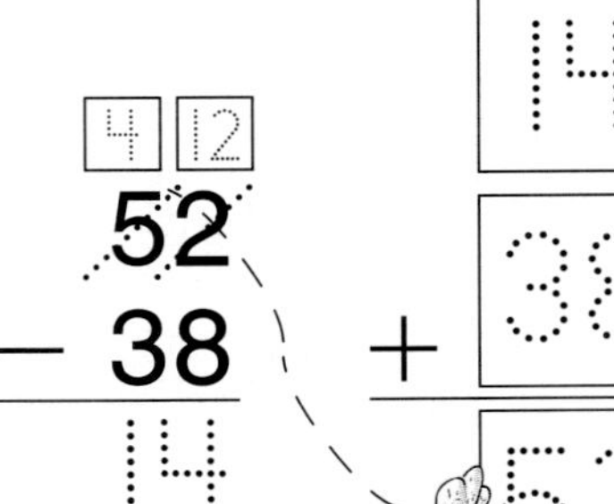

2

$$\begin{array}{r} 52 \\ -\ 38 \\ \hline 14 \end{array} \qquad \begin{array}{r} 14 \\ +\ 38 \\ \hline 52 \end{array}$$

$$\begin{array}{r} 71 \\ -\ 56 \\ \hline \end{array} \qquad +$$

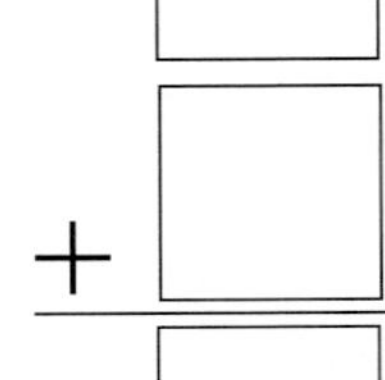

3

$$\begin{array}{r} 80 \\ -\ 40 \\ \hline \end{array} \qquad +$$

$$\begin{array}{r} 35 \\ -\ 24 \\ \hline \end{array} \qquad +$$

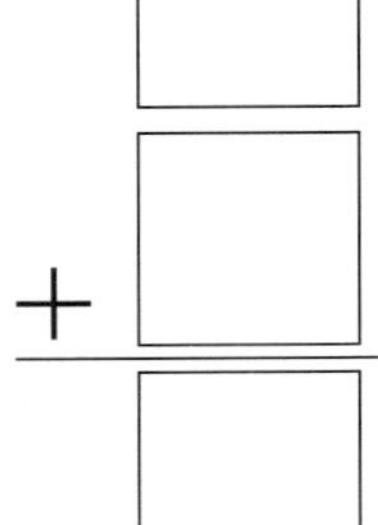

$$\begin{array}{r} 60 \\ -\ 43 \\ \hline \end{array} \qquad +$$

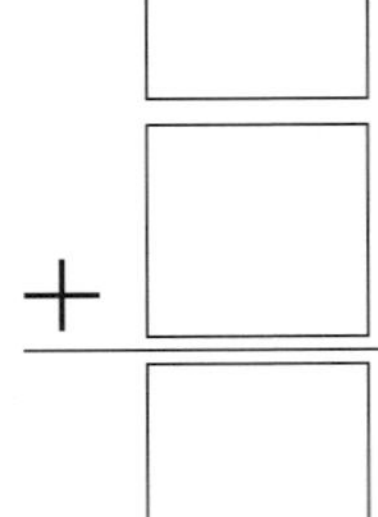

4

$$\begin{array}{r} 57 \\ -\ 9 \\ \hline \end{array} \qquad +$$

$$\begin{array}{r} 99 \\ -\ 62 \\ \hline \end{array} \qquad +$$

$$\begin{array}{r} 42 \\ -\ 25 \\ \hline \end{array} \qquad +$$

Problem Solving Critical Thinking

5 Joe did these subtraction problems.
Use addition to check his work.
Did he do both problems correctly? Explain.

$$\begin{array}{r} 64 \\ -\ 29 \\ \hline 35 \end{array} \qquad \begin{array}{r} 73 \\ -\ 38 \\ \hline 45 \end{array}$$

Notes for Home: Your child checked subtraction by adding. *Home Activity:* Ask your child to subtract and check 74 − 55. (19)

Name ______________________

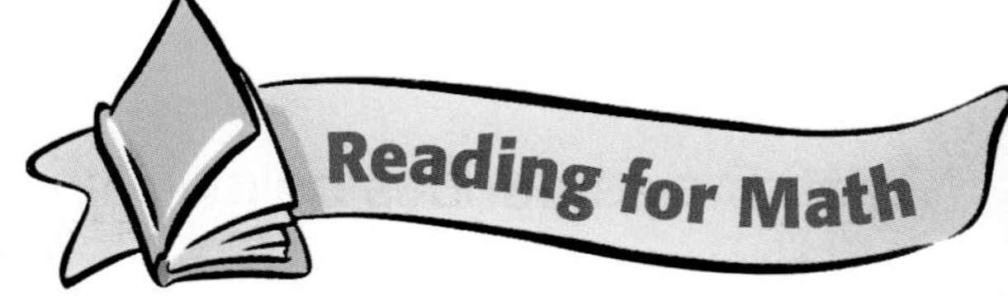

Main Idea and Details

Henry is writing a report about animals. In each paragraph, he writes the main idea and some details. The main idea tells what the paragraph is about. Details tell more about the main idea.

Some animals are fast runners. A cheetah can run 70 miles an hour. A giraffe can run 32 miles an hour.

Some animals are fast runners.

Main Idea

A cheetah can run 70 miles an hour.

Detail

A giraffe can run 32 miles an hour.

Detail

Henry's report got all mixed up. Help him match the sentences below with their main idea.

A lobster has 10 legs.
An alligator can live about 50 years.
A spider has 8 legs.

1. **Some animals have many legs.**

Main Idea

Detail

Detail

Talk About It Which sentence was not a detail for the main idea in Henry's report? Explain.

Notes for Home: Your child identified the details for a main idea. *Home Activity:* Ask your child to tell you which main idea on the page this detail tells about: Insects have 6 legs. (Some animals have many legs.)

Match the sentences below with their main ideas.

Blue whales can weigh 150 tons.

A sailfish can swim 68 miles in one hour.

African elephants can weigh 6 tons.

A giraffe can be 18 feet tall.

A seahorse can swim 1 mile in 10 hours.

2 **Some animals weigh a lot more than we might think.**

Main Idea

Detail

Detail

3 **Some fish swim very fast and some swim very slowly.**

Main Idea

Detail

Detail

Critical Thinking

4 These 2 sentences are details.
What could the main idea be?

African elephants can be 12 feet tall.

Grizzly bears can be 8 feet tall.

Notes for Home: Your child matched details with main ideas. *Home Activity:* Ask your child to tell another detail for one of the main ideas on this page.

Name

Problem Solving: Too Much Information

Learn

PROBLEM SOLVING GUIDE

Understand • Plan • Solve • Look Back

A python can be as long as 32 feet. It can weigh up to 150 pounds. An anaconda snake can be 37 feet long. How much longer can an anaconda snake be than a python?

I don't need to know how much the python weighs. I'll cross out that sentence.

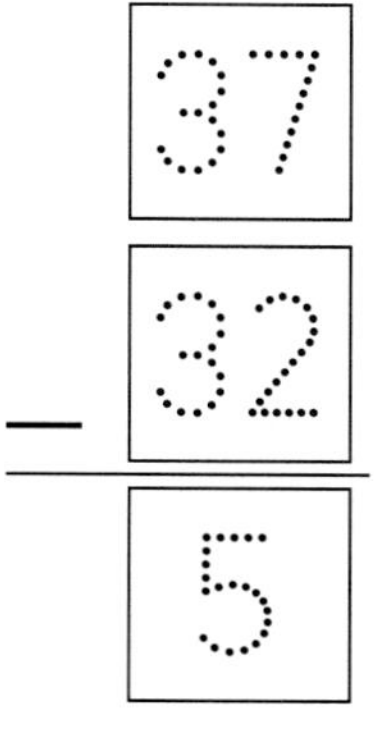

The anaconda snake can be 5 feet longer.

Check

Solve. Cross out the information you do not need.

1. A bushmaster snake can be 12 feet long. It has fangs more than 1 inch long. A cobra can be 18 feet long. How much longer can a cobra be than a bushmaster?

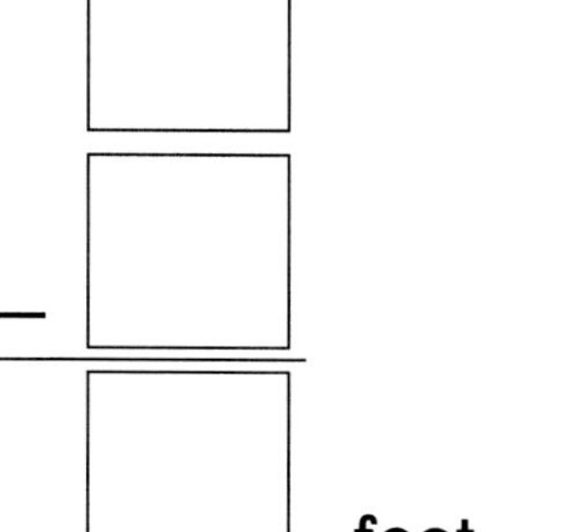

feet

2. A box turtle can live to be 120 years old. Some snakes can live to be 30 years old. An alligator can live to be 60 years old. How much longer can an alligator live than a snake?

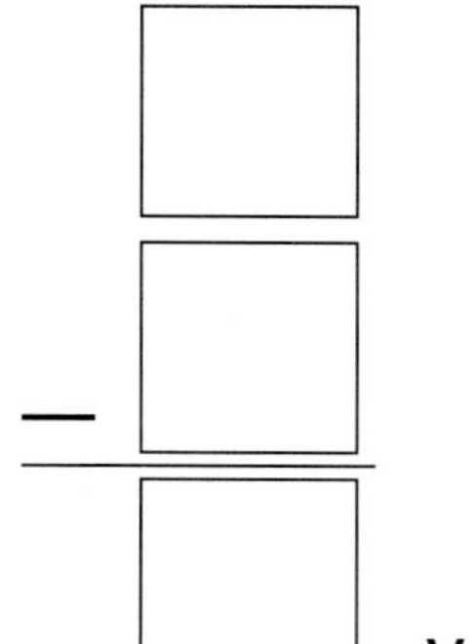

years

Talk About It How did you decide which information you did not need?

Notes for Home: Your child identified unneeded information for solving problems.
Home Activity: Ask your child to explain why the information is unneeded in Exercises 1-2.

PROBLEM SOLVING

Practice

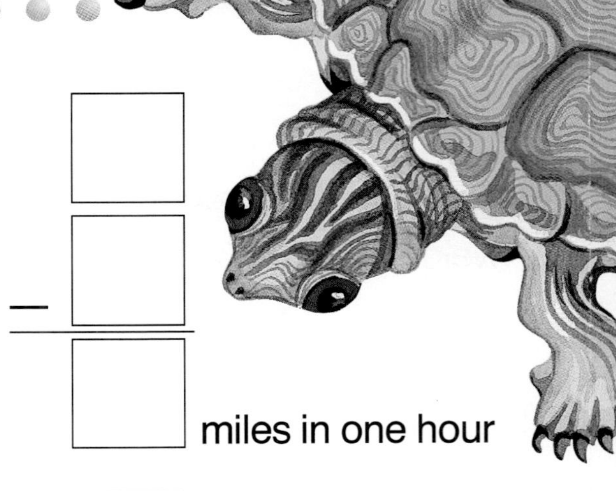

Solve. Cross out the information you do not need.

3. The leatherback turtle travels 22 miles in one hour. The black mamba snake travels 7 miles in one hour. The largest reptile is 16 feet long. How much faster is the leatherback turtle than the black mamba snake?

   ☐
   − ☐
   ☐ miles in one hour

4. A male alligator can grow to be 12 feet long. An alligator can live to be 60 years old. A female alligator can grow to be 9 feet long. How much longer can a male alligator be than a female?

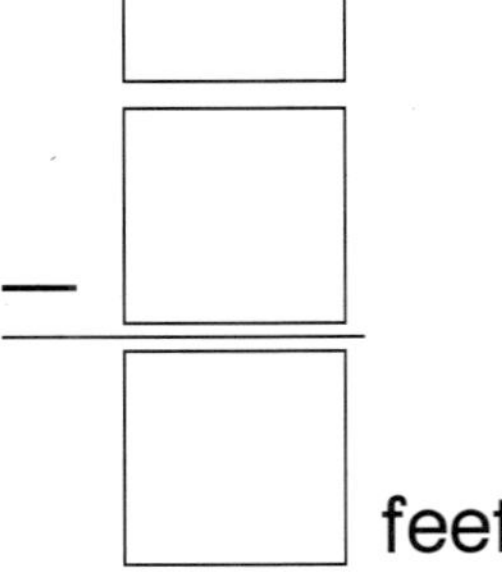

   ☐
   − ☐
   ☐ feet

Journal

5. Write a problem about pythons, turtles, or alligators with too much information. Have a friend solve it.

Pythons

Pythons are among the world's largest snakes.
An African rock python may grow to 32 feet long.
An Indian python may grow to 20 feet long.
A female python may lay up to 100 eggs.

Turtles

There are 7 main types of turtles.
Mud turtles may grow to be 6 inches long.
Pond turtles may grow to be 12 inches long.
Sea turtles may grow to be 28 inches long.

Alligators

Alligators live to be 50 or 60 years old.
Male alligators may grow to 12 feet long.
Female alligators may grow to 9 feet long.
Female alligators can lay 20 to 60 eggs.

Notes for Home: Your child solved problems by identifying unneeded information. *Home Activity:* Ask your child to write a different problem about pythons, turtles, or alligators with too much information.

For additional practice, see Skills Practice Bank, page 534, Set 3.

Name

Mixed Practice

Lessons 8–13

Concepts and Skills

Subtract. Regroup if you need to.

1.

tens	ones
□	□
6	5
− 3	4

tens	ones
□	□
5	2
− 2	9

tens	ones
□	□
4	0
− 2	8

tens	ones
□	□
3	1
− 1	6

2. 87¢ − 14¢   62¢ − 47¢   70¢ − 23¢   59¢ − 18¢   90¢ − 26¢

Subtract. Write an addition problem to check.

3. 38 − 19   + □ □ = □

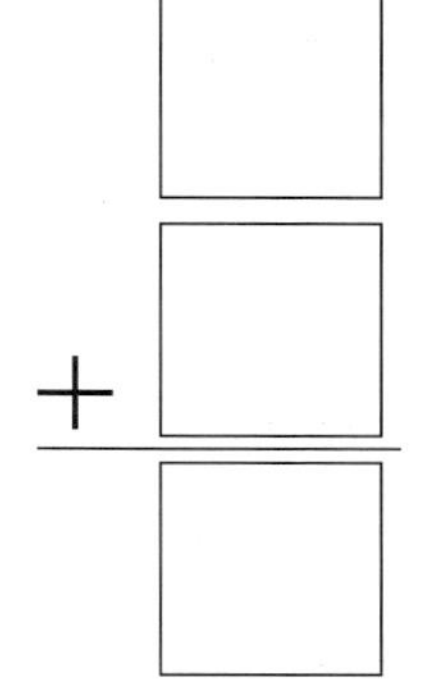

75 − 23   + □ □ = □

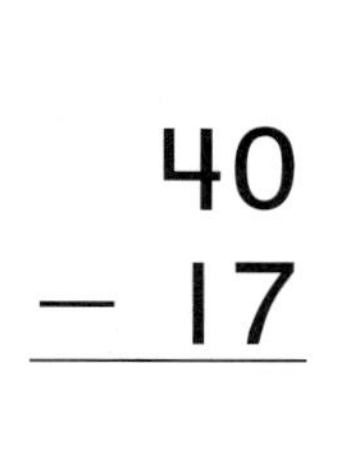

40 − 17   + □ □ = □

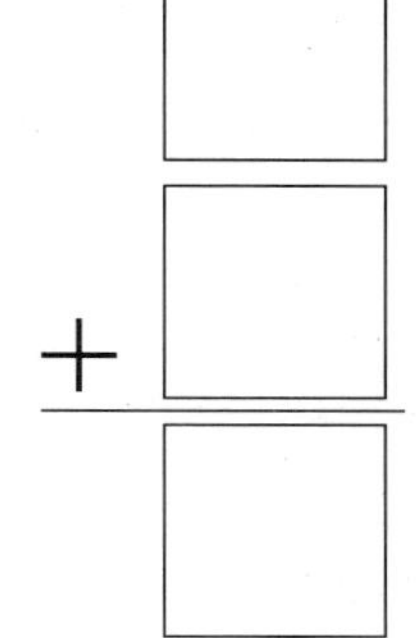

Problem Solving

Solve. Cross out the information you do not need.

4. An Indian python can be 20 feet long. An alligator can live to be 60 years old. A male alligator can be 12 feet long. How much longer can an Indian python be than a male alligator?

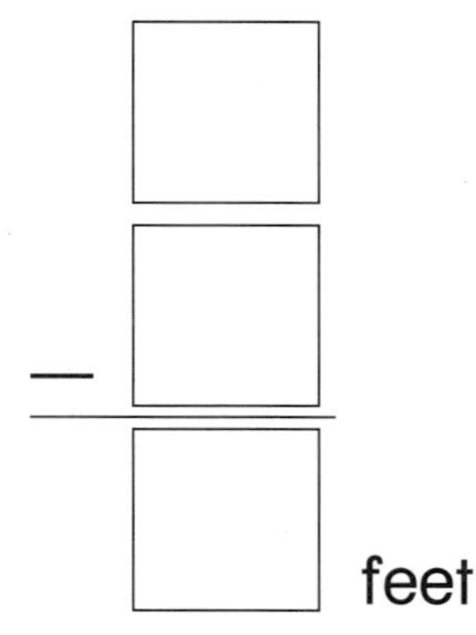

□ − □ = □ feet

Journal

5. Write an addition problem to check this problem: **57 − 8 = 39**
How do you know if the difference is correct or incorrect? Explain.

Notes for Home: Your child practiced subtracting, checking subtraction with addition, and solving problems. *Home Activity:* Ask your child to find 53 − 36 and check the difference by adding. (53 − 36 = 17; 17 + 36 = 53)

MIXED PRACTICE

Name ______________________________

Cumulative Review

Chapters 1–9

Concepts and Skills

Write the time.

1 

_____ o'clock

_____ : _____

2 

_____ : _____

3 

_____ : _____

Problem Solving

Use the chart to solve each problem.

4 Which color of frogs was seen most often?

____

5 How many more **red** frogs than **yellow** frogs were seen?

_____ red frogs

Frogs in the Jungle

Frog Colors	Tally	Total
Blue	𝍸 𝍸	10
Red	𝍸 ll	7
Yellow	𝍸	5

Test Prep

Fill in the ○ for the correct answer.
Use mental math to add.

6 24 + 50 = _____

64 ○ 74 ○ 54 ○ 84 ○

7 59 + 30 = _____

59 ○ 69 ○ 89 ○ 99 ○

Notes for Home: Your child reviewed telling time, solving problems, and adding.
Home Activity: Ask your child where the hour hand and minute hand would be at 12 o'clock. (Both hands would point at 12.)

Name ______________________________

Chapter 9 Review

Concepts and Skills

Subtract. You can use the chart.

1. 46 − 20 = ____
2. 34 − 10 = ____
3. 29 − 20 = ____

1	2	3	4	5	6	7	8	9	10
11	12	13	14	15	16	17	18	19	20
21	22	23	24	25	26	27	28	29	30
31	32	33	34	35	36	37	38	39	40
41	42	43	44	45	46	47	48	49	50

Find the nearest ten.
Estimate the difference.

4. 73 − 19

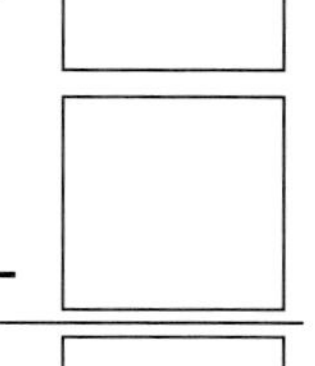

73 − 19 is about ____.

Subtract.
Write an addition problem to check.

5. 90 − 38

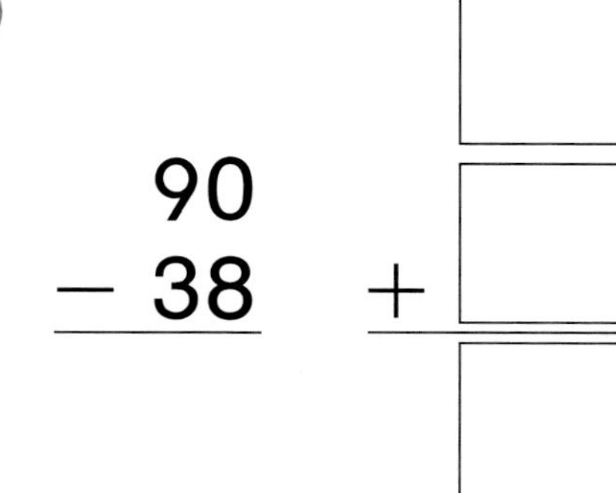

Subtract. Regroup if you need to.

6. 75 − 41   53¢ − 6¢   40¢ − 17¢   68 − 31   50¢ − 9¢   86 − 52

Problem Solving

Solve. Cross out the information you do not need.

7. On Monday, Kevin saw 14 cranes wading in a pond. The cranes were white and grey. On Wednesday, he saw 7 cranes. How many more cranes did he see on Monday than on Wednesday?

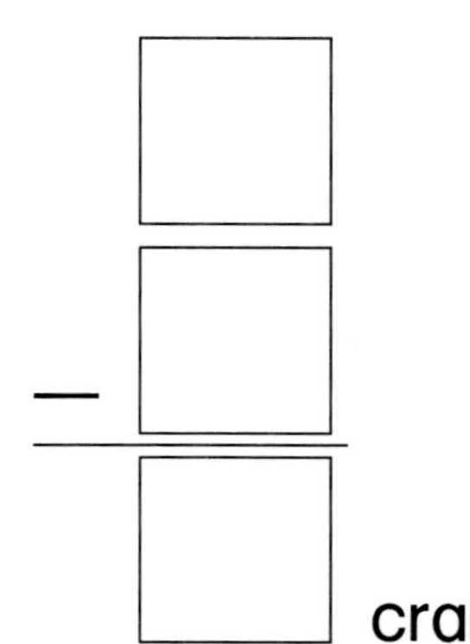

Notes for Home: Your child reviewed Chapter 9 concepts, skills, and problem solving.
Home Activity: Ask your child to explain how to estimate 59 − 23. (60 − 20 = 40)

Name ______________________________

Chapter 9 Test

Subtract.

1. $50 - 30 =$ ____
2. $70 - 20 =$ ____
3. $48 - 10 =$ ____
4. $67 - 20 =$ ____

Find the nearest ten. Estimate the difference.

5. $89 - 21$ is about ____.
6. $72 - 48$ is about ____.

Subtract. Regroup if you need to.

7.

60	37¢	29	50	84	92¢
− 25	− 6¢	− 13	− 19	− 27	− 49¢

Subtract. Write an addition problem to check.

8.

$$\begin{array}{r} 37 \\ -\ 14 \\ \hline \end{array} \qquad \begin{array}{r} \square \\ +\ \square \\ \hline \square \end{array}$$

$$\begin{array}{r} 52 \\ -\ 27 \\ \hline \end{array} \qquad \begin{array}{r} \square \\ +\ \square \\ \hline \square \end{array}$$

$$\begin{array}{r} 86 \\ -\ 39 \\ \hline \end{array}$$

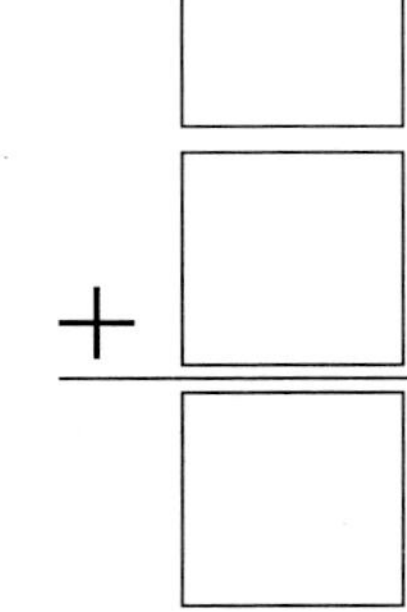

Solve. Cross out the information you do not need.

9. An adult gorilla is about 6 feet tall. A wolf can live about 20 years. A howler monkey is only about 2 feet tall. About how much taller is an adult gorilla than a howler monkey?

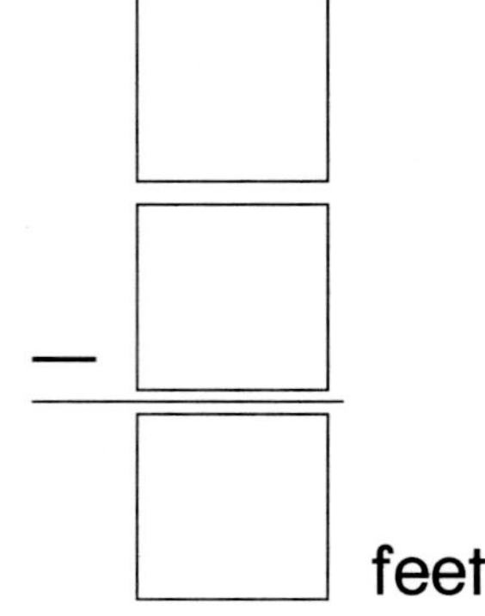

feet

Notes for Home: Your child was tested on Chapter 9 concepts, skills, and problem solving. *Home Activity:* Ask your child to identify one problem in Exercise 7 which requires regrouping and one which does not.

Name

Performance Assessment

Chapter 9

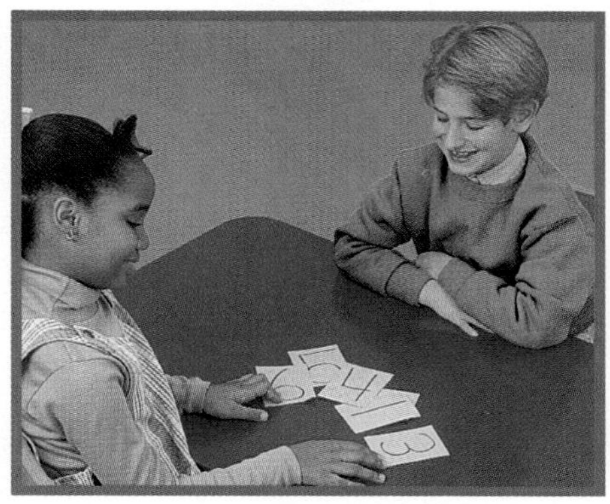

Mix up the number cards. Make a stack.

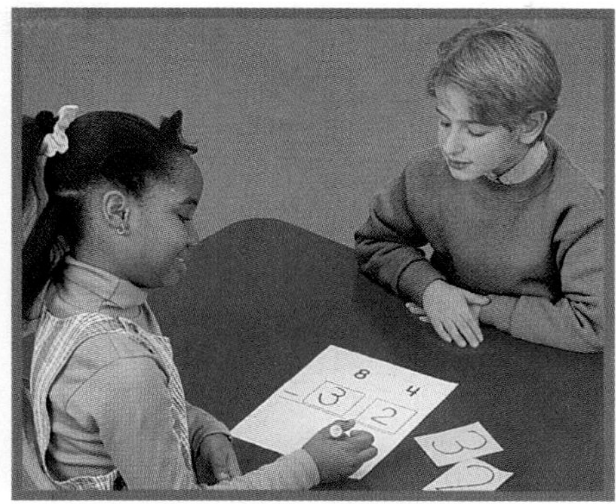

Use the top two cards. Write the numbers in the squares in any order.

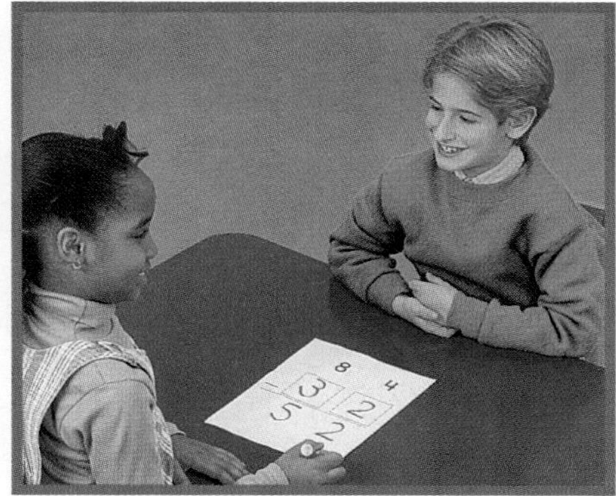

Subtract.

Do the activity again.

1. 6 8
   − ☐☐

2. 7 2
   − ☐☐

3. 8 6
   − ☐☐

4. 8 0
   − ☐☐

5. 9 5
   − ☐☐

6. 7 0
   − ☐☐

Problem Solving Critical Thinking

7. Mario used four numbers from 1 through 9 to write a subtraction problem. The answer to his problem was 47. What numbers could he have used?

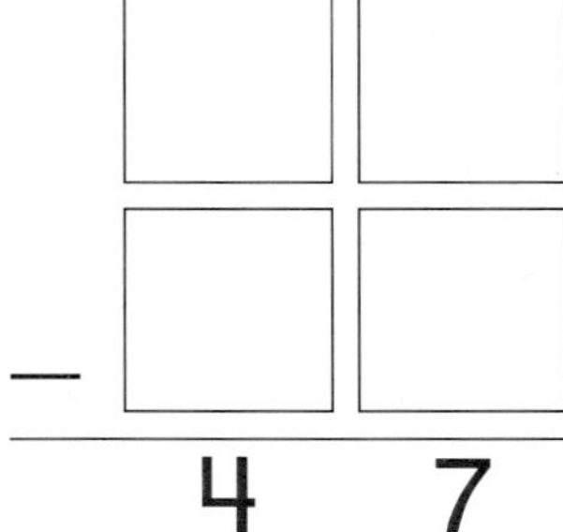

☐☐
− ☐☐
4 7

Notes for Home: Your child did an activity that tested Chapter 9 skills, concepts, and problem solving.
Home Activity: Ask your child to tell you another pair of numbers that could be used to solve Exercise 7.

PERFORMANCE ASSESSMENT

Name ______________________________

Zoom to Zero!

Keys You Will Use

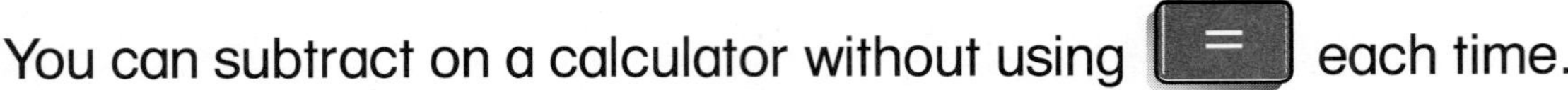

You can subtract on a calculator without using [=] each time.

100 − 24 − 35 − 18 = ?

Press these keys.

[1] [8] [=] 23.

How to Play

1. Play with a partner. Use counters to cover 3 or 4 numbers. Use your [calculator] to subtract those numbers from 100.
2. The player who gets closest to zero wins the round. He or she colors in the numbers that were covered by the counters.
3. For the next round, players move the counters to new numbers and subtract from 100.
4. To win, a player must color 12 numbers on his or her gameboard.

13	24	32	33	12
16	19	10	29	30
15	14	26	11	34
27	23	28	25	12
17	20	31	22	18

Tech Talk How can using a calculator help when you are subtracting more than one number?

Visit our Web site. **www.parent.mathsurf.com**

Speed Spin

The spinner below shows the speeds traveled by some fast animals. Find out how much faster some animals can travel than others.

1 Use a pencil and a paper clip to make a spinner. Then spin twice.

2 Compare the speeds of the two animals.

3 How much faster did one animal travel than the other?

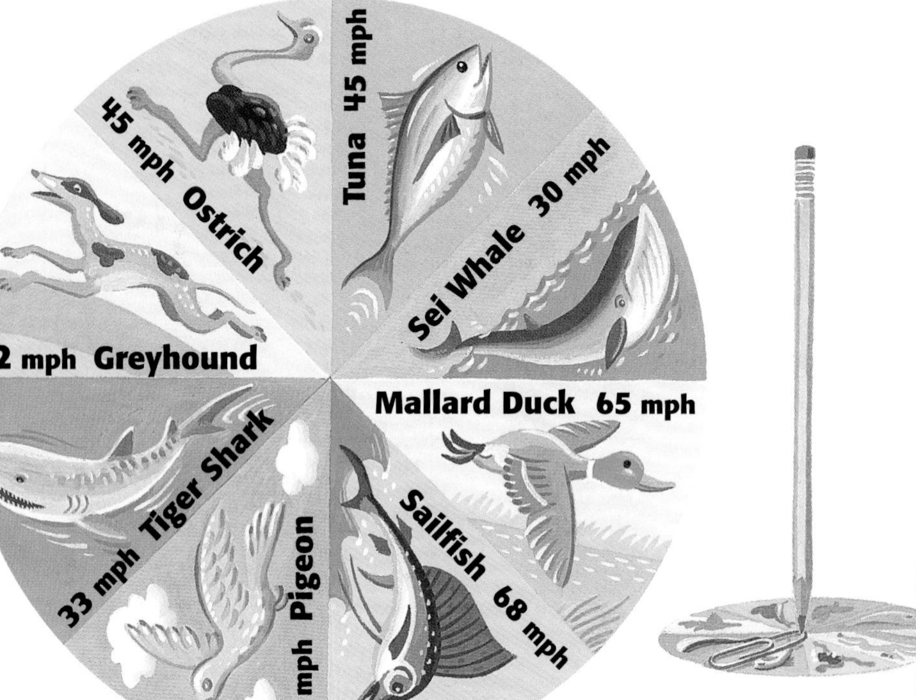

Fold down

MathSoup

Scott Foresman - Addison Wesley My Math Magazine No. 9

Ready, Set...

Boing!

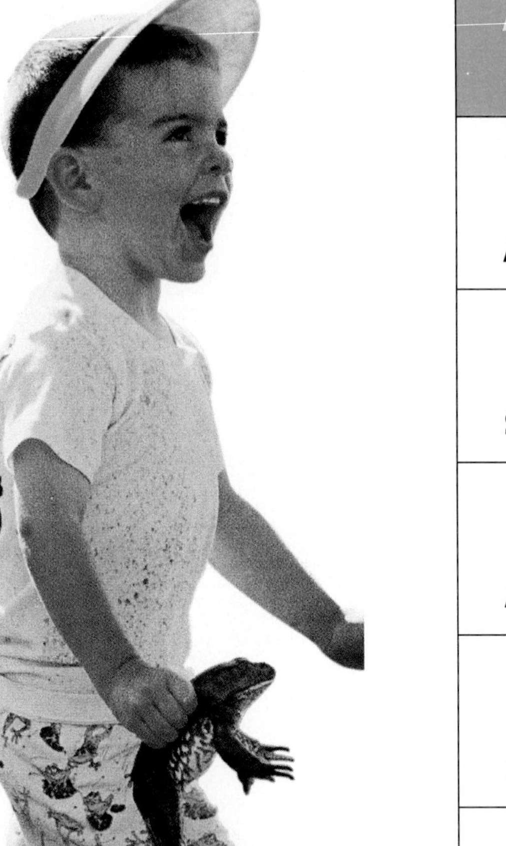

Have you ever won a contest? Have you ever tickled a frog?

Four-year-old Cody Shilts did both. He won a frog jumping contest. His frog jumped about 19 feet in three hops.

People in the contest gave their frogs funny names. Cody called his frog Free Willy. The frog that has the record for the longest jump ever was named Rosie the Ribeter.

Notes for Home: Your child practiced subtraction. *Home Activity:* Ask your child to compare the distance "jumped" by a frog on his or her chart to the distance jumped by Rosie the Ribeter.

Complete the table to show how many hours each of these animals is asleep and awake during one day. Remember that there are 24 hours in one day.

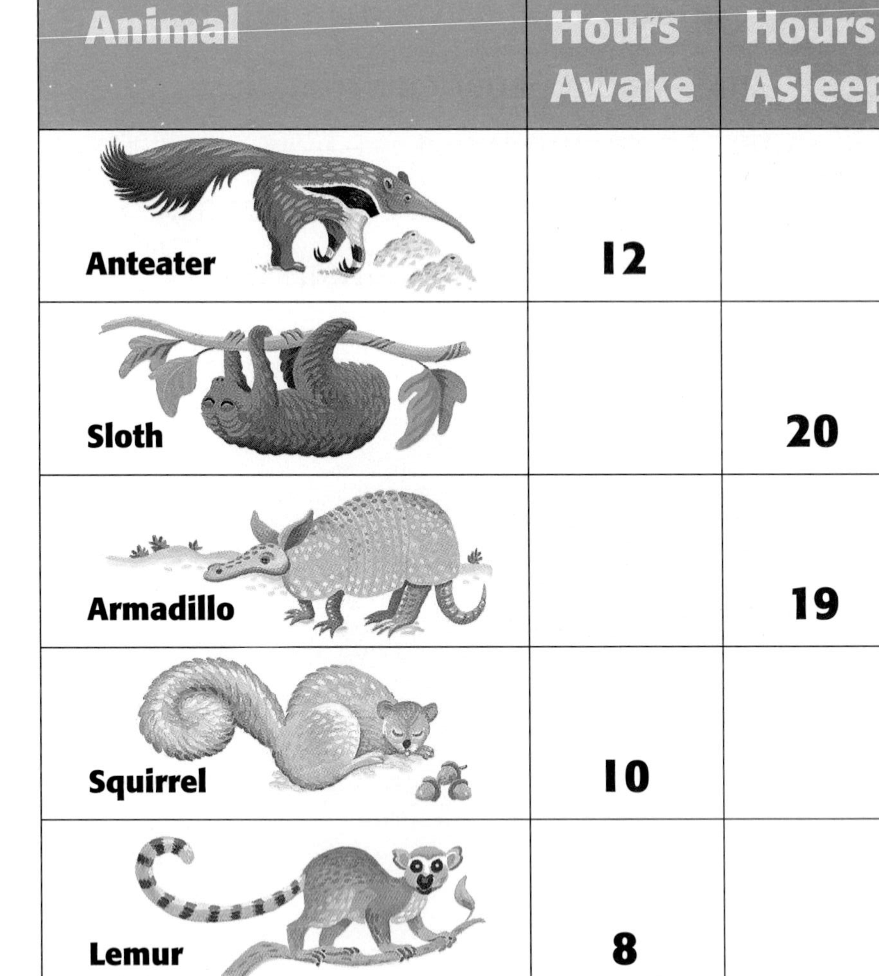

Animal	Hours Awake	Hours Asleep
Anteater	12	
Sloth		20
Armadillo		19
Squirrel	10	
Lemur	8	

Notes for Home: Your child practiced subtraction and completed a table. *Home Activity:* Ask your child how many hours a koala is awake each day. (2)

Snoozzzzzzze

Sleep is very important to good health. You need at least 10 hours of sleep every night.

However, some animals need to sleep much more than you do. For example, a pig sleeps for about 13 hours a day.

A koala spends more time asleep each day than any other animal– 22 hours in all!

1 Rosie the Ribeter jumped about 21 feet. About how much farther is that than Free Willy's jump?

_____ feet farther

2 Fill in the chart below with funny frog names. Roll three number cubes each with 4, 5, 6, 7, 8, and 9 on them. Add the numbers on the cubes to show how far one of the frogs on your chart "jumped." Repeat for the other names on your chart.

Frog Name	Distance Jumped
	feet
	feet
	feet

3 Write your own word problem asking how much farther one frog on your chart jumped than another.

Create a Flap

In order to fly, birds flap their wings very fast. Some birds flap their wings faster than others.

The chart shows how many times some birds flap their wings in 10 seconds.

Type of Bird	Flaps (in 10 seconds)
Heron	**20** times
Pigeon	**60** times
Starling	**70** times

1 You try it! Count how many times you flap your arms in 10 seconds. Record your results.

_____ times

Use your data to answer the questions.

2 Did you flap your arms **more** or **fewer** times in 10 seconds than a heron?

_____ times

3 How many more or fewer times? _____

4 How many more times can a pigeon flap its wings in 10 seconds than you flapped your arms?

_____ more times

Notes for Home: Your child practiced subtraction. *Home Activity:* Ask your child how many more times a starling can flap its wings in10 seconds than he or she flapped his or her arms.

CHAPTER 10

Numbers to 1,000

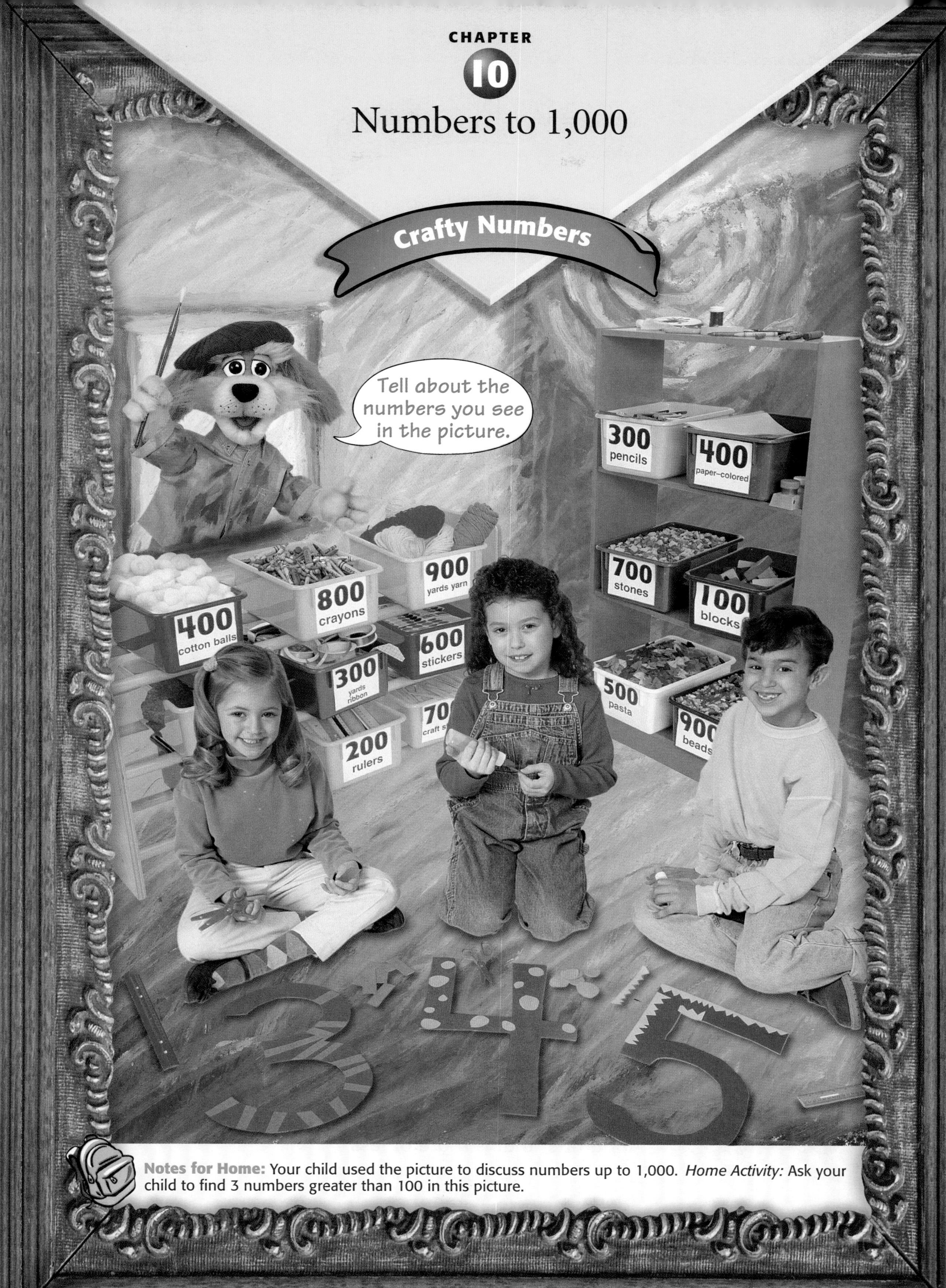

Notes for Home: Your child used the picture to discuss numbers up to 1,000. *Home Activity:* Ask your child to find 3 numbers greater than 100 in this picture.

Dear Family,
Our class is starting Chapter 10. We will be learning about numbers up to 1,000. We will add and subtract larger numbers. Here are some activities we can do together.

Ready, Set, Count!
Have your child find different ways to count to 100. Suggest counting by different numbers such as 10 or 25. Then help him or her count beyond 100.

See and Say
Point out three-digit numbers, such as 592 or 327, in magazines, books, or addresses. Read the numbers aloud. Tell how many hundreds, tens, and ones. Help your child tell what number comes after each number.

Community Connection

Look for three-digit numbers on buildings and signs. Read the numbers aloud. Then have your child tell you a number that is more or less.

Visit our Web site. www.parent.mathsurf.com

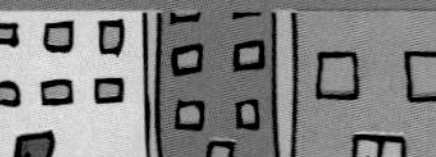

Name

Explore Hundreds

Explore

Show 100 using [tens rod].

Share

How many [ones cubes] do you need to show 100?

How many [tens rod] do you need to show 100?

Notes for Home: Your child explored making 100. *Home Activity:* Help your child explore other ways to show 100, for example, using 10 dimes to show 100 cents.

EXPLORE

Connect

10 tens

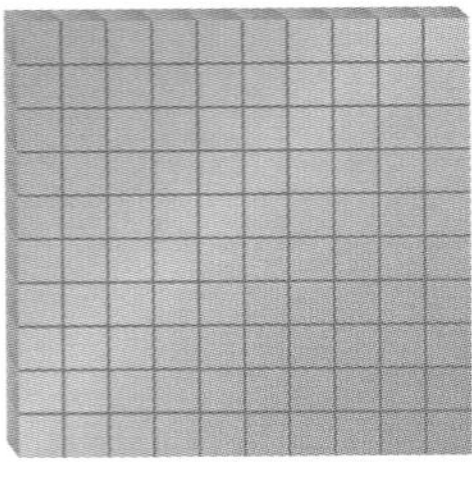

100

Write how many hundreds.
Write the number.

	How many hundreds?	Write the number.
1	2 hundreds	200
2	___ hundreds	___
3	___ hundreds	___
4	___ hundreds	___
5	___ hundreds	___
6	___ hundreds	___

Journal

7 Write five things you know about 100.

Notes for Home: Your child wrote how many hundreds and the number for different hundreds.
Home Activity: Ask your child how many hundreds are in 900. (9)

EXPLORE

Name

Identify Hundreds

Learn

Check

Use [hundreds block] to complete the chart.

	Show this many. Write the number.	Show 100 less. Write the number.	Show 100 more. Write the number.
1	[2 hundreds blocks] 200	100	300
2	[3 hundreds blocks] ____	____	____
3	[4 hundreds blocks] ____	____	____

Talk About It What pattern do you see in the chart?

Notes for Home: Your child showed groups of 100 and wrote the number for different hundreds.
Home Activity: Ask your child what numbers would be 100 less and 100 more than 500. (400, 600)

Practice

Use [hundred block] to complete the chart.

	Show this many. Write the number.	Show 200 less. Write the number.	Show 200 more. Write the number.
4	[5 hundred blocks] 500	300	700
5	[6 hundred blocks] ____	____	____
6	[7 hundred blocks] ____	____	____

Problem Solving Visual Thinking

7 Gina needs 800 beads.
Circle bags to show 800.

Notes for Home: Your child practiced writing numbers for groups of 100. *Home Activity:* Ask your child to write the number that is 200 less than 700 and 200 more than 400. (500, 600)

Name

Write Three-Digit Numbers

Learn

I count hundreds, tens, and ones. Then I write the number.

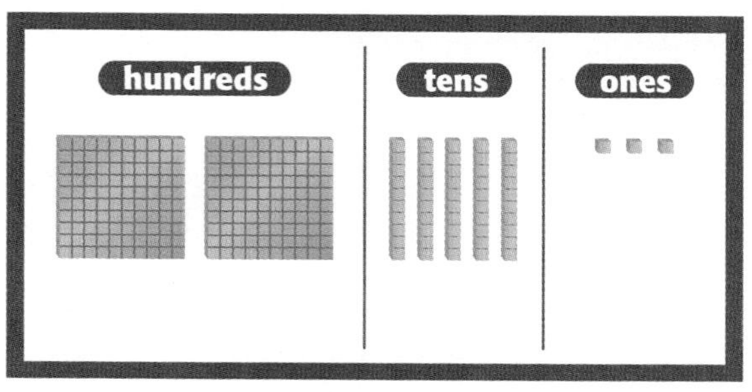

hundreds	tens	ones
2	5	3

253

two hundred fifty-three

Check

Use [place-value mat] and [blocks].

Write how many hundreds, tens, and ones. Then write the number.

1.

hundreds	tens	ones
3	2	4

324

2.

hundreds	tens	ones

______

3.

hundreds	tens	ones

______

4.

hundreds	tens	ones

______

Talk About It What does the 3 stand for in each number?

386 **138** **423**

Notes for Home: Your child wrote three-digit numbers. *Home Activity:* Ask your child what the 2 in 324 stands for. (2 tens)

Practice

Write how many hundreds, tens, and ones. Write the number.

You can use 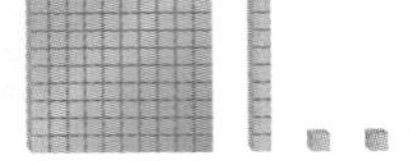 and ▦ ▮ ▪ ▪.

5 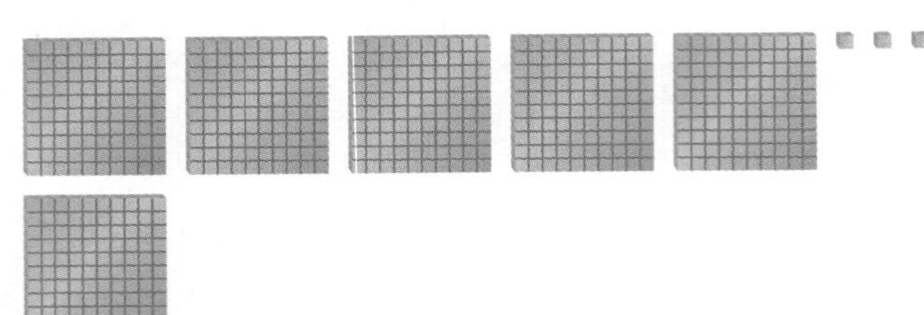

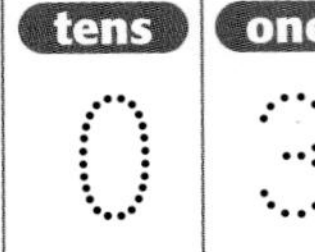

hundreds	tens	ones
6	0	3

603

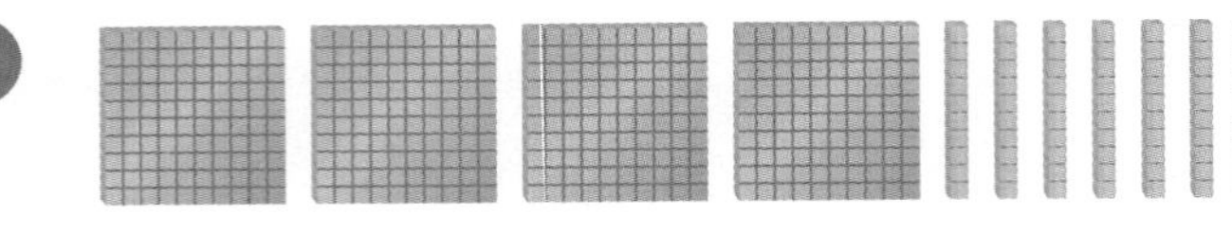

6 

hundreds	tens	ones

____

7 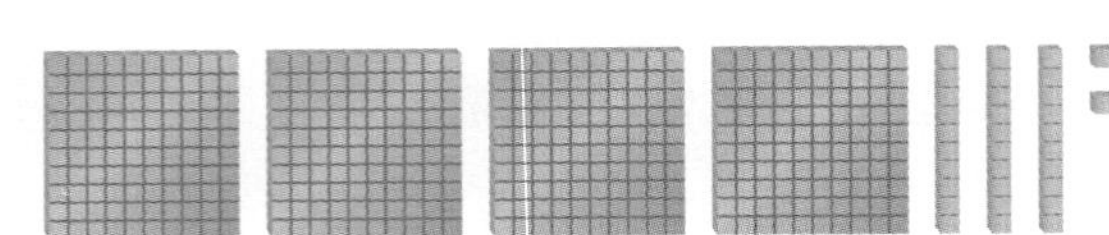

hundreds	tens	ones

____

Write your own. Choose your own number. Draw the ▦ ▮ ▪ ▪. Then write the number.

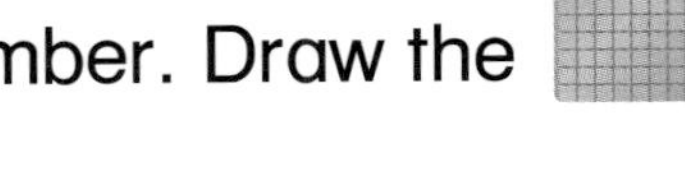

8 

hundreds	tens	ones

____

Problem Solving Patterns

Find each answer. What patterns do you see?

9 How many ▦ in 500? _______

How many ▮ in 500? _______

How many ▪ ▪ in 500? _______

10 How many 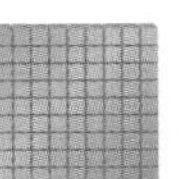 in 700? _______

How many ▮ in 700? _______

How many ▪ ▪ in 700? _______

Notes for Home: Your child practiced writing three-digit numbers. *Home Activity:* Help your child find a three-digit number on a package, can, or jar. Ask him or her to tell how many hundreds, tens, and ones are in the number.

PRACTICE

Name

Before, After, Between

Learn

Check

Write the missing numbers.

1

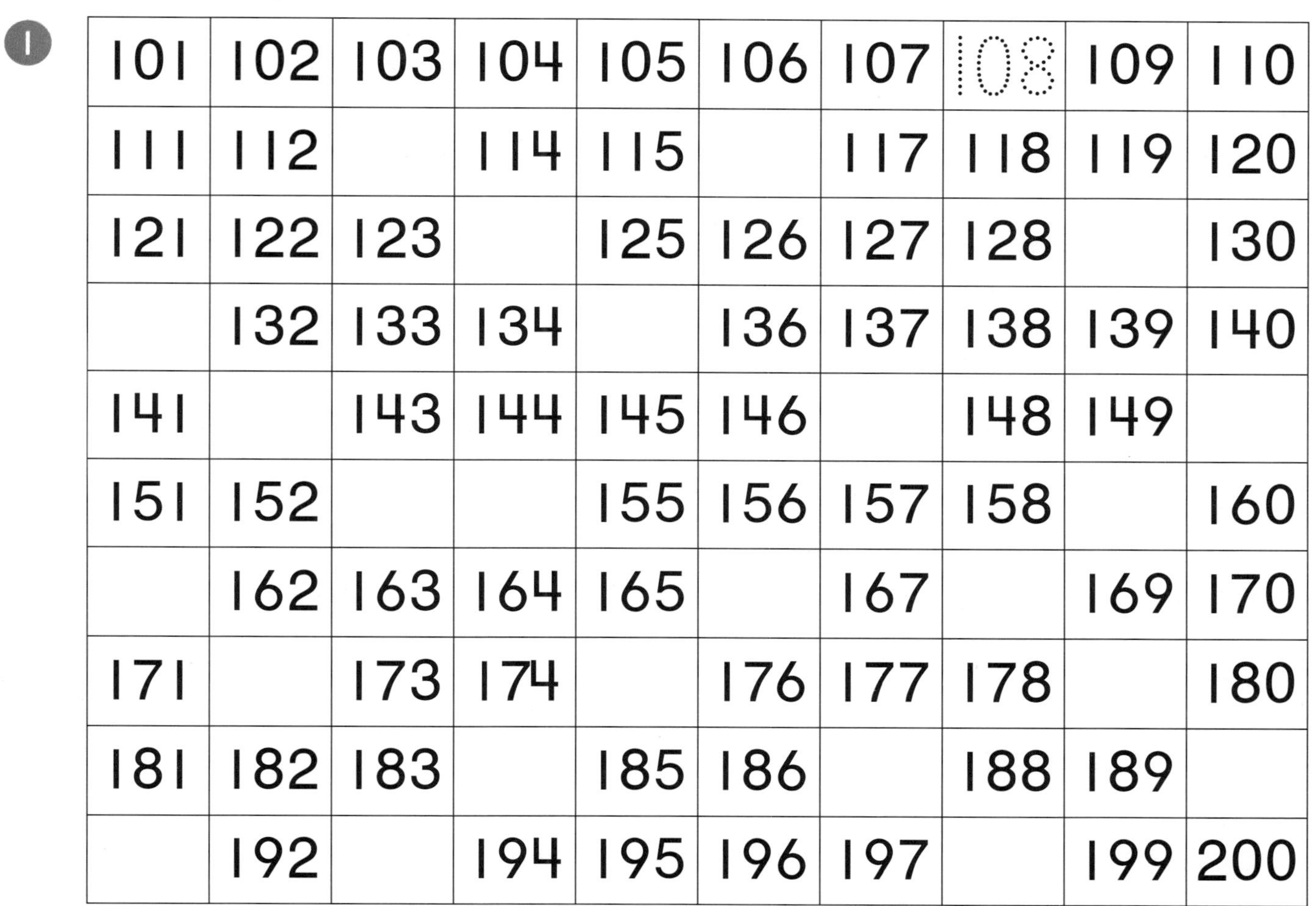

101	102	103	104	105	106	107	108	109	110
111	112		114	115		117	118	119	120
121	122	123		125	126	127	128		130
	132	133	134		136	137	138	139	140
141		143	144	145	146		148	149	
151	152			155	156	157	158		160
	162	163	164	165		167		169	170
171		173	174		176	177	178		180
181	182	183		185	186		188	189	
	192		194	195	196	197		199	200

Talk About It What would the numbers be in the row that would come after 200? What would the numbers be in the row that would come before 101?

Notes for Home: Your child identified numbers that are before, after, and between other numbers. *Home Activity:* Point to a three-digit number. Ask your child to say the numbers that come one before and one after.

Practice

Write the number that comes one before.

2. 184, 185 ____, 131 ____, 116

3. ____, 243 ____, 653 ____, 500

4. ____, 524 ____, 187 ____, 469

Write the number that comes one after.

5. 419, 420 721, ____ 199, ____

6. 112, ____ 578, ____ 989, ____

7. 84, ____ 344, ____ 636, ____

Write the number that comes between.

8. 118, 119, 120 299, ____, 301

9. 350, ____, 352 224, ____, 226

10. 541, ____, 543 695, ____, 697

Problem Solving

11. Write all the even numbers between 340 and 360.

342, 344, ____________________

____

Notes for Home: Your child practiced identifying numbers that are one before, one after, and between other numbers. *Home Activity:* Pick a number between 100 and 200. Ask your child to say the two numbers that the number they picked is between.

PRACTICE

Name

Compare Numbers

Learn

Betty sells hundreds of beads.
She sold 250 large beads.
She sold 175 small beads.
Did she sell more large or small beads?

She sold more  beads.

Symbols can be used to compare numbers.

250 > 175
250 is greater than 175.

175 < 250
175 is less than 250.

250 = 250
250 is equal to 250.

Check

Compare each number.
Write >, <, or =.

1. 423  353   501  489   380  380
2. 141 ◯ 241   677 ◯ 712   447 ◯ 399
3. 168 ◯ 168   750 ◯ 570   126 ◯ 216

Talk About It How would you compare 361 and 327?

Notes for Home: Your child used symbols to compare numbers. *Home Activity:* Ask your child to write the numbers 561 and 651 and then write the symbol to compare the numbers. (561 < 651)

Practice

Compare the numbers.
Write >, <, or =.

> is greater than
< is less than
= is equal to

If the number of hundreds are the same, compare the tens. 2 tens is less than 7 tens.

4. 432 ○ 454   631 ○ 613

5. 327 ○ 516   823 ○ 832

6. 240 ○ 212   409 ○ 409

Write your own. Make true statements.
Use numbers between 200 and 300.

7. ______ > ______   8. ______ > ______

9. ______ < ______   10. ______ < ______

11. ______ = ______   12. ______ = ______

Problem Solving Critical Thinking

Solve the riddle.

13. I am a number less than 345 and greater than 340.
I have 2 ones.
What number am I?

______

14. Write a riddle about a number.
Have a friend solve your riddle.

______

______

______

Notes for Home: Your child practiced comparing numbers. *Home Activity:* Ask your child to pick two numbers between 100 and 999. Ask your child to write the two numbers with a "greater than" or "less than" symbol.

For additional practice, see Skills Practice Bank, page 536, Set 1.

Name ______________________________

Order Numbers

Learn

A book's table of contents has numbers. The numbers tell the order of the pages.

These numbers are in order from least to greatest.

312, 329, 336, 340, 351

These numbers are in order from greatest to least.

351, 340, 336, 329, 312

Check

Write the numbers in order from least to greatest.

1. 140, 235, 318, 96, 421

   96, 140, ______, ______, ______

2. 

   ______, ______, ______, ______, ______

Write the numbers in order from greatest to least.

3. 

   690, ______, ______, ______, ______

Talk About It Where would you put 602 in this list of numbers? Why?

202 502 702 902

Notes for Home: Your child put numbers in order. *Home Activity:* Ask your child to order 160, 43, 215, 189, and 300 from least to greatest. (43, 160, 189, 215, 300)

Practice

Write the numbers in order from least to greatest.

4. 119, 93, 125, 201   93, ____, ____, ____

5. 296, 228, 252, 283   ____, ____, ____, ____

Write the numbers in order from greatest to least.

6. 348, 220, 464, 732   732, ____, ____, ____

7. 605, 973, 751, 489   ____, ____, ____, ____

8. 245, 217, 273, 229   ____, ____, ____, ____

Write your own.

9. List four numbers in order from least to greatest. Choose numbers between 400 and 500. ____, ____, ____, ____

10. List four numbers in order from greatest to least. Choose numbers between 600 and 800. ____, ____, ____, ____

PRACTICE

Problem Solving Estimation

11. These stacks of paper are for the art class. Draw lines to match each number to a stack. Then write the numbers in order from least to greatest.

____, ____, ____, ____

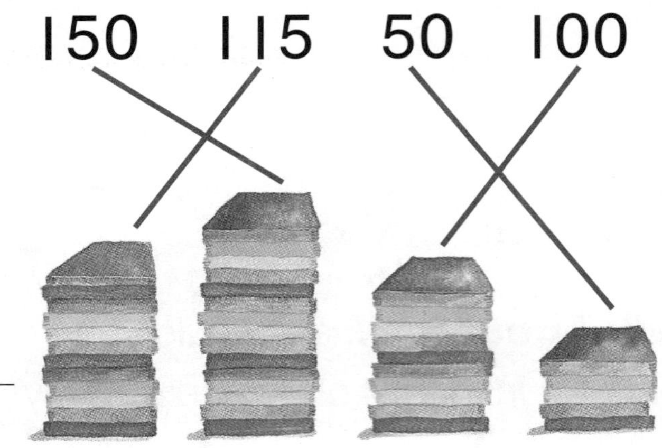

Notes for Home: Your child practiced putting numbers in order. *Home Activity:* Ask your child where he or she would place 255 in Exercise 5. (between 252 and 283)

Name

Problem Solving: Group Decision Making

Learn

PROBLEM SOLVING GUIDE

Understand • Plan • Solve • Look Back

Understand what the problem asks.

Plan how to solve the problem.

Solve the problem.

Look back to check your work.

Use this guide to help you solve problems.

Check

Work with your group to solve the problem. Use the Problem Solving Guide.

1. Grove School sold 74 tickets to the craft fair.
   38 people came in the front door.
   27 people came in the side door.
   How many people bought tickets but did not come?

   Understand What does the problem ask? How many people bought tickets but did not come to the fair?

   Plan How can you solve the problem? ______

   Solve Solve the problem. ______

   Look Back Check your work. ______

Talk About It How did having a guide help your group solve the problem?

Notes for Home: Your child worked with a group and learned how to use the Problem Solving Guide. *Home Activity:* Ask your child to think of another way to solve the story problem on this page.

Practice

Work with your group to solve the problem.

2 Allison and Emma are selling beads at the craft fair.
Emma has 47 beads to sell.
Allison has 36 beads.
Together they sell 29 beads.
How many beads do Allison and Emma have now?

Understand What does the problem ask? How many beads do Allison and Emma have now?

Plan How can you solve the problem? ______________________

Solve Solve the problem. ______________________

Look Back Check your work. ______________________

Write About It

3 Work as a group to write a problem for another group to solve.

____

____

____

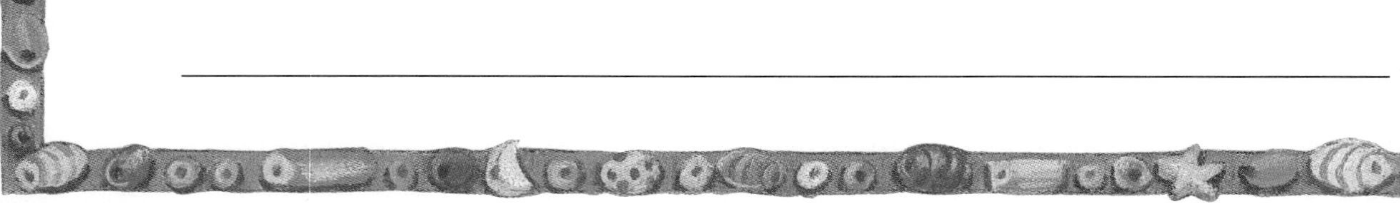

Notes for Home: Your child practiced using the Problem Solving Guide. *Home Activity:* Ask your child how he or she can check the answer to the story problem.

PROBLEM SOLVING

Name

Mixed Practice

Lessons 1–7

Concepts and Skills

Write 100 less and 100 more. You can use 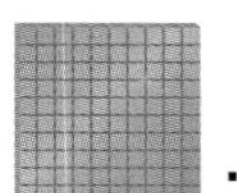 .

	Show this many. Write the number.	Show 100 less. Write the number.	Show 100 more. Write the number.
1	______	______	______

Write how many hundred, tens, and ones. Then write the number.

 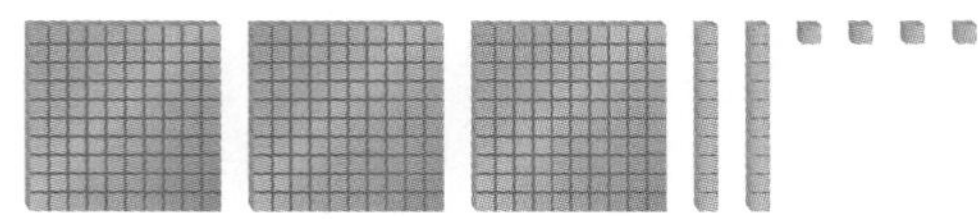

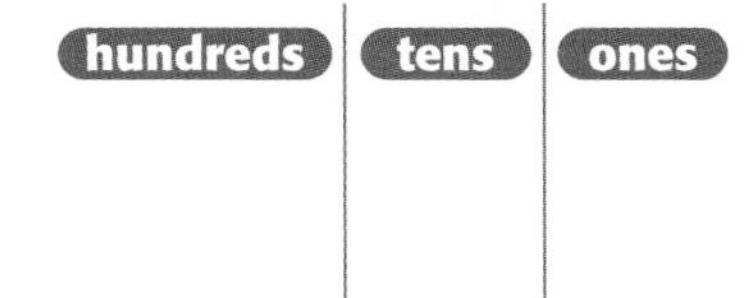

______

Write the number one before, one after, or between.

3 ______, 132   829, ______   499, ______, 501

Compare. Write >, <, or =.

4 650 ◯ 610   330 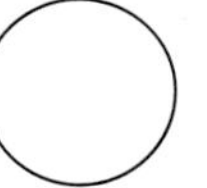 330   897 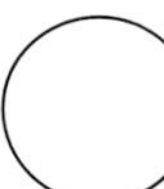 905

Problem Solving

Solve. Use the Problem Solving Guide to help.

5 Lee bought a bag of 50 colored tiles. Later he bought 30 more tiles. He used 62 tiles. How many tiles does he have left? ______ tiles

Journal

6 Think of another way to solve the problem. Write about it.

Notes for Home: Your child practiced writing and comparing three-digit numbers. *Home Activity:* Ask your child to tell you the number one before 132 and the number one after 829. (131, 830)

MIXED PRACTICE

Name ______________________________

Cumulative Review

Chapters 1-10

Concepts and Skills

Count the money.

Write the total amount.

1

______¢

Problem Solving

Use the graph to answer the questions.

2 How many more cards does Calvin have than Lamar?

______ more

3 How many cards do Calvin, Lamar, and Kim have together?

______ cards

Card Collections	
Calvin	
Lamar	
Kim	

Each  means 10 cards.

Test Prep

Fill in the ○ for the correct answer.

Subtract.

4

$$\begin{array}{r} 90 \\ -\ 25 \\ \hline \end{array}$$

55 ○ 65 ○ 75 ○ 115 ○

5

$$\begin{array}{r} 57 \\ -\ 30 \\ \hline \end{array}$$

17 ○ 27 ○ 37 ○ 87 ○

Notes for Home: Your child reviewed counting money, using a graph to solve problems, and subtracting. from earlier chapters. *Home Activity:* Ask your child to look at the graph and tell how many more cards Lamar has than Kim. (20 more)

Name ______________________

That's Sum Toss!

Players 2

What You Need

2 number cubes 

How to Play

1. Toss the number cubes.
2. Use your toss to make a two-digit number. Write it on your chart.
3. Toss again. Write the number.
4. Add the numbers.
5. Take turns. For your next turns, toss the number cubes once. Write the number and add it to the last sum.
6. After 6 turns, the player with the greatest sum wins.

	hundreds	tens	ones
+			
+			
+			
+			
+			
+			

PRACTICE

Notes for Home: Your child played an addition game. *Home Activity:* Ask your child to think of a three-digit number and add it to the last sum on this page.

Name ______________________

Write how many hundreds, tens, and ones. Then write the number.

1 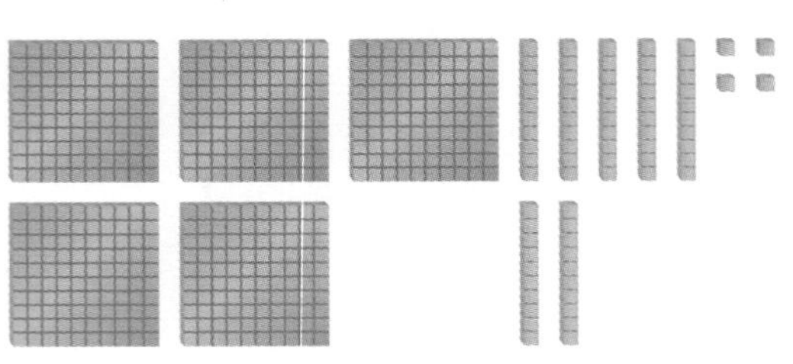

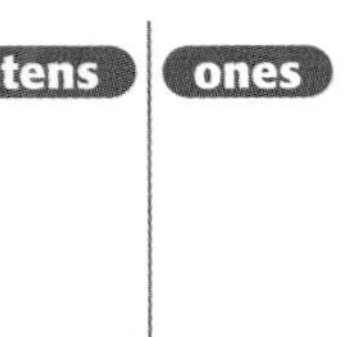

______

Write the number that comes one before, one after, or between.

2 ______, 300 499, ______ 769, ______, 771

Compare. Write >, <, or =.

3 736 ◯ 763 981 ◯ 918 515 ◯ 515

Add or subtract. Use mental math.

4

100	400	60	40	600
+ 600	+ 200	+ 20	− 20	− 100

Add. Regroup if you need to. You can use  and .

5

532	439	480	340	608
+ 134	+ 22	+ 182	+ 430	+ 82

Riddle

6 Solve.

I'm less than 125 and greater than 120.

Add 100 to me and all my digits are the same.

What number am I? ______

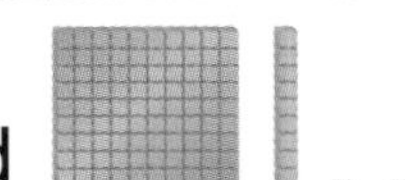

Notes for Home: Your child practiced writing, comparing, adding, and subtracting numbers.
Home Activity: Ask your child to add 300 + 400. (700)

PRACTICE

Name

Subtract Three-Digit Numbers

Learn

The craft store had 657 rolls of yarn in January.
523 rolls were sold during the year.
How many rolls were left at the end of the year?

Subtract the ones first. Then subtract the tens and the hundreds.

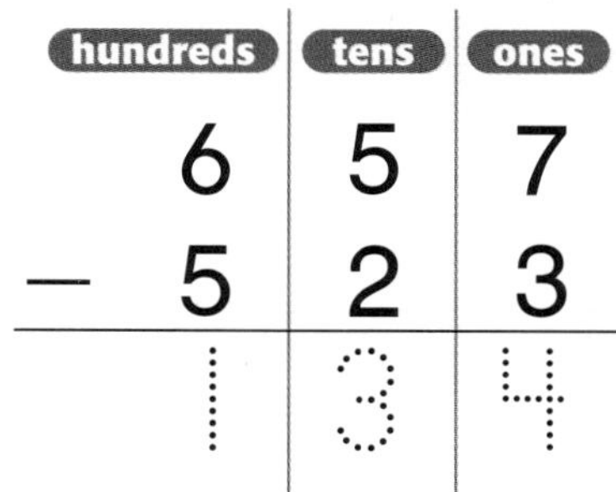

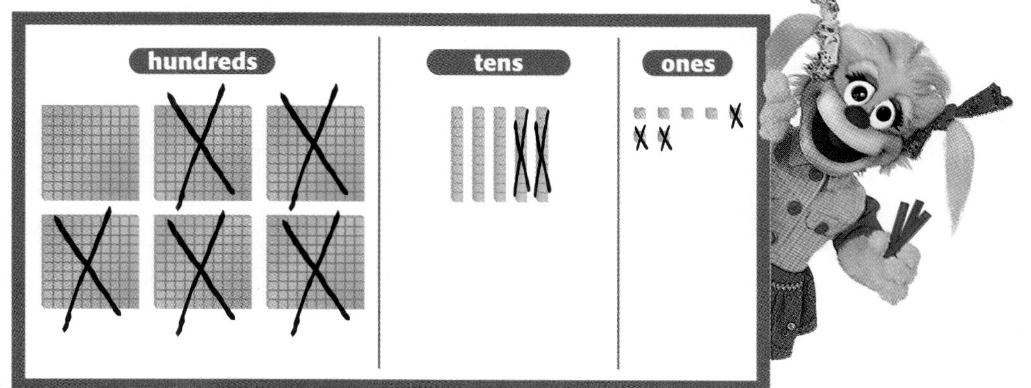

134 rolls are left.

Check

Use [place-value mat] and [hundreds, tens, ones blocks]. Subtract.

1

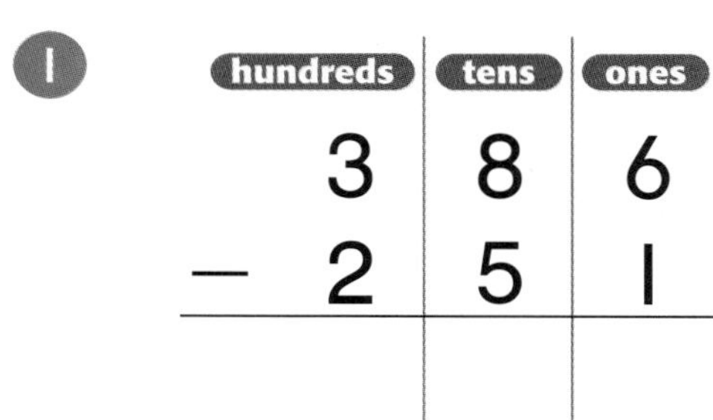

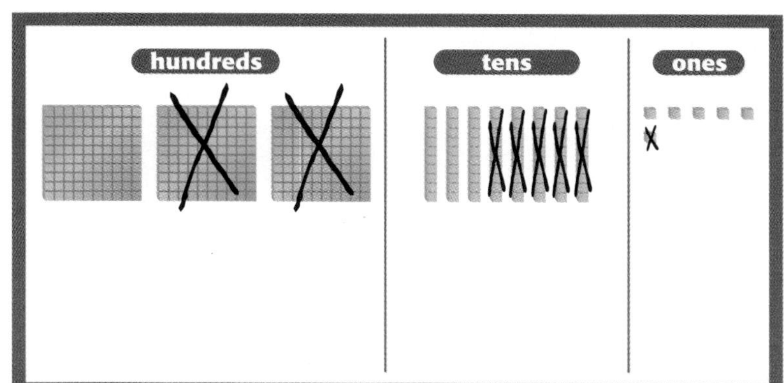

2

	hundreds	tens	ones
	7	2	6
−	1	1	4

	hundreds	tens	ones
	5	8	9
−	4	1	6

	hundreds	tens	ones
	6	9	5
−	1	3	2

Talk About It How is subtracting three-digit numbers like subtracting two-digit numbers?

Notes for Home: Your child learned how to subtract two three–digit numbers without regrouping.
Home Activity: Ask your child to explain how to find the answer to 350-200.

Practice

Show each number. Subtract. You can use  and 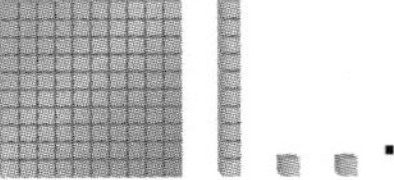.

3

hundreds	tens	ones
5	3	9
− 2	3	5
3	0	4

hundreds	tens	ones
6	2	5
− 4	1	3

hundreds	tens	ones
9	8	5
− 4	0	4

4

$679 - 151$ $487 - 237$ $389 - 64$ $573 - 120$ $759 - 52$

5

$574 - 301$ $215 - 102$ $695 - 12$ $728 - 315$ $956 - 412$

Write About It

6 Use this subtraction problem to write a math story. Then solve.

$796 - 531$

Notes for Home: Your child practiced subtracting three-digit numbers without regrouping. *Home Activity:* Ask your child to write another math story using the problem in Exercise 6.

PRACTICE

Name

Subtract Three-Digit Numbers With or Without Regrouping

Learn

Subtract 427 − 173.

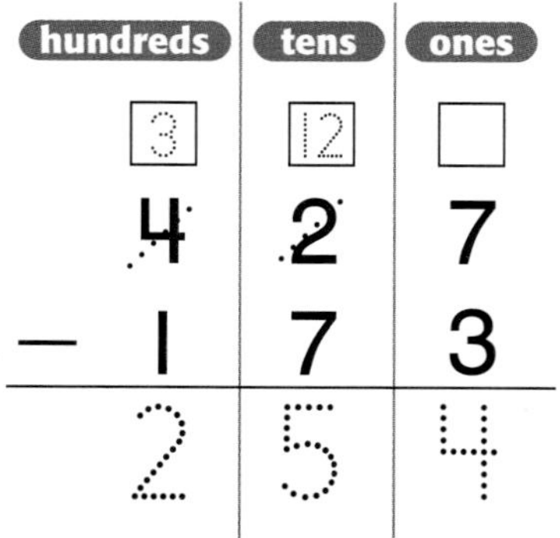

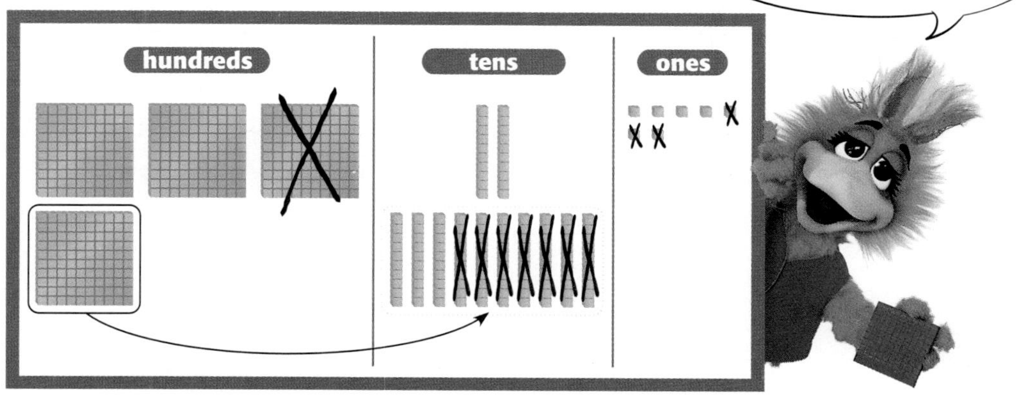

Check

Use [place-value mat] and [blocks].

Subtract. Regroup if you need to.

1

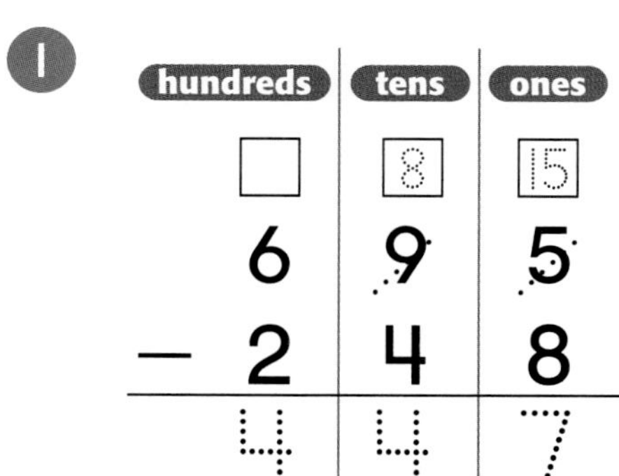

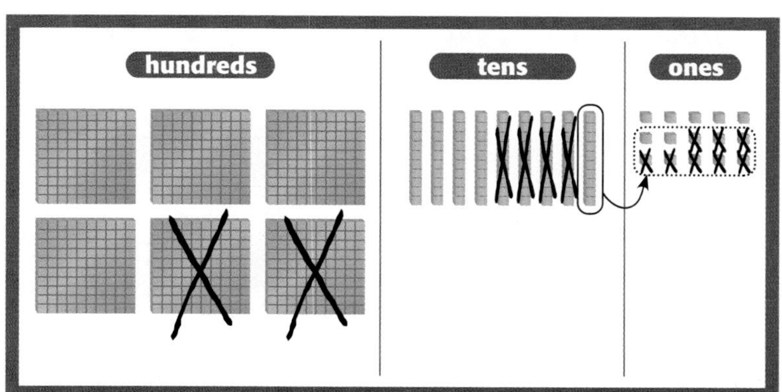

2

hundreds	tens	ones
7	4	5
− 5	3	1

hundreds	tens	ones
5	2	9
− 2	8	3

hundreds	tens	ones
4	6	1
− 2	5	3

Talk About It How are these problems alike? How are they different?

$$\begin{array}{r} 374 \\ -\ 120 \\ \hline \end{array} \qquad \begin{array}{r} 374 \\ -\ 129 \\ \hline \end{array}$$

Notes for Home: Your child learned how to subtract two three-digit numbers with regrouping.
Home Activity: Have your child show you how to find: 827 − 319. (508)

Practice

Subtract. Regroup if you need to. You can use 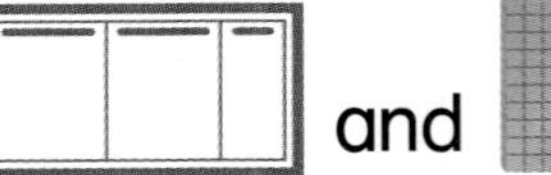 and .

3

hundreds	tens	ones
	2	17
5	3	7
− 3	1	9
2	1	8

hundreds	tens	ones
7	2	1
− 4	1	4

hundreds	tens	ones
4	2	9
− 1	6	1

4 $645 - 218$ $\quad 589 - 16$ $\quad 741 - 230$ $\quad 846 - 92$ $\quad 957 - 427$

5 $759 - 613$ $\quad 537 - 64$ $\quad 372 - 158$ $\quad 450 - 310$ $\quad 725 - 91$

Problem Solving Critical Thinking

6 You need to regroup.
What numbers could you
write in the boxes?

hundreds	tens	ones
5	☐	7
+ 2	4	☐

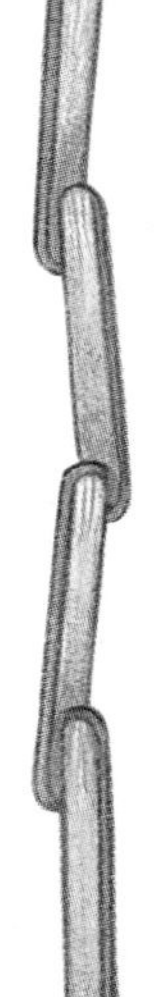

7 You do not need to regroup.
What numbers could you
write in the boxes?

hundreds	tens	ones
5	☐	7
+ 2	4	☐

Notes for Home: Your child practiced subtracting three-digit numbers with and without regrouping . *Home Activity:* Ask your child to write a three-digit subtraction problem that needs regrouping and show you how to solve it.

For additional practice, see Skills Practice Bank, page 536, Set 2.

Name ______________________________

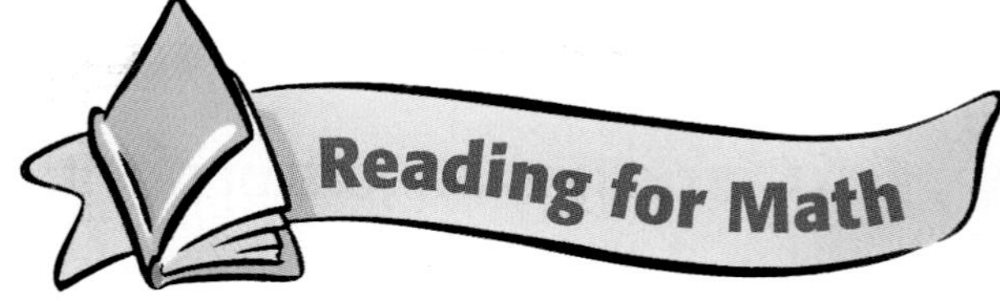

Use Picture Clues

James is shopping for art supplies.
Can you help him find what he needs?

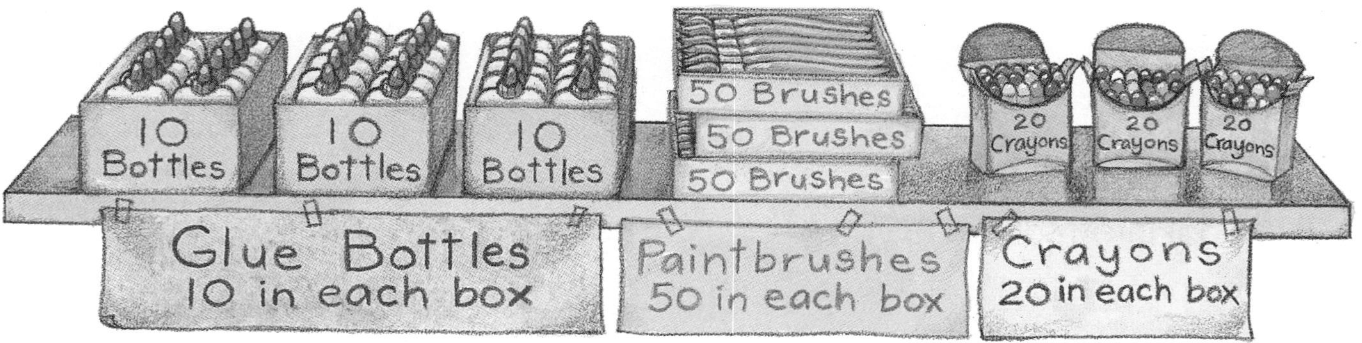

Use the picture to answer the questions.

1. James buys two boxes of glue. How many bottles of glue does he buy?

   ______ bottles

2. How many paint brushes are on the shelf?

   ______ paintbrushes

3. How many crayons are in the picture?

   ______ crayons

4. James needs 40 crayons. Circle 40 crayons in the picture.

5. James wants 150 paintbrushes. How many boxes does he need?

   ______ boxes

6. James buys two boxes of crayons. How many crayons are left on the shelf?

   ______ crayons

Talk About It How did the pictures help you find each of the answers above?

Notes for Home: Your child used details in a picture to answer questions. *Home Activity:* Ask your child how many bottles of glue are in 3 boxes. (30 bottles)

Carrie has 30 jars of paint. She buys 2 more boxes of paint.
How many jars of paint does she have in all?

7. What information do you need from the picture to solve the problem?

____

____

____

____

8. Solve. ______ jars of paint

9. Use the above picture to write a problem. Have a friend solve it.

____

____

____

____

Journal

10. Write about how the picture helped you solve the problems.

Notes for Home: Your child solved a story problem using pictures and addition. *Home Activity:* Ask your child how many colored stones he or she would have in two bags. (400 colored stones)

Name

Problem Solving: Use Data from a Picture

Learn

PROBLEM SOLVING GUIDE

Understand • Plan • Solve • Look Back

You need 250 craft sticks for a project. Which bins could you use? Circle your answer.

Check

Use the picture to answer the questions.

1. Gregory needs 270 colored stones for an art project. Which bags could he use? Circle them in red.

2. Luisa needs 250 stones. Which bags could she use? Circle them in blue.

3. Walt used two bag of stones that each had less than 100. How many stones did he use?

   ______ stones

Talk About It Which other bags of stones could Luisa use?

Notes for Home: Your child used the pictures on this page to solve problems. *Home Activity:* Ask your child to make up his or her own problem using some of the pictures on this page.

Practice

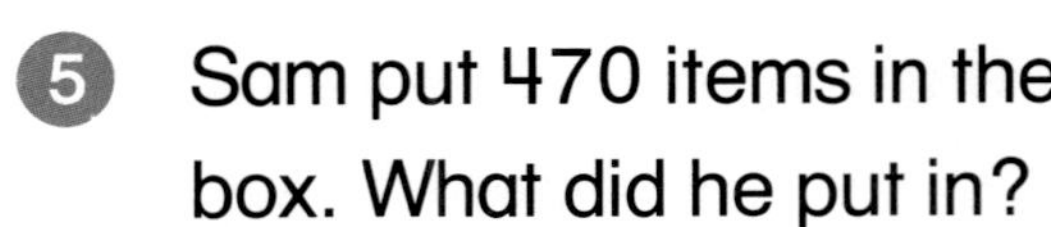

Use the picture to answer the questions.
The box can hold up to 500 items.

4. Jean puts the bin of buttons in the box. What else can she put in?

   craft sticks

5. Sam put 470 items in the box. What did he put in?

   ______

6. Elise put the felt shapes in the box. What else can she put in?

   ______

7. Lucy put 400 items in the box. What did she put in?

   ______

Derrick puts 480 items in the box.
What items did he put in the box?
Give two possible combinations.

8. ______

9. ______

Critical Thinking

10. Are there 3 bins that could be put in the box together? Explain your answer.

Notes for Home: Your child used the numbers in this picture to solve problems.
Home Activity: Ask your child which two items add to make 560. (the buttons and the felt shapes)

PROBLEM SOLVING

For additional practice, see Skills Practice Bank, page 536, Set 3.

Name

Mixed Practice

Lessons 8–13

Concepts and Skills

Add or subtract. Use mental math.

1	300	400	70	600	33
	+ 200	+ 500	− 20	− 300	+ 44

Add or subtract. Regroup if you need to.

2	253	837	394	754	842
	+ 34	− 184	+ 255	− 34	+ 128

MIXED PRACTICE

Problem Solving

Use the picture to answer the questions.

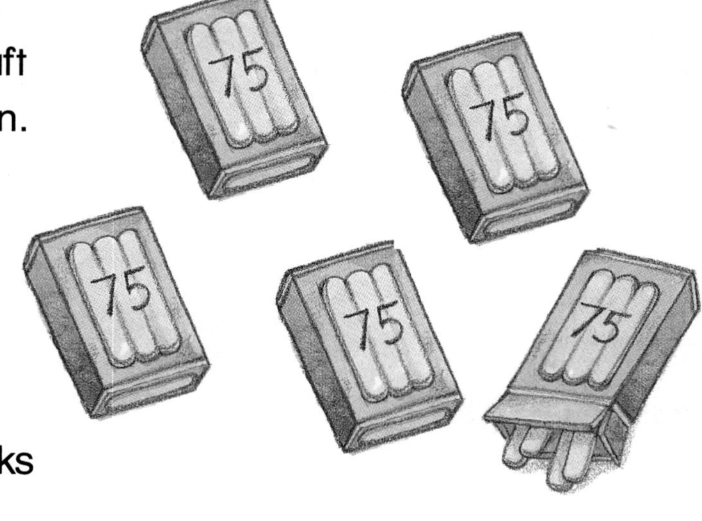

3 Wayne and his father need 375 craft sticks to build a model of a log cabin. How many boxes of craft sticks do they need?

_____ boxes of craft sticks

4 Donald has 3 boxes of craft sticks. How many more boxes of craft sticks does he need to build a model that uses 525 craft sticks?

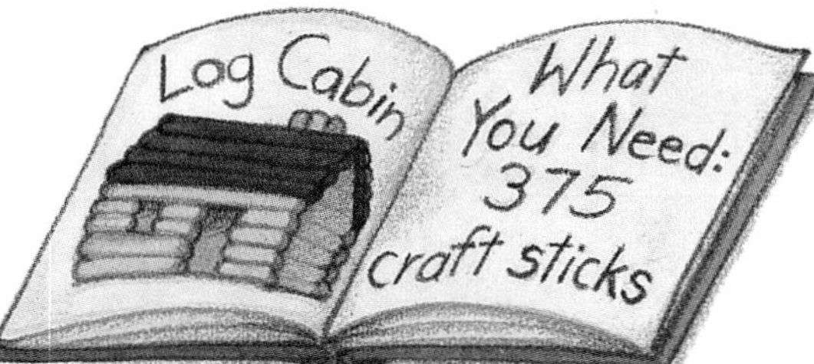

_____ more boxes of craft sticks

Journal

5 How did the pictures help you answer the questions about building model log cabins? Write about it.

Notes for Home: Your child practiced adding and subtracting numbers and solving problems.
Home Activity: Ask your child how many craft sticks there would be in 2 boxes. (150 craft sticks)

Name ______________________________

Cumulative Review

Chapters 1–10

Concepts and Skills

Write the number of tens and ones.

Then write the number.

_____ tens and _____ ones

_____

 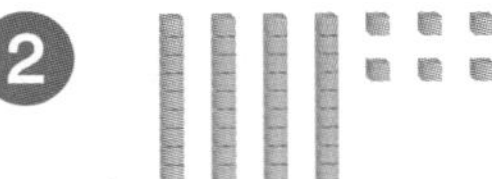

_____ tens and _____ ones

_____

Does the activity take more or less than one minute?

Circle **more** or **less.**

3 taking a bath

more **less**

4 reading a book

more **less**

5 pouring milk

more **less**

6 raking leaves

more **less**

Test Prep

Fill in the ○ for the correct answer.

Add.

7
$$\begin{array}{r} 25¢ \\ +\ 13¢ \\ \hline \end{array}$$

38¢ ○ 28¢ ○ 12¢ ○ 48¢ ○

8
$$\begin{array}{r} 17¢ \\ +\ 35¢ \\ \hline \end{array}$$

32¢ ○ 42¢ ○ 47¢ ○ 52¢ ○

Notes for Home: Your child reviewed identifying and writing tens and ones, estimating if activities take more or less than one minute, and adding amounts of money. *Home Activity:* Ask your child to think of an activity that takes less than one minute and an activity that take more than one minute.

CUMULATIVE REVIEW

Name ______________________

Chapter 10 Review

Vocabulary

Choose from these words to complete each sentence.

greater than	less than	equal to

1. 216 is ____________ 261.
2. 425 is ____________ 385.

Concepts and Skills

Write how many hundreds, tens, and ones. Then write the number.

3. 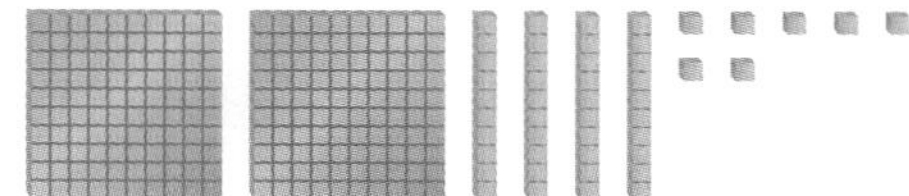

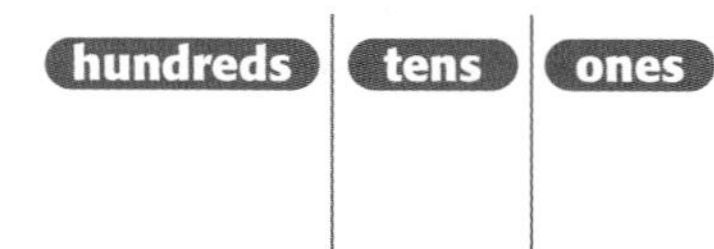

______

Compare the numbers. Write >, <, or =.

4. 294 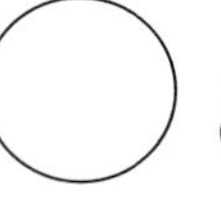 291 83 ◯ 83 516  519

Write the numbers in order from greatest to least.

5. 358, 704, 129, 816 ______, ______, ______, ______

6. Add or subtract. Use mental math.

$$\begin{array}{r} 70 \\ -\ 30 \\ \hline \end{array} \quad \begin{array}{r} 600 \\ +\ 100 \\ \hline \end{array} \quad \begin{array}{r} 400 \\ +\ 200 \\ \hline \end{array}$$

7. Add or subtract. Regroup if you need to.

$$\begin{array}{r} 804 \\ +\ 172 \\ \hline \end{array} \quad \begin{array}{r} 637 \\ -\ 475 \\ \hline \end{array} \quad \begin{array}{r} 418 \\ +\ 173 \\ \hline \end{array}$$

Problem Solving

Use the picture to answer the question.

8. Ms. Silva's class needs exactly 450 beads for a craft project. Circle the bags they could use.

Notes for Home: Your child reviewed Chapter 10 vocabulary, concepts, skills, and problem solving. *Home Activity:* Ask you child to find the bags in the picture that total 300. (Two bags of 150 each, or one bag of 125 and one bag of 175.)

Name ______________________

Chapter 10 Test

Write how many hundreds, tens, and ones. Then write the number.

 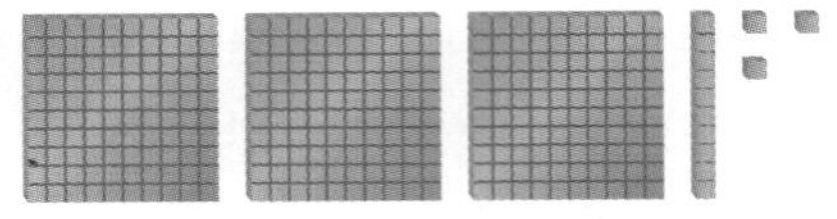

hundreds	tens	ones

______

Write the number that comes one before, one after, or between.

2 ______, 524 839, ______ 212, ______, 214

Compare the numbers. Write >, <, or =.

3 152 ◯ 152 734  741 695  692

Write the numbers in order from least to greatest.

4 514, 827, 279, 613 ______, ______, ______, ______

Add or subtract.
Use mental math.

5 $60 + 20$ $400 - 100$ $700 - 200$

Add or subtract.
Regroup if you need to.

 $524 + 123$ $842 - 224$ $317 + 435$

Use the picture to answer the question.

7 Mr. Simon's class needs exactly 425 colored stones for a craft project. Which bags could they use? Circle the bags.

125

Notes for Home: Your child was tested on Chapter 10 concepts, skills, and problem solving learned in Chapter 10. *Home Activity:* Ask your child to find the bags in the picture that total 525. (Two bags of 200 and one bag of 125.)

Name

Performance Assessment

Chapter 10

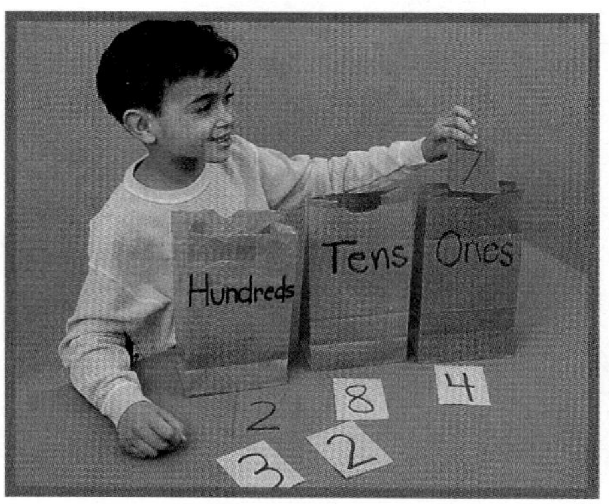

Pick 2 cards from each bag. Write your numbers.

Compare your numbers.

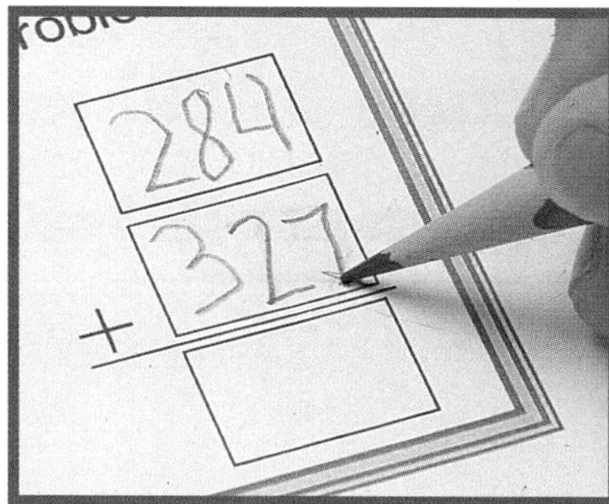

Write an addition problem. Solve.

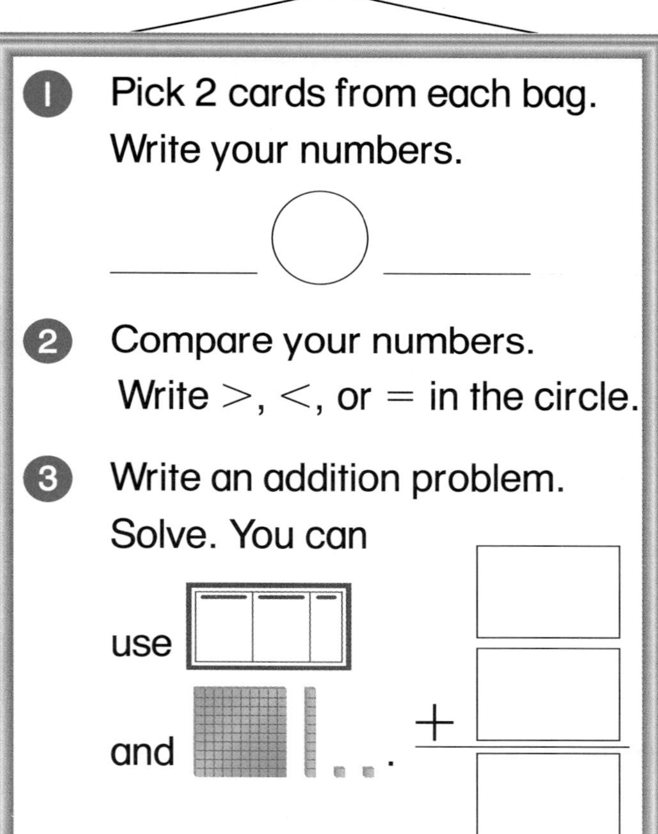

1. Pick 2 cards from each bag. Write your numbers.
2. Compare your numbers. Write >, <, or = in the circle.
3. Write an addition problem. Solve. You can use [place-value chart] and [blocks] . . .

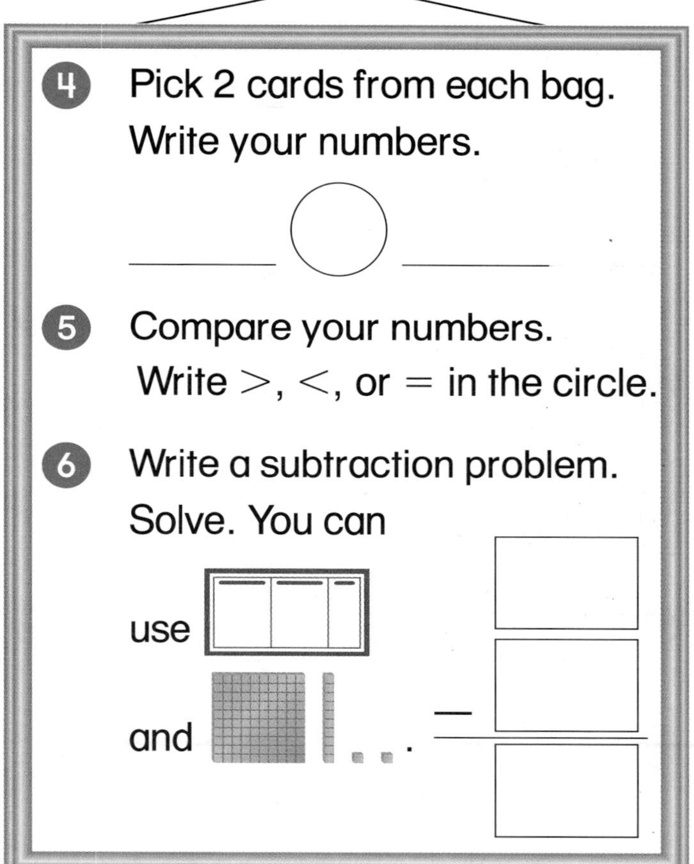

4. Pick 2 cards from each bag. Write your numbers.
5. Compare your numbers. Write >, <, or = in the circle.
6. Write a subtraction problem. Solve. You can use [place-value chart] and [blocks] . . .

Critical Thinking

7. Take all of the numbers out of the bags. Make an addition problem using 2 three-digit numbers with the greatest possible sum. Then use the numbers to make a problem with the smallest possible sum.

Notes for Home: Your child did an activity that tested Chapter 10 concepts, skills, and problem solving. *Home Activity:* Ask your child to think of two three-digit numbers below 500 and write an addition or subtraction problem using them.

Name ____________________

Picture 1,000!

Computer Skills You Will Need

1. Draw a small shape using your computer's drawing program.

2. Copy and paste your shape to make as many shapes as you can. Print your page.

3. How many shapes are on your page? ______ shapes

4. Use your [calculator]. Find the number of shapes one group in your class made.

5. Find the number of shapes your class made.

6. With your class, make a display of your shapes when they total 1,000.

Tech Talk How did you find the number of shapes your class made?

Visit our Web site. www.parent.mathsurf.com

Make a Mosaic

For many years, artists have used colored tiles to make works of art called **mosaics**.

Follow these steps to make a mosaic drawing or pattern.

1 Use a piece of grid paper and at least 3 different colors of crayons.

2 Color squares on the grid paper to make a picture or a pattern.

3 Find how many total squares are in your mosaic picture. Explain how you found out.

red
blue
yellow

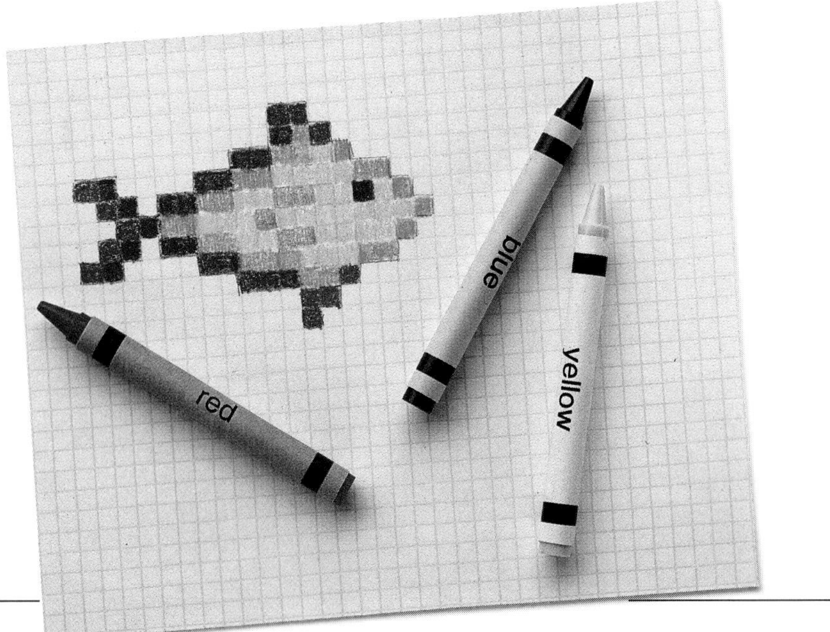

 Visit our Web site. www.parent.mathsurf.com

Fold down

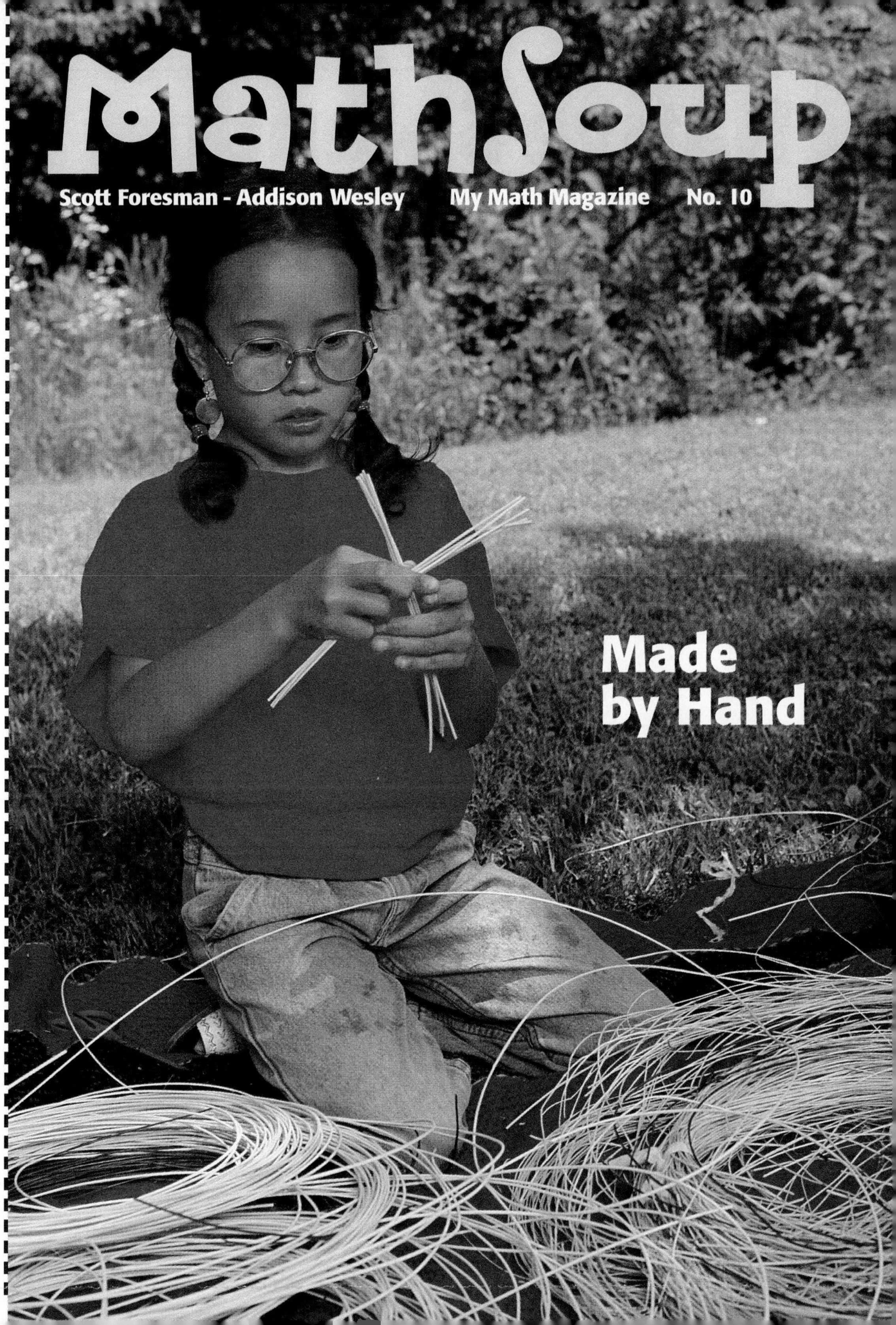
MathSoup
Scott Foresman - Addison Wesley My Math Magazine No. 10
Made
by Hand

Native Splendor

Bridget is a member of the Cherokee nation living in Oklahoma. Bridget's grandparents demonstrate crafts and skills at the Cherokee Heritage Center.

1 Bridget's grandmother weaves baskets using dried vines. To make one basket, she uses 110 vines. To make a second basket, she uses 175 vines. How many more vines does she use for the second basket?

_______ more vines

An art teacher wants to show children's pottery at Open House. The table shows how much pottery each grade made.

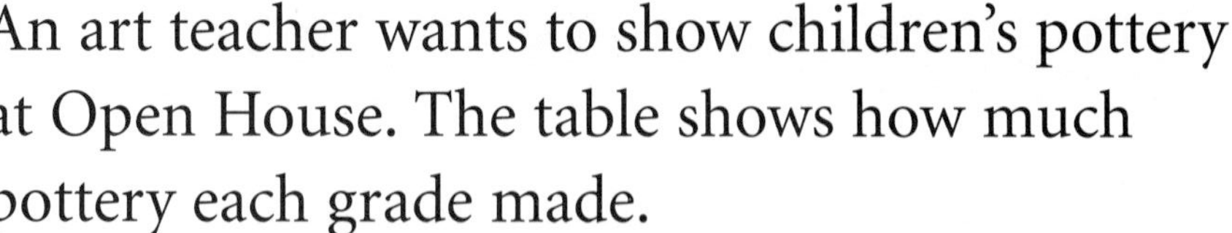

Grade	Pieces Made
1	89
2	117
3	131
4	119
5	142

1 Find the three largest numbers on the table. What is the total number of pieces made by these three grades?

____

2 Write the numbers of pieces made in order from least to greatest.

_______, _______, _______, _______, _______

Notes for Home: Your child practiced subtracting three-digit numbers.
Home Activity: Ask your child to find 415 – 290. (125)

Fired Up About Clay

Travis Owens doesn't study art only at school. He makes clay pottery at home with his mother and father.

A beautiful bowl takes many hours of hard work. First, Travis uses a potter's wheel to form a bowl. Then he lets the clay dry completely. Finally, Travis "fires," or bakes, the clay twice. A coating called glaze is put on the bowl when it is fired.

2 Bridget's grandmother also makes quilts. In January, she spent 125 hours working on a quilt. In February, she worked on the quilt for 115 more hours. How many hours did Bridget's grandmother work in 2 months?

________ hours

Notes for Home: Your child practiced ordering and adding three-digit numbers. *Home Activity:* Ask your child to add to find the total number of pieces made for all the grades. (598)

Patch Patterns

These quilts were made by African American quilters from small patches of cloth.

What patterns do you see? Use a pattern to make your own paper quilt!

What You Need

construction paper   scissors   glue

What You Do

1 Use colored construction paper to make paper patches this size.

2 Use 3 different colors. Cut out 7 squares from each color.

3 Find the answer for each problem. Use the code to match each answer to a color patch. Glue a color patch on top of each square.

Use the color patch shown for answers from:

401-500.

501-600.

601-700.

464 + 221	300 + 290	100 + 406	505 + 100
300 + 201	576 − 132	268 + 220	400 + 190
888 − 280	900 − 350	700 − 120	957 − 321

Notes for Home: Your child practiced adding, subtracting, and ordering three-digit numbers. *Home Activity:* Ask your child to put the following numbers in order from least to greatest: 563, 490, 679. (490, 563, 679)

CHAPTER 11
Measurement

Notes for Home: Your child told stories about size using objects in the picture.
Home Activity: Ask your child to tell a story about the sizes of things in his or her room.

Dear Family,
Our class is starting Chapter 11. We will be learning about measurement. Here are some activities we can do together.

Assistant Chef

When cooking or baking, ask your child to help you by measuring some of the ingredients, especially some of those that are measured with cups.

Measure It

Help your child use a ruler to measure various small household objects. Measure spaces to find if the space can be used to store a certain object.

Community Connection

When you are at the grocery store, help your child estimate how many pounds food items, such as apples, will weigh. Then let your child use a scale to see how much the items actually weigh.

Visit our Web site. **www.parent.mathsurf.com**

Name

Explore Nonstandard Units

Explore

Choose an object in your classroom to measure. Measure its length.

Choose a unit of measure.

Measure the same object with a different unit. Complete the chart.

	What I Measured	Unit of Measure	Measurement
1	______	______ ______	about ______ about ______
2	______	______ ______	about ______ about ______
3	______	______ ______	about ______ about ______

Share

Which units were easiest to use? Why?

Notes for Home: Your child used different objects to measure the lengths of objects in the classroom. *Home Activity:* Ask your child to measure the length of his or her bed with an object such as a spoon or straw.

EXPLORE

Connect

Estimate the lengths.
Use Snap Cubes to measure.
Write the numbers.

4

Estimate: about ______ Snap Cubes Measure: about ______ Snap Cubes

5
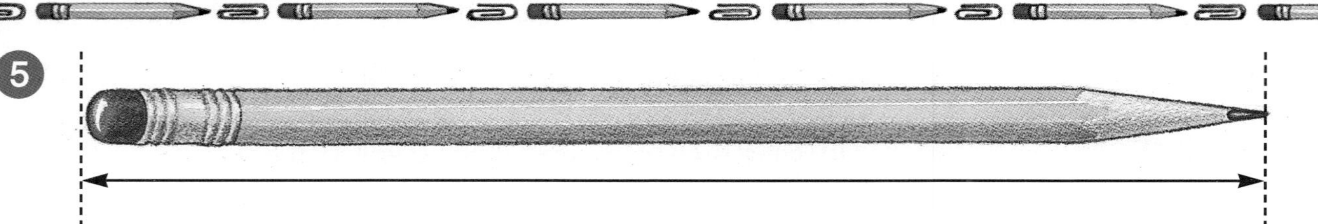

Estimate: about ______ Snap Cubes Measure: about ______ Snap Cubes

6
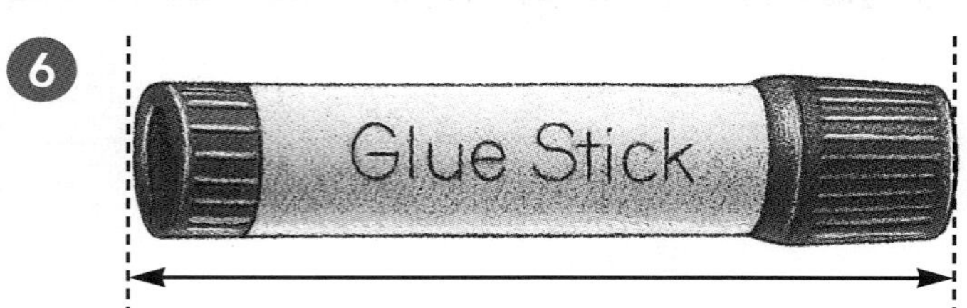

Estimate: about ______ Snap Cubes Measure: about ______ Snap Cubes

Problem Solving Critical Thinking

7 Pablo measured how tall he is.
First he measured with paper clips.
Then he measured with pencils.

Did Pablo need more paper clips or more pencils? Explain.

Notes for Home: Your child estimated and measured the lengths of objects using Snap Cubes. *Home Activity:* Ask your child to use a paper clip or another similar object to measure the lengths of objects in the kitchen.

EXPLORE

Name

Inches and Feet

Learn

The piece of paper
is about 1 inch long.

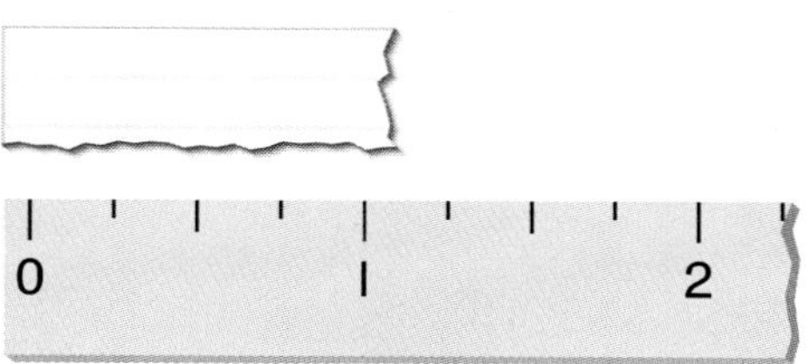

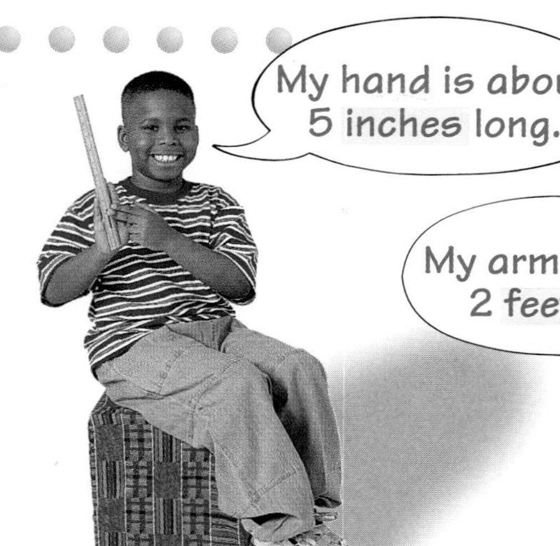

Check

Estimate the length in inches. Measure with your inch ruler.

1	length of your shoe	about ______ inches	about ______ inches

Estimate the length or height in feet. Measure with your yardstick.

	What to Measure	Estimate	Measurement
2	a friend's height	about ______ feet	about ______ feet
3	a friend's arm span	about ______ feet	about ______ feet

Talk About It What are two more objects you would measure using inches? using feet? Explain.

Notes for Home: Your child learned how to measure length and height in inches and feet.
Home Activity: Ask your child to measure the lengths of your arm, foot, arm span, and height using inches or feet.

Practice

Estimate about how many inches.
Measure with your inch ruler.

	What to Measure	Estimate	Measurement
4	length of your finger	about ______ inches	about ______ inches

Estimate about how many feet.
Measure with your yardstick.

	What to Measure	Estimate	Measurement
5	length of your arm	about ______ feet	about ______ feet

PRACTICE

Write your own.

Draw or write what you will measure.
Use inches or feet to measure.

	What You Will Measure	Estimate	Measurement
6		about ____________	about ____________

Problem Solving Visual Thinking

7 Look at the two pieces of ribbon. Circle the piece of ribbon you think is longer. Explain. You can use string to check.

Notes for Home: Your child practiced estimating and measuring lengths in inches and feet. *Home Activity:* Ask your child to estimate and measure the length of an object in inches or feet and tell you the measurement.

Name

Inches, Feet, and Yards

Learn

Yuko just completed a jump.
She wants to find out how long it is.
She can measure length in inches, feet, and yards.

Check

Work with a partner. Use an inch ruler and a yardstick.

1. Find how many inches are in 1 foot.

   There are 12 inches in 1 foot.

2. Find how many inches are in 2 feet.

   There are ______ inches in 2 feet.

3. Find how many inches are in 3 feet.

   There are ______ inches in 3 feet.

4. Find how many feet are in 1 yard.

   There are ______ feet in 1 yard.

Talk About It How did you find the number of inches in 1 foot? the number of feet in 1 yard?

Notes for Home: Your child investigated inches, feet, and yards. *Home Activity:* Ask your child to tell you which is longer—an inch, a foot, or a yard. (yard)

Practice

Complete the chart.

	Estimate. Find an object about this long.	Write or draw your object.	Measure length to check.
5	about 1 inch		about ______
6	about 1 foot		about ______
7	about 1 yard		about ______

Problem Solving Estimation

Circle the best estimate for the length of each object.

about 1 inch

about 1 foot

about 1 yard

9

about 1 inch

about 1 foot

about 1 yard

about 1 inch

about 1 foot

about 1 yard

Notes for Home: Your child found and measured objects that were about 1 inch, 1 foot, and 1 yard long. *Home Activity:* Ask your child to find objects at home that are about 1 inch, 1 foot, and 1 yard long.

Name ______________________

Practice Game 5

Every Inch Counts

Players 2 – 4

What You Need

1 red beanbag for a target
1 blue beanbag for each player
ruler or yardstick

How to Play

1. One player tosses the red beanbag. This will be the target for all players.
2. Each player tosses a blue beanbag as close to the target as possible.
3. After each turn, each player measures the distance in inches from the target to his or her beanbag.
4. Record your score after each turn. Each inch from the target counts as one point.
5. Do the activity 2 more times. Find your total number of points.
6. The player with the **least** number of points, wins!

Turn	Distance from Target	Points
1	_____ inches	_____
2	_____ inches	_____
3	_____ inches	_____

Total _____

PRACTICE

Notes for Home: Your child practiced measuring distances using inches while playing a game. *Home Activity:* Play the game with your child. Use small blocks or crumpled paper if beanbags are not available.

Name ______________________________

Estimate the length of this picture.
Use Snap Cubes to measure.

1 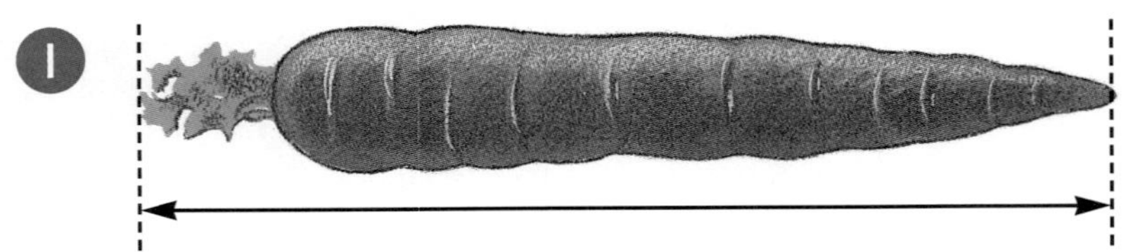

Estimate: about _____ Snap Cubes Measure: about _____ Snap Cubes

Estimate the length of the chalkboard in your classroom. Use a yardstick to measure.

2 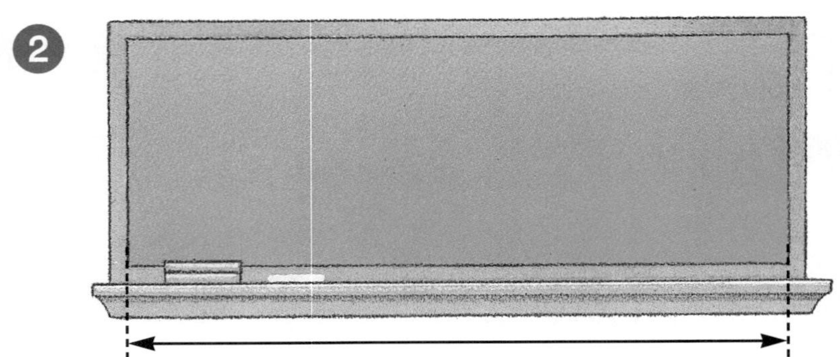

Estimate: about ______ feet

Measure: about ______ feet

Complete the chart. Use an inch ruler and a yardstick to measure.

	What to Measure	Estimate	Measure
3		about ______ inches	about ______ inches
4	Write or draw your own.	about __________	about __________

Notes for Home: Your child practiced estimating and measuring lengths. *Home Activity:* Have your child estimate the length of a favorite toy in inches. Ask your child to measure the length of the toy, then compare the actual length to his or her estimate.

PRACTICE

Name

Centimeters and Meters

Learn

The Snap Cube is 1 centimeter long.

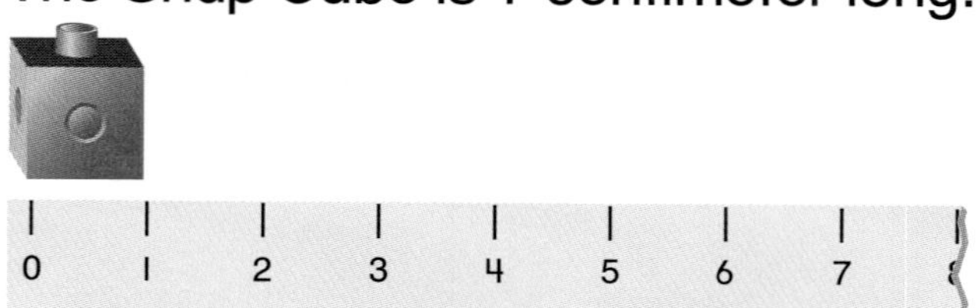

Your finger is about 1 centimeter wide.

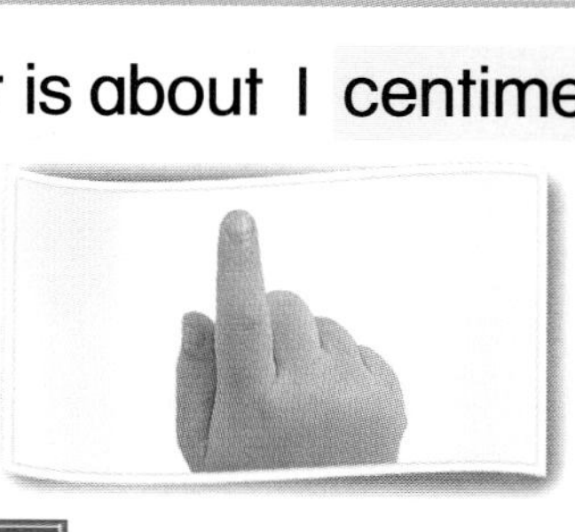

Check

Estimate the length in centimeters.

Measure with a centimeter ruler. Write the numbers.

1. 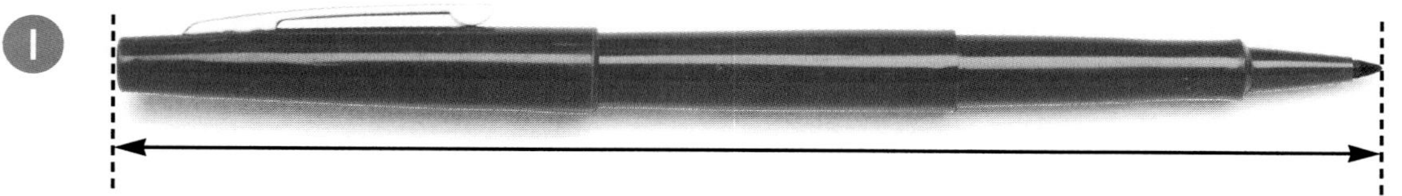

Estimate: about ______ centimeters

Measure: about ______ centimeters

2. 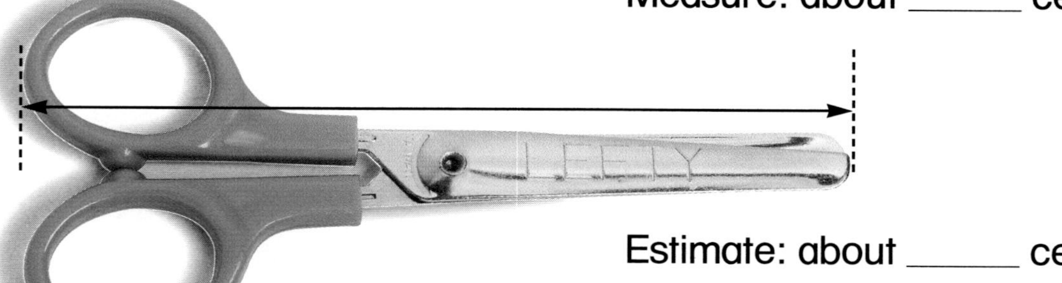

Estimate: about ______ centimeters

Measure: about ______ centimeters

Talk About It Estimate how many centimeters are in a meter. Then find out how many. Explain how you found out.

Notes for Home: Your child estimated and measured length using centimeters. *Home Activity:* Ask your child to use the width of his or her finger to estimate the length of a book in centimeters.

Practice

Estimate about how many meters.
Measure with a meter stick.

	What to Measure	Estimate	Measure
3	width of the doorway	about ______ meters	about ______ meters
4	length of the bulletin board	about ______ meters	about ______ meters
5	distance from the doorway to the other side of your classroom	about ______ meters	about ______ meters

Mental Math

6 Solve.

Cara is 130 centimeters tall.
Maya is 115 centimeters tall.
How much taller is Cara?

______ centimeters taller

Notes for Home: Your child estimated and measured length in meters. *Home Activity:* Ask your child to find something at home that is about 1 meter in length, width, or height.

PRACTICE

Name

Perimeter

Learn

Mark is making a box. He wants to put ribbon around the edge of the box. How much ribbon does he need?

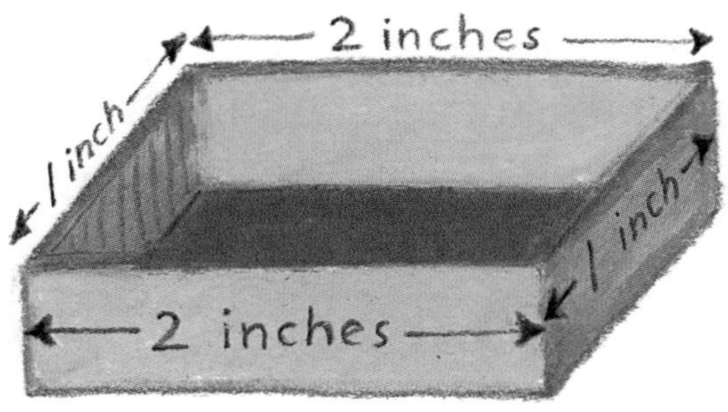

Add the lengths of all the sides.

1 + 2 + 1 + 2 = 6 inches around

Mark needs 6 inches of ribbon.

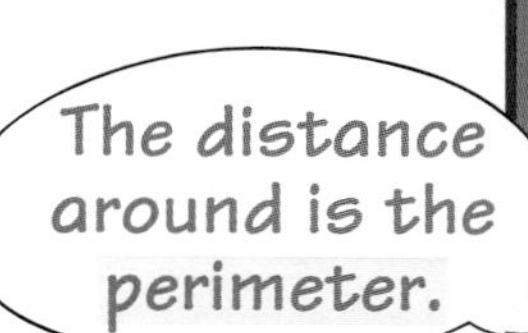

Check

Pick three objects you can measure. Draw them. Measure the lengths of all the sides with your inch ruler. Add to find each perimeter.

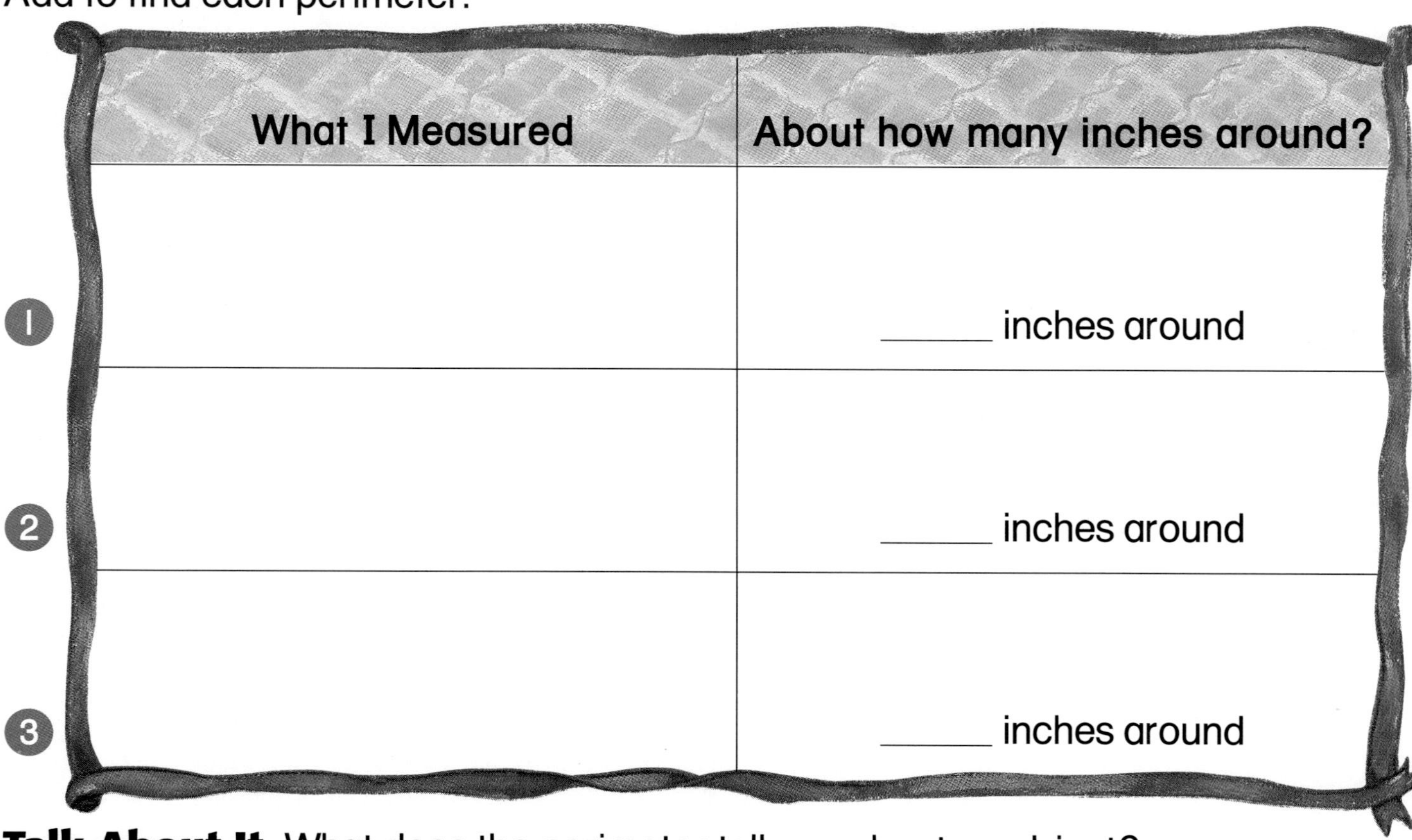

	What I Measured	About how many inches around?
1		____ inches around
2		____ inches around
3		____ inches around

Talk About It What does the perimeter tell you about an object?

Notes for Home: Your child found the perimeter of objects. *Home Activity:* Ask your child to find the perimeter of an object at home, such as a box of cereal.

4 Mark an **X** on the shape that you estimate has the greatest perimeter. Measure the lengths of the sides. Add to find the perimeter. Circle the shape with the greatest perimeter.

____ inches around

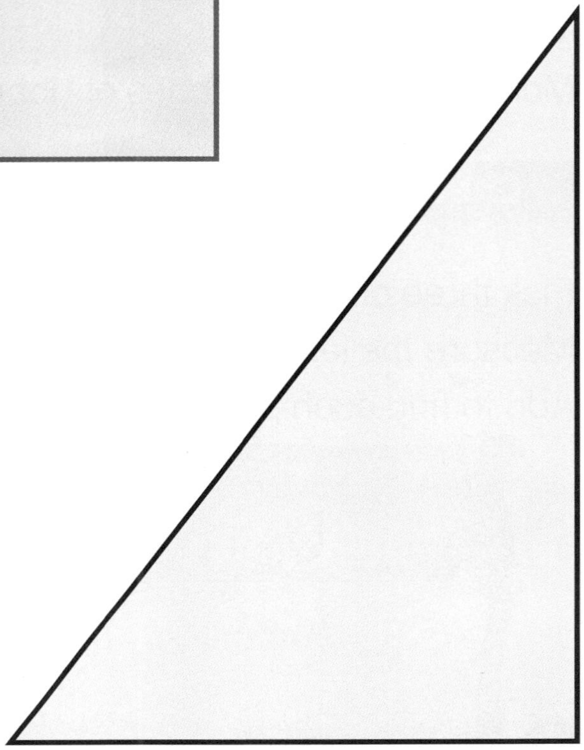

____ inches around

____ inches around

Problem Solving Visual Thinking

5 Do not measure. Which has the greater perimeter, the triangle or the rectangle? Explain why.

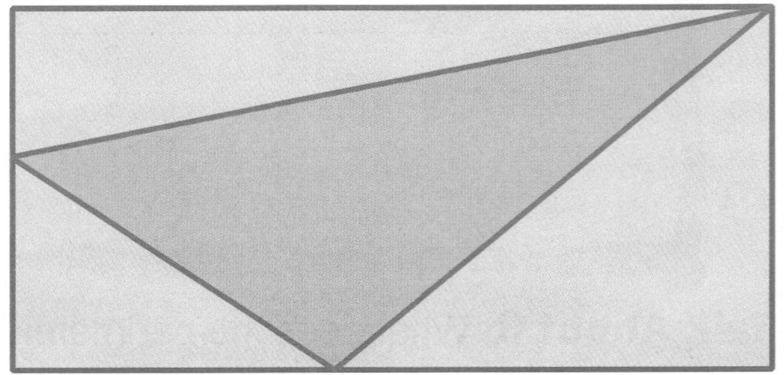

Notes for Home: Your child practiced finding the perimeter of different shapes. *Home Activity:* Ask your child to explain how he or she found each perimeter on the page.

For additional practice, see Skills Practice Bank, page 537, Set 1.

Name

Area

Learn

How many square units will cover the rectangle?

The area is 8 square units.

Check

Estimate how many square units will cover the shape.

Use  to cover the shape. Write how many.

1

Estimate: ______ square units

Measure: ______ square units

Talk About It Could you cover a circle with square units? Explain.

Notes for Home: Your child learned about the area of a rectangle. *Home Activity:* Ask your child to estimate the area of a cookie sheet in graham cracker squares or another square object. Then ask your child to help you cover the cookie sheet with the cracker squares or the other object.

Practice

Estimate how many square units will cover the shape.

Use ▢ to cover the shape. Write how many.

2 

Estimate: ______ square units   Measure: ______ square units

3 Estimate: ______ square units

Measure: ______ square units

Estimate how many ▢ will cover each of these objects.

Use ▢ to check your estimate.

4 the cover of your math book

Estimate: ______ square units

Measure: ______ square units

5 a piece of paper

Estimate: ______ square units

Measure: ______ square units

PRACTICE

Problem Solving Critical Thinking

6 You have squares that are these sizes.
You want to find the area of your notebook's cover. Which would you need more of? Why?
Circle your answer.

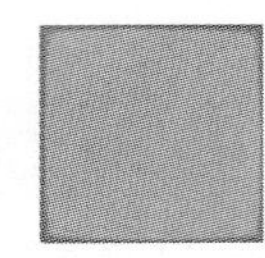

Notes for Home: Your child practiced using square units to measure the area of different shapes.
Home Activity: Ask your child to name things at home that could be measured using square units.

Name

Problem Solving: Use Logical Reasoning

Learn

PROBLEM SOLVING GUIDE

Understand • Plan • Solve • Look Back

Check

Use paper squares. Follow the directions to make each shape. Draw what you make.

1. Make a shape that
   - is a rectangle.
   - has a perimeter of 10 units.
   - has an area of 6 square units.

2. Make a shape that
   - is a square.
   - has a perimeter of 4 units.
   - has an area of 1 square unit.

Talk About It What are 3 different rectangles you can make with an area of 12 square units? What are their perimeters?

Notes for Home: Your child created shapes with a given perimeter and area. *Home Activity:* Work with your child to see how many different rectangles you can make using 6, 8, or 10 paper squares.

PROBLEM SOLVING

Practice

Use paper squares. Follow the directions to make each shape. Draw what you make.

3 Make a shape that
– is not a rectangle.
– has a perimeter of 14 units.
– has an area of 6 square units.

4 Make a shape that
– is a square.
– has a perimeter of 8 units.
– has an area of 4 square units.

Write your own.

5 Draw your own shape.
Describe the shape.
Tell about the perimeter and the area.

My shape

– has ______ sides.

– has a perimeter of ______ units.

– has an area of ______ square units.

Journal

6 Make some shapes that have the same perimeter but different areas. Draw the shapes. Tell about their areas and their perimeters.

Notes for Home: Your child solved problems involving area and perimeter. *Home Activity:* Work with your child to draw 3 different shapes with a perimeter of 12 units. (a 3 × 3 square; a 2 × 4 rectangle; and a 1 × 5 rectangle)

PROBLEM SOLVING

For additional practice, see Skills Practice Bank, page 537, Set 2.

Name

Mixed Practice

Lessons 1–7

Concepts and Skills

Estimate the length.

Measure with a centimeter ruler.

Estimate: about _____ centimeters long

Measure: _____ centimeters long

Estimate the perimeter and area.
Measure with an inch ruler and use  to cover the shape.

2 Perimeter

Estimate: _____ inches around

Measure: _____ inches around

3 Area

Estimate: _____ square units

Measure: _____ square units

Problem Solving

Draw a different shape with the same area.

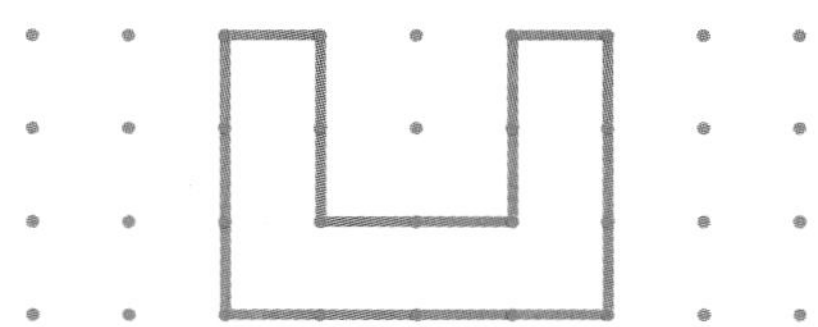

4 Area: _____ square units

Perimeter: _____ units around

5 Area: _____ square units

Perimeter: _____ units around

Journal

6 Draw a shape. Estimate and measure the perimeter and area. Write about how you measured.

Notes for Home: Your child practiced estimating and measuring length, perimeter, and area.
Home Activity: Have your child estimate the length or the perimeter of a small object in your home. Compare the estimate with the measurement.

MIXED PRACTICE

Name

Cumulative Review

Chapters 1–11

Concepts and Skills

Add.

1

23	40	64	16	34	72
+ 18	+ 37	+ 9	+ 15	+ 55	+ 27

Write how many hundreds, tens, and ones.
Then write the number.

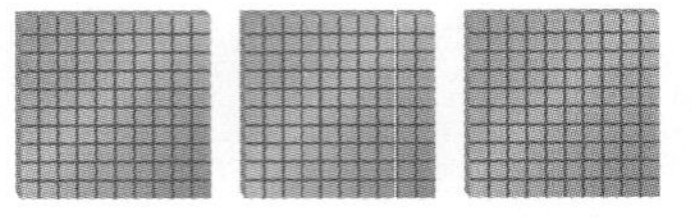
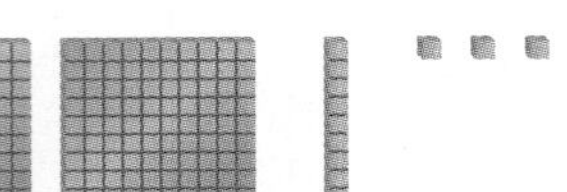

hundreds	tens	ones

______

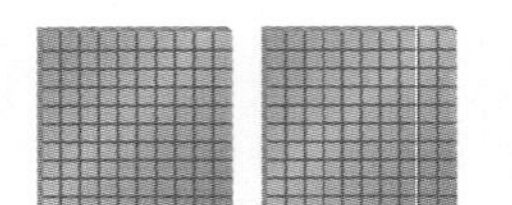
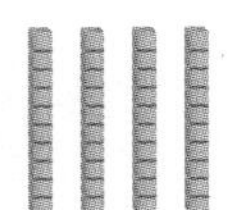

hundreds	tens	ones

______

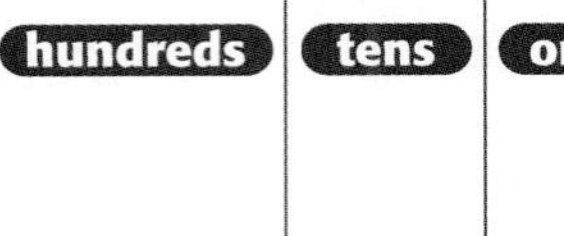
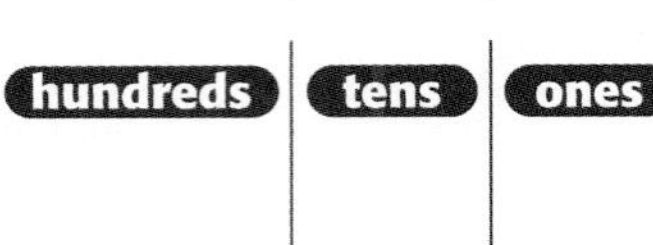

Problem Solving

Solve.

4 The truck took 25 boxes to the grocery store. Then it took 17 boxes to the hardware store. How many boxes did the truck take?

______ boxes

5 46 railroad cars stop at the train station. Another 37 railroad cars hook up to the train. How long is the train now?

______ cars

Test Prep

Fill in the ○ for the correct answer.

6 Choose the number that comes one before 475.

476 ○ 447 ○ 474 ○

7 Choose the number that comes one after 356.

357 ○ 365 ○ 355 ○

Notes for Home: Your child reviewed two-digit addition, writing large numbers, and using addition to solve problems. *Home Activity:* Ask your child what the 6 stands for in 689. (6 hundreds)

CUMULATIVE REVIEW

Name

Explore One Pound

Explore

Find objects you can weigh. Use a balance scale.
Make a list of objects that are lighter than 1 pound.
Make a list of objects that are heavier than 1 pound.

Share

What are some objects that weigh about 1 pound?

Notes for Home: Your child compared the weights of objects to one pound by using a balance scale. *Home Activity:* Look for objects in the kitchen or grocery store that weigh about 1 pound.

Connect

Is each object **heavier than, lighter than,** or **about** 1 pound? Estimate. Then use a pound weight and a balance scale to check. Complete the chart.

	Object	Estimate	Measure
1		_____ 1 pound	_____ 1 pound
2		_____ 1 pound	_____ 1 pound
3		_____ 1 pound	_____ 1 pound
4		_____ 1 pound	_____ 1 pound
5		_____ 1 pound	_____ 1 pound

EXPLORE

Tell a Math Story

6 Write a math story about something you need to weigh.

Notes for Home: Your child estimated whether objects weigh more or less than 1 pound.
Home Activity: Help your child find weights on labels of food products.

Name

Kilograms

Learn

Lighter than 1 kilogram

About 1 kilogram

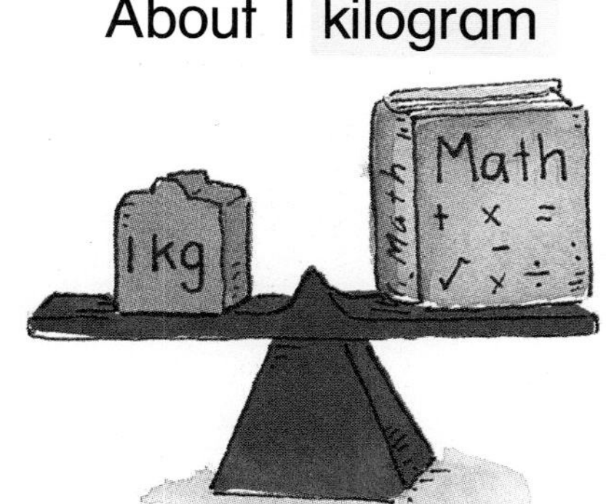

Heavier than 1 kilogram

Check

Find each of these objects. Use a balance scale.
Circle the words that tell about the object.

lighter than 1 kilogram

about 1 kilogram

heavier than 1 kilogram

lighter than 1 kilogram

about 1 kilogram

heavier than 1 kilogram

lighter than 1 kilogram

about 1 kilogram

heavier than 1 kilogram

lighter than 1 kilogram

about 1 kilogram

heavier than 1 kilogram

Talk About It If one object is larger than another object, is it always heavier?

Notes for Home: Your child used a balance scale to find objects that are lighter than, heavier than, or about 1 kilogram. *Home Activity:* Ask your child to find something in your home that weighs about 1 kilogram or about 2 pounds. You can use a bathroom scale to check.

Practice

5 Circle in **red** the objects that are lighter than 1 kilogram.

6 Circle in **blue** the objects that are heavier than 1 kilogram.

Write your own. Choose an object.

7 Is your object lighter than or heavier than 1 kilogram?

My ________________ is ________________ than 1 kilogram.

Problem Solving Critical Thinking

8 Is 1 kilogram of nails heavier than 1 kilogram of feathers? Explain.

Notes for Home: Your child identified objects that are lighter or heavier than 1 kilogram. *Home Activity:* Ask your child to hold objects from your refrigerator and estimate if they are lighter or heavier than 1 kilogram.

Name

Cups, Pints, and Quarts

Learn

There are 2 cups in 1 pint.

There are 2 pints in 1 quart.

Check

Color the containers to answer each question.

1 How many cups fill 1 pint?

2 How many cups fill 2 pints?

3 How many cups fill 1 quart?

4 How many pints fill 1 quart?

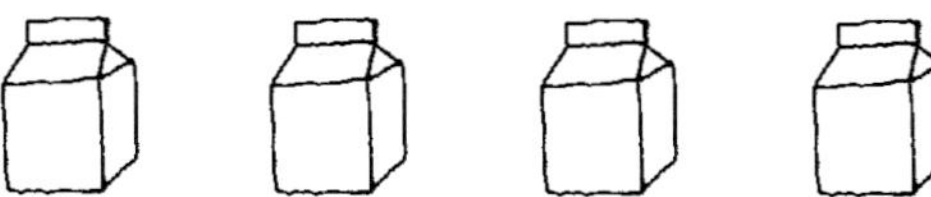

Talk About It What measurements did you find that are the same as one quart?

Notes for Home: Your child learned about cups, pints, and quarts. *Home Activity:* Ask your child to order these units of measure from least to greatest: pint, cup, quart. (cup, pint, quart)

2 cups fill 1 pint.

2 pints fill 1 quart.

Solve each problem.

6 Gina buys 3 pints of milk. Color the number of cups she could fill.

7 Mr. Habib buys 1 quart of yogurt. Color the number of cups he could fill.

8 Simon has 4 pints of juice. Color the number of quarts that holds the same amount.

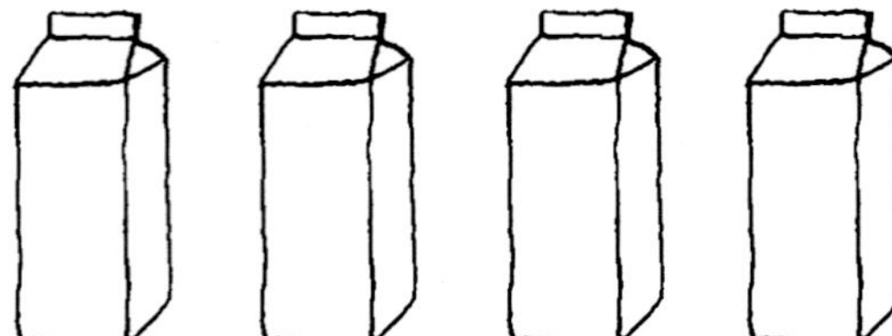

9 Jorge has 2 quarts of juice. Color the number of pints that holds the same amount.

PRACTICE

Problem Solving Visual Thinking

10 Draw cups to solve.

Jess has 2 quarts of milk.
Ed has 6 cups of milk. Who has more?

____________ has more.

Notes for Home: Your child solved problems about cups, pints, and quarts. *Home Activity:* Ask your child to show you some liquids at home that could be measured in cups, pints, or quarts.

For additional practice, see Skills Practice Bank, page 537, Set 3.

Name

Liters

Learn

Check

Use a one-liter container. Check other containers to see if they hold **more** or **less** than one liter.

	Draw your container.	Does it hold **more** or **less** than one liter?
1		______ than one liter
2		______ than one liter
3		______ than one liter

Talk About It Would your class need more or less than one liter of juice for a snack? Explain.

Notes for Home: Your child determined if containers hold more or less than one liter.
Home Activity: Ask your child to find a container at home or at the store and find out if it holds more than one liter, less than one liter, or about one liter.

Practice

4 Which things hold **less** than one liter?
Circle them.

5 Which things hold **more** than one liter?
Mark an **X** on them.

PRACTICE

Mental Math

6 A barrel holds ten liters of apple juice.
How many liters will ten barrels hold? _______

Notes for Home: Your child identified containers that hold more or less than one liter.
Home Activity: Ask your child to find two containers in your home that hold more than one liter and two containers that hold less than one liter.

Name ______________________

Reading for Math

Read for a Purpose

Frosty Fruit Smoothies

4 cups chopped strawberries
4 cups chopped bananas
2 quarts milk
1 pint fresh orange juice
1 cup frozen pineapple juice

Blend all ingredients until smooth.
Serve and enjoy!

Serves 12 people

Use the recipe to answer the questions.

1. How do you know this is a recipe?

____

____

2. What words give you clues that this is a recipe?

____

3. How is a recipe like other things you read?

____

____

4. How is a recipe different from other things you read?

____

____

Talk About It What would you expect to find in all recipes?

Notes for Home: Your child used a recipe to answer questions. *Home Activity:* Ask your child to list the amounts of orange juice, pineapple juice, and milk in the recipe from least to greatest. (pineapple juice, orange juice, milk)

Crunchy Granola

2 cups whole wheat flour
2 cups whole oats
2 cups sesame seeds
2 cups raisins
1 cup honey
4 tablespoons vegetable oil

Mix all ingredients together.
Bake at 300° for 20 minutes.

Serves 18 people

What can I measure with my cup?

Use the recipe to answer the questions.

5. What kinds of information do you find in this recipe?

____

____

6. What do you need to know in order to understand how to use this recipe?

____

____

7. What would you do first if you were going to use this recipe?

____

____

Critical Thinking

8. What would you do if you needed to make this recipe serve 36 people? Explain.

Notes for Home: Your child read a recipe to answer questions. *Home Activity:* Ask your child to read some of the amounts shown in the recipe.

Name

Problem Solving: Group Decision Making

Learn

PROBLEM SOLVING GUIDE

Understand • Plan • Solve • Look Back

Punch for a Bunch

2 quarts orange juice

_____ quarts apple juice

_____ pints pineapple juice

_____ pints cranberry juice

_____ cups lemonade

_____ cups grape juice

4 cups fill 1 quart.

So there would be 8 cups in 2 quarts.

Check

Work in a group to solve. Use some of each ingredient. Fill in the recipe above.

1. You need to make 30 cups of punch. Decide how much of each juice to use. Fill in the recipe.

Talk About It How did you decide how much of each juice to use? How do you know that you made enough punch?

Notes for Home: Your child completed a recipe by filling in juice amounts. *Home Activity:* Ask your child to tell how many cups 3 quarts of grape juice and 2 quarts of apple juice will make. (20 cups)

Practice

PROBLEM SOLVING

Make your own recipe for punch.
You need to make 20 cups.

2. Write your recipe on the card.
Write a name for your punch.

Our Recipe: ____________

How much?	What kind of juice?

Answer these questions about your punch recipe.

3. How many cups of punch does your recipe make? 20 cups

4. How many pints of punch does your recipe make? ______ pints

5. How many quarts of punch does your recipe make? ______ quarts

Journal

6. Write a punch recipe for your family.
Make enough for each person to have 1 cup.

Notes for Home: Your child made decisions with a group to create a recipe. *Home Activity:* Ask your child to estimate how many quarts of juice might be needed to serve 7 people. (about 2)

Name

Temperature

Learn

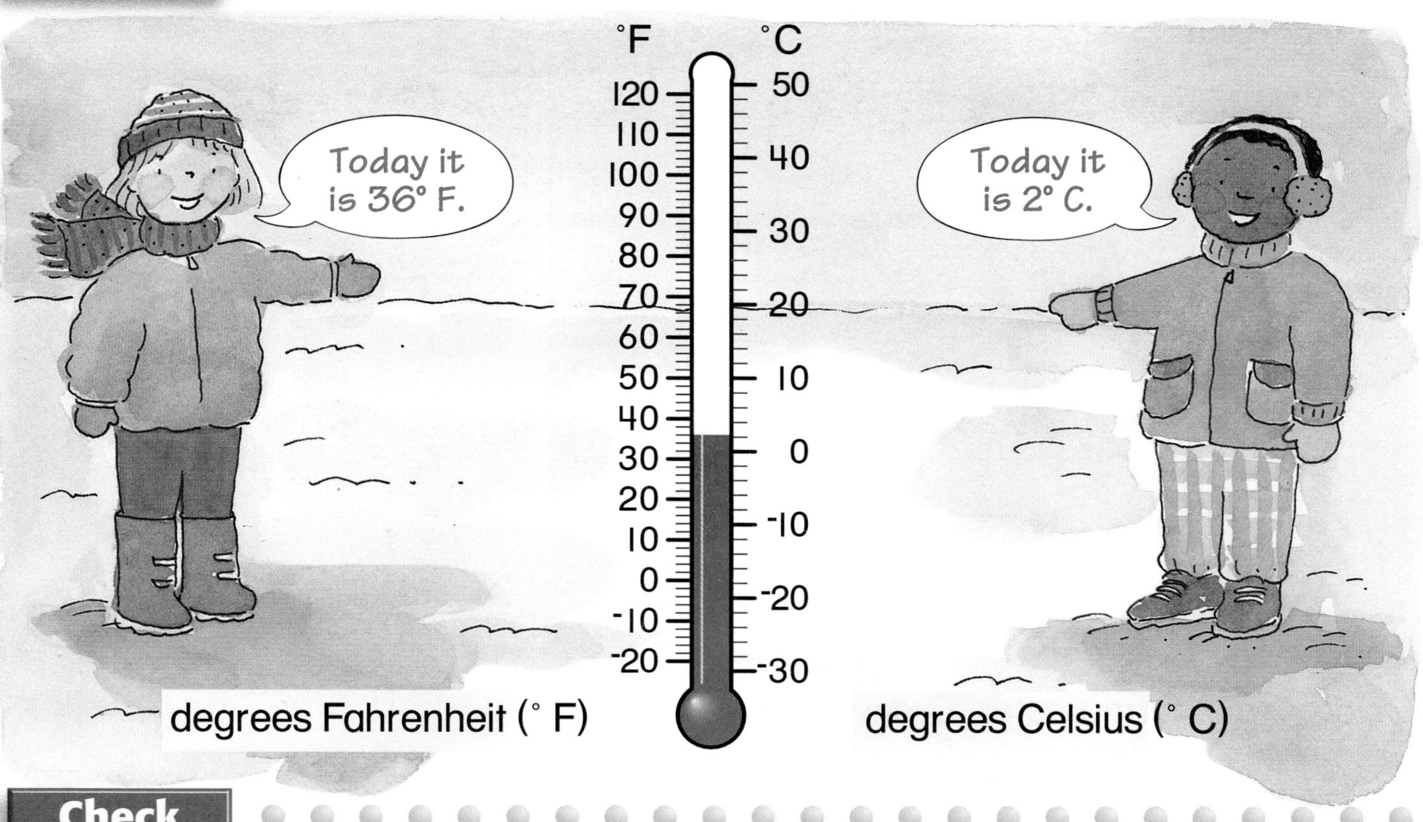

Check

Color to show the temperature.

Talk About It Before school, it is 40° F. After school, it is 65° F. How many degrees did the temperature rise? Explain how you found out.

Notes for Home: Your child learned how to use a thermometer to show the temperature. *Home Activity:* Ask your child to use a newspaper or watch or listen to a weather forecast to find out predicted temperatures for the next few days.

Practice

Color to show the temperature.

3 0° C

4 82° F

Write your own.

Choose and write a temperature.
Color in the thermometer. Draw a picture to show an activity you might do at that temperature.

5 _____° C

6 _____° F

120
110
100
90
80
70
60
50
40
30
20
10
0
-10
-20

Problem Solving Critical Thinking

7 It's 32° and I'm going swimming.
Circle the correct thermometer.

°F
120
110
100
90
80
70
60
50
40
30
20
10
0
-10
-20

°C
50
40
30
20
10
0
-10
-20
-30

Notes for Home: Your child practiced showing different temperatures on thermometers.
Home Activity: Help your child use a thermometer on the page to indicate the current temperature in both Celsius and Fahrenheit degrees.

PRACTICE

Name

Mixed Practice

Lessons 8–13

Concepts and Skills

1. Color to show the temperature.

2. Is the penny heavier or lighter than 1 kilogram? Write **heavier** or **lighter.**

A penny is ____________ than 1 kilogram.

3. Is the bowling ball heavier or lighter than 1 pound? Write **heavier** or **lighter.**

A bowling ball is ____________ than 1 pound.

Problem Solving

Solve.

4. You need to make 1 cup of punch for each of 20 children. Do you have enough? Circle **yes** or **no.**

yes **no**

5. Does the punch recipe use more apple juice or grape juice?

____

Journal

6. Keep track of the temperature in the morning for 5 days. Write about what you find.

Notes for Home: Your child practiced showing temperatures, determining the weight of objects using kilograms and pounds, and reading a recipe. *Home Activity:* Ask your child to estimate how much an object weighs. Weigh the object and compare the result with the estimate.

MIXED PRACTICE

Name ____________________

Cumulative Review

Chapters 1–11

Concepts and Skills

Use the hundred chart to subtract.

1	2	3	4	5	6	7	8	9	10
11	12	13	14	15	16	17	18	19	20
21	22	23	24	25	26	27	28	29	30
31	32	33	34	35	36	37	38	39	40
41	42	43	44	45	46	47	48	49	50
51	52	53	54	55	56	57	58	59	60
61	62	63	64	65	66	67	68	69	70
71	72	73	74	75	76	77	78	79	80
81	82	83	84	85	86	87	88	89	90
91	92	93	94	95	96	97	98	99	100

1. 39 − 20 = ____
2. 55 − 30 = ____
3. 77 − 40 = ____
4. 36 − 10 = ____
5. 83 − 50 = ____
6. 63 − 60 = ____

Problem Solving

Write each number sentence. Solve.

7. 68 boxes are on the truck.
   7 more boxes are loaded on. ____________ boxes

   At the first stop 20 boxes are unloaded.
   How many boxes are on the truck now? ____________ boxes

Test Prep

Fill in the ○ for the correct answer.

8. $\begin{array}{r} 323 \\ +\ 247 \\ \hline \end{array}$

   ○ 76
   ○ 560
   ○ 570
   ○ 670

9. $\begin{array}{r} 145 \\ +\ 194 \\ \hline \end{array}$

   ○ 329
   ○ 331
   ○ 339
   ○ 1,243

Notes for Home: Your child reviewed subtracting tens, multiple-step problems, and adding and subtracting large numbers. *Home Activity:* Ask your child to find 97 − 50 and then add 6. (53)

Name ______________________________

Chapter 11 Review

Vocabulary

1. Circle the picture that is about 1 centimeter long.

2. Circle the object that weighs about 1 pound.

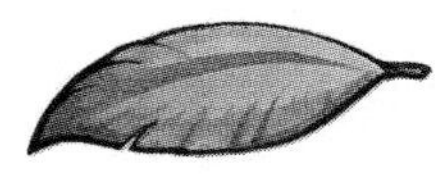

Concepts and Skills

3. Use an inch ruler to measure the length.

Measure: about ______ inches

4. Color to show the temperature.

30° F

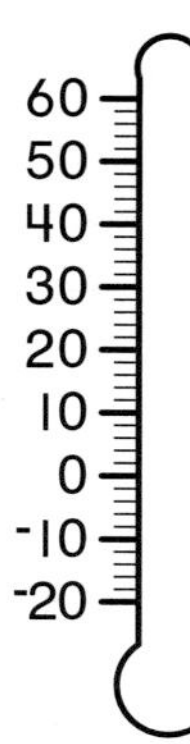

5. Is the orange lighter or heavier than 1 kilogram?

The orange is ______________ than 1 kilogram.

6. Does the pail hold more or less than one liter?

The pail holds ______________ than one liter.

Problem Solving

7. Find the perimeter and area of this shape. Then draw a different shape with the same area.

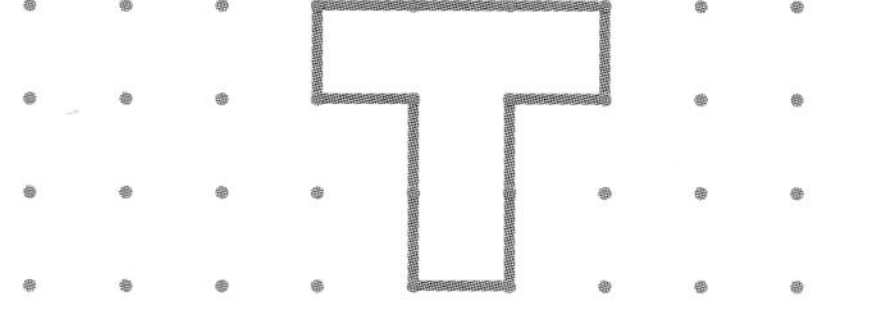

Perimeter: ______ units around

Area: ______ square units

Perimeter: ______ units around

Area: ______ square units

Notes for Home: Your child reviewed Chapter 11 vocabulary, concepts, skills, and problem solving. *Home Activity:* Ask your child to use a ruler to draw a shape with an area of 7 square units.

CHAPTER REVIEW

Name

Chapter 11 Test

How long is each candle?

1 Measure in inches.

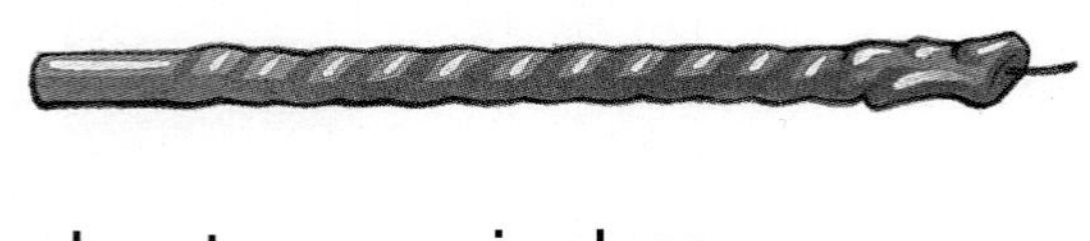

about ______ inches

2 Measure in centimeters.

about ______ centimeters

3 Color to show 27° C.

4 Jarek has 1 quart of milk. Color to show how many cups he can fill.

5 Circle the objects that hold less than one liter.

6 Circle the objects that are lighter than 1 kilogram.

7 Mark an **X** on the objects that are heavier than 1 pound.

8 Draw a rectangle that has a perimeter of 12 units and an area of 8 square units.

Notes for Home: Your child was assessed on Chapter 11 concepts, skills, and problem solving.
Home Activity: Ask your child to name different units that can be used to measure length. (inch, foot, yard, centimeter, meter)

Name

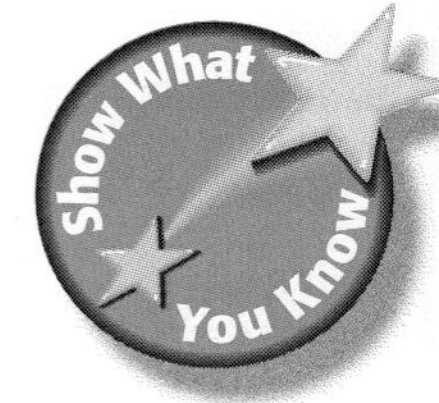

Performance Assessment

Chapter 11

Find a container that is shaped like a box.

1 Draw a picture of your container.

Measure your container in different ways.
Complete the chart.

2	Length	about ______ inches
3	Area of one side	about ______ square units
4	Perimeter	about ______ inches

5 Does your container weigh more or less than 1 pound? __________ than one pound

6 How much does your container hold? about ______ cups

Problem Solving Critical Thinking

7 Describe a day that is 30° F.
Describe a day that is 30° C.
You can use a thermometer to help.

Notes for Home: Your child did an activity that assessed Chapter 11 skills, concepts, and problem solving. *Home Activity:* Estimate the number of small objects in a jar. Estimate how much the filled jar weighs.

Name ______________________________

Shape Up!

Computer Skills You Will Need

Use your drawing program.

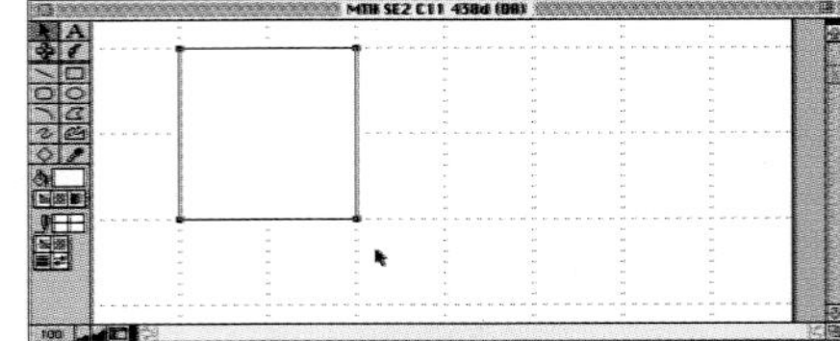

1. Draw a square. Hold down 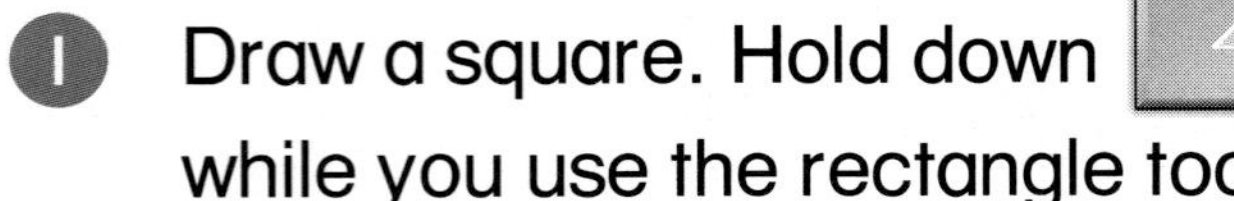 while you use the rectangle tool.

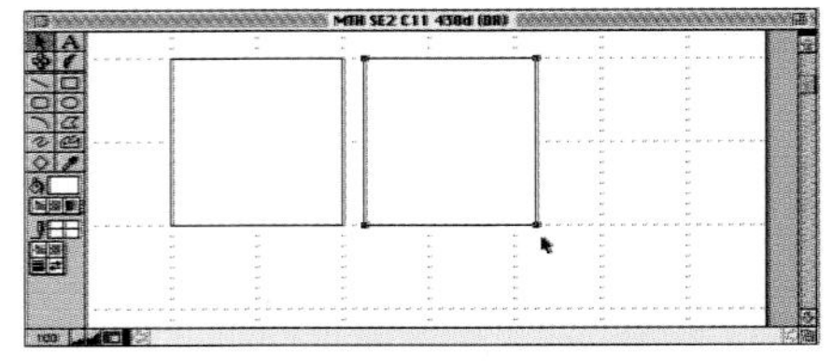

2. Copy and paste your square. Move your new square so that the sides are lined up.
3. Paste more squares, and move them to make a shape.
4. On a separate card, write a riddle about the perimeter and the area of your shape.
5. Work in a group. Make a display of your shapes. Mix up the riddles. Ask another group to solve them.

My perimeter is 14 units.
My area is 8 square units.

Tech Talk A shape has a perimeter of 10 units and an area of 6 square units. How would you use your computer to draw it?

Visit our Web site. **www.parent.mathsurf.com**

Math at Home

Food Finds

With an adult, look through your cupboards and refrigerator at home. Find cans, bottles, and packages of food that show different measurements on the labels.

List or draw foods in the correct box below.

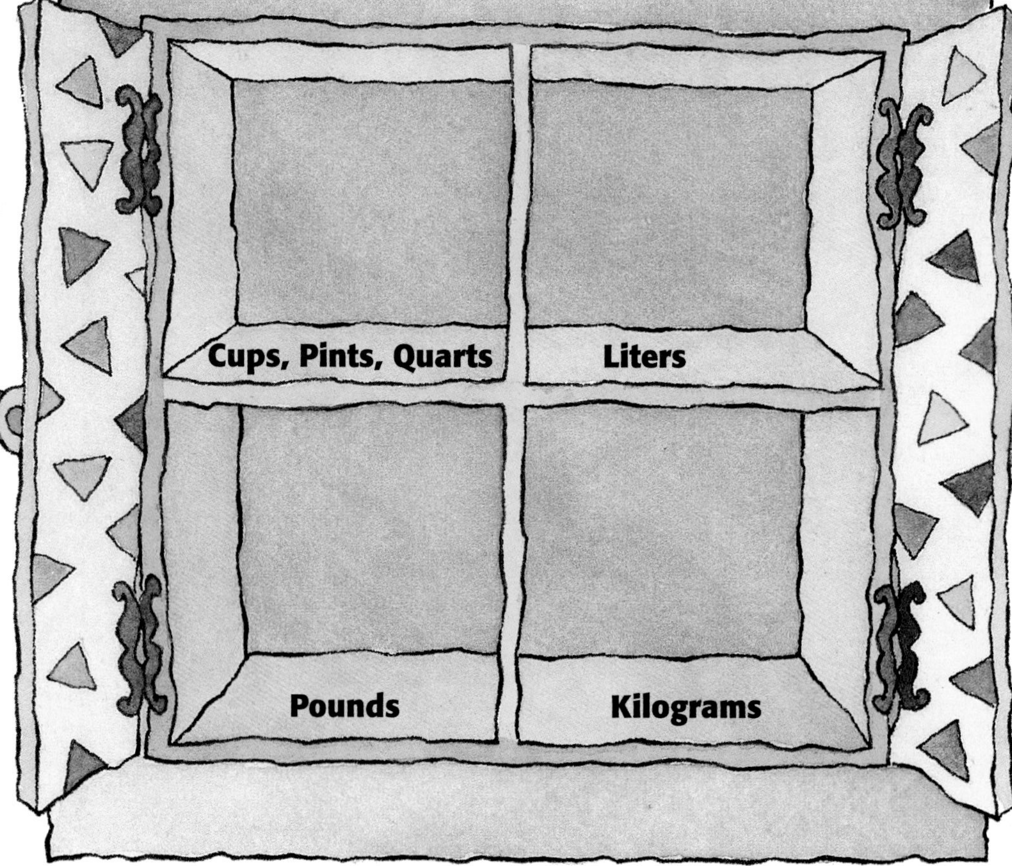

Fold down

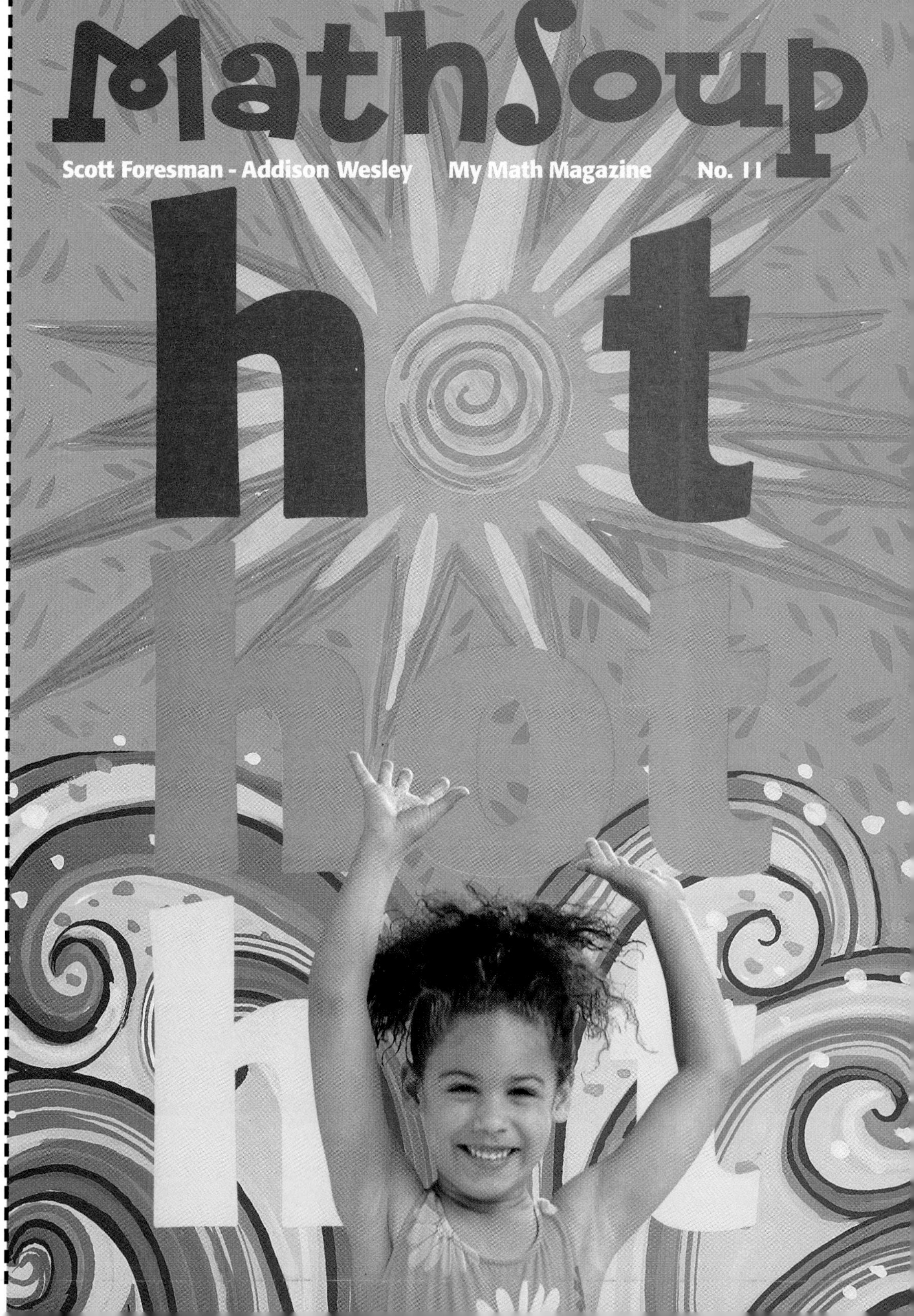

MathSoup

Scott Foresman - Addison Wesley My Math Magazine No. 11

Hot, Hotter, Hottest!

The temperature is different in different places. Even when it is warm where you are, it may be much warmer or cooler somewhere else. This chart shows warm temperatures in different cities.

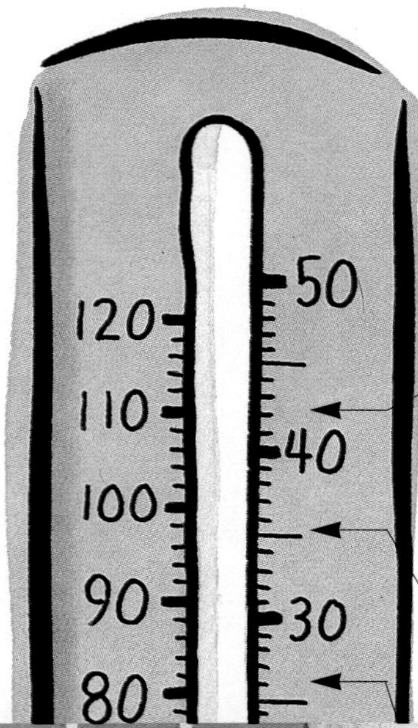

120 110 100 90 80

50 40 30

1 Write the name of each city from the chart next to the correct line on the thermometer.

2 What is today's temperature where you live? Circle that temperature on the thermometer.

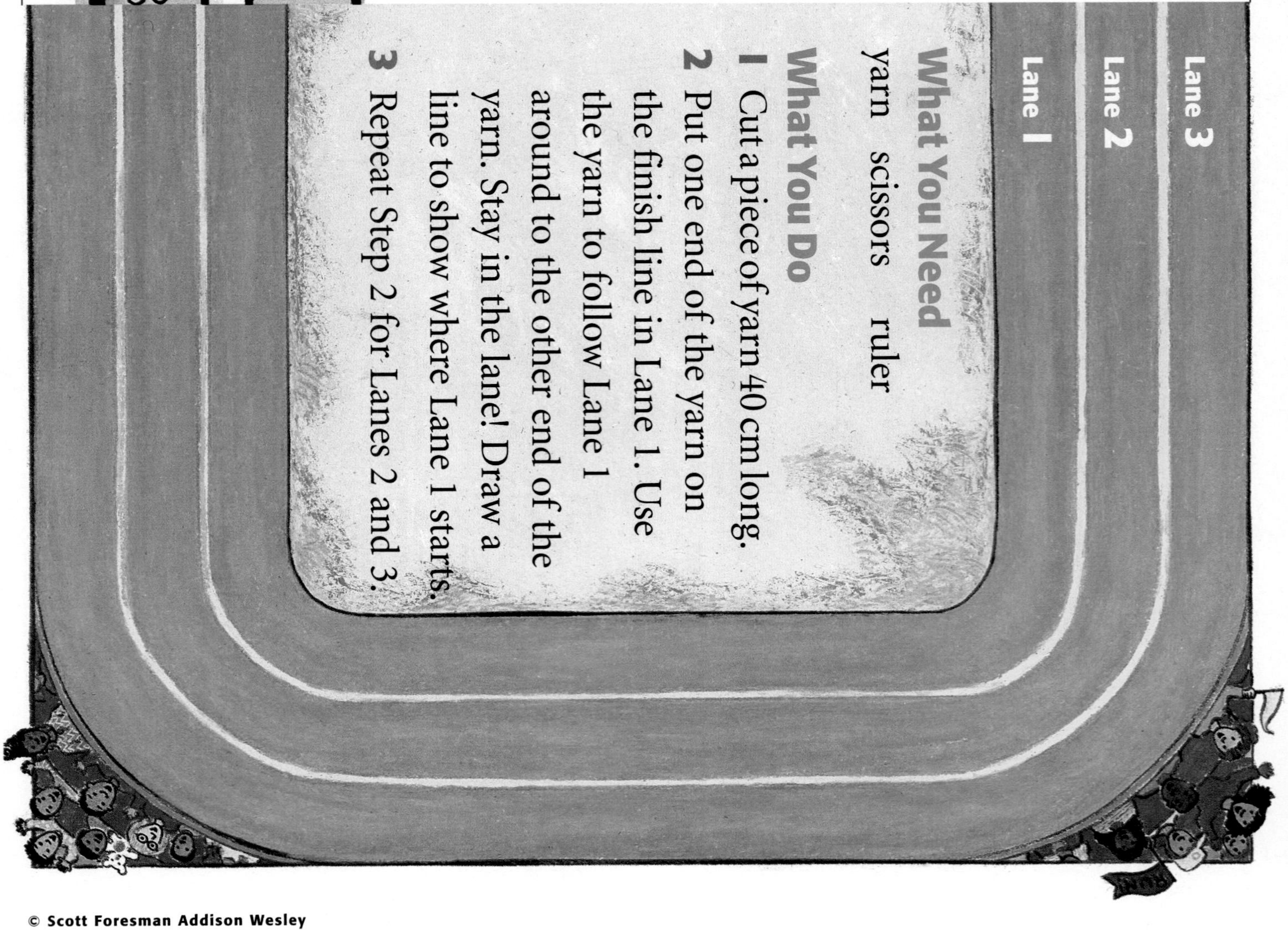

Lane 3

Lane 2

Lane 1

What You Need

yarn scissors ruler

What You Do

1 Cut a piece of yarn 40 cm long.

2 Put one end of the yarn on the finish line in Lane 1. Use the yarn to follow Lane 1 around to the other end of the yarn. Stay in the lane! Draw a line to show where Lane 1 starts.

3 Repeat Step 2 for Lanes 2 and 3.

Stay in Your Lane!

When runners race on a track, they sometimes start at different places so they will all run the same distance and finish at the same place. Use the diagram and follow the directions to draw the starting lines for a race.

City	°F	°C
New York City, U.S.A.	82°	28°
London, England	73°	23°
Reykjavik, Iceland	57°	14°
Khartoum, Sudan	107°	42°
Calcutta, India	96°	36°

Notes for Home: Your child practiced metric measurement. *Home Activity:* Ask your child to find an object that measures about 40 cm in length.

Notes for Home: Your child learned about temperatures in different cities. *Home Activity:* Ask your child to compare the temperatures in Khartoum and Reykjavik. (Khartoum is 50°F warmer, 28°C warmer)

Wrap It Up!

You know how to find the perimeter of rectangles. But how could you find the perimeter of these shapes? Follow these directions to find out.

What You Need

yarn scissors ruler

What You Do

1 Find the circle. Put one end of a piece of yarn on the border of the circle.

2 Curve the yarn around the border of the circle. Cut the piece of yarn when it reaches all the way around the circle.

3 Straighten out the piece of yarn. Measure it to the nearest inch. Measure it to the nearest centimeter. Record your measurements.

4 Repeat the steps for the other shapes.

Perimeter: ______ in. ______ cm

Perimeter: ______ in. ______ cm

Perimeter: ______ in. ______ cm

Perimeter: ______ in. ______ cm

Notes for Home: Your child practiced finding perimeters. *Home Activity:* Ask your child to find the perimeter of a curved object at home using string or yarn and a ruler.

CHAPTER 12

Geometry and Fractions

Notes for Home: Your child matched food containers with different kinds of solids. *Home Activity:* Ask your child to find objects in your home that are solids like those shown in the picture.

Dear Family,
Our class is starting Chapter 12. We will be learning about different shapes and using fractions. Here are some fun things we can do together.

It's in the Bag
Put several food items into a brown grocery bag. Ask your child to reach into the bag without looking, feel an object, and describe the shape. Then ask your child to guess what the object is.

Share Your Lunch
When serving food such as pizza, pie, or casseroles, ask your child how to share the food with four people. Help your child cut it into equal pieces.

Community Connection

Take your child on a shape search around your neighborhood. Look for circles, triangles, and rectangles in buildings or on street signs.

Visit our Web site. **www.parent.mathsurf.com**

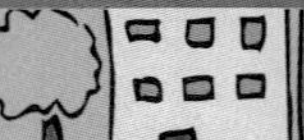

Name

Explore Solid Figures

Explore

Sort solid figures into 2 groups.

Write the names of the solids you sorted.

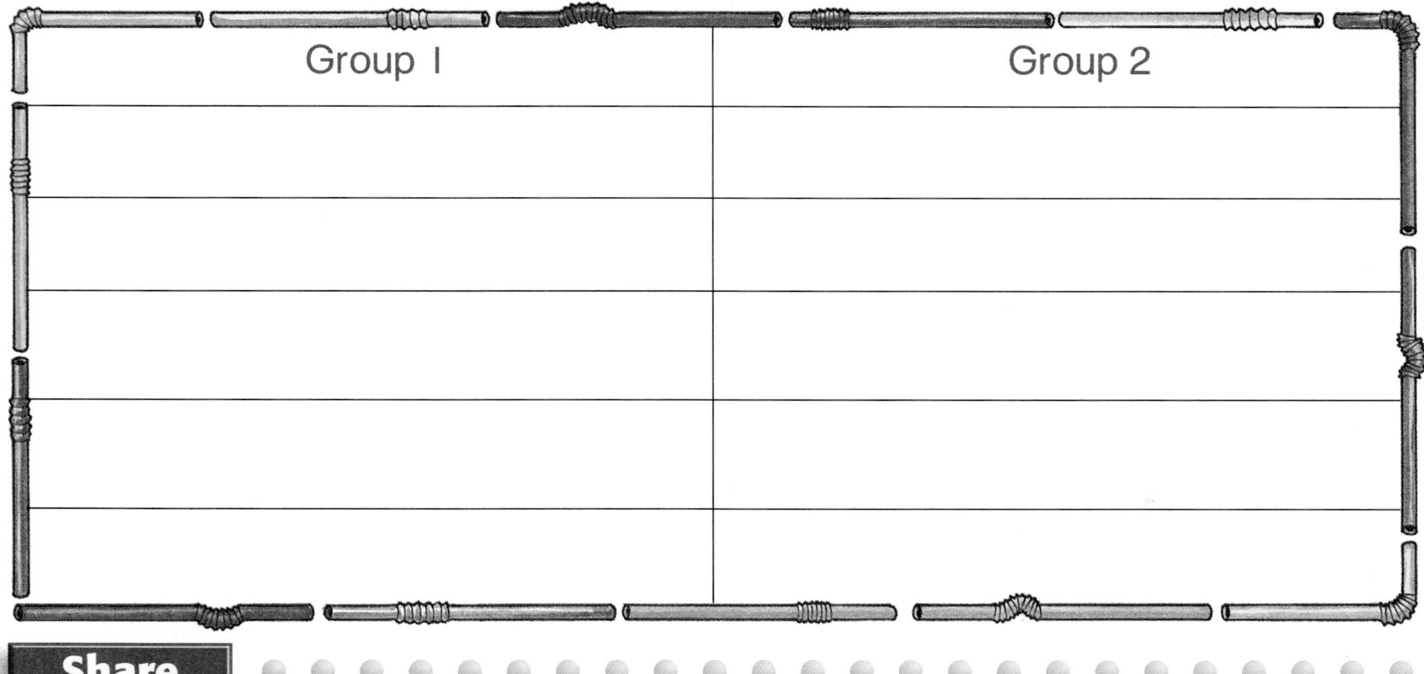

Group 1	Group 2

Share

How did you sort the solid figures?

What other ways could you sort them?

Notes for Home: Your child sorted solid objects into two groups. *Home Activity:* Ask your child to sort objects at home into two groups and explain how he or she sorted them.

EXPLORE

Connect

Use solids. Find how many faces, corners, and edges.

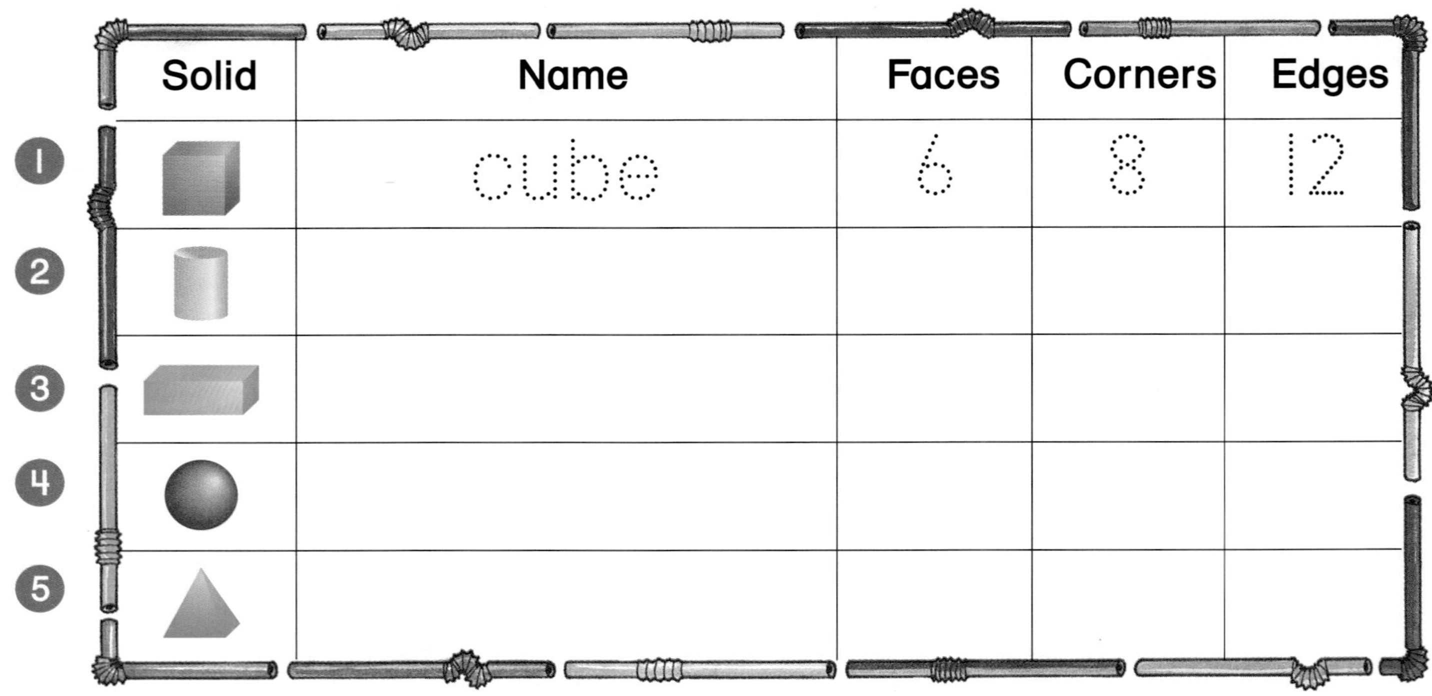

	Solid	Name	Faces	Corners	Edges
1		cube	6	8	12
2					
3					
4					
5					

Problem Solving Critical Thinking

6. How many faces, corners, and edges do these rectangular prisms have? Do you think this is true for all rectangular prisms? Explain.

Notes for Home: Your child found the number of corners, faces, and edges in different solid objects. *Home Activity:* Ask your child to find two objects in your home and tell you how many faces, corners and edges for each object.

Name

Explore Solid and Plane Figures

Explore

Look around. What solids do you see?
What shapes do they have?

Find objects in your classroom.
Trace faces of these solids to make a picture.

Share

What everyday objects could you use to trace a circle?

Notes for Home: Your child traced objects to draw shapes. *Home Activity:* Ask your child to trace two objects in your home and describe the shapes he or she drew.

EXPLORE

EXPLORE

Connect

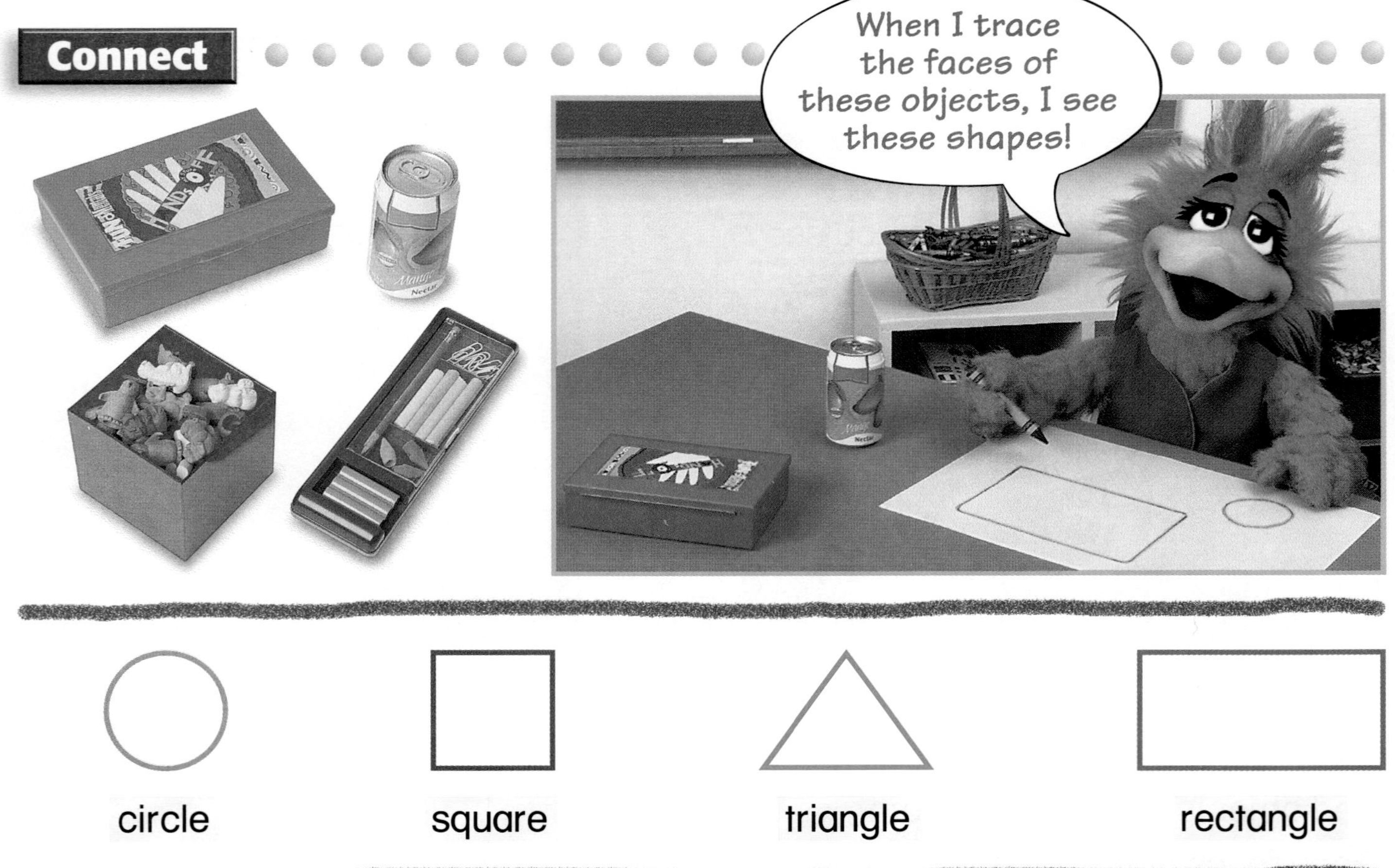

circle square triangle rectangle

Circle the shape you would make if you traced each object.

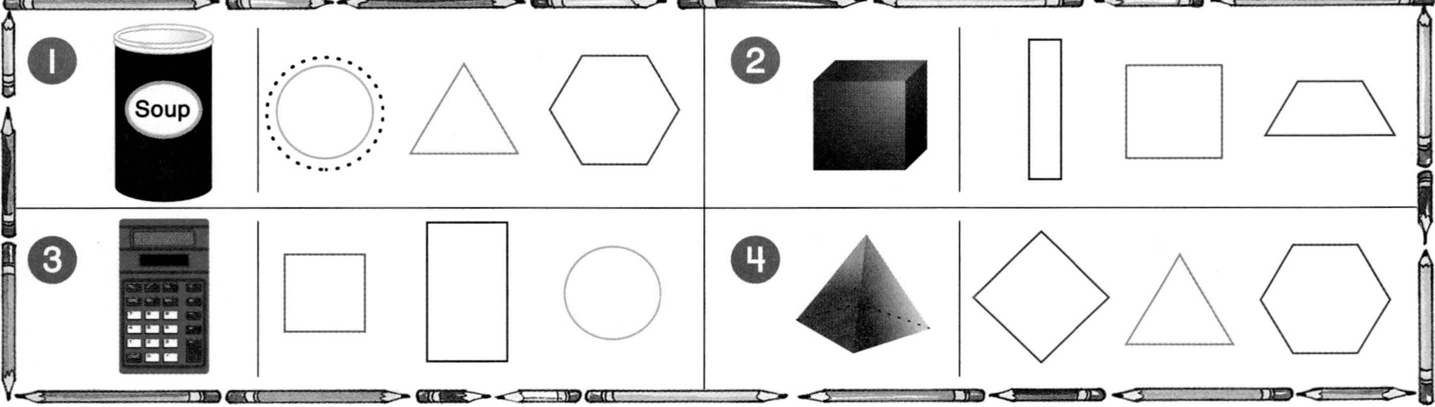

Problem Solving Visual Thinking

5 Draw a picture of shapes you would make if you traced each object.

Notes for Home: Your child identified the shape that would be drawn if different objects were traced. *Home Activity:* Ask your child to tell you what shape would be drawn if he or she traced a box. (rectangle)

Name ____________________

Make Shapes

Learn

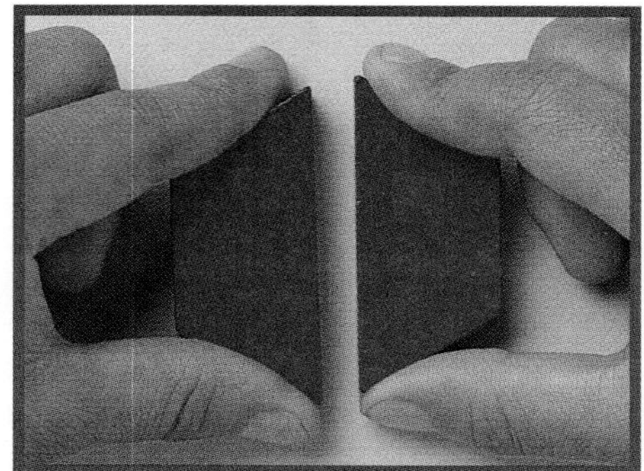

Put pattern blocks together. Be sure the edges match!

Trace your new shape.

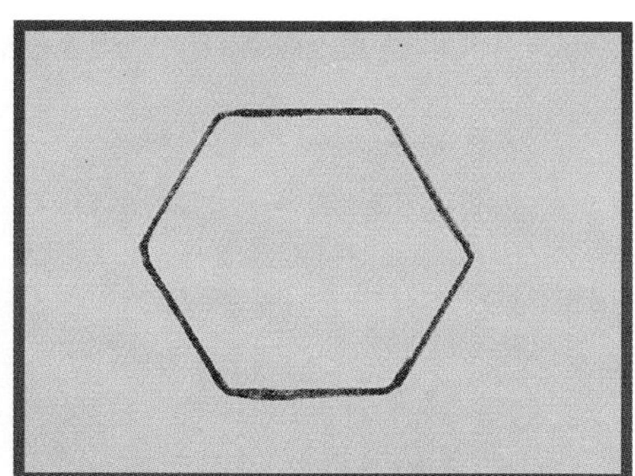

Count the sides and corners.

6 sides 6 corners

Check

Use pattern blocks to make shapes. Complete the chart.

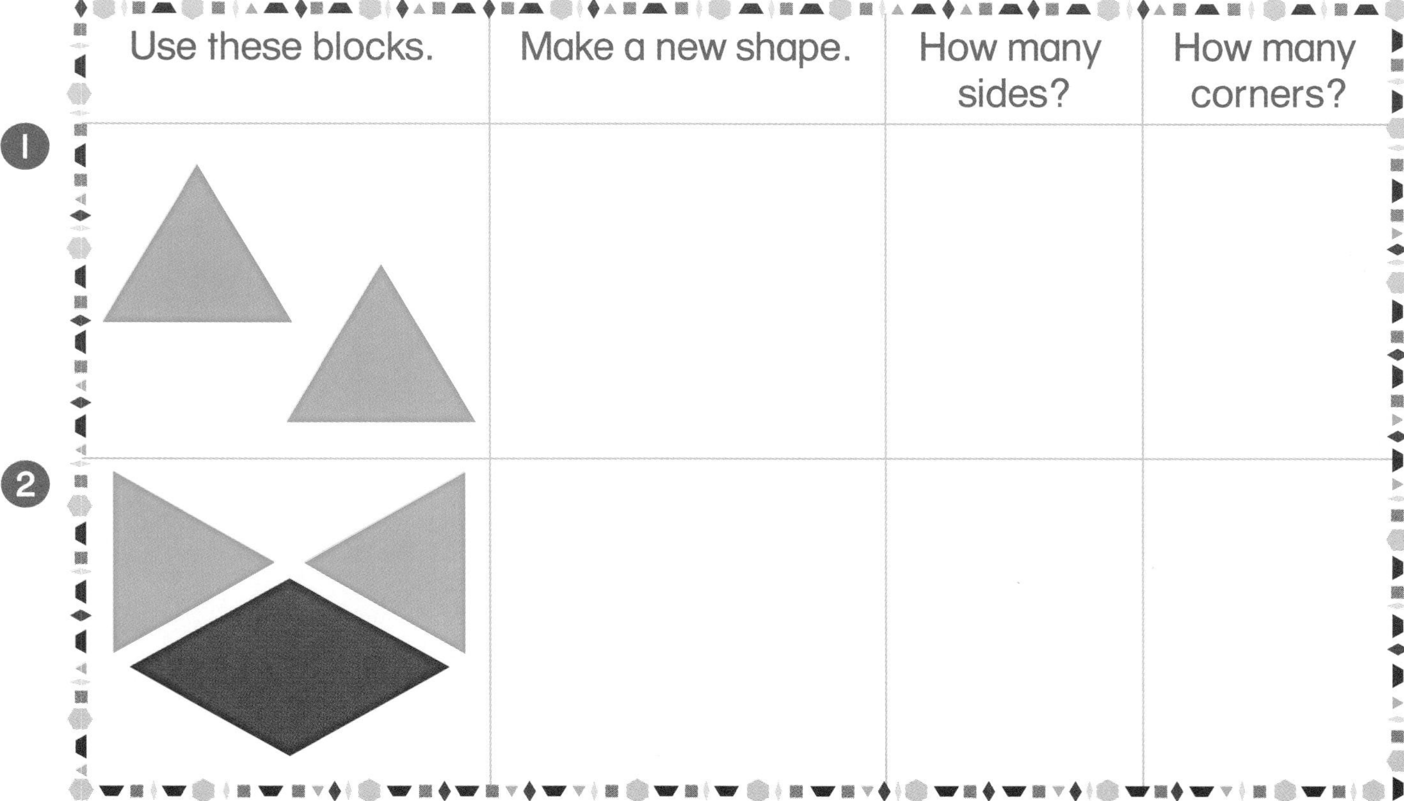

	Use these blocks.	Make a new shape.	How many sides?	How many corners?
1				
2				

Talk About It Can you make a shape that has a different number of sides than corners? Why or why not?

Notes for Home: Your child combined shapes to make other shapes. *Home Activity:* Ask your child to count the edges and corners on a table in your home.

Practice

Write your own. Use pattern blocks.

Make new shapes. Complete the chart.

	Blocks I Used	New Shape I Made	How many sides?	How many corners?
3				
4				

PRACTICE

Problem Solving Patterns

5 Draw what comes next.

Notes for Home: Your child used pattern blocks to make new shapes and found the number of sides and corners for the new shape. *Home Activity:* Ask your child to make a new shape by drawing a square and a triangle together. Ask your child how many sides and corners the new shape has.

Name

Congruent Shapes

Learn

These two shapes match exactly!

They are congruent. That means they are the same size and the same shape.

Check

Circle the shape that is congruent to the first shape.

1

2

Draw a shape that is congruent to each shape.

3

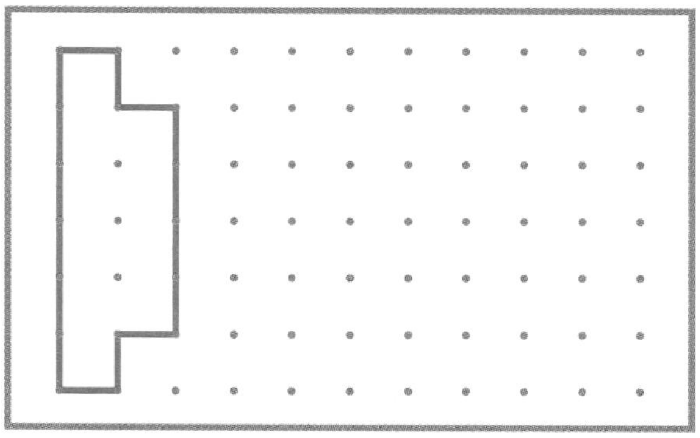

4

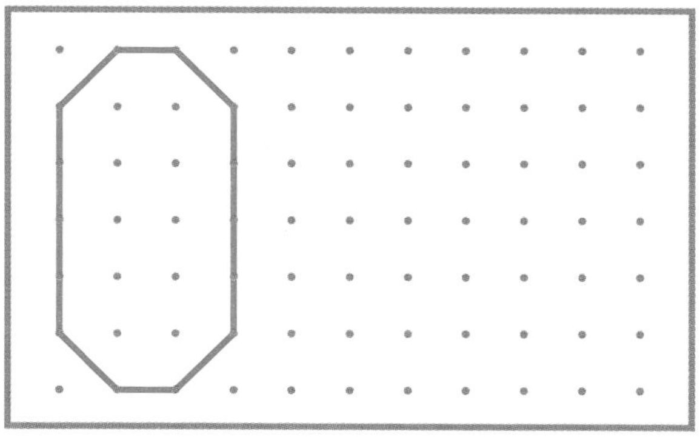

Talk About It How do you know when two shapes are congruent?

Notes for Home: Your child learned about congruent shapes, or shapes that are the same size and shape. *Home Activity:* Show your child a set of plates that are small, medium, and large. Then ask your child to find the plates that are congruent.

Practice

Draw a shape that is congruent to each shape.

5
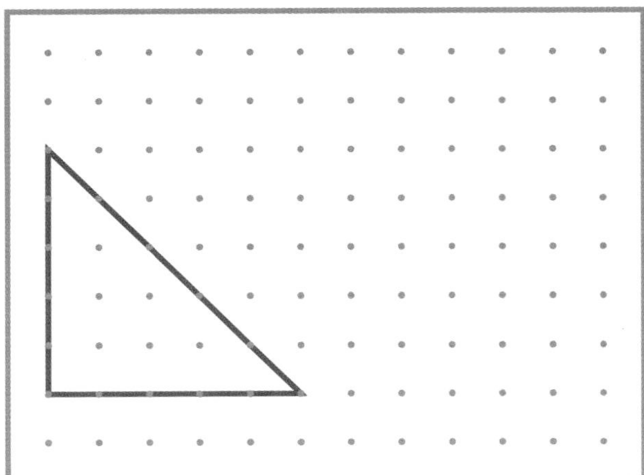

6
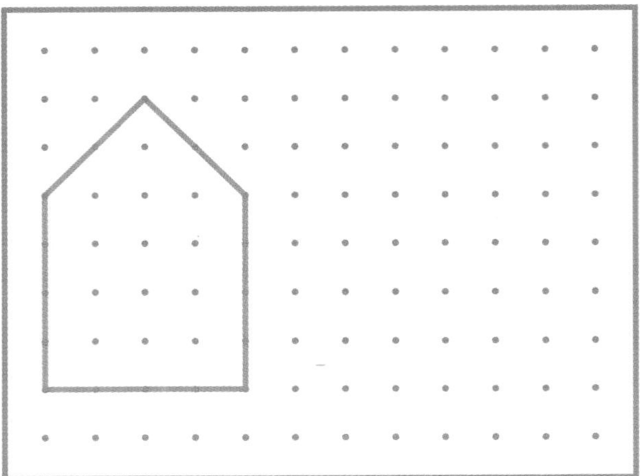

Write your own. Draw a shape. Then have a friend draw a shape that is congruent to your shape.

7
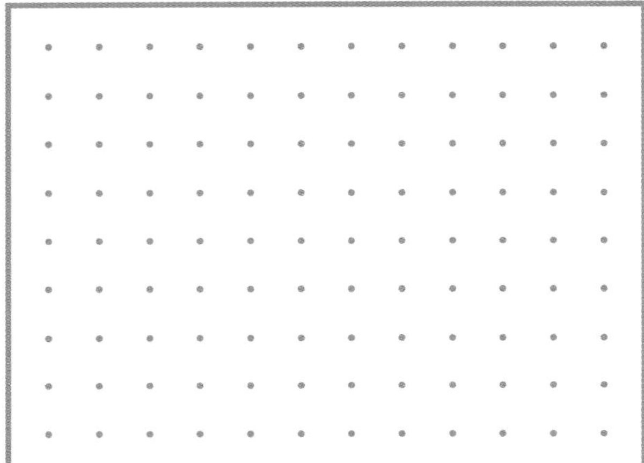

8
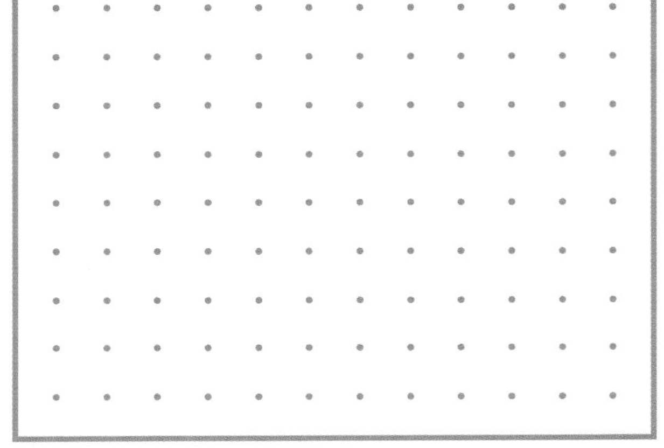

PRACTICE

Problem Solving Visual Thinking

Which fences will keep a pet in the yard? Explain why.
Draw a pet inside those fences.

9

Notes for Home: Your child practiced drawing shapes that are congruent to other shapes.
Home Activity: Show forks, spoons, and knives that are different sizes and shapes. Ask your child to make pairs showing congruent shapes.

For additional practice, see Skills Practice Bank, page 538, Set 1.

Name

Slides, Flips, and Turns

Learn

You can slide, flip, and turn shapes.

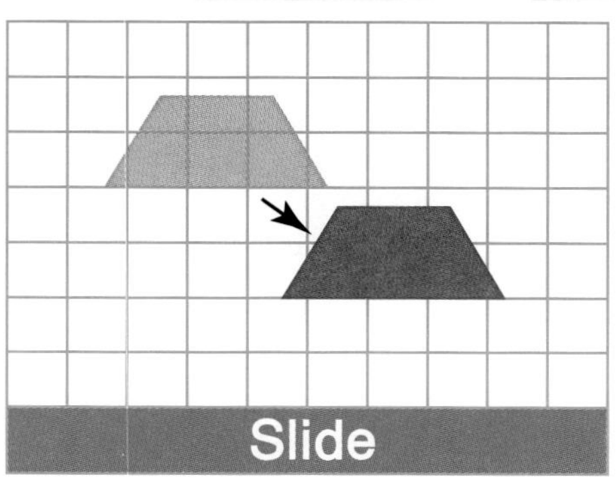

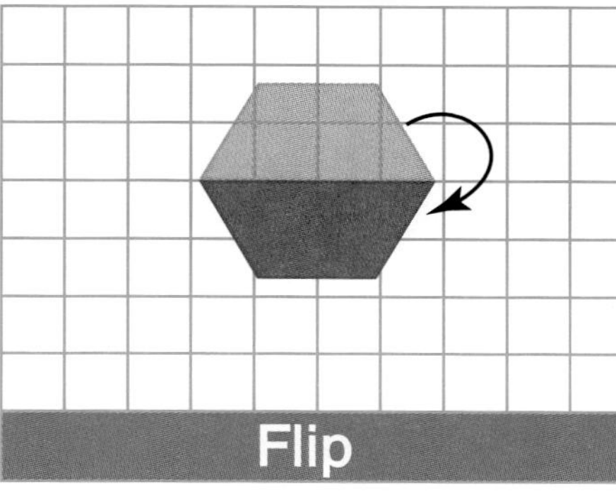

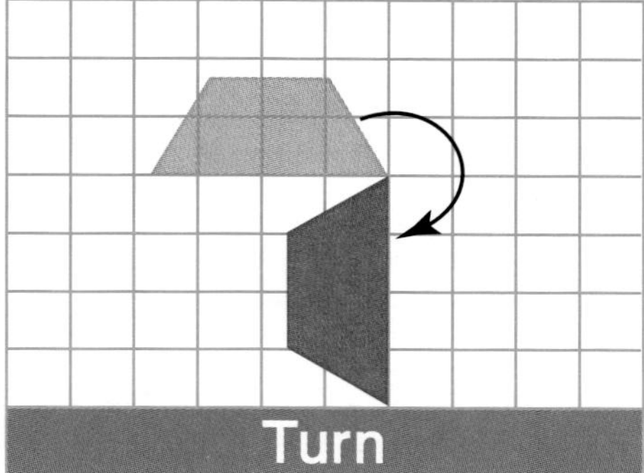

Check

Slide, flip, or turn pattern blocks.
Draw to show how the shape was moved.

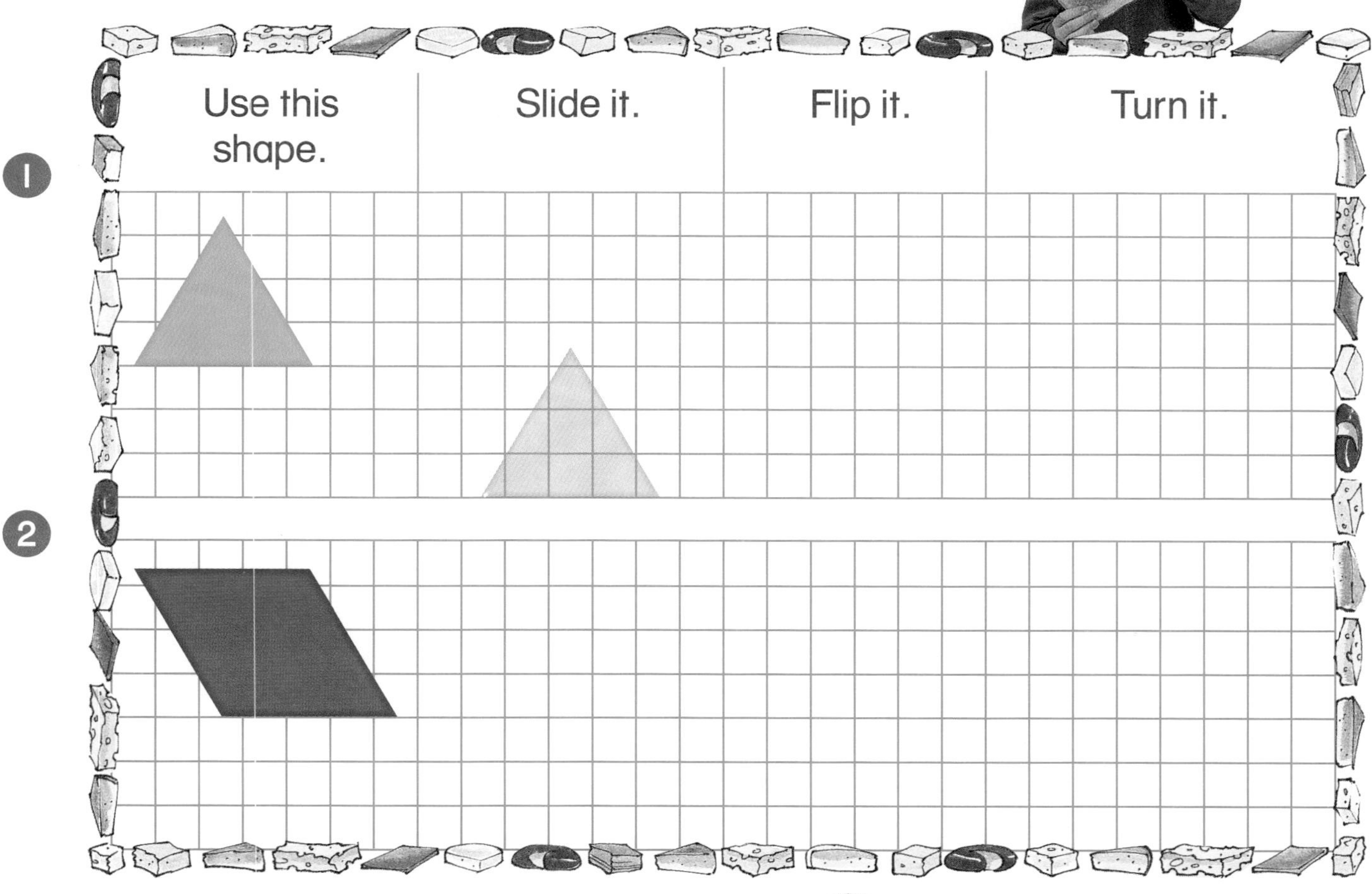

Talk About It Tell how this shape was moved.

Notes for Home: Your child moved shapes by sliding, flipping, or turning them.
Home Activity: Ask your child to use a piece of paper to show you how to slide, flip, and turn a shape.

Practice

Write **slide**, **flip**, or **turn**. Use pattern blocks to check.

3 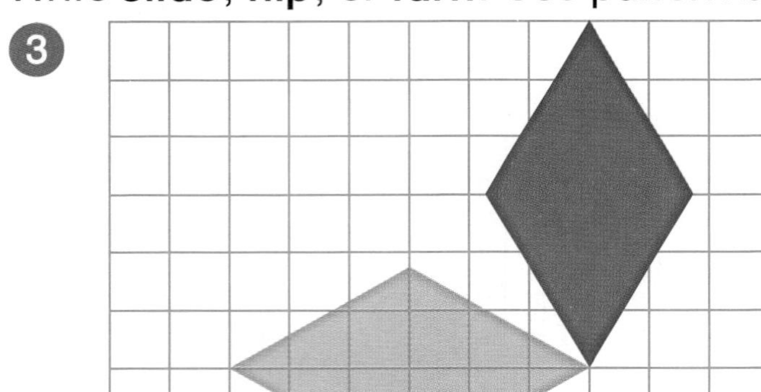

____

4 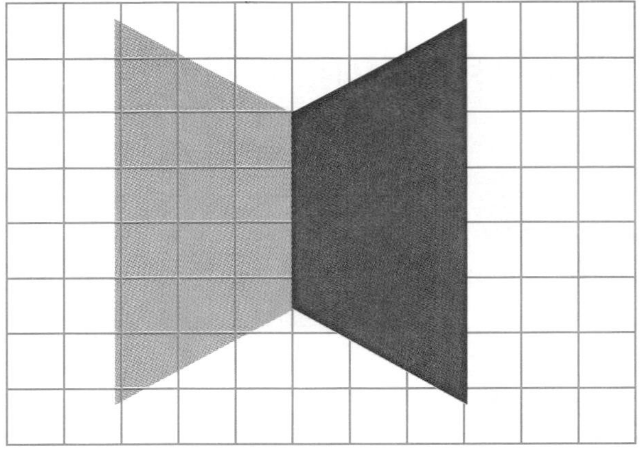

____

5 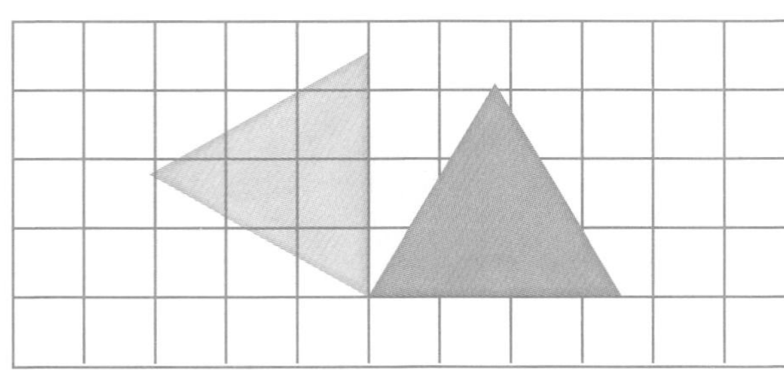

____

6 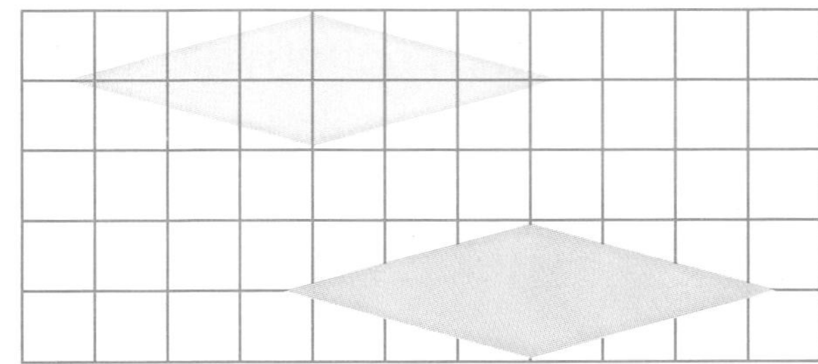

____

PRACTICE

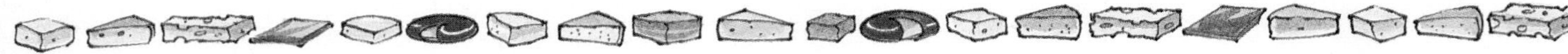

Problem Solving

Use pattern blocks to make the shape. Trace to show the blocks you used.

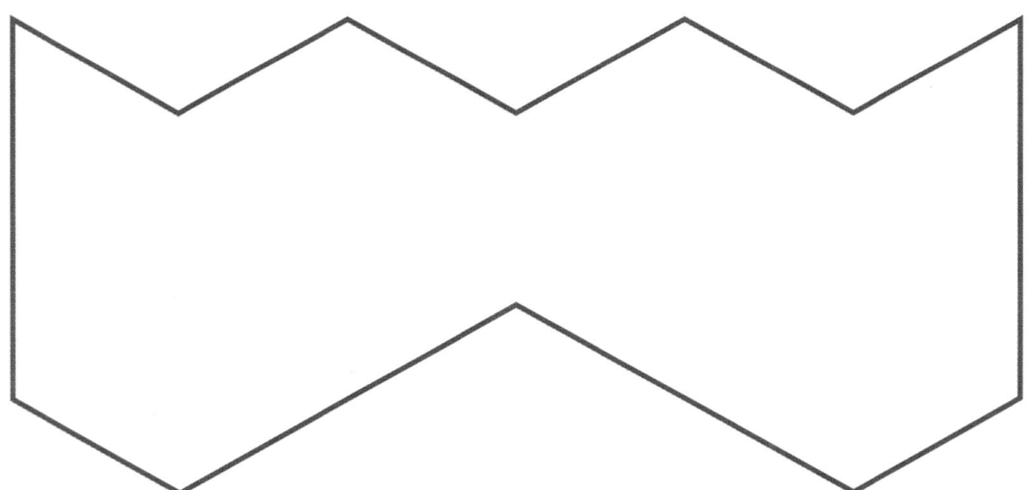

Notes for Home: Your child used blocks to tell whether a shape had been flipped, turned, or slid.
Home Activity: Ask your child to draw a picture of a triangle that has been slid.

Name

Symmetry

Learn

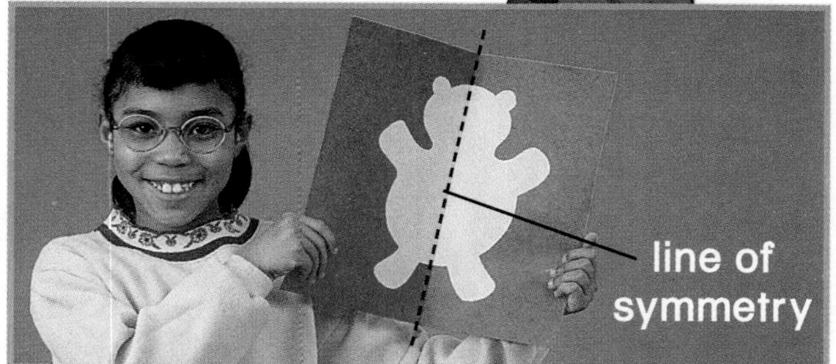

This shape shows a line of symmetry. The parts match when the picture is folded. It looks like a flip!

This shape does not show a line of symmetry. The parts do not match when the picture is folded.

Check

Does the shape show symmetry? Circle **yes** or **no**.
Draw a line of symmetry if there is one.

1. yes no
2. yes no
3. yes no
4. yes no

Make the shapes show symmetry. Draw to show the matching parts.

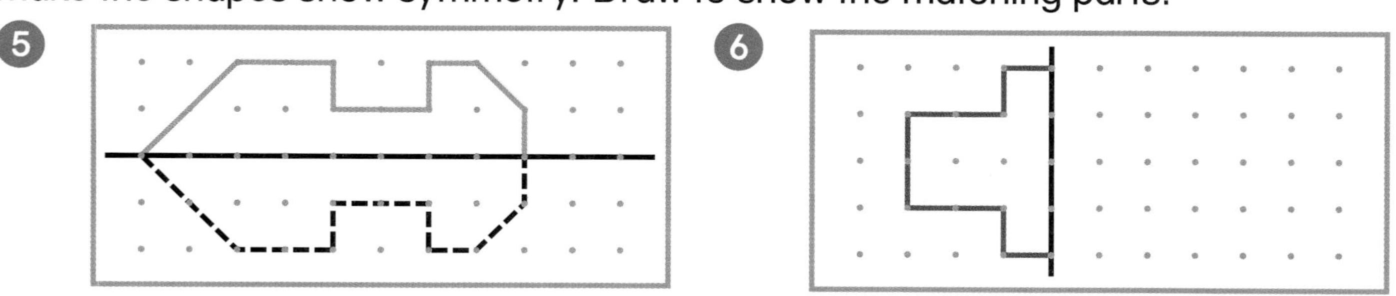

5.
6.

Talk About It What objects in your classroom show symmetry?

Notes for Home: Your child learned how to determine if a shape shows a line of symmetry, or matching parts. *Home Activity:* Ask your child to find a picture in a magazine or newspaper that shows two matching parts.

Practice

Make the shapes show symmetry.

Draw to show the matching part.

7 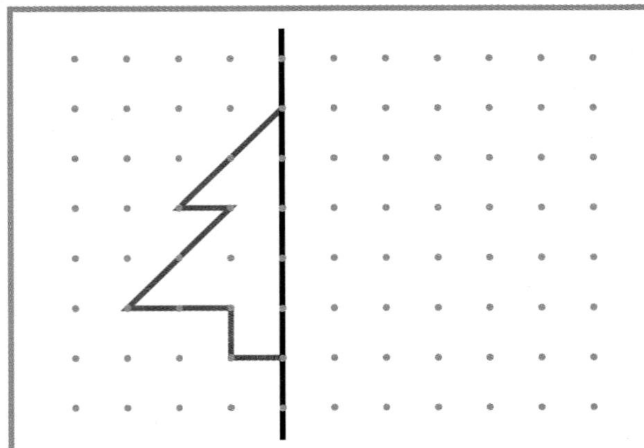

8 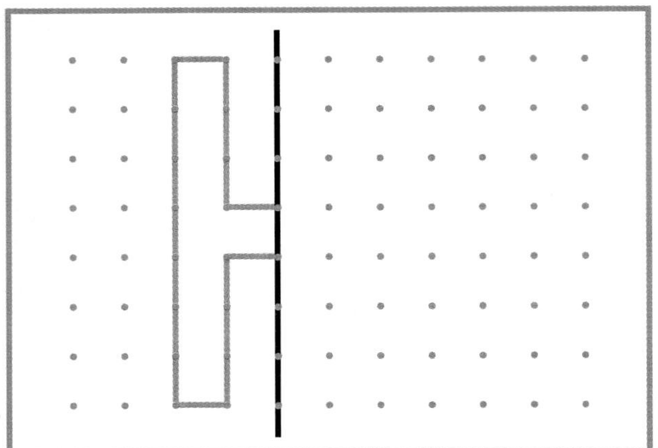

Mixed Practice Trace each shape.

Flip the pattern block. Trace again.

Draw one line of symmetry for the new shape.

9 Use ▬ .

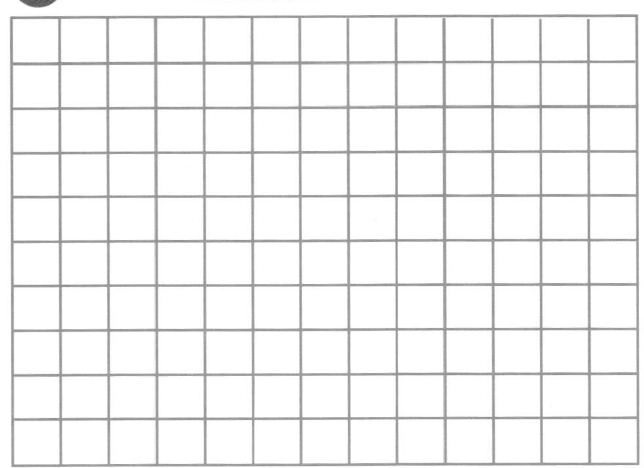

10 Use ▲ .

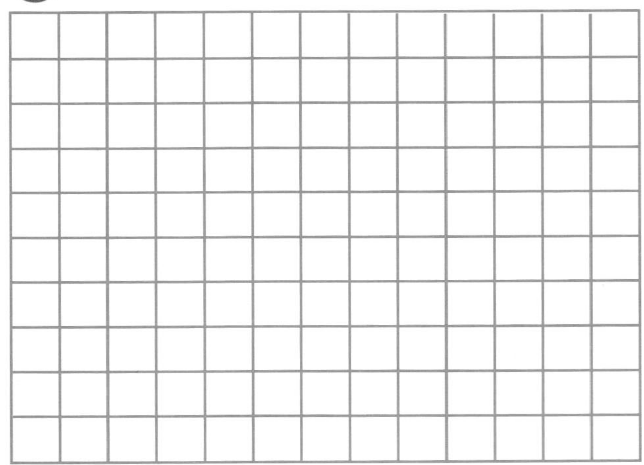

Problem Solving Visual Thinking

Draw as many lines of symmetry as you can.

11 

12 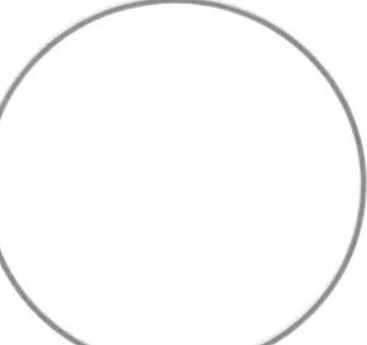

13 

Notes for Home: Your child completed shapes to show symmetry. *Home Activity:* Ask your child to draw a picture of a sandwich to show matching parts.

PRACTICE

Name ______________________

Reading for Math

Use Logical Reasoning

Read the riddle. Then draw the shape it describes.

I read the whole riddle first before I started to draw.

1. I have 3 corners and 3 sides. I am green on the inside with blue dots.

2. There is a pattern block that is my shape. I have 6 sides and 6 corners. I am red on the inside.

3. My shape shows symmetry. I have no corners. I have black and yellow stripes.

Talk About It How does it help to read the whole riddle first before you begin to draw the shape?

Notes for Home: Your child drew shapes to fit a description. *Home Activity:* Describe an object in your home and have your child identify it.

Read the riddle. Then draw the shape it describes.

4. If you traced around the face of a cube, you would draw my shape. I have a line of symmetry drawn through my middle. I am gray.

5. There is a pattern block that is my shape. You can make me by putting 2 triangles together. I am brown all over.

6. I have 5 sides and 5 corners. You can make me by putting a square and a triangle together. I am black.

7. I am not a square, but I have 4 sides and 4 corners. Part of me is yellow, and part is purple.

Journal

8. Draw your own shape. Tell a friend how to draw it. Don't let your friend see your drawing!

Notes for Home: Your child drew shapes to fit a description. *Home Activity:* Ask your child to draw a shape that has 3 sides and is two colors.

Name

Problem Solving: Use Logical Reasoning

Learn

PROBLEM SOLVING GUIDE

Understand • Plan • Solve • Look Back

Which cracker am I?

I am yellow.
I have less than 4 corners.

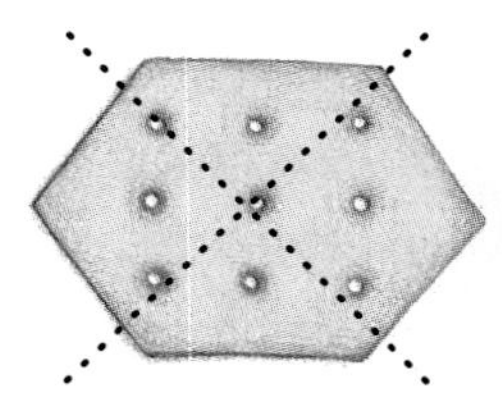
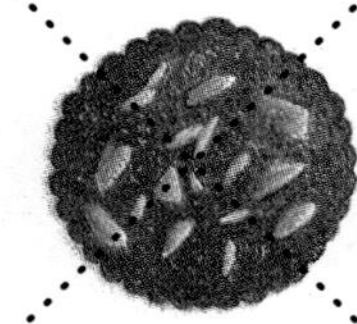
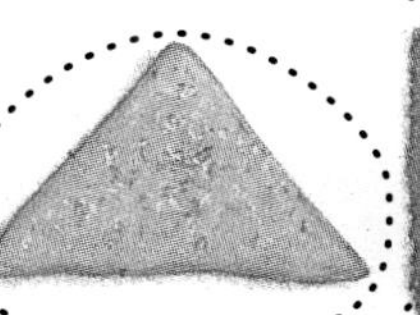
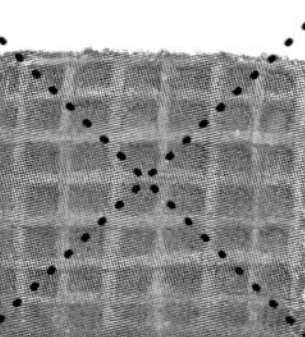

Check

Solve the riddles. Cross out pictures that don't match the clues. Circle the answers.

1. Which cracker am I?
I have more than 3 sides.
I am not yellow.
I have more than 4 corners.

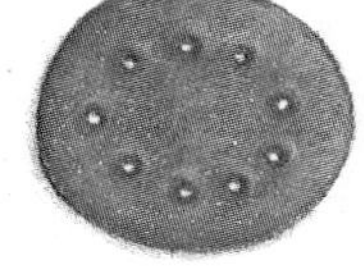
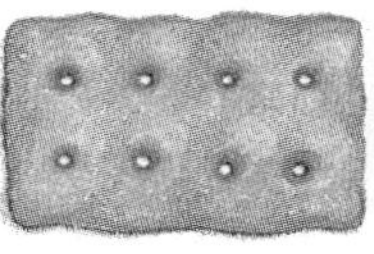
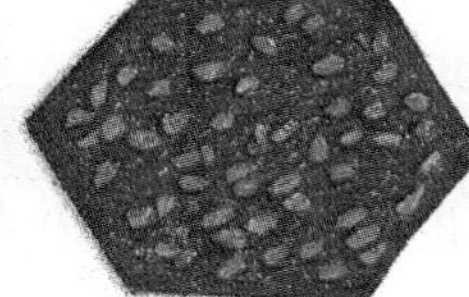

2. Which cracker am I?
My shape shows symmetry.
I have more than 3 corners.

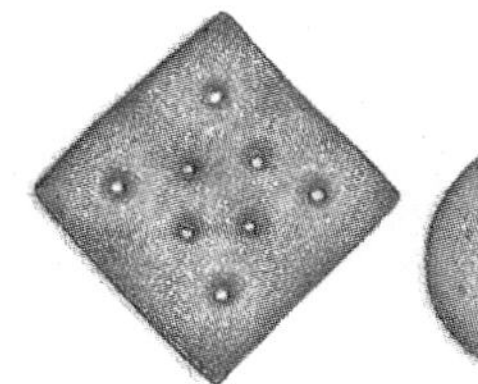
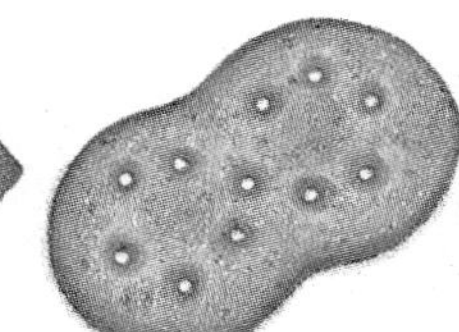

3. Which cracker am I?
I have corners. I am not congruent to another cracker.

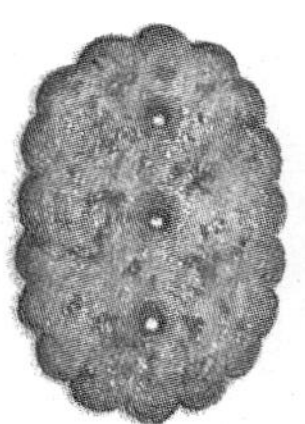

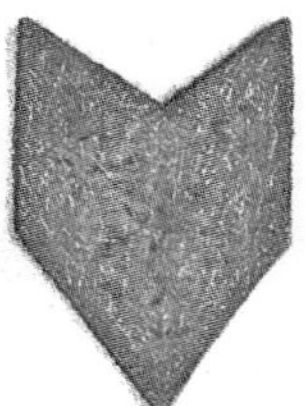
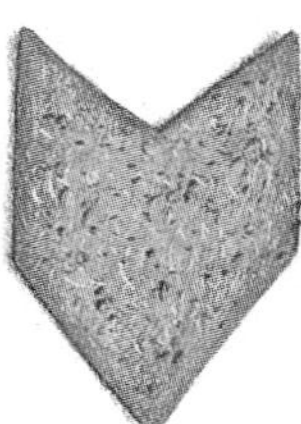

Talk About It How does crossing out pictures help you to solve the riddles?

Notes for Home: Your child used logical reasoning to solve riddles. *Home Activity:* Ask your child to solve this riddle: I have no corners. Am I a circle, square, or triangle? (circle)

PROBLEM SOLVING

Practice

Solve the riddles. Cross out pictures that don't match the clues. Circle the answers.

4 Which cracker am I?
I have more than 3 corners.
I do not have holes.

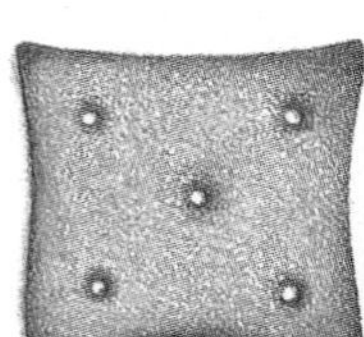

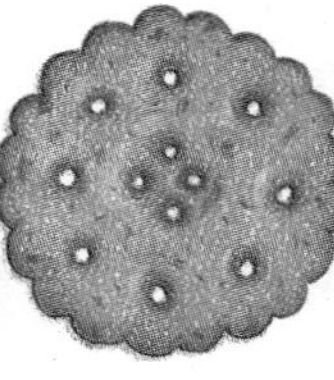

5 Which cracker am I?
I have no corners.
I have no stripes.

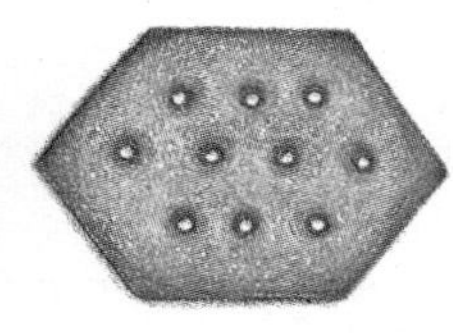

6 Which cracker am I?
I am not a rectangle.
I am brown.
I have 3 sides.

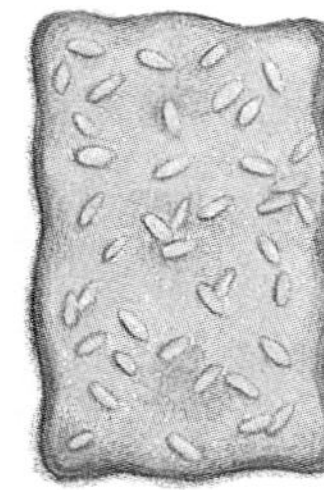

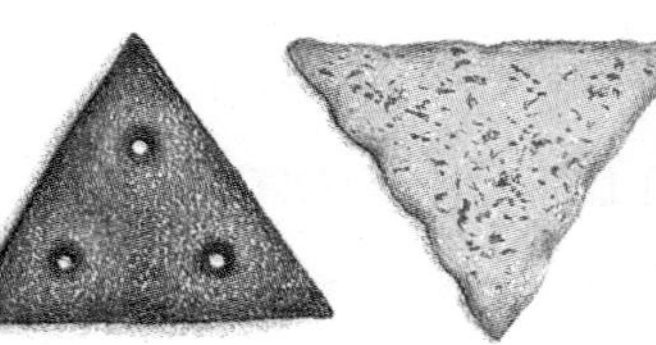
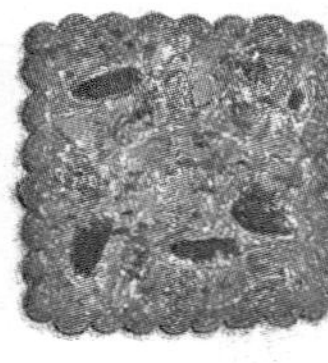

Write About it

7 Write a riddle about 4 different shapes.

Draw your shapes.

PROBLEM SOLVING

Notes for Home: Your child practiced using logical reasoning to solve riddles.
Home Activity: Use different objects and ask your child to tell you a riddle about them.

Name ______

Mixed Practice

Lessons 1–7

Write how many faces, corners, and edges for this solid. 

1 ______ faces
2 ______ corners
3 ______ edges

4 Draw a shape that is congruent.

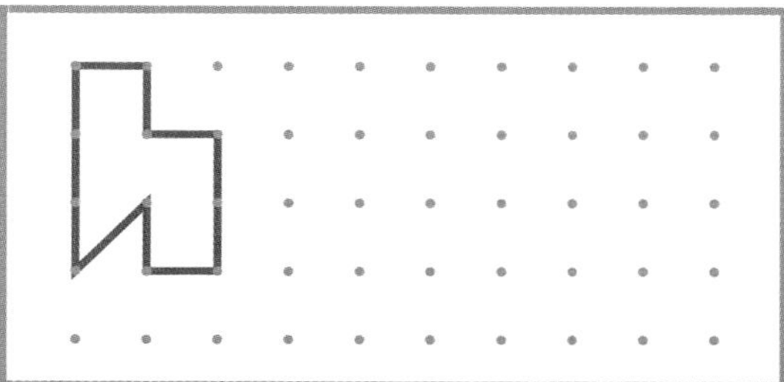

5 Write **slide, flip,** or **turn**.

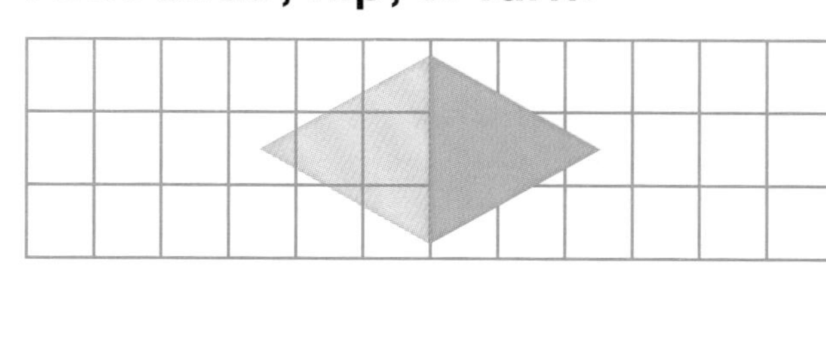

______

Make the shapes show symmetry. Draw matching parts.

6

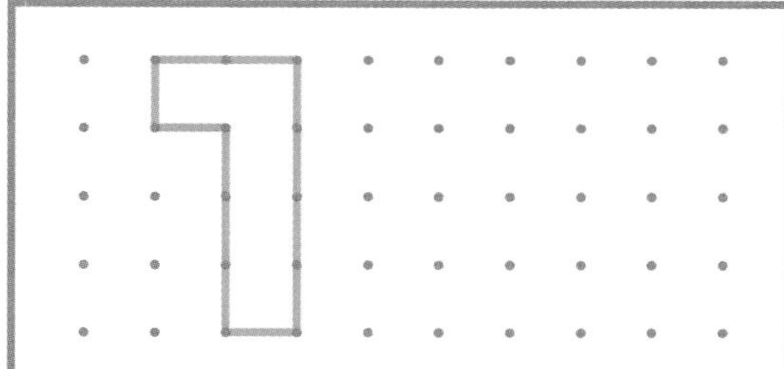

7

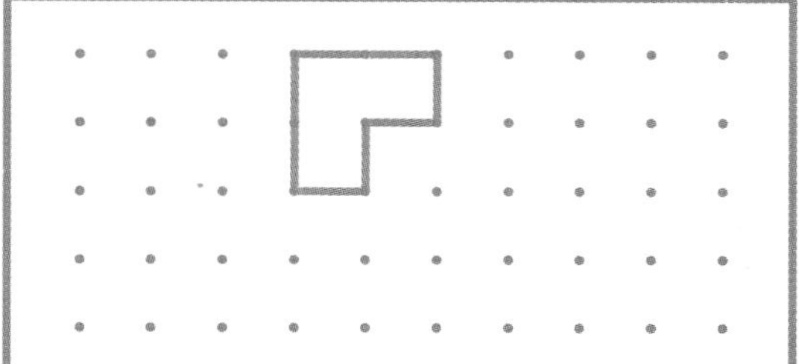

MIXED PRACTICE

Problem Solving

Solve the riddle. Cross out the pictures that don't match the clues. Circle the answer.

8 I have more than 1 side.
I have 4 corners.
I have only 1 line of symmetry.
I have holes.

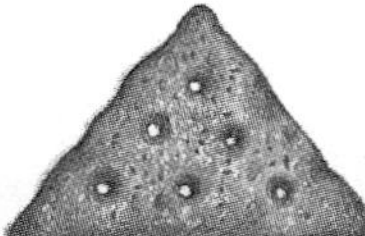

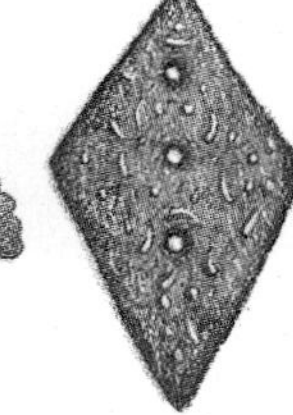

Journal

9 Draw a triangle. Then draw what happens when you flip, slide, and turn the triangle.

Notes for Home: Your child practiced identifying and drawing shapes. *Home Activity:* Ask your child to draw a building that includes a square, a rectangle, a triangle, and a circle.

me ______________________________

Cumulative Review

Chapters 1–12

Concepts and Skills

Write the number.

1 thirty-nine ______ **2** seventy-two ______ **3** sixty ______

Find the nearest ten.

Estimate the sum.

4

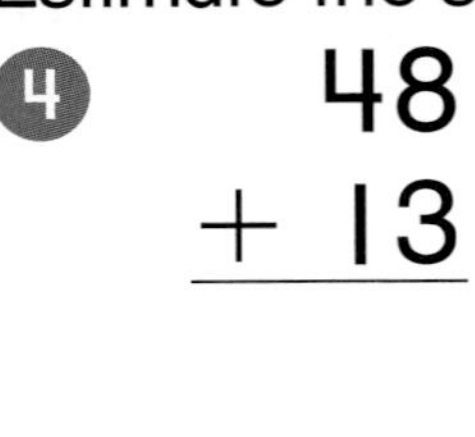

$$\begin{array}{r} 48 \\ +\ 13 \\ \hline \end{array}$$

Think:

48 + 13 is about ______.

5

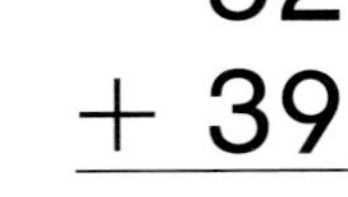

$$\begin{array}{r} 52 \\ +\ 39 \\ \hline \end{array}$$

Think:

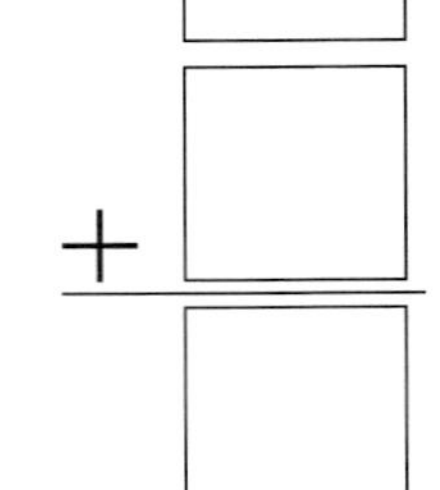

52 + 39 is about ______.

Problem Solving

Solve.

6 Cheese costs 38¢. Crackers cost 29¢. How much would both cheese and crackers cost?

______ ¢

7 You need 18 banana slices and 27 apple slices for a fruit salad. How many slices do you need?

______ slices

Test Prep

Fill in the ○ for the correct answer.

8 Find the length in inches.

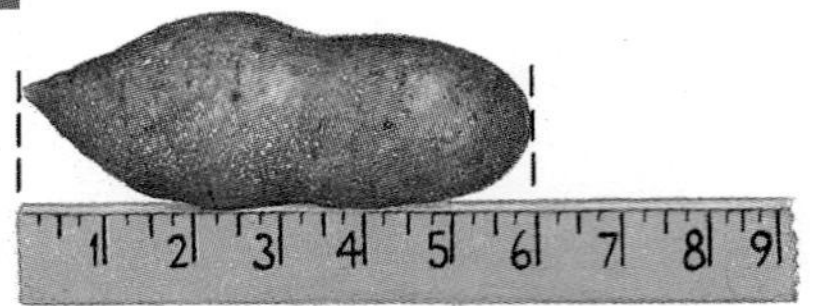

about 3 inches ○ about 4 inches ○ about 6 inches ○ about 9 inches ○

Notes for Home: Your child reviewed reading and writing words, estimating sums, solving problems, and estimating lengths. *Home Activity:* Ask your child to use a ruler to measure the length of a fork and a spoon.

CUMULATIVE REVIEW

Name

Equal and Unequal Parts

Learn

I made 4 equal parts. Everyone will get a piece that is the same size.

Oops! I made 4 parts, but they are not the same size.

Check

Write the number of parts. Then circle **equal** or **not equal.**

1. 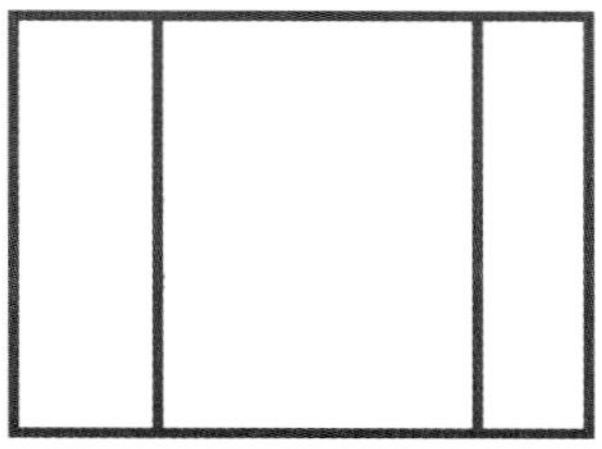 3 parts
   equal
   not equal

2. 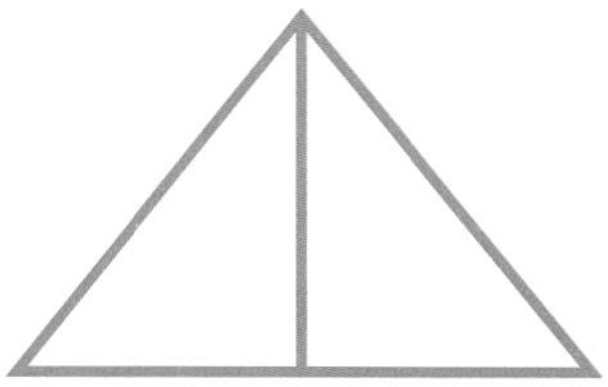 ______ parts
   equal
   not equal

3. 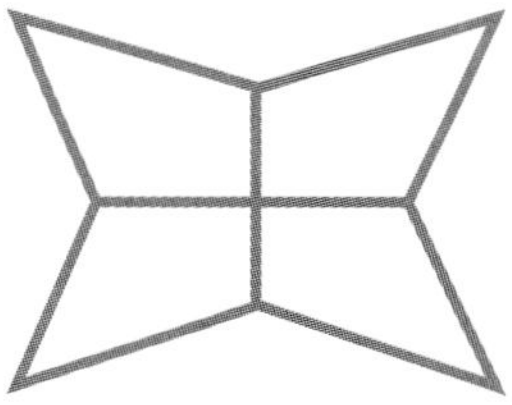 ______ parts
   equal
   not equal

4.  ______ parts
   equal
   not equal

5. 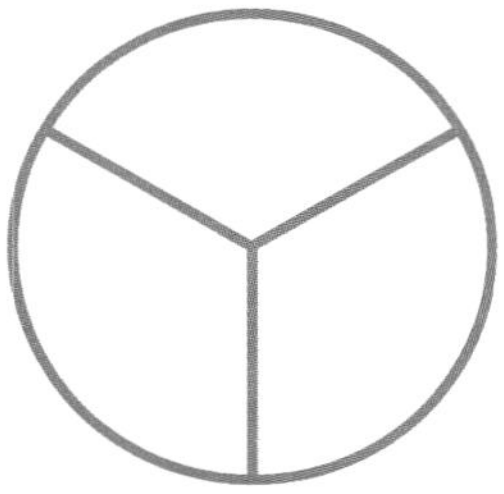 ______ parts
   equal
   not equal

6. ______ parts
   equal
   not equal

Talk About It What are 3 ways you could divide a square into 4 equal parts?

Notes for Home: Your child identified the number of parts in a shape and decided if the parts are equal or not equal. *Home Activity:* Ask your child to draw a circle divided into 4 equal parts and another circle divided into 4 parts that are not equal.

How many equal parts in each shape?

7

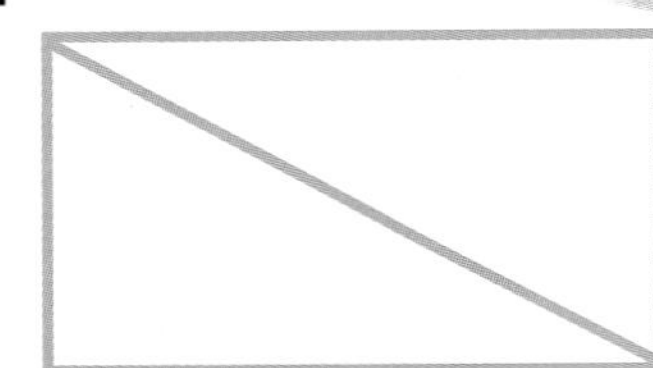

9 equal parts

_____ equal parts

_____ equal parts

Draw equal parts. Color each part a different color.

8

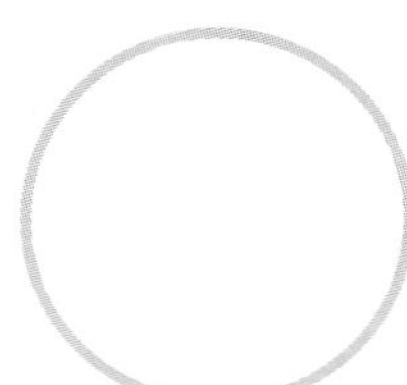

3 equal parts

2 equal parts

4 equal parts

9

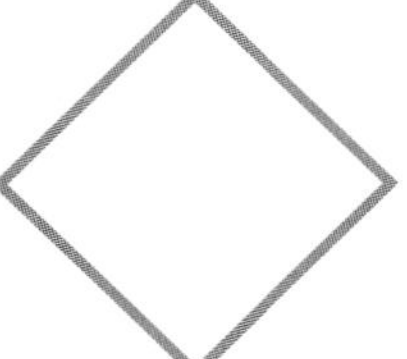

8 equal parts

6 equal parts

2 equal parts

Problem Solving Visual Thinking

10 Use pattern blocks to make this shape.
How many different ways can you find?
Which ways show equal parts?

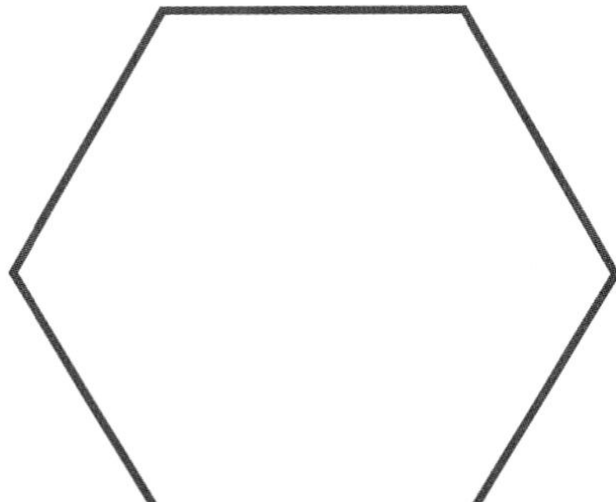

Notes for Home: Your child divided shapes into a number of equal parts. *Home Activity:* Ask your child to draw rectangles divided into 2, 3, 4, and 6 equal parts.

Name

Unit Fractions

Learn

The parts are equal. You can write a fraction.

halves

I of 2 equal parts is blue.

One half is blue. $\frac{1}{2}$ is blue.

thirds

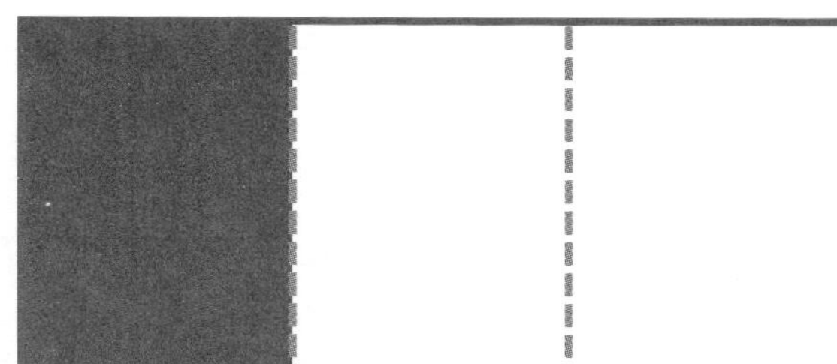

I of 3 equal parts is red.

One third is red. $\frac{1}{3}$ is red.

Check

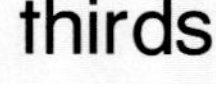

Fold paper to show equal parts. Shade one part.

	How many equal parts?	Draw to show how you folded and shaded.	Write the fraction for the shaded part.
1	4		1 part shaded 4 equal parts in all one fourth is shaded.
2	6		☐ part shaded ☐ equal parts in all ______ sixth is shaded.

Talk About It What does the fraction $\frac{1}{10}$ mean?

Notes for Home: Your child learned about fractions as parts of a whole. *Home Activity:* Ask your child to draw pictures of sandwiches cut into halves and fourths. Ask your child to name the fraction for each part.

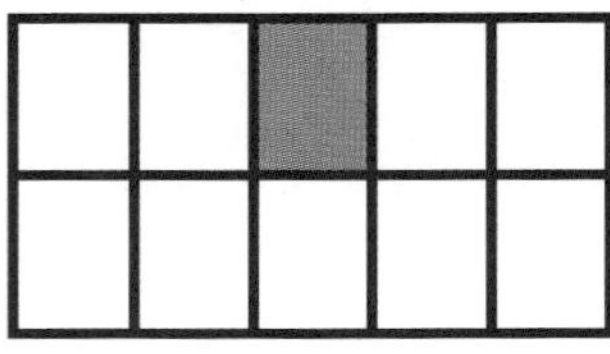
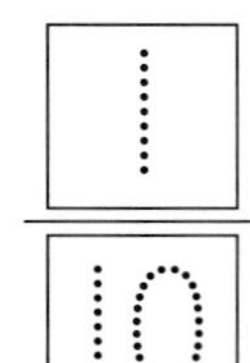

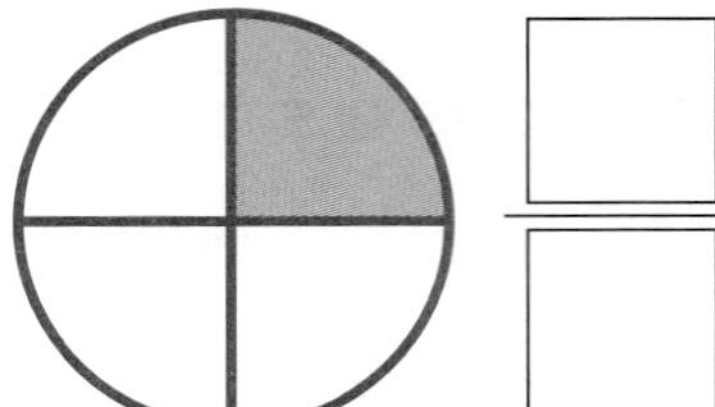

fraction for the part that is shaded.

3  

1 part shaded

10 equal parts in all

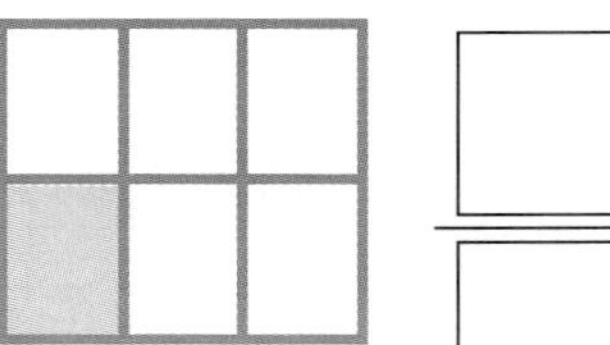

4 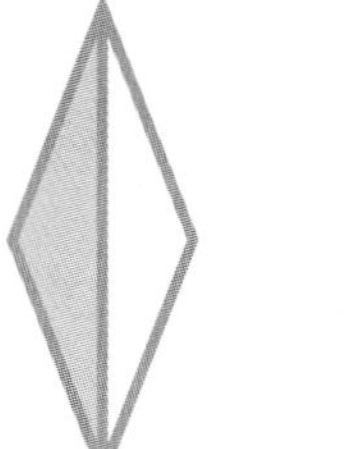 

5  

6  

7  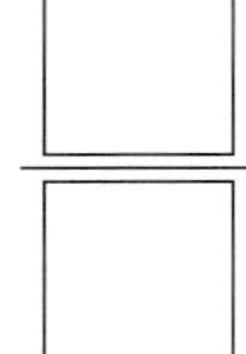

8  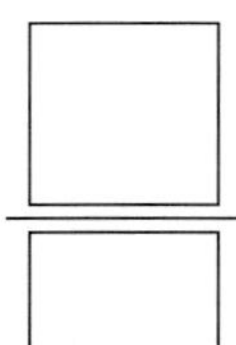

9  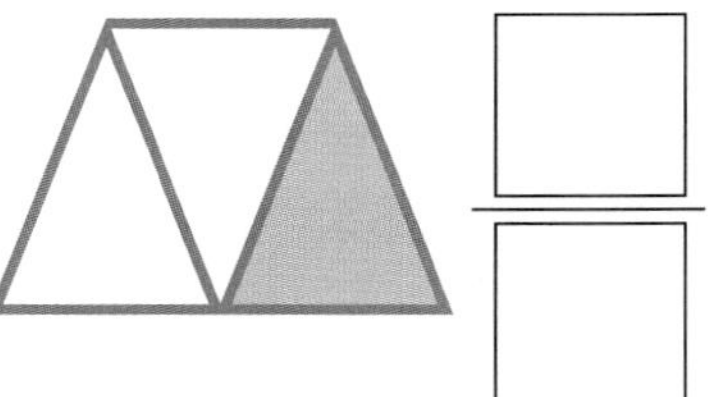

10  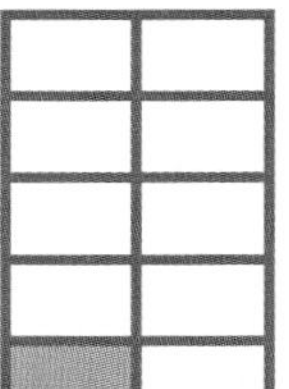 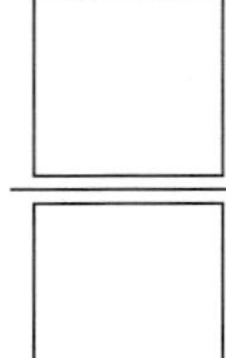

11

12

13

Problem Solving Critical Thinking

14 Each cracker has 4 equal parts.
How are the parts of the two crackers alike?
How are they different?

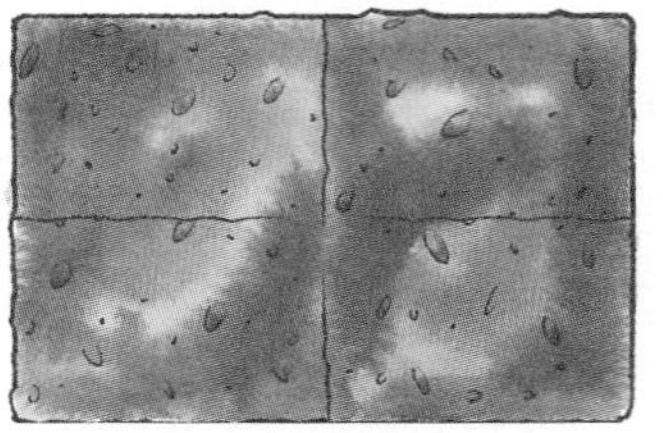
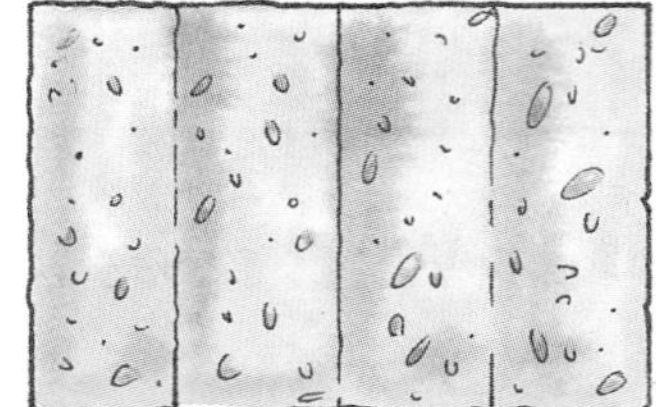

Notes for Home: Your child practiced writing different fractions. *Home Activity:* Ask your child to cut a food item into equal parts, and name the fraction for one of the parts.

PRACTICE

Name

Fraction

Learn

2 parts with jelly

4 equal parts

two fourths of the cracker have jelly.

Check

Write the fraction for the parts that are shaded. Count equal parts first.

1.  $\frac{3}{5}$ — 3 fifths

2. 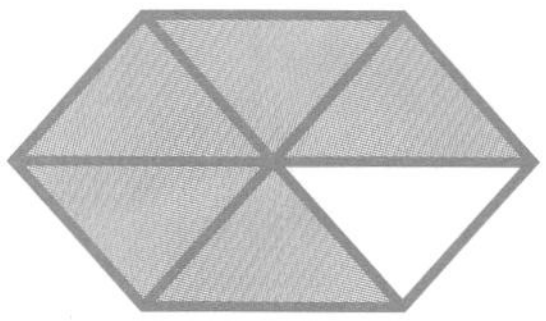 $\frac{\square}{\square}$ — ______ sixths

3. 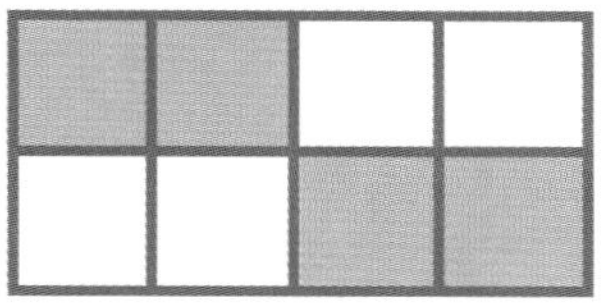 $\frac{\square}{\square}$ — ______ eighths

4. 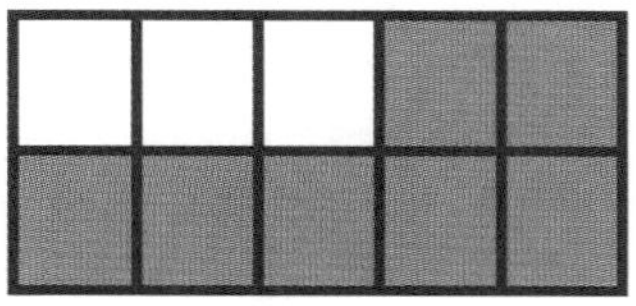 $\frac{\square}{\square}$ — ______ tenths

5. 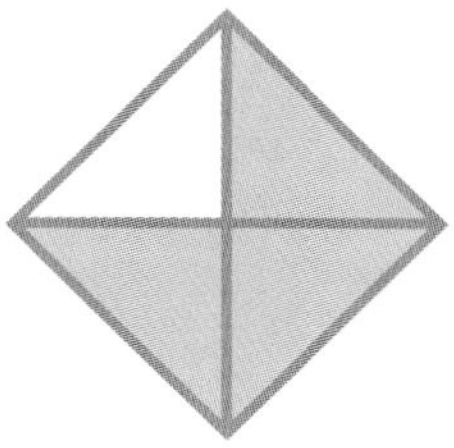 $\frac{\square}{\square}$ — ______ fourths

6. 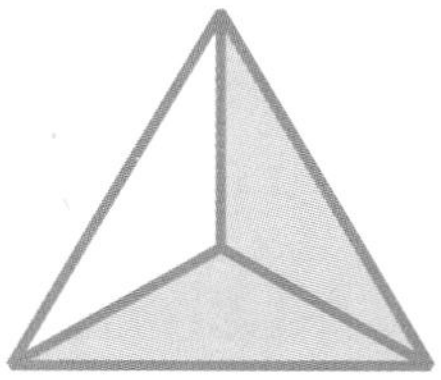 $\frac{\square}{\square}$ — ______ thirds

Talk About It What are 3 ways you could show $\frac{3}{8}$ of this shape?

Notes for Home: Your child wrote fractions to describe the shaded parts of shapes.
Home Activity: Ask your child to tell you what $\frac{5}{6}$ means. (5 out of 6 equal parts)

ɘ of the equal parts.

ɑction for parts that are shaded.

7 Shade 3 parts. $\frac{3}{5}$

8 Shade 2 parts.

9 Shade 6 parts.

10 Shade 9 parts.

11 Shade 1 part.

12 Shade 2 parts.

13 Shade 3 parts.

14 Shade 1 part.

Problem Solving

15 Solve.

You have $\frac{1}{3}$ of a granola bar left. How much did you already eat?

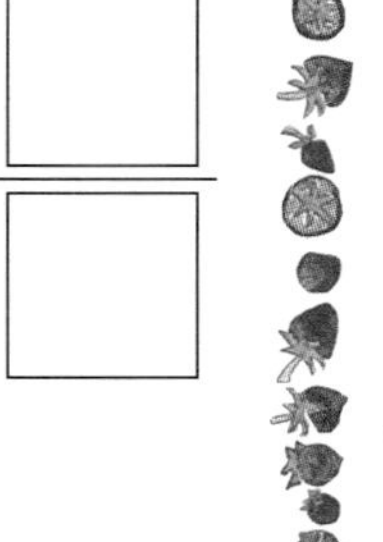

Write your own problem about a fraction of a pizza. Have a friend solve it.

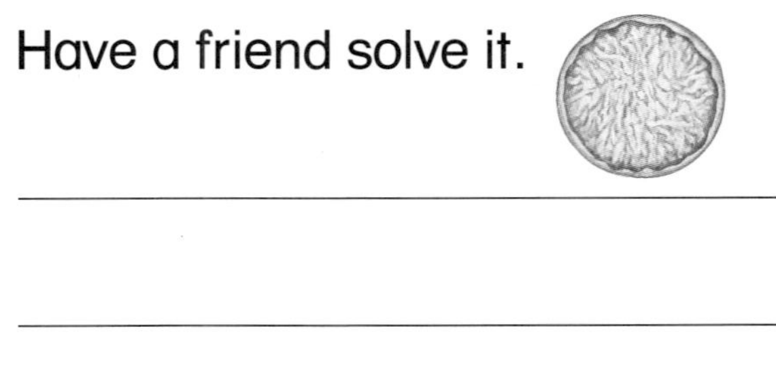

Notes for Home: Your child practiced writing fractions. *Home Activity:* Ask your child to fold a paper into 4 equal parts, color some parts, and name the fraction.

For additional practice, see Skills Practice Bank, page 538, Set 2.

Name ___________________________

Fraction Concentration

Players 2

What You Need

Gameboard

Crayon purple

Cards labeled with one fraction on each card

I can't color in $\frac{1}{3}$ now, so I'll skip my turn.

$\frac{1}{2}$ $\frac{1}{3}$ $\frac{2}{3}$ $\frac{1}{4}$ $\frac{2}{4}$ $\frac{1}{8}$ $\frac{2}{8}$ $\frac{3}{8}$ $\frac{4}{8}$ $\frac{5}{8}$ $\frac{6}{8}$ $\frac{3}{4}$

How to Play

1. Lay out cards facedown.
2. Players take turns. Each player turns one card over and colors that fraction on his or her gameboard. Then the player puts the card back facedown.
3. The player who colors in three rows first wins.

one							

Notes for Home: Your child played a game to practice naming fractions. *Home Activity:* Ask your child to draw pictures to show the fractions $\frac{2}{3}$ and $\frac{3}{4}$.

PRACTICE

Name ________________________________

Write the number of parts.
Then circle **equal** or **not equal.**

1 

______ part

equal

not equal

2 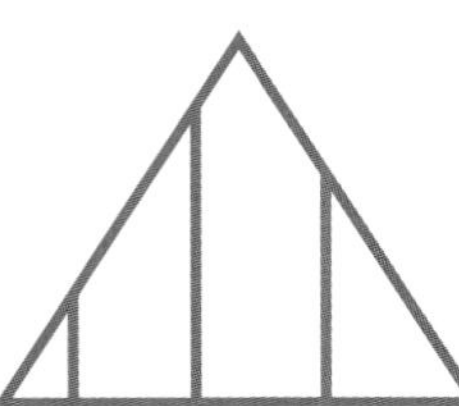

______ parts

equal

not equal

Draw equal parts. Color each part a different color.

3   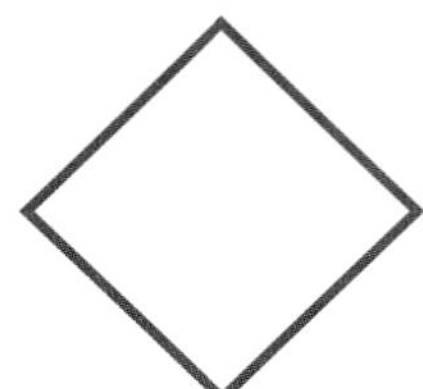

6 equal parts

4 equal parts

2 equal parts

Write the fraction for the parts that are shaded.

4 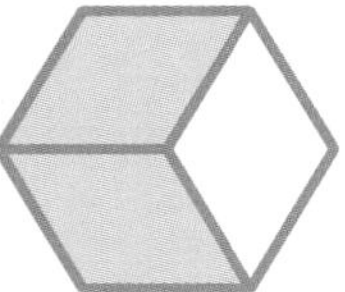

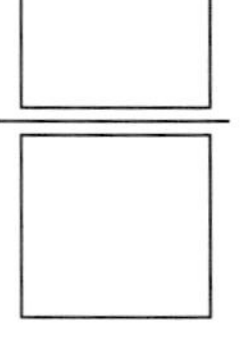

________ thirds

5 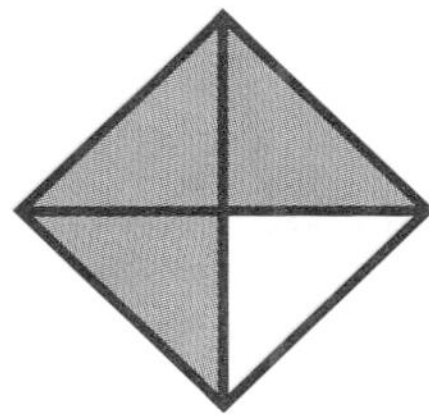

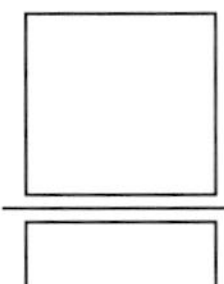

________ fourths

Shade some of the equal parts.
Write the fraction for the shaded parts.

6 Shade 1 part.

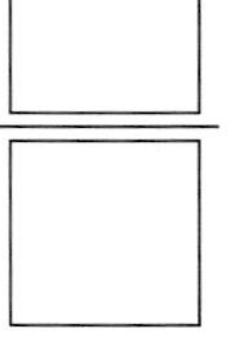

7 Shade 5 parts.

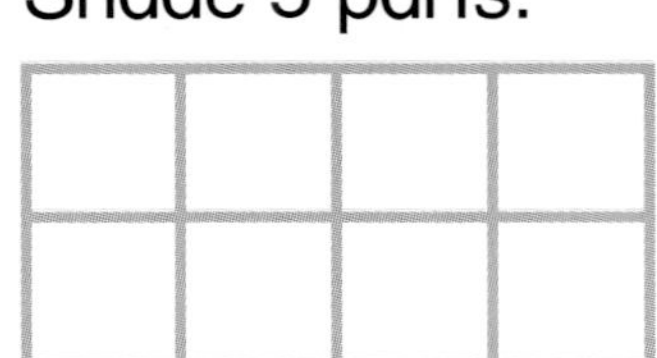

PRACTICE

Notes for Home: Your child practiced writing fractions. *Home Activity:* Ask your child to fold a paper into 8 equal parts, color some parts, and name the fraction.

Name

Estimate Parts of a Whole

Learn

About how much of the tostada is left?

Check

How much is left? Circle the best estimate.

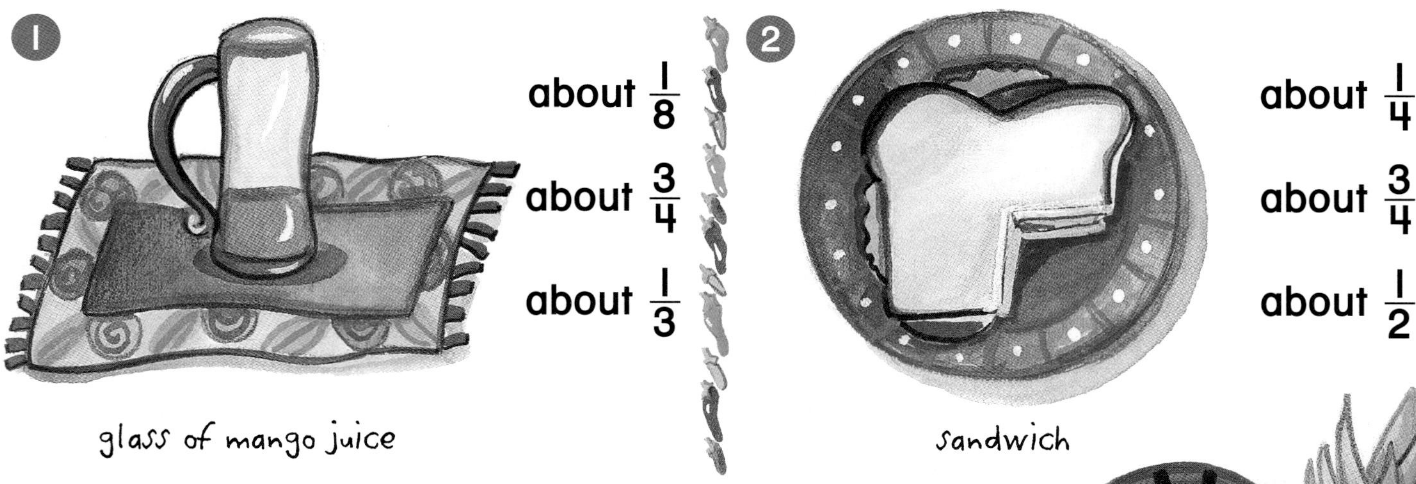

Talk About It About how much of the pineapple slice is left? About how much was eaten? Explain how you know.

Notes for Home: Your child learned to estimate fractions. *Home Activity:* Ask your child to tell you what part is left of a food item using a fraction.

Practice

How much is **left**? Circle the best estimate.

3

pitcher of water

about $\frac{1}{4}$

about $\frac{2}{3}$

about $\frac{1}{6}$

4
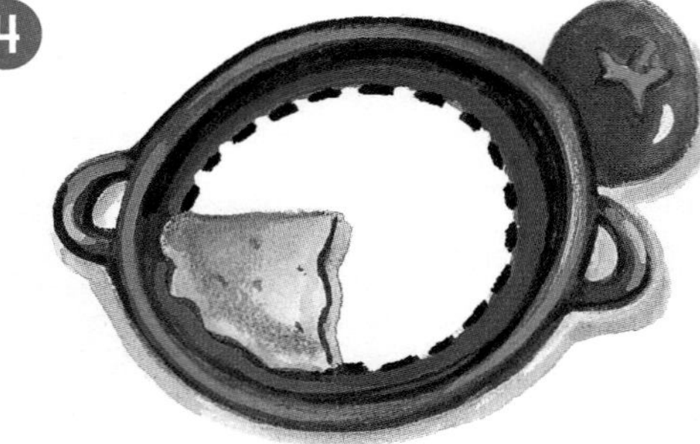
tamale pie

about $\frac{1}{2}$

about $\frac{1}{4}$

about $\frac{3}{4}$

How much **was eaten**? Circle the best estimate.

5

cornbread muffin

about $\frac{3}{4}$

about $\frac{7}{8}$

about $\frac{1}{2}$

6

burrito

about $\frac{1}{3}$

about $\frac{1}{2}$

about $\frac{2}{3}$

Problem Solving Visual Thinking

7 Lena and Jesse had sandwiches that were the same size.

Lena ate 2 parts of her sandwich. Jesse ate 1 part of his. Did Lena eat more than Jesse? Explain.

Lena's Sandwich

Jesse's Sandwich

Notes for Home: Your child estimated what fraction of a food item remains. Ask your child to tell you what part of a slice of bread remains after half of the slice has been eaten.

Name

Explore a Fraction of a Set

Explore

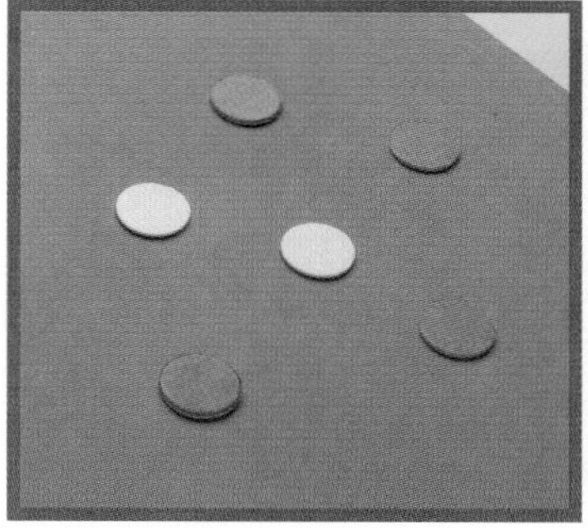

Take some counters.

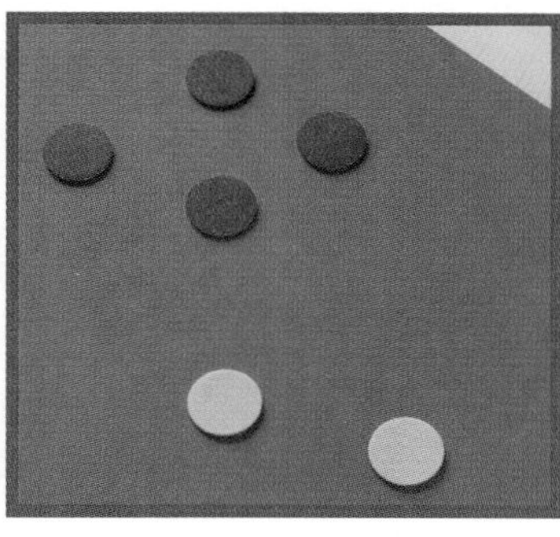

Sort them by color.

4 red counters / 6 counters in all	2 yellow counters / 6 counters in all

Write the fractions.

	Draw the counters.	Write the fractions.	
1		red counters / counters in all	yellow counters / counters in all
2		red counters / counters in all	yellow counters / counters in all
3		red counters / counters in all	yellow counters / counters in all
4		red counters / counters in all	yellow counters / counters in all

EXPLORE

Share

For each picture of counters, add the number of red counters to the number of yellow counters. What pattern do you see?

Notes for Home: Your child explored finding the number of red and yellow counters in a group of counters. *Home Activity:* Ask your child to draw a group of squares in two different colors, and then tell you how many squares of the first color, the second color, and how many squares in all.

Connect

I can write fractions that tell about the group of peppers!

There are 3 green peppers.
There are 4 peppers in all.

$\frac{3}{4}$ of the peppers are green,
and $\frac{1}{4}$ is yellow.

What fraction of each group is green? Write the fraction.

5 

2 green cabbages

3 cabbages in all

$\frac{\square}{\square}$ are green.

6 

____ green

____ apples in all

$\frac{\square}{\square}$ are green.

7 

____ green

____ bananas in all

$\frac{\square}{\square}$ are green.

8 

____ green

____ pears in all

$\frac{\square}{\square}$ are green.

Problem Solving

9 Draw 6 grapes. Color some purple.
Color the rest green.
What fraction is green?

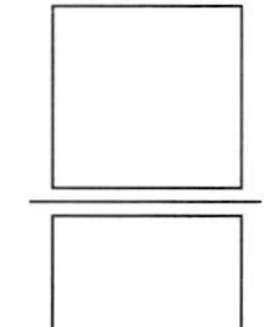

$\frac{\square}{\square}$ are green.

EXPLORE

Notes for Home: Your child wrote fractions to describe how many of a group of objects are one color. *Home Activity:* Ask your child to draw a group of circles in two different colors and write a fraction to tell you how many of the circles are one color.

Name

Fraction of a Set

Learn

There are 3 glasses of **purple** juice.
There are 2 glasses of orange juice.
There are five glasses in all.

$\frac{3}{5}$ are **purple**. $\frac{2}{5}$ are orange.

Check

Color each group to show the fractions.

1.    

$\frac{3}{4}$ orange $\frac{1}{4}$ yellow

2. 
$\frac{2}{6}$ brown $\frac{4}{6}$ red

3. 
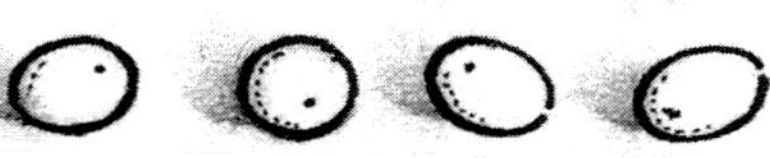
$\frac{4}{8}$ green $\frac{4}{8}$ purple

4.   
$\frac{1}{3}$ blue $\frac{2}{3}$ green

5. 
$\frac{1}{5}$ yellow $\frac{4}{5}$ red

6. 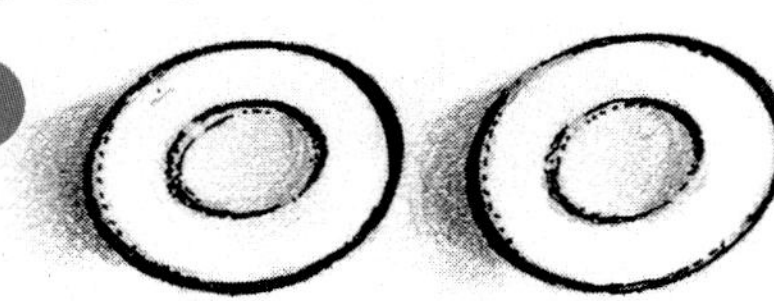
$\frac{1}{2}$ purple $\frac{1}{2}$ yellow

Talk About It $\frac{5}{6}$ of the apples in a bowl are yellow. How many apples are there in all? Explain how you know.

Notes for Home: Your child colored objects to show a fraction. *Home Activity:* Ask your child to draw 5 circles and color $\frac{2}{5}$ red and $\frac{3}{5}$ blue.

Practice

7. Draw a group of apples.
Color $\frac{5}{6}$ yellow. Color $\frac{1}{6}$ red.

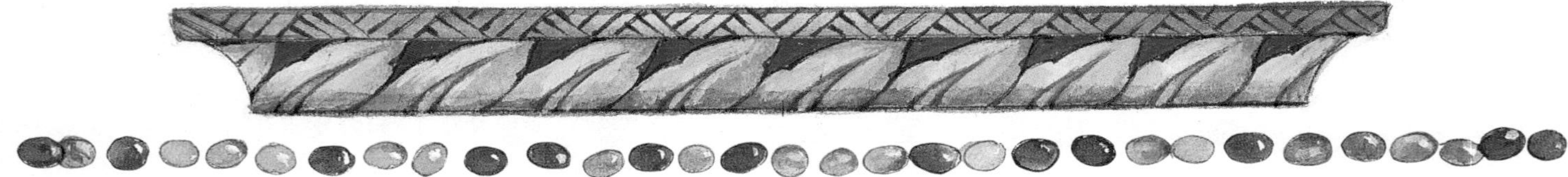

8. Draw a group of muffins.
Color $\frac{1}{4}$ orange. Color $\frac{3}{4}$ brown.

9. Draw a group of crackers.
Color $\frac{1}{3}$ yellow. Color $\frac{2}{3}$ orange.

PRACTICE

Mental Math

Solve.

10. I have 5 eggs. 3 are white and the rest are brown. How many eggs are brown?

_____ eggs

What fraction of my eggs are brown? $\frac{\square}{\square}$ are brown.

Notes for Home: Your child drew groups of objects and colored them to show a fraction. *Home Activity:* Ask your child to draw a group of his or her favorite food item, draw some of them one color, and tell the fraction shown by his or her picture.

Name ______________________________

Explore Probability

Explore

Which color are you more likely to pick?

Put red cubes and yellow cubes in a bag. Reach in and pick one cube. Color the graph to show what you picked. Put the cube back in the bag. Pick 10 times in all. Write your results.

Put 20 red cubes and 10 yellow cubes in a bag.

1  

red										
yellow										

_____ red

_____ yellow

2 Put 20 red cubes and 2 yellow cubes in a bag.

red										
yellow										

_____ red

_____ yellow

3 Put 10 red cubes and 10 yellow cubes in a bag.

red										
yellow										

_____ red

_____ yellow

Share

Compare your results with your classmates. How are they alike? How are they different?

Notes for Home: Your child explored probability by picking cubes from a bag. *Home Activity:* Ask your child to put 15 of one item and 5 of a second item in a bag. Pick an item and return it to the bag. Repeat 10 times. Ask your child to describe the results.

EXPLORE

Connect

4. Put red, blue, and yellow cubes in a bag. Make the yellow cubes more likely to be picked. Use 20 cubes in all.

   Pick 1 cube. Record your results. Put the cube back. Pick 20 times in all.

Number of cubes in my bag	My results
R _____	R _____
B _____	B _____
Y _____	Y _____

5. Put red, blue, and yellow cubes in a bag. Make the blue cubes more likely to be picked. Use 20 cubes in all.

   Pick 1 cube. Record your results. Put the cube back. Pick 20 times in all.

Number of cubes in my bag	My results
R _____	R _____
B _____	B _____
Y _____	Y _____

Journal

6. Suppose you put 10 red cubes, 10 yellow cubes, and 10 blue cubes in a bag. You pick a cube 12 times. Which color do you think you would pick the most? Explain.

Notes for Home: Your child put red, blue, and yellow cubes in a bag so that it would be more likely that one color would be picked. *Home Activity:* Ask your child to put 3 red crayons and 1 blue crayon in a bag. Have your child predict which color is more likely to be picked.

Name

Problem Solving: Make a Prediction

Learn

PROBLEM SOLVING GUIDE

Understand • Plan • Solve • Look Back

How can you predict what is more likely to happen?

The spinner has more green than yellow, so it's more likely to land on green.

Check

1. Look at the red and blue spinner. Predict. If you were to spin once, would this spinner be more likely to land on red or blue? ____________

2. What makes you think so?

____

____

3. Predict. If you were to spin 12 times, how many times would the spinner land on red? _____ On blue? _____

4. Spin 12 times. Color a square for each spin. Write the results.

_____ red

_____ blue

Talk About It How did you predict the number of times the spinner would land on red?

Notes for Home: Your child predicted which colors a spinner would land on, and then tested that prediction. *Home Activity:* Ask your child to draw two spinners using the colors red and yellow. Ask them to make the first spinner more likely to spin red and the second spinner more likely to spin yellow.

PROBLEM SOLVING

Practice

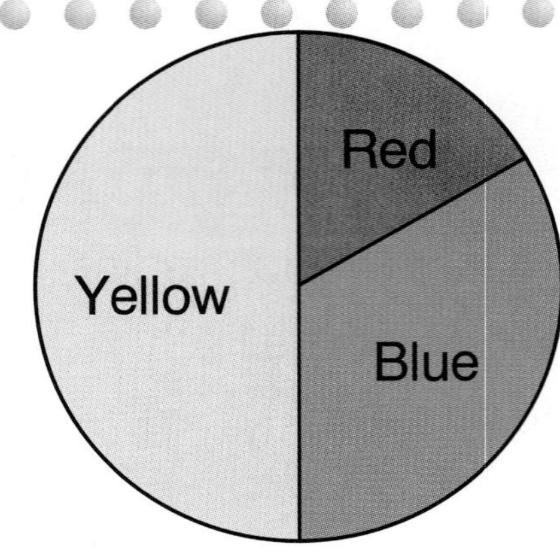

5. Predict. If you were to spin once, would this spinner be most likely to land on red, blue, or yellow?

____

6. What makes you think so?

____

____

7. Predict. If you were to spin 12 times, how many times would the spinner land on red? _____ on blue? _____ on yellow? _____

8. Spin 12 times. Color a square for each spin. Write the results.

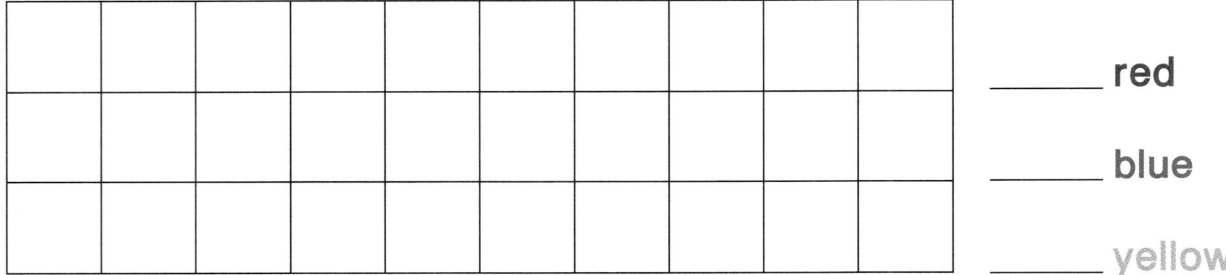

_____ red

_____ blue

_____ yellow

Write About It

9. Name something that is certain to happen in the next 5 minutes. _______________

10. Name something that cannot happen in the next 5 minutes. _______________

11. Name something that is likely to happen in the next 5 minutes. _______________

Notes for Home: Your child practiced making predictions. *Home Activity:* Ask your child to predict which is more likely to happen within the next day: your child will eat a meal or your child will travel to another country.

 For additional practice, see Skills Practice Bank, page 538, Set 3.

Name

Mixed Practice

Lessons 8-15

How many equal parts in each shape?

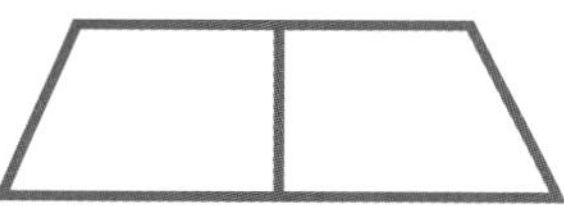

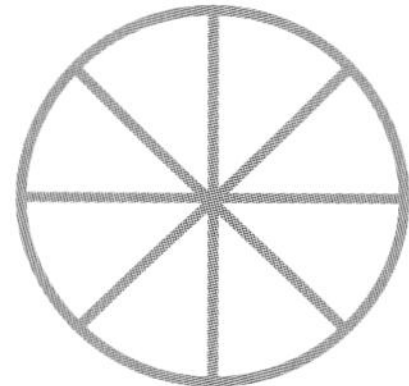

_______ equal parts _______ equal parts _______ equal parts

Write the fraction for the part that is shaded.

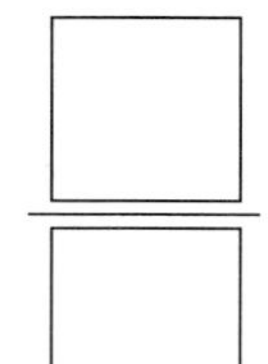

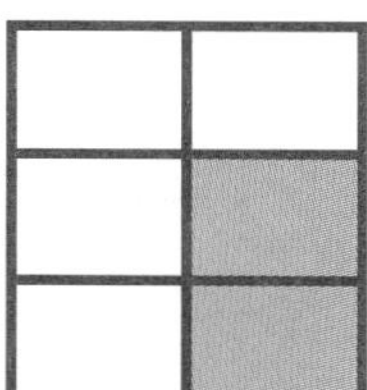

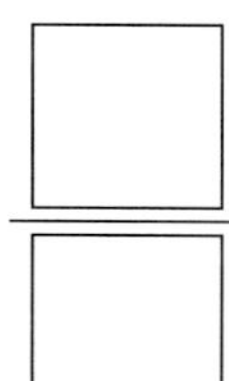

How much is left?

Circle the best estimate.

about $\frac{1}{2}$

about $\frac{1}{4}$

Draw a group of grapes.

Color $\frac{4}{6}$ purple. Color $\frac{2}{6}$ green.

MIXED PRACTICE

Problem Solving

6 Predict. If you were to spin this spinner 20 times, would it be most likely to land on blue, yellow, or red more times? _______________

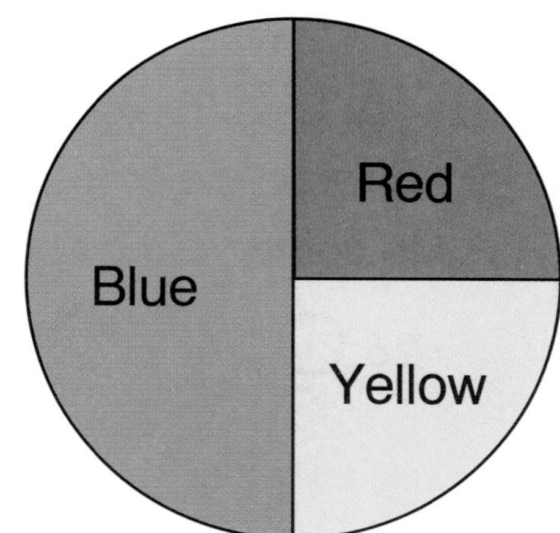

Journal

7 You and a friend cut a cookie in half. Could your friend get a bigger part? Explain.

Notes for Home: Your child practiced finding the number of equal parts, identifying fractions, and making a prediction. *Home Activity:* Ask your child to draw 5 shirts so that $\frac{3}{5}$ of the shirts are blue.

Name ________________________________

Cumulative Review

Chapters 1–12

Concepts and Skills

Add or subtract.

1.

75	23	78	40	60	54
+ 9	+ 18	− 56	+ 30	− 9	− 48

2.

37	45	54	50	66	59
+ 28	− 20	+ 32	+ 18	− 37	− 29

Problem Solving

3. Ramona brought fruit for the class. She brought 24 oranges and 12 bananas. How many pieces of fruit did she bring in all?

_____ pieces of fruit

4. Ralph helped his grandma make green beans. He started with 67 beans. He cut 38 of them. How many more beans did Ralph need to cut?

_____ beans

Test Prep

Fill in the ○ for the correct answer.

5. Choose the correct symbol to compare the numbers.

26  54

○ < ○ = ○ >

6. Which numbers are in order from greatest to least?

○ 17, 109, 38, 342

○ 6, 17, 38, 109, 342

○ 342, 109, 38, 17, 6

Notes for Home: Your child reviewed adding and subtracting two-digit numbers, comparing numbers, ordering numbers, and solving problems. *Home Activity:* Ask your child to order the following numbers from least to greatest: 10, 450, 79, 5, 220. (5, 10, 79, 220, 450)

Name

Chapter 12 Review

Vocabulary

1. Circle the shape you would make if you traced one face of the cube.

 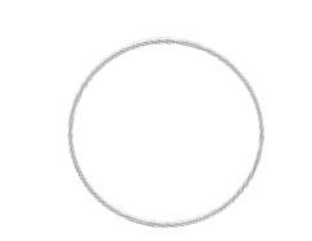 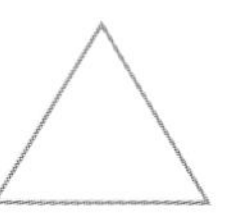 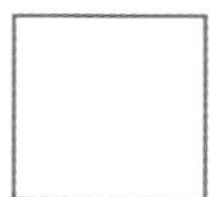

2. Divide the circle into fourths.

Shade $\frac{3}{4}$.

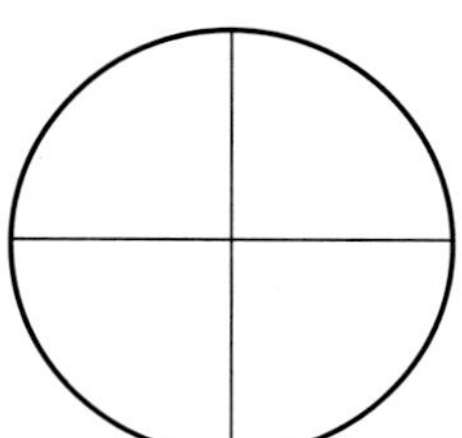

Concepts and Skills

3. Draw a shape that is congruent to this shape. Draw a line of symmetry on your shape.

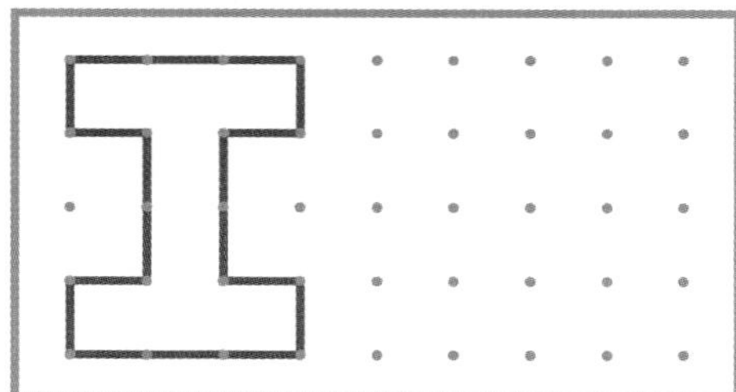

4. How was the shape moved? Write **slide**, **flip**, or **turn**.

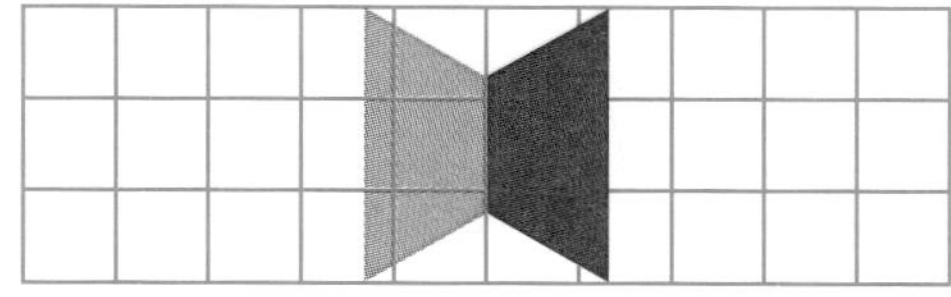

____

Write the fraction for the parts that are shaded.

5. 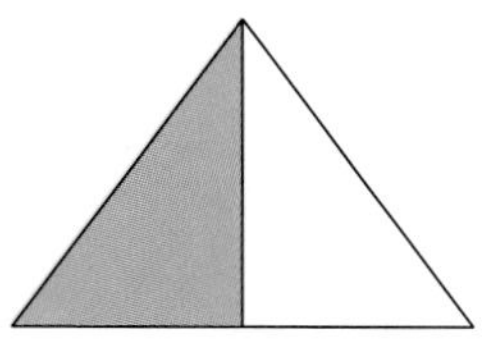 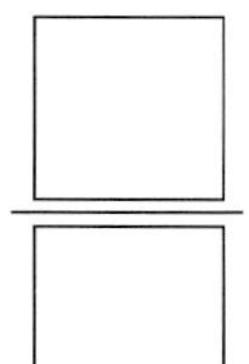 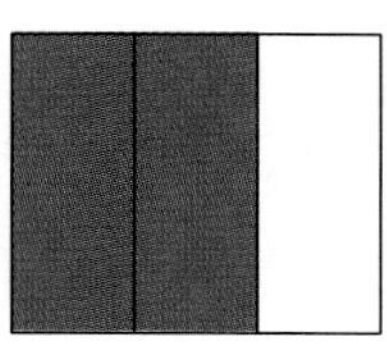 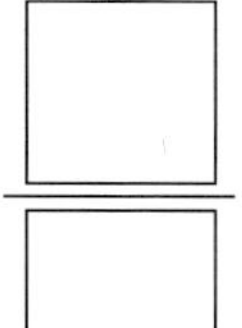 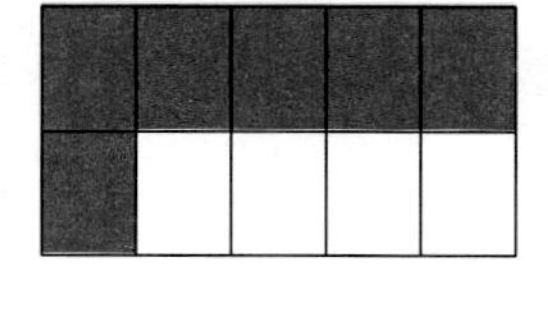 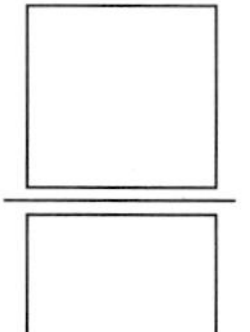

Problem Solving

6. 

Color $\frac{8}{9}$ of the tiles red. Color the rest blue. Are you **more likely** to pick a red tile or a blue tile out of the bag? ______________

7. Solve the riddle. Circle the answer.
I have more than 3 sides.
I am not yellow. I have
more than one line of symmetry.

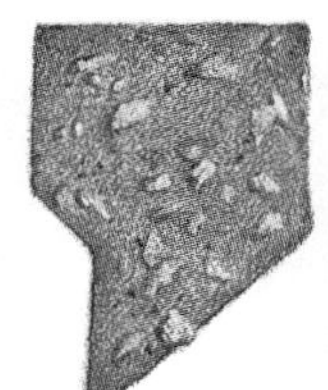  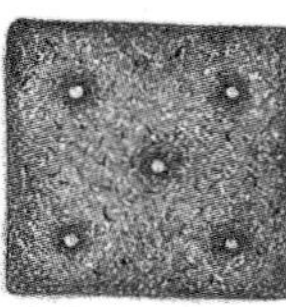 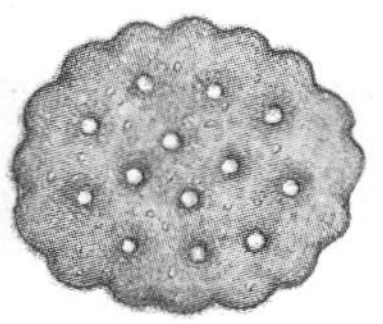

Notes for Home: Your child reviewed vocabulary, concepts, skills, and problem solving from Chapter 12. *Home Activity:* Ask your child to draw a rectangle, divide it into a number of equal parts, and then describe one or more parts using fractions.

Name

Chapter 12 Test

Circle the shape you would make if you traced one face of the objects.

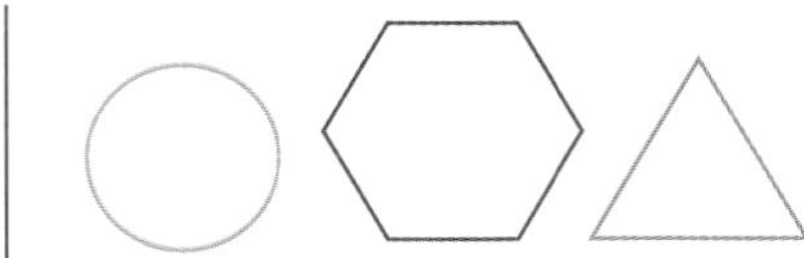

2

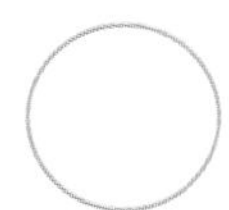

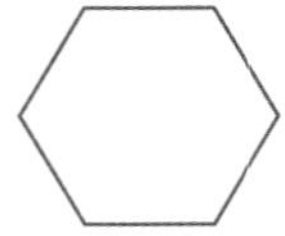

3 Draw a shape that is congruent to this shape. Draw a line of symmetry on your shape.

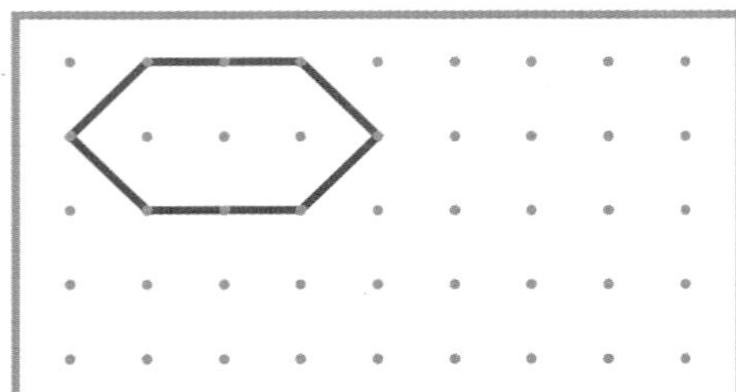

4 How was the shape moved? Write **slide**, **flip**, or **turn**.

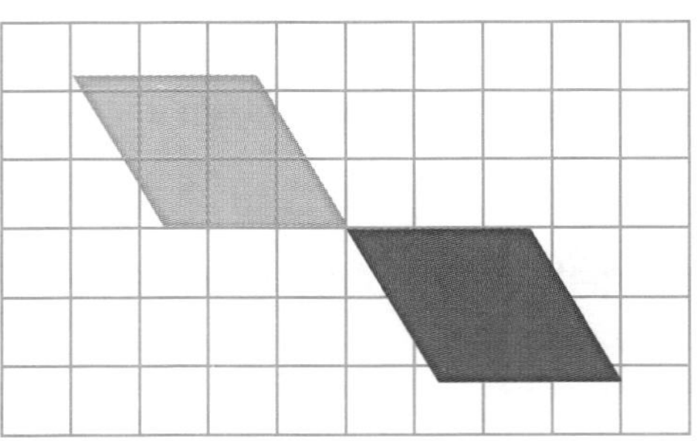

____

5 Write the fraction for the parts that are shaded.

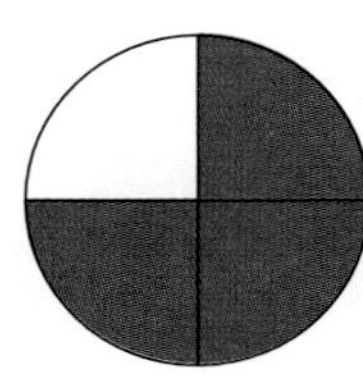

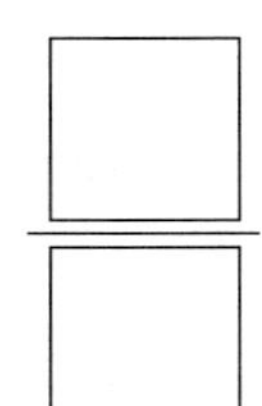

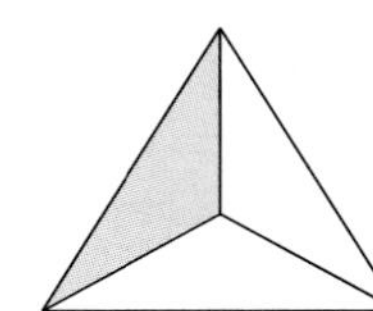

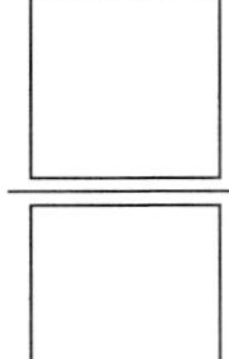

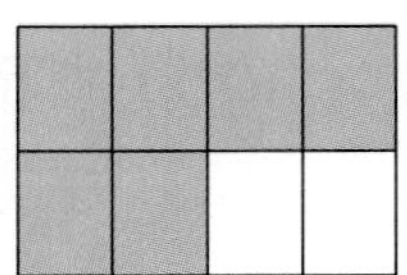

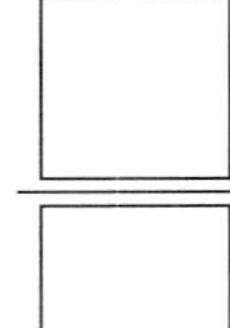

6

Color $\frac{4}{6}$ of the tiles yellow. Color the rest green. Are you **more likely** or **less likely** to pick a green tile out of the bag? ______________

Solve the riddle. Circle the answer.

7 I have fewer than 6 corners.
I have more than 3 sides.
I am not a square.

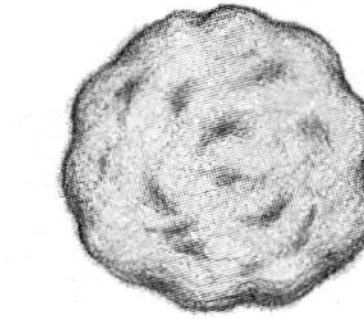

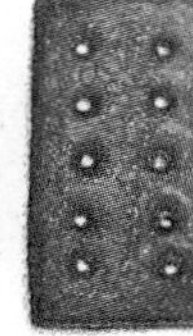

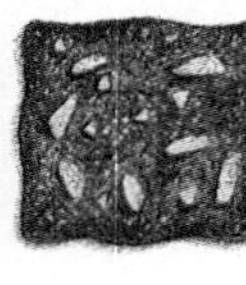

Notes for Home: Your child was tested on Chapter 12 skills concepts, and problem solving. *Home Activity:* Ask your child to draw two shapes, tell you if the shapes have matching parts, and draw a line to show the matching parts if they do.

CHAPTER TEST

Name ____________________

Performance Assessment

Chapter 12

Find an object in your classroom that is a rectangular prism. Tell about your object.

1 My object is a ____________.	2 It has _____ faces.
3 It has ____________ edges.	4 It has _____ corners.
5 Use another piece of paper. Trace a face of your object.	6 Draw 2 lines of symmetry so that your shape has 4 parts that are equal in size.
7 Color 3 of the parts red.	8 Color one part yellow.
9 Write a fraction that tells what part is red. $\frac{\square}{\square}$	10 Write a fraction that tells what part is yellow. $\frac{\square}{\square}$

Problem Solving Critical Thinking

11 Color the tiles so that $\frac{10}{12}$ of the group are green and the rest are blue.

12 What fraction of the tiles are blue? $\frac{\square}{\square}$

13 Would you be more likely to pick a green tile or a blue tile? Explain.

____

____

Notes for Home: Your child did an activity that tested Chapter 12 skills, concepts, and problem solving. *Home Activity:* Ask your child to describe an object in your home that is the shape of a sphere.

Name ____________________

Picture This!

Computer Skills You Will Need

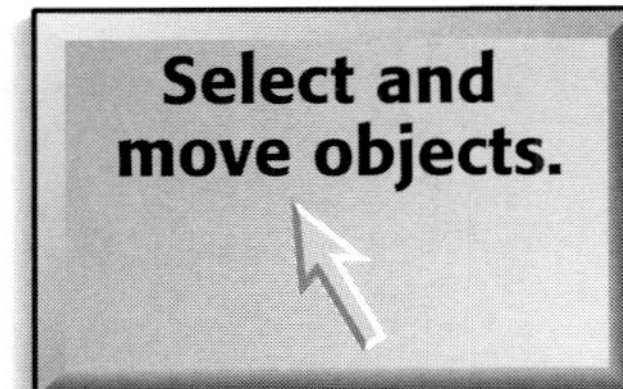

Use your drawing program.

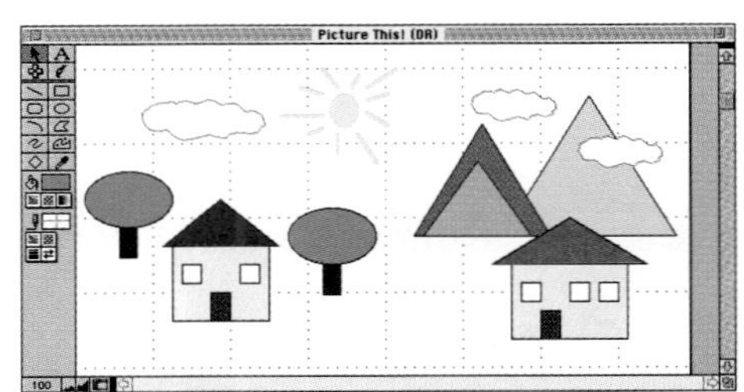

1. Draw a picture using shapes. You can move shapes so that they are inside other shapes. You can *drag* shapes to make them larger or smaller.
2. Ask a friend to use your picture to complete this chart.

Circles	Triangles	Squares	Other Rectangles

3. Make a pattern using shapes. Ask a friend to tell what comes next.

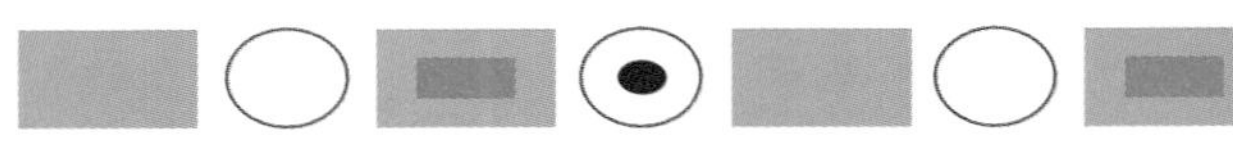

4. Ask a friend to use your picture to complete this chart.

Circles	Triangles	Squares	Other Rectangles

Tech Talk How would you draw this design? Do you think there is more than one way? Explain.

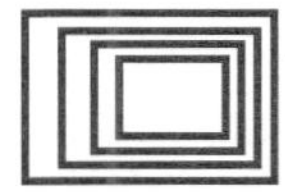

Visit our Web site. **www.parent.mathsurf.com**

Sym-mat-ry!

You can use symmetry to make interesting place mats.

What You Need

colored paper   scissors

What You Do

1 **Take a piece of colored paper. Fold it in half.**

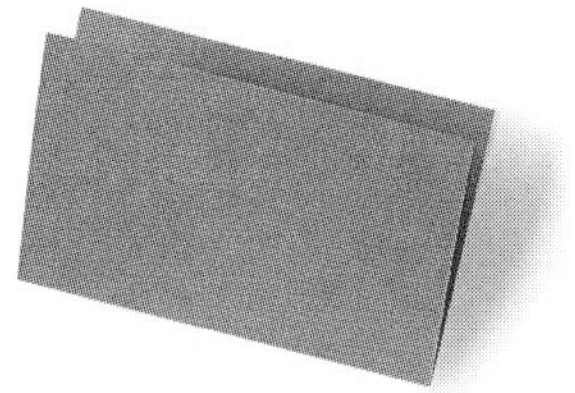

2 **Draw a shape along the edges of one side.**

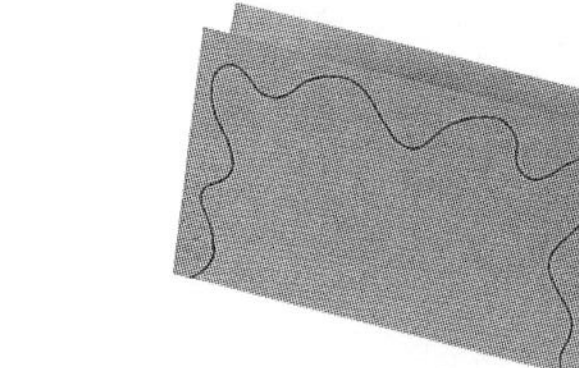

3 **Cut along your line. Unfold the paper.**

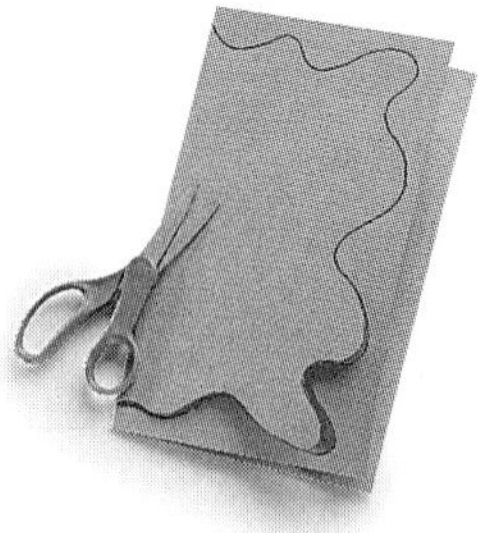

4 **Describe what happened. Find a line of symmetry.**

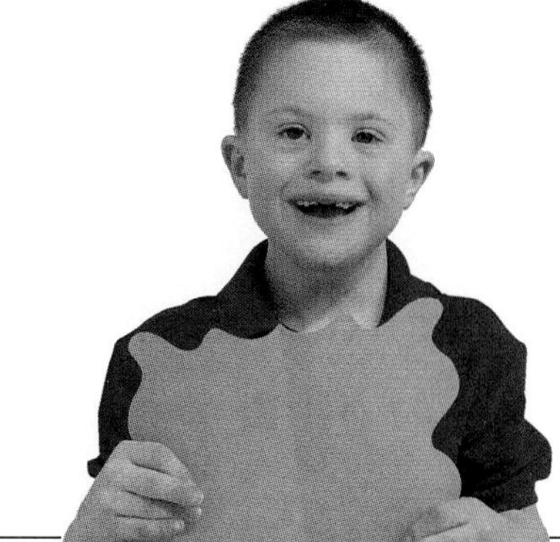

Fold down

MathSoup

Scott Foresman - Addison Wesley My Math Magazine No. 12

Take a Bite!

Putting It All Together

Tangrams are a kind of puzzle from China. A large square is cut into different shapes. The shapes can be arranged to form different pictures.

Cut out the tangram below, then cut along the lines to make pieces. See if you can arrange the pieces to make the pictures shown.

Notes for Home: Your child made pictures using different shapes. *Home Activity:* Ask your child to identify some of the shapes used in the tangram, such as the square and triangles.

Look at the pictures of these "buildings." Tell how many cubes are in each building.

1 ______ cubes

2 ______ cubes

3 ______ cubes

4 ______ cubes

5 Make your own model building with cubes. Ask another person to count the cubes.

Notes for Home: Your child counted the number of cubes used to form shapes. *Home Activity:* Ask your child to compare the number of cubes in the buildings for Exercises 1 and 4.

Cube Count

Many buildings look like rods and cubes that are put together.

This building in Montreal, Canada, looks like many cubes.

The Sears Tower in Chicago looks like rods that are attached.

1 a fish

2 a cat

3 Make up your own picture!
Show it to a friend or family member.
Have them guess what the picture is.

Super Sandwich

What is your favorite sandwich? peanut butter and jelly? How about ham and cheese?

Did you know there is a special day for sandwiches? National Sandwich Day is every year on November 3.

Write the fraction for one part of each sandwich.

1 ______

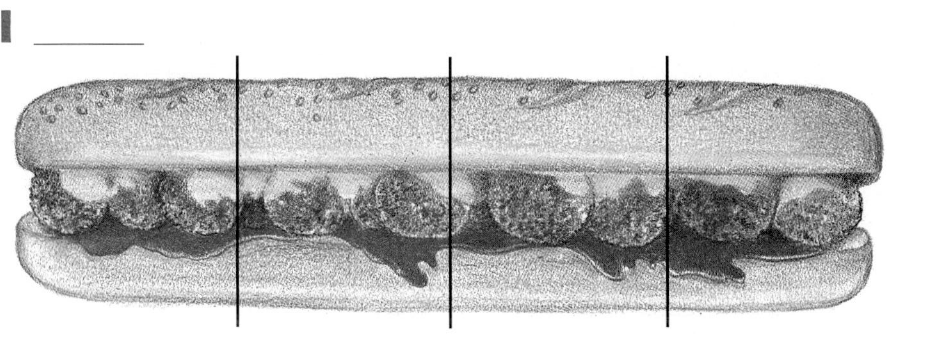

2 ______

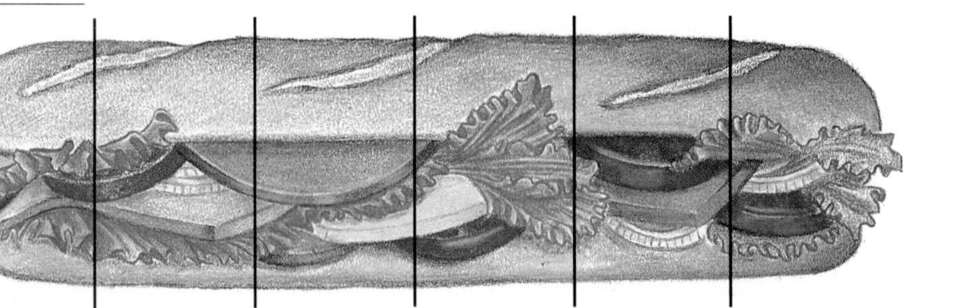

Draw lines to divide each sandwich into the given fraction.

3 **halves**

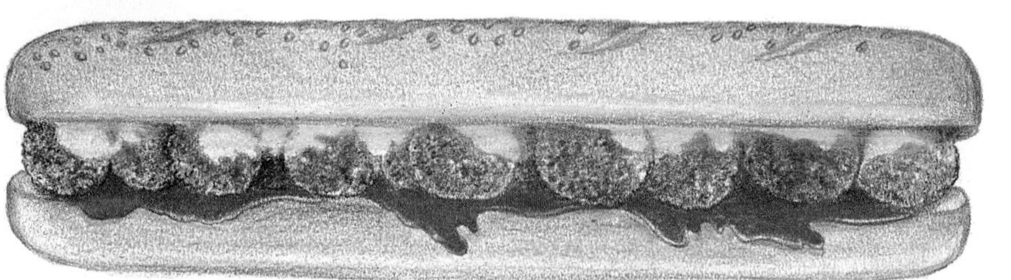

4 **thirds**

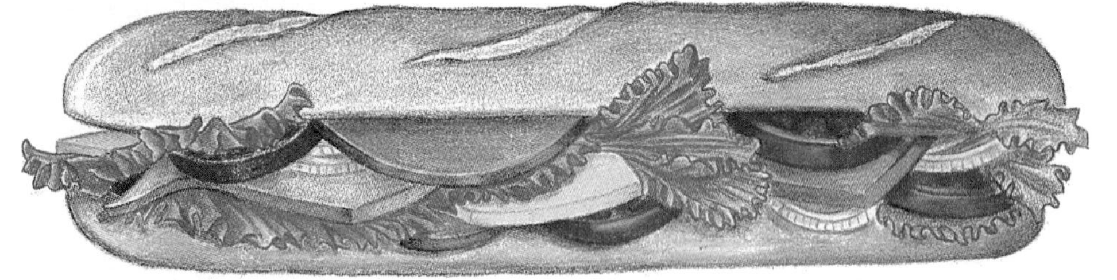

5 Someone ate part of this sandwich. $\frac{1}{3}$ is left. How much was eaten?

______

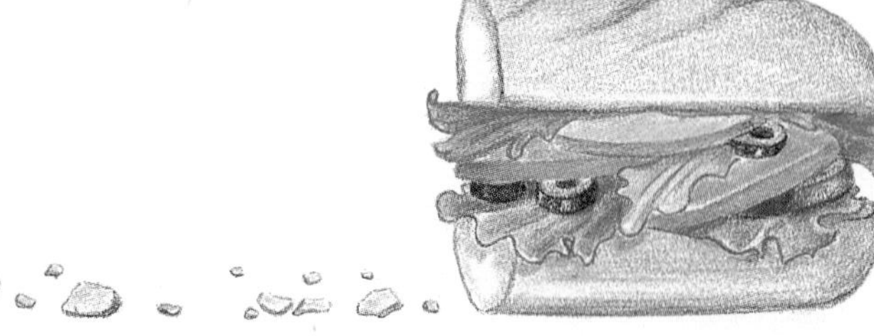

Notes for Home: Your child practiced identifying and making fractional parts of a whole. *Home Activity:* Ask your child to divide a piece of bread into halves, then fourths.

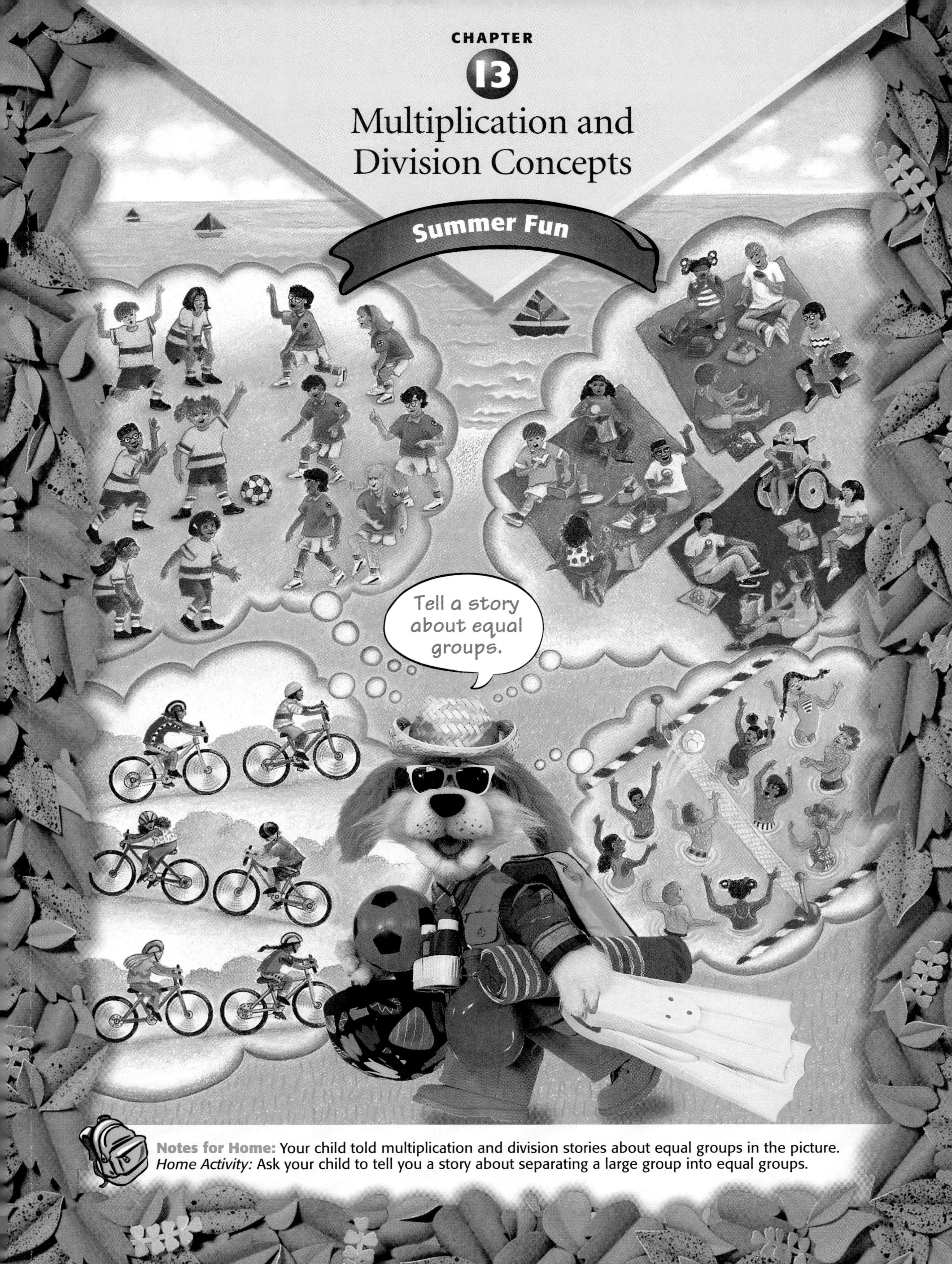

Notes for Home: Your child told multiplication and division stories about equal groups in the picture.
Home Activity: Ask your child to tell you a story about separating a large group into equal groups.

Dear Family,
Our class is starting Chapter 13. We will be multiplying and dividing. Here are some activities we can do together.

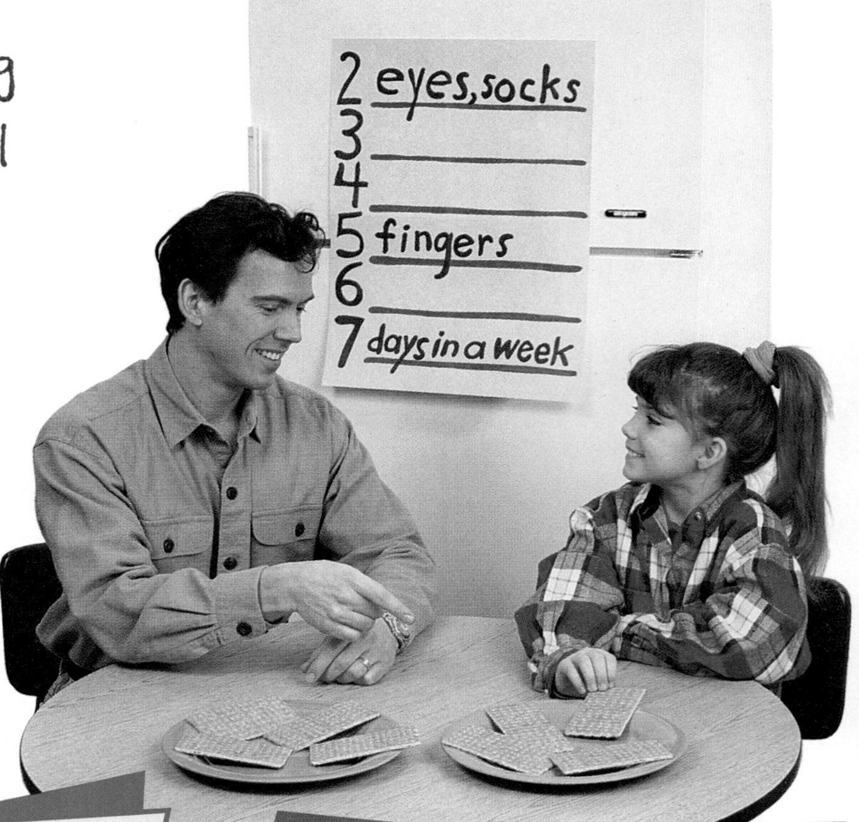

Hunting for Groups
Help your child look around your home and make a list of things that come in groups. Keep the list handy so that your child can continue to add to it.

Snack Time
At snack time, have your child show how to make equal groups. For example, ask your child how to divide 8 crackers equally between 2 people.

Community Connection

When you are outside with your child, look for examples of equal groups. Ask your child to tell how many in all. For example, 5 cars with 4 wheels each is 20 wheels in all.

Visit our Web site. www.parent.mathsurf.com

Name

Explore Joining Equal Groups

Explore

Use pattern blocks to make a design.
Draw it here.

How many pattern blocks did you use? ______

Make the same design more times.

	Make this many.	How many pattern blocks in all?
1	2	
2	3	
3	4	
4	5	

Share

How did you find the total number of pattern blocks when you made your design 5 times?

Notes for Home: Your child used pattern blocks to explore putting together equal groups. *Home Activity:* Ask your child to use objects such as buttons to make 2 groups of 3 and then tell how many in all.

EXPLORE

Connect

EXPLORE

You can add to find how many sails in all.

3 + 3 + 3 + 3 = 12

Use pattern blocks to make the sails.

Find how many sails in all.

		Draw the sails.	How many sails in all?
5	1 boats		3
6	2 boats		3 + 3= _____
7	3 boats		3 + 3 + 3 _____
8	4 boats		3 + 3 + 3 + 3 = _____

Talk About It What patterns do you see in your answers?

Notes for Home: Your child made equal groups and added to find how many in all. *Home Activity:* Ask your child to use objects to make 3 groups of 4 objects each. Ask your child to add to find how many objects in all. (12)

Name ______________________________

Addition and Multiplication

Learn

When groups are equal, you can add or multiply to find how many in all.

How many wheels?

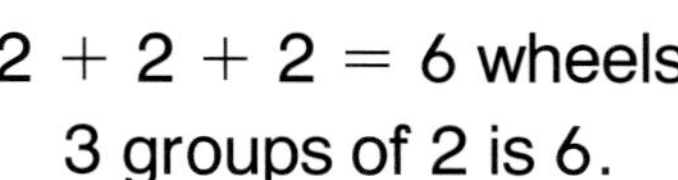

$2 + 2 + 2 = 6$ wheels
3 groups of 2 is 6.

$3 \times 2 = 6$ wheels
3 times 2 is 6.

Check

Use Snap Cubes. Find how many in all. Draw to show your work.

1. 4 water balloons in each pail

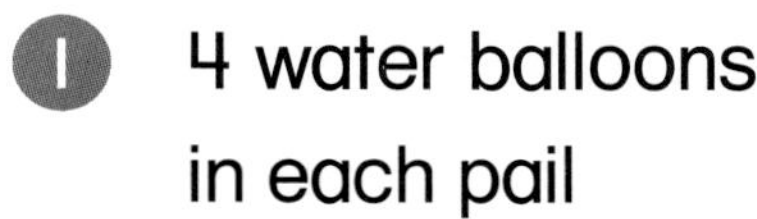
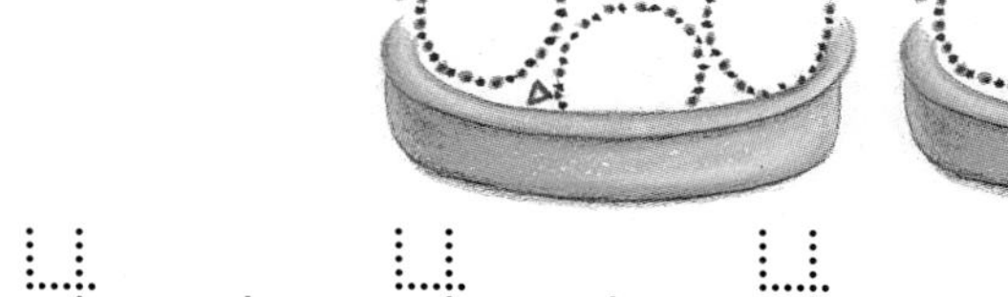
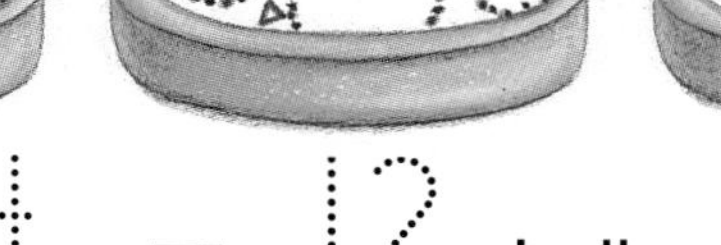

4 + 4 + 4 = 12 balloons

3 groups of 4 is 12. 3 × 4 = 12 balloons

2. 3 tennis balls in each can

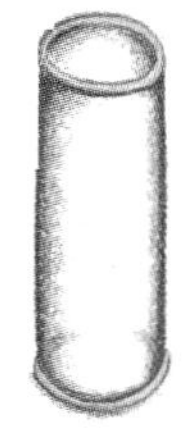
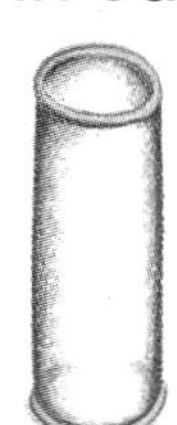
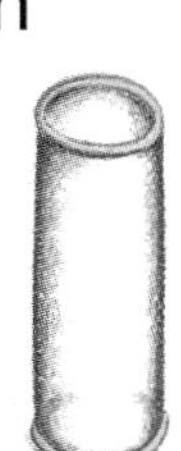
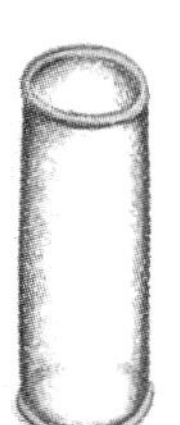
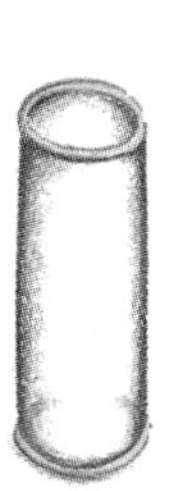

____ + ____ + ____ + ____ + ____ = ____ balls

5 groups of 3 is 15. ____ × ____ = ____ balls

Talk About It Could you write a multiplication sentence for $2 + 2 + 2 + 4$? Explain.

Notes for Home: Your child used addition and multiplication to find how many in several groups. *Home Activity:* Ask your child to find the total numbers of flowers if there are 3 flowers in each of 3 pots.

Practice

Find how many in all. You can use snap cubes.

3 How many legs?
4 groups of 2

____ + ____ + ____ + ____ = ____

____ × ____ = ____ legs

4 How many children?
2 groups of 3

____ + ____ = ____

____ × ____ = ____ children

5 How many kites?
4 groups of 3

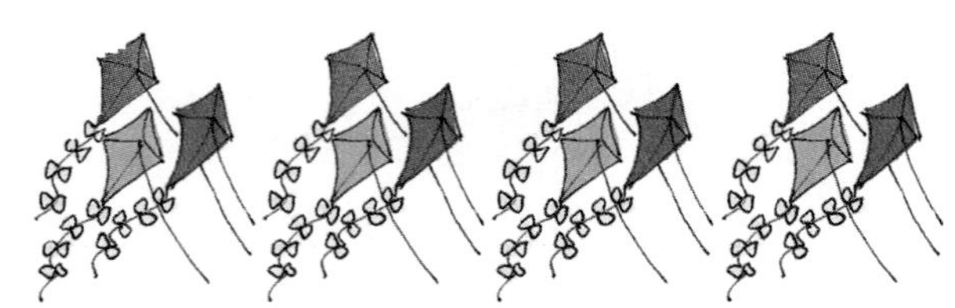

____ + ____ + ____ + ____ = ____

____ × ____ = ____ kites

6 How many balloons?
3 groups of 5

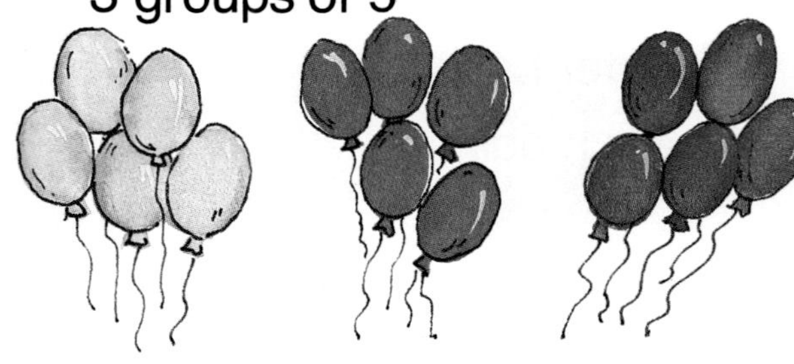

____ + ____ + ____ = ____

____ × ____ = ____ balloons

PRACTICE

Problem Solving Visual Thinking

Can you multiply to find how many in all? Tell why or why not.

7 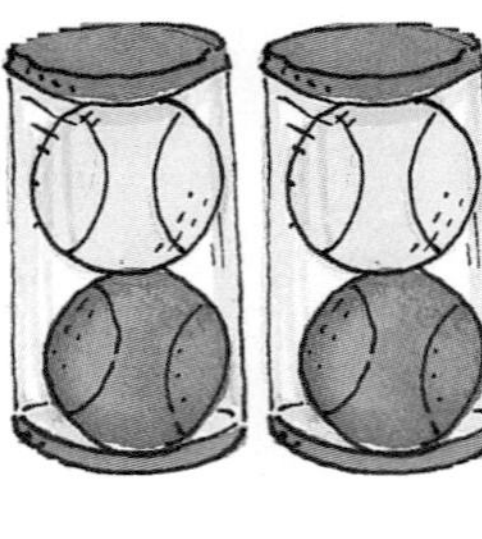

yes no

8 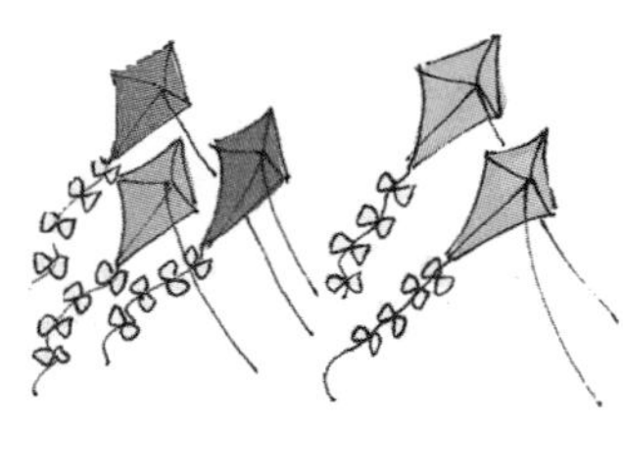

yes no

9  

yes no

Notes for Home: Your child added and multiplied to find the total number in several groups. *Home Activity:* Ask your child to write a multiplication sentence to find the total number of crackers for 2 packs of crackers with 4 crackers in each pack.

Name

Explore Building Arrays

Explore

Use Snap Cubes. Make equal rows.
Color to show your rows.
Write how many.

1 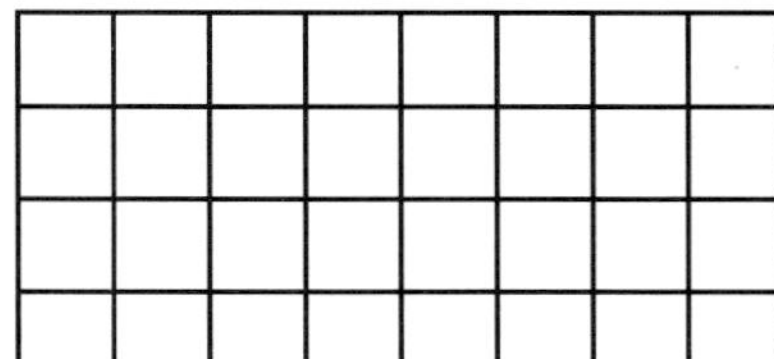

_____ equal rows _____ in each row

_____ in all

2 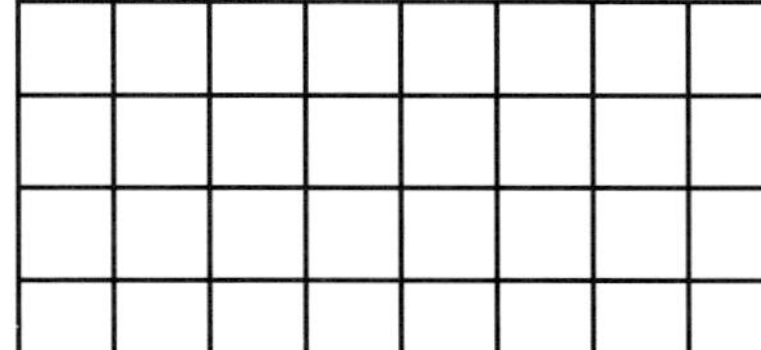

_____ equal rows _____ in each row

_____ in all

3 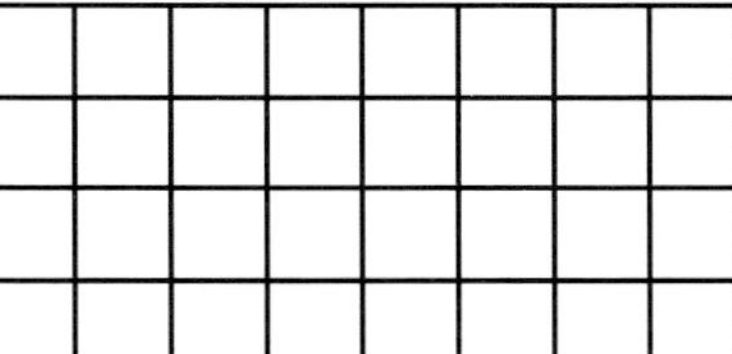

_____ equal rows _____ in each row

_____ in all

4 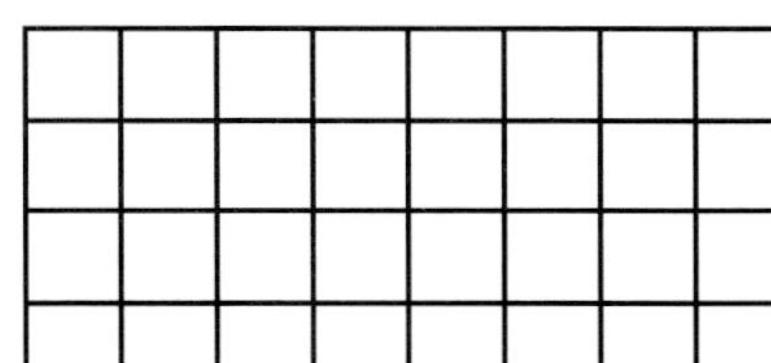

_____ equal rows _____ in each row

_____ in all

Share

How are these alike?
How are they different?

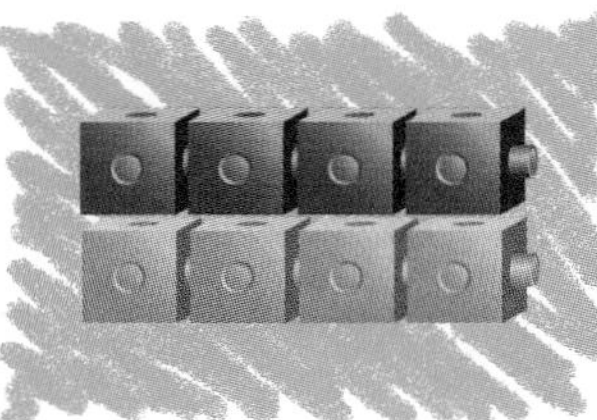

Notes for Home: Your child colored equal rows on a grid and found how many squares in all.
Home Activity: Have your child use objects to show you 2 rows of 6 and then find how many objects in all.

Connect

2 rows of 5 chairs

$2 \times 5 = 10$

There are

10 chairs in all.

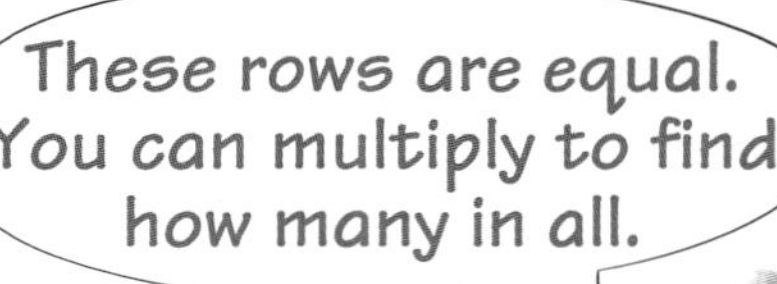

Color equal rows. Write how many. Find the product.

5. Show 3 rows of 4

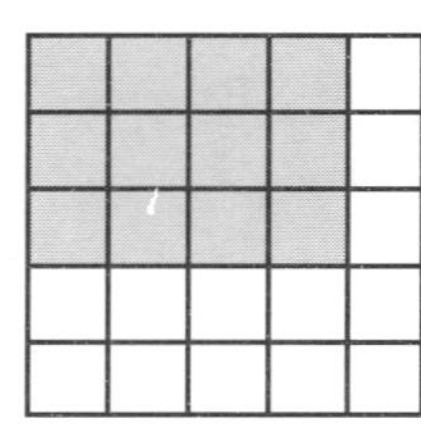

3 rows

4 in each row

$3 \times 4 =$ 12

6. Show 4 rows of 2

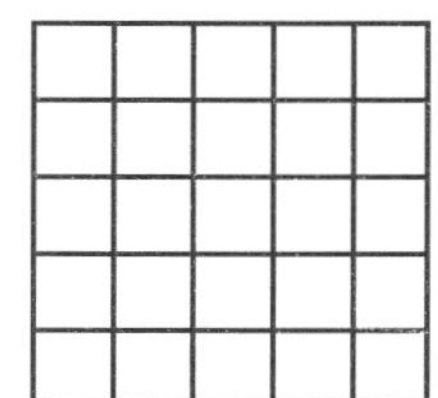

____ rows

____ in each row

$4 \times 2 =$ ____

7. Show 5 rows of 5

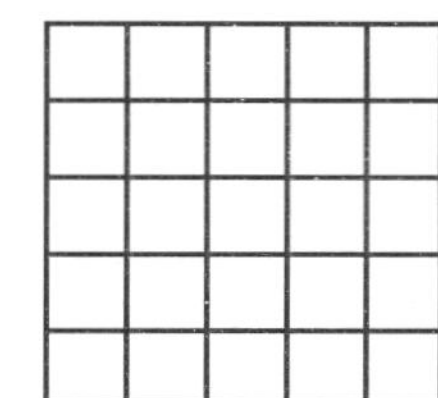

____ rows

____ in each row

$5 \times 5 =$ ____

Problem Solving

8. Draw groups to show 3×5.

How many in all? ____

9. Draw groups to show 5×7.

How many in all? ____

Notes for Home: Your child colored equal rows on a grid and completed a multiplication number sentence. *Home Activity:* Ask your child to draw a picture which shows 6 groups of 4.

EXPLORE

Name

Multiplication in Any Order

Learn

You can multiply the numbers in any order and get the same product.

Both rides hold 6 people!

$3 \times 2 =$ 6

$2 \times 3 =$ 6

Check

You can use Snap Cubes. Make equal rows.
Color each row. Find the product.

1. 3 rows of 5 — 5 rows of 3

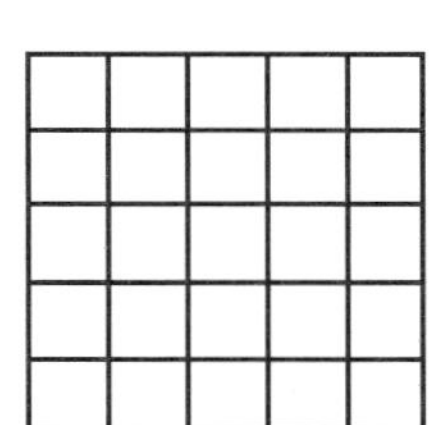

$3 \times 5 =$ ____ $5 \times 3 =$ ____

2. 2 rows of 4 — 4 rows of 2

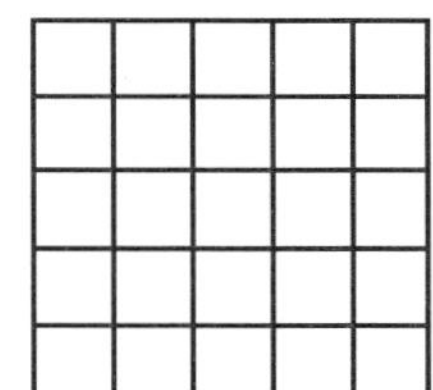

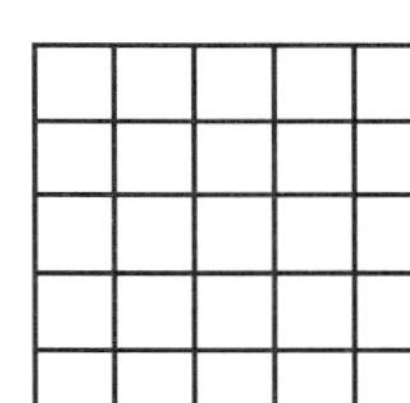

$2 \times 4 =$ ____ $4 \times 2 =$ ____

3. 3 rows of 4 — 4 rows of 3

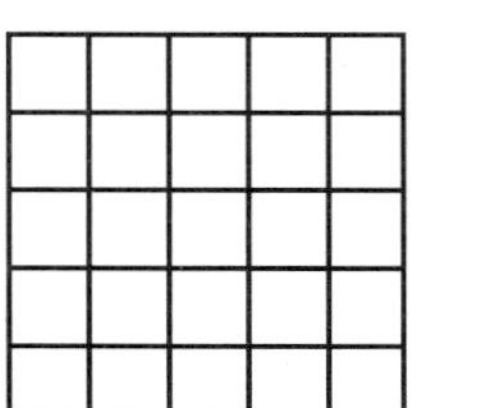

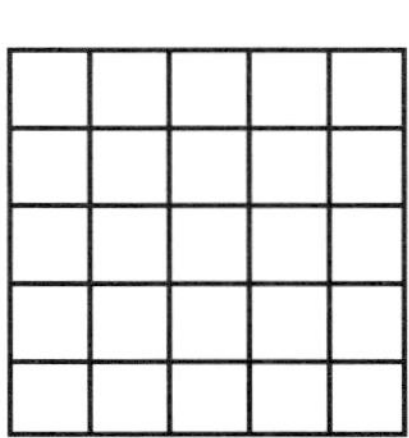

$3 \times 4 =$ ____ $4 \times 3 =$ ____

4. 1 row of 5 — 5 rows of 1

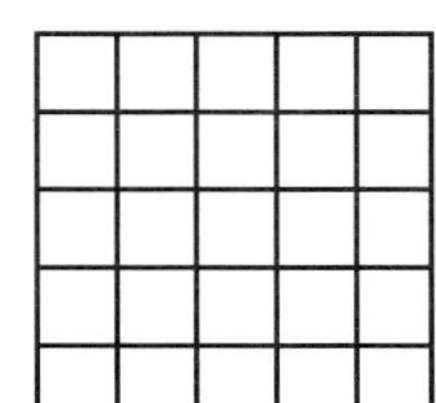

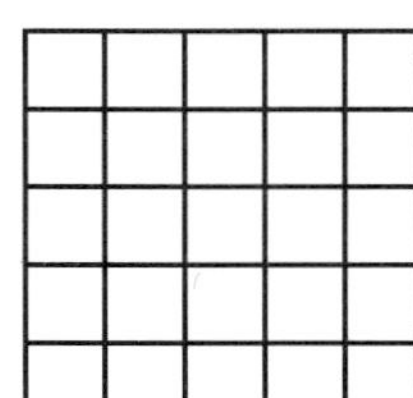

$1 \times 5 =$ ____ $5 \times 1 =$ ____

Talk About It Does 4 rows of 3 Snap Cubes have more Snap Cubes than 3 rows of 4 Snap Cubes? Explain.

Notes for Home: Your child colored rows to show multiplication facts, and completed number sentences. *Home Activity:* Ask your child to arrange small objects such as buttons or beans to show 2×6 and 6×2.

Practice

Find the product. You can use Cubes.

5 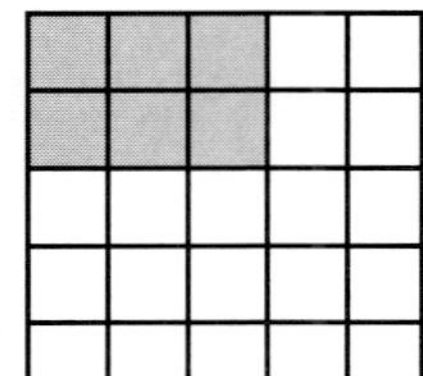 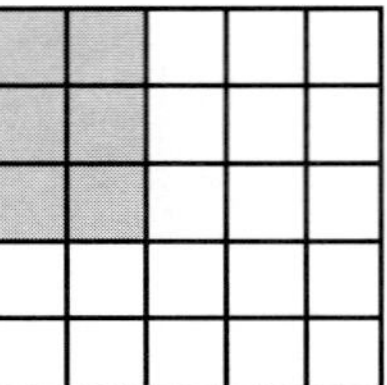

$5 \times 4 =$ _____ $4 \times 5 =$ _____

6 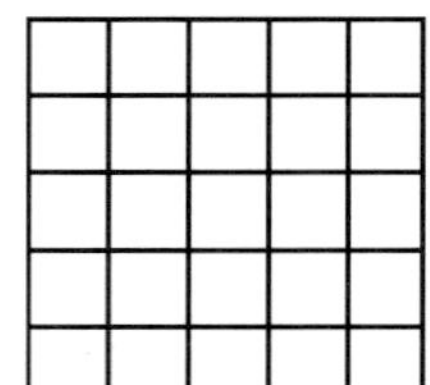 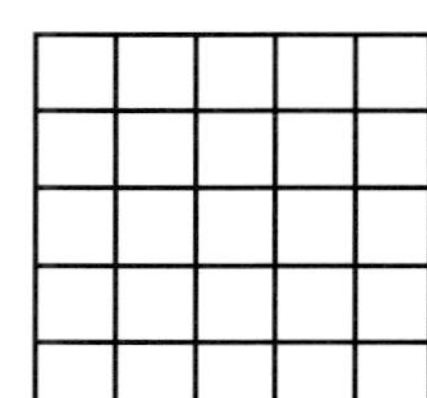

$2 \times 3 =$ _____ $3 \times 2 =$ _____

Write your own. Use the same numbers.
Color different rows. Write different multiplication sentences.

_____ $\times$ _____ $=$ _____ _____ $\times$ _____ $=$ _____

7 $5 \times 4 =$ _____

$4 \times 5 =$ _____

8 $4 \times 6 =$ _____

$6 \times 4 =$ _____

9 $3 \times 8 =$ _____

$8 \times 3 =$ _____

Problem Solving Patterns

10 Find the products. What patterns do you see?

  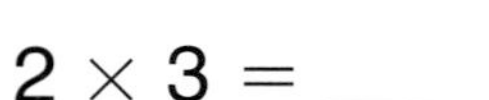  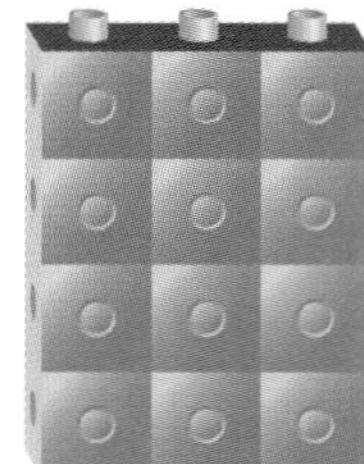

$1 \times 3 =$ _____ $2 \times 3 =$ _____ $3 \times 3 =$ _____ $4 \times 3 =$ _____

Notes for Home: Your child found answers to related multiplication facts. *Home Activity:* Ask your child to use objects to show you 4 groups of 3 and 3 groups of 4.

Name ______________________

Practice Game

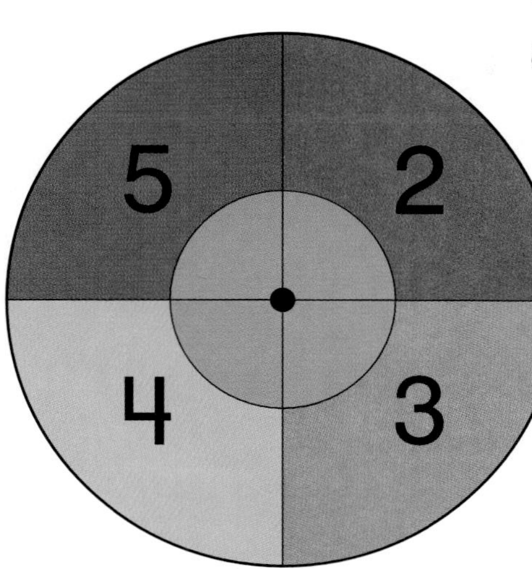

Number of Buckets

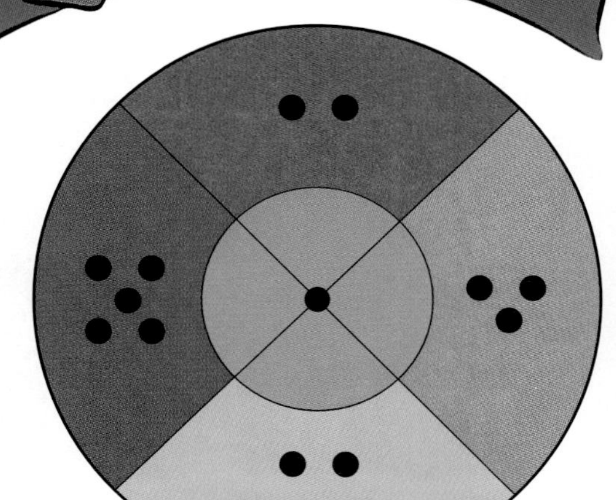

Number of Beans in each Bucket

Players 2 or 3

What You Need

beans or counters 

pencil 

paper clip 

How to Play

1. Spin each spinner.
2. Multiply to find how many beans in all. Write a number sentence.
3. If your product is correct, take that many beans or counters.
4. After each turn, add to find your total number of beans.
5. The first player to get a total of 50 or more wins!

Number Sentence	Total
___ × ___ = ___	
___ × ___ = ___	
___ × ___ = ___	
___ × ___ = ___	
___ × ___ = ___	
___ × ___ = ___	
___ × ___ = ___	
___ × ___ = ___	

PRACTICE

Notes for Home: Your child played a game to practice multiplication facts. *Home Activity:* Ask your child to tell you how he or she found the numbers in the column labeled **Total.**

Name ___________________

Find how many in all. You can use Snap Cubes.

1. How many beach balls?
2 groups of 6

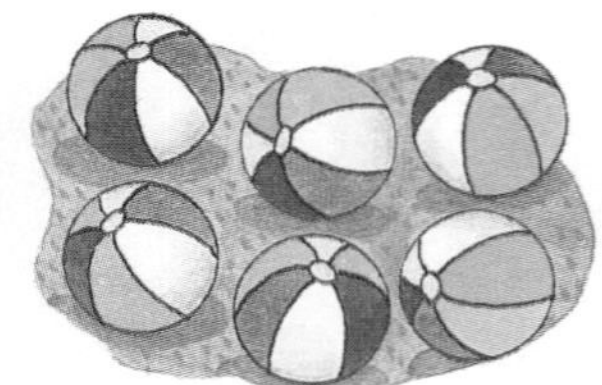
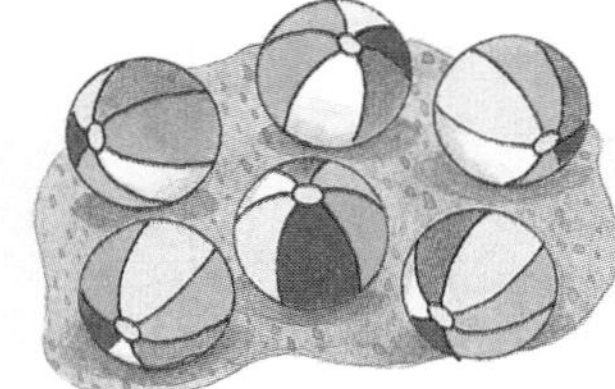

___ + ___ = ___

___ $\times$ ___ = ___

2. How many arms?
3 groups of 5

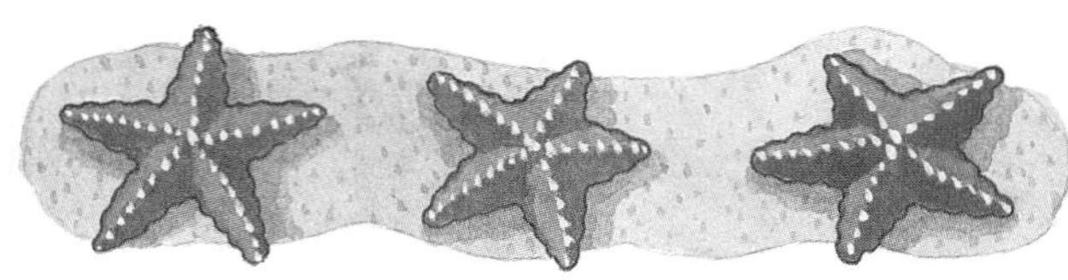

___ + ___ + ___ = ___

___ $\times$ ___ = ___

Find the product. You can use Snap Cubes.

3.

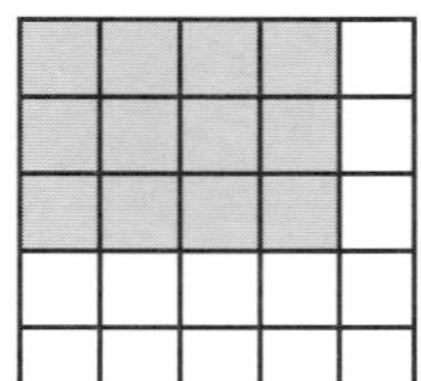
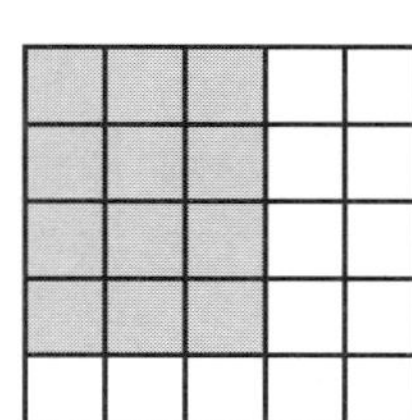

$3 \times 4 =$ ___ $4 \times 3 =$ ___

4.

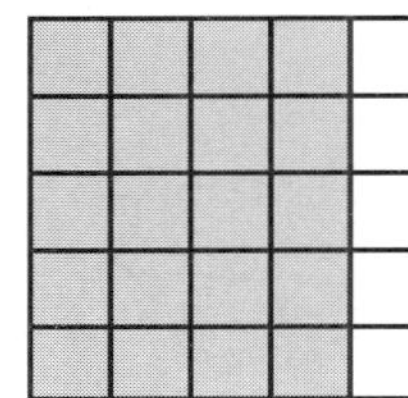
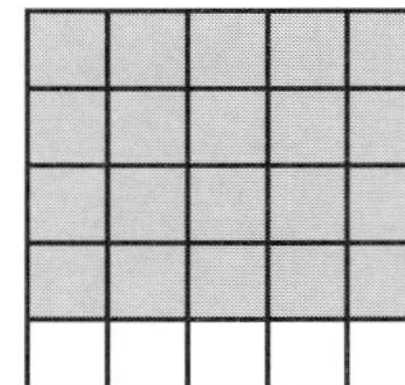

$5 \times 4 =$ ___ $4 \times 5 =$ ___

5. $2 \times 5 =$ ___
$5 \times 2 =$ ___

6. $4 \times 2 =$ ___
$2 \times 4 =$ ___

7. $5 \times 3 =$ ___
$3 \times 5 =$ ___

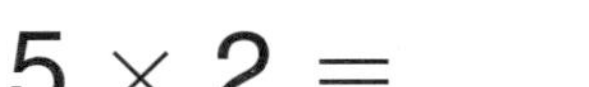

Number Sense

8. Ellen and her friends are jumping rope. How many feet are jumping rope?

___ feet

Notes for Home: Your child practiced using multiplication. *Home Activity:* Ask your child to write and solve a pair of multiplication facts that use the same numbers.

PRACTICE

Name

Multiplication in Vertical Form

Learn

3 × 4 = 
rows, balls in each row, balls in all

$$\begin{array}{r} 4 \\ \times\ 3 \\ \hline 12 \end{array}$$

4 balls in each row
× 3 rows
12 balls in all

Check

Find the products.

1 2 rows of 8

2 × 8 = ____

$$\begin{array}{r} 8 \\ \times\ 2 \\ \hline \end{array}$$ rows

2 4 groups of 2

4 × 2 = ____

$$\begin{array}{r} 2 \\ \times\ 4 \\ \hline \end{array}$$ groups

3 5 groups of 3

5 × 3 = ____

$$\begin{array}{r} 3 \\ \times\ 5 \\ \hline \end{array}$$ groups

4 3 rows of 6

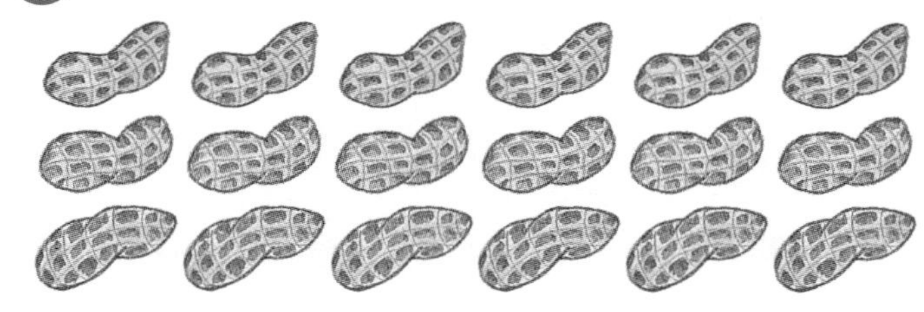

3 × 6 = ____

$$\begin{array}{r} 6 \\ \times\ 3 \\ \hline \end{array}$$ rows

Talk About It

Describe a picture that shows this multiplication fact. **7 × 3 = 21**

Notes for Home: Your child found the answer to multiplication facts written two different ways.
Home Activity: Ask your child to show you two ways to write 6 times 2. (6 × 2; $\begin{array}{r} 2 \\ \times\ 6 \end{array}$)

Practice

Write the number sentence.

5 2 rows of 7

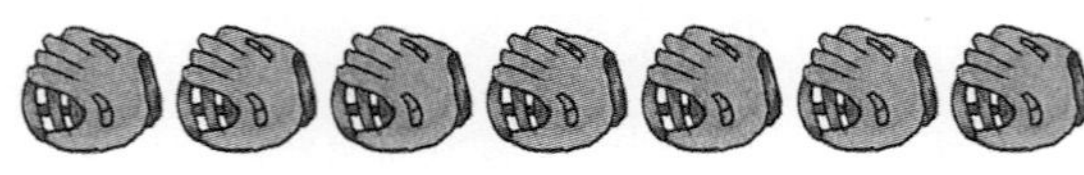

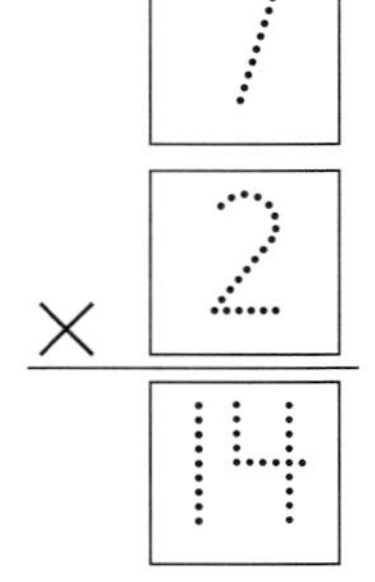

2 × 7 = 14

$$\begin{array}{r} 7 \\ \times\ 2 \\ \hline 14 \end{array}$$

6 4 groups of 5

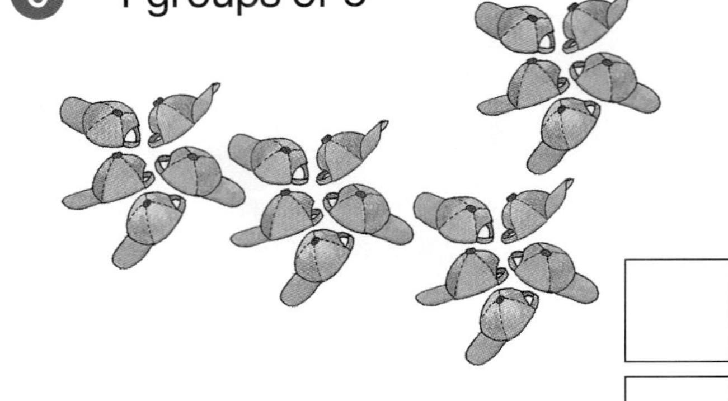

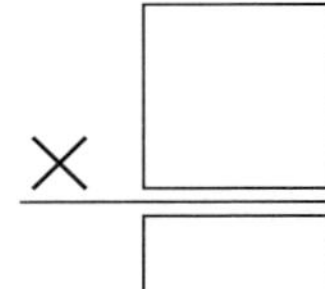

___ × ___ = ___

7 4 rows of 4

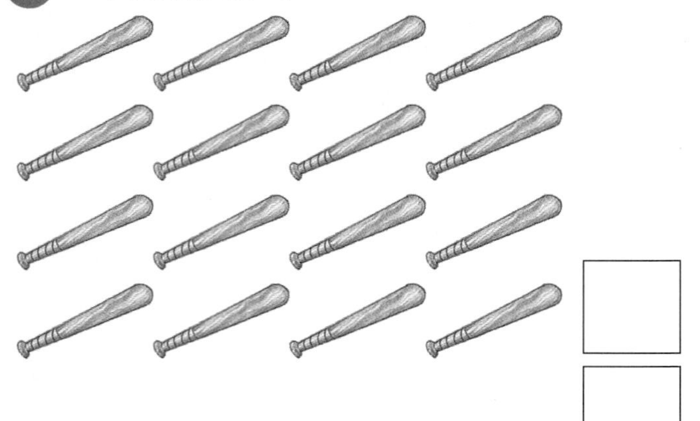

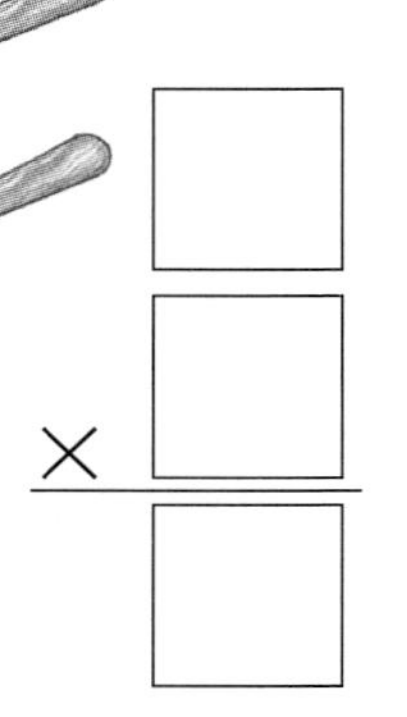

___ × ___ = ___

8 5 rows of 2

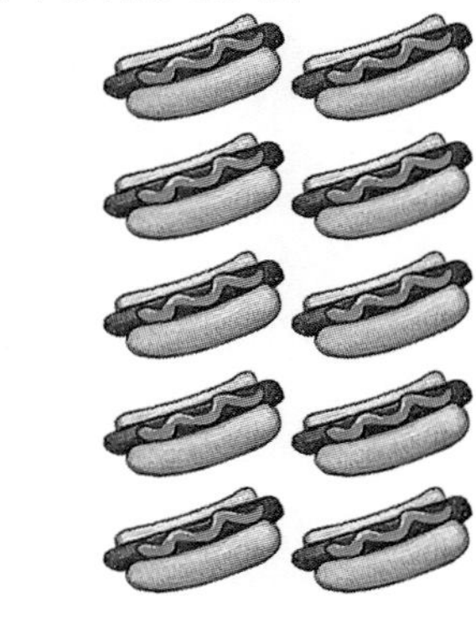

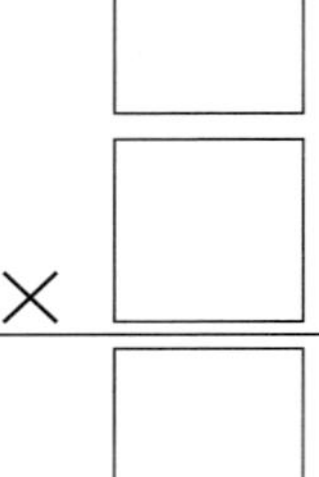

___ × ___ = ___

PRACTICE

Problem Solving Patterns

9 Draw the next larger square. Write the number sentence.

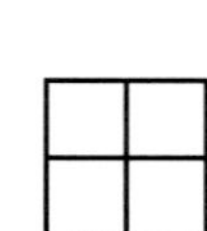

2 × 2 = 4

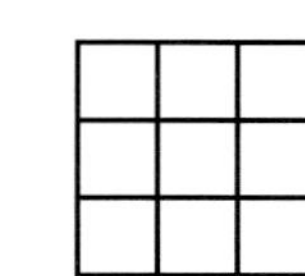

3 × 3 = 9

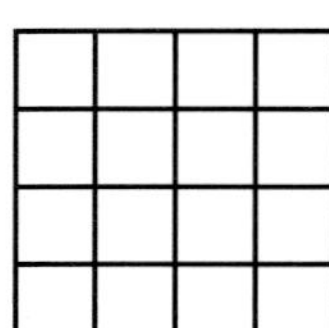

4 × 4 = 16

___ × ___ = ___

Notes for Home: Your child wrote multiplication facts in two different ways. *Home Activity:* Ask your child to draw 3 groups of 5 and then write the multiplication fact for the picture two different ways.

For additional practice, see Skills Practice Bank, page 539, Set 1.

Name

Problem Solving: Draw a Picture

Learn

PROBLEM SOLVING GUIDE

Understand • Plan • Solve • Look Back

Lesley has 4 bean plants,
4 carrot plants, and 4 pepper plants.
How many plants does she have in all?

Check

Draw a picture to solve each problem.
Complete the number sentence.

1. Nolan's garden has 4 rows of corn. Each row has 5 plants. How many corn plants does he have?

   4 × 5 = 20 corn plants

2. Sandra planted 3 seeds in each flower pot. She had 6 pots. How many seeds did she plant?

   ____ × ____ = ____ seeds

Talk About It In the story about Sandra, how could you draw a different picture to solve the problem?

Notes for Home: Your child drew pictures to solve word problems involving multiplication. *Home Activity:* Ask your child to draw a picture to find how many toys in all if there are 4 boxes with 4 toys each.

PROBLEM SOLVING

Practice

Draw a picture to solve each problem.
Complete the number sentence.

3. 5 children pick 2 pumpkins each. How many pumpkins do they pick in all?

   5 × 2 = 10 pumpkins

4. Tamara plants 3 sunflowers in each of 7 pots. How many sunflowers does she plant in all?

   ______ × ______ = ______ sunflowers

5. Leah picks 5 bowls of strawberries. Eric picks 5 bowls of blueberries. Malik picks 5 bowls of blackberries. How many bowls of berries do they pick in all?

   ______ × ______ = ______ bowls of berries

Problem Solving Estimation

6. About how many flowers are in the garden?

   Circle the best estimate.

   about 15 **about 50** **about 90**

Notes for Home: Your child solved problems involving multiplication by drawing pictures. *Home Activity:* Ask your child to explain how he or she chose the answer for Exercise 6.

Name

Mixed Practice

Lessons 1–6

Concepts and Skills

Find how many in all. You can use Snap Cubes.

1 How many shells?

4 groups of 3

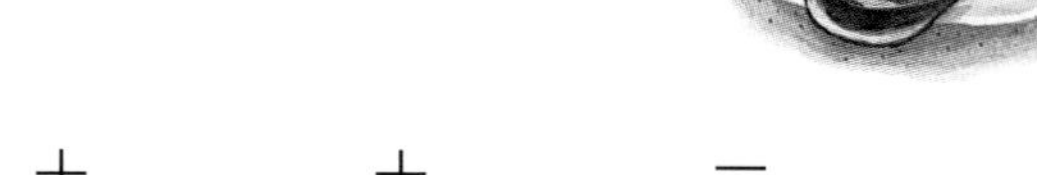

___ + ___ + ___ + ___ = ___

___ $\times$ ___ = ___

Color equal rows. Find the product.

2 4 rows of 5 — 5 rows of 4

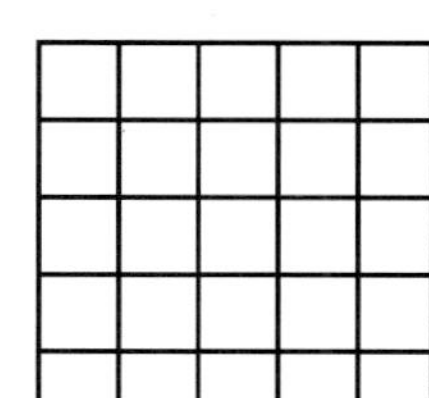

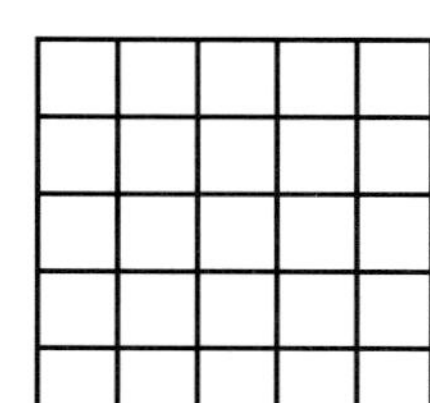

$4 \times 5 =$ ___ $5 \times 4 =$ ___

3 3 rows of 2 — 2 rows of 3

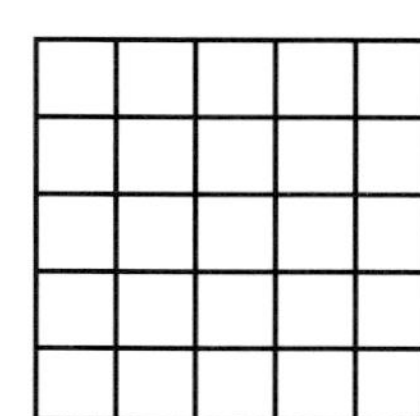

$3 \times 2 =$ ___ $2 \times 3 =$ ___

MIXED PRACTICE

Problem Solving

Draw a picture to solve the problem.

4 There are 6 buckets on a beach blanket.
Each bucket has 3 shovels in it.
How many shovels are there in all?

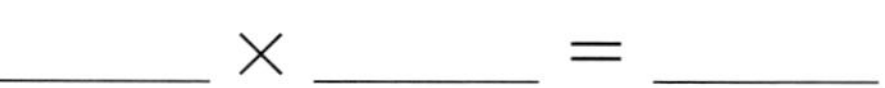

___ $\times$ ___ = ___

Journal

5 Write a story to tell about $3 \times 4 = 12$.

Notes for Home: Your child practiced using pictures and drawing pictures to solve multiplication problems. *Home Activity:* Ask your child how the pictures in Exercise 2 would be different if they showed 4×3 and 3×4.

Name

Cumulative Review

Chapters 1–13

Concepts and Skills

Shade some of the equal parts.

Write the fraction for the parts that are shaded.

1 Shade 6 parts.

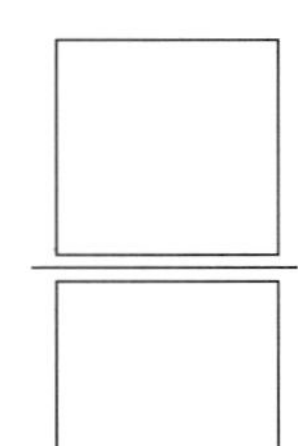

 Shade 2 parts.

Getting Ready for Next Year

Copy each problem on a separate piece of paper. Add or subtract.

3

420	653	592	314	817	617
+ 119	− 428	− 161	+ 227	− 252	+ 212

4

584	216	987	375	714	504
+ 53	− 429	− 654	+ 264	+ 82	+ 162

Test Prep

Fill in the ○ for the correct answer.

Which shape would you make if you traced each object?

5

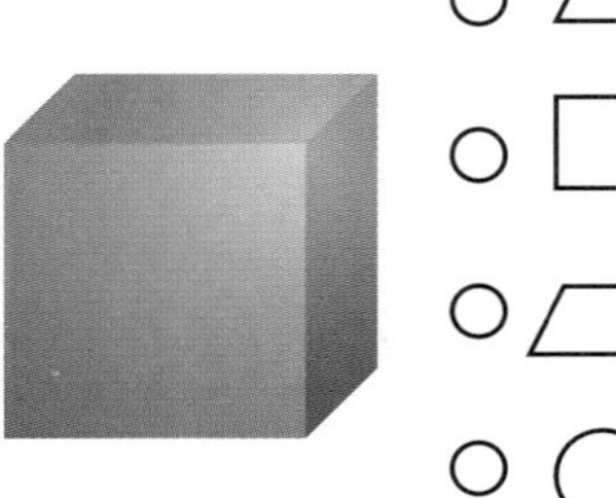

○ △
○ □
○ ⏢
○ ◯

6

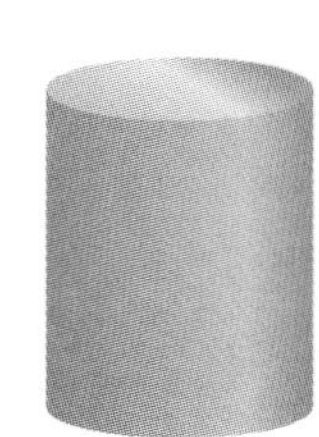

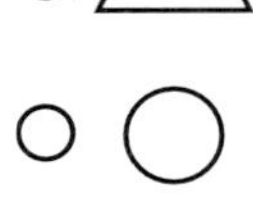

○ △
○ □
○ ⏢
○ ◯

7

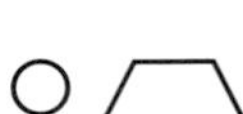

○ ▭
○ △
○ ◯
○ ⏢

Notes or Home: Your child reviewed fractions, solids, and addition and subtraction. *Home Activity:* Ask your child to share a piece of fruit or other food item so that he or she has $\frac{2}{3}$ and you have $\frac{1}{3}$.

Name

Explore Making Equal Groups

Explore

Use 12 counters. How many ways can you make equal groups? Draw one of your ways.

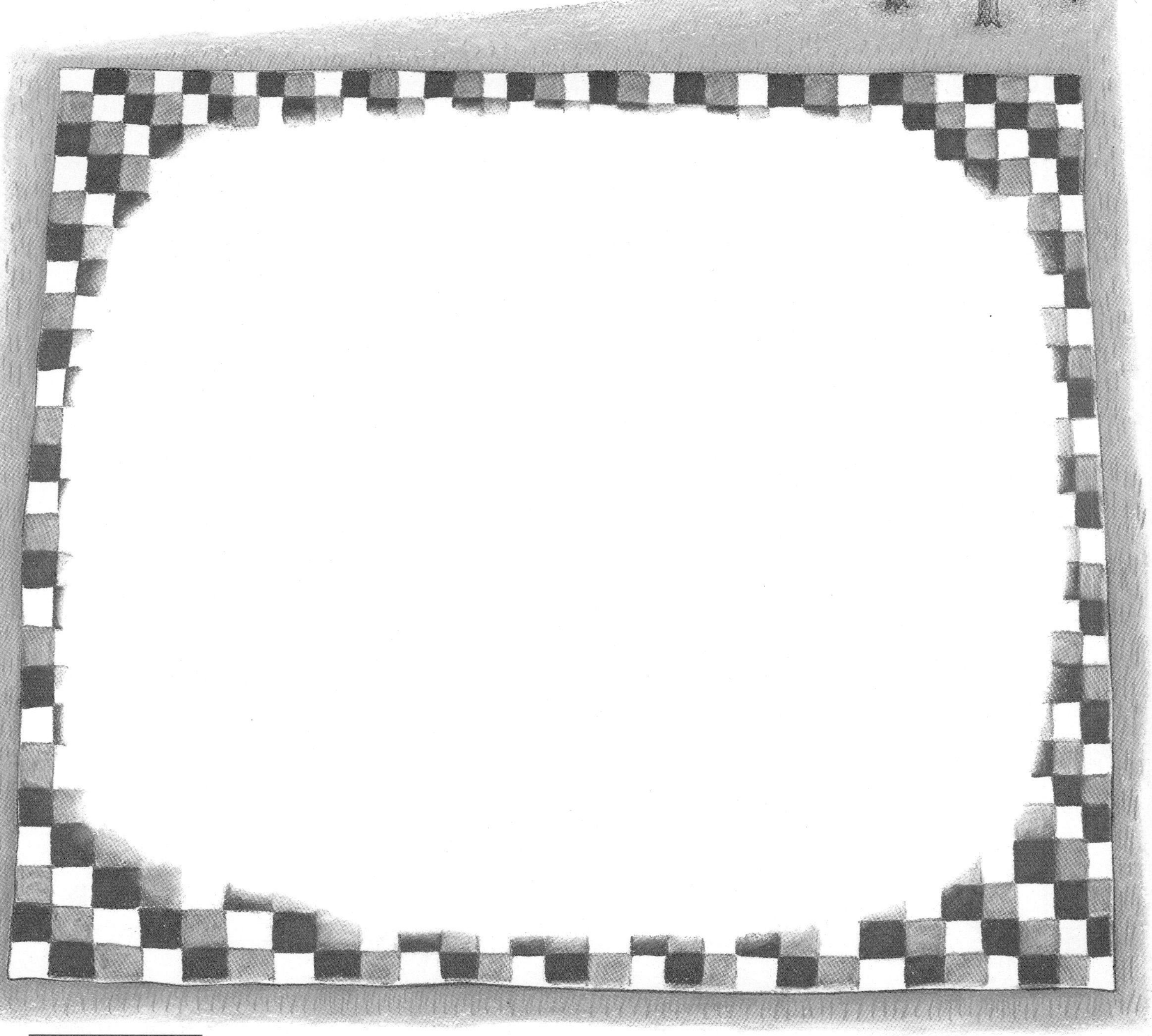

Share

Tell about the other ways you found to make equal groups.

Notes for Home: Your child used counters to make equal groups. *Home Activities:* Ask your child to use 8 objects to make equal groups.

EXPLORE

Connect

On their hike, 3 children picked 18 berries. They shared them equally. How many berries did each child get?

Each child gets __6__ berries.

Start by giving one to each child. Keep sharing until they are gone.

Use counters to make equal groups. Draw a picture to show your work.

1. 12 people share 3 picnic blankets. How many people on each blanket?

__4__ people

2. 8 children share 2 picnic tables. How many children at each table?

_____ children

3. 4 children share 16 water balloons. How many balloons for each child?

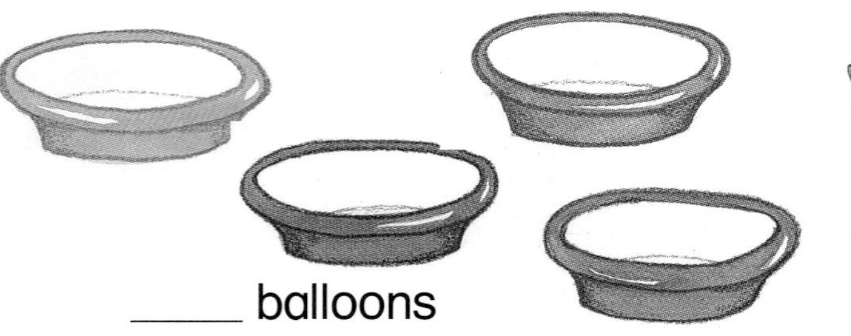

_____ balloons

4. 5 children share 10 hot dogs. How many hot dogs for each child?

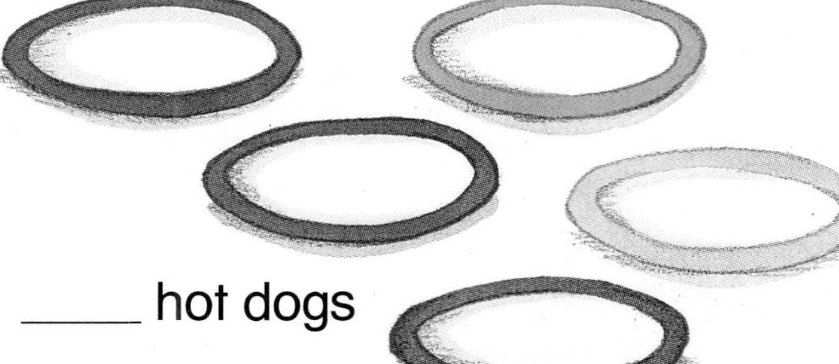

_____ hot dogs

Talk About It Could 4 children share 17 crackers equally? How do you know?

Notes for Home: Your child drew pictures to share amounts equally. *Home Activity:* Ask your child to use 6 objects and show how to share them equally among 6 people.

EXPLORE

Name

Share and Divide

Learn

5 children share 15 hoops equally.
How many hoola hoops will each child get?

15 divided by 5 equals 3

15 ÷ 5 = 3 hoops.

Check

Use counters to make equal groups. Draw to show your work.
Write the number sentence.

1. 12 bean bags in 4 buckets

12 ÷ 4 = 3 bean bags

2. 16 beads on 2 necklaces

____ ÷ ____ = ____ beads

3. 10 balloons shared by 2 children

____ ÷ ____ = ____ balloons

4. 9 yo-yos in 3 boxes

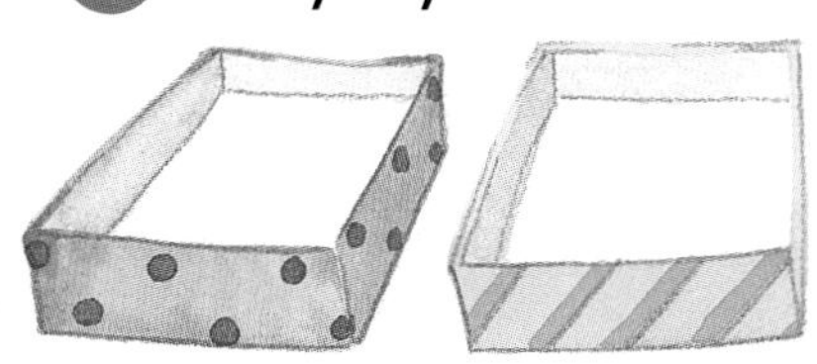

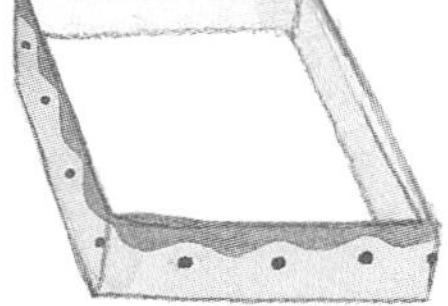

____ ÷ ____ = ____ yo-yos

Talk About It How did you find how many yo-yos went in each box?

Notes for Home: Your child drew pictures to share groups equally and completed division sentences. *Home Activity:* Ask your child to draw a picture and write a division sentence to show 9 balls shared equally by 3 children.

Practice

You can use counters. Draw a picture to show equal groups.
Write the number sentence.

5 20 pieces of chalk in 4 boxes

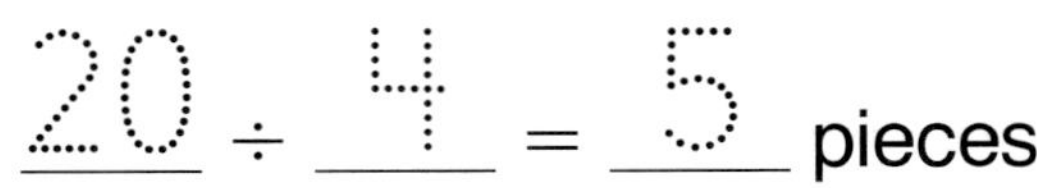

20 ÷ 4 = 5 pieces

6 12 birds on 2 branches.

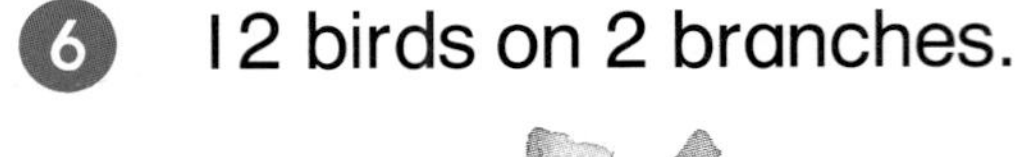

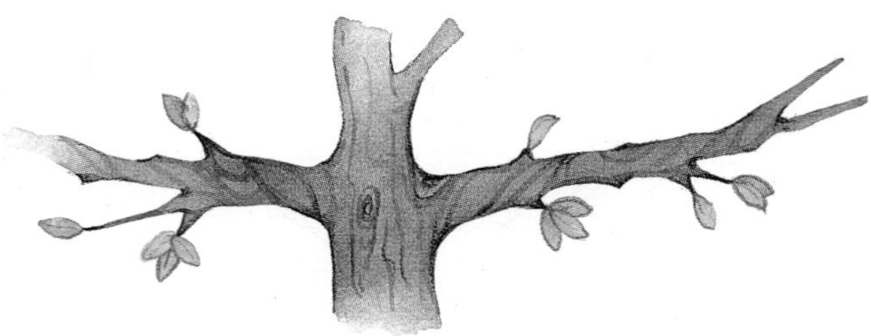

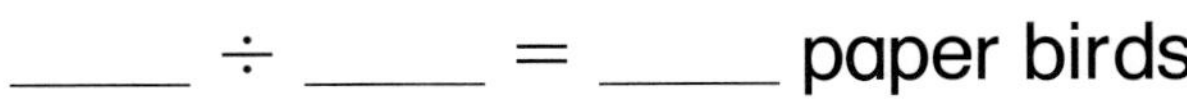

____ ÷ ____ = ____ paper birds

7 25 marbles in 5 bags

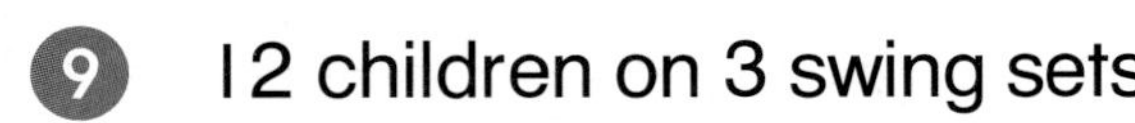

____ ÷ ____ = ____ marbles

8 15 toy cars in 3 cases

____ ÷ ____ = ____ toy cars

9 12 children on 3 swing sets

____ ÷ ____ = ____ children

10 8 kites shared by 2 children

____ ÷ ____ = ____ kites

PRACTICE

Problem Solving

Solve. You can use counters.

11 Tanesha has 18 water balloons to give away. If she gives 2 to each friend, how many friends will get water balloons?

____ friends

Notes for Home: Your child drew pictures and completed number sentences. *Home Activity:* Ask your child to write a division sentence using the numbers 18, 3, and 6.

For additional practice, see Skills Practice Bank, page 539, Set 2.

Name ________________________________

Reading for Math

Compare and Contrast

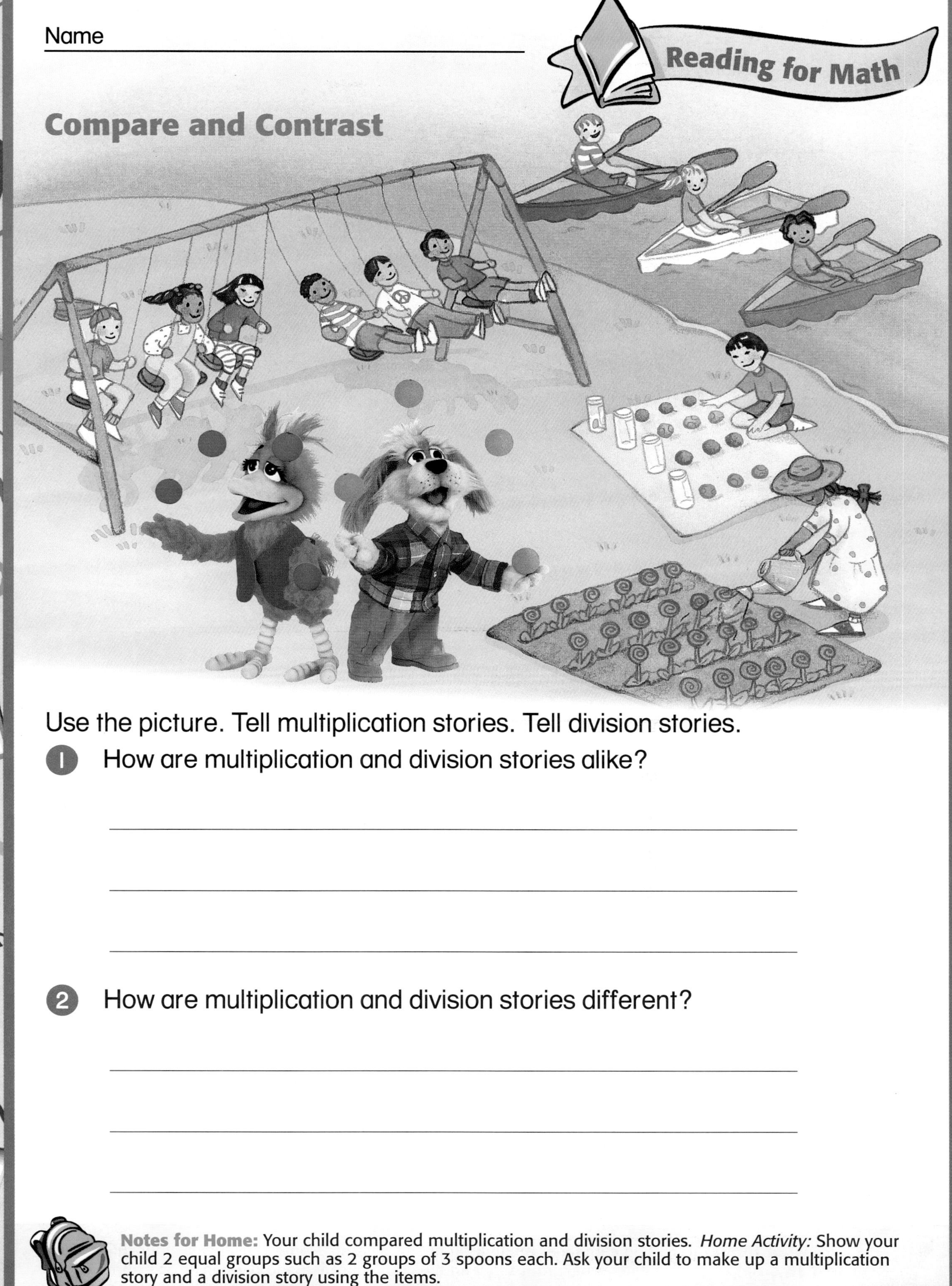

Use the picture. Tell multiplication stories. Tell division stories.

1. How are multiplication and division stories alike?

____

____

____

2. How are multiplication and division stories different?

____

____

____

Notes for Home: Your child compared multiplication and division stories. *Home Activity:* Show your child 2 equal groups such as 2 groups of 3 spoons each. Ask your child to make up a multiplication story and a division story using the items.

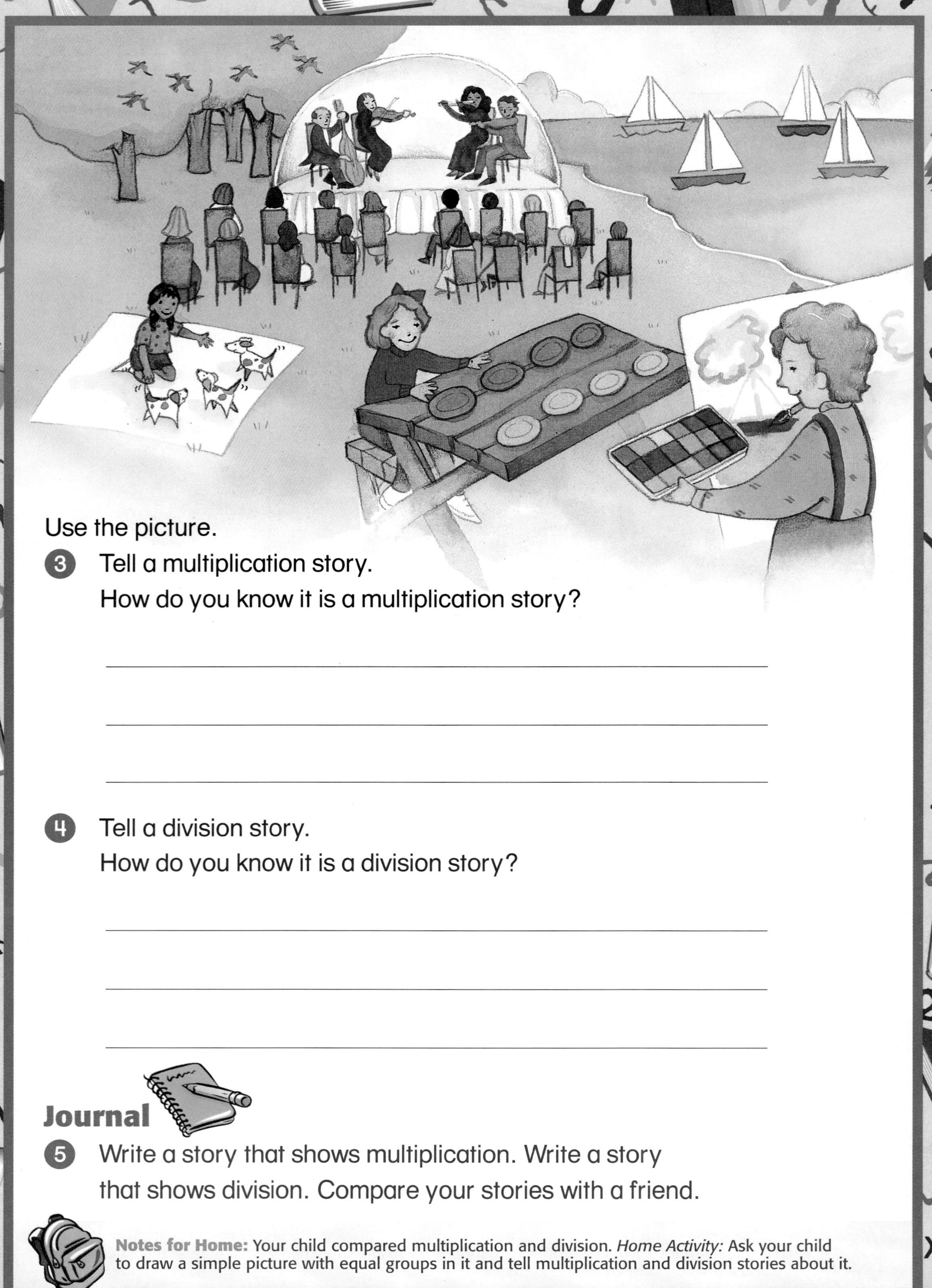

Use the picture.

3. Tell a multiplication story.
   How do you know it is a multiplication story?

4. Tell a division story.
   How do you know it is a division story?

Journal

5. Write a story that shows multiplication. Write a story that shows division. Compare your stories with a friend.

Notes for Home: Your child compared multiplication and division. *Home Activity:* Ask your child to draw a simple picture with equal groups in it and tell multiplication and division stories about it.

Name

Problem Solving: Choose an Operation

Learn

PROBLEM SOLVING GUIDE

Understand • Plan • Solve • Look Back

There are 6 tents.
Each tent has 3 children inside.
How many children are there?

$6 \div 3 = 2$ $\quad$ $6 \times 3 = 18$ $\quad$ $6 - 3 = 3$

Check

Circle the number sentence that solves the problem.

1. 2 children are hiking.
   3 more children join them.
   How many children are hiking?

   $2 \times 3 = 6$ $\quad$ $3 - 2 = 1$ $\quad$ $2 + 3 = 5$

2. On a camping trip, 5 people shared 10 boxes of raisins equally. How many boxes did each person get?

$10 + 5 = 15$ $\quad$ $10 \div 5 = 2$ $\quad$ $2 \times 5 = 10$

Talk About It In the problem about tents, how would you use addition to find the answer? Explain.

Notes for Home: Your child circled the number sentence that solves a word problem.
Home Activity: Ask your child to write a word problem that could be solved by dividing.

Practice

Circle the number sentence that helps you solve the problem.

3. 5 children are fishing. Each child catches 3 fish. How many fish do the children catch in all?

$5 \times 3 = 15$ $5 - 3 = 2$ $15 \div 3 = 5$

4. There are 8 children around a campfire. 2 children go into their tents. How many children are still around the campfire?

$8 + 2 = 10$ $8 \div 2 = 4$ $8 - 2 = 6$

5. 10 people want to share 2 canoes equally. How many people will go in each canoe?

$10 + 2 = 12$ $10 \div 2 = 5$ $10 - 2 = 8$

Tell a Math Story

Tell a story for each number sentence.

6. $4 \times 2 = 8$
7. $12 \div 2 = 6$
8. $17 - 9 = 8$

Notes for Home: Your child identified a number sentence that could be used to solve a word problem. *Home Activity:* Ask your child to write a word problem that could be solved by multiplying.

For additional practice, see Skills Practice Bank, page 539 Set 3.

Name

Mixed Practice

Lessons 7–9

Concepts and Skills

You can use counters to make equal groups.

Draw to show your work. Write the number sentence.

1. 8 people share 2 beach towels. How many people on each towel?

_____ ÷ _____ = _____ people

2. 12 shells go in 3 buckets. How many shells in each bucket?

_____ ÷ _____ = _____ toys

Problem Solving

Circle the number sentence that solves the problem.

3. There are 6 children. Each child has 3 balloons. How many balloons are there?

6 − 3 = 3   **18 ÷ 3 = 6**   **6 × 3 = 18**

4. At a cookout, 4 children share 8 hamburgers equally. How many hamburgers did each child get?

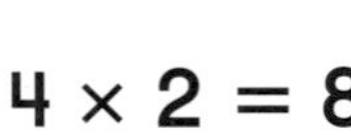

4 × 2 = 8   **8 ÷ 4 = 2**   **8 + 4 = 12**

Journal

5. Write a story for this number sentence. **6 ÷ 2 = 3**

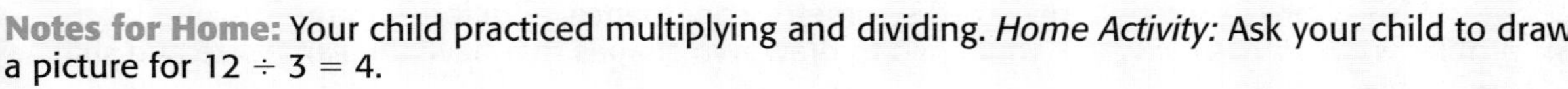

Notes for Home: Your child practiced multiplying and dividing. *Home Activity:* Ask your child to draw a picture for 12 ÷ 3 = 4.

MIXED PRACTICE

Name ______________________________

Cumulative Review

Chapter 1–13

Concepts and Skills

Draw a shape that is congruent to each shape.

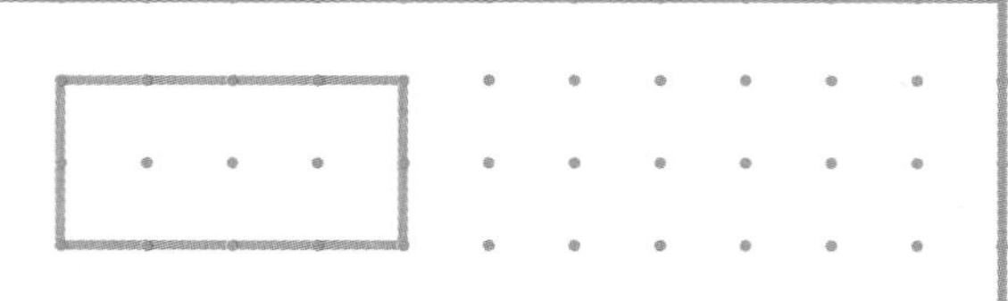

2

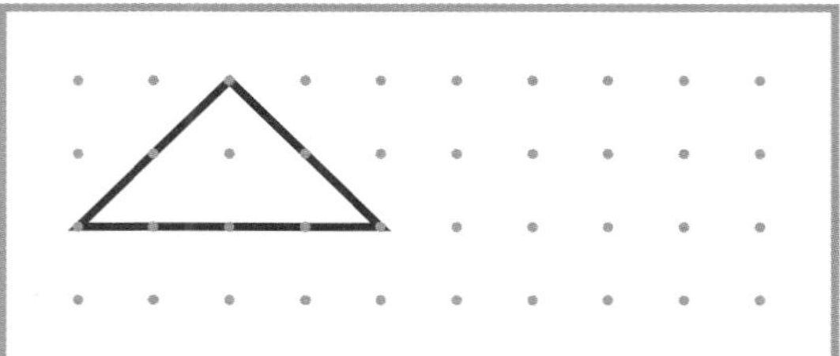

Problem Solving

3 Dan brought 16 oranges and 20 bananas to the picnic. How many pieces of fruit did he bring?

______ pieces of fruit

4 At summer camp, 53 children went canoeing. 27 children went hiking. How many more children went canoeing?

______ children

Getting Ready for Next Year

Copy each problem on a separate piece of paper.
Add.

$\begin{array}{r} 21 \\ 32 \\ +\ 14 \\ \hline \end{array}$ $\begin{array}{r} 15 \\ 12 \\ +\ 45 \\ \hline \end{array}$ $\begin{array}{r} 23 \\ 17 \\ +\ 52 \\ \hline \end{array}$ $\begin{array}{r} 64 \\ 29 \\ +\ 6 \\ \hline \end{array}$ $\begin{array}{r} 18 \\ 48 \\ +\ 10 \\ \hline \end{array}$ $\begin{array}{r} 19 \\ 31 \\ +\ 49 \\ \hline \end{array}$

Test Prep

Fill in the ○ for the correct answer.
Add or subtract.

6 $\begin{array}{r} 415 \\ +\ 386 \\ \hline \end{array}$

○ 701
○ 791
○ 801
○ 811

7 $\begin{array}{r} 526 \\ -\ 352 \\ \hline \end{array}$

○ 174
○ 234
○ 274
○ 284

8 $\begin{array}{r} 982 \\ -\ 657 \\ \hline \end{array}$

○ 335
○ 225
○ 425
○ 325

Notes for Home: Your child reviewed symmetry, congruence, addition, subtraction, and word problems.. *Home Activity:* Ask your child to draw two shapes that have the same size and shape, or that are congruent.

Name ______________________________

Chapter 13 Review

Vocabulary

1 Find the product.
Write the number sentence.

There are 4 trees with 3 children in each tree. How many children are in the trees?

_____ × _____ = _____ children

2 Divide.
Write the number sentence.

12 people share 4 row boats equally. How many people are in each boat?

_____ ÷ _____ = _____ people

Concepts and Skills

3 Color equal rows. Find the product.
4 rows of 3

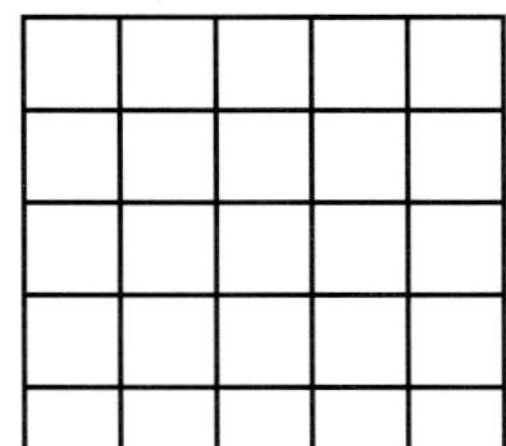

$4 \times 3 =$ _____

4 Find the product.
3 groups of 6

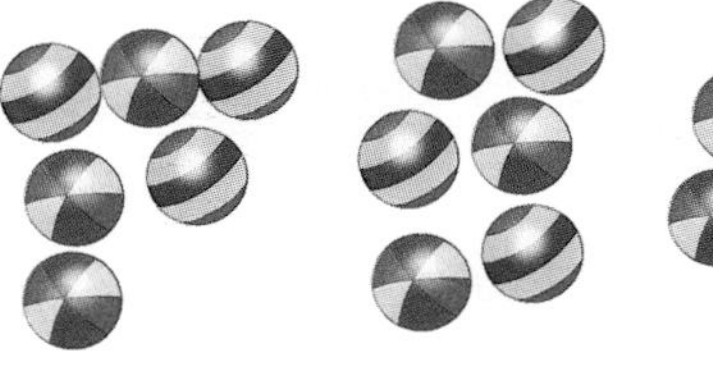

$3 \times 6 =$ _____

$$\begin{array}{r} 6 \\ \times\ 3 \\ \hline \end{array}$$

Problem Solving

5 Draw a picture to solve the problem.
Complete the number sentence.

At the beach, 2 children collect 5 seashells each. How many seashells do they have?

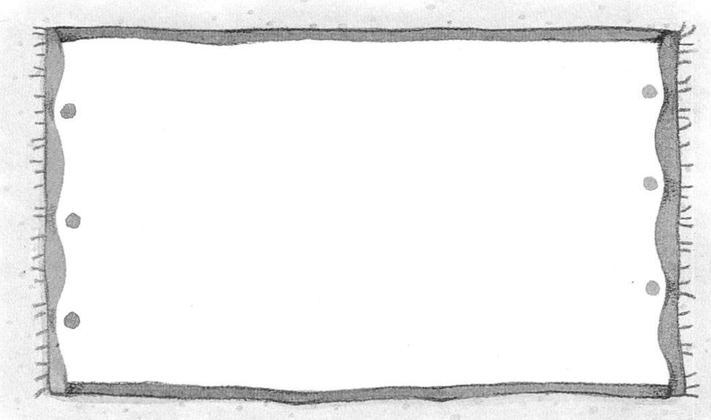

_____ × _____ = _____ seashells

6 Circle the number sentence that solves the problem.

2 friends share 4 boxes of raisins equally.
How many boxes of raisins for each friend?

$4 + 2 = 6$ $\qquad 4 \div 2 = 2$ $\qquad 4 \times 2 = 8$

Notes for Home: Your child reviewed vocabulary, concepts, skills, and problem solving from Chapter 13. *Home Activity:* Ask your child to write a multiplication story and a division story using the numbers 10, 5, and 2.

CHAPTER REVIEW

Name ________________________________

Chapter 13 Test

Find how many in all. Write the number sentence.

1 How many clams?

2 groups of 5

____ + ____ = ____

____ × ____ = ____

2 Color equal rows. Find the product.

3 rows of 5

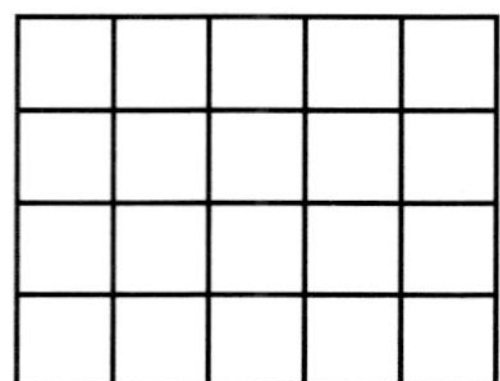

____ × ____ = ____

3 Find the product.

4 groups of 3

$4 \times 3 =$ ____

$$\begin{array}{r} 3 \\ \times\ 4 \\ \hline \end{array}$$

4 You can use counters. Draw a picture to show equal groups. Write the number sentence.

10 children on 2 blankets

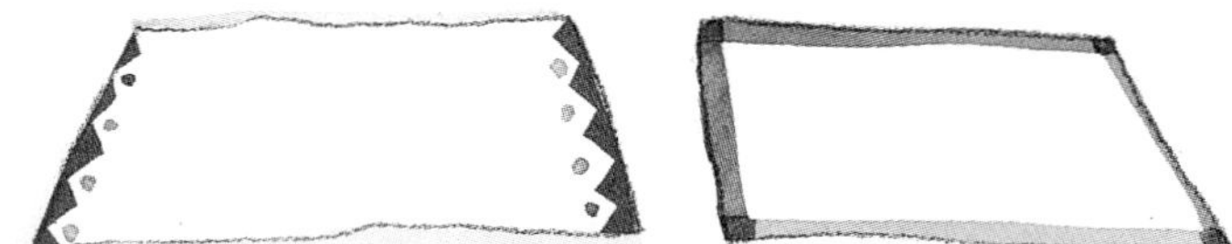

5 Draw a picture to solve the problem.

Calvin plants 3 rows of flowers with 6 flowers in each row. How many flowers does he plant in all?

____ × ____ = ____ flowers

6 Circle the number sentence that solves the problem.

4 children share 16 balloons equally.
How many balloons does each child get?

$4 \times 4 = 16$ $16 + 4 = 20$ $16 \div 4 = 4$

Notes for Home: Your child was tested on Chapter 13 skills, concepts, and problem solving.
Home Activity: Ask your child to tell a word problem that could be solved using the addition number sentence in Exercise 6.

Name

Performance Assessment

Chapter 13

Take number cards.

Write a story.

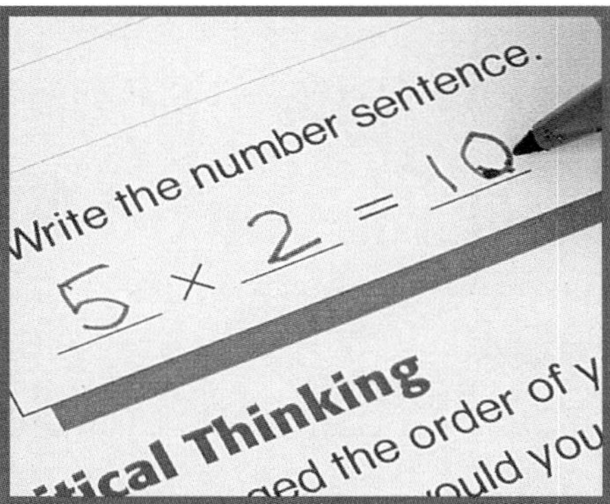

Write the number sentence.

Activity 1	Activity 2
Take two number cards from Bag 1.	Start with the number 12. Pick one number card from Bag 2.
1 Write a multiplication story that uses your numbers.	3 Write a division story that uses your numbers.
2 Write the number sentence. ____ × ____ = ____	4 Write the number sentence. ____ ÷ ____ = ____

Critical Thinking

If you changed the order of your numbers in Activity 1, how would your story change?

Notes for Home: Your child did an activity that tested Chapter 13 skills, concepts, and problem solving. *Home Activity:* Ask your child to write a multiplication story about objects in your home.

PERFORMANCE ASSESSMENT

Name ______________________________

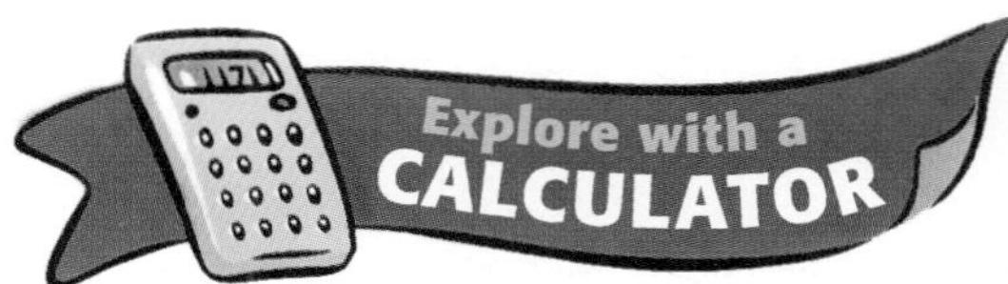

Your Town Counts!

Keys You Will Use ON/C × + =

About how many people do you think are in your city or town? You can use your calculator to help you estimate.

1. Each person in your room stands for a family. Find how many people the students in your class represent. Add to find the total number.
2. Estimate how many people the students in your school represent. Multiply the total number of people your class represents by the number of classes in your school.

______	×	______	=	______
actual people your class represents		actual number of classes		estimated number of people

3. Estimate how many people are in your town. Find out how many schools there are in your city or town. Multiply your estimate of the total number of people your school represents by the number of schools in your city or town.

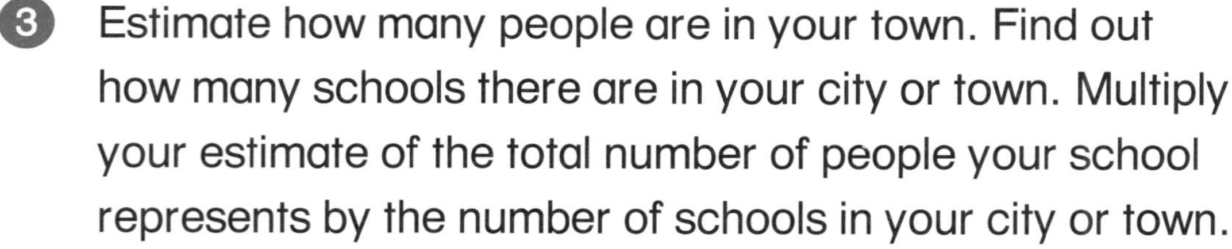

______	×	______	=	______
estimated number of people		actual number of schools		estimated number of people in my town

4. Find out the actual number of people in your city or town. Compare your estimate to the actual number. Was your estimate higher or lower than the actual number?

Tech Talk How could you solve the above problem without the  key?

Visit our Web site. www.parent.mathsurf.com

What a Square!

If you can arrange dots to form an array in the shape of a square, you have formed a square number.

Here are the first four square numbers. Use multiplication to tell about the number of dots.

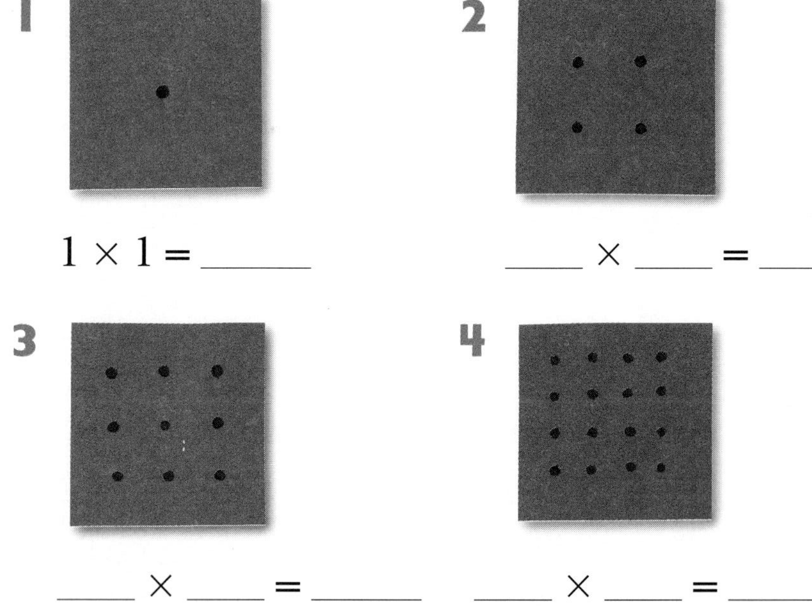

1 $1 \times 1 =$ ______

2 ____ × ____ = ______

3 ____ × ____ = ______

4 ____ × ____ = ______

What do you think the next two square numbers are? Draw an array, then use multiplication to tell about the number of dots.

Fold down

MathSoup

Scott Foresman - Addison Wesley My Math Magazine No. 13

Hot Shot!

Pay Your Way

It's summer! What do you want to do? Go out to eat? To pay for your summer fun, sometimes you have to do summer work.

The advertisements show different jobs you can do to earn money.

Justin began playing in tournaments when he was six years old. He almost always finishes in first, second, or third place! Many hours of practice help Justin enjoy many hours of summer fun!

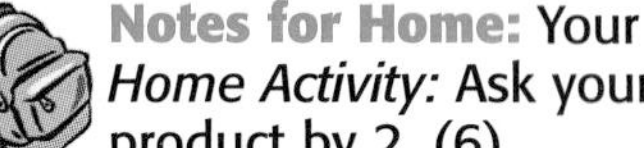

Notes for Home: Your child practiced multiplying and dividing. *Home Activity:* Ask your child to multiply 3×4, then divide the product by 2. (6)

Just Fore Fun!

Have you ever played miniature golf? Justin Carter's favorite game is golf—not miniature golf, but full-sized golf on real golf courses.

Hole	Score
1	6
2	5
3	4
4	3
5	5
6	6
7	4
8	7
9	5

Hole	Score
10	3
11	4
12	5
13	7
14	4
15	5
16	3
17	6
18	5

Suppose Justin got these scores in one round of golf.

1 On how many holes did Justin score 3? Multiply to find his total score for these holes.

2 Multiply to find Justin's total score for the holes where he scored 4, 5, 6, and 7.

3 Add your answers to find Justin's score for the entire round.

Use the advertisements to answer these questions.

1 Your neighbors go on vacation. You water their plants for 5 days. How much do you earn?

_____

2 You and a friend do 1 job of yard work. When you are finished, you divide the money equally. How much do you each earn?

_____

3 You and a friend clean your home for 2 hours. Then you wash 2 cars. How much do both of you earn in all?

_____

Divide the money you earned equally. How much do you each earn?

_____

Notes for Home: Your child practiced multiplication. *Home Activity:* Ask your child to find 3×4. Then ask him or her to state two different facts with the same product. (2×6, 1×12)

It's in the Bank!

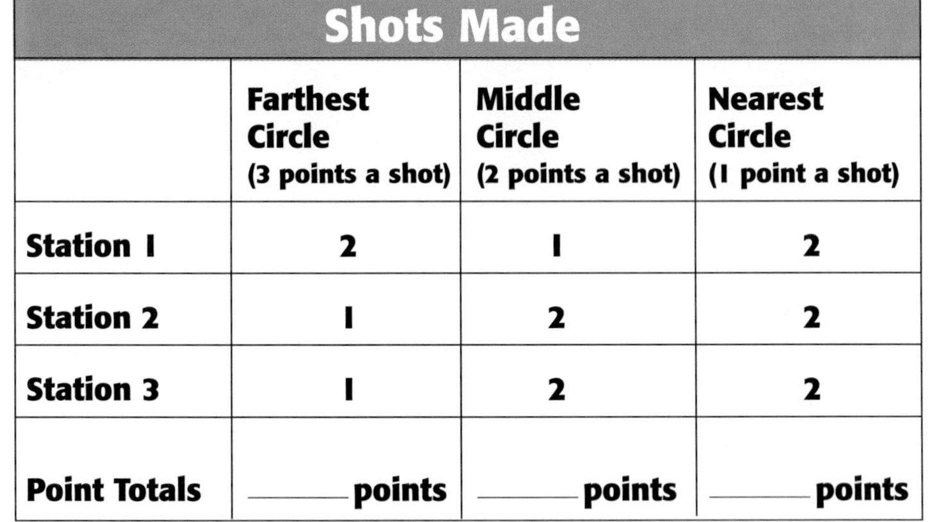

Do you like basketball? How about miniature golf? Here's a game that combines them. It's called Bankshot.

In Bankshot, you must bank, or bounce, the basketball off different backboards.

Each basket, or station, has three circles by it. You shoot twice from each circle and earn different points for each shot.

Shots Made			
	Farthest Circle (3 points a shot)	**Middle Circle** (2 points a shot)	**Nearest Circle** (1 point a shot)
Station 1	2	1	2
Station 2	1	2	2
Station 3	1	2	2
Point Totals	____ points	____ points	____ points

1 Suppose you are playing Bankshot. The table shows the number of shots you made at the first three stations. Find your total points for each circle.

2 Add your point totals to find your total score.

____ points

Notes for Home: Your child practiced multiplying and adding to find totals.
Home Activity: Ask your child to add the products for 3×3 and 4×2. (17)

Name

Skills Practice Bank

Chapter 1

Set 1 Use after page 8.

Count by 2s, 5s, or 10s.

Write the numbers.

1. 2, 4, ____, ____, ____
2. 12, 14, ____, ____, ____
3. 10, 20, ____, ____, ____
4. 15, 20, ____, ____, ____

Set 2 Use after page 12.

Continue the pattern. Color the numbers.

1.

1	2	3	4	5	6	7	8	9	10
11	12	13	14	15	16	17	18	19	20
21	22	23	24	25	26	27	28	29	30
31	32	33	34	35	36	37	38	39	40
41	42	43	44	45	46	47	48	49	50

Set 3 Use after page 22.

1. Use the tally chart to make a bar graph.

Favorite Game	
Jump Rope	IIII
Tag	III
Hide-and-Seek	卌 I

Favorite Game						
Jump Rope						
Tag						
Hide-and-Seek						
	1	2	3	4	5	6

2. How many more children chose **Hide-and-Seek** than **Jump Rope?** ____ more

SKILLS PRACTICE BANK

Name ______________________________

Skills Practice Bank

Chapter 2

Set 1 Use after page 44.

Add.

1

4	7	8	9	5	8	9
+ 1	+ 2	+ 0	+ 2	+ 3	+ 3	+ 1

2

3	5	3	2	3	4	1
+ 9	+ 2	+ 6	+ 9	+ 5	+ 3	+ 7

Set 2 Use after page 58.

Subtract.

1

6	9	7	8	11	12	10
− 1	− 2	− 0	− 2	− 1	− 0	− 2

2

5	12	8	7	10	9	6
− 2	− 1	− 0	− 2	− 1	− 2	− 1

Set 3 Use after page 68.

Circle **add** or **subtract.**

Write the number sentence. Solve.

1 10 children jumped rope.
2 children went home.
How many children were left?

add **subtract**

______ children

2 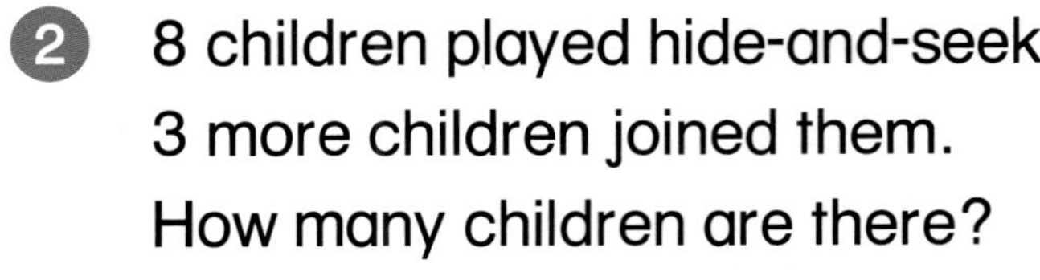
8 children played hide-and-seek.
3 more children joined them.
How many children are there?

add **subtract**

______ children

Name

Skills Practice Bank

Chapter 3

Set 1 Use after page 92.

Add. Write the addition sentence.

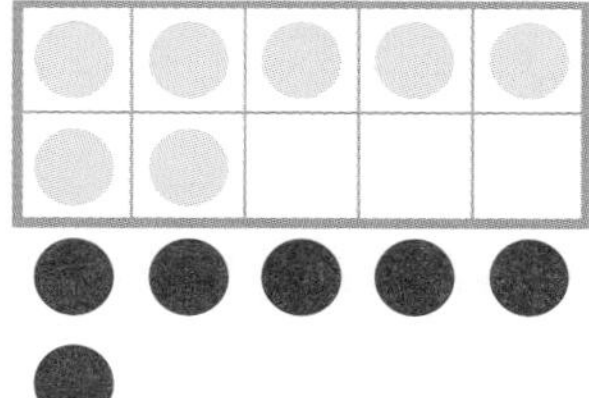

____ + ____ = ____

2

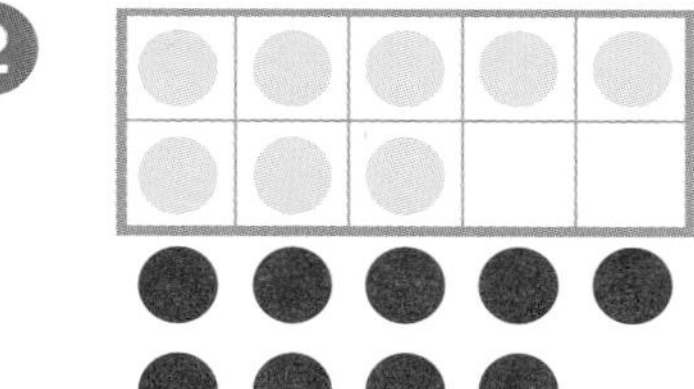

____ + ____ = ____

Set 2 Use after page 94.

1. Malik is cleaning his room. Find all the ways he can put 7 toys in two boxes. Each box can hold up to 6 toys. Write your numbers in the list. You can use ● ○ to help.

Box 1	Box 2

Set 3 Use after page 102.

Write a number sentence. Solve.

1. 8 children were playing a party game. 5 more children joined them. How many children were playing then?

____

2. 13 children were playing a party game. 5 children stopped playing. How many children were playing then?

____

Name ______________________________

Skills Practice Bank

Chapter 4

Set 1 Use after page 122.

Complete each fact family. Add or subtract.

1. $9 + 5 =$ ____
   $5 + 9 =$ ____
   $14 - 5 =$ ____
   $14 - 9 =$ ____

2. $7 + 6 =$ ____
   $6 + 7 =$ ____
   $13 - 6 =$ ____
   $13 - 7 =$ ____

3. $9 + 8 =$ ____
   $8 + 9 =$ ____
   $17 - 8 =$ ____
   $17 - 9 =$ ____

Set 2 Use after page 136.

Add.

1. $5 + 5 + 4 =$ ____
   $4 + 3 + 4 =$ ____

2. $6 + 3 + 2 =$ ____
   $8 + 0 + 2 =$ ____

Set 3 Use after page 144.

Write each number sentence. Solve.

1. There are 14 prizes on the shelf. People win 6 prizes. How many prizes are left?

   ______________ prizes

   4 more prizes are put on the shelf. How many prizes are there now?

   ______________ prizes

2. Joe brings 4 sandwiches to the picnic. Bonnie brings 8 more. How many sandwiches are at the picnic?

   ______________ sandwiches

   6 of the sandwiches are eaten. How many sandwiches are left?

   ______________ sandwiches

Name

Skills Practice Bank

Chapter 5

Set 1 Use after page 162.

Write the number.

1. eight ______
2. seventeen ______
3. forty-five ______

Write the word.

4. 7 ____________
5. 14 ____________
6. 23 ____________

Set 2 Use after page 166.

Use the graph to answer the questions.

1. How many leaves did Bridget collect?

   ______ leaves

2. How many more leaves did Clara collect than Lamar?

   ______ more

Leaf Collections	
Clara	🍁🍁🍁🍁🍁
Lamar	🍁🍁🍁
Bridget	🍁🍁🍁🍁🍁🍁

Each 🍁 means 10 leaves.

Set 3 Use after page 176.

Write the numbers in order from least to greatest.

1. 53 38 47 ______ ______ ______
2. 41 70 28 ______ ______ ______
3. 86 90 82 ______ ______ ______
4. 79 59 97 ______ ______ ______

SKILLS PRACTICE BANK

Name ____________________

Skills Practice Bank

Chapter 6

Set 1 Use after page 206.

Count the money. Write how much in all.

_____ ¢

_____ ¢

Set 2 Use after page 208.

1. Chris needs 25¢ to buy milk for lunch. Complete the list to find all the ways to make 25¢.

Set 3 Use after page 214.

1. Use quarters and dimes to show $1.00. Draw the coins. Write how many.

There are _____ quarters and _____ dimes in $1.00.

Name

Skills Practice Bank

Chapter 7

Set 1 Use after page 240.

Draw the clock hands.
Write the ending time.

1 Start 5:00 

2 hours later

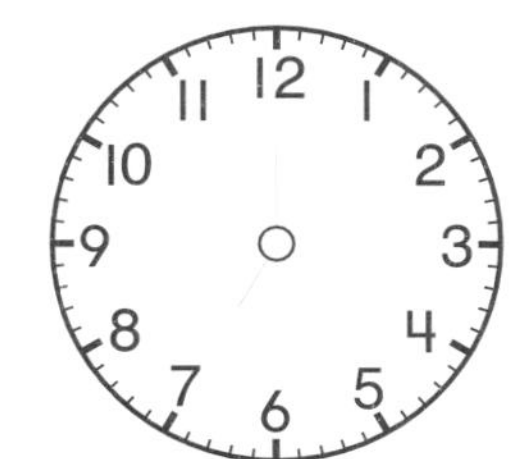 Stop ___:___

Set 2 Use after page 244.

Use the table. Solve the problems.
Write each answer.

Computer Club Schedule		
Day	Starts	Ends
Monday	3:00	4:00
Tuesday	3:00	4:00
Wednesday	3:00	5:00
Thursday	3:00	4:00
Friday	3:00	6:00

1 On how many days does the Computer Club meet for only one hour?

_____ days

2 For how many hours does the Computer Club meet on Friday?

_____ hours

Set 3 Use after page 248.

Write the time for each clock.

1  ___:___

2  ___:___

3  ___:___

4  ___:___

SKILLS PRACTICE BANK

Name ______________________________

Skills Practice Bank

Chapter 8

Set 1 Use after page 286.

Add. Then circle the sum if you regrouped.

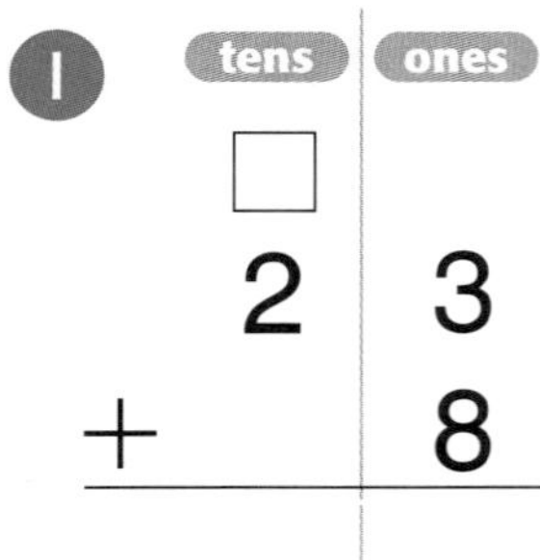

1.

tens	ones
□	
2	3
+	8

2.

tens	ones
□	
5	4
+	5

3.

tens	ones
□	
7	7
+	7

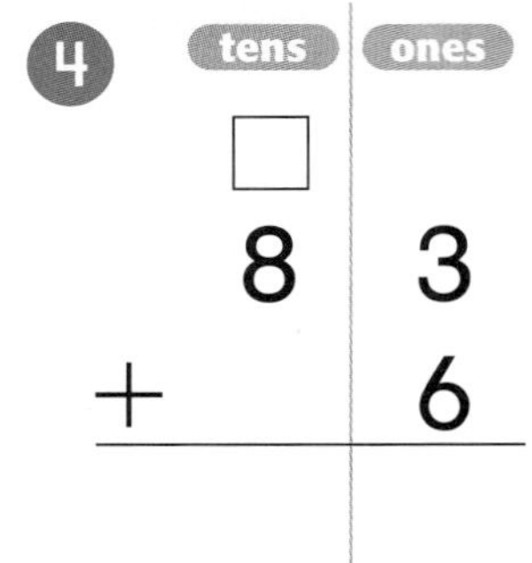

4.

tens	ones
□	
8	3
+	6

Set 2 Use after page 298.

Add.

1.

15	53	40	14	62	20
22	8	12	18	10	9
+ 41	+ 31	+ 38	+ 21	+ 17	+ 47

Set 3 Use after page 300.

Solve. Show each guess. Then check each guess.

1. Brett has 67¢.
He wants to buy 2 toys.
What can he buy?

Brett can buy the ____________________ and the ____________________.

Name ______________________________

Skills Practice Bank

Chapter 9

Set 1 Use after page 324.

Subtract. Circle the difference if you regrouped.

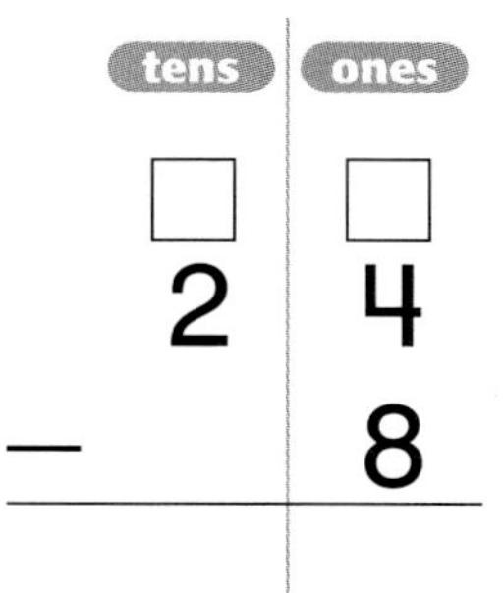

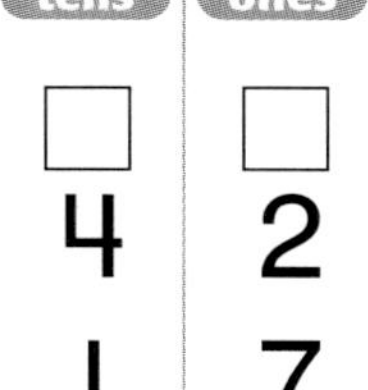

tens	ones		tens	ones		tens	ones		tens	ones
□	□		□	□		□	□		□	□
2	4		4	2		7	5		6	4
−	8		− 1	7		− 3	9		− 5	2

2

tens	ones		tens	ones		tens	ones		tens	ones
□	□		□	□		□	□		□	□
8	7		9	3		7	2		4	9
− 3	6		− 3	9		− 5	5		− 3	8

Set 2 Use after page 336.

Subtract. Regroup if you need to.

1

26	50	62	70	84	96
− 19	− 23	− 41	− 28	− 18	− 62

Set 3 Use after page 344.

Solve. Cross out the information you do not need.

A dolphin can swim about 37 miles per hour.
A trout can swim about 15 miles per hour.

People can swim about 5 miles per hour.
How much faster can a dolphin swim than a trout?

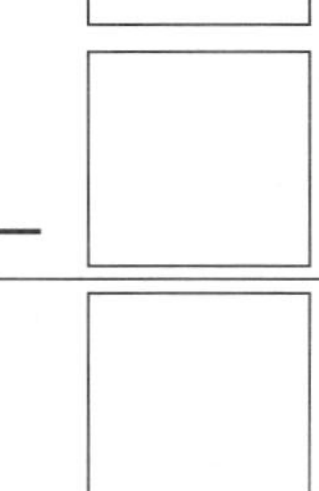

□ − □ = □ miles per hour

SKILLS PRACTICE BANK

Name

Skills Practice Bank

Chapter 10

Set 1 Use after page 366.

Compare the numbers. Write >, <, or =.

1. 132 ◯ 231   418 ◯ 481   642 ◯ 624
2. 770 ◯ 770   301 ◯ 279   883 ◯ 880

Set 2 Use after page 384.

Subtract. Regroup if you need to.

1. $\begin{array}{r} 418 \\ -\ 327 \\ \hline \end{array}$ $\begin{array}{r} 742 \\ -\ 127 \\ \hline \end{array}$ $\begin{array}{r} 415 \\ -\ 210 \\ \hline \end{array}$ $\begin{array}{r} 618 \\ -\ 453 \\ \hline \end{array}$ $\begin{array}{r} 886 \\ -\ 94 \\ \hline \end{array}$

Set 3 Use after page 388.

Use the picture to answer the questions.

1. Reggie needs 250 beads for an art project. Which bags could he choose? Circle them in red.
2. Stephanie needs 175 beads to make a craft. Which bags could she choose? Circle them in blue.

SKILLS PRACTICE BANK

Name

Skills Practice Bank

Chapter 11

Set 1 Use after page 412.

1 Mark an **X** on the shape that you estimate has the greatest perimeter. Measure the lengths of the sides. Add to find the perimeter. Circle the shape with the greatest perimeter.

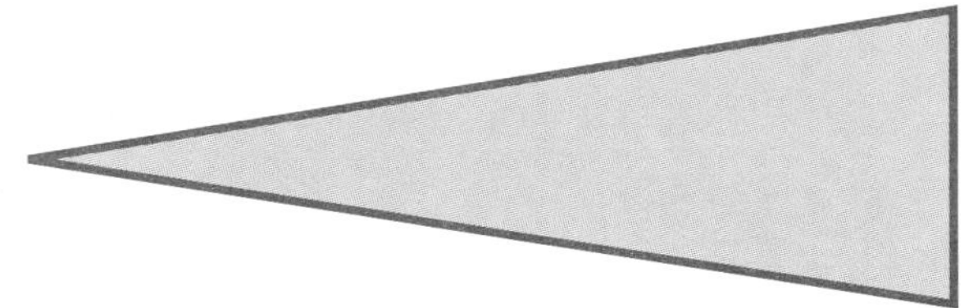

_____ inches around

_____ inches around

Set 2 Use after page 416.

1 Use paper squares.
Draw a shape that
- is a rectangle.
- has a perimeter of 14 units.
- has an area of 12 square units.

Set 3 Use after page 424.

Solve.

1 Dalia needs 2 quarts of milk for a recipe. Color the number of cups she could fill.

2 Bernard has 6 pints of juice. Color the number of quarts that hold the same amount.

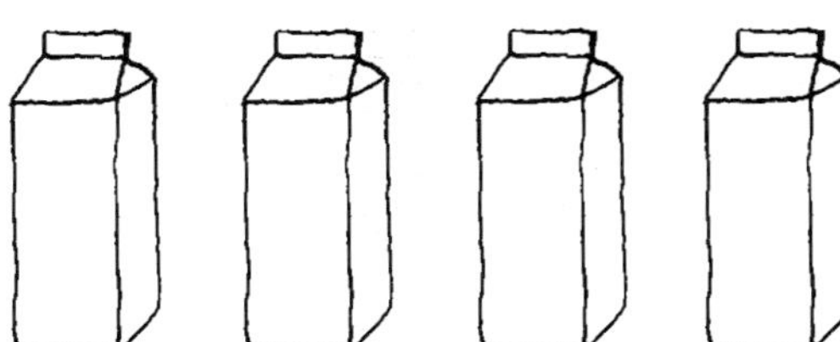

SKILLS PRACTICE BANK

Name

Skills Practice Bank

Chapter 12

Set 1 Use after page 452.

Draw a shape that is congruent to each shape.

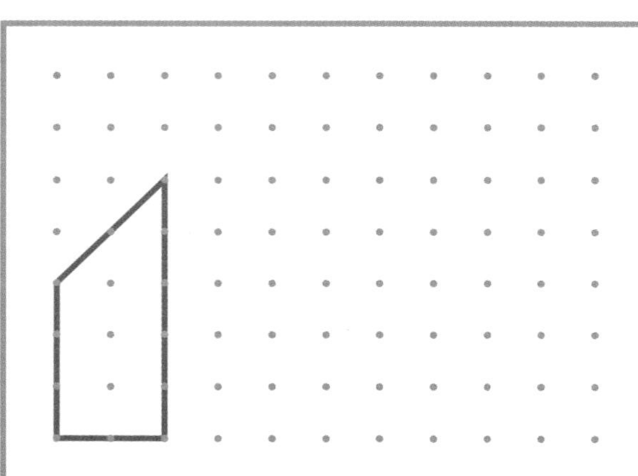

2

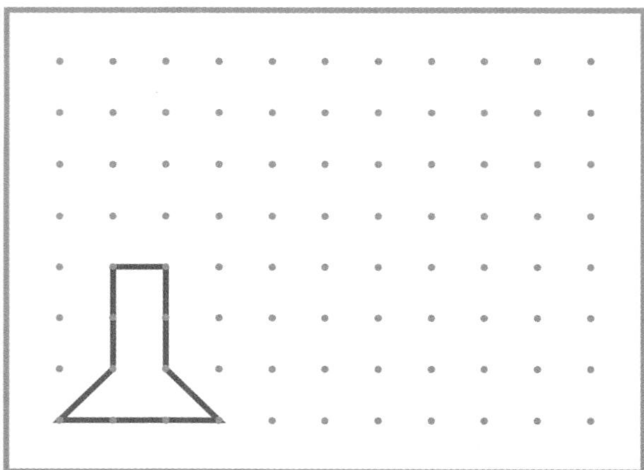

Set 2 Use after page 468.

1 Write the fraction for the shaded parts. Count equal parts first.

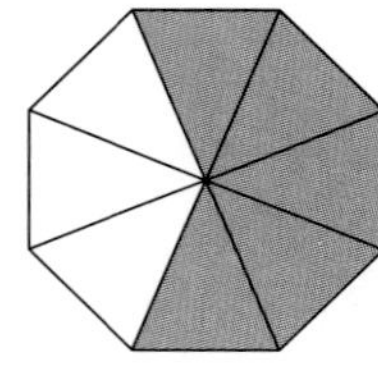

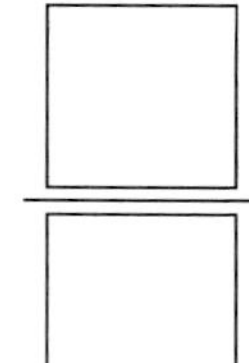

2 Shade some of the equal parts. Write the fraction for the shaded parts. Shade 4 parts.

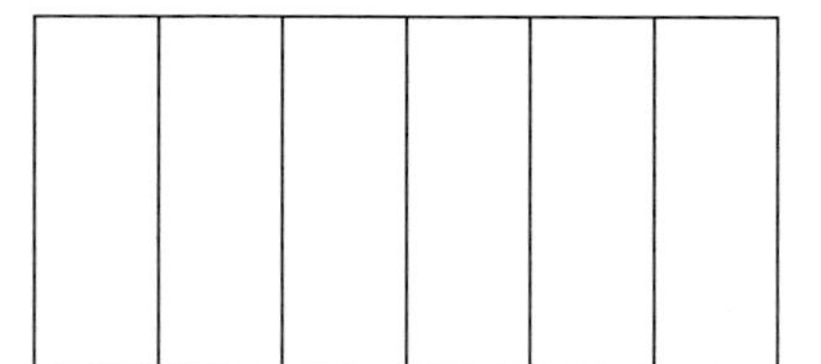

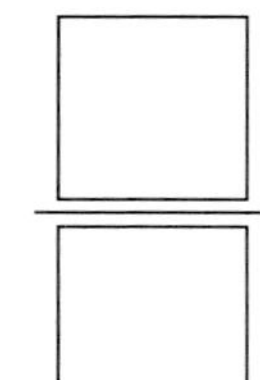

Set 3 Use after page 480.

1 Predict. If you were to spin 12 times, how many times would the spinner land

on orange? ______ on red? ______

on purple? ______

2 Spin 12 times. Write the results.

______ orange ______ red

______ purple

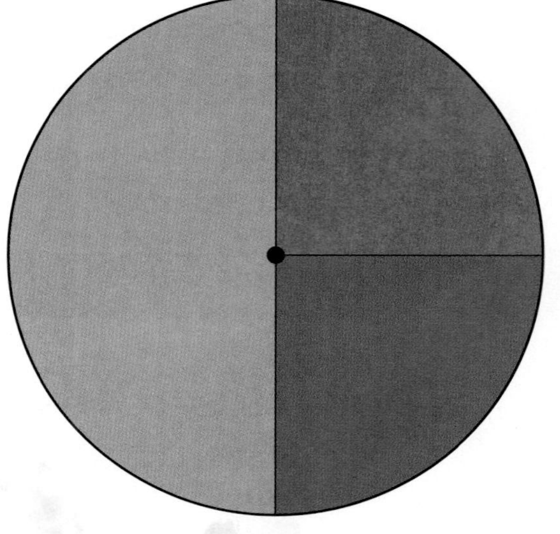

SKILLS PRACTICE BANK

Name ______________________________

Skills Practice Bank

Chapter 13

Set 1 Use after page 504.

Write the number sentence.

1 6 groups of 2 balls

____ × ____ = ____

$\begin{array}{r} \square \\ \times \ \square \\ \hline \square \end{array}$

2 3 rows of 5 Snap Cubes

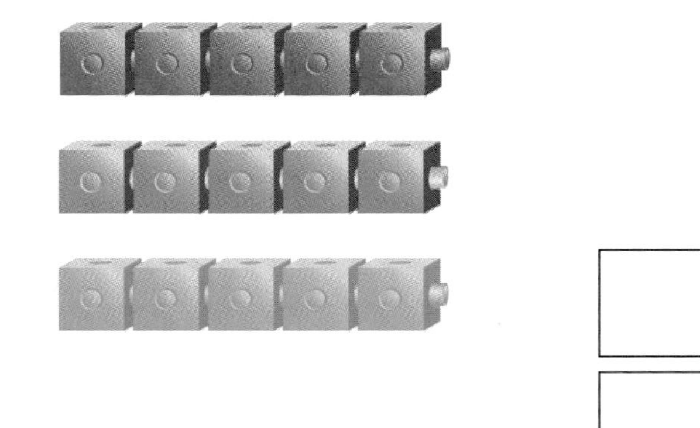

____ × ____ = ____

$\begin{array}{r} \square \\ \times \ \square \\ \hline \square \end{array}$

Set 2 Use after page 512.

You can use counters.

Draw a picture to show equal groups.

Write the number sentence.

1 12 children in 3 wagons

____ ÷ ____ = ____ children

2 16 children in 4 rowboats

____ ÷ ____ = ____ children

Set 3 Use after page 516.

Circle the number sentence that solves the problem.

1 15 children were making crafts.
5 children left to go on a hike.
How many children were still making crafts?

15 + 5 = 20

15 ÷ 5 = 3

15 − 5 = 10

Name ________________________________

Basic Facts Review

Set 1 Use after page 53.

Add.

1.

2	6	9	8	3	2	5
+ 7	+ 3	+ 3	+ 1	+ 7	+ 9	+ 2

2.

10	5	11	2	7	12	9
+ 0	+ 4	+ 1	+ 6	+ 1	+ 0	+ 1

3. $4 + 6 =$ ____ $3 + 5 =$ ____ $7 + 3 =$ ____

4. $2 + 8 =$ ____ $1 + 8 =$ ____ $5 + 6 =$ ____

Set 2 Use after page 69.

Subtract.

1.

7	8	9	11	10	9	10
− 2	− 0	− 2	− 2	− 0	− 1	− 2

2.

12	11	10	9	12	11	9
− 6	− 5	− 7	− 0	− 3	− 4	− 6

3. $8 - 0 =$ ____ $12 - 5 =$ ____ $10 - 3 =$ ____

4. $11 - 6 =$ ____ $8 - 4 =$ ____ $11 - 1 =$ ____

BASIC FACTS REVIEW

Name ______________________

Set 3 Use after page 95.

Add.

1	6 + 6	9 + 4	7 + 5	8 + 8	9 + 3	3 + 7	9 + 1
2	9 + 6	8 + 5	7 + 7	4 + 8	6 + 7	1 + 10	4 + 7
3	4 + 4	9 + 2	8 + 2	7 + 9	3 + 5	5 + 5	8 + 9
4	6 + 8	2 + 10	7 + 5	9 + 9	8 + 4	6 + 5	4 + 7

5. $10 + 0 =$ ____ $5 + 6 =$ ____ $8 + 8 =$ ____
6. $2 + 9 =$ ____ $4 + 4 =$ ____ $5 + 7 =$ ____
7. $6 + 3 =$ ____ $9 + 4 =$ ____ $8 + 9 =$ ____
8. $9 + 9 =$ ____ $5 + 8 =$ ____ $11 + 1 =$ ____
9. $6 + 6 =$ ____ $2 + 7 =$ ____ $4 + 8 =$ ____
10. $5 + 9 =$ ____ $4 + 6 =$ ____ $5 + 5 =$ ____

Name ______________________________

Set 4 Use after page 107.

Add or subtract.

1. $\begin{array}{r}7\\+\ 7\\\hline\end{array}$ $\begin{array}{r}14\\-\ 7\\\hline\end{array}$
2. $\begin{array}{r}9\\+\ 6\\\hline\end{array}$ $\begin{array}{r}15\\-\ 6\\\hline\end{array}$
3. $\begin{array}{r}9\\+\ 5\\\hline\end{array}$ $\begin{array}{r}14\\-\ 5\\\hline\end{array}$
4. $\begin{array}{r}9\\+\ 9\\\hline\end{array}$ $\begin{array}{r}18\\-\ 9\\\hline\end{array}$
5. $\begin{array}{r}6\\+\ 8\\\hline\end{array}$ $\begin{array}{r}14\\-\ 8\\\hline\end{array}$
6. $\begin{array}{r}8\\+\ 8\\\hline\end{array}$ $\begin{array}{r}16\\-\ 8\\\hline\end{array}$
7. $\begin{array}{r}12\\-\ 5\\\hline\end{array}$ $\begin{array}{r}10\\-\ 3\\\hline\end{array}$ $\begin{array}{r}9\\+\ 4\\\hline\end{array}$ $\begin{array}{r}8\\+\ 6\\\hline\end{array}$ $\begin{array}{r}9\\+\ 5\\\hline\end{array}$ $\begin{array}{r}10\\-\ 0\\\hline\end{array}$ $\begin{array}{r}8\\+\ 7\\\hline\end{array}$
8. $\begin{array}{r}9\\+\ 8\\\hline\end{array}$ $\begin{array}{r}7\\+\ 7\\\hline\end{array}$ $\begin{array}{r}15\\-\ 9\\\hline\end{array}$ $\begin{array}{r}13\\-\ 7\\\hline\end{array}$ $\begin{array}{r}6\\+\ 6\\\hline\end{array}$ $\begin{array}{r}11\\-\ 1\\\hline\end{array}$ $\begin{array}{r}10\\-\ 7\\\hline\end{array}$
9. $10 + 0 =$ ____ $12 - 4 =$ ____ $8 + 4 =$ ____
10. $9 + 8 =$ ____ $17 - 8 =$ ____ $6 + 7 =$ ____
11. $2 + 9 =$ ____ $8 + 8 =$ ____ $15 - 9 =$ ____
12. $12 + 0 =$ ____ $9 - 5 =$ ____ $7 + 8 =$ ____
13. $11 - 3 =$ ____ $4 + 8 =$ ____ $4 + 9 =$ ____

BASIC FACTS REVIEW

Name ______________________________

Set 5 Use after page 129.

Complete each fact family.

1. $6 + 7 = \_\_\_$
   $7 + 6 = \_\_\_$
   $13 - 7 = \_\_\_$
   $13 - 6 = \_\_\_$

2. $4 + 8 = \_\_\_$
   $8 + 4 = \_\_\_$
   $12 - 4 = \_\_\_$
   $12 - 8 = \_\_\_$

3. $8 + 7 = \_\_\_$
   $7 + 8 = \_\_\_$
   $15 - 7 = \_\_\_$
   $15 - 8 = \_\_\_$

4. $\begin{array}{r} 9 \\ +\ 9 \\ \hline \end{array}$ $\begin{array}{r} 18 \\ -\ 9 \\ \hline \end{array}$

5. $\begin{array}{r} 7 \\ +\ 7 \\ \hline \end{array}$ $\begin{array}{r} 14 \\ -\ 7 \\ \hline \end{array}$

6. $\begin{array}{r} 6 \\ +\ 6 \\ \hline \end{array}$ $\begin{array}{r} 12 \\ -\ 6 \\ \hline \end{array}$

Set 6 Use after page 145.

Add. Circle the numbers you would add first.

1. $\begin{array}{r} 4 \\ 7 \\ +\ 4 \\ \hline \end{array}$ $\begin{array}{r} 2 \\ 8 \\ +\ 6 \\ \hline \end{array}$ $\begin{array}{r} 3 \\ 4 \\ +\ 5 \\ \hline \end{array}$ $\begin{array}{r} 7 \\ 3 \\ +\ 3 \\ \hline \end{array}$ $\begin{array}{r} 9 \\ 6 \\ +\ 1 \\ \hline \end{array}$ $\begin{array}{r} 3 \\ 5 \\ +\ 5 \\ \hline \end{array}$ $\begin{array}{r} 5 \\ 8 \\ +\ 4 \\ \hline \end{array}$

Find the missing numbers in each fact family.

2. $\_\_\_ + 9 = 17$
   $17 - 9 = \_\_\_$
   $9 + \_\_\_ = 17$
   $17 - \_\_\_ = 9$

3. $\_\_\_ + 6 = 13$
   $13 - 6 = \_\_\_$
   $6 + \_\_\_ = 13$
   $13 - \_\_\_ = 6$

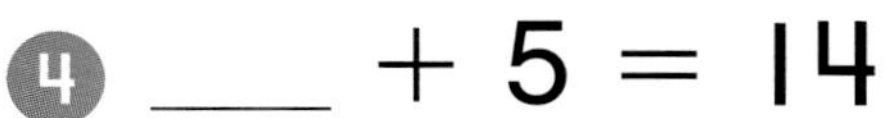

4. $\_\_\_ + 5 = 14$
   $14 - 5 = \_\_\_$
   $5 + \_\_\_ = 14$
   $14 - \_\_\_ = 5$

Picture Glossary

after

1, 2, 3, 4, 5

4 comes **after** 3.

area

The number of square units in a shape

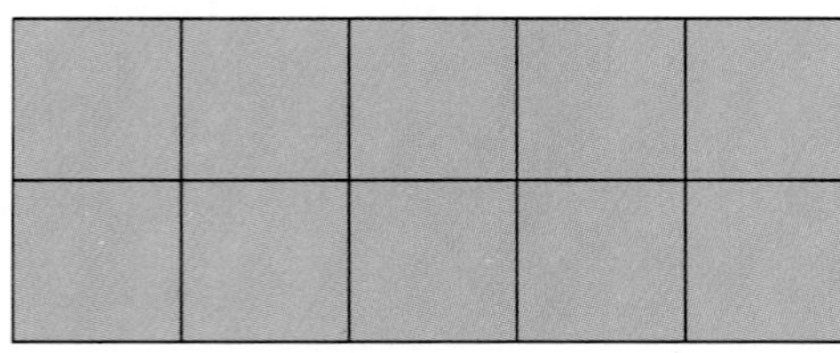

10 square units

bar graph

Sea Animals We Like

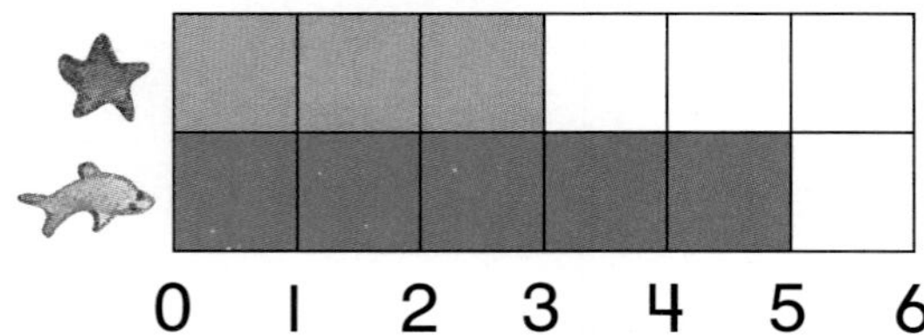

before

1, 2, 3, 4, 5

2 comes **before** 3.

between

1, 2, 3, 4, 5

3 comes **between** 2 and 4.

cent (¢)

A penny is 1 cent.

centimeter

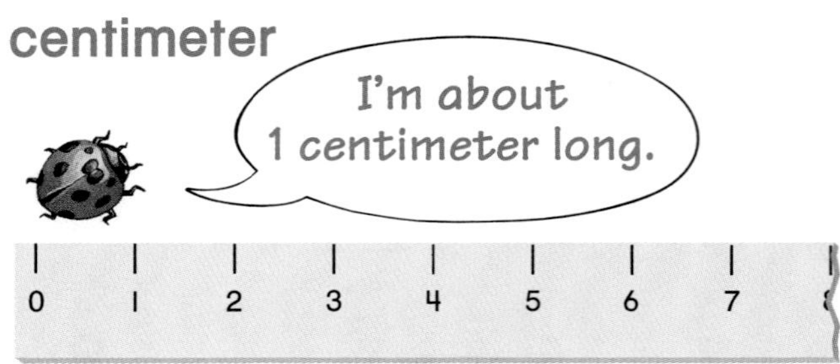

cone

count back

3, **2**

$3 - 1 = 2$

count on

3, **4**

$3 + 1 = 4$

cube

cup

cylinder

difference

$7 - 1 = 6$

$$\begin{array}{r} 7 \\ -\ 1 \\ \hline 6 \end{array}$$

difference

dime

10¢

divide

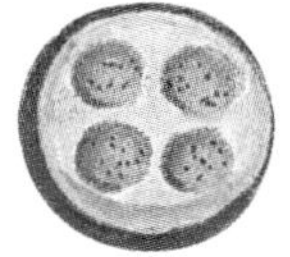

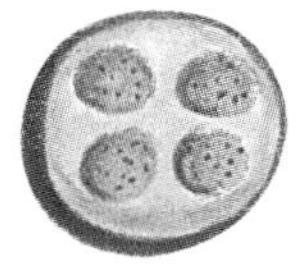

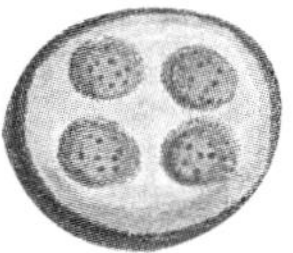

12 ÷ 3 = 4

dollar

$1.00

decimal point

doubles

4 + 4 = 8

8 − 4 = 4

doubles plus one

7 + 7 = 14, so 7 + 8 = 15.

equal sign =

2 + 3 = 5

estimate

42 + 21 is about 60.

even

2, 4, 6, 8, and 10 are **even** numbers.

fact family

2 + 4 = 6   6 − 4 = 2

4 + 2 = 6   6 − 2 = 4

foot

A **foot** is 12 inches.

fraction

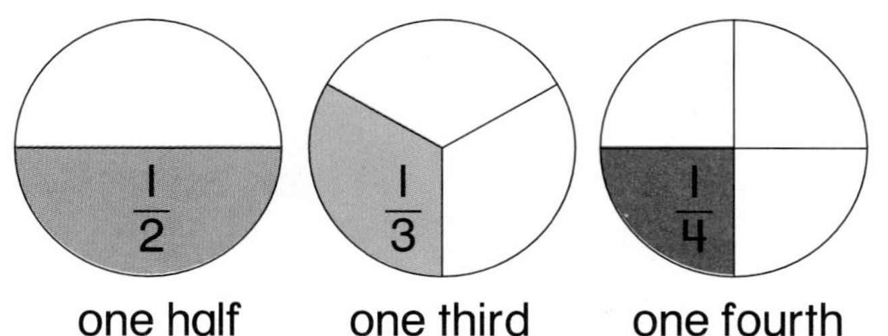

one half   one third   one fourth

greater than >

99 > 32

greatest

47   36   **51**

51 is the **greatest** number.

half dollar

50¢

half hour

PICTURE GLOSSARY

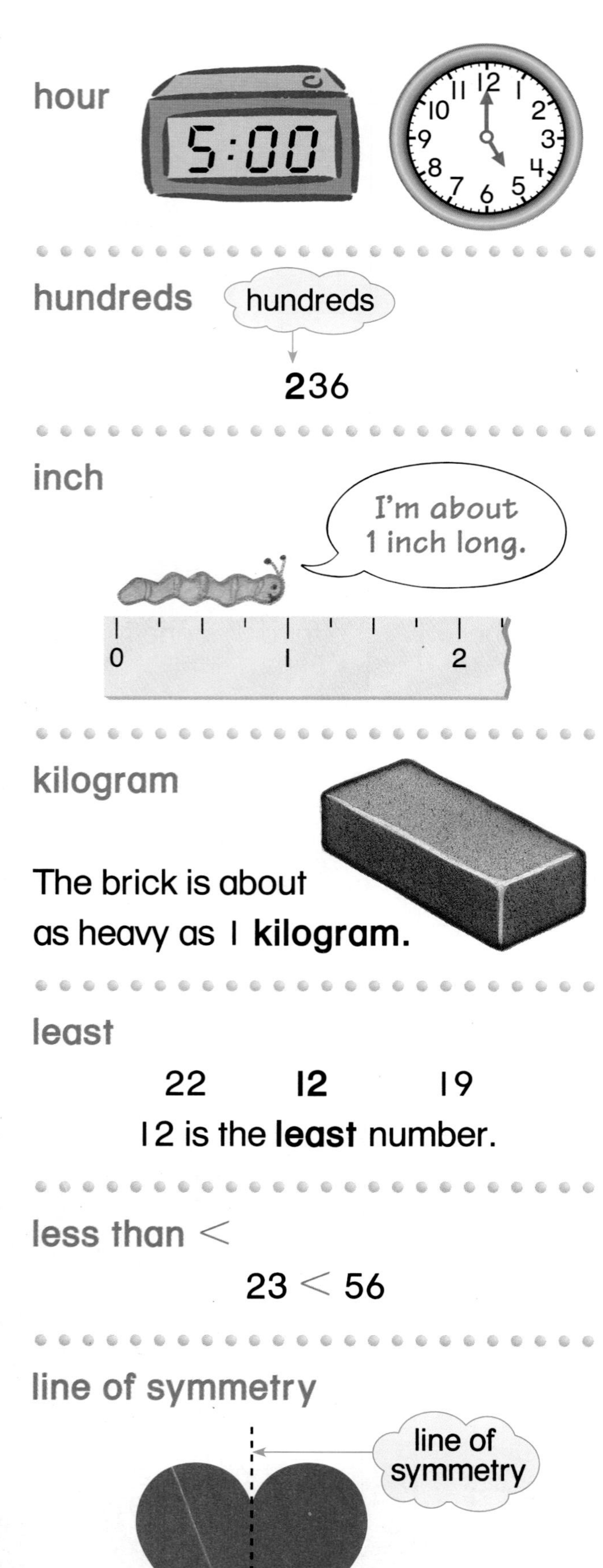

hour

5:00

hundreds

hundreds

236

inch

I'm about 1 inch long.

0 1 2

kilogram

The brick is about as heavy as 1 **kilogram.**

least

22 **12** 19

12 is the **least** number.

less than <

23 < 56

line of symmetry

line of symmetry

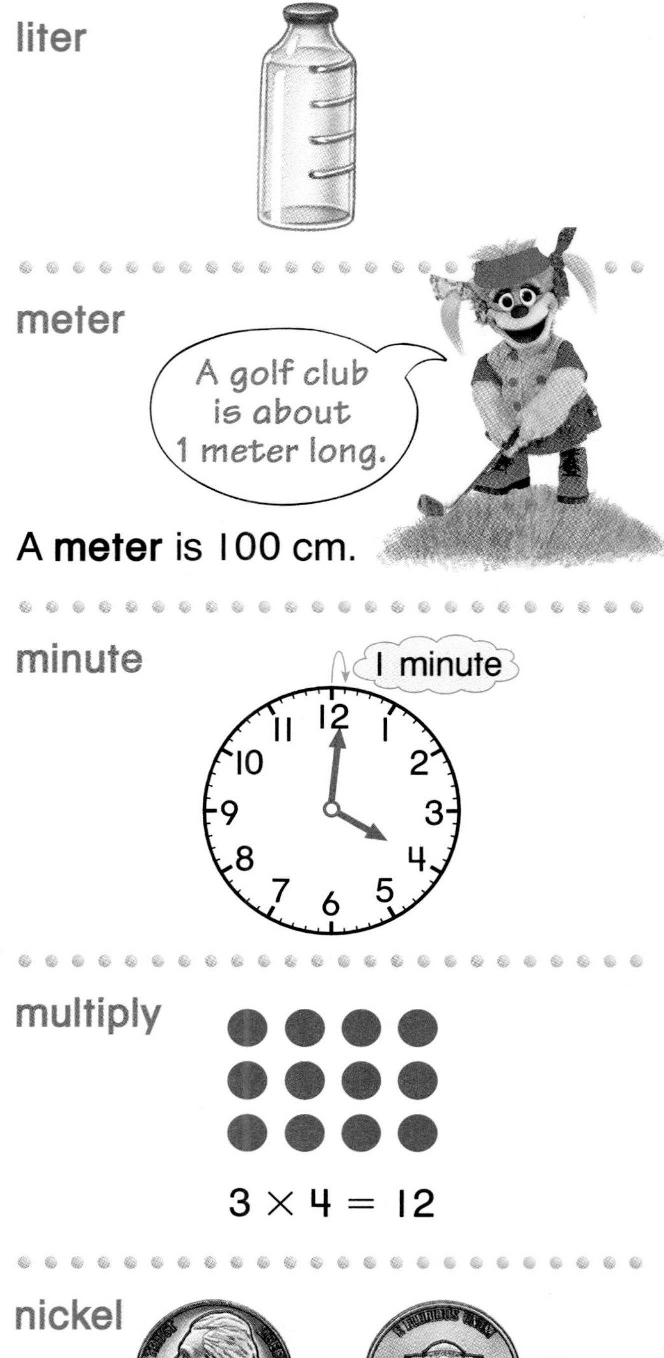

liter

meter

A golf club is about 1 meter long.

A **meter** is 100 cm.

minute

1 minute

multiply

$3 \times 4 = 12$

nickel

5¢

odd

1, 3, 5, 7, and 9 are **odd** numbers.

pattern

penny

1¢

perimeter

The distance around is the **perimeter.**

pictograph

Our Boats

Tim

Maria

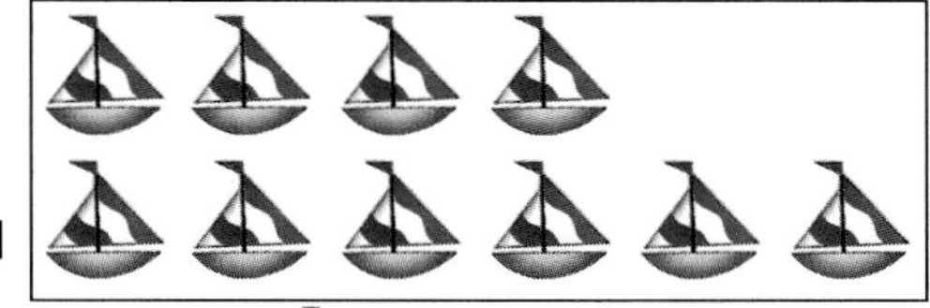

Each ⛵ means 1 boat.

pint

One pint is 2 cups.

pound

The bread weighs about 1 **pound.**

product

$3 \times 4 = 12$ ← **product**

pyramid

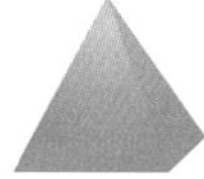

quart

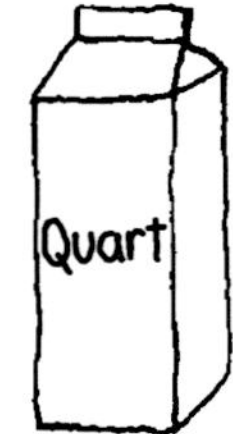

One quart is 4 cups.

quarter

25¢

rectangular prism

sphere

sum

$2 + 3 = 5$ ← **sum** →

$$\begin{array}{r} 2 \\ +\ 3 \\ \hline 5 \end{array}$$

tally marks 𝍸 ||

turnaround facts

$3 + 4 = 7$ $4 + 3 = 7$

yard

A **yard** is 3 feet.

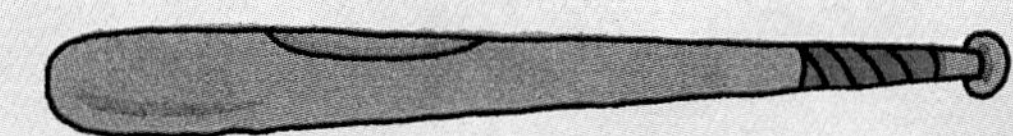

A baseball bat is about 1 **yard** lo

Credits

Illustration

Allen, Elizabeth 51, 52, 67, 68

Becker, Pamela 199, 202, 208, 210

Belcher, Cynthia 40, 273, 311, 317, 333, 344, 373

Berrett, Lisa 40, 41, 42, 51, 54, 56, 60, 62, 63, 64, 67, 69, 70, 103, 104, 105, 165, 166, 167, 182, 189, 190, 271, 285, 286, 303, 304, 313, 317, 318, 340, 346, 402, 433, 435, 436

Bettoli, Delana 474, 475, 476, 481

Bolton, Jennifer 126, 127, 128, 131, 135, 137

Broda, Ron 231

Brooks, Nan 79, 99, 100

Cable, Annette 119, 120, 121, 122, 124, 141, 142, 143, 148, 459, 460, 461, 462, 483, 484, 491, 493, 494, 495, 509

Carter, Abby 211, 212, 221

Dieterichs Morrison, Shelley 37, 47, 431, 432, 433, 436

Dinges, Michael 273, 274, 277, 278, 288

Dugan, Karen 117, 233, 234, 235, 238, 239, 243, 244, 247, 248, 249, 385, 386, 387, 388, 389

Egan, Tim 172, 178, 294

Freeman, Nancy 155

Galkin, Simon 455, 456, 463, 464, 467, 468, 501, 502, 503, 504, 505, 506, 507

Harris, Diane Teske 363, 371, 373, 378

Hirashima, Jean 321, 322

Jeanotilla, Carol 37

Karas, Brian 103, 104, 105

Kotik, Kenneth 1

Laden, Nina 155, 170, 183, 184, 365, 366, 367, 368, 369, 370, 379, 382

Lash-Ruff, Michelle 192, 204, 226

Levine, Melinda 267

Mauterer, Erin 445, 446, 447, 448, 451, 452, 453, 454, 465, 466

Melmon, Deborah Haley 79, 84, 95, 96, 101, 102, 219, 220, 231, 471, 472, 481

Moffatt, Judy 267, 311

Oversat, Laura 79, 90, 92, 108

Parnell, Miles 79, 87, 88, 110

Polfus, Roberta 401, 402, 408, 410

Raymond, Victoria 443

Rockwell, Barry 315, 316, 328, 335, 343

Romero, Javier 32

Roth, Roger 200, 201, 205, 206, 213, 214

Schneider, Jennifer 7, 8, 510, 511, 512, 513, 514, 515, 516, 517, 519, 520

Sheperd, Roni 14, 15, 16, 24, 25

Snider, Jackie 79, 107, 109

Steiger, Terry 155, 171, 399, 407, 419, 421, 422, 426, 496, 497, 498, 499

Sullivan, Don 79, 89, 91, 93, 94, 320, 323, 324, 331, 332, 337, 338

Swan, Susan 79, 98

Thompson, Emily 180, 181, 184, 187, 299, 300, 301, 406, 417, 420, 421

Verzaal, Dale C. 17, 18, 27, 29, 30

Weissman, Bari 89

Williams, Toby 117

Wolf, Elizabeth 39, 40, 42, 47, 48, 56, 59, 60, 62, 64, 65, 66, 156, 161, 162, 166, 167, 179, 186, 189, 190, 197, 269, 270, 279, 280, 284, 287, 292, 293, 298, 355, 399, 401, 403, 404, 409, 411, 415, 419, 423, 424, 425, 427, 428, 429, 430, 437, 540, 541, 542

Math Soup Illustration

Chapter 1
Steve Mach 2, 3, 6, 7
Troy Thomas 4, 5
Nadine Bernard Westcott 1

Chapter 2
Geri Bourget 4, 5
Jennifer Hewitson 1, 2, 3
Laura Oversat 7

Chapter 3
Dusan Petricic 8
Jean and Mou-sien Tseng 4, 5
Nadine Bernard Westcott 6

Chapter 4
Lonni Sue Johnson 8
Steve Mach 6, 7
Dorthy Stott 5

Chapter 5
Geri Bourget 3, 5

Chapter 6
Steve Mach 8
Stanley Martucci 1, 6

Chapter 7
Lonni Sue Johnson 6

Chapter 9
Barry Rockwell 3, 4, 6, 7, 8

Chapter 10
Kate Evans 8

Chapter 11
Mary Lynn Blasuta 2
Jennifer Bolten 1
Abby Carter 8
Ruta Dangavietis 6
Georgia Shola 4

Chapter 12
Stanley Martucci 4
Barry Rockwell 3

Chapter 13
Terri Starrett 2

Photography

Unless otherwise acknowledged, all photos are the property of Scott Foresman - Addison Wesley. Math Soup photography created expressly for Scott Foresman - Addison Wesley by Fritz Geiger and Michael Walker.

Cover Gail Shumway/FPG

Myrleen Ferguson/PhotoEdit 1(Row 2, l)
John Eastcott/YVA Momatiuk/The Image Works, 1(Row 2, c)
David Young-Wolff/PhotoEdit 1(Row 3, cl)
Comstock 1(Row 3, cr)
Roy Morsch/Stock Market 1(Row 3, r)
Paul Conklin/PhotoEdit 1(Row 4, l)
Jim Cummins/FPG 1(Row 4, cl)
Bryan F. Peterson/Stock Market 1(Row 4, r)
Tom Prettyman/PhotoEdit 48(t)
Elena Rooraid/PhotoEdit 48(b)
David Wells/The Image Works 84
Bill Aron/PhotoEdit 106
D. Greco/The Image Works 143
Bob Daemmrich 199(t)
Bob Daemmrich/Stock Boston 202(b)
David Young-Wolff/PhotoEdit 206(l)
Michael Newman/PhotoEdit 206(r)
Richard Pasley/Stock Boston 208(t)
Lawrence Migdale/Stock Boston 212
Comstock 240
Superstock 314, 318, 320, 321, 328(r) 329, 334, 336, 340, 342(l)
Mickey Gibson/ANIMALS ANIMALS 317
Fritz Prenzel/ANIMALS ANIMALS 327(t)
ANIMALS ANIMALS 328(l)
Ken Cole/ANIMALS ANIMALS 342(r)

Math Soup Photography

Chapter 2
HMS Images/Image Bank 4

Chapter 3
Richard T. Nowitz 1, 3

Chapter 4
Randall Hyman 2

Chapter 5
Les Morsillo 4–5
Michael Okoniewski 7(tr)
Michael Gullett 7(bl)

Chapter 6
Paul F. Gero 1, 4–5

Chapter 7
Keith Ayres 2

Chapter 8
National Geographic Society/ Photo: Franklin J. Viola 3
All car photos by Jeffrey Dworin 4–5
I. N. Phelps Stokes Collection/New York Public Library, Astor, Lenox and Tilden Foundations 6(t)
From the Collections of the Henry Ford Museum and Greenfield Village 6(b)
Library of Congress 7(t)
UPI/Corbis-Bettmann 7(b)

Chapter 9
Tim Davis/Tony Stone Images 1
Ted Benson/Modesto Bee 2

Chapter 10
Lawrence Migdale 1, 2, 3
Bob Smith 6, 7

Chapter 12
Jim Cummins/Tony Stone Images 1
Christopher Morrow/Stock Boston 6(t)
Cameramann International 6(b)

Chapter 13
Courtesy of Bankshot 4
K. D. Lawson 7

Workmat 1

Workmat 2

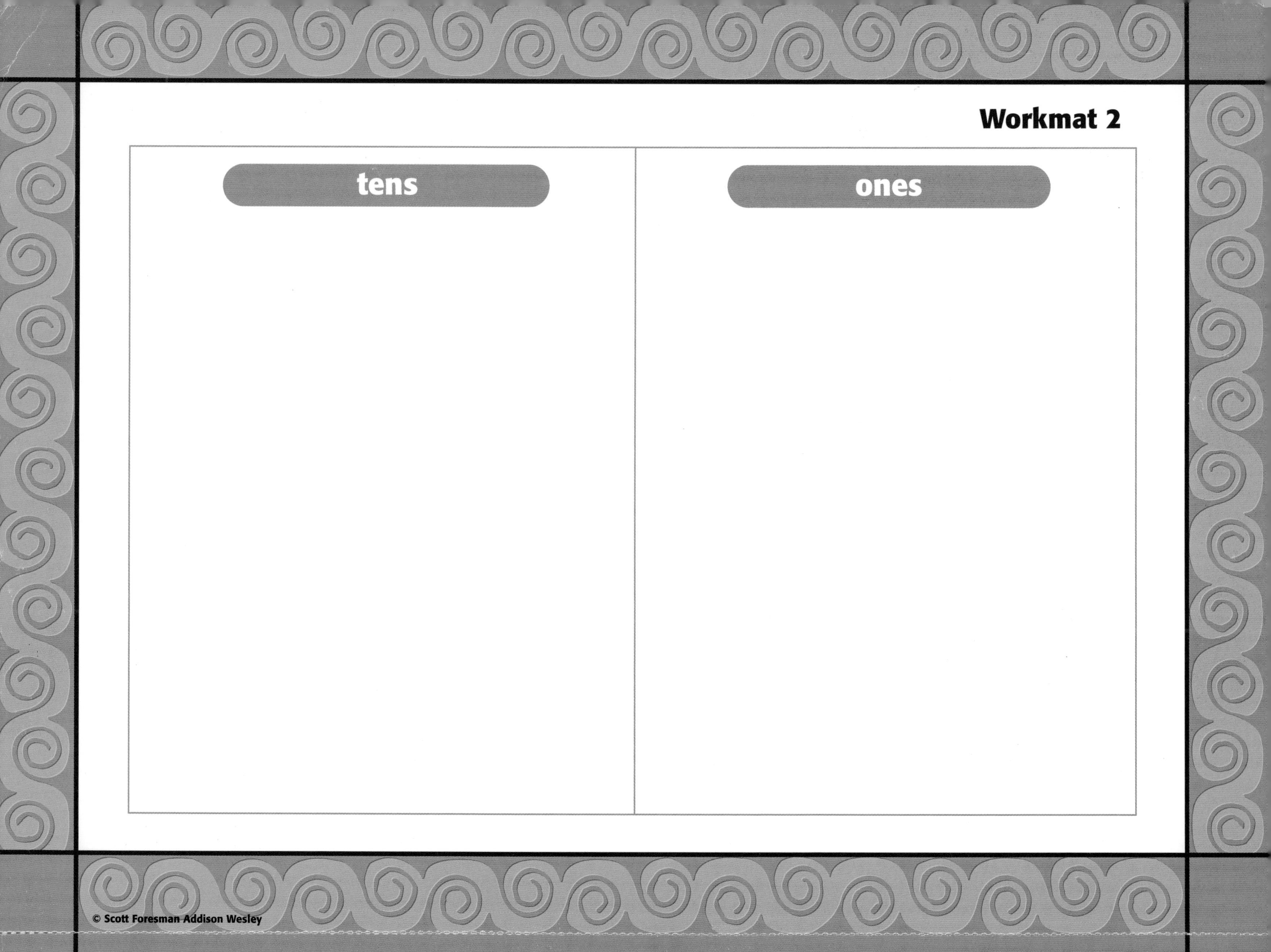

Workmat 3

Workmat 4

1	2	3	4	5	6	7	8	9	10
11	12	13	14	15	16	17	18	19	20
21	22	23	24	25	26	27	28	29	30
31	32	33	34	35	36	37	38	39	40
41	42	43	44	45	46	47	48	49	50
51	52	53	54	55	56	57	58	59	60
61	62	63	64	65	66	67	68	69	70
71	72	73	74	75	76	77	78	79	80
81	82	83	84	85	86	87	88	89	90
91	92	93	94	95	96	97	98	99	100

Workmat 5

hundreds	tens	ones

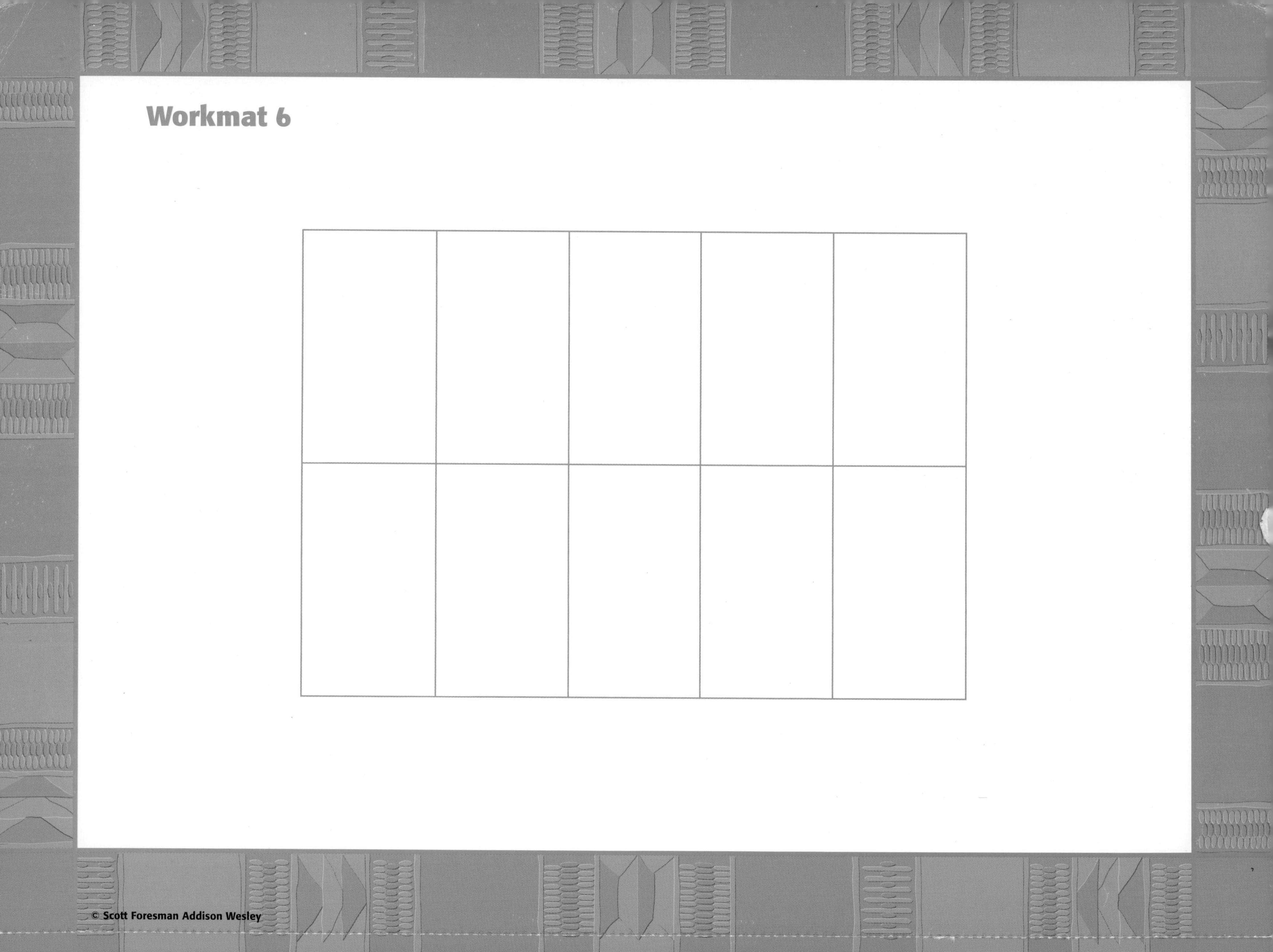

Workmat 6